Longman Annotated English Poets

GENERAL EDITOR: JOHN BARNARD

FOUNDING EDITOR: F. W. BATESON

D1331120

THE POEMS OF

JOHN DRYDEN

– Volume II –
1682 – 1685

EDITED BY
PAUL HAMMOND

Routledge
Taylor & Francis Group

LONDON AND NEW YORK

First published 1995 by Pearson Education Limited

Published 2014 by Routledge
4 Park Square, Milton Park, Abingdon, Oxon OX14 4RN
605 Third Avenue, New York, NY 10017

First issued in paperback 2022

Routledge is an imprint of the Taylor & Francis Group, an informa business

Copyright © 1995, Taylor & Francis.

Publisher's Note
The publisher has gone to great lengths to ensure the quality of this reprint but points out that some imperfections in the original copies may be apparent.

British Library Cataloguing in Publication Data
A CIP catalogue record for this book can be obtained from the British Library

Library of Congress Cataloging in Publication Data
A CIP catalog record for this book can be obtained from the Library of Congress

ISBN 13: 978-1-03-247803-6 (pbk)
ISBN 13: 978-0-582-23944-9 (hbk)

DOI: 10.4324/9781315843353

Contents

Preface

The editorial principles for this edition are set out in the Introduction to Volume I. The acknowledgements printed in Volume I also apply to Volume II, but some copyright acknowledgements which pertain to this volume are repeated here. I am grateful to the Librarian, Leeds University Library, for permission to print 'To Mr L. Maidwell'; and to the University of California Press for permission to quote portions of Dryden's works from *The Works of John Dryden*, edited by H. T. Swedenberg and others, in progress, copyright © 1956–1992 by the Regents of the University of California.

Paul Hammond

List of Illustrations

Chronological Table of Dryden's Life and Publications

For documentation and further details see Winn, Macdonald and *Letters*.

1631   (*9 August*) D. born at Aldwincle, Northamptonshire, the son of Erasmus Dryden and Mary Pickering; brought up in the nearby village of Titchmarsh; probably educated initially at the village school.

1644   Possible date of D.'s entry to Westminster School, London (scholars' conjectures range from 1642 to 1646).

1649   Publication of *Lachrymae Musarum*, a collection of elegies on the death of Lord Hastings, to which D. contributed.

1650   Admitted to Trinity College, Cambridge, as a Westminster scholar; his tutor was John Templer.
      Contributes commendatory verses to John Hoddesdon's *Sion and Parnassus*.

1652   (*19 July*) D. punished by the Master and Seniors for his (unspecified) disobedience to the Vice-Master.
      (*August*) D. writes 'Carmen Lapidarium' on the death of John Smith.

1654   (*February*) D. graduates BA and subsequently leaves Cambridge.
      (*June*) Death of D.'s father, Erasmus (buried *14 June*). He leaves D. a farm, but insufficient income to make him financially independent.

1657   (*19 October*) D. signs a receipt for £50 from John Thurloe, Cromwell's Secretary of State; how long he had been employed by the government is not known, but he was probably introduced by his cousin Sir Gilbert Pickering, Cromwell's Lord Chamberlain.

1657–60   D. has some form of employment with the bookseller Henry Herringman during these years, and may have written occasional prefaces and advertisements for books published by him.

1658   (*3 September*) Death of Cromwell.
      (*23 November*) D. walks in Cromwell's funeral procession along with Milton and Marvell as the Secretaries of the French and Latin Tongues.

1659   (*January*) *Heroic Stanzas* printed in *Three Poems Upon the Death of his late Highness Oliver.*

1660   D. contributes a commendatory poem to Sir Robert Howard's *Poems*; he is lodging with Howard in London at around this time.

(*May*) Restoration of the monarchy and return of Charles Stuart as King Charles II.

(*June*) Publication of *Astraea Redux.*

1661   (*April*) Publication of *To His Sacred Majesty* on the coronation.

1662   (*January*) Publication of *To My Lord Chancellor.*

(*September*) Publication of commendatory verses in Walter Charleton's *Chorea Gigantum* (dated 1663).

(*19 November*) D. elected a Fellow of the Royal Society (proposed by Charleton).

1663   (*5 February*) First performance of D.'s first play, *The Wild Gallant*, at the Theatre Royal, Vere Street; subsequently performed at court *23 February*, probably due to the influence of Lady Castlemaine; D.'s verses 'To the Lady Castlemaine' (circulated in MS) may date from this occasion, or from the play's printing in 1669.

(*1 December*) D. marries Elizabeth Howard, daughter of the Earl of Berkshire, and sister of Sir Robert Howard.

Late in 1663 or early in 1664 *The Rival Ladies* performed at the Theatre Royal, Bridges Street.

1664   (*January*) *The Indian Queen* performed at the Theatre Royal; first recorded performance on *25 January* in the presence of the King.

(*c. November*) *The Rival Ladies* published.

1665   (*February/March*) *The Indian Emperor* performed at the Theatre Royal.

(*March*) *The Indian Queen* published in Sir Robert Howard's *Four New Plays.*

(*5 June*) London theatres close because of the plague. Around this time D. leaves with his wife for her father's country estate at Charlton, Wiltshire. During his year at Charlton D. works on *Secret Love*, *Of Dramatic Poesy* and *Annus Mirabilis.*

1666   (*27 August*) D.'s first son, Charles, born.

(*2–5 September*) Fire of London.

(*November*) London theatres reopen.

(*November/December*) Likely date for the performance of

the revised version of *The Wild Gallant*, with a new Prologue and Epilogue.

1667 (*January*) *Annus Mirabilis* published.

(*March*) *Secret Love* performed at the Theatre Royal.

(*15 August*) *Sir Martin Mar-All* performed at Lincoln's Inn Fields.

(*Autumn*) *Of Dramatic Poesy* and *The Indian Emperor* published.

(*7 November*) *The Tempest* performed at Lincoln's Inn Fields.

1668 D.'s second son, John, born.

(*January*) *Secret Love* published.

(*February*) 'Prologue to *Albumazar*' spoken.

(*13 April*) D. appointed Poet Laureate.

(*Spring*) D. signs contract with the King's Company to write three plays a year in return for a share of the profits.

(*12 June*) *An Evening's Love* performed at the Theatre Royal.

(*Autumn*) *Sir Martin Mar-All* published. Shadwell's *The Sullen Lovers* published with a preface attacking D.'s remarks on Jonson. Sir Robert Howard's *The Duke of Lerma* published with a preface attacking D.'s views on the use of rhyme in plays. D. replies in 'A Defence of An Essay of Dramatic Poesy' prefixed to the second edition of *The Indian Emperor* (*early September*).

1669 (*Spring*) *The Wild Gallant* published.

(*2 May*) D.'s third son, Erasmus-Henry, born.

(*June*) *Tyrannic Love* performed at the Theatre Royal.

1670 (*c. February*) *The Tempest* published.

(*18 August*) D. appointed Historiographer Royal.

(*Autumn*) *Tyrannic Love* published.

(*December*) *The First Part of The Conquest of Granada* performed at the Theatre Royal.

1671 (*January*) *The Second Part of The Conquest of Granada* performed at the Theatre Royal.

(*c. February*) *An Evening's Love* published.

(*November*) *Marriage A-la-Mode* performed at the Theatre Royal.

(*7 December*) First performance of Buckingham's *The Rehearsal*, in which D. is satirized as Mr Bayes.

1672 The song 'Farewell, fair Armida' appears in various printed miscellanies.

(*25 January*) Theatre Royal destroyed by fire.
(*February*) *The Conquest of Granada* published.
(*26 February*) 'Prologue to *Wit without Money*' spoken.
(*Summer: after 4 July*) 'Prologue and Epilogue to *Secret Love*, Spoken by the Women'.
(*Summer or Autumn*) *The Assignation* performed at Lincoln's Inn Fields.

1673   (*Spring*) 'Prologue to *Arviragus* revived' spoken. Probable date of first performance of *Amboyna*. D.'s poems and plays extensively attacked in *The Censure of the Rota* and *The Friendly Vindication*; he is defended in *Mr Dreyden Vindicated* and *A Description of the Academy of the Athenian Virtuosi*.
(*June*) *Marriage A-la-Mode* and *The Assignation* published.
(*July*) 'Prologue and Epilogue at Oxford' spoken.
(*Autumn*) *Amboyna* published.

1674   *Notes and Observations on the Empress of Morocco* published (written jointly by D., Crowne and Shadwell).
(*26 March*) 'Prologue and Epilogue Spoken at the Opening of the New House'.
(*Spring*) *The State of Innocence* written, but not staged, because of the expense.
(*July*) 'Prologue and Epilogue at Oxford' spoken.

1675   (*February*) Epilogue written for a performance of *Calisto* at court.
(*17 November*) *Aureng-Zebe* performed at Drury Lane.
(*Winter*) Rochester's *An Allusion to Horace* (which includes an attack on D.) circulates in MS.

1676   (*February*) *Aureng-Zebe* published.
(*11 March*) 'Epilogue to *The Man of Mode*' spoken.
(*June*) Death of D.'s mother (buried *14 June*).
(*July*) 'Prologue at Oxford' spoken. Publication of Shadwell's *The Virtuoso*; its Dedication has an implicit attack on D.
(*July/August*) *Mac Flecknoe* composed, and put into circulation in MS.

1677   (*February*) *The State of Innocence* published.
(*12 May*) 'Prologue to *Circe*' spoken.
(*Autumn*) 'To Mr Lee, on his *Alexander*' published in Lee's *The Rival Queens*. D. writes 'Heads of an Answer to Rymer' on the endpapers of Thomas Rymer's *The Tragedies of the Last Age* (1677).

(December) All for Love performed at the Theatre Royal.

1678   *(c. February)* 'Epilogue to *Mithridates*' spoken.
(11 March) The Kind Keeper performed at Dorset Garden.
(March) 'Prologue to *A True Widow*' spoken. All for Love published.
(Autumn) Oedipus (by D. and Lee) performed at Dorset Garden.

1679   *(March)* Oedipus published.
(c. April) Troilus and Cressida performed at Dorset Garden.
(July) 'Prologue at Oxford' spoken.
(Summer) 'Prologue to *Caesar Borgia*' spoken.
(Autumn) Troilus and Cressida published by Tonson, marking the beginning of his association with D. The Kind Keeper published dated 1680.
(c. December) 'Prologue to *The Loyal General*' spoken.
(18 December) D. attacked and badly injured in Rose Alley, probably because he was thought to have written An Essay upon Satire (by Mulgrave).

1680   *(February)* Ovid's Epistles published, with Preface and three translations by D.
(July) 'Prologue at Oxford' spoken.
(November) The Spanish Friar performed at Dorset Garden.

1681   *(c. February)* 'Epilogue to *Tamerlane the Great*' spoken.
(March) The Spanish Friar published.
(19 March) 'Epilogue Spoken to the King' at the Oxford Parliament.
(Spring) 'Prologue and Epilogue to *The Unhappy Favourite*' spoken.
(June) His Majesties Declaration Defended published.
(July) 'Prologue at Oxford' spoken.
(October) 'Prologue and Epilogue spoken at *Mithridates*'.
(November) Absalom and Achitophel published, followed by many rejoinders.

1682   *(February)* 'Prologue and Epilogue to *The Loyal Brother*' spoken.
(15/16 March) The Medal published, followed by rejoinders.
(21 April) 'Prologue to His Royal Highness' spoken.
(May) Publication of The Medal of John Bayes, an outspoken attack on D., probably by Shadwell.
(31 May) 'Prologue to the Duchess' spoken.

(*July*) *The Duke of Guise* ready for performance, but banned by the Lord Chamberlain.

(*October*) *Mac Flecknoe* printed in a pirated edition.

(*November*) *The Second Part of Absalom and Achitophel* published. *Religio Laici* published. 'Prologue and Epilogue to the King and Queen' spoken.

(*28 November*) *The Duke of Guise* performed at the Theatre Royal.

(*c. December*) 'Prologue and Epilogue to *The Princess of Cleves*' spoken.

1683 Song 'High state and honours' printed in *Choice Ayres and Songs*.

(*February*) *The Duke of Guise* published, followed by pamphlets attacking it.

(*Spring*) *The Vindication of The Duke of Guise* published.

(*May*) Vol. I of *Plutarch's Lives* published, containing D.'s 'Life of Plutarch'.

(*Autumn*) Soame's *The Art of Poetry* published, with revisions by D.

(*November*) 'Epilogue to *Constantine the Great*' spoken.

1684 'To the Earl of Roscommon' published in Roscommon's *Essay on Translated Verse*. 'To Mr L. Maidwell' written and left in MS. First version of *King Arthur* composed.

(*February*) *Miscellany Poems* published, with contributions by D.

(*March*) Probable date of D.'s letter to Laurence Hyde, asking for help in securing payment of his salary.

(*April*) 'Prologue to *The Disappointment*' spoken.

(*July*) *The History of the League* published.

(*Autumn*) 'To the Memory of Mr Oldham' published in Oldham's *Remains*. *Albion and Albanius* staged before the King.

1685 (*January*) *Sylvae* published, with contributions by D.

(*6 February*) Death of Charles II; accession of James II.

(*March*) *Threnodia Augustalis* published.

(*3 June*) Revised version of *Albion and Albanius* performed at Dorset Garden.

(*11 June*) Duke of Monmouth lands at Lyme Regis; defeated at the Battle of Sedgemoor (*6 July*), and executed (*15 July*).

(*Summer*) Publication of commendatory verses in Northleigh's *The Triumph of our Monarchy*.

(*November*) Publication of 'To the Pious Memory of Mrs Anne Killigrew' in her *Poems*.

1686 D.'s conversion to the Church of Rome is not precisely datable, but probably occurred in 1685; on *19 January 1686* Evelyn recorded: '*Dryden* the famous play-poet & his two sonns, & Mrs. *Nelle* (Misse to the late . . .) were said to go to Masse; & such purchases were no greate losse to the Church.'

D. contributes to *A Defence of the Papers*, a work defending papers on catholicism attributed to Charles II and Anne Hyde.

1687 (*May*) *The Hind and the Panther* published. D. says in the address 'To the Reader' that it had been written 'during the last Winter and the beginning of this Spring; though with long interruptions of ill health, and other hindrances'.

(*Summer*) Publication of commendatory verses in Higden's *A Modern Essay on the Tenth Satyr of Juvenal*.

(*July*) Publication of Montague and Prior's satirical *The Hind and the Panther Transvers'd*.

(*22 November*) St Cecilia's Day celebration, at which D.'s 'A Song for St Cecilia's Day' was performed; the printed text appeared around this time, and was probably distributed at the performance.

(*December*) Composition of 'On the Marriage of Anastasia Stafford'.

1688 Lines on Milton printed in Tonson's new edition of *Paradise Lost*.

Publication of Tom Brown's attack on D., *The Reasons of Mr Bays Changing his Religion*.

(*June*) Publication of *Britannia Rediviva*, celebrating the birth of a son to James II and Queen Mary (on *10 June*).

(*July*) Publication of D.'s translation of Bouhours' *The Life of St Francis Xavier*.

(*5 November*) Prince William of Orange lands at Torbay.

(*11 December*) James II flees London, but is captured and returned; finally escapes to France.

1689 (*January*) Convention Parliament offers the crown to William and Mary. As a result of the revolution D. loses his offices as Poet Laureate and Historiographer Royal (replaced by Shadwell); he returns to the theatre to make a living.

(replaced by Shadwell); he returns to the theatre to make a living.

	(November) Contributes Prologue for performance of Behn's *The Widow Ranter*.
	(4 December) *Don Sebastian* performed at the Theatre Royal.
1690	Tom Brown publishes another attack on D., *The Late Converts Expos'd*.
	(January) *Don Sebastian* published.
	(May) Politically controversial Prologue for Beaumont and Fletcher's *The Prophetess* spoken and immediately suppressed.
	(October) *Amphitryon* performed at the Theatre Royal; printed at the end of the month.
	(December) Prologue for Harris's *The Mistakes* spoken.
1691	D. contributes Preface to Walsh's *A Dialogue concerning Women*.
	(February/March) Publication of Purcell's music for *The Prophetess*, with a dedication to the Duke of Somerset drafted for Purcell by D.
	(May/June) *King Arthur* performed at Dorset Garden (originally written in 1684); published *early June*.
1692	*(c. February)* Publication of commendatory verses in Southerne's *The Wives' Excuse*.
	(March) Publication of *Eleonora*, mourning the Countess of Abingdon.
	(April) *Cleomenes* performed at the Theatre Royal; it is published in *May*. D. contributes a 'Character of Saint-Evremond' to a translation of his *Miscellaneous Essays*.
	(September) Contributes Prologue to the anonymous *Henry the Second*.
	(October) Publication of *The Satires of Juvenal and Persius* (dated 1693).
1693	D. contributes 'A Character of Polybius' to *The History of Polybius*.
	(July) Publication of *Examen Poeticum*, with contributions by D.
	(December) 'To My Dear Friend Mr Congreve' published in Congreve's *The Double Dealer* (dated 1694).
1694	*(January)* *Love Triumphant* performed at the Theatre Royal.
	(March) *Love Triumphant* published.
	(15 June) D. signs contract with Tonson for a complete translation of Virgil, which occupies most of the next three years.

(*July*) *Annual Miscellany for the Year 1694* published with contributions by D.

1695 (*June*) D.'s translation of Du Fresnoy's *De Arte Graphica* published.

1696 (*February*) Contributes Epilogue to *The Husband his own Cuckold* by his son John, and adds a Preface when it is printed in *July*.

(*Spring: before June*) *An Ode on the Death of Mr Henry Purcell* published (Purcell died *21 November 1695*).

1697 (*July*) Publication of *The Works of Virgil*.

(*22 November*) *Alexander's Feast* performed at the St Cecilia's Day celebration; the printed text appeared about this time, and was probably distributed at the performance.

1698 (*February*) Commendatory verses published in Granville's *Heroick Love*.

(*March*) Publication of Jeremy Collier's *A Short View of the Immorality and Profaneness of the English Stage* including criticism of D.'s plays.

(*June*) Commendatory verses published in Motteux's *Beauty in Distress*. D.'s translation of Annals Book I published in *The Annals and History of Cornelius Tacitus*.

1699 (*20 March*) Contract for *Fables* drawn up with Tonson.

(*October*) D. plans to translate Homer and seeks patronage for the project.

1700 (*March*) *Fables Ancient and Modern* published.

(*April*) *The Pilgrim* performed (adapted from a play by Fletcher).

(*1 May*) Death of D.; buried on *2 May* in St Anne's Church, Soho; reburied in Chaucer's grave in Westminster Abbey, *13 May*.

(*June*) *The Pilgrim* published.

Various poems published in memory of D., including *Luctus Britannici* (*June*) and *The Nine Muses*, by women admirers (*September*).

1704 *Poetical Miscellanies: The Fifth Part* includes material by D.

1709 *Ovid's Art of Love* includes Book I translated by D. (written in 1693).

1711 D.'s 'The Life of Lucian' (written *c.* 1696) published in *The Works of Lucian*.

1717 D.'s 'Aesacus transformed into a Cormorant' (written *c.* 1692) published in *Ovid's Metamorphoses*.

Abbreviations

The Works of Dryden

AA	*Absalom and Achitophel*
2AA	*The Second Part of Absalom and Achitophel*
AM	*Annus Mirabilis*
EDP	*Of Dramatic Poesy, An Essay*
EP	*Examen Poeticum* (1693)
HP	*The Hind and the Panther*
MF	*Mac Flecknoe*
MP	*Miscellany Poems* (1684)
RL	*Religio Laici*

Journals

BJRL	*Bulletin of the John Rylands University Library of Manchester*
BNYPL	*Bulletin of the New York Public Library*
CQ	*Cambridge Quarterly*
DUJ	*Durham University Journal*
EA	*Etudes Anglaises*
ECS	*Eighteenth-Century Studies*
EIC	*Essays in Criticism*
ELH	*English Literary History* (now known as 'ELH')
ELN	*English Language Notes*
EMS	*English Manuscript Studies*
ES	*English Studies*
HJ	*Historical Journal*
HLB	*Harvard Library Bulletin*
HLQ	*Huntington Library Quarterly*
JEGP	*Journal of English and Germanic Philology*
JHI	*Journal of the History of Ideas*
JWCI	*Journal of the Warburg and Courtauld Institutes*
MLN	*Modern Language Notes*
MLQ	*Modern Language Quarterly*
MLR	*Modern Language Review*
MPh	*Modern Philology*
N & Q	*Notes and Queries*
PBSA	*Papers of the Bibliographical Society of America*
PLL	*Papers on Language and Literature*
PLPLS	*Proceedings of the Leeds Philosophical and Literary Society (Literary and Historical Section)*

PMLA	*Publications of the Modern Language Association of America* (now known as 'PMLA')
PP	*Past and Present*
PQ	*Philological Quarterly*
PTRS	*Philosophical Transactions of the Royal Society*
RECTR	*Restoration and Eighteenth-Century Theatre Research*
RES	*Review of English Studies*
RS	*Renaissance Studies*
SB	*Studies in Bibliography*
SC	*The Seventeenth Century*
SECC	*Studies in Eighteenth-Century Culture*
SEL	*Studies in English Literature 1500–1900*
SP	*Studies in Philology*
SRev	*Southern Review*
TCBS	*Transactions of the Cambridge Bibliographical Society*
TN	*Theatre Notebook*
TRHS	*Transactions of the Royal Historical Society*
YES	*Yearbook of English Studies*

Other abbreviations

Aen.	Virgil, *Aeneid*
BodL	Bodleian Library, Oxford
BL	British Library, London
Carm.	Horace, *Carmina* ('Odes')
CSPD	*Calendar of State Papers Domestic*
Ecl.	Virgil, *Eclogues*
Ed.	The present editor
Eds	The general consensus among previous editors
FQ	Spenser, *The Faerie Queene*
Geo.	Virgil, *Georgics*
HMC	Historical Manuscripts Commission
LS	*The London Stage* (see Bibliography for details)
Met.	Ovid, *Metamorphoses*
NT	New Testament
OT	Old Testament
PL	Milton, *Paradise Lost*
POAS	*Poems on Affairs of State* (see Bibliography for details)
PR	Milton, *Paradise Regained*
s.d.	stage direction
Serm.	Horace, *Sermones* ('Satires')
SR	*The Stationers' Register*
TC	*The Term Catalogues*

tr.'   translated by
UL   University Library

Note on the use of abbreviated titles for Dryden's poems
Each poem has been given a standardized short title which is used throughout, except that the full original title is given at the beginning of each poem.

Bibliography

This bibliography lists only the editions used for principal references and quotations, and those works of scholarship and criticism which are cited by author or short title. In this bibliography the place of publication is London unless otherwise stated, but in the rest of this edition the place of publication is not given. Throughout the edition the date given for plays is the date of their appearance in print, unless first performance is specified.

The Works of Dryden

Christie	*The Poetical Works of John Dryden*, edited by W. D. Christie (1870)
Day	*The Songs of John Dryden*, edited by Cyrus Lawrence Day (New York, 1932)
Ker	*Essays of John Dryden*, edited by W. P. Ker, 2 vols (Oxford, 1900)
Kinsley	*The Poems of John Dryden*, edited by James Kinsley, 4 vols (Oxford, 1958)
Letters	*The Letters of John Dryden*, edited by Charles E. Ward (Durham, NC, 1942)
Malone	*The Critical and Miscellaneous Prose Works of John Dryden*, edited by Edmond Malone, 3 vols (1800)
Noyes	*The Poetical Works of Dryden*, edited by George R. Noyes (Boston, Mass., 1909; second edition 1950)
Scott	*The Works of John Dryden*, edited by Walter Scott, 18 vols (1808)
Watson	John Dryden, *Of Dramatic Poesy and other critical essays*, edited by George Watson, 2 vols (1962)
Works	*The Works of John Dryden*, edited by H. T. Swedenberg et al., 20 vols (Berkeley, Calif., 1956–)

Dryden's writings are generally cited from *Works*, while pieces which have not yet appeared in *Works* are cited from Kinsley or from the first printed editions. References to *Works* are given by line numbers for the poetry (e.g. ll. 12–34), by act, scene and line numbers for the plays (e.g. I ii 34–56), and by volume and page number for the prose and for the editorial commentary (e.g. i 2–3). When a note in the present edition draws upon or discusses material in the equivalent note in *Works*, this is signalled by a simple citation (*Works*) without further references. The same applies to the citation of other editors.

Classical works
Classical writers are quoted from the Loeb Library, unless there is a particular reason for citing the editions which Dryden is known to have used (for these see Bottkol's article, and the headnotes to Dryden's translations). Translations are generally based on the Loeb versions, but are adapted where necessary.

Seventeenth-century works

Boileau	*Oeuvres complètes de Boileau*, edited by Charles-H. Boudhors, 7 vols (Paris, 1934–43)
Buckingham	George Villiers, Duke of Buckingham, *The Rehearsal*, edited by D. E. L. Crane (Durham, 1976)
Burnet	*Burnet's History of my Own Time, Part I: The Reign of Charles the Second*, edited by Osmund Airy, 2 vols (Oxford, 1897–1900)
Burton	Robert Burton, *The Anatomy of Melancholy*, Everyman's Library (1932)
Carew	*The Poems of Thomas Carew*, edited by Rhodes Dunlap (Oxford, 1949)
Cowley	Abraham Cowley, *Poems*, edited by A. R. Waller (Cambridge, 1905)
	Abraham Cowley, *Essays, Plays and Sundry Verses*, edited by A. R. Waller (Cambridge, 1906)
Danchin	*The Prologues and Epilogues of the Restoration 1660–1700*, edited by Pierre Danchin, *Part One: 1660–1676*, 2 vols (Nancy, 1981) *Part Two: 1677–1690*, 2 vols (Nancy, 1984)
Denham	*The Poetical Works of Sir John Denham*, edited by Theodore Howard Banks, second edition (n.p., 1969)
Downes	John Downes, *Roscius Anglicanus* [first published 1708], edited by Judith Milhous and Robert D. Hume (1987)
Etherege	*The Dramatic Works of Sir George Etherege*, edited by H. F. B. Brett-Smith, 2 vols (Oxford, 1927)
Evelyn	*The Diary of John Evelyn*, edited by E. S. de Beer, 6 vols (Oxford, 1955)
Godwyn	Thomas Godwyn, *Romanae Historiae Anthologia*, revised edition (Oxford, 1631)
Grey	*Debates of the House of Commons, From the Year 1667 to the Year 1694*, edited by Anchitell Grey, 10 vols (1763)

Jonson	*Ben Jonson*, edited by C. H. Herford, Percy and Evelyn Simpson, 11 vols (Oxford, 1925–52)
Langbaine	Gerard Langbaine, *An Account of the English Dramatick Poets* (1691)
Luttrell	Narcissus Luttrell, *A Brief Historical Relation of State Affairs 1678–1714*, 6 vols (1857)
Marvell	*The Poems and Letters of Andrew Marvell*, edited by H. M. Margoliouth; third edition revised by Pierre Legouis and E. E. Duncan-Jones, 2 vols (Oxford, 1971)
Milton	*The Poems of John Milton*, edited by John Carey and Alastair Fowler (1968)
	The Complete Prose Works of John Milton, edited by Don M. Wolfe et al., 8 vols (New Haven, Conn., 1953–82)
Montaigne	Montaigne, *Œuvres complètes*, edited by Maurice Rat (Paris, 1962)
Oldham	*The Poems of John Oldham*, edited by Harold F. Brooks with Raman Selden (Oxford, 1987)
Otway	*The Works of Thomas Otway*, edited by J. C. Ghosh, 2 vols (Oxford, 1932)
Pepys	*The Diary of Samuel Pepys*, edited by Robert Latham and William Matthews, 11 vols (1970–83)
POAS	*Poems on Affairs of State*, edited by George De F. Lord et al., 7 vols (New Haven, Conn., 1963–75)
Rochester	*The Complete Poems of John Wilmot, Earl of Rochester*, edited by David M. Vieth (New Haven, Conn., 1968)
Ross	Alexander Ross, *Mystagogus Poeticus, or The Muses Interpreter* (1647)
Rymer	*The Critical Works of Thomas Rymer*, edited by Curt A. Zimansky (New Haven, Conn., 1956)
Shadwell	*The Complete Works of Thomas Shadwell*, edited by Montague Summers, 5 vols (1927)
Shakespeare	*The Arden Edition of the Works of William Shakespeare*, 39 vols (1949–)
	William Shakespeare, *The Sonnets and A Lover's Complaint*, edited by John Kerrigan (Harmondsworth, 1986)
Southerne	*The Works of Thomas Southerne*, edited by Robert Jordan and Harold Love, 2 vols (Oxford, 1988)
Spence	Joseph Spence, *Observations, Anecdotes, and Characters*

	of Books and Men, edited by James M. Osborn, 2 vols (Oxford, 1966)
Spenser	*Spenser's Faerie Queene*, edited by J. C. Smith, 2 vols (Oxford, 1909)
	Spenser's Minor Poems, edited by Ernest de Selincourt (Oxford, 1910)
Spingarn	*Critical Essays of the Seventeenth Century*, edited by J. E. Spingarn, 3 vols (Oxford, 1908–9)
Sprat	Thomas Sprat, *The History of the Royal-Society of London* (1667)
Waller	*The Poems of Edmund Waller*, edited by G. Thorn Drury, 2 vols (1901)
Wycherley	*The Plays of William Wycherley*, edited by Arthur Friedman (Oxford, 1979)

Modern scholarship and criticism

This list is not intended to be even a basic bibliography of Dryden studies; it simply provides the details of those works which it has been convenient to cite in this edition by author or short title. Readers wishing to find listings of Dryden scholarship and criticism might consult *John Dryden: A Survey and Bibliography of Critical Studies, 1895–1974*, edited by David J. Latt and Samuel Holt Monk (Minneapolis, Minn., 1976); more recent work is listed in regular bibliographies in the periodicals *Restoration*, *The Scriblerian* and *The Year's Work in English Studies*. A selective bibliography is included in Paul Hammond, *John Dryden: A Literary Life* (Basingstoke, 1991).

Ashcraft	Richard Ashcraft, *Revolutionary Politics and Locke's 'Two Treatises of Government'* (Princeton, NJ, 1986)
Beal	Peter Beal, *Index of English Literary Manuscripts*, vol. 2, part 1 (1987)
Bottkol	J. McG. Bottkol, 'Dryden's Latin Scholarship', *MPh* xl (1943) 241–54
Garrison	James D. Garrison, *Dryden and the Tradition of Panegyric* (Berkeley, Calif., 1975)
Gillespie	Stuart Gillespie, 'Dryden's *Sylvae*: A study of Dryden's translations from the Latin in the second Tonson miscellany, 1685' (unpublished PhD thesis, Cambridge 1987)
	Stuart Gillespie, 'A Checklist of Restoration English Translations and Adaptations of

Classical Greek and Latin Poetry, 1660–1700',
Translation and Literature i (1991) 52–67

Haley   K. H. D. Haley, *The First Earl of Shaftesbury* (Oxford, 1968)

Harth   Phillip Harth, *Contexts of Dryden's Thought* (Chicago, Ill., 1968)

Hawkins   Edward Hawkins, *Medallic Illustrations of the History of Great Britain to the Death of George II*, 2 vols (1885)

Highfill   Philip H. Highfill, Jr, Kalman A. Burnim and Edward A. Langhans, *A Biographical Dictionary of Actors, Actresses, Musicians, Dancers, Managers and other stage personnel in London, 1660–1800* (Carbondale, Ill., 1973–)

Hoffman   Arthur W. Hoffman, *John Dryden's Imagery* (Gainesville, Fla., 1962)

Hotson   Leslie Hotson, *The Commonwealth and Restoration Stage* (Cambridge, Mass., 1928)

Hume   Robert D. Hume, *The Development of English Drama in the Late Seventeenth Century* (Oxford, 1976)

Hutton   Ronald Hutton, *The Restoration: A Political and Religious History of England and Wales 1658–1667* (Oxford, 1985)

Ronald Hutton, *Charles the Second: King of England, Scotland, and Ireland* (Oxford, 1989)

LS   *The London Stage 1660–1800*, Part I: 1660–1700, edited by William van Lennep (Carbondale, Ill., 1965)

Macdonald   Hugh Macdonald, *John Dryden: A Bibliography of Early Editions and of Drydeniana* (Oxford, 1939). (For corrections and additions to Macdonald's bibliography see James M. Osborn, *MPh* xxxix (1941) 69–98, 197–212.)

McFadden   George McFadden, *Dryden the Public Writer 1660–1685* (Princeton, NJ, 1978)

Mason   J. R. Mason, 'To Milton through Dryden and Pope' (unpublished PhD thesis, Cambridge 1987)

Milhous and Hume   Judith Milhous and Robert D. Hume, 'Dating Play Premieres from Publication Data, 1660–1700', *HLB* xxii (1974) 374–405

Miner   Earl Miner, *Dryden's Poetry* (Bloomington, Ind., 1971)

Ogg   David Ogg, *England in the Reign of Charles II*, second edition (Oxford, 1956)

Osborn   James M. Osborn, *John Dryden: Some Biographical Facts and Problems*, revised edition (Gainesville, Fla., 1965)

Owen   Susan Owen, 'Drama and Politics in the Exclusion Crisis: 1678–83' (unpublished PhD thesis, Leeds 1992)

Price   Curtis A. Price, *Music in the Restoration Theatre: With a Catalogue of Instrumental Music in the Plays 1665–1713* (Ann Arbor, Mich., 1979)
                 Curtis Alexander Price, *Henry Purcell and the London Stage* (Cambridge, 1984)

Spurr   John Spurr, *The Restoration Church of England, 1646–1689* (New Haven, Conn., 1991)

Tilley   M. P. Tilley, *A Dictionary of the Proverbs in England in the Sixteenth and Seventeenth Centuries* (Ann Arbor, Mich., 1950)

Verrall   A. W. Verrall, *Lectures on Dryden* (Cambridge, 1914)

Winn   James Anderson Winn, *John Dryden and his World* (New Haven, Conn., 1987) (cited as 'Winn')
                 James Anderson Winn, *'When Beauty Fires the Blood': Love and the Arts in the Age of Dryden* (Ann Arbor, Mich., 1992) (cited with short title)

Zwicker   Steven N. Zwicker, *Dryden's Political Poetry: The Typology of King and Nation* (Providence, R.I., 1972)

THE POEMS

68 Prologue and Epilogue to *The Loyal Brother*

Date and publication. Spoken early February 1682 (the first recorded performance of the play was on 4 February (*LS*)). The poems were first printed in a
folio half-sheet headed *A Prologue Written by Mr Dryden, to a New Play, call'd,
The Loyal Brother, &c.*, and published by Tonson (no date, but Luttrell dated
his copy (now in the Huntington) 7 February 1681/2). They were then
printed anonymously with the play *The Loyal Brother or the Persian Prince. A
Tragedy*, published by William Cademan in 1682 (*TC* May), dedicated to the
Duke of Richmond. The present text follows Tonson's publication.

Context. This was the first play by the Irish dramatist Thomas Southerne
(1660–1746). It was performed by the King's Company at the Theatre Royal,
and was a Tory play as the title suggests. In his dedication Southerne says:
'Nor durst I have attempted thus far into the World, had not the Laureats
own Pen secur'd me, maintaining the out-works, while I lay safe intrencht
within his Lines; and malice, ill nature, and censure were forc'd to grinn at a
distance' (sig. A2ʳ). Southerne told Pope that at this time D. 'was so famous
for his Prologues, that the players would act nothing without that decor-
ation. His usual price till then had been four guineas: But when Southern
came to him for the Prologue he had bespoke, Dryden told him he must have
six guineas for it, "which (said he) young man, is out of no disrespect to you,
but the Players have had my goods too cheap" ' (*Works of Alexander Pope*,
edited by Warburton, 9 vols (1751) vi 81; Johnson's version of the story has
two and three guineas). Later D. wrote a Prologue for Southerne's *The
Disappointment* (1684) and 'To Mr Southerne on his comedy called *The Wives
Excuse*' (1692). When he was ill in 1691 D. asked Southerne to help him finish
Cleomenes (Winn 451), and he refers to Southerne and Congreve as his friends
in letters of 1693 (*Letters* 54, 60).

A Prologue
written by Mr Dryden
to a new play called
The Loyal Brother

Poets like lawful monarchs ruled the stage,
Till critics like damned Whigs debauched our age.

Mark how they jump: critics would regulate ⎤
Our theatres, and Whigs reform our state: ⎬
5   Both pretend love, and both (plague rot 'em) hate. ⎦
The critic humbly seems advice to bring,
The fawning Whig petitions to the King:
But one's advice into a satire slides,
T' other's petition a remonstrance hides.
10 These will no taxes give, and those no pence:
Critics would starve the poet, Whigs the prince.
The critic all our troops of friends discards;
Just so the Whig would fain pull down the guards.
Guards are illegal that drive foes away,
15 As watchful shepherds that fright beasts of prey:
Kings who disband such needless aids as these
Are safe—as long as e'er their subjects please;
And that would be till next Queen Bess's night,
Which thus grave penny chroniclers endite.
20 Sir Edmund Berry first in woeful wise
Leads up the show, and milks their maudlin eyes:
There's not a butcher's wife but dribs her part,
And pities the poor pageant from her heart;

¶**68.** *Prologue*.
3. jump] coincide, tally (*OED* 5).
7. See 'Prologue Spoken at *Mithridates*' l. 4*n*.
9. remonstrance] a list of grievances presented to the King by a Parliament.
10. no pence] For methods of avoiding payment at theatres see 'Epilogue Spoken to the King and Queen' l. 26*n*.
13. On 30 November 1678 Charles rejected a bill disbanding the militia.
18–40. The anniversary of the accession of Elizabeth I on 17 November was celebrated with annual Pope-burnings, which developed into great processions in 1679, 1680 and 1681. For a description see Sheila Williams, *JWCI* xxi (1958) 104–18.
19. penny chroniclers] The processions were described in several pamphlets (cited by Williams 105–6).
20. Sir Edmund Berry] Sir Edmund Berry Godfrey, a magistrate, was murdered in October 1678 shortly after receiving Oates's first testimony about the Popish Plot. The processions began with 'A Dead Body Representing Sir *Edmundbury Godfrey*, in the Habit he usually Wore, the Cravat wherewith he was Murdered, about his Neck, with spots of Blood on his Wrists, Shirt, and white Gloves that were on his Hands, his Face Pale and Wan, Riding on a White Horse, and one of his Murderers behind him to keep him from falling' (1679 broadside, quoted by Williams 107).
22. dribs] dribbles, weeps.

Who to provoke revenge rides round the fire,
25 And with a civil congee does retire.
But guiltless blood to ground must never fall:
There's Antichrist behind to pay for all.
The punk of Babylon in pomp appears,
A lewd old gentleman of seventy years,
30 Whose age in vain our mercy would implore,
For few take pity on an old cast whore.
The devil, who brought him to the shame, takes part, ⎫
Sits cheek by jowl, in black, to cheer his heart, ⎬
Like thief and parson in a Tyburn cart. ⎭
35 The word is given, and with a loud huzzaw
The mitred moppet from his chair they draw:
On the slain corpse contending nations fall;
Alas, what's one poor pope among 'em all!
He burns; now all true hearts your triumphs ring,
40 And next (for fashion) cry, 'God save the King.'
A needful cry in midst of such alarms,
When forty thousand men are up in arms.

24–5. When the procession reached Temple Bar the villains were thrown into a huge fire (Williams 115).

25. *congee*] farewell.

27–33. The climax of the procession was the float carrying the Pope, represented as Antichrist or the Whore of Babylon (from Revelation xvii) accompanied by the devil: he appeared 'in a Lofty Glorious Pageant, Representing a Chair of State, covered with Scarlet, the Chair Richly Imbroydered, Fringed, and bedeckt with Golden Balls and Crosses; . . . on his Head a Triple Crown of Gold, and a Glorious Collor of Gold and precious Stones, St. *Peters* Keys, a number of Beads, *Agnus Dei*'s, and other *Catholick* Trumpery; at his Back stood his *Holiness*'s Privy Councellor, the *Devil*, frequently Caressing, Hugging and Whispering, and oft-times Instructing him aloud, to destroy His Majesty' (1679 broadside, quoted in Williams 113).

29. *seventy years*] The right age for Innocent XI (1611–89); he was actually to disapprove of Louis XIV's revocation of the Edict of Nantes in 1685 (which had protected French Protestants), and of James II's aggressive promotion of Roman Catholicism.

34. Criminals were accompanied by a priest on their journey to execution at Tyburn.

36. *moppet*] rag doll (*OED* 2).

42. Titus Oates had alleged that a secret Catholic army of 20,000 men was ready to rise in London (*A True Narrative of the Horrid Plot* (1679) 39); Henry Care put the figure at 50,000 (*The History of the Damnable Popish Plot* (1680) 108); on the other side, Sir Roger L'Estrange said that 40,000 armed men had

But after he's once saved, to make amends
In each succeeding health they damn his friends:
45   So God begins, but still the devil ends.
What if some one inspired with zeal should call,
'Come, let's go cry "God save him" at Whitehall'?
His best friends would not like this over-care,
Or think him e'er the safer for that prayer.
50   Five praying saints are by an Act allowed,
But not the whole church militant in crowd.
Yet should heaven all the true petitions drain
Of Presbyterians who would kings maintain,
Of forty thousand, five would scarce remain.

The Epilogue
by the same hand

Spoken by Mrs Sarah Cooke

A virgin poet was served up today,
Who till this hour ne'er cackled for a play:
He's neither yet a Whig nor Tory boy,
But, like a girl whom several would enjoy,
5   Begs leave to make the best of his own natural toy.
Were I to play my callow author's game,
The King's House would instruct me, by the name:
There's loyalty to one: I wish no more—
A commonwealth sounds like a common whore.

---

been mobilized by the Whigs to seize the King at Oxford (*Notes upon Stephen College* (1681) 47), and D. refers to 'forty thousand true Protestants' having attended a Pope-burning (*The Vindication* (1683) 15) (Southerne, *Works*, edited by Robert Jordan and Harold Love (1988)).
50–1. The Conventicle Act (1664) prohibited nonconformist meetings of more than five people.

Epilogue.
Title. Sarah Cooke (d. 1688) was described by the Count de Grammont as 'the prettiest, but also the worst actress in the realm'. She was introduced to the stage by the Earl of Rochester *c.* 1667; after some roles in touring companies she performed with the King's Company from 1677, joined the United Company in 1682, and left the stage in 1687. She also spoke the Epilogue to *The Duke of Guise* (Highfill iii 473–5).

10 Let husband or gallant be what they will,
    One part of woman is true Tory still.
    If any factious spirit should rebel,
    Our sex with ease can every rising quell.
    Then as you hope we should your failings hide,
15 An honest jury for our play provide.
    Whigs at their poets never take offence,
    They save dull culprits who have murthered sense:
    Though nonsense is a nauseous heavy mass,
    The vehicle called faction makes it pass.
20 Faction in play's the commonwealthsman's bribe,
    The leaden farthing of the canting tribe:
    Though void in payment laws and statutes make it,
    The neighbourhood that knows the man will take it.
    'Tis faction buys the votes of half the pit;
25 Theirs is the Pension Parliament of wit.
    In city clubs their venom let 'em vent,
    For there 'tis safe in its own element.
    Here where their madness can have no pretence,
    Let 'em forget themselves an hour in sense.

12. spirit] seventeenth-century slang for 'erect penis'; cp. *Romeo and Juliet* II i
24 and Hugh Ormsby-Lennon, *Swift Studies* iii (1988) 9–78, esp. 23–5.
15. An honest jury] London juries were selected by the sheriffs and often
returned politically motivated verdicts (cp. 'Prologue to *The Duke of Guise*'
l. 43*n*).
16–19. Defending *The Duke of Guise* D. wrote: 'Or what if it were a little
insipid, there was no Conjuring that I remember in *Pope Joan* [Settle's *The
Female Prelate* (1680)]: And the *Lancashire Witches* [by Shadwell (1681)] were
without doubt, the most *insipid* Jades that ever flew upon a Stage; and yet
even *These* by the favour of a *Party* made a shift to hold up their heads' (*The
Vindication* (1683) 5).
21. leaden farthing] a token issued by a tradesman, not legal tender.   *canting
tribe*] nonconformists.
25. Pension Parliament] The name given by the Whigs to the Parliament of
1661–79, many of whose Members had received substantial bribes both from
the court and from Louis XIV's ambassador Barrillon; *Flagellum Parliamentar-
ium* (in MS, 1679) listed 178 Members of Parliament alleged to have received
bribes (Ogg 483–5).
26. city clubs] Whig political clubs, the most famous of which was the Green
Ribbon Club (see *The Medal*, 'Epistle to the Whigs' ll. 46–8).

30   In one poor isle, why should two factions be? ⎤
     Small diff'rence in your vices I can see: ⎬
     In drink and drabs both sides too well agree. ⎦
     Would there were more preferments in the land:
     If places fell, the party could not stand.
35   Of this damned grievance every Whig complains,
     They grunt like hogs till they have got their grains.
     Meantime you see what trade our plots advance:
     We send each year good money into France,
     And they that know what merchandise we need
40   Send o'er true Protestants to mend our breed.

32. drabs] prostitutes.
34. i.e. if lucrative government offices fell to the Whigs, their oppositional stance would not be maintained.
40. Refugees from Louis XIV's persecution of the Huguenots, which began in 1681; also alluding to the Whig habit of calling themselves 'True Protestants'.

69 The Medal

Date and publication. When Shaftesbury was indicted on a charge of high treason at the Old Bailey on 24 November 1681 the jury returned the bill marked *ignoramus* ('we do not know'). To celebrate, a medal (see Plate 1) was struck by George Bower, embosser in ordinary to the Mint since 1664, who had previously produced medals for Charles II's restoration, his marriage, and the Popish Plot. The date of issue of the medal is uncertain, but it seems to be alluded to in Christopher Nesse's *A Key* (Luttrell's copy is dated 13 January 1682; Macdonald 225) and so probably appeared in mid-December 1681. Edmund Hickeringill (*The Mushroom* (March 1682) 16) says that D.'s poem is of 'three months birth' (Winn 601). The medal carried a bust of Shaftesbury on the obverse, with the inscription 'Antonio Comiti de Shaftesbury', and on the reverse a view of London Bridge and the Tower, with the rising sun breaking through a cloud, and the inscriptions 'Laetamur' ('we rejoice') and '24 Nov 1681'. Spence reported (from a priest whom he met at Pope's house) that the idea for the poem was suggested to D. by Charles: 'One day as the King was walking in the Mall and talking with Dryden, he said: "If I were a poet (and I think I'm poor enough to be one) I would write a poem on such a subject in the following manner—"; and then gave him the plan for it. Dryden took the hint, carried the poem as soon as it was written to the King, and had a present of a hundred broadpieces [pound coins] for it' (Spence i 28). Politically, by early 1682 the tide was turning against the Whigs: 'A month before the verdict, the court had succeeded in promoting the election of a moderate Tory, Sir John Moore, as Lord Mayor; ten members of Shaftesbury's jury were defeated in the December elections for the Common Council of London; and the King now felt strong enough to begin an action of *quo warranto* that would allow him to alter the City's charter . . . the Duke of York was recalled from Scotland; he arrived at Yarmouth a week before the publication of *The Medall*' (Winn 365). *The Medall. A Satyre Against Sedition. By the Author of Absalom and Achitophel* was published by Jacob Tonson in 1682 (16 March according to Malone (I i 163) citing Luttrell; a letter from Lenthall Warcupp to his father dated 15 March says 'wee expect the Poem vpon my Lord S. Meddall to come out this morning' (G. Thorn-Drury, *RES* i (1925) 324)). Some press corrections were made; the present text is taken from a corrected copy of *1682*. The poem was reprinted in Edinburgh, 1682; Dublin, 1682; in *MP* 1684 and 1692; and in 1692. The first edition carried anonymous commendatory verses by Nahum Tate and T. Adams: see Appendix B.

Authorship. The poem appeared anonymously, but by now D.'s authorship of *AA* was no secret; see *AA*, headnote ('*Authorship*'). *The Medal* was attributed to D. on the contents page of *MP* (1692), but not in the text.

Sources. W. O. S. Sutherland showed that many images in the poem are paralleled in contemporary pamphlets and newspapers (*University of Texas Studies in English* xxxv (1956) 123–34). A. E. Wallace Maurer pointed out that the design of the poem echoes the design of the medal, so that D. is coining his own medal. After an introduction (ll. 1–21), on the obverse D.'s portrait of Shaftesbury (ll. 22–144); then on the reverse, not one but five emblematic scenes: Shaftesbury's followers in confusion (ll. 145–66), London in a precarious condition (ll. 167–204), the Association (ll. 205–55), Shaftesbury corrupting the nation (ll. 256–86), and the future should the Whigs succeed (ll. 287–322). The poem concludes with a Latin motto, a rejoinder to *Laetamur* on the medal. Maurer notes that D. draws on the 'Advice to a Painter' convention of satire, and also on the emblem tradition for many of his images, e.g. ll. 27, 31, 35, 79–80, 119–22 (Maurer, *PLL* ii (1966) 293–304). M. A. Doody suggests that D. may have recalled the Interregnum ballad 'The States New Coyne', printed in *Rump* (1662) i 289–90 (*The Daring Muse* (1985) 40).

Reception. There were several swift replies: *The Mushroom* [by Edmund Hickeringill] (Luttrell's copy dated 23 March according to Malone); *The Medal Revers'd* [by Samuel Pordage] (Luttrell's copy (Dyce Collection) dated 31 March); *The Loyal Medal Vindicated* (Luttrell's copy (Huntington) dated 6 April); and *The Medal of John Bayes*, almost certainly by Shadwell (Luttrell's copy (Dyce Collection) dated 15 May). Pordage doubted whether the author of *AA* also wrote *The Medal*, 'since the stile and painting is far different, and their *Satyrs*, are of a different hew, the one being a much slovenlier Beast than the other' (2–3). Shadwell said that D. had mistaken the difference between satire and libel: 'For Libel and true *Satyr* different be; / This must have *Truth*, and *Salt*, with *Modesty*. / Sparing the Persons, this does tax the Crimes, / Gall's not great Men, but Vices of the Times / With Witty and Sharp, not blunt and bitter rimes. / Methinks the Ghost of *Horace* there I see, / Lashing this *Cherry-cheek'd Dunce* of Fifty three; / Who, at that age, so boldly durst profane, / With base hir'd Libel, the free *Satyr*'s Vein. / Thou stil'st it Satyr, to call Names, Rogue, Whore, / Traytor, and Rebel, and a thousand more' (2). BodL MS Firth c 16 has an anonymous poem 'Uppon the Author of the Poem ye Medall' (pp. 50–1).

The Medal
A Satire against Sedition

Per Graiûm populos, mediaeque per Elidis urbem
Ibat ovans; divumque sibi poscebat honores.

¶69. *Epigraph.* 'Through the Greek people, and through the city in the heart of Elis, he went triumphant, claiming for himself the honours due to the gods' (*Aen.* vi 588–9, of Salmoneus who sought to emulate Jove).

Epistle to the Whigs

For to whom can I dedicate this poem with so much
justice as to you? 'Tis the representation of your own
hero: 'tis the picture drawn at length which you admire
and prize so much in little. None of your ornaments are
5 wanting, neither the landscape of the Tower, nor the
rising sun, nor the *anno domini* of your new sovereign's
coronation. This must needs be a grateful undertaking
to your whole party, especially to those who have
not been so happy as to purchase the original. I
10 hear the graver has made a good market of it: all his
kings are bought up already, or the value of the remainder so enhanced that many a poor Polander who would
be glad to worship the image is not able to go to the cost
of him, but must be content to see him here. I must
15 confess I am no great artist, but signpost painting will
serve the turn to remember a friend by, especially when

---

12. Polander] The sixteenth- and seventeenth-century debate over the advantages of elective and hereditary monarchies cited the ancient custom among
the Germanic tribes of electing their rulers; Denmark, Sweden and Poland
were current examples of this practice. But by 1660 Denmark and Sweden
had become hereditary monarchies, leaving Poland as the only example of an
elective monarchy (E. R. Wasserman, *MLN* lxxiii (1958) 165–7). Tory
propaganda alleged that Shaftesbury had sought election to the throne of
Poland in 1674 when Jan Sobiewski was chosen, thus implying that he
favoured an elective monarchy for England. There seems to be no historical
basis for this report, and he would have been ineligible anyway, since the
Poles chose only from reigning European houses. The story is carried in *A
Modest Vindication of the Earl of S—y* (1681), where his poet laureate is to be
'John Drydenurtzitz . . . for writing Panegyricks upon *Oliver Cromwel*, and
Libels against his present Master King *Charles* II' (4). In Aphra Behn's *The
City Heiress* (*c*. April 1682) Sir Timothy Treat-all has his head measured for
the crown of Poland; cp. also Otway's Prologue to *Venice Preserv'd* (February
1682) ll. 36–9; *Scandalum Magnatum: or, Potapski's Case. A Satyr against Polish
Oppression* (which has echoes of *AA*, and an attack on Shadwell); and 'The
Last Will and Testament of Anthony King of Poland' (BL MS Burney 390).
15. signpost painting] Maurer 298 suggests an echo of Marvell's *Last Instructions
to a Painter* (in MS, 1667; *POAS* i 99): 'canst thou daub a sign-post, and that
ill? / 'Twill suit our great debauch and little skill' (ll. 7–8).

better is not to be had. Yet for your comfort the linea-
ments are true, and though he sate not five times to me,
as he did to B., yet I have consulted history, as the
20   Italian painters do when they would draw a Nero or a
Caligula: though they have not seen the man, they can
help their imagination by a statue of him, and find out
the colouring from Suetonius and Tacitus. Truth is,
you might have spared one side of your medal: the head
25   would be seen to more advantage if it were placed on a
spike of the Tower, a little nearer to the sun, which
would then break out to better purpose. You tell us in
your preface to the *No Protestant Plot* that you shall be
forced hereafter to leave off your modesty: I suppose
30   you mean that little which is left you, for it was worn to
rags when you put out this medal. Never was there
practised such a piece of notorious impudence in the
face of an established government. I believe when he is
dead you will wear him in thumb-rings as the Turks did
35   Scanderbeg, as if there were virtue in his bones to pre-

---

18. he sate not five times] Cp. *Last Instructions*: 'After two sittings, now, our
Lady State, / To end her picture, does the third time wait' (ll. 1–2; Maurer).
19. B.] George Bower (see headnote).
20–1. Nero . . . Caligula] Nero Claudius Caesar, Emperor AD 54–68, and
Gaius Julius Caesar Germanicus ('Caligula'), Emperor AD 37–41, were two
of the most cruel and tyrannical of Roman emperors.
23. Suetonius and Tacitus] Suetonius (b. *c.* AD 69) was the author of *De Vita
Caesarum*, which included lives of Nero and Caligula. Tacitus (b. *c.* AD 56)
included accounts of Caligula and Nero in his *Annales*, though the former is
lost.
28. No Protestant Plot] The Whig tract *No Protestant Plot* (three parts, 1681–
2) by Robert Ferguson; the address to the reader in part three (published
February 1682 (Haley 691)) says: 'if our Enemies persevere in their ways of
impudence, we hope all mankind will acquit us, if from henceforth we lay
aside bashfulness and modesty' (sig. A4ᵛ).
35. Scanderbeg] George Castriota *alias* Iskander Beg (*c.* 1404–67), an Albanian
who deserted the Turkish service and fought for his country's independence.
'The Turkes hauing gotten the towne of *Lissa*, did with a vehement and
earnest desire search out the bodie of *Scanderbeg*: . . . ioyfull was he that could
get or cary away any peece of his bodie were it neuer so litle: and those that
had any part thereof, caused the same most religiously to be set and curiously
enchased, some in siluer, some in golde, bearing it about them vpon some
part of their bodies as a thing most holy, diuine, and fatall' (*The Historie of
George Castriot* (1596) 496; Kinsley).

serve you against monarchy. Yet all this while you
pretend not only zeal for the public good, but a due
veneration for the person of the King. But all men who
can see an inch before them may easily detect those
40 gross fallacies. That it is necessary for men in your
circumstances to pretend both is granted you, for without them there could be no ground to raise a faction.
But I would ask you one civil question: what right has
any man among you, or any Association of men (to
45 come nearer to you), who out of Parliament cannot be
considered in a public capacity, to meet, as you daily
do, in factious clubs, to vilify the government in your
discourses and to libel it in all your writings? Who made
you judges in Israel? Or how is it consistent with your
50 zeal of the public welfare to promote sedition? Does
your definition of loyal, which is to serve the King
according to the laws, allow you the licence of traduc-
ing the executive power with which you own he is
invested? You complain that His Majesty has lost the
55 love and confidence of his people, and by your very
urging it you endeavour what in you lies to make him
lose them. All good subjects abhor the thought of arbitrary power, whether it be in one or many: if you were
the patriots you would seem, you would not at this rate
60 incense the multitude to assume it; for no sober man can
fear it, either from the King's disposition or his practice,
or even, where you would odiously lay it, from his
ministers. Give us leave to enjoy the government and the
benefit of laws under which we were born, and which
65 we desire to transmit to our posterity. You are not the

44. *Association*] In 1680 the Whigs in Parliament proposed a Protestant Association against popery and the succession of the Duke of York; a paper
outlining such an association was discovered in Shaftesbury's rooms and used
at his trial (cp. 'Prologue to *The Duke of Guise*' l. 14).
47. *factious clubs*] There were many Whig clubs in London, most importantly
the Green Ribbon Club, through which Whig activities were co-ordinated
(see J. R. Jones, *DUJ* xlix (1956) 17–20; D. Allen, *HJ* xix (1976) 561–80;
Ashcraft 143–5; 2AA ll. 524–33).
49. *judges in Israel*] The judges were the rulers of Israel in the period between
Joshua and the kings; this reference echoes the application of OT history to
contemporary politics in *AA* (cp. ll. 119, 177–8 below).
59. *patriots*] See *AA* l. 179n.

trustees of the public liberty, and if you have not right
to petition in a crowd, much less have you to intermed-
dle in the management of affairs, or to arraign what you
do not like—which in effect is everything that is done
70   by the King and Council. Can you imagine that any
reasonable man will believe you respect the person of
His Majesty, when 'tis apparent that your seditious
pamphlets are stuffed with particular reflections on
him? If you have the confidence to deny this, 'tis easy to
75   be evinced from a thousand passages, which I only forbear to quote because I desire they should die and be
forgotten. I have perused many of your papers, and to
show you that I have, the third part of your *No Protestant Plot* is much of it stolen from your dead author's
80   pamphlet called *The Growth of Popery*, as manifestly as
Milton's *Defence of the English People* is from Buchanan
De Jure Regni apud Scotos, or your first Covenant and
new Association from the Holy League of the French

66–7. you have not right to petition in a crowd] In 1661 Parliament passed an Act
against tumultuous petitioning, making it illegal to obtain more than twenty
signatures, or for more than ten persons to present a petition to Parliament
(Kinsley).

79–80. your dead author's pamphlet] *An Account of the Growth of Popery and
Arbitrary Government in England* (1677) by Andrew Marvell (1621–78). Ferguson's pamphlet does not seem particularly indebted to Marvell's, though they
share basic assumptions about a papist threat to English liberties. Allegations
of plagiarism were standard polemical devices: Marvell was accused of lifting
The Rehearsal Transpros'd from Milton's pamphlets (George F. Sensabaugh,
That Grand Whig Milton (1952) 37; cp. 77–88).

81. Milton . . . Buchanan] Milton's *Defensio pro populo Anglicano* (1651) and
Defensio Secunda (1654) are defences of the new English republic against the
attack mounted by Salmasius. It is particularly in *The Tenure of Kings and
Magistrates* (1649) that Milton follows George Buchanan (1506–82) who in his
De Jure Regni apud Scotos (1579) argued that the people only entrust power to
their ruler, and may remove or kill a tyrant if that trust is abused. Buchanan's
work appeared in an English translation in 1680, and is discussed in Sir
William Dugdale's *A Short View of the Late Troubles in England* (1681), on
which D. may have been drawing (J. H. Smith, *HLQ* xx (1957) 233–43).
Milton's work had a significant influence upon Whig political thought: see
Sensabaugh. Milton, Buchanan and Suarez (see l. 201n below) are cited
together as advocates of the killing of tyrants in George Hickes, *A Sermon
preached before the Lord Mayor . . . 30th of January, 1681/2* (1682) 17–19.

82–3. Covenant . . . Holy League] Dugdale 600–50 compared the Holy League

Guisards. Anyone who reads Davila may trace your
85 practices all along. There were the same pretences for
reformation and loyalty, the same aspersions of the
King, and the same grounds of a rebellion. I know not
whether you will take the historian's word, who says it
was reported that Poltrot, a Huguenot, murthered
90 Francis Duke of Guise by the instigations of Theodore
Beza; or that it was a Huguenot minister, otherwise
called a Presbyterian (for our church abhors so devilish
a tenent) who first writ a treatise of the lawfulness of
deposing and murthering kings of a different persuasion
95 in religion. But I am able to prove from the doctrine of
Calvin and principles of Buchanan that they set the
people above the magistrate, which if I mistake not is
your own fundamental, and which carries your loyalty
no farther than your liking. When a vote of the House
100 of Commons goes on your side, you are as ready to
observe it as if it were passed into a law; but when you
are pinched with any former and yet unrepealed Act of

of the sixteenth-century Guisards with the opposition to Charles I, which
produced the Solemn League and Covenant. D. exploited the parallel further
in *The Duke of Guise* (see 'Prologue' ll. 1–2*nn*).

84. Davila] Historian of the French civil wars; D. used the translation of his
work, *The Historie of the Civill Warres of France* (1647–8) for *The Duke of
Guise*.

90–1. Theodore Beza] Beza (1519–1605) was Calvin's associate and successor
as leader of the Genevan Protestants. The allegation that he persuaded Poltrot
to kill the Duke of Guise is reported by Davila (*Historie* i 176; *Works*).

91. a Huguenot minister] Davila reports that a Huguenot minister 'printed a
book in which he maintained, That the people of France were no longer
obliged to be obedient to the King, because he was turned Idolator; and for
this reason affirmed, that it was lawful to kill him' (*Historie* i 216–17; *Works*).

93. tenent] tenet.

96. Calvin . . . Buchanan] Calvinist political theory, exemplified by Calvin
himself, Beza and Buchanan, developed the argument that it was lawful to
resist and kill a tyrant, particularly one who persecuted the godly (see Quentin Skinner, *The Foundations of Modern Political Thought*, 2 vols (1978) ii 302–
48).

99–102. vote . . . unrepealed Act] The Bill to exclude James from the succession, and the Bill to exempt Protestant dissenters from the Elizabethan and
Jacobean statutes still in force against dissenters, which passed the Commons
but did not become law, were reprinted as part of Whig propaganda in *A
Collection of the Substance of several Speeches and Debates* (1681).

Parliament, you declare that in some cases you will not
be obliged by it. The passage is in the same third part of
105   the *No Protestant Plot*, and is too plain to be denied. The
late copy of your intended Association you neither
wholly justify nor condemn, but, as the papists when
they are unopposed fly out into all the pageantries of
worship, but in times of war, when they are hard
110   pressed by arguments, lie close entrenched behind the
Council of Trent, so now, when your affairs are in a
low condition, you dare not pretend that to be a legal
combination, but whensoever you are afloat I doubt not
but it will be maintained and justified to purpose. For
115   indeed there is nothing to defend it but the sword: 'tis
the proper time to say anything when men have all
things in their power.
      In the meantime you would fain be nibbling at a
parallel betwixt this Association and that in the time of
120   Queen Elizabeth. But there is this small difference
betwixt them, that the ends of the one are directly
opposite to the other: one with the Queen's approbation
and conjunction, as head of it; the other without either
the consent or knowledge of the King, against whose
125   authority it is manifestly designed. Therefore you do
well to have recourse to your last evasion, that it was
contrived by your enemies, and shuffled into the papers
that were seized: which yet you see the nation is not so
easy to believe as your own jury; but the matter is not
130   difficult, to find twelve men in Newgate who would
acquit a malefactor.

104. The passage] Ferguson argues that dissenters are not bound by the Acts
which *'prevent and suppress Seditious Conventicles'* since their meetings are not
seditious; and also that if the Parliament which met on 8 May 1673 were
found to have assembled after the statutory interval between sessions, then
'the Laws by which the Phanaticks are Disturbed, Fined and Imprisoned, will
not be found to have the Legality, Force and Power that some men do
imagine' (*The Third Part of No Protestant Plot* (1682) 34–5).
111. Council of Trent] The Council (1545–63) which renewed Roman Catholic doctrine and discipline in response to the attacks made on the church by
Protestantism.
120. Queen Elizabeth] The Whigs' proposed Association echoed that of 1585,
which was designed to protect Elizabeth against assassination by promising
to avenge her death on the Catholics.

I have one only favour to desire of you at parting,
that when you think of answering this poem, you
would employ the same pens against it who have com-
135 bated with so much success against *Absalom and Achito-*
phel: for then you may assure yourselves of a clear victory, without the least reply. Rail at me abundantly,
and, not to break a custom, do it without wit. By this
method you will gain a considerable point, which is
140 wholly to waive the answer of my arguments. Never
own the bottom of your principles, for fear they should
be treason. Fall severely on the miscarriages of government, for if scandal be not allowed, you are no freeborn
subjects. If God has not blessed you with the talent of
145 rhyming, make use of my poor stock and welcome: let
your verses run upon my feet, and for the utmost refuge
of notorious blockheads, reduced to the last extremity
of sense, turn my own lines upon me, and in utter
despair of your own satire, make me satirize myself.
150 Some of you have been driven to this bay already; but
above all the rest commend me to the nonconformist
parson who writ the *Whip* and *Key*. I am afraid it is not
read so much as the piece deserves, because the bookseller is every week crying help at the end of his gazette
155 to get it off. You see I am charitable enough to do him a
kindness, that it may be published as well as printed,
and that so much skill in Hebrew derivations may not
lie for waste paper in the shop. Yet I half suspect he
went no farther for his learning than the index of
160 Hebrew names and etymologies which is printed at the
end of some English bibles. If Achitophel signify the
brother of a fool, the author of that poem will pass with
his readers for the next of kin. And perhaps 'tis the
relation that makes the kindness. Whatever the verses
165 are, buy 'em up, I beseech you, out of pity; for I hear

134. *the same pens*] For the replies to *AA* see the headnote to that poem.
148. *turn my own lines upon me*] as in Pordage's *Azaria and Hushai*.
151–2. *the nonconformist parson*] Christopher Nesse, author of *A Whip* and *A*
Key.
161–2. *the brother of a fool*] Nesse says that 'Achitophel' in Hebrew means 'A
Foole my Brother' (*A Key* 24).

the conventicle is shut up, and the brother of Achitophel out of service.

Now footmen, you know, have the generosity to
make a purse for a member of their society who has had
170   his livery pulled over his ears, and even protestant socks
are bought up among you out of veneration to the
name. A dissenter in poetry from sense and English will
make as good a protestant rhymer as a dissenter from
the Church of England a protestant parson. Besides, if
175   you encourage a young beginner, who knows but he
may elevate his style a little above the vulgar epithets of
'profane', and 'saucy Jack' and 'atheistic scribbler' with
which he treats me when the fit of enthusiasm is strong
upon him: by which well-mannered and charitable ex-
180   pressions I was certain of his sect before I knew his
name. What would you have more of a man? He has
damned me in your cause from Genesis to the Revelations, and has half the texts of both the testaments
against me, if you will be so civil to yourselves as to
185   take him for your interpreter, and not to take them for
Irish witnesses. After all, perhaps you will tell me that
you retained him only for the opening of your cause,
and that your main lawyer is yet behind. Now if it so
happen he meet with no more reply than his pre-
190   decessors, you may either conclude that I trust to the
goodness of my cause, or fear my adversary, or disdain
him, or what you please; for the short on't is, 'tis indifferent to your humble servant whatever your party says
or thinks of him.

176. *vulgar epithets*] *A Key* calls *AA* 'that *Prophane,* and *Blasphemous Poem*'
('To the King') and 'Sawcy Satyr Verse' (25).
178. *enthusiasm*] See 'To John Hoddesdon' l. 82*n*.
186. *Irish witnesses*] See *AA* l. 1012*n*. After Shaftesbury's trial the witnesses
left in guarded coaches, 'and it was but necessary, for a rabble of above six
hundred men followed them very tumultuously, and with very ill language'
(*HMC Ormonde* n.s. vi 237). The Whigs attempted to discredit these turncoat
informers: 'their *Notorious Adventures,* their *Swearing, Counter-swearing, Quarrels* amongst themselves, *Suborning,* and being *Suborn'd,* Endeavours to *drop*
the Popish Plot, and *Sham* another upon Protestants, &c. are become the
Common themes of every Table-talk, and the Subject matter of *Play-House
Drolls*' ([William Hetherington], *The Irish-Evidence Convicted by their Own
Oaths* (1682) 3; Kinsley). *The Third Part of No Protestant Plot* attacks the
credibility of these witnesses in great detail.

The Medal
A Satire against Sedition

Of all our antic sights and pageantry
Which English idiots run in crowds to see,
The Polish medal bears the prize alone:
A monster, more the favourite of the town
5 Than either fairs or theatres have shown.
Never did art so well with nature strive,
Nor ever idol seemed so much alive;
So like the man: so golden to the sight,
So base within, so counterfeit and light.
10 One side is filled with title and with face,
And, lest the king should want a regal place,
On the reverse a tower the town surveys,
O'er which our mounting sun his beams displays.
The word, pronounced aloud by shrieval voice,
15 *Laetamur*, which in Polish is 'rejoice'.
The day, month, year to the great act are joined,
And a new canting holiday designed.
Five days he sate for every cast and look,
Four more than God to finish Adam took.

1. *antic*] grotesque, bizarre (*OED* 2).

3–16. The medal is illustrated in Plate 1; for a description see headnote, and also S. A. Golden, *N & Q* ccvii (1962) 383–4.

3. *Polish*] See 'Epistle' l. 12n.

8. *golden*] Surviving examples of the medal are in silver, but some must have been silver gilt: Richard Duke writing to Otway calls it 'a fine gilt Thing' (Macdonald 26).

10. *face*] also meaning 'impudence, effrontery' (*OED* 7).

11. *the king*] i.e. Shaftesbury.   *place*] residence (*OED* 5b).

13. *mounting sun*] The sun is in the east, therefore rising (S. A. Golden).

14. *shrieval*] The Whig sheriffs were responsible for the selection of the jury which returned the *ignoramus* verdict on Shaftesbury (cp. *AA* ll. 584–629n; 'Prologue to *The Duke of Guise*' ll. 42n, 43n).

15. The Latin *laetamur* means 'we rejoice'.

17. Days of fasting and prayer were proclaimed by Parliament in the 1640s in thanksgiving for victories over the King (Schless, *POAS* iii 47).   *canting*] using religious language affectedly, esp. of puritans.

19. God created Adam on the sixth day (Genesis i 27).

20   But who can tell what essence angels are,
      Or how long heaven was making Lucifer?
      O could the style that copied every grace
      And ploughed such furrows for an eunuch face,
      Could it have formed his ever-changing will,
25   The various piece had tired the graver's skill!
      A martial hero first, with early care
      Blown like a pigmy by the winds to war:
      A beardless chief, a rebel ere a man
      (So young his hatred to his Prince began).
30   Next this (how wildly will ambition steer!)
      A vermin wriggling in th' usurper's ear:
      Bart'ring his venal wit for sums of gold,
      He cast himself into the saint-like mould:
      Groaned, sighed and prayed, while godliness was gain,
35   The loudest bagpipe of the squeaking train.

21. Lucifer] For the application of satanic imagery to Shaftesbury see *AA* l. 373*n*.

22. style] engraving tool (*OED* 2).

23. furrows] Bower's portrait shows deep lines from the side of the nose down to the chin (Schless).   *eunuch*] reworking the idea of Shaftesbury's unproductive sexuality from *AA* ll. 170–2.

24. ever-changing will] Cp. *AA* ll. 152–5*n*. For a summary of Shaftesbury's career, which is discussed in the following lines, see *AA* ll. 150–99*n*.

25. various] changeable in character and opinions (*OED* 2a, b); cp. *AA* l. 545*n*.

27. pigmy] Cp. *AA* l. 157*n*.

28–9. Shaftesbury fought for Parliament in the Civil War, holding various military and civil posts in Dorset while in his twenties.

30–1. From 1653 to 1655 Shaftesbury served on Cromwell's Council of State.

30. For the image cp. *AA* l. 162.

31. 'Earwig' was a common metaphor for a parasite or whisperer (*OED* 2; Kinsley).

32–3. 'It is quite unnecessary to suppose that Ashley Cooper had to put on any hypocritical act in order to impress Cromwell, and there is no evidence to suggest that he did in fact pretend to be one of the "Saints". Dryden's lines refer to nothing more than the common Tory view that the Barebones Parliament was composed entirely of extreme religious enthusiasts, and that any member of it must have been either a religious maniac or a hypocrite' (Haley 67).

35. bagpipe] Alluding to puritan claims to speak by inspiration of the Holy Spirit. Cp. L'Estrange: [Whig] 'Common Pamphleteers . . . [are] no more

But as 'tis hard to cheat a juggler's eyes,
His open lewdness he could ne'er disguise.
There split the saint: for hypocritic zeal
Allows no sins but those it can conceal.
40 Whoring to scandal gives too large a scope:
Saints must not trade, but they may interlope.
Th' ungodly principle was all the same,
But a gross cheat betrays his partner's game.
Besides, their pace was formal, grave and slack:
45 His nimble wit outran the heavy pack.
Yet still he found his fortune at a stay,
Whole droves of blockheads choking up his way.
They took, but not rewarded, his advice:
Villain and wit exact a double price.
50 Power was his aim, but thrown from that pretence
The wretch turned loyal in his own defence,
And malice reconciled him to his Prince.
Him in the anguish of his soul he served,
Rewarded faster still than he deserved.
55 Behold him now exalted into trust,
His counsel's oft convenient, seldom just:
Ev'n in the most sincere advice he gave
He had a grudging still to be a knave;

---

then the Caballs Bag-Pipe to the Faction' (*Observator* lxxxii (21 December 1681); W. O. S. Sutherland, *University of Texas Studies in English* xxxv (1956) 123–34). Maurer 299 notes that in *The Ship of Fools* the bagpipe is chosen over the lute and the harp by the impatient fool who will not abide correction (*Stultifera Nauis . . . The Ship of Fooles*, tr. Alexander Barclay (1570) 100).

36. juggler] L'Estrange called the Whigs spiritual jugglers (*Observator* lxvii (2 November 1681), lxxii (19 November 1681); Sutherland).

37. lewdness] Enemies frequently accused Shaftesbury of lewdness, especially after the tide had turned against the Whigs in 1682, but Haley 211–15 finds no actual evidence to support these allegations.

41. interlope] trade without a licence (*OED* 1).

44. slack] slow (*OED* 4).

46. at a stay] at a standstill.

51–2. At the Restoration, Shaftesbury was appointed a Privy Councillor and served Charles as Chancellor of the Exchequer, Commissioner of the Treasury, and Lord Chancellor, until his dismissal in November 1673.

58. grudging] secret inclination (*OED* 4).

The frauds he learned in his fanatic years
60   Made him uneasy in his lawful gears;
       At best as little honest as he could,
       And like white witches mischievously good;
       To his first bias longingly he leans,
       And rather would be great by wicked means.
65   Thus framed for ill, he loosed our triple hold
       (Advice unsafe, precipitous and bold).
       From hence those tears! that Ilium of our woe!
       Who helps a powerful friend forearms a foe.
       What wonder if the waves prevail so far
70   When he cut down the banks that made the bar?
       Seas follow but their nature to invade,
       But he by art our native strength betrayed.
       So Samson to his foe his force confessed,
       And to be shorn lay slumbering on her breast.
75   But when this fatal counsel, found too late,
       Exposed its author to the public hate,
       When his just sovereign by no impious way
       Could be seduced to arbitrary sway,

60. *gears*] harness (*OED* 3b).
62. *white witches*] ones who use witchcraft benevolently.
63. *bias*] Cp. *AA* l. 79.
65. *loosed our triple hold*] broke the Triple Alliance; see *AA* l. 175*n*.
67. *Ilium*] Troy, which was betrayed by the duplicity of Sinon.
68. The breaking of the Triple Alliance helped France (always thought of as England's principal potential enemy) in its war against Holland.
73–4. Samson told Delilah that his strength depended on his never having cut his hair; then as he slept on her knees Delilah had his hair cut off (Judges xvi 17–19).
77–80. On 15 March 1672 Charles issued the Declaration of Indulgence suspending the execution of all penal laws against nonconformists and recusants; when the Commons objected to the King's suspending power Shaftesbury defended it, but Charles decided to cancel the Declaration in March 1673. Shaftesbury's strong support later that month for the Test Act (which excluded all but Anglicans from public office) established his reputation as 'a Protestant hero' (Haley 323).

Forsaken of that hope he shifts the sail,
80   Drives down the current with a pop'lar gale,
And shows the fiend confessed without a veil. ⎫
He preaches to the crowd that power is lent,
But not conveyed, to kingly government;
That claims successive bear no binding force;
85   That coronation oaths are things of course;
Maintains the multitude can never err,
And sets the people in the papal chair.
The reason's obvious: interest never lies;
The most have still their interest in their eyes; ⎫
90   The power is always theirs, and power is ever wise. ⎭
Almighty crowd, thou shorten'st all dispute,
Power is thy essence, wit thy attribute!
Nor faith nor reason make thee at a stay,
Thou leap'st o'er all eternal truths in thy Pindaric way!
95   Athens, no doubt, did righteously decide
When Phocion and when Socrates were tried;

79–80. Cp. *AA* ll. 159–62*n.* Maurer 299 notes that in *The Ship of Fools* 224 a fool guilty of 'the despising of misfortune' tugs frantically at the sail of a boat which is cracking in the middle.

80. Drives] drifts (*OED* 26).

81. confessed] revealed.

82–7. See *AA* ll. 759–810*nn.*

85. things of course] matters of mere custom.

87. i.e. makes the people infallible.

88. interest never lies] The Tory paper *Heraclitus Ridens* used this phrase as the motto for the issue reporting the *ignoramus* verdict (no. xliv, 29 November 1681; W. O. S. Sutherland). Cp. *AA* l. 501*n*, and *His Majestie's Declaration Defended* (1681; *Works* xvii 205).

92. wit] cleverness, ingenuity (*OED* 5); here a suspect attribute, as in *AA* ll. 153, 162–3.

94. A fourteener. Tom Brown has D. say: 'I measur'd it not by my Fingers, but a pair of Compasses; and I dare safely say 'tis the longest line except one in Christendom' (*The Reasons of Mr. Bays Changing his Religion* (1688) 17; *Works*).   *Pindaric*] The poems of Pindar (Greek, 518–438 BC), with their apparently inexplicable versification and lack of connections, were thought of as quintessential examples of poetic inspiration untrammelled by reason; the link between irrational 'enthusiasm' in poetry and in religion had been made by Thomas Rymer in *The Tragedies of the Last Age Consider'd* (1678) 8: 'Those who object against reason are the Fanaticks in Poetry, and are never to be sav'd by their good works' (see also Oldham, *Poems* 414, 456).

95–7. The Athenians executed the philosopher Socrates for impiety (399 BC)

As righteously they did those dooms repent:
Still they were wise, whatever way they went.
Crowds err not, though to both extremes they run,
100   To kill the father and recall the son.
Some think the fools were most, as times went then,
But now the world's o'erstocked with prudent men.
The common cry is ev'n religion's test:
The Turk's is, at Constantinople, best,
105   Idols in India, Popery at Rome,
And our own worship only true at home:
And true but for the time: 'tis hard to know
How long we please it shall continue so;
This side today, and that tomorrow burns,
110   So all are God-a'mighties in their turns.
A tempting doctrine, plausible and new:
What fools our fathers were, if this be true!
Who to destroy the seeds of civil war
Inherent right in monarchs did declare,

and the general Phocion for treason (317 BC); on each occasion they repented
and punished the accusers of the condemned men. Plutarch noted that 'Phocion's fate reminded the Greeks anew of that of Socrates; they felt that the sin
and misfortune of Athens were alike in both cases' (*Phocion* 38).
100. The execution of Charles I in 1649, and the recall of his son in 1660.
103–6. Martin Clifford (an associate of the Duke of Buckingham) wrote in
his *A Treatise of Humane Reason* (1674) that every man should be allowed
quietly to follow his own religion, and that each religion is mistaken in
thinking its own sacred texts to be an infallible guide to the truth: 'The Jew
says, I cannot err, for I follow the Old Testament, which is infallible, and
only that. The Christian assures himself of the Truth as long as he is guided
by the Evangelists and Apostles, whose Writings are the infallible dictates of
the Holy Ghost. The Turk assumes the same from the Alcoran; and the
Heathen from Oracles, Sybill's Books, and the like. What shall I do? None of
all these Books can be believed by their own Light, for there are things
equally strange in them all' (79, 87–8). The nonconformist and future Whig
pamphleteer Robert Ferguson replied: 'I know not an Opinion more pernicious in its Consequences, than that Men may be as safe in the Event by
embracing Turcism as Christianity. . . . Should Persons conspire to overthrow all Revelation, they could not fall upon a Method more likely to effect
it, than by endeavouring to persuade the World that there are things equally
as strange in the Bible as in the Alcoran' (*The Interest of Reason in Religion*
(1675) sig. a4ᵛ) (*Works*).
103. i.e. popular opinion is the arbiter even of the truth of religion.

115 And that a lawful power might never cease
Secured succession to secure our peace.
Thus property and sovereign sway at last
In equal balances were justly cast:
But this new Jehu spurs the hot-mouthed horse,
120 Instructs the beast to know his native force,
To take the bit between his teeth and fly
To the next headlong steep of anarchy.
Too happy England, if our good we knew,
Would we possess the freedom we pursue!
125 The lavish government can give no more,
Yet we repine, and plenty makes us poor.
God tried us once: our rebel fathers fought;
He glutted 'em with all the power they sought,
Till mastered by their own usurping brave
130 The free-born subject sunk into a slave.
We loathe our manna, and we long for quails;
Ah, what is man, when his own wish prevails!

117–18. The Whigs, however, argued that the actions of the King were encroaching upon the property and freedom of the people: see *AA* ll. 536*n*, 777–94*n*.

119. Jehu] leader of a revolt against King Joram; 'and the driving is like the driving of Jehu the son of Nimshi; for he driveth furiously' (2 Kings ix 20). Cp. Settle: 'besides the specious flattery, *That Kings can do no ill*, and *That all Crimes are cancelled in a Crown*, he has Religion to drive the Royal Jehu on' (*The Character of a Popish Successour* (1681) 11; W. O. S. Sutherland). The story of Jehu had generally been used in the seventeenth century to show that revolt against a ruler could be justified on religious grounds; D. reinterprets Jehu as an anarchic revolutionary (see Laura B. Kennelly, *Restoration* xiv (1990) 91–6). D.'s lines also draw upon the traditional image of the ruler controlling the people like a rider controlling a horse, as in Renaissance equestrian statues and paintings; the image of horse and rider also serves traditionally for the control of the passions by reason. Maurer 299 notes that one of Alciati's emblems shows a driver of a wagon who has lost control of the reins and bits of two furious horses who are dragging him over a cliff (*Emblematum Flumen* (1551) no. 63).

122. steep] precipice (*OED* B 1).

123. Echoes Virgil: *O fortunatos nimium, sua si bona norint, / agricolas!* ('O too happy farmers, if they knew their good!'; *Geo.* ii 458–9).

129. usurping brave] Oliver Cromwell.   *brave*] bravo, bully, assassin (*OED* 1b).

131. During their journey through the wilderness the Israelites were given manna from heaven to eat; when they complained at the lack of meat, God provided quails, but punished the people with a plague (Numbers xi).

How rash, how swift to plunge himself in ill,
Proud of his power, and boundless in his will!
135   That kings can do no wrong we must believe:
None can they do, and must they all receive?
Help heaven! or sadly we shall see an hour
When neither wrong nor right are in their power!
Already they have lost their best defence,
140   The benefit of laws which they dispense;
No justice to their righteous cause allowed,
But baffled by an arbitrary crowd;
And medals graved their conquest to record,
The stamp and coin of their adopted lord.
145   The man who laughed but once, to see an ass
Mumbling to make the cross-grained thistles pass,
Might laugh again to see a jury chaw
The prickles of unpalatable law.
The witnesses that, leech-like, lived on blood,
150   Sucking for them were med'cinally good;
But when they fastened on *their* festered sore, ⎤
Then justice and religion they forswore,   ⎬
Their maiden oaths debauched into a whore. ⎦
Thus men are raised by factions, and decried,
155   And rogue and saint distinguished by their side.

142. The Whigs charged that Charles's government had become arbitrary (as
in Marvell's *An Account of the Growth of Popery and Arbitrary Government*
(1677); cp. *AA* ll. 212, 330, 701, 762). D. replies here that power granted to
the crowd will produce arbitrary government (cp. *AA* ll. 777–94*n*).
144. *stamp*] medal (*OED* 15).   *coin*] device, impress (*OED* 4).
145–6. The story is told of Crassus by Lucillius (see Thomas Browne, *Pseudo-
doxia Epidemica* VII xvi 2; Saintsbury).
146. *Mumbling*] chewing softly (*OED* 3).
147–8. As Charles gained mastery of the political situation in 1681–2 he used
the law increasingly to the discomfort of the Whigs, e.g. in the trial of
Stephen College (executed August 1681) and the legal attack on the charters
by which London and other cities were governed.
149–53. See 'Epistle to the Whigs' l. 186*n*.
151. *festered sore*] With an allusion to the open wound in Shaftesbury's side,
left after an operation in 1668 to remove a hydatid cyst of the liver, which
was drained through a pipe. Tory propagandists called him 'Tapski', and the
final scene in D.'s *Albion and Albanius* (1685) shows a man 'incompast by
several Phanatical Rebellious Heads, who suck poyson from him, which runs
out of a Tap in his Side' (III ii).
154–5. Cp. *AA* 'To the Reader' ll. 5–6.

They rack ev'n scripture to confess their cause,
And plead a call to preach in spite of laws.
But that's no news to the poor injured page:
It has been used as ill in every age,
160 And is constrained, with patience, all to take,
For what defence can Greek and Hebrew make?
Happy who can this talking trumpet seize,
They make it speak whatever sense they please!
'Twas framed at first our oracle t' enquire,
165 But since our sects in prophecy grow higher
The text inspires not them, but they the text inspire. ⎤
    London, thou great emporium of our isle,
O thou too bounteous, thou too fruitful Nile,
How shall I praise or curse to thy desert,
170 Or separate thy sound from thy corrupted part!
I called thee Nile; the parallel will stand:
Thy tides of wealth o'erflow the fattened land,
Yet monsters from thy large increase we find
Engendered on the slime thou leav'st behind.

156–7. Nonconformist preachers claimed the authority of divine inspiration, against Anglican insistence that only ministers ordained in the legally established Church of England had authority to preach.

158–9. Cp. *RL* ll. 400–8.

162. talking trumpet] megaphone.

164. enquire] seek information from (*OED* 3a; citing this as its last example).

167. London] London was the seat of Whig opposition to the court, and the theatre in which much of the drama of the Popish Plot and Exclusion Crisis took place. Charles Blount's Whig pamphlet *An Appeal from the Country to the City* (1679) opens with an encomium of London as 'the great Metropolis and Soul of our once flourishing and glorious Kingdom' and continues with a lurid vision of the destruction of the city by papists (1–3). *emporium*] principal centre of commerce; cp. *AM* l. 1205*n*.

168. Cp. *AM* ll. 183–4.

169–70. desert . . . part] a perfect rhyme in seventeenth-century pronunciation.

173–4. Ovid recounts that monstrous half-live forms were discovered in the slime left by the receding Nile (*Met.* i 422–9). D. reverses Settle's application of the image: 'the very Name of a Popish Monarch has the Influence of the Sun in *Egypt*, and daily warms our Mud into Monsters, till they are become our most threatening and most formidable *Enemies*' (*The Character of a Popish Successour* (1681) 3; W. O. S. Sutherland).

174. Engendered on] *1682 corrected state*; Enlivened by *1682 uncorrected state*.

175   Sedition has not wholly seized on thee,
       Thy nobler parts are from infection free:
       Of Israel's tribes thou hast a numerous band,
       But still the Canaanite is in the land;
       Thy military chiefs are brave and true,
180   Nor are thy disenchanted burghers few;
       The head is loyal which thy heart commands,
       But what's a head with two such gouty hands?
       The wise and wealthy love the surest way,
       And are content to thrive and to obey,
185   But wisdom is to sloth too great a slave;
       None are so busy as the fool and knave.
       Those let me curse; what vengeance will they urge
       Whose ordures neither plague nor fire can purge,
       Nor sharp experience can to duty bring,
190   Nor angry heaven, nor a forgiving King!
       In gospel phrase their chapmen they betray,
       Their shops are dens, the buyer is their prey.
       The knack of trades is living on the spoil;
       They boast ev'n when each other they beguile.
195   Customs to steal is such a trivial thing,
       That 'tis their charter to defraud their King.
       All hands unite of every jarring sect,
       They cheat the country first, and then infect.
       They for God's cause their monarchs dare dethrone,
200   And they'll be sure to make his cause their own.

178. Canaanite] zealot, fanatic (*OED* 2, citing Matthew x 4).
179–82. Control of the City of London was being wrested from the Whigs during 1681–2 (see 'Prologue to *The Duke of Guise*' l. *3n*). Some of London's *burghers* had become disenchanted with the Whig cause; its *head* was the Tory Lord Mayor Sir John Moore (elected September 1681), but its two *gouty hands* were the Whig sheriffs Thomas Pilkington and Benjamin Shute (elected June 1681). In *1682 uncorrected state* the present ll. 179–80 follow ll. 181–2.
182. a] *1682 corrected state*; the *1682 uncorrected state*.
187. urge] provoke (*OED* 7a).
188. The plague of 1665 and the fire of 1666.
191. i.e. they cheat their customers ('chapmen': *OED* 4) while using phrases from the gospels.
195. Customs duties were often evaded, and in 1680 the soldiers assisting customs officers in seizing contraband were themselves imprisoned by the Lord Mayor of London (Ogg 422).

Whether the plotting Jesuit laid the plan
Of murthering kings, or the French Puritan,
Our sacrilegious sects their guides outgo,
And kings and kingly power would murther too.
205   What means their trait'rous combination less,
Too plain t' evade, too shameful to confess.
But treason is not owned when 'tis descried:
Successful crimes alone are justified.
The men who no conspiracy would find,
210   Who doubts, but had it taken, they had joined:
Joined in a mutual cov'nant of defence,
At first without, at last against their Prince.
If sovereign right by sovereign power they scan,
The same bold maxim holds in God and man:
215   God were not safe, his thunder could they shun
He should be forced to crown another son.
Thus when the heir was from the vineyard thrown,
The rich possession was the murtherers' own.

201. *Jesuit*] The Spanish Jesuit Juan Mariana (1536–1623) justified tyrannicide
in his *De Rege et Regis Institutione* (1559), and another Spanish Jesuit Francisco
Suarez (1548–1617) in his treatise *Defensio Catholicae Fidei contra Anglicanae
Sectae Errores* (1613) argued that a heretical king, once deposed by decree
from the Pope, could be killed by a private individual; the murder of kings
was popularly regarded as a Jesuit speciality, e.g. in John Oldham's *Satyrs
upon the Jesuits* (1681). The similar regicidal tenets of Jesuits and Protestant
fanatics were often noted, e.g. in the sermons on the anniversary of Charles
I's execution, 30 January 1682, by Henry Maurice (*A Sermon Preached* . . .
(1682) 32) and Edward Pelling (*A Sermon Preached* . . . (1682) 13–14).
202. *French Puritan*] See 'Epistle to the Whigs' ll. 90–1n.
205. *combination*] The Association (see 'Epistle to the Whigs' l. 44n).   *less*]
less than tyrannicide.
207. i.e. traitors do not admit their plans to be treason when they are discovered.
209. *The men*] the jury who rejected the charge of treason against Shaftesbury.
213. i.e. if they define sovereignty by its power rather than its legitimacy.
217–18. In the parable of the wicked husbandmen the owner of a vineyard
sent his son to receive the fruits of it, but the husbandmen said, 'This is the
heir; come, let us kill him, and let us seize on his inheritance. And they caught
him, and cast him out of the vineyard, and slew him' (Matthew xxi 33–41).

In vain to sophistry they have recourse: ⎤
220   By proving theirs no plot they prove 'tis worse— ⎬
      Unmasked rebellion, and audacious force; ⎦
      Which though not actual, yet all eyes may see
      'Tis working in th' immediate power to be:
      For from pretended grievances they rise,
225   First to dislike, and after to despise;
      Then Cyclop-like in human flesh to deal,
      Chop up a minister at every meal;
      Perhaps not wholly to melt down the King,
      But clip his regal rights within the ring;
230   From thence t' assume the power of peace and war,
      And ease him by degrees of public care.
      Yet to consult his dignity and fame ⎤
      He should have leave to exercise the name, ⎬
      And hold the cards while Commons played the game. ⎦
235   For what can power give more than food and drink,
      To live at ease, and not be bound to think?
      These are the cooler methods of their crime,
      But their hot zealots think 'tis loss of time:
      On utmost bounds of loyalty they stand, ⎤
240   And grin and whet like a Croatian band ⎬
      That waits impatient for the last command. ⎦
      Thus outlaws open villainy maintain:
      They steal not, but in squadrons scour the plain,
      And if their power the passengers subdue,
245   The most have right, the wrong is in the few.
      Such impious axioms foolishly they show,
      For in some soils republics will not grow:

220. As in *No Protestant Plot* (see 'Epistle to the Whigs' l. 28*n*).
226-7. The Cyclopes were giants who had no assemblies or laws; one of them cut up and ate two of Odysseus' companions at each meal (*Odyssey* ix 113, 289–344; cp. *Astraea Redux* l. 45*n*). D. refers here to the Commons' attacks on Charles's ministers, e.g. the moves to impeach Clarendon in 1667 and Danby in 1679, recalling also the Act of Attainder against Charles I's minister Strafford, who was executed in 1641.
229. Coins which were clipped within the ring or circle surrounding the King's head were not legal tender.
230. Only the King could declare war and make peace treaties.
243. *scour*] move across, looking for enemies.
244. *passengers*] travellers, passers-by.

Our temperate isle will no extremes sustain
Of pop'lar sway or arbitrary reign,
250 But slides between them both into the best,
Secure in freedom, in a monarch blessed:
And though the climate, vexed with various winds,
Works through our yielding bodies on our minds,
The wholesome tempest purges what it breeds
255 To recommend the calmness that succeeds.
   But thou, the pander of the people's hearts
(O crookèd soul, and serpentine in arts),
Whose blandishments a loyal land have whored,
And broke the bonds she plighted to her lord,
260 What curses on thy blasted name will fall,
Which age to age their legacy shall call;
For all must curse the woes that must descend on all.
Religion thou hast none: thy mercury
Has passed through every sect, or theirs through thee;

252–5. Cp. Halifax: 'Our Government is like our climate. There are winds which are sometimes loud and unquiet, and yet with all the trouble they give us, we owe great part of our health unto them; they clear the air, which else would be like a standing pool, and instead of refreshment would be a disease unto us. There may be fresh gales of asserting liberty, without turning into such storms or hurricanes, as that the state should run any hazard of being cast away by them. These strugglings, which are natural to all mixed governments, while they are kept from growing into convulsions do by a mutual agitation from the several parts rather support and strengthen than weaken or maim the constitution; and the whole frame, instead of being torn or dis-jointed, cometh to be the better and closer knit by being thus exercised.' ('The Character of a Trimmer' (in MS, 1684–5) in *Complete Works*, edited by J. P. Kenyon (1969) 63; cp. Burton, *Anatomy of Melancholy* I ii 2.5; II ii 3; Kinsley).

263. This was a common charge against Shaftesbury: cp. 'There is no body swears against my L. *Shaftesbury* . . . for being a Protestant, or being pub-lickly engaged against *Popery*; I never heard that he was accused for being of any Religion' (*Heraclitus Ridens* xxxvii (11 October 1681); Kinsley); and 'Being a Gentleman of no Religion himself, he seems for all that, to Espouse every Devision, and Sub-division of it; every Faction, and Person, who are bold enough, to stand stiff in opposition to the *Ancient* and *Well Setled Government*' (*The Character of a Disbanded Courtier* (1682) 3; *Works*). In his later years, Shaftesbury inclined to Deism (Haley 67, 732).   *mercury*] This is the OED's first example of the metal being used figuratively for liveliness, vola-tility and inconstancy (*OED* 9). Mercury was used in the treatment of syph-ilis (cp. l. 266). W. O. S. Sutherland 128 notes a pun on mercury meaning

265   But what thou giv'st, that venom still remains,
      And the poxed nation feels thee in their brains.
      What else inspires the tongues and swells the breasts
      Of all thy bellowing renegado priests,
      That preach up thee for God, dispense thy laws,
270   And with thy stum ferment their fainting cause,
      Fresh fumes of madness raise, and toil and sweat
      To make the formidable cripple great?
      Yet should thy crimes succeed, should lawless power
      Compass those ends thy greedy hopes devour,
275   Thy canting friends thy mortal foes would be:
      Thy God and theirs will never long agree.
      For thine (if thou hast any) must be one
      That lets the world and humankind alone;
      A jolly God that passes hours too well
280   To promise heaven, or threaten us with hell,
      That unconcerned can at rebellion sit,
      And wink at crimes he did himself commit.
      A tyrant theirs; the heaven their priesthood paints
      A convent'cle of gloomy sullen saints,

---

newspaper (as in the Whig papers *The True Protestant Mercury* and *The Impartial Protestant Mercury*), citing the pun in *Heraclitus Ridens* (no. iii; 15 February 1681): 'whether taking so much *Mercury* so ill prepared by the Quacks of *Goatham*-Colledg, is not the reason why so many People are troubled with Ulcers in their Mouths, and a continual Salivation of Sedition'.

268. renegado priests] Nonconformist ministers, formerly Anglican clergy, who could not accept the Act of Uniformity (1662) or the Test Act (1673) (Schless).

270. stum] must used for renewing vapid wine (*OED* 1b).

271–2. Cp. 'Lucretius: Against the Fear of Death' ll. 204–5.

272. cripple] For other denigrations of Shaftesbury's physical form see *AA* ll. 156–8n.

278–82. A caricature of the Epicurean notion of the gods as explained by Lucretius: *omnis enim per se divom natura necessest / immortali aevo summa cum pace fruatur / semota ab nostris rebus seiunctaque longe; / nam privata dolore omni, privata periclis, / ipsa suis pollens opibus, nil indiga nostri, / nec bene promeritis capitur neque tangitur ira.* (*De Rerum Natura* i 44–9: 'For whatsoere's *Divine* must live in Peace, / In undisturb'd and everlasting ease: / Not care for us, from fears and dangers free, / Sufficient to its own felicity: / Nought here below, Nought in our power it needs; / Nere smiles at good, nere frowns at wicked deeds', tr. Creech (1682)).

282. Zeus rebelled against and deposed his father Chronos (Pierre Legouis, *TLS* (15 July 1965) 602).

285 A heaven, like Bedlam, slovenly and sad,
    Foredoomed for souls with false religion mad.
        Without a vision poets can foreshow
    What all but fools by common sense may know:
    If true succession from our isle should fail,
290 And crowds profane with impious arms prevail,
    Not thou, nor those thy factious arts engage ⎤
    Shall reap that harvest of rebellious rage   ⎟
    With which thou flatt'rest thy decrepit age. ⎦
        The swelling poison of the several sects
295 Which, wanting vent, the nation's health infects,
    Shall burst its bag, and fighting out their way
    The various venoms on each other prey.
        The presbyter, puffed up with spiritual pride,
    Shall on the necks of the lewd nobles ride,
300 His brethren damn, the civil power defy,
    And parcel out republic prelacy.
        But short shall be his reign: his rigid yoke
    And tyrant power will puny sects provoke,
    And frogs and toads and all the tadpole train
305 Will croak to heaven for help from this devouring
        crane.

286. Foredoomed] according to the Calvinist doctrine that the godly elect are predestined to eternal salvation.
293. decrepit age] Shaftesbury was sixty and in poor health.
297. Cp. *AA* ll. 1012–15.
298. presbyter] Puritan ministers preferred this Greek NT term (meaning 'elder') to 'priest'.
299. lewd nobles] e.g. the Duke of Buckingham (*AA* ll. 544–68*n*), the Earl of Huntingdon (*AA* l. 574*n*), Lord Howard of Escrick (*AA* ll. 575–6*n*).
301. republic prelacy] quasi-republican government of the church by presbyters instead of hierarchical government by bishops.
303. puny] later, i.e. newly emerging (*OED* 2); small, feeble (*OED* 4).
304–5. In Aesop's fable the frogs ask Jove for a king, and he gives them a log; dissatisfied, they ask for an active leader, and he sends a stork, which devours them. They ask Jove to remove 'This cruel Prince that made his Will a Law', but Jove refuses. The moral is that 'No Government can th' unsetled Vulgar please, / Whom Change delights, think Quiet a disease. / Now Anarchy and Armies they maintain, / And wearied, are for King and Lords again' (*The Fables of Æsop*, tr. John Ogilby, second edition (1668) 32). Settle also uses this story (*The Character of a Popish Successour* (1681) 16; W. O. S. Sutherland), as do other writers against royal power (see *POAS* i 189, 251, 281, ii 343).

The cut-throat sword and clamorous gown shall jar
In sharing their ill-gotten spoils of war:
Chiefs shall be grudged the part which they pretend, ⎤
Lords envy lords, and friends with every friend   ⎬
310 About their impious merit shall contend.   ⎦
The surly Commons shall respect deny,
And jostle peerage out with property.
Their general either shall his trust betray
And force the crowd to arbitrary sway,
315 Or they suspecting his ambitious aim   ⎤
In hate of kings shall cast anew the frame,   ⎬
And thrust out Collatine that bore their name. ⎦
　　Thus inborn broils the factions would engage,   ⎤
Or wars of exiled heirs, or foreign rage,   ⎬
320 Till halting vengeance overtook our age,   ⎦
And our wild labours, wearied into rest,
Reclined us on a rightful monarch's breast.
　　　　　　　—*Pudet haec opprobria, vobis*
Et dici potuisse, et non potuisse refelli.

---

308. pretend] claim (*OED* 4b).

311. surly] haughty, arrogant (*OED* 2).

317. Lucius Tarquinius Collatinus took part in the expulsion from Rome of
the King Tarquinius Superbus, and was elected consul. Later when a law was
passed banishing the entire Tarquin family, he too went into exile (Livy i 50,
ii 2). D. suggests that a similar fate awaits the Duke of Monmouth should he
become King. Kinsley notes that D. makes the same point in *His Majesties
Declaration Defended* (1681; *Works* xvii 212).

320. halting] limping.

323–4. Added in *1682 corrected state*. From Ovid, *Met.* i 758–9: 'It is shameful
that this opprobrium could be said of you, and that it could not be answered'
(D. changes *nobis* ('us') to *vobis* ('you')).

70 Prologue to His Royal Highness

Date and publication. James arrived in London from Scotland on 8 April 1682; on 20 April he was given a dinner in the City, and on 21 April attended a performance of *Venice Preserv'd* at the Duke's Theatre. The specially written Prologue by D. and Epilogue by Otway were immediately printed, and on 27 April were advertised in *The Observator* as 'recommended *to All Men of Sense and Loyalty*'. Otway's play (first staged in February) has reflections on the Plot and on Shaftesbury, which made it a natural choice, and Otway's Epilogue is strongly partisan (Danchin no. 322). A single folio half-sheet headed *Prologue To His Royal Highness, Upon His first appearance at the Duke's Theatre since his Return from Scotland* was published by Tonson in 1682 (MS date 20 April on Ashley copy (BL), 21 April on Luttrell's (Huntington)); there were two issues.

Prologue to His Royal Highness

Upon his first appearance at the Duke's Theatre
since his return from Scotland

Spoken by Mr Smith

In those cold regions which no summers cheer,
When brooding darkness covers half the year,
To hollow caves the shivering natives go,
Bears range abroad, and hunt in tracks of snow:
5 But when the tedious twilight wears away,
And stars grow paler at th' approach of day,
The longing crowds to frozen mountains run,
Happy who first can see the glimmering sun!
The surly salvage offspring disappear,
10 And curse the bright successor of the year.

¶70. *Title. Mr Smith*] William Smith (d. 1695), one of the most successful speakers of prologues, and a strong adherent of James. A member of the Duke's Company, he became co-manager of the United Company in 1682. His roles included Sir John Swallow in *Sir Martin Mar-all*, Hector in *Troilus and Cressida*, Lorenzo in *The Spanish Friar* and Crillon in *The Duke of Guise*.

Yet, though rough bears in covert seek defence, ⎫
White foxes stay, with seeming innocence: ⎬
That crafty kind with daylight can dispense.   ⎭
Still we are thronged so full with Reynard's race
15 That loyal subjects scarce can find a place:
Thus modest truth is cast behind the crowd,
Truth speaks too low, hypocrisy too loud.
Let 'em be first to flatter in success,
Duty can stay, but guilt has need to press.
20 Once when true zeal the sons of God did call
To make their solemn show at heaven's Whitehall,
The fawning devil appeared among the rest,
And made as good a courtier as the best.
The friends of Job who railed at him before
25 Came cap in hand when he had three times more.
Yet late repentance may, perhaps, be true;
Kings can forgive if rebels can but sue.
A tyrant's power in rigour is expressed,
The father yearns in the true Prince's breast.
30 We grant an o'ergrown Whig no grace can mend,
But most are babes that know not they offend.
The crowd, to restless motion still inclined,
Are clouds that rack according to the wind.
Driven by their chiefs they storms of hailstones pour,
35 Then mourn, and soften to a silent shower.
O welcome to this much offending land
The Prince that brings forgiveness in his hand!
Thus angels on glad messages appear,
Their first salute commands us not to fear.
40 Thus heaven, that could constrain us to obey ⎫
(With rev'rence if we might presume to say),   ⎬
Seems to relax the rights of sovereign sway: ⎭
Permits to man the choice of good and ill,
And makes us happy by our own freewill.

11–15. Echoing the beast fables which had become a medium of Exclusion Crisis propaganda, such as *The Badger in the Fox Trap* (1681) (see Paul Hammond, *N & Q* ccxxvii (1982) 55–7).

20–5. Job i and xlii.

33. rack] drive.

34–5. For the rhyme cp. *Threnodia Augustalis* ll. 294, 297.

39. Luke i 30 and ii 10.

71 Prologue to the Duchess

Date and publication. When James returned to London in April 1682 (see previous poem) his Duchess, who was pregnant, remained in Edinburgh. In May he returned to Scotland to escort her to London; they arrived on 27 May, and 'at night were ringing of bells, and bonefires in severall places, and other publick expressions of joy' (Luttrell i 189). On 31 May there was another special performance of *Venice Preserv'd* at the Duke's Theatre (date noted on Luttrell's copy of D.'s Prologue) for which D. again wrote a Prologue and Otway an Epilogue (Danchin no. 325). The Newdigate news-letters, however, report that the play was D'Urfey's *The Royalist* (LS 309). Lee similarly wrote a prologue for a performance at the King's Theatre (Danchin no. 324); for other poems see *POAS* iii 387–91. *Prologue to The Dutchess, On Her Return from Scotland* was published as a single folio half-sheet by Tonson in 1682 (MS date 1 June on Luttrell's copy (Huntington)). It was reprinted without changes in *EP*. The present text follows the first edition.

Prologue to the Duchess
On her return from Scotland

When factious rage to cruel exile drove
The Queen of beauty and the court of love,
The Muses drooped with their forsaken arts,
And the sad Cupids broke their useless darts.
5 Our fruitful plains to wilds and deserts turned,
Like Eden's face when banished man it mourned.
Love was no more when loyalty was gone,
The great supporter of his awful throne.
Love could no longer after beauty stay,
10 But wandered northward to the verge of day
As if the sun and he had lost their way.

¶**71.** *1–2.* D. praised the Duchess's beauty in his Dedication of *The State of Innocence* (1677): 'You render Mankind insensible to other Beauties: and have destroy'd the Empire of Love in a Court which was the seat of his Dominion. You have subverted (may I dare to accuse you of it) even our Fundamental Laws; and Reign absolute over the hearts of a stubborn and Free-born people tenacious almost to madness of their Liberty' (sig. A2ᵛ). See further Winn, *When Beauty* 413–18 for D.'s relations with the Duchess.
8, 35. awful] inspiring awe.

But now th' illustrious nymph returned again
Brings every grace triumphant in her train:
The wondering Nereids, though they raised no storm,
15   Foreslowed her passage to behold her form:
Some cried a Venus, some a Thetis passed,
But this was not so fair, nor that so chaste.
Far from her sight flew Faction, Strife and Pride,
And Envy did but look on her, and died.
20   Whate'er we suffered from our sullen fate,
Her sight is purchased at an easy rate:
Three gloomy years against this day were set,
But this one mighty sum has cleared the debt.
Like Joseph's dream, but with a better doom,
25   The famine past, the plenty still to come.
For her the weeping heavens become serene,
For her the ground is clad in cheerful green,
For her the nightingales are taught to sing,
And nature has for her delayed the spring.
30   The Muse resumes her long-forgotten lays,   ⎤
And Love, restored, his ancient realm surveys, ⎬
Recalls our beauties, and revives our plays;   ⎦
His waste dominions peoples once again,
And from her presence dates his second reign.
35   But awful charms on her fair forehead sit,
Dispensing what she never will admit;
Pleasing, yet cold, like Cynthia's silver beam,
The people's wonder and the poet's theme.
Distempered Zeal, Sedition, cankered Hate
40   No more shall vex the church and tear the state;

---

14. Nereids] Greek sea-nymphs.
15. Foreslowed] delayed.
16. Thetis] a Nereid, mother of Achilles.
22. Three gloomy years] Since James's departure for the Netherlands in March 1679 at the height of the Popish Plot.
24–5. In Genesis xli Joseph interprets Pharaoh's dream as foretelling seven years of plenty followed by seven of famine.   *doom*] destiny (*OED* 4).
26–9. Cp. Lucretius i 1–20 and D.'s translation, 'Lucretius: The Beginning of the First Book'.
37. Cynthia] the moon.
38. Cp. *AA* l. 238.

No more shall Faction civil discords move,
Or only discords of too tender love:
Discord like that of music's various parts,
Discord that makes the harmony of hearts,
45 Discord that only this dispute shall bring—
Who best shall love the Duke, and serve the King.

72 The Second Part of Absalom and Achitophel

Date and publication. Probably composed April–May 1682 (D.'s lines respond to attacks on *The Medal*). Howard H. Schless (*POAS* iii 278–9) notes that except for the last ten lines the poem refers solely to events which occurred before the end of May 1682, and 'seems to culminate in the panegyric to the Duke and Duchess of York upon their return to London on 7 May'. He suggests that the publication of *2AA* was delayed pending the outcome of the shrieval elections in July, referred to in ll. 1131–40. Winn 370–1 observes that *The Duke of Guise* was banned in the summer of 1682 in order not to provoke Monmouth, but was cleared for performance in November when the political climate had changed and the court party was confident of its strength. *The Second Part of Absalom and Achitophel. A Poem* was published by Tonson in November 1682 (Luttrell's copy (Huntington) dated 10 November): siglum '*1682a*'. Some press corrections were made, and the poem was reprinted with some verbal revisions in 1682 ('*1682b*'); reprinted Dublin 1682. The present text is based on *1682a* incorporating the revisions from *1682b*.

Authorship. In *The Second Part of Miscellany Poems* (1716) sig. B1ʳ⁻ᵛ Tonson said that after the success of *AA* 'several Persons pressing him to write a Second Part, he, upon declining it himself, spoke to Mr. Tate to write one, and gave him his Advice in the Direction of it; and that Part beginning [l. 310] . . . and ending [l. 509] . . . were intirely Mr. Dryden's Compositions, besides some Touches in other places.' Scott detected D.'s hand in the passages on Corah (ll. 69–102), the Green Ribbon Club (ll. 522–33) and Arod (ll. 534–55) but this is purely subjective. Schless 279–80 notes that the whole of *2AA* is 'impregnated with phrases found elsewhere in D.', both in *AA* and other works, and conjectures that some passages may be discarded from *AA*. But the former point does not affect the question of authorship, merely confirming Tate's dependence on D., while there is no evidence for the latter speculation. The bulk of the poem is unquestionably by Tate, and accordingly only D.'s known contribution is fully annotated here (for ampler notes to Tate's part see *POAS* iii 281–338). Nahum Tate (1652–1715) had contributed commendatory verses to *AA* and *The Medal*; in 1679 D. had written a Prologue to Tate's *The Loyal General*, and Tate had also contributed to *Ovid's Epistles* (1680).

The Second Part of Absalom and Achitophel
A Poem

—Si quis tamen haec quoque, si quis
Captus amore leget—

Since men like beasts each other's prey were made,
Since trade began, and priesthood grew a trade,
Since realms were formed, none sure so cursed as
    those
That madly their own happiness oppose;
5   There heaven itself and godlike kings in vain
Shower down the manna of a gentle reign,
While pampered crowds to mad sedition run,
And monarchs by indulgence are undone.
Thus David's clemency was fatal grown,
10 While wealthy faction awed the wanting throne.
For now their sov'reign's orders to contemn
Was held the charter of Jerusalem;
His rights t' invade, his tributes to refuse
A privilege peculiar to the Jews,
15 As if from heavenly call this licence fell,
And Jacob's seed were chosen to rebel!
    Achitophel with triumph sees his crimes
Thus suited to the madness of the times;
And Absalom, to make his hopes succeed,
20 Of flattering charms no longer stands in need;
While fond of change, though ne'er so dearly bought,
Our tribes outstrip the youth's ambitious thought;
His swiftest hopes with swifter homage meet,
And crowd their servile necks beneath his feet.
25 Thus to his aid while pressing tides repair,
He mounts and spreads his streamers in the air.
The charms of empire might his youth mislead,
But what can our besotted Israel plead?

¶72. *Epigraph.* 'However if there is anyone to read these also, anyone who has been won by love of the theme' (Virgil, *Ecl.* vi 9–10).
9. *clemency was*] *1682b*; Goodness was e'en *1682a*.
20. *flattering*] *1682b*; Flatterie's *1682a*.

Swayed by a monarch whose serene command
30   Seems half the blessing of our promised land,
Whose only grievance is excess of ease,
Freedom our pain, and plenty our disease!
Yet, as all folly would lay claim to sense,
And wickedness ne'er wanted a pretence,
35   With arguments they'd make their treason good,
And righteous David's self with slanders load:
That arts of foreign sway he did affect,
And guilty Jebusites from law protect,
Whose very chiefs, convict, were never freed;
40   Nay, we have seen their sacrificers bleed!
Accusers' infamy is urged in vain,
While in the bounds of sense they did contain,
But soon they launched into th' unfathomed tide,
And in the depths they knew disdained to ride;
45   For probable discoveries to dispense
Was thought below a pensioned evidence;
Mere truth was dull, nor suited with the port
Of pampered Corah, when advanced to court.
No less than wonders now they will impose,
50   And projects void of grace or sense disclose.
Such was the charge on pious Michal brought,
Michal that ne'er was cruel e'en in thought,
The best of queens, and most obedient wife,
Impeached of cursed designs on David's life!
55   His life, the theme of her eternal prayer,
'Tis scarce so much his guardian angel's care.
Not summer morns such mildness can disclose,
The Hermon lily nor the Sharon rose.
Neglecting each vain pomp of majesty,
60   Transported Michal feeds her thoughts on high.
She lives with angels, and as angels do
Quits heaven sometimes to bless the world below,
Where cherished by her bounty's plenteous spring
Reviving widows smile, and orphans sing.

33. as] 1682b; since 1682a.
48. Corah] Titus Oates (see AA ll. 632–77n).
51. Michal] Queen Catherine (see AA ll. 11n, 672–3n).
58. Hermon] a mountain in Palestine.   Sharon rose] from The Song of
Solomon ii 1.

65 O! when rebellious Israel's crimes at height
  Are threatened with her Lord's approaching fate,
  The piety of Michal then remain
  In heaven's remembrance, and prolong his reign.
  Less desolation did the pest pursue
70 That from Dan's limits to Beersheba slew;
  Less fatal the repeated wars of Tyre,
  And less Jerusalem's avenging fire.
  With gentler terror these our state o'erran
  Than since our evidencing days began!
75 On every cheek a pale confusion sat,
  Continued fear beyond the worst of fate!
  Trust was no more, art, science useless made,
  All occupations lost but Corah's trade.
  Meanwhile a guard on modest Corah wait,
80 If not for safety, needful yet for state.
  Well might he deem each peer and prince his slave,
  And lord it o'er the tribes which he could save:
  E'en vice in him was virtue—what sad fate
  But for his honesty had seized our state?
85 And with what tyranny had we been cursed
  Had Corah never proved a villain first?
  T' have told his knowledge of th' intrigue in gross
  Had been alas to our deponent's loss:
  The travelled Levite had th' experience got
90 To husband well and make the best of 's plot;
  And therefore like an evidence of skill
  With wise reserves secured his pension still;
  Nor quite of future power himself bereft,
  But limbos large for unbelievers left.
95 And now his writ such reverence had got
  'Twas worse than plotting to suspect his plot.
  Some were so well convinced they made no doubt
  Themselves to help the foundered swearers out;

---

66. *fate*] death (OED 4b).
69–70. See 2 Samuel xxiv 15; alluding to the plague of 1665.
71. Nebuchadnezzar besieged Tyre for thirteen years (*Works*); alluding to the Dutch wars (1665–7, 1672–4).
72. Nebuchadnezzar destroyed Jerusalem in 586 BC (*Works*); alluding to the Fire of London (1666).
95. *And*] 1682b; For 1682a.

Some had their sense imposed on by their fear,
100   But more for int'rest sake believe and swear.
E'en to that height with some the frenzy grew,
They raged to find their danger not prove true.
    Yet than all these a viler crew remain,
Who with Achitophel the cry maintain;
105   Not urged by fear, nor through misguided sense,
(Blind zeal and starving need had some pretence)
But for the Good Old Cause that did excite
Th' original rebels' wiles, revenge and spite;
These raise the plot to have the scandal thrown
110   Upon the bright successor of the crown,
Whose virtue with such wrongs they had pursued
As seemed all hope of pardon to exclude.
Thus while on private ends their zeal is built
The cheated crowd applaud and share their guilt.
115   Such practices as these, too gross to lie
Long unobserved by each discerning eye,
The more judicious Israelites unspelled,
Though still the charm the giddy rabble held.
Ev'n Absalom amidst the dazzling beams
120   Of empire, and ambition's flattering dreams,
Perceives the plot (too foul to be excused)
To aid designs no less pernicious used;
And, filial sense yet striving in his breast,
Thus to Achitophel his doubts expressed:
125   'Why are my thoughts upon a crown employed,
Which once obtained, can be but half enjoyed?
Not so when virtue did my arms require,
And to my father's wars I flew entire.
My regal power how will my foes resent,
130   When I myself have scarce my own consent?
Give me a son's unblemished truth again,
Or quench the sparks of duty that remain.
How slight to force a throne that legions guard
The task to me; to prove unjust, how hard!

117. *unspelled*] freed from a spell (*OED* 2).
121–2. i.e. 'perceives that the Popish Plot is being used to promote designs
that are equally pernicious'.
133–4. i.e. 'how slight a task it is for me to seize the throne by force; how
hard a task to prove Charles an unjust king.'

135 And if th' imagined guilt thus wound my thought,
    What will it when the tragic scene is wrought?
    Dire war must first be conjured from below:
    The realm we'd rule we first must overthrow.
    And when the civil furies are on wing
140 That blind and undistinguished slaughters fling,
    Who knows what impious chance may reach the
       King?
    O rather let me perish in the strife
    Than have my crown the price of David's life!
    Or if the tempest of the war he stand,
145 In peace some vile officious villain's hand
    His soul's anointed temple may invade;
    Or, pressed by clamorous crowds, myself be made
    His murtherer—rebellious crowds, whose guilt
    Shall dread his vengeance till his blood be spilt:
150 Which if my filial tenderness oppose,
    Since to the empire by their arms I rose,
    Those very arms on me shall be employed,
    A new usurper crowned, and I destroyed.
    The same pretence of public good will hold,
155 And new Achitophels be found, as bold
    To urge the needful change—perhaps the old.'
    He said. The statesman with a smile replies
    (A smile that did his rising spleen disguise):
    'My thoughts presumed our labours at an end,
160 And are we still with conscience to contend?
    Whose want in kings as needful is allowed
    As 'tis for them to find it in the crowd.
    Far in the doubtful passage you are gone,
    And only can be safe by pressing on.
165 The crown's true heir, a Prince severe and wise,
    Has viewed your motions long with jealous eyes,
    Your person's charms, your more prevailing arts,
    And marked your progress in the people's hearts;
    Whose patience is th' effect of stinted power,
170 But treasures vengeance for the fatal hour;

142. O] Oh *1682b;* Or *1682a.*
152–6. See *The Medal* l. 317*n.*
165–70. Cp. *AA* ll. 441–6.

And if remote the peril he can bring,
Your present danger's greater from the King.
Let not a parent's name deceive your sense,
Nor trust the father in a jealous Prince!
175 Your trivial faults if he could so resent
To doom you little less than banishment,
What rage must your presumption since inspire,
Against his orders your return from Tyre?
Nor only so, but with a pomp more high
180 And open court of popularity,
The factious tribes'—'And this reproof from thee?',
The Prince replies, 'O statesman's winding skill,
They first condemn that first advised the ill!'
'Illustrious youth', returned Achitophel,
185 'Misconstrue not the words that mean you well.
The course you steer I worthy blame conclude,
But 'tis because you leave it unpursued.
A monarch's crown with fate surrounded lies,
Who reach lay hold on death that miss the prize.
190 Did you for this expose yourself to show,
And to the crowd bow popularly low?
For this your glorious progress next ordain,
With chariots, horsemen, and a numerous train,
With fame before you like the morning star,
195 And shouts of joy saluting from afar?
O from the heights you've reached but take a view,
Scarce leading Lucifer could fall like you!
And must I here my shipwracked arts bemoan?
Have I for this so oft made Israel groan,
200 Your single int'rest with the nation weighed,
And turned the scale where your desires were laid?
Ev'n when at helm a course so dang'rous moved
To land your hopes, as my removal proved.'
'I not dispute', the royal youth replies,
205 'The known perfection of your policies,
Nor in Achitophel yet grudge or blame
The privilege that statesmen ever claim,

178. Tyre] Holland; Monmouth returned from a brief exile there in November
1679.
190–5. See *AA* ll. 729–38*n.*

Who private int'rest never yet pursued,
But still pretended 'twas for others' good.
210 What politician yet e'er scaped his fate,
Who saving his own neck not saved the state?
From hence on every hum'rous wind that veered
With shifted sails a several course you steered.
What form of sway did David e'er pursue
215 That seemed like absolute, but sprung from you?
Who at your instance quashed each penal law
That kept dissenting factious Jews in awe;
And who suspends fixed laws may abrogate;
That done, form new, and so enslave the state.
220 Ev'n property, whose champion now you stand,
And seem for this the idol of the land,
Did ne'er sustain such violence before
As when your counsel shut the royal store:
Advice that ruin to whole tribes procured,
225 But secret kept till your own bank's secured.
Recount with this the triple cov'nant broke,
And Israel fitted for a foreign yoke.
Nor here your counsel's fatal progress stayed,
But sent our levied powers to Pharaoh's aid.
230 Hence Tyre and Israel low in ruins laid,
And Egypt, once their scorn, their common terror
    made.
Ev'n yet of such a season we can dream
When royal rights you made your darling theme,
For power unlimited could reasons draw,
235 And place prerogative above the law;
Which on your fall from office grew unjust,
The laws made king, the King a slave in trust,
Whom with statecraft, to int'rest only true,
You now accuse of ills contrived by you.'

216–17, 232–6. See *The Medal* ll. 77–80n.
223–5. In January 1672 the Exchequer stopped repayment of the government's debts to City banks. Though proposed by Clifford and opposed by Shaftesbury, the latter was blamed for it. There is apparently no evidence for the charge that Shaftesbury withdrew his money from the bankers in advance of the Stop (Haley 294–6).
226–31. See *AA* l. 175n.
229. *Pharaoh*] Louis XIV.
237. See *AA* ll. 765–76n.

240   To this hell's agent: 'Royal youth fix here;
         Let int'rest be the star by which I steer.
         Hence to repose your trust in me was wise,
         Whose int'rest most in your advancement lies;
         A tie so firm as always will avail
245   When friendship, nature and religion fail.
         On ours the safety of the crowd depends:
         Secure the crowd and we obtain our ends,
         Whom I will cause so far our guilt to share
         Till they are made our champions by their fear.
250   What opposition can your rival bring
         While Sanhedrins are jealous of the King?
         His strength as yet in David's friendship lies,
         And what can David's self without supplies?
         Who with exclusive bills must now dispense,
255   Debar the heir, or starve in his defence:
         Conditions which our elders ne'er will quit,
         And David's justice never can admit.
         Or forced by wants his brother to betray,
         To your ambition next he clears the way;
260   For if succession once to nought they bring,
         Their next advance removes the present King:
         Persisting else his senates to dissolve,
         In equal hazard shall his reign involve.
         Our tribes, whom Pharaoh's power so much alarms,
265   Shall rise without their Prince t' oppose his arms;
         Nor boots it on what cause at first they join,
         Their troops once up are tools for our design.
         At least such subtle covenants shall be made
         Till peace itself is war in masquerade.
270   Associations of mysterious sense
         Against, but seeming for, the King's defence,
         Ev'n on their courts of justice fetters draw,
         And from our agents muzzle up their law.
         By which, a conquest if we fail to make,
275   'Tis a drawn game at worst, and we secure our stake.'
             He said; and for the dire success depends
             On various sects, by common guilt made friends,

269. Cp. *AA* l. 752.
270–1. See *The Medal*, 'Epistle' l. *120n.*

Whose heads, though ne'er so diff'ring in their creed,
I' th' point of treason yet were well agreed.
280 'Mongst these, extorting Ishban first appears,
Pursued b' a meagre troop of bankrupt heirs.
Blessed times, when Ishban, he whose occupation
So long has been to cheat, reforms the nation!
Ishban of conscience suited to his trade,
285 As good a saint as usurer e'er made.
Yet Mammon has not so engrossed him quite
But Belial lays as large a claim of spite;
Who for those pardons from his Prince he draws
Returns reproaches, and cries up the cause.
290 That year in which the city he did sway
He left rebellion in a hopeful way.
Yet his ambition once was found so bold
To offer talents of extorted gold,
Could David's wants have so been bribed to shame
295 And scandalise our peerage with his name;
For which his dear sedition he'd forswear,
And e'en turn loyal to be made a peer.
Next him let railing Rabsheka have place,
So full of zeal he has no need of grace;
300 A saint that can both flesh and spirit use,
Alike haunt conventicles and the stews;
Of whom the question difficult appears,
If most i' th' preacher's or the bawd's arrears.
What caution could appear too much in him
305 That keeps the treasure of Jerusalem!
Let David's brother but approach the town,
'Double our guards', he cries, 'we are undone.'

280–97. *Ishban*] Sir Robert Clayton (1629–1707), wealthy London merchant
and Whig Lord Mayor 1679–80; there seems to be no biblical counterpart.
298–309. *Rabsheka*] Sir Thomas Player (d. 1686), Chamberlain of the City,
and a patron of its brothels. On 13 September 1679 he asked for the guard to
be doubled as a protection against the Duke of York and the papists (see
'Prologue to *The Loyal General*' l. 5n); in October 1678, in the first weeks of
the Popish Plot, Player justified placing chains across London's streets by
saying 'He did not know but the next morning they might all rise with their
throats cut' (J. P. Kenyon, *The Popish Plot* (1972, 1974) 92). The biblical
Rabshakeh incited the people to revolt against King Hezekiah (2 Kings xviii
17–37).

Protesting that he dares not sleep in's bed
'Lest he should rise next morn without his head.'
310   Next these a troop of busy spirits press,
Of little fortunes, and of conscience less;
With them the tribe whose luxury had drained
Their banks, in former sequestrations gained;
Who rich and great by past rebellions grew,
315   And long to fish the troubled streams anew.
Some future hopes, some present payment draws,
To sell their conscience and espouse the cause;
Such stipends those vile hirelings best befit,
Priests without grace, and poets without wit.
320   Shall that false Hebronite escape our curse,
Judas that keeps the rebels' pension-purse;
Judas that pays the treason-writer's fee,
Judas that well deserves his namesake's tree;
Who at Jerusalem's own gates erects
325   His college for a nursery of sects;
Young prophets with an early care secures,
And with the dung of his own arts manures.
What have the men of Hebron here to do?
What part in Israel's promised land have you?
330   Here Phaleg the lay Hebronite is come,
'Cause like the rest he could not live at home;

310–509. This is the section attributed to D. by Tonson.

313. sequestrations] i.e. of royalists' estates after the Civil War.

315. streams] *1682b*; Waves *1682a*.

320. Hebronite] Scot.

321–7. Judas] Robert Ferguson (d. 1714), major Whig controversialist and plotter. He taught at Islington, and became prominent as a spokesman for the dissenters in the debate with Samuel Parker in the 1670s. During the Exclusion Crisis he was in Shaftesbury's inner circle, fled with him to Holland and received £40 in his will. Ferguson was the author of *No Protestant Plot* (1681–2; see *The Medal*, 'Epistle' l. 28*n*). According to Burnet (ii 358) he 'had the management of a secret press, and of a purse that maintained it'. See Ashcraft *passim*.

330–49. Phaleg] James Forbes, according to the 1716 key. Scott identified him as the travelling companion to the Earl of Derby, who was roughly used by the Earl and returned home. There seems to be no evidence as to his politics or his lechery (on the complications see Schless 297). The biblical Peleg was so named because 'in his days the earth was divided' (Genesis x 25).

Who from his own possessions could not drain
An omer ev'n of Hebronitish grain;
Here struts it like a patriot, and talks high
335 Of injured subjects, altered property;
An emblem of that buzzing insect just
That mounts the wheel and thinks she raises dust.
Can dry bones live? or skeletons produce
The vital warmth of cuckoldizing juice?
340 Slim Phaleg could, and at the table fed
Returned the grateful product to the bed.
A waiting man to trav'lling nobles chose,
He his own laws would saucily impose,
Till bastinadoed back again he went
345 To learn those manners he to teach was sent.
Chastised he ought to have retreated home,
But he reads politics to Absalom:
For never Hebronite, though kicked and scorned,
To his own country willingly returned.
350 But leaving famished Phaleg to be fed
And to talk treason for his daily bread,
Let Hebron, nay let hell produce a man
So made for mischief as Ben-Jochanan.
A Jew of humble parentage was he,
355 By trade a Levite, though of low degree:
His pride no higher than the desk aspired,
But for the drudgery of priests was hired
To read and pray in linen ephod brave,
And pick up single shekels from the grave.
360 Married at last, and finding charge come faster,
He could not live by God, but changed his master;

333. *omer*] Hebrew measure of capacity, 5·1 pints.
334. *patriot*] See *AA* l. 179*n*.
335. *property*] See *AA* l. 536*n*.
336–7. As in La Fontaine, *Fables* vii 9 (Kinsley).
338–9. See Ezekiel xxxvii 1–10.
353–99. *Ben-Jochanan*] Revd Samuel Johnson (1649–1703), chaplain to the Whig leader Lord Russell, and author of *Julian the Apostate* (1682), which argues that the early Christians did not try to exclude Julian from succeeding to the throne because they were unaware of his apostasy until he became Emperor; subsequently they were hostile to him, and prayed for his death. The work is implicitly an argument for Exclusion. The name *Ben-Jochanan* is probably a quasi-Hebrew version of 'Johnson' (Noyes).

Inspired by want was made a factious tool,
They got a villain and we lost a fool.
Still violent, whatever cause he took,
365   But most against the party he forsook;
For renegadoes, who ne'er turn by halves,
Are bound in conscience to be double knaves.
So this prose-prophet took most monstrous pains
To let his masters see he earned his gains.
370   But as the dev'l owes all his imps a shame,
He chose th' apostate for his proper theme;
With little pains he made the picture true,
And from reflection took the rogue he drew.
A wondrous work to prove the Jewish nation
375   In every age a murmuring generation;
To trace 'em from their infancy of sinning,
And show 'em factious from their first beginning;
To prove they could rebel, and rail and mock,
Much to the credit of the chosen flock;
380   A strong authority, which must convince
That saints own no allegiance to their Prince:
As 'tis a leading-card to make a whore,
To prove her mother had turned up before.
But tell me, did the drunken patriarch bless
385   The son that showed his father's nakedness?
Such thanks the present church thy pen will give,
Which proves rebellion was so primitive.
Must ancient failings be examples made?
Then murtherers from Cain may learn their trade.
390   As thou the heathen and the saint hast drawn,
Methinks th' apostate was the better man,
And thy hot father (waiving my respect)
Not of a mother church, but of a sect.

382. leading-card] one which is played first, setting a precedent (Schless).
383. turned up] prostituted herself; cp. 'Epilogue to 1 Conquest of Granada'
l. 12n.
384. patriarch] 1682b; Patriot 1682a. The reference is to Noah (Genesis ix 18–
27).
392. father] St Gregory Nazianzen, whose invective against Julian is used by
Johnson (Noyes).

And such he needs must be of thy inditing;
395 This comes of drinking ass's milk and writing.
If Balack should be called to leave his place
(As profit is the loudest call of grace)
His temple, dispossessed of one, would be
Replenished with seven devils more by thee.
400   Levi, thou art a load, I'll lay thee down,
And show rebellion bare, without a gown;
Poor slaves in metre, dull and addle-pated,
Who rhyme below ev'n David's psalms translated.
Some in my speedy pace I must outrun,
405 As lame Mephibosheth the wizard's son:
To make quick way I'll leap o'er heavy blocks,
Shun rotten Uzza as I would the pox,

394. inditing] writing, composing.
395. ass's milk] taken by invalids (cp. Pope, *Epistle to Dr Arbuthnot* l. 306).
396. Balack] Gilbert Burnet (1643–1715), according to the 1716 key; but the lines 'offer so brief and so general a portrait that even the contemporary Luttrell was unable to gloss them' (Schless). Burnet's *History of the Reformation of the Church of England* (1679–81) had been hailed by the Whigs, and he had associates among their leaders. Currently chaplain to the Rolls chapel, Burnet had been offered the see of Chichester by Charles II on condition that he served the court interest, and the mastership of the Temple on condition that he severed links with the Whigs; Burnet declined. See further *HP* iii 1141–91. Biblically Balack was the King of Moab who tried to persuade Balaam to curse the children of Israel (Numbers xxii–xxiii).
398–9. Matthew xii 43–5.
403. David's psalms translated] the much-derided version by Sternhold and Hopkins (1562).
405. Mephibosheth] Samuel Pordage (1633–91?), son of the mystic and astrologer John Pordage; author of *Azaria and Hushai* (1682), an answer to *AA*, and of *The Medal Revers'd* (1682). L'Estrange called him 'limping Pordage' (*Observator* cxix (5 April 1682); Schless). See 2 Samuel iv 4.
407. Uzza] Identified in the 1716 key only as 'J.H.', but by Noyes as John Grubham Howe (1659–1722), a writer of scurrilous verses, 'smutty jests and downright lies', whose 'whole design is to be thought a wit' ('An Answer to the Satire on the Court Ladies' (in MS, 1680) ll. 28, 33, in *Court Satires*, edited by Wilson 42, q.v. 254–6 for Howe's life; see also Schless 302). Schless conjectures plausibly that the biblical reference is not to Uzza (who was killed when he touched the ark: 1 Chronicles xiii 7–11), but, in view of *rotten*, to King Uzziah, who was struck with leprosy for opposing the priests (2 Chronicles xxvi 16–23).   *rotten*] Cp. 'Adorned with pimples and a stinking breath. / . . . His poisoned corpse wrapped in a wicker skin, / Dismal without and ten times worse within' ('An Answer' ll. 50–4).

And hasten Og and Doeg to rehearse,
Two fools that crutch their feeble sense on verse,
410   Who by my Muse to all succeeding times
Shall live, in spite of their own doggerel rhymes.
    Doeg, though without knowing how or why,
Made still a blundering kind of melody;
Spurred boldly on, and dashed through thick and
    thin,
415   Through sense and nonsense, never out nor in;
Free from all meaning, whether good or bad,
And in one word, heroically mad.
He was too warm on picking work to dwell, ⎫
But faggotted his notions as they fell,   ⎬
420   And if they rhymed and rattled all was well. ⎭
Spiteful he is not, though he wrote a satire,
For still there goes some thinking to ill nature;

412–56. Doeg] Elkanah Settle (1648–1724). His *The Empress of Morocco* (1673) was severely handled by D., Crowne and Shadwell in their joint *Notes and Observations on The Empress of Morocco* (1674). Settle became a Whig and devised the Pope-burning ceremonies in 1679 and 1680. In 1680 he produced two anti-Catholic plays, *The Female Prelate* and *Fatal Love*, along with the Whig tract *The Character of a Popish Successor*. The Prologue to his *The Heir of Morocco* on 11 March 1682 referred contemptuously to the Rose Alley attack on D., and to D.'s plays (ll. 7–16; Danchin no. 320); and in April appeared *Absalom Senior*, his reply to *AA*, which included a malicious personal attack on D. (34; *POAS* iii 164–6). Settle became a Tory in 1683, publishing his *Narrative* (1683), and a Whig again in 1688. Kinsley notes that 'the name of the Edomite traitor Doeg ("fearful, uneasy"; 1 Samuel xxii) accords with what is known of his character'.

413. blundering] Echoes *Notes and Observations* sig. aʳ: 'he by his blundering hobling Verse, disagreeing and (to imitate his non-sense) almost never-riming rime, has made all Verse ridiculous'. Rochester then called him 'blundering Settle' (*An Allusion to Horace* (in MS, 1675–6) l. 18).

414–20. Cp. 'our Poet writes by chance, is resolv'd upon the Rhime before hand, and for the rest of the Verse has a Lottery of words by him, and draws them that come next, let them make sense or non-sense when they come together he matters not that . . . he would perswade us he is a kind of Phanatick in Poetry, and has a light within him; and writes by an inspiration which (like that of the Heathen Prophets) a man must have no sense of his own when he receives' (*Notes and Observations* 2, 71; Noyes, Kinsley).

418. picking work] the work of picking out the good from the bad.

419. Cp. Flecknoe: a schoolboy's learning is 'all *capping* verses, and *Faggotting Poets* looser lines, which fall from him as disorderly as Faggott-sticks, when the band is broak' (*Enigmaticall Characters* (1658) 77; Malone).

He needs no more than birds and beasts to think,
All his occasions are to eat and drink.
425   If he call 'rogue' and 'rascal' from a garret
He means you no more mischief than a parrot.
The words for friend and foe alike were made,
To fetter 'em in verse is all his trade.
For almonds he'll cry 'whore' to his own mother,
430   And call young Absalom King David's brother.
Let him be gallows-free by my consent,
And nothing suffer since he nothing meant.
Hanging supposes human soul and reason;
This animal's below committing treason.
435   Shall he be hanged who never could rebel?
That's a preferment for Achitophel.
The woman that committed buggery
Was rightly sentenced by the law to die,
But 'twas hard fate that to the gallows led
440   The dog that never heard the statute read.
Railing in other men may be a crime,
But ought to pass for mere instinct in him.
Instinct he follows, and no farther knows,
For to write verse with him is to transprose.
445   'Twere pity treason at his door to lay,
Who 'makes heaven's gate a lock to its own key'.

---

429. *almonds*] proverbially rewards given to parrots for speaking (Tilley A 220).   *cry 'whore'*] When Otway challenged Settle to a duel over the character of him in *A Session of the Poets*, Settle penned an apology: '*I confess I Writ the Session of the Poets, and am very sorry fo't and am the Son of a Whore* for doing it; Witness my hand E.S.' (*A Character of the True Blue Protestant Poet* (1682); Kinsley; cp. Macdonald 239–40).

430. Settle identifies Absalom with the Duke of York in *Absalom Senior*.

437–40. The story is told in the ballad *The Four Legg'd Elder* (1647; reprinted 1677; in *Rump* (1662) i 350–4; and in *Wit and Mirth* (1682) 76ff.).

444. *transprose*] Refers to *Absalom Senior: or, Achitophel Transpros'd*. The word originates in *The Rehearsal*, where Bayes (i.e. D.) says: 'my first Rule is the Rule of Transversion, or *Regula Duplex*: changing Verse into Prose, or Prose into verse . . . I take a book in my hand . . . if there be any Wit in't, as there is no book but has some, I Transverse it; that is, if it be Prose put it into Verse, . . . and if it be Verse, put it into Prose. *Johnson*. Methinks, Mr. Bayes, that putting Verse into Prose should be call'd Transprosing' (I i 96–107).

446. Mocking *Absalom Senior*: 'In Gloomy Times, when Priestcraft bore the sway, / And made Heav'ns Gate a Lock to their own Key' (ll. 1–2).

Let him rail on, let his invective Muse
Have four and twenty letters to abuse,
Which if he jumbles to one line of sense
450   Indict him of a capital offence.
In fireworks give him leave to vent his spite,
Those are the only serpents he can write;
The height of his ambition is we know
But to be master of a puppet show:
455   On that one stage his works may yet appear,
And a month's harvest keeps him all the year.
    Now stop your noses, readers, all and some,   ⎫
For here's a tun of midnight-work to come,   ⎬
Og from a treason-tavern rolling home.   ⎭

448. four and twenty letters] because i/j and u/v were forms of the same letter until the seventeenth century.

451. fireworks] Alluding to Settle's contributions to the Whig celebrations. Kinsley cites *Heraclitus Ridens* l (10 January 1682): 'I know a lusty Fellow, that would not willingly be thought Valiant, who has an indifferent Hand at making of Crackers, Serpents, Rockets, and the other Play-things, that are proper on the Fifth of *November*; and has for such his Skill received Applause and Victuals from the munificent Gentlemen about *Temple Bar* . . . he forsooth is design'd *Poet Laureat* too . . . his Squibs and his Poems have much what the same Fortune; they crack and bounce, and the Boys and Girls laugh at 'em.'

452. serpents] kind of firework which burns with a serpentine motion or flame (*OED* 6); playing on the serpent as a symbol of malice (*OED* 3).

454. puppet show] In 1681 Settle contracted to write 'a certain Interlude or Stage Play' for Elizabeth Leigh, daughter of Mrs Mynn who kept booths at Bartholomew and Southwark fairs (Hotson 274–6). In *The Vindication . . . of . . . The Duke of Guise* (1683) D. says that the Whigs 'must take up with *Settle*, and such as they can get: *Bartholomew-Fair Writers*' (45); Kinsley.

458. tun] large cask for wine, ale or beer.   *midnight-work*] production of excrement (cp. *MF* ll. 47, 103).

459–509. Og] Thomas Shadwell (see *MF* headnote); probable author of *The Medal of John Bayes* (May 1682). In *The Vindication* (1683) D. wrote: '*Og* may write against the King if he pleases, so long as he *Drinks* for him; and his *Writings* will never do the Government so much *harm*, as his *Drinking* does it *good*: for true Subjects, will not be much perverted by his *Libels*; but the Wine *Duties* rise considerably by his *Claret*. He has often call'd me an *Atheist* in Print, I would believe more charitably of him; and that he only goes the *broad way*, because the other is too *narrow* for him. He may see by this, I do not delight to meddle with his course of *Life*, and his *Immoralities*, though I have a long *Bead-roll* of them. I have hitherto contented my self with the *Ridiculous* part of him, which is enough in all conscience to employ one man: even

THE SECOND PART OF ABSALOM AND ACHITOPHEL

460   Round as a globe, and liquored every chink,
       Goodly and great he sails behind his link;
       With all this bulk there's nothing lost in Og,
       For every inch that is not fool is rogue:
       A monstrous mass of foul corrupted matter,
465   As all the devils had spewed to make the batter.
       When wine has given him courage to blaspheme
       He curses God, but God before cursed him;
       And if man could have reason, none has more
       That made his paunch so rich, and him so poor.
470   With wealth he was not trusted, for heaven knew
       What 'twas of old to pamper up a Jew;
       To what would he on quail and pheasant swell,
       That ev'n on tripe and carrion could rebel?
       But though heaven made him poor (with rev'rence
          speaking)
475   He never was a poet of God's making.
       The midwife laid her hand on his thick skull
       With this prophetic blessing: 'Be thou dull.'

---

without the story of his late fall at the *Old Devil*, where he *broke no Ribbs*, because the hardness of the Stairs cou'd reach *no Bones*; and for my part, I do not wonder how he came to *fall*, for I have always known him heavy; the Miracle is, how he got *up again*. I have heard of a *Sea-Captain* as *fat* as he, who to scape Arrests, would lay himself flat upon the ground, and let the *Bayliffs* carry him to *Prison*, if they could. If a Messenger or two, nay, we may put in three or four, should come, he has friendly Advertisement how to scape them. But to leave him, who is not worth any further consideration, now I have done laughing at him, Wou'd every man knew his own Tallent, and that they who are only born for *drinking*, wou'd let both *Poetry* and *Prose* alone' (25–6). The biblical Og, King of Bashan, was renowned for his bulk (Deuteronomy iii 1–11).

461. link] torch.

464–5. matter / . . . batter] As Kinsley notes, D. in his 'Discourse Concerning Satire' (1693) says that 'double Rhyme, (a necessary Companion of Burlesque Writing) is not so proper for Manly Satire, for it turns Earnest too much to Jest, and gives us a Boyish kind of Pleasure' (*Works* iv 81); cp. *AM*, 'Account' ll. 77–80.

473. A satire on Edward Howard (1671) attributes the discrepancy between his mind and body to his diet: 'With lights and livers and with stinking fish, / Ox-cheek, tripe, garbage, thou dost treat thy brain' (*POAS* i 341; Ken Robinson and Clare Wenley, *DUJ* lxxv (1983) 29).

477. Be thou dull] Since only these words are italicized in *1682* the midwife's

Drink, swear and roar, forbear no lewd delight
Fit for thy bulk, do anything but write.
480 Thou art of lasting make like thoughtless men,
A strong nativity—but for the pen.
Eat opium, mingle arsenic in thy drink,
Still thou may'st live avoiding pen and ink.
I see, I see 'tis counsel given in vain,
485 For treason botched in rhyme will be thy bane.
Rhyme is the rock on which thou art to wreck,
'Tis fatal to thy fame and to thy neck.
Why should thy metre good King David blast?
A psalm of his will surely be thy last.
490 Dar'st thou presume in verse to meet thy foes,
Thou whom the penny pamphlet foiled in prose?
Doeg, whom God for mankind's mirth has made,
O'ertops thy talent in thy very trade;
Doeg to thee—thy paintings are so coarse—
495 A poet is, though he's the poet's horse.
A double noose thou on thy neck dost pull
For writing treason, and for writing dull:
To die for faction is a common evil,
But to be hanged for nonsense is the devil.
500 Hadst thou the glories of thy King expressed,
Thy praises had been satire at the best;
But thou in clumsy verse, unlicked, unpointed,
Hast shamefully defied the Lord's Anointed.
I will not rake the dunghill of thy crimes,
505 For who would read thy life that reads thy rhymes?

---

blessing seems confined to them (Noyes).   *dull*] The word had been
branded on Shadwell in *MF*.
478. Drink, swear and roar] Echoes D.'s 'Prologue to [Shadwell's] *A True
Widow*' (1678) l. 25 (*Works*).
480. make] constitution (*OED* 2b).
481. nativity] horoscope.
489. Schless suggests that Psalm xxiii was read by the chaplain to the condemned man on the scaffold.
502. unlicked] as a bear was supposed to lick her formless cubs into shape.
504. Unlike Shadwell, who in *The Medal of John Bayes* had catalogued D.'s
supposed misdemeanours.

But of King David's foes be this the doom,
May all be like the young man Absalom;
And for my foes may this their blessing be,
To talk like Doeg, and to write like thee.
510   Achitophel each rank, degree and age
For various ends neglects not to engage;
The wise and rich for purse and counsel brought,
The fools and beggars for their number sought:
Who yet not only on the town depends,
515 For ev'n in court the faction had its friends.
These thought the places they possessed too small,
And in their hearts wished court and King to fall;
Whose names the Muse disdaining holds i' th' dark,
Thrust in the villain herd without a mark,
520 With parasites and libel-spawning imps,
Intriguing fops, dull jesters and worse pimps.
Disdain the rascal rabble to pursue,
Their set cabals are yet a viler crew;
See where involved in common smoke they sit,
525 Some for our mirth, some for our satire fit.
These gloomy, thoughtful and on mischief bent,
While those for mere good fellowship frequent
Th' appointed club, can let sedition pass,
Sense, nonsense, anything t' employ the glass;
530 And who believe in their dull, honest hearts
The rest talk treason but to show their parts,
Who ne'er had wit or will for mischief yet,
But pleased to be reputed of a set.
    But in the sacred annals of our Plot,
535 Industrious Arod never be forgot:
The labours of this midnight-magistrate
May vie with Corah's to preserve the state;
In search of arms he failed not to lay hold
On war's most powerful, dang'rous weapon, gold;

506–7. 'The enemies of my lord the king, and all that rise against thee to do thee hurt, be as that young man is' (2 Samuel xviii 32; Kinsley).

528. *Th' appointed club*] e.g. the Green Ribbon Club (see *The Medal*, 'Epistle' l. 47*n*).

535–55. *Arod*] Sir William Waller (d. 1699), a Middlesex justice; 'a great Inquisitor of Priests and Jesuits, and Gutter (as the Term was for Stripping) of Popish Chapels. In which he proceeded with that scandalous Rigor, as to bring forth the Pictures, and other Furniture of great Value, and burn them

540   And last, to take from Jebusites all odds,
       Their altars pillaged, stole their very gods.
       Oft would he cry, when treasure he surprised,
       ' 'Tis Baalish gold in David's coin disguised',
       Which to his house with richer relicts came,
545   While lumber idols only fed the flame;.
       For our wise rabble ne'er took pains t' enquire
       What 'twas he burnt, so 't made a rousing fire;
       With which our elder was enriched no more
       Than false Gehazi with the Syrian's store:
550   So poor that when our choosing tribes were met
       Ev'n for his stinking votes he ran in debt;
       For meat the wicked, and as authors think
       The saints he choused for his electing drink.
       Thus every shift and subtle method passed,
555   And all to be no Zaken at the last.
            Now, raised on Tyre's sad ruins, Pharaoh's pride
       Soared high, his legions threat'ning far and wide;
       As when a batt'ring storm engendered high
       By winds upheld hangs hov'ring in the sky,
560   Is gazed upon by every trembling swain,
       This for his vineyard fears, and that his grain;
       For blooming plants and flowers new opening, these
       For lambs eaned lately, and far-lab'ring bees;
       To guard his stock each to the gods does call,
565   Uncertain where the fire-charged clouds will fall:
       Ev'n so the doubtful nations watch his arms,
       With terror each expecting his alarms.

---

publicly; which gave Occasion to suspect, and some said positively, that, under this Pretence, he kept good Things for himself' (Roger North, *Examen* (1740) 277; Kinsley). The biblical Arod was a son of Gad (Numbers xxvi 17–18).

540. Jebusites] Roman Catholics.

549. Elisha cured Naaman the Syrian of leprosy, and refused payment; when Naaman left, Elisha's servant Gehazi followed him and got money from him by lying. For this he was struck with leprosy (2 Kings v 20–7).

553. choused] cheated.

555. Zaken] elder. The reference is either to his being deprived of his magistracy in spring 1680 (Kinsley, citing Luttrell i 39), or to his failure to win election to Parliament until 15 November 1680 (Schless).

563. eaned] born.

Where Judah, where was now thy lion's roar?
Thou only couldst the captive lands restore;
570   But thou with inbred broils and faction pressed
From Egypt need'st a guardian with the rest.
Thy Prince from Sanhedrins no trust allowed,
Too much the representers of the crowd,
Who for their own defence give no supply
575   But what the crown's prerogatives must buy:
As if their monarch's rights to violate
More needful were than to preserve the state!
From present dangers they divert their care,
And all their fears are of the royal heir,
580   Whom now the reigning malice of his foes
Unjudged would sentence, and ere crowned depose.
Religion the pretence, but their decree
To bar his reign whate'er his faith shall be!
By Sanhedrins and clam'rous crowds thus pressed,
585   What passions rent the righteous David's breast,
Who knows not how t' oppose, or to comply,
Unjust to grant, and dangerous to deny!
How near in this dark juncture Israel's fate,
Whose peace one sole expedient could create,
590   Which yet th' extremest virtue did require,
Ev'n of that Prince whose downfall they conspire!
His absence David does with tears advise;
T' appease their rage, undaunted he complies;
Thus he who prodigal of blood and ease
595   A royal life exposed to winds and seas,
At once contending with the waves and fire,
And heading danger in the wars of Tyre,
Inglorious now forsakes his native sand,
And like an exile quits the promised land.
600   Our monarch scarce from pressing tears refrains,
And painfully his royal state maintains,
Who now embracing on th' extremest shore
Almost revokes what he enjoined before;
Concludes at last more trust to be allowed
605   To storms and seas than to the raging crowd.

---

592. In February 1679 Charles reluctantly asked James to go to Holland, where he stayed until September.

Forbear, rash Muse, the parting scene to draw,
With silence charmed as deep as theirs that saw!
Not only our attending nobles weep,
But hardy sailors swell with tears the deep.
610 The tide restrained her course, and more amazed
The twin stars on the royal brothers gazed,
While this sole fear——
Does trouble to our suff'ring hero bring
Lest next the popular rage oppress the King.
615 Thus parting, each for th' other's danger grieved,
The shore the King, and seas the Prince received.
Go, injured hero, while propitious gales
Soft as thy consort's breath inspire thy sails;
Well may she trust her beauties on a flood,
620 Where thy triumphant fleets so oft have rode!
Safe on thy breast reclined, her rest be deep,
Rocked like a Nereid by the waves asleep,
While happiest dreams her fancy entertain,
And to Elysian fields convert the main.
625 Go, injured hero, while the shores of Tyre
At thy approach so silent shall admire,
Who on thy thunder still their thoughts employ,
And greet thy landing with a trembling joy.
On heroes thus the prophet's fate is thrown,
630 Admired by every nation but their own;
Yet while our factious Jews his worth deny,
Their aching conscience gives their tongue the lie.
Ev'n in the worst of men the noblest parts
Confess him, and he triumphs in their hearts,
635 Whom to his King the best respects commend
Of subject, soldier, kinsman, prince and friend:
All sacred names of most divine esteem,
And to perfection all sustained by him.
Wise, just and constant, courtly without art,
640 Swift to discern and to reward desert;
No hour of his in fruitless ease destroyed,
But on the noblest subjects still employed;

611. *twin stars*] Castor and Pollux.
622. *Nereid*] sea nymph.

Whose steady soul ne'er learned to separate
Between his monarch's int'rest and the state,
645 But heaps those blessings on the royal head
Which he well knows must be on subjects shed.
   On what pretence could then the vulgar rage
Against his worth and native rights engage?
Religious fears their argument are made,
650 Religious fears his sacred rights invade!
Of future superstition they complain,
And Jebusitic worship in his reign;
With such alarms his foes the crowd deceive,
With dangers fright which not themselves believe.
655   Since nothing can our sacred rites remove
Whate'er the faith of the successor prove,
Our Jews their ark shall undisturbed retain,
At least while their religion is their gain;
Who know by old experience Baal's commands
660 Not only claimed their conscience but their lands.
They grutch God's tithes; how therefore shall they
    yield
An idol full possession of the field?
Grant such a Prince enthroned, we must confess
The people's suff'rings than that monarch's less,
665 Who must to hard conditions still be bound,
And for his quiet with the crowd compound.
Or should his thoughts to tyranny incline,
Where are the means to compass the design?
Our crown's revenues are too short a store,
670 And jealous Sanhedrins would give no more!
   As vain our fears of Egypt's potent aid;
Not so has Pharaoh learned ambition's trade,
Nor ever with such measures can comply
As shock the common rules of policy;
675 None dread like him the growth of Israel's King,
And he alone sufficient aids can bring;
Who knows that Prince to Egypt can give law,
That on our stubborn tribes his yoke could draw,

659. *Baal*] Cromwell.
661. *grutch*] begrudge.

At such profound expense he has not stood,
680   Nor dyed for this his hands so deep in blood;
Would ne'er through wrong and right his progress
    take,
Grudge his own rest, and keep the world awake,
To fix a lawless prince on Judah's throne,
First to invade our rights, and then his own;
685   His dear-gained conquests cheaply to despoil,
And reap the harvest of his crimes and toil.
We grant his wealth vast as our ocean's sand,
And curse its fatal influence on our land,
Which our bribed Jews so num'rously partake
690   That ev'n an host his pensioners would make.
From these deceivers our divisions spring,
Our weakness, and the growth of Egypt's King;
These with pretended friendship to the state
Our crowd's suspicion of their Prince create,
695   Both pleased and frightened with the specious cry
To guard their sacred rights and property;
To ruin thus the chosen flock are sold
While wolves are ta'en for guardians of the fold;
Seduced by these we groundlessly complain,
700   And loathe the manna of a gentle reign.
Thus our forefathers' crooked paths are trod,
We trust our Prince no more than they their God.
But all in vain our reasoning prophets preach
To those whom sad experience ne'er could teach,
705   Who can commence new broils in bleeding scars,
And fresh remembrance of intestine wars;
When the same household mortal foes did yield,
And brothers stained with brothers' blood the field;
When sons' cursed steel the fathers' gore did stain,
710   And mothers mourned for sons by fathers slain!
When thick as Egypt's locusts on the sand
Our tribes lay slaughtered through the promised
    land,
Whose few survivors with worse fate remain
To drag the bondage of a tyrant's reign;
715   Which scene of woes unknowing we renew,
And madly ev'n those ills we fear pursue,
While Pharaoh laughs at our domestic broils,
And safely crowds his tents with nations' spoils.

Yet our fierce Sanhedrin in restless rage
720   Against our absent hero still engage,
And chiefly urge (such did their frenzy prove)
The only suit their Prince forbids to move;
Which till obtained they cease affairs of state,
And real dangers waive for groundless hate.
725   Long David's patience waits relief to bring
With all th' indulgence of a lawful king,
Expecting till the troubled waves would cease
But found the raging billows still increase.
The crowd, whose insolence forbearance swells,
730   While he forgives too far, almost rebels.
At last his deep resentments silence broke,
Th' imperial palace shook, while thus he spoke:
    'Then Justice wake, and Rigour take her time,
For lo! our mercy is become our crime.
735   While halting Punishment her stroke delays,
Our sov'reign right, heaven's sacred trust, decays;
For whose support ev'n subjects' interest calls,
Woe to that kingdom where the monarch falls.
That Prince who yields the least of regal sway
740   So far his people's freedom does betray.
Right lives by law, and law subsists by power,
Disarm the shepherd, wolves the flock devour.
Hard lot of empire o'er a stubborn race
Which heaven itself in vain has tried with grace.
745   When will our reason's long-charmed eyes unclose,
And Israel judge between her friends and foes?
When shall we see expired deceivers' sway,
And credit what our God and monarchs say?
Dissembled patriots bribed with Egypt's gold
750   Ev'n Sanhedrins in blind obedience hold;
Those patriots' falsehood in their actions see,
And judge by the pernicious fruit the tree.
If aught for which so loudly they declaim—
Religion, laws and freedom—were their aim,
755   Our senates in due methods they had led,
T' avoid those mischiefs which they seemed to dread;
But first, ere yet they propped the sinking state,
T' impeach and charge as urged by private hate
Proves that they ne'er believed the fears they pressed,
760   But barb'rously destroyed the nation's rest.

O whither will ungoverned senates drive,
And to what bounds licentious votes arrive?
When their injustice we are pressed to share,
The monarch urged t' exclude the lawful heir.
765 Are princes thus distinguished from the crowd,
And this the privilege of royal blood?
But grant we should confirm the wrongs they press,
His sufferings yet were than the people's less;
Condemned for life the murd'ring sword to wield,
770 And on their heirs entail a bloody field:
Thus madly their own freedom they betray,
And for th' oppression which they fear make way;
Succession fixed by heaven the kingdom's bar
Which once dissolved admits the flood of war;
775 Waste, rapine, spoil without th' assault begin,
And our mad tribes supplant the fence within.
Since then their good they will not understand,
'Tis time to take the monarch's power in hand,
Authority and force to join with skill
780 And save the lunatics against their will.
The same rough means that swage the crowd appease
Our senates, raging with the crowd's disease.
Henceforth unbiassed measures let 'em draw
From no false gloss, but genuine text of law;
785 Nor urge those crimes upon religion's score
Themselves so much in Jebusites abhor.
Whom laws convict, and only they, shall bleed,
Nor pharisees by pharisees be freed.
Impartial justice from our throne shall shower,
790 All shall have right, and we our sov'reign power.'
He said; th' attendants heard with awful joy,
And glad presages their fixed thoughts employ.
From Hebron now the suffering heir returned,
A realm that long with civil discord mourned,
795 Till his approach, like some arriving god,
Composed and healed the place of his abode,

762. *licentious*] unrestrained by law, decorum or morality (*OED* 2).
781. *swage*] appease.
793. James was in Scotland from November 1679 to February 1680, and from November 1680 to March 1682; the poem has reached the latter date.

The deluge checked that to Judaea spread,
And stopped sedition at the fountain's head.
Thus in forgiving David's paths he drives,
800 And chased from Israel, Israel's peace contrives.
The field confessed his power in arms before,
And seas proclaimed his triumphs to the shore;
As nobly has his sway in Hebron shown
How fit t' inherit godlike David's throne.
805 Through Zion's streets his glad arrivals spread,
And conscious faction shrinks her snaky head;
His train their sufferings think o'erpaid, to see
The crowd's applause with virtue once agree.
Success charms all, but zeal for worth distressed
810 A virtue proper to the brave and best;
'Mongst whom was Jothran, Jothran always bent
To serve the crown, and loyal by descent;
Whose constancy so firm, and conduct just
Deserved at once two royal masters' trust;
815 Who Tyre's proud arms had manfully withstood
On seas, and gathered laurels from the flood;
Of learning yet no portion was denied,
Friend to the Muses, and the Muses' pride.
Nor can Benaiah's worth forgotten lie,
820 Of steady soul when public storms were high;
Whose conduct while the Moor fierce onsets made
Secured at once our honour and our trade.
Such were the chiefs who most his suff'rings
        mourned,
And viewed with silent joy the Prince returned;
825 While those that sought his absence to betray
Press first their nauseous false respects to pay:
Him still th' officious hypocrites molest,
And with malicious duty break his rest.
    While real transports thus his friends employ,
830 And foes are loud in their dissembled joy,

811–18. Jothran] George Legge (1648–91), created Earl of Dartmouth in
December 1682; a loyal follower of James, and son of a royalist colonel.
There is no biblical Jothran.
819–22. Benaiah] Col. Edward Sackville, who distinguished himself at Tan-
gier. The biblical Benaiah was loyal and brave (2 Samuel xxiii 20–3).
829. Editorial paragraph.

His triumphs so resounded far and near
Missed not his young ambitious rival's ear;
And as when joyful hunters' clam'rous train
Some slumb'ring lion wakes in Moab's plain,
835   Who oft had forced the bold assailants yield,
And scattered his pursuers through the field,
Disdaining furls his mane, and tears the ground,
His eyes inflaming all the desert round,
With roar of seas directs his chasers' way,
840   Provokes from far, and dares them to the fray:
Such rage stormed now in Absalom's fierce breast,
Such indignation his fired eyes confessed;
Where now was the instructor of his pride?
Slept the old pilot in so rough a tide,
845   Whose wiles had from the happy shore betrayed
And thus on shelves the cred'lous youth conveyed?
In deep revolving thoughts he weighs his state,
Secure of craft, nor doubts to baffle fate;
At least, if his stormed bark must go adrift
850   To baulk his charge, and for himself to shift;
In which his dext'rous wit had oft been shown,
And in the wreck of kingdoms saved his own;
But now with more than common danger pressed,
Of various resolutions stands possessed,
855   Perceives the crowd's unstable zeal decay,
Lest their recanting chief the cause betray,
Who on a father's grace his hopes may ground,
And for his pardon with their heads compound.
Him therefore, ere his Fortune slip her time,
860   The statesman plots t' engage in some bold crime
Past pardon, whether to attempt his bed,
Or threat with open arms the royal head,
Or other daring method, and unjust
That may confirm him in the people's trust.
865   But failing thus t' ensnare him, nor secure
How long his foiled ambition may endure,
Plots next to lay him by, as past his date,
And try some new pretender's luckier fate;

864. confirm] 1682b; secure 1682a.

Whose hopes with equal toil he would pursue,
870 Nor cares what claimer's crowned, except the true.
Wake Absalom, approaching ruin shun,
And see, O see for whom thou art undone!
How are thy honours and thy fame betrayed,
The property of desp'rate villains made!
875 Lost power and conscious fears their crimes create,
And guilt in them was little less than fate;
But why shouldst thou, from every grievance free,
Forsake thy vineyards for their stormy sea?
For thee did Canaan's milk and honey flow,
880 Love dressed thy bowers, and laurels sought thy
    brow;
Preferment, wealth and power thy vassals were,
And of a monarch all things but the care.
O should our crimes again that curse draw down
And rebel arms once more attempt the crown,
885 Sure ruin waits unhappy Absalon,
Alike by conquest or defeat undone.
Who could relentless see such youth and charms
Expire with wretched fate in impious arms,
A Prince so formed with earth's and heaven's
    applause
890 To triumph o'er crowned heads in David's cause?
Or grant him victor, still his hopes must fail,
Who conquering would not for himself prevail;
The faction whom he trusts for future sway
Him and the public would alike betray,
895 Amongst themselves divide the captive state,
And found their hydra-empire in his fate.
Thus having beat the clouds with painful flight,
The pitied youth with sceptres in his sight
(So have their cruel politics decreed)
900 Must by that crew that made him guilty bleed!
For could their pride brook any prince's sway,
Whom but mild David would they choose t' obey?
Who once at such a gentle reign repine
The fall of monarchy itself design:
905 From hate to that their reformations spring,
And David not their grievance, but the King.
Seized now with panic fear the faction lies,
Lest this clear truth strike Absalom's charmed eyes;

   Lest he perceive, from long enchantment free,
910 What all beside the flattered youth must see.
   But whate'er doubts his troubled bosom swell,
   Fair carriage still became Achitophel,
   Who now an envious festival installs,
   And to survey their strength the faction calls,
915 Which fraud religious worship too must gild;
   But O how weakly does sedition build!
   For lo! the royal mandate issues forth
   Dashing at once their treason, zeal and mirth!
   So have I seen disastrous chance invade
920 Where careful emmets had their forage laid;
   Whether fierce Vulcan's rage the furzy plain
   Had seized, engendered by some careless swain,
   Or swelling Neptune lawless inroads made
   And to their cell of store his flood conveyed,
925 The commonwealth broke up distracted go,
   And in wild haste their loaded mates o'erthrow:
   Ev'n so our scattered guests confus'dly meet
   With boiled, baked, roast all jostling in the street,
   Dejected all and ruefully dismayed
930 For shekel without treat or treason paid.
    Sedition's dark eclipse now fainter shows,
   More bright each hour the royal planet grows,
   Of force the clouds of envy to disperse
   In kind conjunction of assisting stars.
935 Here, lab'ring Muse, those glorious chiefs relate
   That turned the doubtful scale of David's fate;
   The rest of that illustrious band rehearse
   Immortalized in laurelled Asaph's verse.
   Hard task! yet will not I thy flight recall;
940 View heaven and then enjoy thy glorious fall.
    First write Bezaliel, whose illustrious name
   Forestalls our praise and gives his poet fame.

913–30. When the Duke of York was invited to dine with the Artillery
Company on 20 April 1682, the Whigs organized a rival dinner of thanksgiving for deliverance from the papists, with tickets a guinea each; the Whig
feast was prohibited by the King (see *POAS* iii 174–82).
938. *Asaph*] D. himself. The biblical Asaph was one of those appointed by
David 'to record, and to thank and praise the Lord God of Israel' (1 Chronicles xvi 4). See also *Threnodia Augustalis* ll. 1–8n.
941–56. *Bezaliel*] Henry Somerset (1629–1700), Marquis of Worcester and

The Kenites' rocky province his command,
A barren limb of fertile Canaan's land,
945 Which for its gen'rous natives yet could be
Held worthy such a president as he!
Bezaliel with each grace and virtue fraught,
Serene his looks, serene his life and thought,
On whom so largely Nature heaped her store,
950 There scarce remained for arts to give him more.
To aid the crown and state his greatest zeal,
His second care that service to conceal;
Of dues observant, firm in every trust,
And to the needy always more than just;
955 Who truth from specious falsehood can divide,
Has all the gownmen's skill without their pride.
Thus crowned with worth from heights of honour
        won
Sees all his glories copied in his son,
Whose forward fame should every Muse engage,
960 Whose youth boasts skill denied to others' age.
Men, manners, language, books of noblest kind
Already are the conquest of his mind;
Whose loyalty before its date was prime,
Nor waited the dull course of rolling time.
965 The monster faction early he dismayed,
And David's cause long since confessed his aid.
        Brave Abdael o'er the prophets' school was placed,
Abdael with all his father's virtue graced;
A hero who, while stars looked wond'ring down,
970 Without one Hebrew's blood restored the crown.

(from 1682) Duke of Beaufort; Lord President of the Council of Wales; active
in the King's campaign against borough charters (Ogg 635). The biblical
Bezaleel was filled 'with the spirit of God, in wisdom, and in understanding,
and in knowledge' (Exodus xxxi 3).
943. Kenites] Welsh; of the biblical Kenites it was said: 'Strong is thy dwell-
ingplace, and thou puttest thy nest in a rock' (Numbers xxiv 21).
958–66. his son] Charles Somerset (1661–98) co-operated with his father in
the suppression of nonconformists in their region (Schless).
967–84. Abdael] Christopher Monck (1653–88), son of George, Duke of
Albemarle, who was instrumental in the Restoration of Charles II; Chancellor of Cambridge University from 1682; the biblical Abdael was son of Guni
(1 Chronicles v 15).

That praise was his; what therefore did remain
For following chiefs, but boldly to maintain
That crown restored; and in this rank of fame
Brave Abdael with the first a place must claim.
975   Proceed, illustrious, happy chief, proceed,
Foreseize the garlands for thy brow decreed,
While th' inspired tribe attend with noblest strain
To register the glories thou shalt gain:
For sure, the dew shall Gilboah's hills forsake,
980   And Jordan mix his stream with Sodom's lake,
Or seas retired their secret stores disclose,
And to the sun their scaly brood expose,
Or swelled above the cliffs their billows raise,
Before the Muses leave their patron's praise.
985   Eliab our next labour does invite,
And hard the task to do Eliab right:
Long with the royal wanderer he roved,
And firm in all the turns of Fortune proved.
Such ancient service and desert so large
990   Well claimed the royal household for his charge.
His age with only one mild heiress blessed
In all the bloom of smiling nature dressed,
And blessed again to see his flower allied
To David's stock, and made young Othniel's bride!
995   The bright restorer of his father's youth,
Devoted to a son's and subject's truth;
Resolved to bear that prize of duty home
So bravely sought (while sought) by Absalom.
Ah Prince! th' illustrious planet of thy birth
1000   And thy more powerful virtue guard thy worth,
That no Achitophel thy ruin boast:
Israel too much in one such wreck has lost.
    Ev'n envy must consent to Helon's worth,
Whose soul, though Egypt glories in his birth,

976. *Foreseize*] seize in advance (*OED*'s example).
985–1002. *Eliab*] Henry Bennet (1618–85), Earl of Arlington; companion of
Charles in exile, and after 1660 one of his chief ministers. In 1672 his daughter
Isabella married Charles's illegitimate son the Duke of Grafton ('Othniel':
Joshua xv 17). The biblical Eliab was David's brother (1 Samuel xvii 28).
988. *Fortune*] Noyes; Fortunes *1682a,b*.
994. *Othniel's*] Noyes; Othriel's *1682a,b*.
1003–12. *Helon*] Louis de Duras (?1640–1709), Earl of Feversham, a Hugue-

1005 Could for our captive ark its zeal retain,
And Pharaoh's altars in their pomp disdain:
To slight his gods was small; with nobler pride
He all th' allurements of his court defied,
Whom profit nor example could betray,
1010 But Israel's friend and true to David's sway.
What acts of favour in his province fall
On merit he confers, and freely all.
   Our list of nobles next let Amri grace,
Whose merits claimed the Abbethdin's high place;
1015 Who with a loyalty that did excel
Brought all th' endowments of Achitophel.
Sincere was Amri, and not only knew
But Israel's sanctions into practice drew;
Our laws, that did a boundless ocean seem,
1020 Were coasted all, and fathomed all by him:
No Rabbin speaks like him their mystic sense,
So just, and with such charms of eloquence;
To whom the double blessing does belong,
With Moses' inspiration Aaron's tongue.
1025   Than Sheva none more loyal zeal have shown,
Wakeful as Judah's lion for the crown,
Who for that cause still combats in his age
For which his youth with danger did engage.
In vain our factious priests the cant revive,
1030 In vain seditious scribes with libels strive
T' enflame the crowd, while he with watchful eye
Observes, and shoots their treasons as they fly.
Their weekly frauds his keen replies detect,
He undeceives more fast than they infect.

---

not and nephew of Marshall Turenne; he held positions in the royal household. The biblical Helon ('valorous') was the father of Eliab (Numbers i 9).
1013–24. Amri] Heneage Finch (1621–82), Earl of Nottingham; he succeeded Shaftesbury as Lord Keeper in 1673 and Lord Chancellor in 1674.
1014. Abbethdin] See *AA* l. 189*n*.
1025–36. Sheva] Sir Roger L'Estrange (1616–1704); served the King in the Civil War; became licenser of the press in 1663, and during the Exclusion Crisis a Tory pamphleteer and journalist, combating Whig propaganda in his periodical *The Observator*. The biblical Sheva was one of David's scribes (2 Samuel xx 25).

1035 So Moses when the pest on legions preyed
Advanced his signal and the plague was stayed.
Once more, my fainting Muse, thy pinions try,
And strength's exhausted store let love supply.
What tribute, Asaph, shall we render thee?
1040 We'll crown thee with a wreath from thy own tree!
Thy laurel grove no envy's flash can blast,
The song of Asaph shall for ever last!
With wonder late posterity shall dwell
On Absalom and false Achitophel;
1045 Thy strains shall be our slumb'ring prophets' dream,
And when our Zion virgins sing, their theme.
Our jubilees shall with thy verse be graced,
The song of Asaph shall for ever last!
How fierce his satire loosed, restrained how tame,
1050 How tender of th' offending young man's fame!
How well his worth and brave adventures styled,
Just to his virtues, to his error mild.
No page of thine that fears the strictest view,
But teems with just reproof, or praise as due.
1055 Not Eden could a fairer prospect yield,
All paradise without one barren field;
Whose wit the censure of his foes has passed,
The song of Asaph shall for ever last!
What praise for such rich strains shall we allow?
1060 What just rewards the grateful crown bestow?
While bees in flowers rejoice, and flowers in dew,
While stars and fountains to their course are true,
While Judah's throne and Zion's rock stand fast,
The song of Asaph and the fame shall last.
1065 Still Hebron's honoured, happy soil retains
Our royal hero's beauteous dear remains;
Who now sails off with winds nor wishes slack
To bring his suff'rings' bright companion back:
But ere such transport can our sense employ,
1070 A bitter grief must poison half our joy;

1035–6. Moses lifted up a serpent of brass in the wilderness to avert the
plague of serpents (Numbers xxi 6–9).
1065–102. In May 1682 the Duke of York set out for Scotland to bring home
the Duchess; the ship in which he was embarked foundered with great loss of
life, though the Duke escaped.

Nor can our coasts restored those blessings see
Without a bribe to envious destiny!
Cursed Sodom's doom for ever fix the tide
Where by inglorious chance the valiant died.
1075   Give not insulting Askelon to know,
Nor let Gath's daughters triumph in our woe!
No sailor with the news swell Egypt's pride,
By what inglorious fate our valiant died!
Weep Arnon! Jordan, weep thy fountains dry,
1080   While Zion's rock dissolves for a supply.
Calm were the elements, night's silence deep,
The waves scarce murm'ring, and the winds asleep;
Yet fate for ruin takes so still an hour,
And treacherous sands the princely bark devour.
1085   Then death unworthy seized a gen'rous race,
To virtue's scandal, and the stars' disgrace.
O had th' indulgent powers vouchsafed to yield
Instead of faithless shelves a listed field,
A listed field of heaven's and David's foes,
1090   Fierce as the troops that did his youth oppose,
Each life had on his slaughtered heap retired,
Not tamely and unconqu'ring thus expired;
But destiny is now their only foe,
And dying ev'n o'er that they triumph too;
1095   With loud last breaths their master's scape applaud,
Of whom kind force could scarce the fates defraud;
Who for such followers lost, O matchless mind,
At his own safety now almost repined!
Say, royal sir, by all your fame in arms,
1100   Your praise in peace, and by Urania's charms,
If all your suff'rings past so nearly pressed
Or pierced with half so painful grief your breast?
Thus some diviner Muse her hero forms,
Not soothed with soft delights, but tossed in storms.
1105   Not stretched on roses in the myrtle grove,
Nor crowns his days with mirth, his nights with
      love,

1075–6. From 2 Samuel i 20; no specific parallels seem intended.
1088. listed] converted into lists for tilting (OED).
1100. Urania] the heavenly Venus, i.e. Duchess of York.

But far removed in thund'ring camps is found,
His slumbers short, his bed the herbless ground.
In tasks of danger always seen the first,
1110 Feeds from the hedge, and slakes with ice his thirst.
Long must his patience strive with Fortune's rage,
And long opposing gods themselves engage,
Must see his country flame, his friends destroyed,
Before the promised empire be enjoyed;
1115 Such toil of fate must build a man of fame,
And such to Israel's crown the godlike David came.
　　What sudden beams dispel the clouds so fast,
Whose drenching rains laid all our vineyards waste?
The spring so far behind her course delayed
1120 On th' instant is in all her bloom arrayed;
The winds breathe low, the element serene,
Yet mark what motion in the waves is seen!
Thronging and busy as Hyblæan swarms,
Or straggled soldiers summoned to their arms.
1125 See where the princely bark in loosest pride
With all her guardian fleet adorns the tide!
High on her deck the royal lovers stand,
Our crimes to pardon ere they touched our land.
Welcome to Israel and to David's breast!
1130 Here all your toils, here all your suff'rings rest.
　　This year did Ziloah rule Jerusalem,
And boldly all sedition's surges stem,
Howe'er encumbered with a viler pair
Than Ziph or Shimei to assist the chair;
1135 Yet Ziloah's royal labours so prevailed
That faction at the next election failed,
When ev'n the common cry did 'justice' sound,
And merit by the multitude was crowned.
With David then was Israel's peace restored,
1140 Crowds mourned their error, and obeyed their lord.

1131. Ziloah] Sir John Moore, a Tory, was elected Lord Mayor of London in September 1682.
1133. viler pair] Pilkington and Shute, Whig sheriffs for 1681–2.
1134–5. Ziph . . . Shimei] Cornish and Bethel, Whig sheriffs for 1680–1 (see *AA* ll. 584–629n).
1135–6. In July Moore secured the election of two Tory sheriffs for 1682–3 (see 'Prologue to *The Duke of Guise*' l. 3n).

73 Prologue and Epilogue to the King and Queen

Date and publication. The decline of the factious King's Company culminated in its merger with the dominant Duke's Company which was agreed on 4 May 1682; the union seems to have become fully effective by the time of a performance at court on 15 November (*LS* 309, 315). The new company was called the King's Company and moved into the Theatre Royal, Drury Lane. The date of the opening performance is not known; the date on Luttrell's copy (see below) could be that of either the performance or his purchase. A folio pamphlet headed *Prologue. To The King and Queen, At The Opening Of Their Theatre*, containing D.'s Prologue and Epilogue, was published by Tonson dated 1683 (MS date 16 November 1682 on Luttrell's copy (Huntington)). There is also an undated broadside with the same title. The present text follows the folio pamphlet.

Prologue to the King and Queen at the Opening of their Theatre

Spoken by Mr Betterton

Since faction ebbs, and rogues grow out of fashion,
Their penny-scribes take care t' inform the nation
How well men thrive in this or that plantation;

¶73. *Prologue.*
Title. Betterton] Thomas Betterton (see 'Prologue to *Troilus and Cressida*' Title *n*) had been the actor-manager of the successful Duke's Company, and with William Smith (who spoke the Epilogue) now took the dominant role in the united company.
1. By mid-November 1682 the Whig opposition was virtually defeated. The City of London, normally a Whig stronghold, had elected Tory sheriffs and a Tory Lord Mayor (see 'Prologue to *The Duke of Guise*' l. 3*n*); Shaftesbury was in hiding, and left secretly for Holland *c.* 20 November; and Whig newspapers were banned.
2–5. During 1682 the proprietors of Carolina (who included Shaftesbury) made special efforts to promote emigration to the colony. Their secretary Samuel Wilson wrote an *Account of the Province of Carolina in America* (1682), and in the same year appeared R.F.'s *The Present State of Carolina* and Thomas Ash's *Carolina*, pamphlets which stressed the colony's natural advantages. The Whig *True Protestant Mercury* (14–18, 21 October) reported letters from Carolina describing how the colony was flourishing. Pennsylvania was also promoted in *A Brief Account of the Province of Pennsylvania* (1682) by the

How Pennsylvania's air agrees with Quakers,
5 And Carolina's with Associators:
Both e'en too good for madmen and for traitors.

Truth is, our land with saints is so run o'er,
And every age produces such a store,
That now there's need of two New Englands more.

10 What's this, you'll say, to us and our vocation?
Only thus much, that we have left our station
And made this theatre our new plantation.

The factious natives never could agree,
But aiming, as they called it, to be free,
15 Those playhouse Whigs set up for property.

Some say they no obedience paid of late,
But would new fears and jealousies create,
Till topsy-turvey they had turned the state.

Plain sense without the talent of foretelling
20 Might guess 'twould end in downright knocks and
    quelling:
For seldom comes there better of rebelling.

When men will needlessly their freedom barter
For lawless power, sometimes they catch a Tartar:
(There's a damned word that rhymes to this called
    'charter').

Quaker William Penn, who wrote that 'The Air is generally clear and sweet'
(5) (*Works*).
5. *Associators*] See 'Prologue to *The Duke of Guise*' l. 14*n*.
6. *madmen . . . traitors*] Quakers . . . Whigs.
13–15. The last years of the King's Company were marked by many disputes, including lawsuits over who owned costumes and props (Hotson 266–73; *LS* 307).
14. Cp. *AA* ll. 50–1.
15. *property*] See *AA* l. 536*n*.
17. *jealousies*] suspicions.
20. *quelling*] killing, destruction.
23. *catch a Tartar*] tackle one who proves too formidable (*OED* 4).
24. *charter*] See 'Prologue to *The Duke of Guise*' headnote and l. 43*n*.

25 But since the victory with us remains,
    You shall be called to twelve in all our gains,
    If you'll not think us saucy for our pains.

    Old men shall have good old plays to delight 'em,
    And you, fair ladies and gallants that slight 'em,
30 We'll treat with good new plays, if our new wits can
        write 'em.

    We'll take no blundering verse, no fustian tumour,
    No dribbling love from this or that presumer;
    No dull fat fool shammed on the stage for humour.

    For, faith, some of 'em such vile stuff have made
35 As none but fools or fairies ever played;
    But 'twas, as shopmen say, to force a trade.

    We've giv'n you tragedies, all sense defying,
    And singing men in woeful metre dying;
    This 'tis when heavy lubbers will be flying.

---

26. *called to twelve*] invited to share.

28. *old plays*] The merger brought the united company the rights to many pre-Restoration plays which had belonged to Killigrew (cp. 'Epilogue at the Opening of the New House' ll. 33–4*n*). But in 1690 George Powell recalled that 'the reviveing of the old stock of Plays, so ingrost the study of the House, that the Poets lay dorment; and a new Play cou'd hardly get admittance, amongst the more precious pieces of Antiquity, that then waited to walk the Stage' (*LS* 316).

31. *blundering*] Cp. 2*AA* l. 413*n*.   *tumour*] bombast.

33. Shadwell, who had been ridiculed in D'Urfey's *Sir Barnaby Whigg* (*c.* November 1681); an unauthorized first printed text of *MF* had been published in October 1682. He did not have another new play performed until *The Squire of Alsatia* (1688).   *fat*] Cp. *MF* ll. 25, 193–5.   *shammed*] imitated, impersonated (*OED* 4a).   *humour*] playing on Shadwell's devotion to the Jonsonian comedy of humours.

35. *fairies*] Perhaps alluding to Shadwell's *The Lancashire Witches* (performed September 1681; printed 1682) or *Psyche* (1675; perhaps revived 19 January 1682). Both were staged by the Duke's Company.

39. *flying*] soaring artistically; also alluding to the flying witches in *The Lancashire Witches*.

40   All these disasters we well hope to weather;
     We bring you none of our old lumber hether:
     Whig poets and Whig sheriffs may hang together.

Epilogue

Spoken by Mr Smith

New ministers when first they get in place
Must have a care to please; and that's our case.
Some laws for public welfare we design,
If you, the power supreme, will please to join.
5   There are a sort of prattlers in the pit,
Who either have, or who pretend to wit.
These noisy sirs so loud their parts rehearse
That oft the play is silenced by the farce.
Let such be dumb, this penalty to shun,
10   Each to be thought my lady's eldest son.
But stay: methinks some vizard mask I see
Cast out her lure from the mid gallery.
About her all the flutt'ring sparks are ranged,
The noise continues though the scene is changed;
15   Now growling, sputtering, wauling, such a clutter
'Tis just like puss defendant in a gutter:
Fine love no doubt, but ere two days are o'er ye
The surgeon will be told a woeful story.

41. *hether*] hither.
42. *Whig sheriffs*] See 'Prologue to *The Duke of Guise*' l. 3n.   *sheriffs*]
probably monosyllabic ('shreve' was a common seventeenth-century form).

Epilogue.
Title. *Mr Smith*] See 'Prologue to His Royal Highness' Title *n.*
5–8. For the noise of the wits in the pit cp. 'Epilogue Spoken at the Opening
of the New House' ll. 7–24.
10. *my lady's eldest son*] i.e. a spoilt, talkative child (cp. *Much Ado About
Nothing* II i 9).
11. *vizard mask*] See 'Prologue to *2 Conquest of Granada*' l. 13n.
12. *mid gallery*] For the middle gallery as a haunt of rakes and prostitutes cp.
'Prologue to *The Disappointment*' ll. 57–8.
15. *clutter*] turmoil (*OED* 4).

Let vizard mask her naked face expose,
20 On pain of being thought to want a nose:
Then for your lackeys, and your train beside
(By whate'er name or title dignified)
They roar so loud you'd think behind the stairs
Tom Dove and all the brotherhood of bears:
25 They're grown a nuisance beyond all disasters—
We've none so great but their unpaying masters.
We beg you, sirs, to beg your men, that they
Would please to give you leave to hear the play.
Next, in the playhouse spare your precious lives;
30 Think, like good Christians, on your bairns and wives:
Think on your souls—but by your lugging forth
It seems you know how little they are worth.
If none of these will move the warlike mind,
Think on the helpless whore you leave behind!
35 We beg you last, our scene-room to forbear,
And leave our goods and chattels to our care.
Alas, our women are but washy toys,
And wholly taken up in stage employs;
Poor willing tits they are, but yet I doubt
40 This double duty soon will wear 'em out.
Then you are watched besides, with jealous care;
What if my lady's page should find you there?
My lady knows t' a tittle what there's in ye;
No passing your gilt shilling for a guinea.

20. to want a nose] to have lost a nose through syphilis.

23. behind the stairs] At Drury Lane the stairs to the side boxes were close to
the stage, and servants waiting there would have been clearly audible.

24. Tom Dove] a bear exhibited at the Bear Garden.

26. unpaying masters] Theatregoers could see a single Act free if they either
paid or left at the end; some patrons avoided paying by changing their seats;
and gentlemen were also admitted on credit (*LS* lxxi–lxxiv; Pepys 7 January
1668).

29–34. Playhouse brawls were common: cp. 'Prologue to *The Spanish Friar*'
l. 40*n* and 'Another Epilogue to *The Duke of Guise*' ll. 5–6*n*.

31. lugging forth] drawing swords.

35. scene-room] The scene-room was found useful for meetings between
patrons and actresses: cp. 'Epilogue to *The Assignation*' ll. 20–1 and 'Epilogue
to *Henry the Second*' ll. 21–4.

37. washy] weak (*OED* 6), perhaps with a pun on 'wash' meaning cosmetics
(*OED* 3b).

39. tits] girls (*OED* sb.³ 2).

45   Thus, gentlemen, we have summed up in short
     Our grievances from country, town and court:
     Which humbly we submit to your good pleasure;
     But first vote money, then redress at leisure.

48. Parliament normally voted the King money after discussing the redress of grievances.

74 Religio Laici

Date and publication. Religio Laici or A Laymans Faith. A Poem was published by Tonson in late November 1682: Luttrell's copy is dated 28 November (Macdonald 33), and the poem was advertised in *The Observator* on 30 November. There were three issues of the first edition (siglum: '*1682a*'), and reprints in 1682 ('*1682b*') and 1683. The present text is from *1682a*, second issue, which includes revisions in the Preface and l. 456. The first edition includes two commendatory poems, one anonymous (apparently by John Vaughan: see Richard H. Perkinson, *PQ* xxviii (1949) 517–18), and one by Thomas Creech; *1683* adds one by Roscommon (see Appendix B). Although D. considered including *RL* in *Sylvae* (see *Letters* 23), it was not reprinted in D.'s lifetime.

Context. The immediate occasion of *RL* was the publication of *A Critical History of the Old Testament*, a translation by Henry Dickinson of the *Histoire Critique du Vieux Testament* (1678) by the French Catholic priest Richard Simon (1638–1712). This pioneering work of biblical criticism studied the textual problems of the OT, discussing the corruptions which had crept into the text in the process of its transmission, and evaluating modern translations. Simon thought that this demonstration of the unreliability of the text of scripture had grave consequences for the Protestant reliance on scripture as the sole authoritative source of Christian teaching (see ll. 276–81*n*). But Simon had criticized Catholic as well as Protestant authorities, and copies of the first edition of the book were seized and burnt in Paris before it was officially published. It was reprinted in 1680 in Amsterdam (three impressions). Rejoinders soon appeared: Charles Marie Du Veil (1678) pointed out the dangerous implications of Simon's work for Protestant reliance on the Bible, and Friedrich Spanheim (1679) argued that Simon's work was dangerous to Christianity generally. For Simon see further Jean Steinmann, *Richard Simon et les origines de l'exégèse biblique* (1960) and Paul Auvray, *Richard Simon* (1974). For the relationship of *RL* to Simon's work see Phillip Harth, *Contexts of Dryden's Thought* (1968), which provides a detailed and authoritative discussion of the poem's contexts and arguments, and Gerard Reedy, *The Bible and Reason* (1985) 90–118.

Around May 1681 Tonson began negotiations with Dickinson for a translation of Simon's work, but after the translation was complete he withdrew from what he now considered to be a dangerous project; the English version was published with the imprint of Walter Davis late in 1681 (dated 1682). After poor sales, Tonson took the book over and reissued it with his own name on the title page, adding Dickinson's translation of Simon's reply to Spanheim, and including commendatory poems from Richard Duke, Nathaniel Lee and Nahum Tate; another appeared in *Sylvae* (1685). Harth 194 suggests that *RL* may have originated as D.'s commendatory poem for this volume (perhaps the extant ll. 228–51). D. might have been motivated not only by his intellectual interest in the work, and loyalty to Tonson, but also by the Cambridge connection with Dickinson, who was a graduate of D.'s college, Trinity (matric. 1673, LLB 1678). For the publishing history of the translation see Charles E. Ward, *MLN* lxi (1946) 407–12. Dickinson saw the translation as a means of combating deism, by 'giving in English a Piece of so much Learning, and from whence we may draw convincing Arguments for the confuting of all the atheistical Opinions of our Age. There are a sort of half-learned men ... searching out of the Bible those things onely which at the first sight seem to destroy the authority of it. ... We have a fresh example of what I have been saying in the person of him, who, not many years ago, occasion'd the publishing of that excellent Piece, intituled, *A Letter to A Deist*' (sig. A2^{r-v}). Reaction to the translation included a letter from John Evelyn to John Fell, Bishop of Oxford, on 19 March 1682, expressing concern that Simon's book would be seen as undermining the Protestant claim to rest faith on scripture alone (*Diary and Correspondence of John Evelyn*, edited by William Bray, 4 vols (1854) iii 264–7; Harth 185–6). Dissenters were also worried, and William Lorimer's *An Examination of a Considerable Part of Pere Simon's Critical History of the Old Testament* appeared in 1682 with a preface by Richard Baxter.

The wider context for *RL* is that of religious controversy in the Restoration period. The principal guide to this is Harth's book, though Sanford Budick's *Dryden and the Abyss of Light* (1970) and Victor M. Hamm's article on D. and Catholic apologists, *PMLA* lxxx (1965) 190–8, are also useful. (Louis I. Bredvold's *The Intellectual Milieu of John Dryden* (1934) includes interesting material, but his argument that *RL* is almost Catholic in spirit is misguided, and has been refuted by Thomas H. Fujimura, *PMLA* lxxvi (1961) 205–17.) Four questions of particular concern to *RL* may be distinguished. (i) The poem places great emphasis upon the right use of reason in religious matters. Anglican theology had come to stress the importance of rational inquiry as an aid to religious understanding: in different ways this was a concern of the Tew Circle in the 1630s (whose members included Viscount Falkland and William Chillingworth), the Cambridge Platonists in the 1650s (including Benjamin Whichcote, Ralph Cudworth, Henry More and John Smith), and the group which were now being called Latitudinarians (including Edward Stillingfleet and John Tillotson: for their beliefs see Simon Patrick, *A Brief Account of the New Sect of Latitude-Men* (1662)). For discussions of the importance of reason in Restoration religion see R. W. McHenry, *Mosaic* vii (1974) 69–86; Spurr 249–69 (a useful brief context for the debates in *RL*) and in *JHI* xlix (1988) 563–85; Lotte Mulligan in *Occult and Scientific Mentalities in the Renaissance*, edited by Brian Vickers (1984) 375–401; Gillian Manning, *SC* viii (1993) 99–121; and *Philosophy, Science and Religion in England 1640–1700*, edited by Richard Kroll et al. (1992). D. argues that reason has an important place in the understanding of religious matters, but it cannot produce all the answers, and has to give way to faith at the appropriate point. (ii) The poem combats the deist position, according to which human reason is sufficient to discover that there is a God, and that man is to serve him through worship. Deism in England is generally traced back to Lord Herbert of Cherbury and his treatises *De Veritate* (1624) and *De Religione Laici* (1645; edited by and tr. Harold R. Hutcheson (1944)). In Restoration England deist ideas had some currency, but not in printed form until *The Oracles of Reason* (1693), a collection of tracts edited by Charles Blount, though Harth notes that two of the pieces in this collection are found in MS (bound with printed tracts in BL 873.b.3) and might therefore have been available to D. in MS form when writing *RL*. For a discussion of seventeenth-century deism see Hutcheson 55–81 and Harth 56–94, and for contemporary views of deism see Edward Stillingfleet's *A Letter to a Deist* (1677), and William Stephens's *An Account of the Growth of Deism in England* (1696). D. argues against the deist that human intuition is insufficient, and only supernatural revelation can inform us truly and fully of God and his will; in any case, human reasoning is itself only the afterglow of revelation. (iii) The poem combats the Roman Catholic position that church tradition, specifically that embodied in the papacy, provides the only authoritative guide which God has given mankind. Against this claim D. argues that scripture is the only authoritative word of God, and that this, carefully interpreted, gives man all he needs to know. This is the common tenor of Protestant apologetics throughout the seventeenth century. (iv) The poem also combats the nonconformists, who rely upon the inspiration of the spirit to guide them in interpreting scripture, and who will admit no human authority external to themselves. Although the dissenting sects had been marginalized and contained by the Restoration settlement, they still flourished, and the upheaval of the Exclusion Crisis in 1680–2 had been fuelled partly by adherents to 'the Good Old Cause', who combined republicanism in politics with nonconformity in religion. All in all, *RL* argues for a non-Calvinist, Anglican position, which insists that the use of reason in matters of religion is necessary but insufficient; man's natural reason and intuition need to be corrected and completed by revelation; God's revelation is found definitively in the Bible; the Bible may be troubled by textual errors but is clear from doubt at all important points; interpretation should take tradition into account, but cannot rely upon it; and private reason or inspiration must be checked by tradition and consensus.

Structure. These topics are organized into a carefully-designed argument, the first part of which Harth (96) outlines thus:

I. *Necessity of Revelation* (ll. 1–125).
    (a) Inadequacy of natural religion (ll. 1–92).
    (b) Our dependence on revelation for the means of atonement (ll. 93–125).
II. *Proofs that this Revelation is Contained in the Bible* (ll. 126–67).
    (a) Superiority of its teachings to those of other religions in answering the ends of human life (ll. 126–33).
    (b) Antiquity of its laws (ll. 134–7).

(c) Character and circumstances of its authors (ll. 138–45).
(d) Confirmation of its doctrines by miracles (ll. 146–51).
(e) Its remarkable reception, in spite of so many hindrances, internal and external (ll. 152–67).

III. *Answer to the Objection of the Deist* (ll. 168–223).

At this point D. turns to Simon's book, and we may summarize the argument of the rest of the poem thus:

ll. 224–51: Commendation of Simon's book and Dickinson's translation.

ll. 252–75: If the text of the Bible (upon which Protestants rely) has suffered through the process of transmission over the centuries, all the more so has oral tradition (upon which Catholics rely).

ll. 276–81: Interjection of the Catholic argument that only church tradition can provide a reliable guide when the text of the Bible is uncertain.

ll. 282–369: The Anglican rejoinder that the text of the Bible is sufficiently clear at all essential points, and if it needs to be interpreted by reference to tradition, the most reliable tradition is the most ancient one, i.e. the interpretations of scripture provided by the early church fathers, not by the modern papacy.

ll. 370–97: During the Middle Ages the Catholic church kept the Bible in the hands of the priests; at the Reformation the people discovered what it was of which they had been deprived.

ll. 398–426: The widespread availability of the Bible had the unfortunate effect of permitting individual interpretations of scripture, and encouraging the proliferation of sects.

ll. 427–50: The safest way to proceed is to rely upon the clear passages of scripture, and to seek guidance from authoritative tradition, setting aside idiosyncratic personal opinions in the interests of public harmony.

Sources. Many of the arguments in *RL* are commonplaces of seventeenth-century religious debate, but Harth established that D. made extensive use of Sir Charles Wolseley's *The Reasonablenes of Scripture-Belief* (1672), which he followed closely in the arguments against deism in the first half of *RL*. D. may also have used Wolseley's *The Unreasonablenesse of Atheism Made Manifest* (1669). Other likely sources were Richard Burthogge's *Causa Dei* (1675) (see Budick 85–92) and Hamon L'Estrange's *Considerations, upon Dr Bayly's Parenthetical Interlocution* (1651) (Sanford Budick, *N & Q* ccxiv (1969) 375–9). D.'s knowledge of deism might have derived from reading Lord Herbert of Cherbury, but Harth showed that D.'s formulation of the seven catholic articles is closest to that found in the tract 'Of Natural Religion', first printed in 1693 but possibly available to D. in MS (see above and ll. 42–61n). Since Stephens in *An Account of the Growth of Deism in England* says that he has gained his knowledge of deist principles from inquiry and conversation

among acquaintances in London, rather than from reading, D. may likewise
have been able to draw upon personal contacts. For the second part of *RL*,
which discusses the issues raised by Simon's book, D. evidently read at least
some parts of the *Critical History* attentively. D.'s passages defending the
Protestant reliance on the authority of scripture against the Catholic adherence to church tradition draw upon a debate in which many writers had been
embroiled for decades (see Harth 199–200); since most of their arguments
had become commonplaces, it is impossible to establish D.'s sources here
with any confidence, though he evidently knew Hooker (see Preface l. 324).
The records of D.'s purchases at book auctions on 19 April 1680 and 15 May
1682 show that he was reading extensively in Protestant and Catholic theology: for details see T. A. Birrell, *ES* xlii (1961) 193–217. K. W. Gransden
(*SEL* xvii (1977) 397–406) argues for the general influence of Latin satire on
RL.

Reception. Contemporary reception seems to have been muted. Luttrell wrote
'Atheisticall' on his copy (Macdonald 33). For Henry Care's response see
Preface l. 300*n*. Charles Blount's *Religio Laici* (1683) is addressed to D. and
commends *RL*, but is largely derived from Herbert of Cherbury (see Harth
92–4). Two poems in *MP* (1684) commend *RL*, one by Roscommon and the
other anonymous. Robert Gould in *The Laureat* [1687] derides D.'s discussion of Athanasius, and J. R.'s *Religio Laici* (1688) borrows D.'s title for an
attack on his change of religion. William Lowth's *A Vindication of the Divine
Authority and Inspiration of the Writings of the Old and New Testaments* (1692)
refers to D.'s treatment of Simon in *RL* (sigs. b^r–b2^r).

Religio Laici
or
A Layman's Faith
A Poem

Ornari res ipsa negat; contenta doceri.

¶74. *Title. Religio Laici*] 'The religion of a layman'. The title has precedents in
Lord Herbert of Cherbury's *De Religione Laici* (1645; its running title is
Religio Laici (Harth 62)), Sir Thomas Browne's *Religio Medici* (1642) and Sir
George Mackenzie's *Religio Stoici* (1665).
Epigraph. 'The subject itself refuses to be ornamented; it is content to be
explained' (Manilius, *Astronomica* iii 39). In the 'Dedication of the *Aeneis*'
(1697) (*Works* v 318) D. quotes this line again, and applies it to Horace's
satires and epistles.

The Preface

A poem with so bold a title, and a name prefixed from
which the handling of so serious a subject would not be
expected, may reasonably oblige the author to say
somewhat in defence both of himself and of his under-
5 taking. In the first place, if it be objected to me that
being a layman I ought not to have concerned myself
with speculations which belong to the profession of
divinity, I could answer that perhaps laymen, with
equal advantages of parts and knowledge, are not the
10 most incompetent judges of sacred things; but in the
due sense of my own weakness and want of learning, I
plead not this: I pretend not to make myself a judge of
faith in others, but only to make a confession of my
own; I lay no unhallowed hand upon the ark, but wait
15 on it, with the reverence that becomes me, at a distance.
In the next place, I will ingenuously confess that the
helps I have used in this small treatise were many of
them taken from the works of our own reverend
divines of the Church of England, so that the weapons
20 with which I combat irreligion are already consecrated;
though I suppose they may be taken down as lawfully
as the sword of Goliah was by David, when they are to
be employed for the common cause against the enemies
of piety. I intend not by this to entitle them to any of
25 my errors, which yet I hope are only those of charity to
mankind; and such as my own charity has caused me to
commit, that of others may more easily excuse. Being
naturally inclined to scepticism in philosophy, I have no

9. parts] abilities, talents.

14. lay no unhallowed hand upon the ark] Uzzah was struck dead by God for touching the ark in order to stop it toppling (1 Chronicles xiii 9–10; cp. *AA* l. 804*n*).

22. sword of Goliah] David, fleeing from Saul, took the sword of Goliath
whom he had killed (1 Samuel xxi 8–9; cp. *HP* ii 599–600).

24. entitle them to] impute to them (*OED* 5c).

28. scepticism] Harth 1–31 argues convincingly that this refers to modesty and
diffidence in inquiry, as advocated by the Royal Society and by others in the
Restoration, rather than to the sceptical approach to epistemology which
derives from Greek philosophy and is exemplified in Montaigne. The
opposite to *scepticism* in this Restoration sense would be dogmatism. 'He is
drawing our attention to his way of reasoning, not to his theory of knowl-

reason to impose my opinions in a subject which is
30 above it; but whatever they are I submit them with all
reverence to my mother church, accounting them no
further mine than as they are authorized, or at least
uncondemned, by her. And indeed, to secure myself on
this side, I have used the necessary precaution of show-
35 ing this paper before it was published to a judicious and
learned friend, a man indefatigably zealous in the service of the church and state, and whose writings have
highly deserved of both. He was pleased to approve the

---

edge' (Harth 7). Cp. D.'s *Defence of EDP* (1667): 'my whole Discourse was
Sceptical, according to that way of reasoning which was used by *Socrates*,
Plato, and all the Academiques of old, which *Tully* and the best of the
Ancients followed, and which is imitated by the modest Inquisitions of the
Royal Society . . . it is a Dialogue sustain'd by persons of several opinions, all
of them left doubtful, to be determined by the Readers' (*Works* ix 15). In the
'Life of Plutarch' prefixed to *Plutarchs Lives* (1683), D. writes approvingly of
Plutarch's rejection of both the dogmatism of the Epicureans and Stoics, and
the excessive scepticism of the Pyrrhonists: he 'was content . . . only to
propound and weigh opinions, leaving the Judgment of his Readers free
without presuming to decide Dogmatically. Yet it is to be confess'd, that in
the midst of this moderation, he oppos'd the two extreams of the *Epicurean*
and *Stoick* Sects: Both which he has judiciously combatted in several of his
treatises, and both upon the same account, because they pretend too much to
certainty, in their Dogma's; and to impose them with too great arrogance;
which he, who (following the *Academists*,) doubted more and pretended less,
was no way able to support. The *Pyrrhonians*, or grosser sort of *Scepticks*,
who bring all certainty in question, and startle even at the notions of
Common sense, appear'd as absurd to him on the other side; for there is a
kind of positiveness in granting nothing to be more likely on the one part
than on another, which his Academy avoided by inclining the ballance to that
hand, where the most weighty reasons, and probability of truth were visible'
(*Works* xvii 249).
29–30. a subject which is above it] i.e. theology.
35–6. a judicious and learned friend] Identified as John Tillotson (1630–94) by
David Nichol Smith (*John Dryden* (1950) 88–9); see further David D.
Brown, *MLR* lvi (1961) 66–9. Tillotson was a notable preacher, Dean of
Canterbury 1672–89, Dean of St Paul's 1689–91, and Archbishop of Canterbury 1691–4. (Kinsley and *Works* follow Smith in giving wrong dates here.)
His treatise *The Rule of Faith* (1666) was a work of Protestant apologetics
which stressed the role of reason in matters of religion, and his many pub-
lished sermons traversed similar ground. He was not comfortable with the
Athanasian Creed, and in a letter to Gilbert Burnet in 1694 said 'I wish we
were well rid of it' (BodL MS Add D. 23 f. 62; Kinsley).

body of the discourse, and I hope he is more my friend
40   than to do it out of complaisance. 'Tis true he had too
good a taste to like it all, and amongst some other faults
recommended to my second view what I have written,
perhaps too boldly, on St Athanasius, which he advised
me wholly to omit. I am sensible enough that I had
45   done more prudently to have followed his opinion, but
then I could not have satisfied myself that I had done
honestly not to have written what was my own. It has
always been my thought that heathens who never did,
nor without miracle could hear of the name of Christ,
50   were yet in a possibility of salvation. Neither will it
enter easily into my belief, that before the coming of
our Saviour, the whole world, excepting only the Jewish nation, should lie under the inevitable necessity of
everlasting punishment, for want of that revelation
55   which was confined to so small a spot of ground as that
of Palestine. Among the sons of Noah we read of one
only who was accursed, and if a blessing in the ripeness
of time was reserved for Japhet (of whose progeny we
are), it seems unaccountable to me why so many gener-

40. *complaisance*] mere desire to please.

43. *Athanasius*] See Preface ll. 130–75.

44. *sensible*] conscious, aware.

48–50. *heathens . . . were yet in a possibility of salvation*] Christian theologians
had long been divided on the question of whether virtuous heathens who had
had no opportunity to learn of Christ could be saved. The view taken by D.
had some support from contemporaries, e.g. Martin Clifford: 'Certainly in
the two contrary excesses of belief in this matter, that on the side of Mercy
hath the appearance of greater safety; and I had rather think with *Origen, That
the Devils themselves, by the excessive kindness of their Judge, shall at last be
exempted from damnation*, than that he himself shall be damn'd for that
Opinion'; furthermore, 'so small a part of Mankind hath submitted to the
Obedience of the Christian Faith: Now to condemn all those Millions of
persons . . . is so wild an uncharitableness, that few have been so barbarously
severe, as to be guilty of it' (*A Treatise of Humane Reason* (1675) 30–2); cp.
also Tillotson, Wilkins and Burthogge, quoted in Harth 163–4, and Harth's
discussion generally, 156–73.

56. *sons of Noah*] After the flood God blessed the sons of Noah, though Ham
was subsequently cursed because he saw his father's nakedness (Genesis ix 1,
22–5). Noah's son Japheth was said to be the ancestor of the Gentiles, and
their knowledge to be the dimly remembered instructions of Noah to his
sons (see Don Cameron Allen, *The Legend of Noah* (1949) 116 and Harth 121).

60 ations of the same offspring as preceded our Saviour in
the flesh should be all involved in one common con-
demnation, and yet that their posterity should be en-
titled to the hopes of salvation: as if a Bill of Exclusion
had passed only on the fathers, which debarred not the
65 sons from their succession. Or that so many ages had
been delivered over to hell, and so many reserved for
heaven, and that the devil had the first choice and God
the next. Truly I am apt to think that the revealed
religion which was taught by Noah to all his sons might
70 continue for some ages in the whole posterity: that
afterwards it was included wholly in the family of Sem
is manifest, but when the progenies of Cham and Japhet
swarmed into colonies, and those colonies were subdiv-
ided into many others, in process of time their descend-
75 ants lost by little and little the primitive and purer rites
of divine worship, retaining only the notion of one
deity, to which succeeding generations added others
(for men took their degrees in those ages from conquer-
ors to gods). Revelation being thus eclipsed to almost
80 all mankind, the light of nature as the next in dignity
was substituted, and that is it which St Paul concludes
to be the rule of the heathens, and by which they are
hereafter to be judged. If my supposition be true, then
the consequence which I have assumed in my poem
85 may be also true, namely, that deism, or the principles
of natural worship, are only the faint remnants or dying
flames of revealed religion in the posterity of Noah, and
that our modern philosophers, nay, and some of our
philosophizing divines, have too much exalted the

63. Bill of Exclusion] Alluding to the Whig attempts in 1680–1 to pass a bill
excluding James, Duke of York, from the succession to the throne.
78. took their degrees] graduated (i.e. successful conquerers were deified).
81. St Paul] In Romans ii 14–15: 'For when the Gentiles, which have not the
law, do by nature the things contained in the law, these, having not the law,
are a law unto themselves: Which shew the work of the law written in their
hearts, their conscience also bearing witness'.
85. deism] Belief in the existence of a God, based upon the testimony of reason, but rejecting revelation (*OED*'s first example). See headnote, '*Context*'.
88–9 our modern philosophers ... philosophizing divines] Those thinkers who
emphasized the capacity of unaided human reason to form some conception

90 faculties of our souls, when they have maintained that
    by their force mankind has been able to find out that
    there is one supreme agent or intellectual being which
    we call God, that praise and prayer are his due worship,
    and the rest of those deducements, which I am confi-
95 dent are the remote effects of revelation, and unattain-
    able by our discourse—I mean as simply considered,
    and without the benefit of divine illumination. So that
    we have not lifted up ourselves to God by the weak
    pinions of our reason, but he has been pleased to de-
100 scend to us; and what Socrates said of him, what Plato
    writ, and the rest of the heathen philosophers of several
    nations, is all no more than the twilight of revelation,

---

of God. Among such philosophers would be the deist Lord Herbert of
Cherbury (see headnote); René Descartes, whose *Meditationes de Prima Philo-
sophia* (1641) argued that the concept of a supremely perfect being proved the
existence of that being; and Walter Charleton, D.'s friend, and a follower of
Gassendi (see 'To Dr Charleton', headnote). The philosophizing divines
would primarily be the Cambridge Platonists, such as Ralph Cudworth, who
thought that religious truths, once they were revealed by God, were amen-
able to rational inquiry. D. is arguing that reason, while having its proper
place in religious discourse, is ultimately incapable of understanding religious
truths fully. See further Harth 129–34.

90. faculties of our souls] Renaissance philosophers, developing Aristotle's *De
Anima*, divided the soul into the vegetative, the sensitive and the intellective,
each with its appropriate faculties; the intellective soul had the faculties of
intellect, will and memory (see *The Cambridge History of Renaissance Philosophy*, edited by Charles B. Schmitt (1988) 455–534, esp. 466–7).

92. intellectual being] a being who can be apprehended only by the intellect,
not by the senses (*OED* 2).

93. praise and prayer are his due worship] For these, and the other inferences of
natural religion, see headnote, '*Context*', and ll. 42–61*n*.

94. deducements] deductions.

95–7. Cp. Wolseley: 'So *Plato* and others having spoken somewhat of *One
God* (Though it ought to be noted that the Being of *One God* was never
generally and distinctly acknowledged in any *Heathen Country*, nor was there
ever a *Law* made in any *Heathen State* to establish the Being and Worship of
one God. Nay, some have supposed that no particular *Person* did ever purely
by *Natural Light*, determine that there was *but one God*: But that such who
have spoken of it had it from a *Tradition* originated in *Revelation*)' (*Reasonablenes* 109–10; Harth 124–5).

96. discourse] reasoning (*OED* 2); the word is used frequently by Wolseley
(e.g. 83).

99. pinions] wings.

after the sun of it was set in the race of Noah. That there
is something above us, some principle of motion, our
105 reason can apprehend, though it cannot discover what it
is by its own virtue. And indeed 'tis very improbable
that we, who by the strength of our faculties cannot
enter into the knowledge of any being, not so much as
of our own, should be able to find out by them that
110 supreme nature which we cannot otherwise define than
by saying it is infinite, as if infinite were definable, or
infinity a subject for our narrow understanding. They
who would prove religion by reason do but weaken the
cause which they endeavour to support: 'tis to take
115 away the pillars from our faith, and to prop it only with
a twig; 'tis to design a tower like that of Babel, which if
it were possible (as it is not) to reach heaven, would
come to nothing by the confusion of the workmen. For
every man is building a several way, impotently
120 conceited of his own model and his own materials:
reason is always striving, and always at a loss, and of
necessity it must so come to pass, while 'tis exercised
about that which is not its proper object. Let us be
content at last to know God by his own methods, at
125 least so much of him as he is pleased to reveal to us in
the sacred scriptures; to apprehend them to be the word
of God is all our reason has to do, for all beyond it is the
work of faith, which is the seal of heaven impressed
upon our human understanding.

104. principle of motion] Aristotle introduced the idea of a first mover, the
origin of all motion in the universe, which is itself unmoved. This became the
first of Aquinas' five ways of deducing the existence of God from general
facts about the universe. The point applies not to a creator who initiates the
universe and then leaves it (e.g. to run like a clock), but to one who continues
as a sustaining cause of the universe, for according to Aristotelian physics (in
contrast to Newton's physics, to be described in his *Principia* (1687)), the
continuation of motion requires explanation, just as much as its initiation
does.   *principle*] fundamental source, cause (*OED* 3).
106. virtue] strength.
116. Babel] The builders of the tower of Babel intended it to reach to heaven;
God decided to 'confound their language, that they may not understand one
another's speech' (Genesis xi 1–9).
119. several] different.
120. conceited of] possessed with a good opinion of (*OED* 2b).
128. seal] D. adapts and reapplies the image of sealing which was common in

130   And now for what concerns the holy bishop Athana-
        sius, the preface of whose creed seems inconsistent with
        my opinion, which is that heathens may possibly be
        saved. In the first place, I desire it may be considered
        that it is the preface only, not the creed itself, which (till
135   I am better informed) is of too hard a digestion for my
        charity. 'Tis not that I am ignorant how many several
        texts of scripture seemingly support that cause, but
        neither am I ignorant how all those texts may receive a
        kinder and more mollified interpretation. Every man
140   who is read in church history knows that belief was
        drawn up after a long contestation with Arius concern-
        ing the divinity of our blessed Saviour, and his being
        one substance with the Father; and that thus compiled it
        was sent abroad among the Christian churches as a kind
145   of test, which whosoever took was looked on as an
        orthodox believer. 'Tis manifest from hence that the
        heathen part of the empire was not concerned in it, for
        its business was not to distinguish betwixt pagans and
        Christians, but betwixt heretics and true believers. This
150   well considered takes off the heavy weight of censure

Calvinist writing to indicate those whom God had predestined for eternal
salvation (based on Ephesians iv 30 and Revelation vii 4).
130–75. Athanasius] St Athanasius (*c.*296–373) was Bishop of Alexandria, and
the leading opponent of Arianism (which denied the divinity of Christ, and
taught that the Son of God was not eternal, but created by the Father). The
Athanasian Creed (no longer attributed to the saint following the researches
of Gerard Voss (1642)), is prefaced by the assertion: 'Whosoever will be
saved: before all things it is necessary that he hold the Catholick Faith. Which
Faith except every one do keep whole and undefiled: without doubt he shall
perish everlastingly'. Various seventeenth-century divines were troubled by
the damnatory clauses in this creed. Harth 172–3 notes that D.'s arguments
here are paralleled by (and may derive from) those of the distinguished
Anglican divine Henry Hammond, quoted by Gabriel Towerson in his *A
Briefe Account of Some Expressions in Saint Athanasius His Creed* (1663) 8–9: 'I
suppose they must be interpreted by their *opposition* to those *Heresies* that had
invaded the *Church* ... against the *Apostolick Doctrine* ... and were therefore
to be *anathematiz'd* after this manner and with *detestation* branded and
banished out of the *Church*; Not that it was hereby defin'd to be a *damnable
sin*, to faile in the *understanding*, or *believing* the full matter of any of those
explications before they were *propounded*'.
141. contestation] disputation, controversy.

which I would willingly avoid from so venerable a
man, for if this proportion, 'whosoever will be saved',
be restrained only to those to whom it was intended,
and for whom it was composed (I mean the Christians),
155 then the anathema reaches not the heathens, who had
never heard of Christ, and were nothing interessed in
that dispute. After all, I am far from blaming even that
prefatory addition to the creed, and as far from cavilling
at the continuation of it in the liturgy of the church,
160 where on the days appointed 'tis publicly read: for I
suppose there is the same reason for it now, in opposition to the Socinians, as there was then against the
Arians, the one being a heresy which seems to have
been refined out of the other, and with how much more
165 plausibility of reason it combats our religion, with so
much more caution to be avoided, and therefore the
prudence of our church is to be commended which has
interposed her authority for the recommendation of this
creed. Yet to such as are grounded in the true belief,
170 those explanatory creeds, the Nicene and this of Athanasius, might perhaps be spared; for what is supernatural will always be a mystery in spite of exposition, and
for my own part the plain Apostles' Creed is most
suitable to my weak understanding, as the simplest diet
175 is the most easy of digestion.

151. *avoid*] remove (*OED* 4).
152. *proportion*] part of the whole.
153. *restrained*] restricted.
156. *interessed*] implicated, involved (*OED* 2).
160. *on the days appointed*] The *Book of Common Prayer* (1662) prescribes the
use of the Athanasian Creed in place of the Apostles' Creed at Morning
Prayer on thirteen holy days.
162. *Socinians*] Unitarian belief, which dates from the Reformation, rejects
the doctrines of the Trinity and the divinity of Christ; it became particularly
associated with the names of Lelio and Fausto Socini (uncle and nephew,
1525–62 and 1539–1604). See H. J. McLachlan, *Socinianism in Seventeenth-
Century England* (1951). D. bought Johan Crell's Socinian treatise *Ethica Aris-
totelia*. *Ethica Christiana* (1681) in 1682 (T. A. Birrell, *ES* xlii (1961) 209).
170. *Nicene*] The Nicene Creed was drawn up at the Council of Nicaea (325)
to defend the orthodox faith against the Arians; a longer version of this creed
is commonly used in the eucharist. Its statements on the person of Christ and
the work of the Holy Spirit are more explanatory than those of the terser
Apostles' Creed.

I have dwelt longer on this subject than I intended,
and longer than perhaps I ought; for having laid down,
as my foundation, that the scripture is a rule, that in all
things needful to salvation it is clear, sufficient and
180 ordained by God Almighty for that purpose, I have left
myself no right to interpret obscure places such as concern the possibility of eternal happiness to heathens,
because whatsoever is obscure is concluded not necessary to be known.
185   But, by asserting the scripture to be the canon of our
faith, I have unavoidably created to myself two sorts of
enemies: the papists, indeed, more directly, because
they have kept the scripture from us, what they could,
and have reserved to themselves a right of interpreting
190 what they have delivered under the pretence of infallibility; and the fanatics more collaterally, because they
have assumed what amounts to an infallibility in the
private spirit, and have detorted those texts of scripture
which are not necessary to salvation to the damnable
195 uses of sedition, disturbance and destruction of the civil
government. To begin with the papists, and to speak
freely, I think them the less dangerous (at least, in
appearance) to our present state, for not only the penal
laws are in force against them, and their number is
200 contemptible, but also their peerage and commons are
excluded from parliaments, and consequently those
laws in no probability of being repealed. A general and

185. canon] standard of judgement or authority (*OED* 2c).
188. kept the scripture from us] Translation of the Bible into English was
forbidden at the Council of Oxford (1407); Tyndale's translation of the NT
was printed abroad in 1525–6, and of the Pentateuch in 1529–30. As the
Reformation took hold in England several translations were made; the first
one authorized by Henry VIII appeared in 1537.   *what they could*] as far as
they could.
191–3. fanatics . . . private spirit] Members of extreme Protestant sects claimed
to be directly and individually inspired by the Holy Spirit.
191. collaterally] secondarily, indirectly.
193. detorted] twisted.
198–9. penal laws] See *AA* ll. 94–5n.
199. number] See *AA* l. 123n.
201. excluded from parliaments] The Test Act of 1673 excluded all but adherents
to the Church of England from public office, and that of 1678 imposed an
affirmation of Anglican belief on Members of both Houses of Parliament.

uninterrupted plot of their clergy ever since the Reformation, I suppose all Protestants believe; for 'tis not
205 reasonable to think but that so many of their orders as
were outed from their fat possessions would endeavour
a re-entrance against those whom they account heretics.
As for the late design, Mr Coleman's letters, for aught I
know, are the best evidence, and what they discover,
210 without wire-drawing their sense, or malicious glosses,
all men of reason conclude credible. If there be anything
more than this required of me, I must believe it as well
as I am able, in spite of the witnesses, and out of a
decent conformity to the votes of Parliament. For I
215 suppose the fanatics will not allow the private spirit in
this case: here the infallibility is at least in one part of the
government, and our understandings as well as our
wills are represented. But to return to the Roman Catholics, how can we be secure from the practice of Jesuited
220 papists in that religion? For not two or three of that

203. plot] Many seventeenth-century Protestants supposed that Roman Catholic clergy (esp. the Jesuits) were plotting to overthrow Protestantism in
England; episodes such as the Gunpowder Plot (1605) and the Popish Plot
(1678–9) fuelled such fears.
206 outed] ousted. *fat possessions*] After the dissolution of the monasteries,
abbey lands were sold or given to laymen. The supposed desire of the Roman
Catholic religious orders to recover them was a standard topic in seventeenth-century Protestant polemic.
208. the late design] The Popish Plot to kill Charles II and impose Catholicism
by force; it was uncovered (but largely invented) by Titus Oates in the
autumn of 1678. *Mr Coleman's letters*] Edward Coleman, secretary to the
Duchess of York and previously to the Duke, corresponded with Louis
XIV's Jesuit confessor François La Chaise and others on the ways of promoting 'the conversion of three kingdoms, and by that perhaps the subduing of a
pestilent heresy which has domineered over a greater part of.this northern
world a long time' (J. P. Kenyon, *The Popish Plot* (1972) 101). The letters
were discovered during the Popish Plot crisis; Coleman was found guilty of
treason, and executed on 3 December 1678.
210. wire-drawing] straining, forcing by subtle argument (*OED* 3c).
213 witnesses] The witnesses at the Popish Plot and Exclusion Crisis trials
were frequently suborned: see *AA* l. 922n.
219–20. Jesuited papists] The Jesuits were regarded as the leading proponents
of the idea that rulers could be resisted, deposed or even killed in the interests
of the Roman Catholic church. They were suspected of masterminding the
assassination of Henri IV of France, the Gunpowder Plot, and the Popish

order, as some of them would impose upon us, but
almost the whole body of them, are of opinion that
their infallible master has a right over kings, not only in
spirituals but temporals. Not to name Mariana, Bellar-
225 mine, Emmanuel Sa, Molina, Santarel, Simancha, and
at the least twenty others of foreign countries, we can
produce of our own nation Campion, and Doleman or
Parsons, besides many are named whom I have not
read, who all of them attest this doctrine, that the Pope
230 can depose and give away the right of any sovereign
prince, *si vel paulum deflexerit*, if he shall never so little
warp; but if he once comes to be excommunicated, then
the bond of obedience is taken off from subjects, and
they may and ought to drive him like another Nebu-
235 chadnezzar, *ex hominum Christianorum dominatu*, from

Plot. For a contemporary Protestant view of them see John Oldham, *Satyrs
upon the Jesuits* (1681). D. bought John Barnes's anti-Jesuit book *Dissertatio
contra Aequivocationes* (1625) in 1680 (Birrell 199).
224. Mariana] Juan Mariana (1536–1623), Spanish Jesuit, whose book *De Rege
et Regis Institutione* (1559) justified tyrannicide.   *Bellarmine*] Roberto Bel-
larmino (1542–1621), Italian Jesuit, who was one of the most prominent
Roman Catholic controversialists. Although he defended the temporal authority of the Pope, he held that the Pope had only an indirect power in
temporal matters. D. bought his *Dottrina Christiana* (1603) in Italian in 1680
(Birrell 208).
225. Emmanuel Sa] Manoel Sa (*c.*1530–96), Portuguese Jesuit, whose works
included a manual of casuistry.   *Molina*] Luis de Molina (1535–1600),
Spanish Jesuit, whose *De Justitia et Jure* (1592) argued that rulers' actions are
limited by natural law.   *Santarel*] Anton Santarelli (1569–1649), Italian
Jesuit, whose *Tractatus de haeresi* (1625) created a storm at the University of
Paris because of his remarks on the power of popes over kings.   *Simancha*]
Jacobus Simancas, late-sixteenth-century Spanish theologian and jurist.
227. Campion] Edmund Campion (1540–81), who was part of the first Jesuit
mission to England in 1580; he was arrested and executed in 1581 for conspiracy against the crown.   *Doleman or Parsons*] Robert Parsons (1546–1610),
who led the mission of 1580 with Campion; he escaped to the continent in
1581. His book *A Conference about the Next Succession to the Crowne of Ingland*
(1594), published under the name of R. Doleman, argued that bad kings may
lawfully be deposed by their people, and that the church has power over
rulers; it was reprinted in 1681.
234. Nebuchadnezzar] The king of Babylon, who was driven out from human
society and made to eat grass, because he would not acknowledge that God

exercising dominion over Christians: and to this they
are bound by virtue of divine precept, and by all the ties
of conscience under no less penalty than damnation. If
they answer me (as a learned priest has lately written)
240 that this doctrine of the Jesuits is not *de fide*, and that
consequently they are not obliged by it, they must
pardon me if I think they have said nothing to the
purpose, for 'tis a maxim in their church, where points
of faith are not decided, and that doctors are of contrary
245 opinions, they may follow which part they please, but
more safely the most received and most authorized.
And their champion Bellarmine has told the world in
his *Apology* that the King of England is a vassal to the
Pope, *ratione directi dominii*, and that he holds in villei-
250 nage of his Roman landlord: which is no new claim put
in for England. Our chronicles are his authentic witnesses that King John was deposed by the same plea,
and Philip Augustus admitted tenant. And, which
makes the more for Bellarmine, the French King was

'ruleth in the kingdom of men, and giveth it to whomsoever he will' (Daniel
iv 31–7).
239. a learned priest] Probably Peter Walsh, an Irish Franciscan, who wrote
that the Jesuits' 'deposing Doctrine is not a point of Faith' (*An Answer to
Three Treatises Publisht under the Title of The Jesuites Loyalty* (1678) 83; see
Richard H. Perkinson, *PQ* xxviii (1949) 517–18).
240. de fide] a matter of faith.
248. Apology] Bellarmine's *Apologia . . . pro responsione sua ad librum Jacobi
Magnae Britanniae Regis* (1610), a reply to James I's defence of the oath of
allegiance of subjects to their sovereign in *Triplici Nodo, Triplex Cuneus*
(1607). Bellarmine argues, from a series of medieval examples, that English
kings acknowledged that they were subject to the Pope (*Opera Omnia*, 12 vols
(1870–4) xii 126–8).
249. ratione directi dominii] 'by reason of the right of seignory': i.e. the King
holds his kingdom from the Pope just as a vassal holds his lands 'in villeinage'
from his feudal lord.
252. King John] In 1208 Pope Innocent III placed England under an interdict
(which excluded the people from the benefits of the church's offices), because
King John refused to recognize his appointment of Stephen Langton to the
see of Canterbury. In 1212 the Pope issued a bull excommunicating John and
deposing him from the throne, and entrusted its execution to Philip of
France. The following year John submitted to the Pope and placed the kingdom under his suzerainty.

255   again ejected when our King submitted to the church,
       and the crown received under the sordid condition of a
       vassalage.
         'Tis not sufficient for the more moderate and well-
       meaning papists (of which I doubt not there are many)
260   to produce the evidences of their loyalty to the late
       King, and to declare their innocency in this plot: I will
       grant their behaviour in the first to have been as loyal
       and as brave as they desire, and will be willing to hold
       them excused as to the second (I mean, when it comes
265   to my turn, and after my betters, for 'tis a madness to be
       sober alone, while the nation continues drunk), but that
       saying of their Father Cress. is still running in my head,
       that they may be dispensed with in their obedience to an
       heretic prince while the necessity of the times shall
270   oblige them to it: for that (as another of them tells us) is
       only the effect of Christian prudence, but when once
       they shall get power to shake him off, an heretic is no
       lawful king, and consequently to rise against him is no
       rebellion. I should be glad therefore that they would
275   follow the advice which was charitably given them by a
       reverend prelate of our church, namely that they would
       join in a public act of disowning and detesting those

260–1. *loyalty to the late King*] In *An Apology for the Catholics* (1666; revised
1674) Roger Palmer, Earl of Castlemaine, listed the Catholic gentry and lords
who were killed fighting for Charles I.
267. *Father Cress.*] Hugh Paulinus Cressy (1605–74), Benedictine monk and
servant to Queen Catherine; his *Exomologesis* (1647) gave an account of his
conversion to Rome. He wrote various historical and controversial works,
and the *Reflexions upon the Oathes of Supremacy and Allegiance* (1661) was
attributed to him. In this book (60–78) he denies that the Pope's power to
depose princes is held as an article of faith (*de fide*), and observes that books by
Suarez, Mariana, Bellarmine and Santarelli 'which maintained the *Popes temporal Jurisdiction* and *power to deprive Princes*, and *to absolve Subjects from their
Obedience*' have been condemned in Catholic countries (65). He says that
while some Catholics are prepared to renounce this view, they cannot swear
that this position is actually heretical.
270. *another*] unidentified.
276. *prelate of our church*] *Works* plausibly suggests Edward Stillingfleet (1635–
99), Dean of St Paul's since 1678, although as a dean he was not a *prelate*. In
the Preface to *The Jesuits Loyalty* (1677), a collection of Catholic tracts,
Stillingfleet challenges Catholics to renounce the Pope's power of deposing
princes, and to take the oath of allegiance, but he also argues that the Catholic

Jesuitic principles, and subscribe to all doctrines which
deny the Pope's authority of deposing kings and releas-
280 ing subjects from their oath of allegiance: to which I
should think they might easily be induced, if it be true
that this present Pope has condemned the doctrine of
king-killing (a thesis of the Jesuits) amongst others *ex
cathedra* (as they call it) or in open consistory.
285   Leaving them, therefore, in so fair a way (if they
please themselves) of satisfying all reasonable men of
their sincerity and good meaning to the government, I
shall make bold to consider that other extreme of our
religion, I mean the fanatics or schismatics of the Eng-
290 lish church. Since the Bible has been translated into our
tongue, they have used it so as if their business was not
to be saved but to be damned by its contents. If we
consider only them, better had it been for the English
nation that it had still remained in the original Greek
295 and Hebrew, or at least in the honest Latin of St Jerome,
than that several texts in it should have been prevaricated to the destruction of that government which put it
into so ungrateful hands.
         How many heresies the first translation of Tyndale
300 produced in few years, let my Lord Herbert's *History of*

tracts which he reprints are a sufficiently clear indication of Catholics' real
beliefs, and that the country cannot afford to relax its legal tests against them.
282. this present Pope] Innocent XI (1611–89) condemned sixty-five prop-
ositions from casuist moral theology in his bull *Sanctissimus Dominus* (1679),
including some which allowed equivocation under questioning about crimes,
and mental reservations when taking an oath of allegiance (*A Decree made at
Rome* (1679) 11–13).
283–4. ex cathedra] 'from the throne': used of pronouncements made by the
Pope with the full weight of his office.
284. consistory] the assembly of cardinals convoked by the Pope.
295. Latin of St Jerome] St Jerome (*c.*342–420) produced a Latin text of the
Bible, partly by revising the Old Latin text, and partly by translating afresh
from the Hebrew and Greek. This formed the basis of the Vulgate, the
standard Latin text used by the Roman Catholic church.
296–7. prevaricated] twisted from their true meaning (*OED* 6).
299. Tyndale] William Tyndale (*c.*1494–1536) published translations of the
NT (1525), the Pentateuch (1530) and Jonah (1531). His translations were
banned in 1543.
300. Herbert] In his *The Life and Raigne of King Henry the Eighth* (1649;
reprinted 1682) Lord Herbert of Cherbury reports Henry VIII's speech of

Henry the Eighth inform you, insomuch that for the
gross errors in it, and the great mischiefs it occasioned,
a sentence passed on the first edition of the Bible too
shameful almost to be repeated. After the short reign of
305 Edward the Sixth (who had continued to carry on the
Reformation on other principles than it was begun)
everyone knows that not only the chief promoters of
that work but many others whose consciences would
not dispense with popery, were forced for fear of
310 persecution to change climates; from whence returning
at the beginning of Queen Elizabeth's reign, many of

1545: 'And be not Judges of your selves, of your phantastical opinions and
vain Expositions. In such high Causes you may lightly erre; and although
you be permitted to read holy Scriptures, and to have the Word of God in
your Mother-Tongue, you must understand, that it is licensed you so to do,
onely to inform your own consciences, and to instruct your children and
Family; and not to dispute, and make Scripture a railing or taunting stock
against Priests and Preachers, as many light persons do. I am very sorry to
know and hear, how unreverently that most precious Jewel, the Word of
God, is disputed, rimed, sung, and jangled in every Ale-house and Tavern'
(1649 edn. 536; *Works*). The Whig propagandist Henry Care objected that
any Protestant should 'dare brand this good and holy mans endeavours with
causless *Aspersions*, as Mr. *Dryden* (the *Play-maker*) has lately done in a *Preface*
to a Pamphlet which he calls *Religio Laici*, wherein he suggests many *Haere-
sies* produced in few years by *Tyndals* Translation, and that for the *gross
Errours and the great mischiefs it occasion'd, a sentence pass'd on the first Edition of
the Bible, too shameful* (he says) *almost to be repeated.* – Too *shameful!* I pray, Sir!
to whom? If to those that gave it, why then have you no more Manners to
Authority, no more Respect to Truth, than to revive the memory of a thing
so *shameful* and better buried in Oblivion? If to *Tindal*, or his *Work*, why is
not *one* Haéresie named that it produced, or one of those *shameful* passages
Instanc'd in? The World is not unacquainted with a certain mercenary *Versifi-
cator*, whose *Obscure* and *Atheistical* Sheets (and yet half *Stoln* too, as this very
Preface is from a little Pamphlet of *George Cranmers*, publisht about 41.) has
done abundantly more *shameful mischief* than ever *Tyndals* Translation of the
Holy Bible.... 'Tis perhaps *necessary* that *Cromwels Panegyrist* and so passion-
ate an Admirer of *Pere Simon*, should cast a *Squint Eye* not only on Poor
Tyndal, but all English *Bibles*, and in a word the whole *Reformation*' (*The
Weekly Pacquet of Advice from Rome* v 21 (12 January 1682/3) 165–6; *Works*).
306. on other principles] During the reign of Edward VI (1547–53) the Reformation was promoted vigorously in a Calvinist direction; the subsequent
reign of the Catholic Queen Mary (1553–8) saw the persecution and martyrdom of many Protestants, including Archbishop Cranmer and Bishops
Latimer and Ridley.

them who had been in France and at Geneva, brought
back the rigid opinions and imperious discipline of Calvin to graff upon our Reformation: which, though they
315   cunningly concealed at first (as well knowing how nauseously that drug would go down in a lawful monarchy
which was prescribed for a rebellious commonwealth)
yet they always kept it in reserve, and were never wanting to themselves either in court or Parliament, when
320   either they had any prospect of a numerous party of
fanatic members in the one, or the encouragement of
any favourite in the other, whose covetousness was
gaping at the patrimony of the church. They who will
consult the works of our venerable Hooker, or the
325   account of his life, or more particularly the letter
written to him on this subject by George Cranmer, may
see by what gradations they proceeded: from the dislike
of cap and surplice, the very next step was admonitions
to the Parliament against the whole government ecclesi-
330   astical; then came out volumes in English and Latin in
defence of their tenets; and immediately practices were
set on foot to erect their discipline without authority.
Those not succeeding, satire and railing was the next,

312. Geneva] The city of John Calvin (1509–64), whose theology included the
doctrine of predestination. Opposition from some citizens to his exercise of
dictatorial power over Geneva was met by torture and executions.
314. graff] graft.
324. Hooker] Richard Hooker (*c.*1554–1600) was the principal apologist for
the Elizabethan Church of England. *The Works of Mr. Richard Hooker* (1666)
included his *Laws of Ecclesiastical Polity*, Walton's *Life* and Cranmer's *Letter* of
1598. Cranmer wrote: 'the first degree was only some small difference about
Cap and Surplice.... This was peaceable; the next degree more stirring.
Admonitions were directed to the Parliament in peremptory sort against our
whole Form of Regiment; in defence of them, Volumes were published in
English, and in Latin; yet this was no more than writing, Devices were set on
foot to erect the Practice of the Discipline without Authority: yet herein some
regard of Modesty, some moderation was used; Behold, at length it brake
forth into open outrage, first in writing by *Martin* . . . it was imagined that by
open rayling (which to the vulgar is commonly most plausible) the State
Ecclesiastical might have been drawn in to such contempt and hatred, as the
overthrow thereof should have been most grateful to all Men' (32; *Works*).

and Martin Mar-Prelate (the Marvell of those times)
335   was the first Presbyterian scribbler who sanctified libels
and scurrility to the use of the Good Old Cause, which
was done (says my author) upon this account, that,
their serious treatises having been fully answered and
refuted, they might compass by railing what they had
340   lost by reasoning; and when their cause was sunk in
court and Parliament, they might at least hedge in a
stake amongst the rabble: for to their ignorance all
things are wit which are abusive; but if church and state
were made the theme, then the doctoral degree of wit
345   was to be taken at Billingsgate: even the most saintlike
of the party, though they durst not excuse this contempt and villifying of the government, yet were
pleased, and grinned at it with a pious smile, and called
it a judgement of God against the hierarchy. Thus sec-
350   taries, we may see, were born with teeth, foul-mouthed
and scurrilous from their infancy, and if spiritual pride,
venom, violence, contempt of superiors and slander had
been the marks of orthodox belief, the presbytery and
the rest of our schismatics, which are their spawn, were
355   always the most visible church in the Christian world.

'Tis true, the government was too strong at that time
for a rebellion, but to show what proficiency they had
made in Calvin's school, even then their mouths
watered at it: for two of their gifted brotherhood
360   (Hacket and Coppinger) as the story tells us, got up into

334. *Martin Mar-Prelate*] The pen-name of the author of scurrilous puritan
tracts against episcopacy published in 1588–9.   *Marvell*] Andrew Marvell
(1621–78) wrote for the Whig cause, especially in his *An Account of the Growth
of Popery and Arbitrary Government in England* (1677); cp. *The Medal*, 'Epistle
to the Whigs' ll. 79–80n.
336. *Good Old Cause*] Presbyterianism, and, more generally, puritan republicanism.
341–2. *hedge in a stake*] secure oneself against loss in one speculation by
betting on the other side (*OED* 8).
345. *Billingsgate*] the London fishmarket; a by-word for foul language.
360. *Hacket and Coppinger*] In 1591 Edmund Coppinger and Henry Arth-
ington proclaimed that William Hacket had come as Christ's representative
to establish the gospel and rule over Europe. Hacket was executed. Cranmer
writes: 'Certain Prophets did arise, who deeming it not possible that God
should suffer that to be undone, which they did so fiercely desire to have
done, Namely, that his holy Saints, the favourers and Fathers of the Disci-

a pease-cart and harangued the people to dispose them
to an insurrection, and to establish their discipline by
force; so that however it comes about that now they
celebrate Queen Elizabeth's birthnight as that of their
365 saint and patroness, yet then they were for doing the
work of the Lord by arms against her, and in all probability they wanted but a fanatic Lord Mayor and two
sheriffs of their party to have compassed it.

Our venerable Hooker, after many admonitions
370 which he had given them, toward the end of his preface
breaks out into this prophetic speech: 'There is in every
one of these considerations most just cause to fear, lest
our hastiness to embrace a thing of so perilous consequence' (meaning the Presbyterian discipline) 'should
375 cause posterity to feel those evils which as yet are more
easy for us to prevent than they would be for them to
remedy'.

How fatally this Cassandra has foretold we know too
well by sad experience: the seeds were sown in the time
380 of Queen Elizabeth, the bloody harvest ripened in the
reign of King Charles the Martyr, and because all the
sheaves could not be carried off without shedding some
of the loose grains, another crop is too like to follow;
nay, I fear 'tis unavoidable if the conventiclers be
385 permitted still to scatter.

A man may be suffered to quote an adversary to our

pline, should be enlarged, and delivered from persecution; and seeing no
means of deliverance Ordinary, were fain to perswade themselves that God
must needs raise some extraordinary means; and being perswaded of none so
well as of themselves, they forthwith must needs be the instruments of this
great work. Hereupon they framed unto themselves an assured hope that
upon their Preaching out of a Pease Cart, all the multitude would have
presently joyned unto them' (*Works of Hooker* 32; *Works*).
361. pease] pea.
364. Queen Elizabeth's birthnight] Elizabeth I's accession day, 17 November,
was celebrated with processions by the more Whiggish Protestants: see 'Prologue to *The Loyal Brother*' ll. 18–40n.
367–8. Lord Mayor and two sheriffs] The Lord Mayor of London and the two
sheriffs played important parts in the Exclusion Crisis: see 'Prologue to *The
Duke of Guise*' l. 3n.
371–7. 'There is ... remedy'] *Works of Hooker* sig. D4ʳ.
384. conventiclers] The nonconformist Protestants who gathered for worship
in separate congregations or conventicles.

religion when he speaks truth; and 'tis the observation
of Maimbourg in his *History of Calvinism*, that wherever
that discipline was planted and embraced, rebellion,
390 civil war and misery attended it. And how indeed
should it happen otherwise? Reformation of church and
state has always been the ground of our divisions in
England. While we were papists, our holy father rid us,
by pretending authority out of the scriptures to depose
395 princes; when we shook off his authority, the sectaries
furnished themselves with the same weapons, and out
of the same magazine, the Bible. So that the scriptures,
which are in themselves the greatest security of
governors, as commanding express obedience to them,
400 are now turned to their destruction, and never since the
Reformation has there wanted a text of their interpreting to authorize a rebel. And 'tis to be noted by the
way, that the doctrines of king-killing and deposing,
which have been taken up only by the worst party of
405 the papists, the most frontless flatterers of the Pope's
authority, have been espoused, defended and are still
maintained by the whole body of nonconformists and
republicans. 'Tis but dubbing themselves the people of
God, which 'tis the interest of their preachers to tell
410 them they are, and their own interest to believe; and
after that they cannot dip into the Bible but one text or

388. Maimbourg] Louis Maimbourg, in his *Histoire du Calvinisme* (1682). D.'s
translation of another work by Maimbourg, *The History of the League*, was
published in 1684; in his Postscript D. says that the political tenets of Jesuits
and of Protestant sectaries are similar (*Works* xviii 399).
393. our holy father] the Pope.   *rid*] rode.
396. princes] *1682a (second and third issues)*; Princes, (a Doctrine which, though
some Papists may reject, no Pope has hitherto deny'd, nor ever will,) *1682a*
(first issue). The reason for this change is unclear.
399. commanding express obedience] e.g. 'Let every soul be subject unto the
higher powers. For there is no power but of God: the powers that be are
ordained of God. Whosoever therefore resisteth the power, resisteth the
ordinance of God' (Romans xiii 1–2).
402. to authorize a rebel] Calvinist political thought authorized subjects to
resist an ungodly ruler: see Quentin Skinner, *The Foundations of Modern
Political Thought*, 2 vols (1978) ii 189–348; and cp. *AA* ll. 765–76n.
405. frontless] brazen, shameless.

another will turn up for their purpose. If they are under
persecution (as they call it) then that is a mark of their
election; if they flourish, then God works miracles for
415 their deliverance, and the saints are to possess the earth.
They may think themselves to be too roughly
handled in this paper, but I who know best how far I
could have gone on this subject, must be bold to tell
them they are spared; though at the same time I am not
420 ignorant that they interpret the mildness of a writer to
them as they do the mercy of the government: in the
one they think it fear, and conclude it weakness in the
other. The best way for them to confute me is, as I
before advised the papists, to disclaim their principles
425 and renounce their practices. We shall all be glad to
think them true Englishmen when they obey the King,
and true Protestants when they conform to the church
discipline.
It remains that I acquaint the reader that the verses
430 were written for an ingenious young gentleman my
friend, upon his translation of *The Critical History of the
Old Testament*, composed by the learned Father Simon:
the verses therefore are addressed to the translator of
that work, and the style of them is, what it ought to be,
435 epistolary.
If anyone be so lamentable a critic as to require the
smoothness, the numbers and the turn of heroic poetry
in this poem, I must tell him that if he has not read
Horace, I have studied him, and hope the style of his
440 *Epistles* is not ill imitated here. The expressions of a
poem designed purely for instruction ought to be plain

414. election] as those predestined by God ('elected') to eternal salvation,
according to Calvinist teaching.
427. true Protestants] 'True Protestant' was a title assumed by the Whigs.
430–2. young gentleman . . . Father Simon] See headnote, 'Context'.
432. composed] *1682a* (second and third issues); written *1682a* (first issue).
437. numbers] harmonious rhythms.   *turn*] particular style (*OED* 31, 32).
439. Horace] Cp. Epigraph *n* and *RL* ll. 453–4*n*. However, K. W. Gransden
argues that the manner of *RL* is more akin to that of Juvenal or Lucretius,
who argue a particular case, and offer a *consolatio*, a way of understanding life
philosophically (*SEL* xvii (1977) 397–406).

and natural, and yet majestic, for here the poet is presumed to be a kind of law-giver, and those three qualities which I have named are proper to the legislative
445   style. The florid, elevated and figurative way is for the
passions, for love and hatred, fear and anger are begotten in the soul by showing their objects out of their true
proportion, either greater than the life, or less; but
instruction is to be given by showing them what they
450   naturally are. A man is to be cheated into passion, but to
be reasoned into truth.

Religio Laici

Dim as the borrowed beams of moon and stars

450–1. Echoes Wolseley, who says that belief in Christianity 'is not to be
imposed upon any man, but all men reasoned and discoursed into an assent to
it' (*Reasonablenes of Scripture-Belief* 78).

1–11. The use of the imagery of light in spiritual writing is very ancient; John
i 1–14 is the starting-point for the image of Christ as the light of the world,
and behind this stands a tradition of Jewish and Hellenistic mysticism (see C.
H. Dodd, *The Interpretation of the Fourth Gospel* (1953)). Light is widely used
as an image for spiritual understanding in man: the Cambridge Platonists
frequently quoted Proverbs xx 27: 'The spirit of man is the candle of the
Lord' (see *The Cambridge Platonists*, edited by C. A. Patrides (1969) 11–13).
The image of reason as a light is a commonplace of the seventeenth century,
and those who would dissuade from too great a reliance upon reason sometimes liken reason to an *ignis fatuus*, the phosphorescent light which hovers
over marshy ground and leads travellers astray (e.g. Rochester, *Satire Against
Reason and Mankind* (in MS, *c*.1675) ll. 12–15 (noted by P. J. C. Field, *N & Q*
ccxv (1970) 259–60); and Martin Clifford, *A Treatise of Humane Reason* (1675)
3–4, 63). The comparison which D. makes here between the light of nature
within human beings and that of the moon, and of revealed Christian religion
to that of the sun, is also found in Donne: 'That Light which issues from the
Moone doth best represent and expresse that which in our selves we call the
Light of Nature; For as that in the Moone is permanent and ever there, and
yet it is unequall, various, pale, and languishing, So is our Light of Nature
changeable. . . . And then those artificiall Lightes, which our selves make for
our use and service here, as Fires, Tapers, and such, resemble the light of
Reason. . . . But because of these two kindes of light, the first is too weake,
and the other false . . . we have therefore the Sunne; which is the fountayne
and treasure of all created Light, for an Embleme of that third best light of
our understanding, which is the Word of God' (*Biathanatos* [1647], edited by
Ernest W. Sullivan (1984) 109; Kinsley). Harth 117 also compares Richard

To lonely, weary, wandering travellers
Is reason to the soul; and as on high
Those rolling fires discover but the sky

Burthogge: 'All the *Light* before Christ, whether that among the Jews, or that among the Gentiles, was but *Moon*, or *Star-light*, designed only for the *night* preceding; but it is the *Sun* must Rule by *Day*, and *Christ* the Sun that makes it; by whose Alone Light we must walk. For as in Nature, the *Light* afforded by the Moon and Stars, which is of great Advantage, and very much administers to our Direction, and Comfort in a Journey by night, yet in the day is *none*; The Moon and Stars that shine by night, and then make other things Visible, they are Invisible themselves, and Dark by day; So in the *Moral* world, not only the *Law* of *Moses* to the Jews, but that *Philosophy* and *Wisdom* among the Gentiles, that before the coming of the Lord Christ, while it was yet extream Dark, was of extraordinary Use and Benefit, *It* is no longer *now* of any to them, nor to be insisted on, since He is come. For now 'tis *broad Day*. One would be glad of Moon-light, or Star-light, that is to travel by night; but he delires, and is out of his Wits, that would preferr it before the Sun by Day' (*Causa Dei* (1675) 195–6). Sanford Budick, *N & Q* ccxiv (1979) 375–9, cites a comparable passage in Henry More's *Conjectura Cabbalistica* (1662) 31. Wolseley says that no man who 'searches by the Candle-light of *Nature*' will find answers to spiritual questions (*Reasonablenes* 153). Jeanne H. Welcher, *SEL* viii (1968) 391–6, suggests that these lines also echo Virgil, *Aen.* vi 268–72, where Aeneas and the Sibyl begin their descent to the underworld: *ibant obscuri, sola sub nocte per umbram/ perque domos Ditis vacuas et inania regna:/ quale per incertam lunam sub luce maligna/ est iter in silvis, ubi caelum condidit umbra/ Iuppiter, et rebus nox abstulit atra colorem* ('Obscure they went thro dreery Shades, that led/ Along the waste Dominions of the dead:/ Thus wander Travellers in Woods by Night,/ By the Moon's doubtful, and malignant Light:/ When *Jove* in dusky Clouds involves the Skies;/ And the faint Crescent shoots by fits before their Eyes': 'The Sixth Book of the *Aeneis*' ll. 378–83).

1–3. D. is not dismissing reason, but assigning it to a secondary role in matters of religion, where divine revelation must be the primary guide to our understanding. For the imagery cp. the Catholic apologist John Serjeant's description of reason as 'like a dimsighted man who us'd his Reason to find a trusty Friend to lead him in the twi-light, and then reli'd on his guidance rationally without using his own Reason at all about the Way it self' (*Sure-Footing in Christianity* (1665) 183; quoted by Tillotson in *The Rule of Faith* 153).

2. Perhaps an echo of Spenser's Mutability Cantos, where the moon and the evening star light the way 'to weary wandring travailers' (*FQ* VII vi 9.9; Budick). *travellers*] Herbert of Cherbury describes his enquiring layman as a *viator* ('traveller') (*De Religione Laici* 86 etc).

4. rolling] performing a periodic revolution (*OED* 15). *fires*] stars (*OED* 10b). *discover but the sky*] afford a view only of the sky.

 5   Not light us here, so reason's glimmering ray ⎫
     Was lent, not to assure our doubtful way,   ⎬
     But guide us upward to a better day: ⎭
     And as those nightly tapers disappear
     When day's bright lord ascends our hemisphere,
10   So pale grows reason at religion's sight,
     So dies, and so dissolves in supernatural light.
     Some few, whose lamp shone brighter, have been led
     From cause to cause, to nature's secret head,

5–7. This argument is denied by A.W. in the deist tract 'Of Natural Religion': 'The next Objection against the Sufficiency of Natural Religion to Happiness eternal, is only a bare Affirmation of our Adversaries, That Natural Religion is but an imperfect Light, which God gives us so far, as that by improving it, we may arrive at a Supernatural Knowledge.... But I wholly deny any Natural Light can lead one to a Supernatural; there is no proportion betwixt those two extreams: There is a Gulph betwixt, a μέγα χάσμα' (*The Oracles of Reason* (1693) 201–2).

5. reason's glimmering ray] Cp. 'Our glim'ring knowledge, like the wandring Light/ In Fenns, doth to incertainties direct' (Davenant, 'The Philosophers Disquisition' ll. 261–2, in his *Works* (1673)).

8–11. In *The Indian Emperor* (1667), Montezuma argues that Christian teaching is like a taper, an unnecessary addition to the sunlight, while the Christian priest sees it as a heavenly beam: the priest says, 'That which we worship, and which you believe,/ From Natures common hand we both receive:/ All under various names, Adore and Love/ One power Immense, which ever rules above./ ... But here our Worship takes another way./ *Mont.* Where both agree 'tis there most safe to stay:/ For what's more vain then Publick Light to shun,/ And set up Tapers while we see the Sun?/ *Chr. Pr.* Though Nature teaches whom we should Adore,/ By Heavenly Beams we still discover more' (V ii 61–72).

12–22. This passage refers to the attempts of classical philosophers to understand the origins of the universe.

12–14. Cp. Wolseley: 'The single exercise of natural reason, in such an inquiry, will safely conduct a man to the conclusion of some *first cause*, and some one *Supreme Being* the cause of all Beings, which we call God.... If we can happily bring mankind to God by this high-way of their reason, and light a man to his Creator by this *Lamp* that continually burns in his own soul, we shall then prove *Atheism* a very lye' (*Unreasonablenesse* 45).

13. D.'s interest in how man may understand the secret origins of life, and the often inscrutable causes of events, is evident in many poems, e.g. in the account of the naval war and the causes of the Fire of London in *AM* ll. 137–44, 661–4, 797–800, 849–68; in the injunction to leave alone those things which God has hidden ('Horace: *Odes* III xxix' ll. 40–9); in the encomium of the knowledgeable farmer in 'The Second Book of the *Georgics*': 'Happy the

And found that one first principle must be;
15 But what, or who that universal he—
Whether some soul encompassing this ball,
Unmade, unmoved, yet making, moving all,
Or various atoms' interfering dance
Leaped into form, the noble work of chance,

Man, who, studying Nature's Laws,/ Thro' known Effects can trace the secret Cause' (ll. 698–9); throughout 'Of the Pythagorean Philosophy', which celebrates Pythagoras who 'discours'd of Heav'ns mysterious Laws,/ The World's Original, and Nature's Cause' (ll. 89–90); and in Theseus' philosophical summation of life in 'Palamon and Arcite' iii 1024–83. *head*] source (*OED* 16).

14. one first principle] The prime mover, which creates the world and sets it in motion; cp. Preface l. 104*n*. The idea derives from Aristotle (*Metaphysics* XII 1071b–1073a), who argued that the prime mover is eternal, and cannot itself change or move (cp. l. 17).

15. Cp. Wolseley: 'That God is, and that he is to be *Served*, my *Reason* will tell me; But *What* he is! and after what *Manner* he *Exists* . . . I must be taught from *above*' (*Reasonablenes* 128–9; Harth 126).

16. soul] Plato thought of the soul as the primary source of all things: 'Of all the planets, of the moon, of years and months and all seasons, what other story shall we have to tell than just this same, that since soul, or souls, and those souls good with perfect goodness, have proved to be the causes of all, these souls we hold to be gods, whether they direct the universe by inhabiting bodies, like animated beings, or whatever the manner of their action?' (*Laws* 899b; tr. A.E. Taylor).

18–19. Epicurus taught that the world was brought about by the chance collocation of atoms; see headnote to 'Lucretius: The Beginning of the First Book'. He is cited repeatedly by Christian apologists in the Restoration, who use him as the chief atheistic adversary who must be refuted: e.g. Edward Stillingfleet, *Origines Sacrae* (1662) *passim*, John Tillotson, *The Wisdom of Being Religious* (1664) 18–20, and Wolseley in *Reasonablenes*, who has an extensive refutation of Epicureanism.

18. interfering] colliding (*OED* 2).   *dance*] Wolseley uses this image when writing scathingly of Epicurus' theory: 'If the *dancing motion* of these *Atoms*, in this fancied space, did by chance first dance the world into this *form*; and caper'd the Sun, and the Moon, and the Stars into their stations above us; and placed every thing in the posture it is in about us, and below us; what is the reason these *Atoms* never danced themselves into any thing since?' (*Unreasonablenesse* 91).

19. Leaped] Lucretius says that the atoms 'leap' (*dissiliant*: *De Rerum Natura* ii 87).

20   Or this great all was from eternity— ⎫
      Not ev'n the Stagirite himself could see; ⎬
      And Epicurus guessed as well as he.   ⎭
      As blindly groped they for a future state,
      As rashly judged of providence and fate.

20. Aristotle (in *De Caelo*) argued that the world is eternal, and cannot be said ever to have been generated. His view was much contested by Restoration writers, e.g. Stillingfleet in *Origines Sacrae* 423–40, Tillotson in *The Wisdom of being Religious* 17–18 and Wolseley, who devotes much of *The Unreasonablenesse of Atheism* to contesting the argument that the world is eternal, seeing it as supporting atheism: 'The Atheist usually objects, in this matter, and pleads for the worlds eternity, by urging that *maxim* of *Aristotle*, so much renowned by him, that he saies, all *Philosophers* did agree to it; which is, that *ex nihilo nihil fit*, out of *nothing, nothing can be produced*. And therefore they infer from thence, either an eternity in the world, or in some pre-existing matter' (63). Wolseley regards this as one of the dangerous elements in pagan philosophy which are leading astray contemporary youth: 'Whatever can be fetched from *Aristotle* and others to make good the worlds eternity, is greedily embraced: and all the notions of *Epicurus*, to make good the *Hypothesis of Atoms*, are not only revived and justified, but improved, to the total denial of a God, in the height of all Atheistical principles ... that he is thought a freshman in the highest sort of learning, that has not imbibed some of this kind of Philosophy' (37–8).
21. Stagirite] Aristotle, who was born at Stagira in Macedonia.
23. future state] Plato's ideas concerning the future state are set out in the *Phaedo*, in which Socrates argues that the soul is immortal because it can perceive and share in truth, goodness and beauty, which are eternal; moreover, only in another life can God's justice be shown. Aristotle, however, argued in *De Anima* that the soul is simply the form of organization of a living body, and therefore it is nonsensical to suggest that this might survive the dissolution of the body. Epicurus thought that after death the body dissolved into its constituent atoms (see 'Lucretius: Against the Fear of Death'). Charles Blount surveys classical opinion on this issue in *Anima Mundi: or, an Historical Narration of the Opinions of the Ancients Concerning Mans Soul after this Life: According to unenlightened Nature* [1679].
24. providence and fate] Although Plato sometimes uses the idea of God as providence (e.g. *Letters* VIII 353b), and Aristotle argues that the good is present in the universe both as the order of the parts and as their ruler (*Metaphysics* XIII 1074b–1076a), these ideas are far removed from the Christian understanding of the operation of God in the world. Epicurus taught that the universe was a collection of atoms in random motion, without any guiding principle.

25   But least of all could their endeavours find   *Opinions of*
      What most concerned the good of human kind: *the several*
      For happiness was never to be found,   *sects of*
      But vanished from 'em like enchanted ground.   *philo-*
      One thought content the good to be enjoyed: *sophers*
                                                             concerning
30   This every little accident destroyed.   *the*
      The wiser madmen did for virtue toil,   *summum*
      A thorny, or at best a barren soil.   *bonum*
      In pleasure some their glutton souls would steep,   ⎤
      But found their line too short, the well too deep, ⎬
35   And leaky vessels which no bliss could keep.   ⎦

25–35. This passage considers the attempts of classical philosophers to establish the highest good. Although Stoics, Aristotelians and Epicureans seem to
be aimed at, the representation of their positions is somewhat imprecise.
25 marginal note] begins by l. 24 in *1682*; positioned here by this edition.
summum bonum] highest good.
29. content] Not 'satisfaction, pleasure' (*OED* 1) but 'acceptance of conditions
or circumstances' (*OED* 2). This is probably an allusion to the Stoic philosophy
(propounded originally by Zeno *c.*300 BC), which taught that the supreme
good was to live in consistency with Nature; in its Roman form (e.g. with
Epictetus) it taught detachment from everything which is not in our power,
and this became an influential philosophy in the Renaissance (e.g. with Lip-
sius): peace of mind can only be achieved through control of one's emotions.
But *pace* D. in l. 30, the true Stoic would not have his peace of mind destroyed
by every little accident (quite the opposite), and would have regarded his aim as
being virtue rather than content in any solipsistic or hedonistic sense. A
sympathy for true Stoic values is seen in D.'s praise of Persius' Stoicism in his
'Discourse Concerning Satire' (1693; *Works* iv 55–7), though he criticizes
Stoicism in the Dedication to *Don Sebastian* (1690; *Works* xv 62).
30. accident] unexpected occurrence.
31. virtue] Probably a reference to Aristotelianism: Aristotle in his *Nicomachean
Ethics* argues that man should pursue the golden mean which is the virtue which
lies between two opposite vices.
32. The imagery comes from the parable of the sower: some seeds 'fell upon
stony places, where they had not much earth: and forthwith they sprung up,
because they had no deepness of earth: And when the sun was up, they were
scorched; and because they had no root they withered away. And some fell
among thorns; and the thorns sprung up, and choked them.' (Matthew xiii 5–
7).
33. pleasure] Clearly a reference to Epicureanism, though a tendentious and pe-
jorative interpretation of the Epicurean notion of pleasure, which was properly
a state of bodily and mental tranquillity (see headnote to 'Lucretius: The
Beginning of the First Book', and Paul Hammond, *MLR* lxxviii (1983) 5–6).
35. leaky vessels] See 'Lucretius: Against the Fear of Death' l. 220n.

Thus anxious thoughts in endless circles roll,
Without a centre where to fix the soul:
In this wild maze their vain endeavours end.
How can the less the greater comprehend,
40   Or finite reason reach infinity?
For what could fathom God were more than he.
    The deist thinks he stands on firmer ground, *System of*
Cries, 'εὕρηκα, the mighty secret's found: *deism*

36. anxious thoughts] The anxiety of the unsatisfied search for knowledge is a
theme of *Sylvae*: see 'Horace: *Odes* III xxix' l. 44; 'Horace: *Epode* II' l. 55.
38. Wolseley says that 'the more Refined part lost themselves in a Wilderness
of Abstracted Speculations about what they could never distinctly comprehend' (*Reasonablenes* 113).   *wild*] desolate (*OED* 4); wayward, unruly
(*OED* 7); going beyond reasonable limits (*OED* 13).   *maze*] The rebel
angels, debating philosophical problems in hell, end 'in wandering mazes
lost' (*PL* ii 561).
39–40. Cp. Tiresias in *Oedipus* (1679): 'But how can Finite measure Infinite?/
Reason! alas, it does not know it self!/ Yet Man, vain Man, wou'd with this
short-lin'd Plummet,/ Fathom the vast Abysse of Heav'nly justice' (III i 240–
3); and cp. *HP* i 104–5. Wolseley says: 'This is to measure out *Infiniteness*
(which can have no measure) by *Finiteness*. 'Tis in short, to measure out God
to our selves by our *own Line*' (*Reasonablenes* 52).
42–61. For the history of deism, see headnote, '*Context*'. D.'s account of the
principles of deism follows the catholic articles originally propounded by
Lord Herbert of Cherbury in *De Veritate* (1624) and *De Religione Laici* (1645),
but (as Harth points out, 84–94) the order and wording of D.'s passage are
closest to the version of the articles set out in the essay by 'A.W.' called 'Of
Natural Religion, as opposed to Divine Revelation', which was first printed
in *The Oracles of Reason* (1693) 195–209. Since this tract also survives in MS
(BL 873.b.3), it is possible that D. had access to it, or to a similar MS
account, when composing *RL*. The articles in this version are: '*Natural
Religion is the Belief we have of an eternal intellectual Being, and of the Duty
which we owe him, manifested to us by our Reason, without Revelation or
positive Law: The chief Heads whereof seem contain'd in these few Particu-
lars. 1. That there is one infinite eternal God, Creator of all Things. 2. That he
governs the World by Providence. 3. That 'tis our Duty to worship and obey him as
our Creator and Governor. 4. That our Worship consists in Prayer to him, and Praise
of him. 5. That our Obedience consists in the Rules of Right Reason, the Practice
whereof is Moral Virtue. 6. That we are to expect Rewards and Punishments
hereafter, according to our Actions in this Life; which includes the Soul's Immortality,
and is proved by our admitting Providence. Seventhly, That when we err from the
Rules of our Duty, we ought to Repent, and trust in God's mercy for Pardon.*' (*The
Oracles of Reason* 195–6).
43. εὕρηκα] *Eds.* ἕυρεκα *1682.* 'I have found it' (the cry attributed to Archimedes); pronounced 'héureká' here. The correct spelling is εὕρηκα, with an

God is that spring of good, supreme and best,
45 We made to serve, and in that service blessed;
If so, some rules of worship must be given,
Distributed alike to all by heaven,
Else God were partial, and to some denied
The means his justice should for all provide.
50 This general worship is to praise and pray,
One part to borrow blessings, one to pay;
And when frail nature slides into offence,
The sacrifice for crimes is penitence.
Yet since th' effects of providence we find
55 Are variously dispensed to human kind,
That vice triumphs, and virtue suffers here
(A brand that sovereign justice cannot bear)
Our reason prompts us to a future state,
The last appeal from Fortune, and from fate,
60 Where God's all-righteous ways will be declared,
The bad meet punishment, the good reward.'
   Thus man by his own strength to heaven would
      soar,   *Of revealed*
And would not be obliged to God for more.   *religion*
Vain, wretched creature, how art thou misled
65 To think thy wit these godlike notions bred!
These truths are not the product of thy mind,
But dropped from heaven, and of a nobler kind.

---

eta rather than an epsilon before the kappa. As Kinsley notes, the spelling in
1682 and the metre of the line show that D.'s pronunciation of Greek was
based on accent rather than quantity; this was common in the seventeenth
century (see *Ben Jonson* ix 486). Herbert said that in formulating the articles of
deism he thought himself happier than Archimedes (*De Religione Gentilium*
(1663) 218; Hutcheson 57).

51. borrow] obtain by request (*OED* 2).   *pay*] render something which is
due (*OED* 7a).
52. slides] lapses morally (*OED* 9).
56. triumphs] The verb was often accented on the second syllable in the
seventeenth century (cp. *PL* ix 948, x 572, and many of *OED*'s quotations).
57. brand] mark of disgrace (*OED* 4b).
59. Fortune] Fortune is a capricious power which awards and withdraws gifts
arbitrarily, with no concern for justice: for D.'s interest in fortune see 'Horace: *Odes* III xxix' ll. 73–87n.   *fate*] Here probably 'death' (*OED* 4b) rather
than 'destiny'.
62–3. i.e., the deist relies upon his own reason, and rejects revelation.
66–71. For the argument that the principles of natural religion are not dis-

Revealed religion first informed thy sight,
And reason saw not till faith sprung the light.
70 Hence all thy natural worship takes the source:
'Tis revelation what thou think'st discourse.
Else how com'st thou to see these truths so clear
Which so obscure to heathens did appear?
Not Plato these, nor Aristotle found,
75 Nor he whose wisdom oracles renowned.   *Socrates*
Hast thou a wit so deep, or so sublime,
Or canst thou lower dive, or higher climb?
Canst thou by reason more of godhead know
Than Plutarch, Seneca or Cicero?
80 Those giant wits, in happier ages born,
When arms and arts did Greece and Rome adorn,
Knew no such system, no such piles could raise
Of natural worship, built on prayer and praise,
To one sole God.

---

covered by the unaided reason, but instead are the traces of revelation, see
Preface ll. 95–7n.

69. sprung] caused to appear (*OED* 17).

70–1. Cp. Wolseley: 'some have supposed that no particular *Person* did ever
purely by *Natural Light*, determine that there was *but one God*: But that
such who have spoken of it had it from a *Tradition* originated in *Revelation*'
(*Reasonablenes* 110).

71. discourse] reasoning (*OED* 2).

75. Socrates' follower Chaerephon asked the Delphic oracle whether anyone
was wiser than Socrates, and was told that no one was (Plato, *Apology* 21a).

76. wit] intellect.

79. Plutarch] Greek philosopher (*c.* AD 50–*c.* AD 120), whose works include
moral treatises and dialogues of religious speculation.   *Seneca*] The
Roman Stoic philosopher (*c.* AD 1–AD 65), author of moral essays.   *Cicero*] The Roman philosopher (106–43 BC), author of moral and theological
treatises, including *De Natura Deorum* ('On the nature of the gods').

80. From Virgil: *magnanimi heroes nati melioribus annis* ('high-minded heroes,
born in better years'; *Aen.* vi 649; Kinsley).   *wits*] men of intellect.

82. piles] heaps of wood on which sacrifices are burnt (*OED* 3e); large
buildings, e.g. temples (*OED* 4).

85   Nor did remorse to expiate sin prescribe,
     But slew their fellow creatures for a bribe:
     The guiltless victim groaned for their offence,
     And cruelty and blood was penitence.
     If sheep and oxen could atone for men,
90   Ah, at how cheap a rate the rich might sin!
     And great oppressors might heaven's wrath beguile
     By offering his own creatures for a spoil!
       Dar'st thou, poor worm, offend infinity,
     And must the terms of peace be given by thee?
95   Then thou art justice in the last appeal:
     Thy easy God instructs thee to rebel,
     And like a king remote and weak must take
     What satisfaction thou art pleased to make.
       But if there be a power too just and strong
100 To wink at crimes, and bear unpunished wrong,

86–8. Greeks and Romans tended to regard sacrifice as a gift to the gods (thus Plato, *Euthyphro* 14c), and although some sacrifices were propitiatory or purificatory, they were not normally conducted out of remorse for sin in the way D. implies: that was a Jewish understanding of sacrifice, according to which the animal sacrificed took upon itself the sins of the penitent who offered it.

86. bribe] i.e. to the gods.

89–90. D. adapts Wolseley: 'What a *trifle* is the *Blood* of a *Sheep* or an *Oxe* to satisfie for an Offence against an Infinite Justice! At how *easie* and *cheap* a rate might men *Sin*, and God be *satisfied*! And what a publick *tolleration* of evil were it, if the Blood of Bulls and Goats might take away sin, and the lives of *unreasonable* Creatures *Commute* for the sins of *Men*!' (*Reasonablenes* 162; Harth).

93–110. Cp. Wolseley: 'the terms of our pardon must come from God. 'Tis not in man to find out how God shall forgive him, or to Chalk out the Tracks of Divine Justice and Mercy toward himself; nor will his guilt be removed, nor his thoughts be at rest, till he know Gods mind about it. Nothing can assure us of reconciliation with God, but what is from Heaven appointed as the means of it. No natural knowledg can give us any certain direction about it' (*Reasonablenes* 160).

93. worm] a biblical expression of the humility of man: cp. Psalm xxii 6: 'But I am a worm, and no man'.

95. justice] judge.

98. satisfaction] performance by a penitent of the acts prescribed as payment of the temporal punishment for sin.

100. wink at] close their eyes to.

Look humbly upward, see his will disclose
The forfeit first, and then the fine impose:
A mulct thy poverty could never pay
Had not eternal wisdom found the way,
105   And with celestial wealth supplied thy store:
His justice makes the fine, his mercy quits the score.
See God descending in thy human frame,
Th' offended suffering in th' offender's name;
All thy misdeeds to him imputed see,
110   And all his righteousness devolved on thee.
        For granting we have sinned, and that th' offence
Of man is made against omnipotence,
Some price that bears proportion must be paid,
And infinite with infinite be weighed.
115   See then the deist lost, remorse for vice
Not paid, or, paid, inadequate in price.
What farther means can reason now direct,
Or what relief from human wit expect?
That shows us sick, and sadly are we sure
120   Still to be sick, till heaven reveal the cure.
If then heaven's will must needs be understood
(Which must, if we want cure, and heaven be good),

---

102. forfeit] transgression (*OED* 1).

103. mulct] fine.

105–10. This passage refers to the Christian doctrine of the atonement, that mankind is redeemed through the incarnation and death of Christ, who took man's sins upon him, and whose death provided the only possible satisfaction to God the Father for man's sinfulness.

107. i.e. God becomes incarnate as a man in Christ.

109–10. The vocabulary here invokes the Lutheran version of the doctrine of atonement, according to which man is justified by the imputation of the righteousness of Christ, without becoming possessed of any personal righteousness of his own.

111–14. The development of the doctrine of atonement made by Anselm in *Cur Deus Homo* (1098), and followed by the scholastic theologians, stressed that since sin is an infinite offence against God, it requires an infinite satisfaction; since no finite being, man or angel, could offer such satisfaction, it was necessary for an infinite being, God himself, to take the place of man, and through his death to make complete satisfaction to divine justice. Wolseley says: 'nothing of less Dignity then the *Offender* can compensate for the *Offence*, if any thing but the *Offender himself*' (*Reasonablenes* 159).

119. That] i.e. human intellect.

Let all records of will revealed be shown, ⎫
With scripture all in equal balance thrown, ⎬
125 And our one sacred book will be that one. ⎭
      Proof needs not here, for whether we compare
      That impious, idle, superstitious ware
      Of rites, lustrations, offerings (which before
      In various ages, various countries bore)
130 With Christian faith and virtues, we shall find
      None answ'ring the great ends of human kind
      But this one rule of life: that shows us best
      How God may be appeased, and mortals blessed.
      Whether from length of time its worth we draw
135 (The world is scarce more ancient than the law;

123–5. Cp. Wolseley: 'If it be acknowledged there is any where extant a *Revelation* from *God* to the *World*, let it be produced. Let the best *rival* to the *Bible* upon that account, or all its *Competitors* together be brought forth ... and the *Bible* must needs be *Predominant*, and prevail against all *Competition*' (*Reasonablenes* 178; Harth).

123. records] accented on the second syllable in the seventeenth century.

126–67. D. now turns to arguments for the reliability of the Bible. Harth 141–5 argues that D. is drawing on Wolseley's *The Reasonablenes of Scripture-Belief* for this material; the arguments are also paralleled in other contemporary writers (see Harth's footnotes). Sanford Budick (1969) argues that D.'s awareness that the status of scripture cannot be proved may be indebted to Hamon L'Estrange's *Considerations, upon Dr Bayly's Parenthetical Interlocution* (1651), which D. bought at auction in May 1682 (Birrell 215). L'Estrange says: 'I do not exclude reason, as a guide.... Arguments she hath many, and ponderous to perswade that the Scriptures are of Divine inspiration; that they are not so, to diswade she hath and can frame none. But yet those Arguments are but soluble, no Demonstrations; for in Demonstrations the understanding is so clearly convinced by reason, that it can possibly incline no other way then one ... so that impossible it is for us to *know* that the Scriptures are the word of God' (85–6; Budick).

127. idle] worthless (*OED* 2).   ware] trash (*OED* 4).

128. lustrations] expiatory sacrifices, purificatory rites.

131. Wolseley argues that the Bible best answers 'all the great *Ends* of *Mankind* relating to *this life* and a *future*' (*Reasonablenes* 181).

135. Wolseley points to 'the *Antiquity* of those things it relates to us, and informs us of: And Secondly, the *Antiquity* of this *Book* it self. ... If we consider the Revelation Historically contained in this Book, 'tis what was from the *beginning*, and of the same *Date* with the *World* it self' (*Reasonablenes* 200). Budick (1969) 378 cites a similar argument from L'Estrange 90–1.

Heaven's early care prescribed for every age,
First in the soul, and after in the page),
Or whether more abstractedly we look
Or on the writers, or the written book,
140   Whence but from heaven could men unskilled in arts,
In several ages born, in several parts,
Weave such agreeing truths? Or how, or why
Should all conspire to cheat us with a lie?
Unasked their pains, ungrateful their advice,
145   Starving their gain, and martyrdom their price.
            If on the book itself we cast our view,
Concurrent heathens prove the story true;
The doctrine, miracles, which must convince,
For heaven in them appeals to human sense;

136. Wolseley supposes that 'Gods Revelations were as early as mans *necessi-ties*, That there was no time wherein man stood in need of Supernatural Instruction and help, but that God affords it to him' (*Reasonablenes* 223).

137. Many seventeenth-century theologians thought that certain innate ideas were inscribed by God on man's heart or soul: see Budick 46–72.

139. Or . . . or] Either . . . or.

140. Cp. Wolseley: 'Many of the *Prophets*, and most of the *Apostles* were men Illiterate, and of Parts and Education so *mean*, that they seem no way *capable* to write so profoundly, to lay so *deep* a Contrivement of mischief, or by the single strength of their own abilities to bid so fair to delude the World' (*Reasonablenes* 229).

141–3. Cp. Wolseley: 'The world affords not an instance, that ever so many *Men* that lived in so many several and *distinct Ages*, so exactly agreed about *any one thing*, much less to *cheat* and *abuse* the *World*' (*Reasonablenes* 233).

141. several] separate.

144–5. Cp. Wolseley: 'The most of those that God imploied in that work actually exposed themselves by the doing of it to all the *Persecutions, Hazards*, and *Contempts* imaginable; And some of them . . . with the *loss* of their own *Lives* published their Doctrine' (*Reasonablenes* 230–1).

144. ungrateful] disagreeable (*OED* 2).

145. price] reward.

147. Wolseley 325–47 adduces the testimony of pagan writers to corroborate the historical material in the Bible.

148–51. Wolseley discusses the question 'whether *Miracles* simply in them-selves are always an unquestionable proof of that Doctrine they are brought in to Confirme', and concludes that if the doctrine is not 'opposite to that Natural Duty we owe [God], They *are*. But if otherwise, if they come in direct Competition with the Law of Nature, They are *not*' (*Reasonablenes* 243).

148. i.e. miracles prove the doctrine to be true.

150   And though they prove not, they confirm the cause
       When what is taught agrees with nature's laws.
          Then for the style: majestic and divine,
       It speaks no less than God in every line,
       Commanding words, whose force is still the same
155   As the first fiat that produced our frame.
       All faiths beside or did by arms ascend,
       Or sense indulged has made mankind their friend:
       This only doctrine does our lusts oppose,
       Unfed by nature's soil in which it grows,
160   Cross to our int'rests, curbing sense and sin;
       Oppressed without, and undermined within,
       It thrives through pain, its own tormentors tires,
       And with a stubborn patience still aspires.
       To what can reason such effects assign
165   Transcending nature, but to laws divine?

152–5. Wolseley says: 'no Book nor Writing has so much as attempted to *Command* the world in so *Majestick* a way, nor indeed in any way becoming the *Greatness* and *Sovereignty* of *God*. . . . Not one of them having been clothed with such a *Divine & Majestick Authority'* (*Reasonablenes* 180; and cp. 179, 291).

155. first fiat] 'Fiat lux' is the Latin form of God's command 'Let there be light' (Genesis i 3). Longinus cites this phrase as an example of the sublime (*On the Sublime* ch. 9; widely read in the translations by Boileau (1674) and John Pulteney (1680)).   *frame*] the universe, regarded as a structure (*OED* 8).

156–7. or . . . Or] either . . . Or.

156–63. Cp. Wolseley: 'Never was there at first any Force used to compel men, nor any Arts practised to deceive men about this matter. No man can prove out of any story that ever the Apostles or the Primitive Professors of this Religion raised Arms to introduce or promote it.' Internally it was 'a Religion directly opposite to the whole corrupt interest of humane Nature, and calling men to the highest Mortification and Self-denial, upon the account of an Invisible World to come'; externally 'all the force of the *Roman Empire* was every where violently at work for its total Suppression and Extirpation'; never 'was any Religion so begun and propagated by such indefatigable sufferings' (*Reasonablenes* 289–91).

157. sense] sensuality.

158. This only doctrine] this doctrine alone.

160. Cross to] counter to.

164–5. Cp. Wolseley: 'To no other Cause, but its own Innate worth, and the Divine evidence from Heaven attending it, can it with any tolerable colour of reason be ascribed' (*Reasonablenes* 290).

Which in that sacred volume are contained,
Sufficient, clear, and for that use ordained.
But stay: the deist here will urge anew   *Objection*
No supernatural worship can be true,   *of the deist*
170   Because a general law is that alone
Which must to all and everywhere be known;
A style so large as not this book can claim,
Nor aught that bears revealed religion's name.
'Tis said the sound of a messiah's birth
175   Is gone through all the habitable earth,
But still that text must be confined alone
To what was then inhabited and known;
And what provision could from thence accrue
To Indian souls, and worlds discovered new?
180   In other parts it helps that ages past
The scriptures there were known, and were embraced,
Till sin spread once again the shades of night;
What's that to these who never saw the light?
Of all objections this indeed is chief   *The*
185   To startle reason, stagger frail belief.   *objection*
                                                                                answered

168–83. The deist objects that Christianity cannot be definitive because not
all times and places have had access to the Bible, and so many generations and
races are excluded from the salvation which it promises. Harth 87 points out
that the arguments are similar to those in the essay 'Of Natural Religion' (see
ll. 42–61*n*; D. may have taken the arguments from a MS version of the tract,
or met them elsewhere in a form which no longer survives): 'That Rule
which is necessary to our future Happiness, ought to be generally made
known to all men. But no Rule of Revealed Religion was, or ever could be
made known to all men. Therefore no Revealed Religion is necessary to
future Happiness ... the Minor of the . . . Syllogism is matter of Fact, and
uncontrovertible, that no Religion supernatural has been conveyed to all the
World; witness the large Continent of *America*, not discover'd till within this
two Hundred Years; where if there were any Reveal'd Religion, at least it was
not the *Christian*' (*The Oracles of Reason* 196). The problem of the salvation of
those who had had no opportunity to learn of Christ is discussed in the
Preface: see ll. 48–50*n*.
172. style] title, designation (*OED* 18).
179. D. explored the religion of the American Indians, and their clash with
European Christianity, in *The Indian Queen* (1665) and *The Indian Emperor*
(1667).
182. shades of night] From *PL* iv 1015, where they are associated with Satan.
185. startle ... stagger] Both mean 'cause to waver, unsettle' (*OED* startle 7d;
stagger 6).

We grant, 'tis true, that heaven from human sense
Has hid the secret paths of providence,
But boundless wisdom, boundless mercy may
Find ev'n for those bewildered souls a way:
190   If from his nature foes may pity claim,
Much more may strangers who ne'er heard his name;
And though no name be for salvation known
But that of his eternal Son's alone,
Who knows how far transcending goodness can
195   Extend the merits of that Son to man?
Who knows what reasons may his mercy lead,
Or ignorance invincible may plead?
Not only charity bids hope the best,
But more the great apostle has expressed:
200   That if the gentiles (whom no law inspired)
By nature did what was by law required,
They who the written rule had never known
Were to themselves both rule and law alone;
To nature's plain indictment they shall plead,
205   And by their conscience be condemned or freed.

186–7. Cp. 'Horace: Odes III xxix' ll. 45–7n.

189. bewildered] lost in pathless places; OED's first example is from 'Lucretius: The Beginning of the Second Book' l. 11.

192–3. 'Neither is there salvation in any other: for there is none other name under heaven given among men, whereby we must be saved' (Acts iv 12).

193. Son's] Noyes; Sons 1682, 1683. This is a pleonastic genitive, not a plural.

194–5. Cp. Martin Clifford: 'I may very well believe withal, that there are secret and wonderful waies, by which God may be pleased to apply his [i.e. Christ's] Merits to mankind, besides those direct, open, and ordinary ones of Baptism and Confession' (A Treatise of Humane Reason (1675) 34).

195. merits] The work of man's salvation performed by Christ through the cross (cp. ll. 105–10n).

199–205. For the apostle (St Paul) see Preface l. 81n. The law in l. 200 is the law given to Moses by God, which prescribed the terms on which the behaviour of the Jewish people would be acceptable to God. According to Christian teaching, the demands of the Mosaic law are replaced through the atonement, which establishes a different way in which man's sins may be forgiven. D. suggests that the gentiles who are not subject to the Jewish law, and do not partake in the salvation wrought through the atonement, may be judged in terms of whether they have acted in accordance with that law which was available to them (i.e. the law of nature), and may be saved if they have honestly followed it. Lines 200–5 are italicized in 1682, indicating that they are a paraphrase of St Paul.

Most righteous doom! because a rule revealed
Is none to those from whom it was concealed.
Then those who followed reason's dictates right,
Lived up, and lifted high their natural light,
210 With Socrates may see their Maker's face,
While thousand rubric-martyrs want a place.
  Nor does it balk my charity to find
Th' Egyptian bishop of another mind;
For though his creed eternal truth contains,
215 'Tis hard for man to doom to endless pains
All who believed not all his zeal required,
Unless he first could prove he was inspired.
Then let us either think he meant to say
This faith, where published, was the only way,
220 Or else conclude that, Arius to confute,
The good old man, too eager in dispute,
Flew high, and as his Christian fury rose,
Damned all for heretics who durst oppose.
  Thus far my charity this path has tried
225 (A much unskilful, but well-meaning guide),
Yet what they are, ev'n these crude thoughts were
    bred
By reading that which better thou hast read—
Thy matchless author's work; which thou, my friend,
By well translating better dost commend.
230 Those youthful hours which, of thy equals most
In toys have squandered, or in vice have lost,

*Digression
to the
translator of
Father
Simon's*
Critical
History of
the Old
Testament

206. *doom*] decree (OED 1).
209. *Lived up*] lived on a high level, took a high moral position (OED 4f (first example)).
211. *rubric-martyrs*] Those who have become martyrs for some fine point of ecclesiastical procedure. The rubrics are the passages in prayer books and missals, properly printed in red, which give directions governing the performance of the liturgy.
212. *balk*] place an obstacle in the way of.
213. *th' Egyptian bishop*] Athanasius: see Preface ll. 130–75n.
220. *Arius*] Christian theologian, *c.*250–*c.*336. For Arianism see Preface ll. 130–75n.
224. *charity*] Christian love of one's fellow men (OED 1c).
228. *author . . . friend*] For Richard Simon and his translator Henry Dickinson see headnote.
230. *equals*] contemporaries (OED B 1c).
231. *toys*] things of no value, trifles (OED 5).

Those hours hast thou to nobler use employed,
And the severe delights of truth enjoyed.
Witness this weighty book, in which appears
235 The crabbèd toil of many thoughtful years
Spent by thy author in the sifting care
Of rabbins' old sophisticated ware
From gold divine, which he who well can sort
May afterwards make algebra a sport;
240 A treasure which if country curates buy,
They Junius and Tremellius may defy,
Save pains in various readings and translations,
And without Hebrew make most learned quotations;
A work so full with various learning fraught,
245 So nicely pondered, yet so strongly wrought,
As nature's height and art's last hand required,
As much as man could compass uninspired;
Where we may see what errors have been made
Both in the copier's and translator's trade,
250 How Jewish, Popish interests have prevailed,
And where infallibility has failed.

233. severe] serious (*OED* 5, a Latin sense). Cp. *Musas colimus severiores* ('we cultivate more serious Muses': Martial IX xi 17).

235. crabbèd] difficult, intricate (*OED* 7).

236. sifting care] careful sifting.

237. rabbins] rabbis, chief Jewish authorities on law and doctrine.   *sophisticated*] mixed (*OED* 1), falsified (*OED* 3).

241. Junius and Tremellius] Franciscus Junius (1545–1602) and John Immanuel Tremellius (1510–80) were Protestant scholars who translated the Bible into Latin (NT 1569, OT 1575–9). Simon criticizes the translation in his *Critical History* 155. D. repeats his joke in the 'Dedication of the *Aeneis*': 'If I desired to appear more Learned than I am, it had been as easie for me to have taken their Objections and Solutions [from Macrobius and Pontanus], as it is for a Country Parson to take the Expositions of the Fathers out of *Junius* and *Tremellius*' (*Works* v 309; Harth).

244–5. Echoes Richard Duke's commendatory poem: 'With various learning, knowledge, strength of thought,/ Order and art, and solid judgment fraught;' (*Critical History*, unsigned preliminary pages).

244. fraught] loaded.

245. nicely] carefully, exactly.

246. last hand] final touch, finishing stroke (*OED* 6b).

247. uninspired] without divine inspiration.

250. Simon discusses the ways in which various Jewish and Christian scholars have made the text and interpretation of the Bible serve sectional interests.

          For some who have his secret meaning guessed
          Have found our author not too much a priest:
          For fashion sake he seems to have recourse
255   To Pope and councils, and tradition's force,
          But he that old traditions could subdue
          Could not but find the weakness of the new:
          If scripture, though derived from heavenly birth,
          Has been but carelessly preserved on earth,
260   If God's own people (who of God before
          Knew what we know, and had been promised more,
          In fuller terms, of heaven's assisting care,
          And who did neither time nor study spare
          To keep this book untainted, unperplexed)
265   Let in gross errors to corrupt the text,
          Omitted paragraphs, embroiled the sense,
          With vain traditions stopped the gaping fence,
          Which every common hand pulled up with ease,
          What safety from such brushwood helps as these?
270   If written words from time are not secured,
          How can we think have oral sounds endured?

253. Simon was attacked for undermining the Christian faith both by the
Catholic Bossuet and the Calvinist Spanheim (Harth 180–2). In England,
Evelyn was worried about the implications of the book (see letter cited in
headnote, above). Dickinson in his Preface says: 'I could wish this Criticism
had been made by some of our own Communion, who might have alter'd
nothing of the substance of it, but have left out onely some small reflexions
upon the Protestants; Father *Simon* however is less inveterate and makes
fewer of his reflexions than could be expected from a Roman Catholick
Doctour; which thing is yet more pardonable in him in that he spares not
even them of his own Church' (*Critical History* sig. A2ᵛ; Harth).
260. God's own people] the Jews.
264. unperplexed] without doubts or difficulties.
266. embroiled] confused, made unintelligible (*OED* 1).
271. oral sounds] Simon points out that 'the Gospel was established in many
Churches before any thing of it was writ', and notes that the Council of Trent
'made the not written Traditions to be of equal authority with the word of
God contain'd in the Holy Scriptures, because it suppos'd that those Traditions which were not writ proceeded from our Saviour who communicated
them to his Apostles, and from thence they at last came down to us' (*Critical
History* sigs. (b)ʳ, bᵛ). The Council of Trent (1545–63) declared that unwritten (*non scripta*) tradition shared equal authority with scripture, but this
tradition was understood to be 'unwritten' in the special sense that its doctrines were not originally written down by their authors. D. follows many

Which thus transmitted, if one mouth has failed,
Immortal lies on ages are entailed;
And that some such have been is proved too plain,
275 If we consider interest, church and gain.
'O but', says one, 'tradition set aside,
Where can we hope for an unerring guide?
For since th' orig'nal scripture has been lost,
All copies disagreeing, maimed the most,
280 Or Christian faith can have no certain ground,
Or truth in church tradition must be found.'
Such an omniscient church we wish indeed,
'Twere worth both testaments, and cast in the creed:
But if this mother be a guide so sure
285 As can all doubts resolve, all truth secure,
Then her infallibility as well
Where copies are corrupt or lame can tell,
Restore lost canon with as little pains
As truly explicate what still remains;

*Of the
infallibility
of tradition
in general*

English theologians (both Catholic and Protestant) in assuming that this
unwritten tradition is an oral tradition (Harth 202–4; Tillotson, *The Rule of
Faith* 7–10).

276–81. This speaker urges a Catholic position, that church tradition
provides a reliable guide when scripture fails because of its textual corruption. Cp. Simon: 'The great alterations which have happened, as we have
shewn in the first Book of this Work, to the Copies of the Bible since the first
Originals have been lost, utterly destroy the Protestants and Socinians Principle, who consult onely these same Copies of the Bible as we at present have
them. If the truth of Religion remain'd not in the Church, it would be unsafe
to search for it at present in Books which have been subject to so many
alterations, and have in many things depended upon the pleasure of Trans-
cribers' (*Critical History* sig. (a)4ᵛ).

280–1. Or . . ./ Or] Either . . . Or.

282–9. Line 282 does not suggest that D. is already longing for the infallible
guide which he was later to find in Rome. Rather, as Harth argues, D. is
contesting the Catholic Church's claim to *infallibility* (i.e. to be an unerring
guide in matters of faith) by equating it with *omniscience* (i.e. the ability to
know and pronounce truly upon every matter) (Harth 208–9). John Serjeant
had claimed that tradition provided the Roman Church with an infallible
guide by which to interpret scripture: 'Tradition establisht, the Church is
provided of a certain and Infallible Rule to preserve a Copy of the Scripture's
Letter truly significative of Christs sence' (*Sure-Footing in Christianity* 116–17;
a similar passage is quoted by Tillotson in *The Rule of Faith* 13).

283. cast in] throw in, add (*OED* 78b).

290 Which yet no council dare pretend to do, ⎤
    Unless like Esdras they could write it new. ⎬
    Strange confidence, still to interpret true, ⎦
    Yet not be sure that all they have explained
    Is in the blessed original contained.
295 More safe, and much more modest 'tis, to say
    God would not leave mankind without a way,
    And that the scriptures, though not everywhere
    Free from corruption, or entire, or clear,
    Are uncorrupt, sufficient, clear, entire
300 In all things which our needful faith require.
    If others in the same glass better see,
    'Tis for themselves they look, but not for me:

291. Esdras] Simon notes that the extensive editorial work performed by Esdras on the text of the OT after the books had been corrupted during the Babylonian captivity went beyond the usual degree of collation and correction: 'For *Esdras* could not re-establish those Books, which ... had been corrupted in time of Captivity, but in quality of Prophet or publick Writer' (*Critical History* 23, and cp. 32–3).

295–304. Against the Catholic adherence to church tradition, D. now proposes the standard Protestant reliance upon scripture and private judgement (but cp. ll. 447–50*n*).

296. Harth 210 notes that the argument that Providence would have preserved the essential parts of scripture from corruption was familiar in Anglican apologetics. William Chillingworth wrote that 'the watchfull eye of divine providence ... will never suffer, that the Scripture should be depraved and corrupted, but that in them should alwaies be extant a conspicuous and plain way to eternall happinesse' (*The Religion of Protestants a Safe Way to Salvation* (1638) 61; cp. Tillotson, *The Rule of Faith* 25).

299–300. This is a standard Protestant position; cp. Tillotson: 'the Books of Scripture are sufficiently plain, as to all things necessary to be believed, and practised' (*The Rule of Faith* 20). Simon disagreed: 'Those Protestants without doubt are either ignorant or prejudic'd who affirm that the Scripture is plain of it self. As they have laid aside the Tradition of the Church, and will acknowledge no other principle of Religion but the Scripture it self, they were obliged to suppose it plain and sufficient for the establishing the truth of Faith without any Tradition. But if we but consider the conclusions which the Protestants and Socinians draw from the same principle, we shall be convinc'd that their principle is not so plain as they imagin, since these conclusions are so different and the one absolutely denies what the other affirms' (*Critical History* sig. (*b*)ʳ).

300. i.e. in all things which we are required to believe, as necessary to salvation.

For my salvation must its doom receive
Not from what others, but what I believe.

305 Must all tradition then be set aside?
This to affirm were ignorance or pride.
Are there not many points, some needful sure
To saving faith, that scripture leaves obscure?
Which every sect will wrest a several way

310 (For what one sect interprets, all sects may).
We hold, and say we prove from scripture plain,
That Christ is God; the bold Socinian
From the same scripture urges he's but man.
Now what appeal can end th' important suit?

315 Both parts talk loudly, but the rule is mute.
Shall I speak plain, and in a nation free
Assume an honest layman's liberty?
I think (according to my little skill,
To my own mother church submitting still)

320 That many have been saved, and many may,
Who never heard this question brought in play.
Th' unlettered Christian, who believes in gross,
Plods on to heaven, and ne'er is at a loss:

Objection in behalf of tradition, urged by Father Simon

303. *doom*] judgement.

305–15. D. adopts, but to a different purpose, an argument from Simon:
'There is no Religion which is not at least in appearance, grounded upon the
pure Word of God. Upon this Foundation all the new Heresies are grounded,
and it is strange that all the Patriarchs of these new Sects agree in their
Principle, and yet draw such different Conclusions from the same Principle.
The *Socinians* agree with the Protestants, whether *Lutherans, Zuinglians,* or
Calvinists, that the Holy Scripture is the only true Principle of Religion, and
that we ought to search for it only in the Old and New Testament, and that
there is no need of having recourse either to Tradition or the Fathers. But
when any Fundamental Point in Religion comes to be decided by this Principle, the latter are as much wide from the former, as Heaven from Earth.
Which is a certain sign that the Principle they make use of, is not sufficient for
the deciding of the differences which daily arise about Matters of Religion,
and therefore that we ought with the Catholicks to have recourse to something else' (*Critical History* 114).

309. *several*] separate.

312. *Socinian*] See Preface l. 162*n.*

315. *rule*] the biblical text, considered to be the rule of life.

318. *skill*] knowledge, understanding (*OED* 7).

322. *in gross*] in a general way, without going into details (*OED* B 2).

For the strait gate would be made straiter yet
325   Were none admitted there but men of wit.
The few, by nature formed, with learning fraught,
Born to instruct, as others to be taught,
Must study well the sacred page, and see
Which doctrine, this or that, does best agree
330   With the whole tenor of the work divine,
And plainliest points to heaven's revealed design;
Which exposition flows from genuine sense,
And which is forced by wit and eloquence.
Not that tradition's parts are useless here,
335   When general, old, disinteressed and clear:
That ancient fathers thus expound the page
Gives truth the reverend majesty of age,
Confirms its force by biding every test,
For best authorities next rules are best,

324. strait gate] From Matthew vii 14: 'strait is the gate, and narrow is the
way, which leadeth unto life, and few there be that find it'.   *strait*] narrow.
325. wit] intellect.
334–41. D. adopts the usual Anglican view that ancient church traditions are
a useful guide to faith and to the interpretation of scripture. Kinsley cites
Hooker to exemplify this position: 'Lest therefore the name of Tradition
should be offensive to any, considering how far by some it hath been, and is
abused, we mean by Traditions, Ordinances made in the prime of Christian
Religion, established with that Authority which Christ hath left to his
Church for matters indifferent; and in that consideration requisite to be
observed, till like authority see just and reasonable cause to alter them' (*Of the
Lawes of Ecclesiasticall Politie* v 65; Hooker, *Works* (1666) 245). Similarly the
Restoration Latitudinarians based their teaching upon scripture interpreted
through the early church Fathers: 'they derive it . . . from the Sacred writings
of the Apostles and Evangelists, in interpreting whereof, they carefully
attend to the sense of the ancient Church, by which they conceive the modern
ought to be guided: and therefore they are very conversant in all the genuine
Monuments of the ancient Fathers, those especially of the first and purest
ages' (Simon Patrick, *A Brief Account of the New Sect of Latitude-Men* (1662) 9).
334. parts] roles (*OED* 9b); capacities (*OED* 12).
335. disinteressed] disinterested.
339. Ed. For best *Authority's* next *Rules* are *best* 1682. The reading *Authority's*
could be understood either as *authorities* or *authorities'* or *authority's*. The first
is probably preferable, so that the line means 'next to the rules, the best
guides are the best authorities' (thus *Works*), rather than 'the rules of the best
authority, nearest ('next') in time to the original text, are best' (thus Noyes;
Kinsley).

340 And still the nearer to the spring we go
More limpid, more unsoiled the waters flow.
Thus first traditions were a proof alone,
Could we be certain such they were, so known;
But since some flaws in long descent may be,
345 They make not truth, but probability.
Ev'n Arius and Pelagius durst provoke
To what the centuries preceding spoke.
Such difference is there in an oft-told tale,
But truth by its own sinews will prevail.
350 Tradition written therefore more commends
Authority than what from voice descends;
And this, as perfect as its kind can be,
Rolls down to us the sacred history,
Which, from the universal church received,
355 Is tried, and after for itself believed.

The partial papists would infer from hence   *The second*
Their church in last resort should judge the sense;   *objection*
But first they would assume, with wondrous art,   *Answer to*
Themselves to be the whole, who are but part   *the*
360 Of that vast frame, the church. Yet grant they were   *objection*
The handers down, can they from thence infer
A right t' interpret? Or would they alone
Who brought the present claim it for their own?
The book's a common largess to mankind,
365 Not more for them than every man designed;
The welcome news is in the letter found,
The carrier's not commissioned to expound;

---

346. Arius] See l. *220n.*   *Pelagius*] British theologian active in the late fourth and early fifth centuries AD, who taught that man can take the initial steps towards salvation by his own efforts, independently of divine grace. Opposed by St Augustine, his views were condemned as heretical.   *provoke*] appeal (*OED* 2, citing this example); not 'challenge' as *Works* says.

349. From *magna est veritas et praevalet* ('Great is truth and it prevails': 3 Esdras iv 41 (Vulgate)). For the idea that truth is strong in itself, cp. Cicero: *O magna vis veritatis, quae . . . facile se per se ipsa defendat!* ('O great is the power of truth, which may easily defend itself on its own': *Pro Caelio* xxvi 63).

350. commends] invites acceptance [of its] (approximately *OED* 2).

353. Rolls down] causes to flow onwards (*OED* 3).

355. tried] tested.

356. partial] favouring their own party, biased.

It speaks itself, and what it does contain
In all things needful to be known is plain.
370   In times o'ergrown with rust and ignorance,
A gainful trade their clergy did advance,
When want of learning kept the laymen low,
And none but priests were authorized to know,
When what small knowledge was, in them did dwell,
375   And he a god who could but read or spell;
Then mother church did mightily prevail,
She parcelled out the Bible by retail,
But still expounded what she sold or gave,
To keep it in her power to damn and save.
380   Scripture was scarce, and as the market went
Poor laymen took salvation on content,
As needy men take money, good or bad:
God's word they had not, but the priest's they had.
Yet whate'er false conveyances they made,
385   The lawyer still was certain to be paid.
In those dark times they learned their knack so well
That by long use they grew infallible.
At last a knowing age began t' enquire
If they the book, or that did them inspire;
390   And making narrower search they found, though late,
That what they thought the priest's, was their estate;
Taught by the will produced (the written word)
How long they had been cheated on record.

370. rust] moral corruption (*OED* 2); deteriorating influence of inactivity
upon character and abilities (*OED* 5).
377. retail] in small quantities (*OED* 4b).
381. on content] without question or examination (*OED* 2).
382. Much of the coinage circulating in the Restoration was clipped or
adulterated; D. himself had difficulty with the bad coinage in which Tonson
paid him (*Letters* 75, 77, 80–2).
384. whate'er] accented on the first syllable.   *conveyances*] legal documents
by which property is transferred. Harth 219 notes that William Laud's *Relation of a Conference betweene William Lawd and Mr. Fisher the Jesuite* (1639) 194
cites the use of this legal metaphor by several early church Fathers, who
(unlike the Roman clergy) 'appeale to the *Written* Will, and make that the
Judge without any Exception, when a matter of Faith comes in Question.'
389. Cp. *The Medal* l. 166.
391. estate] Cp. *HP* ii 384.
393. record] written evidence of legal proceedings (*OED* 1). The word was
accented on the second syllable in the seventeenth century.

Then every man who saw the title fair
395 Claimed a child's part, and put in for a share,
Consulted soberly his private good,
And saved himself as cheap as e'er he could.
'Tis true, my friend (and far be flattery hence),
This good had full as bad a consequence;
400 The book thus put in every vulgar hand
Which each presumed he best could understand,
The common rule was made the common prey,
And at the mercy of the rabble lay.
The tender page with horny fists was galled,
405 And he was gifted most that loudest bawled.
The spirit gave the doctoral degree,
And every member of a company
Was of his trade, and of the Bible free.
Plain truths enough for needful use they found,
410 But men would still be itching to expound;
Each was ambitious of th' obscurest place,
No measure ta'en from knowledge, all from grace.
Study and pains were now no more their care,
Texts were explained by fasting and by prayer.
415 This was the fruit the private spirit brought,
Occasioned by great zeal, and little thought.

394. fair] clear (*OED* 17).
398. my friend] Dickinson.
400–22. This passage is directed at the nonconformist Protestant sects.
400. vulgar] of the common people (*OED* 8); coarse, uncultured (*OED* 13b; first example 1678).
406. Cp. *AA* ll. 657–9.
407. company] the trade and craft guilds.
408. i.e. as free to interpret the Bible as to practise his trade.
411. ambitious of] eager for the credit [to be gained by interpreting].
412. Kinsley cites Hooker to exemplify the Anglican position: 'An opinion hath spred it self very far in the World; as if the way to be ripe in Faith, were to be raw in Wit and Judgment; as if Reason were an enemy unto Religion, childish simplicity the Mother of Ghostly and Divine Wisdom.... The Apostle teacheth ... that Nature hath need of Grace, whereunto I hope we are not opposit, by holding, that Grace hath use of Nature' (*Of the Lawes of Ecclesiasticall Politie* iii 8; Hooker, *Works* (1666) 73–4).

While crowds unlearned, with rude devotion warm
About the sacred viands buzz and swarm,
The fly-blown text creates a crawling brood,
420 And turns to maggots what was meant for food.
A thousand daily sects rise up, and die,
A thousand more the perished race supply.
So all we make of heaven's discovered will
Is not to have it, or to use it ill.
425 The danger's much the same, on several shelves
If others wreck us, or we wreck ourselves.
    What then remains, but waiving each extreme,
The tides of ignorance and pride to stem?
Neither so rich a treasure to forgo,
430 Nor proudly seek beyond our power to know.
Faith is not built on disquisitions vain:
The things we must believe are few, and plain;

417–20. Cp. Samuel Butler, *Hudibras* (1678): 'The Learned Write, *An Insect Breeze*,/ Is but a Mungrel Prince of *Bees*,/ That Falls, before a Storm, on Cows,/ And stings the Founders of his House;/ From whose Corrupted Flesh, that Breed/ Of Vermine, did at first proceed:/ So ere the Storm of war broke out/ Religion spawn'd a various Rout,/ Of Petulant Capricious Sects,/ The Maggots of Corrupted Texts,/ That first Run all Religion down,/ And after every swarm its own' (III ii 1–12). For the association of 'Sects, and Insects' cp. Denham, 'The Progress of Learning' l. 161. Budick 153 notes that Francisco Redi's recent experiments with blow-flies had destroyed the hypothesis of spontaneous generation (reported in *Philosophical Transactions of the Royal Society* v (1670) 1175–6).
418. *viands*] The image of the Bible as meat which nourishes believers was much used by nonconformists; it derives from Hebrews v 12–14.
420. *maggots*] with a play on the meaning of *maggot* as 'whimsical fancy' (*OED* 2).
425–6. For the image cp. 'Horace: *Epode* II' l. 101n.
428. *stem*] make headway against (*OED* v³ 1b).
430. Cp. 'Horace: *Odes* III xxix' ll. 44–7nn.
431–2. Cp. St Catharine in *Tyrannic Love* (1670): 'Faith's necessary Rules are plain and Few;/ We, many, and those needless Rules pursue:/ Faith from our hearts into our heads we drive;/ And make Religion all Contemplative./ You, on Heav'ns will may witty glosses feign;/ But that which I must practise here, is plain:' (IV i 548–53). Harth 222–3 notes that the Latitudinarians considered that there were few things which had to be believed: 'They made this one of their main Doctrines; That *The principles which are necessary to Salvation are very few, and very plain, and generally acknowledg'd among Christians. . . .* They saw . . . That *Papism* . . . would drop to the ground, if it were believed, That the *necessary principles of Religion were few*, and *plain*, and those

But since men will believe more than they need,
And every man will make himself a creed,
435 In doubtful questions 'tis the safest way
To learn what unsuspected ancients say;
For 'tis not likely we should higher soar
In search of heaven than all the church before;
Nor can we be deceived, unless we see
440 The scripture and the fathers disagree.
If after all they stand suspected still
(For no man's faith depends upon his will)
'Tis some relief that points not clearly known
Without much hazard may be let alone;
445 And after hearing what our church can say,
If still our reason runs another way,
That private reason 'tis more just to curb,
Than by disputes the public peace disturb.
For points obscure are of small use to learn,
450 But common quiet is mankind's concern.
　　　　Thus have I made my own opinions clear,
Yet neither praise expect, nor censure fear;
And this unpolished, rugged verse I chose,
As fittest for discourse, and nearest prose.

---

agreed on: For then there would be no need of an *Infallible Interpreter*, and *Judge*' (Joseph Glanvill, *Essays on Several Important Subjects* (1676) 25–6).
436. unsuspected] not regarded with suspicion.
447–50. Harth 224 observes that even after the Act of Uniformity (1662) expelled dissenters from the Church of England, Anglican clerics continued to stress the need for private judgement to be restrained, as their predecessors had done: 'Wee teach all Inferiors . . . when they finde cause of doubt or question . . . to instruct their owne reason, and rather rely upon the publick Judgement then their owne in every doubtfull case. . . . If they cannot finde satisfaction so, as inwardly to acquiesce, yet to yeild externall obedience, and peaceable subjection' (Henry Ferne, *Of the Division between the English and Romish Church* (1652) 49–50).
450. Herbert ends *De Religione Laici* by hoping that his work will help *Pacem Communem stabiliendam* ('to establish the common peace': edited by Hutcheson 132). Cp. *AA* ll. 795–810.
453–4. Cp. Wolseley: 'Thus, *my Lord*, I have led you through . . . a discourse unpolished' (*Unreasonablenesse* 189). Horace says that he writes lines which are more fitted for prose (*sermoni propriora: Serm.* I iv 42). Cp. Preface ll. 433–
51.   *discourse*] rational argument.

455   For while from sacred truth I do not swerve,
    Tom Sternhold's or Tom Sha—ll's rhymes will serve.

456. Sternhold] Thomas Sternhold (d. 1549), author with John Hopkins of a
metrical translation of the Psalms (cp. *2AA* l. 403). Settle had called Shadwell
'our *Hopkin Rhimer*' (Preface to *Ibrahim* (1677) sig. a3ᵛ).   *Sha—ll*] *1682a*
(second and third issues), 1682b, 1683; Shadwell 1682a (first issue). For Shadwell
see headnote to *MF*. His attack on D., *The Medal of John Bayes*, had appeared
in May 1682.   *rhymes*] verses (*OED* 1).

75 Prologue, Epilogues and Songs from *The Duke of Guise*

Date and publication. The play was ready for performance in July 1682, but was banned by the Lord Chamberlain because it was thought to reflect on the Duke of Monmouth; Act IV, where the French King rebukes the Duke of Guise for returning to Paris without his permission, parallels Charles's rebuke to Monmouth in 1679 for returning to London. One newsletter said: 'though His Majesty be displeased with the Duke yet he will not suffer others to abuse him' (*LS* 310). D. provided the Lord Chamberlain with the source for the scene in D'Avila's *History of the League* as evidence that no such reflections were intended. The Lord Chamberlain returned the play without comment in September, but the political climate was changing and at the end of October he gave permission for it to be acted. It was performed by the King's Company at the Theatre Royal on 28 November; the Queen saw it on 1 December. See further Macdonald 124–6; *LS* 310, 317; Winn 370–1. Immediately after the play's première a folio pamphlet headed *Prologue, To The Duke of Guise* was published by Tonson, dated 1683 (Luttrell's copy (Huntington) has the MS dates 30 November and 4 December [i.e. 1682], perhaps the dates of performance and purchase; Cambridge UL copy dated 30 November). It contains the Prologue and Epilogue, with 'Another Epilogue, Intended to have been Spoken to the Play, before it was forbidden, last Summer.' A single sheet containing Song II, headed *Love and Jealousie: Or, A Song in the Duke of Guies* [*sic*] was published by P. Brooksby in 1683. The play itself, *The Duke of Guise, A Tragedy*, was published by Bentley and Tonson in 1683 (advertised in *The Observator* 13 February); reprinted 1687, 1699 (two issues). This included the Prologue and Epilogue but not Another Epilogue. The play was dedicated to Lawrence Hyde, Earl of Rochester. The Prologue (but called 'Epilogue') is found in BL MS Add 27408, with one extra couplet after l. 42 which probably derives from the playhouse, though its authorship is uncertain. Song II was printed in *Choice Ayres and Songs* (1683) set by Capt. Pack (facsimile in Day 62–3). The present text of the Prologue, Epilogue and Another Epilogue is taken from the 1683 pamphlet; that of the songs is from the first edition of the play.

Context. The play also touched upon another topical question, the King's attempt to gain control of the City of London through the surrender of its charter; a writ of *Quo Warranto* (requiring the City to demonstrate the legal basis of its freedoms) was issued in November 1681, but the courts did not decide the case in the King's favour until June 1683.

Authorship. The play was written jointly by D. and Lee, but the Prologue and Epilogue are attributed to D. in both pamphlet and play. In *The Vindication* (3) D. says that he wrote only the first scene, Act IV and the first half of Act V. This suggests that D. wrote the second song but not the first; however, both are printed here for the sake of completeness.

Reception. The play was attacked by supporters of the City's independence in several pamphlets: Thomas Hunt, *A Defence of the Charter, and Municipal Rights of the City of London* (1683; SR 13 January); [Shadwell], *Some Reflections upon the Pretended Parallel in the Play called The Duke of Guise* (1683); Anon, *The True History of the Duke of Guise* (1683; SR 27 February); and the anonymous verses *Sol in opposition to Saturn* (1683). A verse defence of D. appeared: Anon, *An Epode To his worthy Friend Mr. John Dryden* (1683; SR 8 March). D. intended to reply to these attacks in a preface to the play, but the booksellers pressed him to publish the play promptly, and the defence appeared separately as *The Vindication* (1683; SR 2 April), which replied to the pamphlets and was particularly caustic about Shadwell.

Prologue

Spoken by Mr Smith

Our play's a parallel: the Holy League
Begot our Cov'nant, Guisards got the Whig;
Whate'er our hot-brained sheriffs did advance
Was, like our fashions, first produced in France;

¶75. *Prologue*.
Title. Mr Smith] William Smith, who played Grillon; see 'Prologue to His Royal Highness', Title *n*.
1–2. Recalling these lines in *The Vindication* D. says that the play is 'a Parallel, betwixt the *Holy League* plotted by the House of *Guise* and its *Adhærents*, with the *Covenant* plotted by the *Rebels* in the time of King *Charles* the *First*, and those of the *new Association*, which was the Spawn of the *old Covenant*' (7). But he denies that there was any parallel intended between Guise and Monmouth: 'the *One* was manifestly the *Leader*, the *Other*, at the worst, is but *misled*. The *Designs* of the *One* tended openly to *Usurpation*: those of the *Other* may yet be interpreted more fairly . . . it is not . . . a Parallel of the *Men*, but of the *Times*' (6–7). John Northleigh in *The Parallel* (1682) draws a comparison between the Association and both the Holy League and the Solemn League and Covenant. See also *Astraea Redux* ll. 98–104*n*.
1. Holy League] The Catholic League, led by the Duke of Guise, which opposed the Protestant King Henri IV of France from his accession in 1589 to his conversion to Rome in 1593. D.'s translation of Maimbourg's *History of the League* was published in 1684.
2. our Cov'nant] The Solemn League and Covenant, the agreement between the Scots and English Parliaments in 1643 to establish presbyterian church government.   *got*] begot.
3. sheriffs] London had two sheriffs, one normally appointed by the Lord Mayor, the other elected, and their duties included the politically sensitive

 5   And when worn out, well scourged, and banished
         there,
     Sent over like their godly beggars here.
     Could the same trick, twice played, our nation gull?
     It looks as if the devil were grown dull,
     Or served us up in scorn his broken meat,
10   And thought we were not worth a better cheat.
     The fulsome cov'nant one would think in reason
     Had given us all our bellies-full of treason;
     And yet, the name but changed, our nasty nation
     Chaws its own excrement, th' Association.
15   'Tis true we have not learned their pois'ning way,
     For that's a mode but newly come in play;
     Besides, your drug's uncertain to prevail, ⎤
     But your true Protestant can never fail   ⎬
     With that compendious instrument, a flail. ⎦

---

one of nominating grand juries. At the election on 24 June 1682 the Whigs disputed the Tory Lord Mayor's right of nomination, and tried to elect two Whigs, the Huguenots Papillon and Dubois, who had served on the 'ignor-amus' jury (see l. 43*n*). The outgoing Whig sheriffs, Pilkington and Shute, were committed to the Tower for irregularities in their conduct of the poll, and a new election produced two Tory sheriffs. A Tory Lord Mayor was elected in October 1682. In November a jury selected now by the Tory sheriffs found Pilkington guilty of *scandalum magnatum* for having said that the Duke of York burnt the city in 1666; he was fined £100,000. Subsequently he and the other Whig ex-sheriffs Shute, Cornish and Bethel were convicted of riot at the June election (Ogg 636–7; Haley 699–704). A sign of the change in the political climate was the performance in January 1683 of Crowne's *The City Politiques* which satirized the London Whigs. For poems on the shrieval elections see *POAS* iii 207–73.

6. godly beggars] the Huguenots; cp. l. 3*n* and 'Epilogue to *The Loyal Brother*' l. 40*n*.

9. broken meat] fragments of food left after a meal.

11. fulsome] sickening, wearisome from repetition (*OED* 3).

14. Chaws] chews.   *Association*] In 1680 proposals were made by Whigs in both Houses of Parliament for an Association of those pledged to protect Protestantism and the King, and to prevent, by force if necessary, James or any other Catholic from succeeding to the throne. A draft for such an Associ-ation was produced as evidence against Shaftesbury at his trial in November 1681.

15. their pois'ning way] See 'Prologue to *The Spanish Friar*' l. 46*n*.

18. true Protestant] The Whigs called themselves 'True Protestants'.

19. compendious] direct, summary, economical (*OED* 2).   *flail*] 'Protestant

20   Go on, and bite, ev'n though the hook lies bare,
     Twice in one age expel the lawful heir;
     Once more decide religion by the sword,
     And purchase for us a new tyrant lord.
     Pray for your King, but yet your purses spare,
25   Make him not two pence richer by your prayer.
     To show you love him much, chastise him more,
     And make him very great, and very poor.
     Push him to wars, but still no pence advance,
     Let him lose England to recover France.
30   Cry freedom up with popular noisy votes,
     And get enough to cut each other's throats;
     Lop all the rights that fence your monarch's throne,
     For fear of too much power, pray leave him none.
     A noise was made of arbitrary sway,   ⎫
35   But in revenge you Whigs have found a way   ⎬
     An arbitrary duty now to pay.   ⎭
     Let his own servants turn to save their stake,
     Glean from his plenty, and his wants forsake;
     But let some Judas near his person stay
40   To swallow the last sop and then betray.
     Make London independent of the crown,
     A realm apart, the Kingdom of the Town.

Flails' were weapons carried during the Popish Plot for protection against papist assailants; see the illustration in *POAS* ii opposite 12.

24–8. Parliaments dominated by the Whigs had refused to grant Charles revenue before the passage of an Exclusion Bill.

34. As in Marvell's *An Account of the Growth of Popery and Arbitrary Government in England* (1677); cp. also *AA* ll. 759–64*n*.

37–40. Alan Roper (*HLQ* liv (1991) 43–72, esp. 49) suggests that this refers to Robert Spencer (1640–1702), Earl of Sunderland, Charles's Secretary of State from 1679; in November 1680 he voted for the exclusion of James from the succession. This is said by Roper to have prompted Charles to exclaim 'The kiss of Judas!', though Haley 602*n* says that the remark actually referred to Monmouth. He was dismissed in January 1681, and was in severe financial difficulties, particularly from gambling debts (cp. image in l. 37).

42. After this line MS adds: 'And let their Majesties the Shreeves, take care/ To hang all Tories, and all Whiggs to spare.'

Let ignoramus juries find no traitors,
And ignoramus poets scribble satires.
45 And that your meaning none may fail to scan, ⎫
Do what in coffee-houses you began: ⎬
Pull down the master and set up the man.   ⎭

Epilogue

Spoken by Mrs Cooke

Much time and trouble this poor play has cost,
And, faith, I doubted once the cause was lost.

43. ignoramus juries] In November 1681 a Middlesex jury had returned a verdict of *ignoramus* ('we do not know') on a charge of high treason against Shaftesbury, and this prompted Charles's attack on the charters by which London and many other towns enjoyed their civic rights (Ogg 634).
44. ignoramus poets] e.g. Shadwell.
46. coffee-houses] These were regarded by the government as nurseries of sedition: on 29 December 1675 a royal proclamation for their suppression was issued, though not executed; in 1677 twenty coffee-house keepers lost their licences for allowing newspapers into their premises; and during the Exclusion Crisis coffee-houses were ideal places to collect signatures for Whig petitions—at the rate of 4s. per hundred names, according to L'Estrange (Ogg 101–2). On 8 November 1682 Mr Justice James told a Grand Jury 'to take care to prevent the spreading of written and printed libels, particularly those spread in coffee-houses, where people met and talked seditiously, so much that he was told there were discrimination tables, one of them called the treason table' (*CSPD 1682* 533). Cp. D'Urfey's 'Prologue spoken before the King' at *Sir Barnaby Whigg* (*c*. November 1681; Danchin no. 308): 'In a Coffee-house, just now amongst the Rabble,/ I bluntly askt, which is the Treason-Table?/ The Fellow pointed, and faith down I sate,/ To hear two hard'ned *Brumicham* Rascals prate;/ Who very busie were in Disputation,/ And setling with great vehemence the Nation;/ Aiming at Politics, though void of Reason,/ And Lacing Coffee with large Lumps of Treason./ Zooks, says the first, (that much deserv'd the Gallows)/ These *Jury-men* of ours are heavenly fellows;' (ll. 1–10). Cp. also *The Character of a Coffee-House* (1673), and 'A Libell on the Coffee-Houses' (early 1676, in BodL MS Don. b. 8 p.557).

Epilogue.
Title. Mrs Cooke] See 'Epilogue to *The Loyal Brother*' Title *n*.

Yet no one man was meant, nor great nor small:
Our poets, like frank gamesters, threw at all.
5 They took no single aim——
But like bold boys, true to their Prince and hearty,
Huzza'd, and fired broadsides at the whole party.
Duels are crimes, but when the cause is right
In battle every man is bound to fight.
10 For what should hinder me to sell my skin ⎤
Dear as I could, if once my hand were in? ⎬
Se defendendo never was a sin. ⎦
'Tis a fine world, my masters, right or wrong,
The Whigs must talk and Tories hold their tc˙ ʒue.
15 They must do all they can——
But we, forsooth, must bear a Christian mind,
And fight like boys with one hand tied behind;
Nay, and when one boy's down 'twere wondrous wise
To cry, 'Box fair', and give him time to rise.
20 When Fortune favours, none but fools will dally: ⎤
Would any of you sparks, if Nan or Mally ⎬
Tipped you th' inviting wink, stand 'shall I, shall I?'? ⎦
A Trimmer cried (that heard me tell this story)
'Fie, Mistress Cooke! faith, you're too rank a Tory!
25 Wish not Whigs hanged, but pity their hard cases;
You women love to see men make wry faces.'

3. See Prologue ll. *1–2n.*
4. frank] lavish.
12. Se defendendo] self-defence.
13. Echoing the proverbial 'a mad world, my masters' (Tilley W880).
21. Nan] common name for a servant girl.   *Mally*] presumably 'Molly',
used both as a proper name and to mean 'wench', or sometimes 'prostitute'.
23. Trimmer] The *OED*'s first example, though the word is not D.'s coinage:
it entered the language of politics in summer 1682 as a term for religious and
political moderates who would not align themselves with either Whigs or
Tories, and came to be used abusively by Tories about those they thought
covertly sympathetic to the Whigs (see Donald R. Benson, *HLQ* xxvii
(1963–4) 115–34, and Roper). In the anonymous pamphlet *The Character of a
Trimmer* (1682) he is described as 'a true Loyal-hearted Protestant, a Well-
wisher and a Well-willer both to his *King* and *Country* . . . one that stands fast
and firm to his Principles. . . . He is no Coffee-Statesman; seldom goes
thither, except now and then by chance, and then for his Health's sake; not
for to read the News, or Pamphlets, being no *News-monger.* . . . He utterly
abominates all scurrilous Names of *WHIGG* and *TORY*, or the like' (1–2).
L'Estrange attacked Trimmers in his *Observator*, beginning on 13 November

'Pray, sir,' said I, 'don't think me such a Jew:
I say no more, but give the devil his due.'
'Lenitives', says he, 'suit best with our condition.'
30   'Jack Ketch', says I, ''s an excellent physician.'
'I love no blood—' 'Nor I, sir, as I breathe,
But hanging is a fine dry kind of death.'
'We Trimmers are for holding all things even.'
'Yes—just like him that hung 'twixt hell and heaven.'
35   'Have we not had men's lives enow already?'
'Yes sure—but you're for holding all things steady:
Now since the weight hangs all on one side, brother,
You Trimmers should, to poise it, hang on t'other.'
Damned neuters, in their middle way of steering,
40   Are neither fish, nor flesh, nor good red-herring:

1682. There 'Trimmer' says: 'When a Vessell does not *Row Even*, they'll cry, *Trimm the Boat*: And so when *One* side is *Lower* then *t'other*, 'tis our way to *Lean* to the *Upper side*'; but L'Estrange denounces this apparent moderation between court and country parties as merely covert Whiggism, and rejects the Trimmer's plea for Tories to refrain from debate (cp. D.'s ll. 13–19). Similarly the anonymous *The Trimmer Catechised* (1683) represents the Trimmer as a shifty dissenter. Benson notes that several passages in D.'s Epilogue parallel, and perhaps derive from, passages in *The Observator*. D.'s attack on Trimmers continued in *The Vindication* (1683), the Dedication of *Plutarchs Lives* (1683), the 'Epilogue to *Constantine the Great*' (November 1683) and the Postscript to *The History of the League* (1684). Halifax's *The Character of a Trimmer* began to circulate in MS *c.* December 1684, after the main controversy was over.

29. Cp. '*Trim.* I am for . . . Gaining upon people by the ways of *Lenity*, and *Indulgence*' (*Observator* 13 November).

30. Jack Ketch] the hangman.

34. Erasmus, who criticized both Luther and the Papacy. Cp. 'what left in *Erasmus* Paradise, between Heav'n and Hell?' (Otway, *The Souldiers Fortune* (1681) iv 536–7).

35. enow] enough.

39. neuters] neutrals.

40–4. Cp. 'A *Trimmer* is a kind of *State-Otter*, neither *Fish*, nor *Flesh*, and yet he smells of *Both*' (*Observator* 15 November; Benson). The imagery of monstrous, amphibious creatures was taken up in *The Character of a Trimmer* (1683), where the Trimmer is called a 'State *Hermaphrodite*': 'this same *Land-Fish* with his *Feather'd-Finns*/ Commits both *Air*, and *Earth*, and *Water-Sins*,/ Complies with those that *Fly*, and *Walk*, and *Dive*,/ But fastens only upon those that *Thrive*.'

Not Whigs nor Tories they, nor this nor that;
Not birds nor beasts, but just a kind of bat;
A twilight animal, true to neither cause,
With Tory wings, but Whiggish teeth and claws.

Another Epilogue

Intended to have been spoken to the play before it was forbidden last summer

Two houses joined, two poets to a play?
You noisy Whigs will sure be pleased today—
It looks so like two shrieves the City way.
But since our discords and divisions cease,
5   You bilbo gallants, learn to keep the peace.
Make here no tilts: let our poor stage alone;
Or if a decent murther must be done
Pray take a civil turn to Marybone.
If not, I swear we'll pull up all our benches,
10 Not for your sakes, but for our orange-wenches':
For you thrust wide sometimes, and many a spark
That misses one can hit the other mark.

---

42. Cp.'He plays the very *Bat*; He flutters with the *Bird*; and he *Creeps* with the Mouse:' (*Observator*, 22 November; Benson).

Another Epilogue.
1. Two houses joined] The King's and Duke's companies had merged on 4 May 1682; see 'Prologue and Epilogue to the King and Queen'.
3. See 'Prologue' l. 3*n*.
5–6. Brawls in the playhouses were common: see 'Prologue to *The Spanish Friar*' l. 40*n*. Recently, on 27 April 1682 Charles Deering and Mr Vaughan 'quarrelled in the Duke's Playhouse, and presently mounted the stage and fought, and Mr D. was dangerously wounded, and Mr V. secured lest it should prove mortal' (*Impartial Protestant Mercury*; LS 308).
5. bilbo] a sword noted for the temper and elasticity of its blade (from Bilbao in Spain).
8. Marybone] Marylebone Fields, often used as a duelling ground.
9. benches] the form of seating used in the pit (cp. 'Prologue for the Women' l. 14; 'Epilogue Spoken at the Opening of the New House' l. 9).

This makes our boxes full, for men of sense
Pay their four shillings in their own defence,
15   That safe behind the ladies they may stay,
Peep o'er the fan, and judge the bloody fray.
But other foes give beauty worse alarms:
The *posse poetarum*'s up in arms.
No woman's fame their libels has escaped;
20   Their ink runs venom, and their pens are clapped.
When sighs and prayers their ladies cannot move
They rail, write treason, and turn Whigs to love.
Nay, and I fear they worse designs advance:
There's a damned love-trick new brought o'er from
        France.
25   We charm in vain, and dress, and keep a pother,
While those false rogues are ogling one another.
All sins besides admit some expiation,
But this against our sex is plain damnation.
They join for libels too, these women-haters,
30   And as they club for love, they club for satires.
The best on't is, they hurt not, for they wear
Stings in their tails, their only venom's there.
'Tis true, some shot at first the ladies hit
Which able marksmen made, and men of wit;
35   But now the fools give fire, whose bounce is louder,
And yet like mere train-bands they shoot but powder.

---

14. four shillings] the price of admission to the boxes.
18. posse poetarum] 'force of poets': from *posse comitatus*, 'the force of the country', the body of men which could be raised by a sheriff to suppress a riot.
25. pother] trouble, fuss.
26. ogling] The *OED*'s first example is from Shadwell's *The Lancashire Witches* (performed 1681), 'Epilogue' l. 24, where it is glossed in the margin as 'a foolish word among the Canters for glancing'.
30–6. Satires against women had proliferated in 1680–1 (cp. 'Epilogue to *The Unhappy Favourite*' ll. 26–37n). On 20 April 1682 Lady Campden wrote, 'There are sad lampoons made of all the ladies, but I cannot get a copy of them' (*Court Satires of the Restoration*, edited by J. H. Wilson (1976) 81). For satires on court ladies from mid-1682 see Wilson 76–85; he also prints (92–5) 'A Ballad' (*c.*August 1682) which attacks the writers of libels who are 'To Court and to cunt disaffected' (l. 6).
35. bounce] noise of an explosion (*OED* 2).
36. train-bands] volunteer citizen soldiers.

Libels, like plots, sweep all in their first fury,
Then dwindle like an ignoramus jury.
Thus age begins with tousing and with tumbling,
40   But grunts and groans, and ends at last in fumbling.

Songs

I

Malicorn, Malicorn, Malicorn, ho!
If the Guise resolves to go,
I charge, I warn thee let him know,
Perhaps his head may lie too low.

II

Shepherdess.   Tell me Thirsis, tell your anguish,
Why you sigh, and why you languish;
When the nymph whom you adore
Grants the blessing of possessing,
5   What can love and I do more?
What can love, what can love and I do
more?

Shepherd.   Think it's love beyond all measure
Makes me faint away with pleasure;
Strength of cordial may destroy,
10   And the blessing of possessing
Kills me with excess of joy.

Shepherdess.   Thirsis, how can I believe you?
But confess, and I'll forgive you.
Men are false, and so are you;
15   Never Nature framed a creature
To enjoy and yet be true;

---

39. tousing] amorous horseplay.

Song I. From Act III, sung by a 'Spirit within'; probably not by D.
Song II. From Act V, sung at the banquet of Malicorne.
9. cordial] medicine to stimulate the heart.

Never Nature framed a creature
To enjoy and yet be true,
To enjoy and yet be true,
20   *soft*   And yet be true.

Shepherd.   Mine's a flame beyond expiring,
Still possessing, still desiring,
Fit for love's imperial crown;
Ever shining and refining,
25   Still the more 'tis melted down.

Chorus together.   Mine's a flame beyond expiring,
Still possessing, still desiring,
Fit for love's imperial crown;
Ever shining and refining
30   Still the more 'tis melted down.

76 Prologue and Epilogue to *The Princess of Cleves*

Date and publication. Performed between September 1680 and December 1682 (between the first season after the death of Rochester on 26 July 1680, alluded to in the play, and the date on Thomas Farmer's music for the play in BL MSS Add 19183–5). Robert D. Hume argues for a first performance in December 1682 (*JEGP* lxxv (1976) 117–38), and this is supported by the suggestion in Winn 603 that Prologue l. 12 shows that D. had recently been reading Simon's *Critical History*. The pieces were first printed in *MP* (1684; reprinted 1692); not included when Lee published his play in 1689.

Context. For D.'s association with Lee see 'To Mr Lee, on his *Alexander*'.

Prologue to *The Princess of Cleves*

    Ladies! (I hope there's none behind to hear)
    I long to whisper something in your ear,
    A secret which does much my mind perplex:
    There's treason in the play against our sex.
5   A man that's false to love, that vows and cheats,
    And kisses every living thing he meets!
    A rogue in mode, I dare not speak too broad,
    One that does something to the very bawd.
    Out on him, traitor, for a filthy beast!
10 Nay, and he's like the pack of all the rest;
    None of 'em stick at mark: they all deceive; ⎞
    Some Jew has changed the text, I half believe, ⎬
    Their Adam cozened our poor grandame Eve. ⎠
    To hide their faults they rap out oaths and tear:
15 Now, though we lie, we're too well-bred to swear,

¶76. *Prologue.*
Title. Cleves] The place is spelt 'Cleve' in the first edition of Lee's play.
1–6. Lee's play concerns the passion of the libertine Nemours for the virtuous Princess of Cleves.
8. bawd] Tournon, Nemours' bawd and former mistress.
11. stick at mark] remain constant to their object.
12. See *RL* ll. 248–50.
14. tear] rant.

So we compound for half the sin we owe,
But men are dipped for soul and body too;
And when found out, excuse themselves, pox cant 'em,
With Latin stuff, *perjuria ridet amantum*.
20 I'm not book-learned, to know that word in vogue,
But I suspect 'tis Latin for a rogue.
I'm sure I never heard that screech owl hollowed
In my poor ears, but separation followed.
How can such perjured villains e'er be savèd?
25 Achitophel's not half so false to David.
With vows and soft expressions to allure,
They stand like foremen of a shop, demure,
No sooner out of sight, but they are gadding,
And for the next new face ride out a-padding.
30 Yet, by their favour, when they have been kissing,
We can perceive the ready money missing.
Well! we may rail, but 'tis as good e'en wink,
Something we find, and something they will sink.
But since they're at renouncing, 'tis our parts
35 To trump their diamonds, as they trump our hearts.

Epilogue to *The Princess of Cleves*

A qualm of conscience brings me back again
To make amends to you bespattered men!
We women love like cats, that hide their joys
By growling, squalling, and a hideous noise.
5   I railed at wild young sparks, but without lying
Never was man worse thought on for high-flying;

16. *compound*] come to terms and pay for an offence.
17. *dipped*] mortgaged.
18. *cant*] overturn (*OED* v² 2), with a pun on *cant* (v³), to talk in jargon.
19. perjuria ridet amantum] '[Jupiter] smiles at the perjuries of lovers' (Ovid, *Ars Amatoria* i 633).
22. *screech owl*] an omen of death.
29. *padding*] searching like highwaymen for new victims.
33. *sink*] make away with.
34. *renouncing*] failing to follow suit, though having the right card.

Epilogue.
6. *high-flying*] aiming high; wide-ranging (i.e. in the object of his passions).

The prodigal of love gives each her part,
And squandering shows at least a noble heart.
I've heard of men who in some lewd lampoon
10   Have hired a friend to make their valour known:
That accusation straight this question brings,
What is the man that does such naughty things?
The spaniel lover, like a sneaking fop,
Lies at our feet; he's scarce worth taking up.
15   'Tis true, such heroes in a play go far,
But chamber practice is not like the bar.
When men such vile, such faint petitions make,
We fear to give, because they fear to take.
Since modesty's the virtue of our kind,
20   Pray let it be to our own sex confined:
When men usurp it from the female nation,
'Tis but a work of supererogation.
We showed a Princess in the play, 'tis true,
Who gave her Caesar more than all his due,
25   Told her own faults; but I should much abhor
To choose a husband for my confessor.
You see what fate followed the saint-like fool
For telling tales from out the nuptial school.
Our play a merry comedy had proved,
30   Had she confessed as much to him she loved.
True Presbyterian wives the means would try,
But damned confessing is flat popery.

---

16. *chamber practice*] giving legal opinions in private.
23–8. The Princess discloses her love for Nemours to her husband, who dies of grief; she then renounces Nemours and retires from court.
24. Luke xx 25.
31. means] (i) strategem (ii) means of grace.

77 Song ('High state and honours to others impart')

Date and publication. Printed in John Shurley's *The Compleat Courtier* (1683), and in a setting by John Abell in *Choice Ayres and Songs* (1683; facsimile in Day 134); not collected until *Poetical Miscellanies: The Fifth Part* (1704). There are MS copies of the words in BL MS Add 30303, and of the setting in BL MSS Add 19759 and 29397. The present text comes from *Choice Ayres*, emended at l. 5. *The Compleat Courtier* ('*CC*') prints the song as three six-line stanzas; substantive variants in that text and in *1704* are recorded in the notes.

Song

High state and honours to others impart,
    But give me your heart;
That treasure, that treasure alone
    I beg for my own.
5 So gentle a love, so fervent a fire
    My soul does inspire.
That treasure, that treasure alone
    I beg for my own.

Your love let me crave,
10   Give me in possessing
    So matchless a blessing,
That empire is all I would have.

    Love's my petition,
    And all my ambition;
15 If e'er you discover
    So faithful, so faithful a lover,
    So real a flame,
    I'll die, I'll die, I'll die,
    So give up my game.

¶77. *1. state*] thoughts *CC.*   *honours*] honour *CC.*
2. your] thy *CC.*
5. fervent] *CC*; *1704*; MSS; frequent *1683*.
14. And all] All *1704.*
16. so faithful] once in *1704.*
18. I'll die] twice in *1704* and *CC.*
19. So] and *CC.*   *game*] name *CC.*

78 An Epigram of Agathias

Date and publication. Printed in vol. i of *Plutarchs Lives*. *Translated from the Greek by Several Hands*, published by Tonson in 1683 (*SR* 25 April; advertised in *The London Gazette* 30 April and in *The Observator* 2 May).

Context. D.'s 'The Life of Plutarch' concludes: 'The Epigram of *Agathias*, deserves also to be remember'd: This Author flourish'd about the year five hundred, in the Reign of the Emperour *Justinian*: The Verses are extant in the *Anthologia*, and with the Translation of them, I will conclude the praises of our Author; having first admonish'd you, that they are suppos'd to be written on a Statue erected by the *Romans* to his memory' (*Works* xvii 287). There then follow the Greek text and D.'s translation.

Source. The lines by the historian and epigrammatist Agathias (*c*.AD 531–80) are part of the Greek Anthology (xvi 331), and also appear in Rualdus's edition of Plutarch (1624) (*Works* xvii 471).

An Epigram on Plutarch by Agathias

> Chaeronean Plutarch, to thy deathless praise
> Does martial Rome this grateful statue raise;
> Because both Greece and she thy fame have shared
> (Their heroes written, and their lives compared);
> 5 But thou thyself couldst never write thy own:
> Their lives have parallels, but thine has none.

¶**78**. *Title. Ed.; not in 1683*.
1. Chaeronean] Plutarch (*c*.AD 50–120) was born at Chaeronea in Boeotia, a region in central Greece.
3–4. Plutarch's parallel lives match prominent figures from Greek and Roman history.

79 The Art of Poetry

Date and publication. Drafted by Soame in 1680. The date of D.'s revision is not known, but an echo of Boileau's original in 'Virgil's Ninth Eclogue' (l. 45*n*) suggests that D. may have been working on these two poems simultaneously in 1683. *The Art of Poetry, Written in French by The Sieur de Boileau, Made English* was published in 1683 by R. Bentley and S. Magnes (*TC* November). For a revision made during press correction, see ll. 203–4*n*.

Context. The poem is a translation of *L'Art Poétique* (1674), a reworking of Horace's *Ars Poetica* by Nicolas Boileau-Despréaux (1636–1711), author of satires, epistles, and the mock-heroic poem *Le Lutrin*. Boileau was already recognized in England as a major poet and critic. Etherege had translated his *Satire* i, substituting English names for Boileau's French references (this is now lost, but is referred to by D. in 1673: see *Letters* 10); Rochester had drawn on *Satires* iii and viii in writing *Timon* and *A Satire Against Reason and Mankind* (both *c.*1674); John Pulteney's translation of the *Traité du Sublime* was published in 1680; and a translation of *Le Lutrin* by N.O. appeared in 1682. Oldham was a particularly close student of Boileau: he translated parts of *Le Lutrin* (in 1678, in BodL MS Rawlinson Poet. 123), drew on *L'Art Poétique* for his translation of Horace's *Ars Poetica* in *Some New Pieces* (1681), and translated *Satires* v and viii in *Poems, and Translations* (1683). D. refers to Boileau as a critic in 'The Authors Apology for Heroique Poetry; and Poetique Licence', prefixed to *The State of Innocence* (1677) sig. b2^v, and praises him highly several times in the 'Discourse Concerning Satire' (1693), saying: 'I might find in *France* a living *Horace* and a *Juvenal*, in the Person of the admirable *Boileau*: Whose Numbers are Excellent, whose Expressions are Noble, whose Thoughts are Just, whose Language is Pure, whose Satire is pointed, and whose Sense is close; What he borrows from the Ancients, he repays with Usury of his own: in Coin as good, and almost as Universally valuable' (*Works* iv 12). For Boileau in Restoration England see further A. F. B. Clark, *Boileau and the French Classical Critics in England 1660–1830* (1925), and Paul Hammond, *John Oldham and the Renewal of Classical Culture* (1983) 63–73, 182–207.

The Art of Poetry is one of a series of Restoration verse treatises on this subject: others include the translations of Horace's *Ars Poetica* by Roscommon (1680), Oldham (1681) and Creech (1684), Mulgrave's *An Essay on Satire* (in MS, 1679) and *An Essay upon Poetry* (1682), and Roscommon's *An Essay on Translated Verse* (1684). Oldham's renderings of Horace and Boileau had already adapted the originals to refer to contemporary English culture, and Rochester had done the same in *An Allusion to Horace* (in MS, 1675–6; printed 1680).

Authorship. The poem was first published anonymously. When Tonson reprinted it in the second edition of *The Annual Miscellany: For the Year 1694.*

Being *The Fourth Part of Miscellany Poems* (1708) it was described as 'Made
English by Sir *William Soame*, Bart. And Revis'd and Alter'd, by Mr. *John
Dryden*', with this additional note from Tonson: 'This Translation of Monsr.
Boileau's *Art of Poetry* was made in the Year *1680*, by Sir *William Soame*, of
Suffolk, Bar^t. who being very intimately acquainted with Mr. *Dryden*, desired
his Revisal of it. I saw the Manuscript lye in Mr. *Dryden*'s Hands for above
Six Months, who made very considerable Alterations in it, particularly, the
beginning of the 4th *Canto*; and it being his Opinion that it would be better to
apply the Poem to *English* Writers, than keep to the *French* Names, as it was
first Translated, Sir *William* desired he wou'd take the Pains to make that
Alteration, and accordingly that was entirely done by Mr. *Dryden*' (sig. A2^r).
Nothing more is known of the collaboration. Sir William Soame (*c.*1644–86)
was Sheriff of Suffolk 1672–3 and Ambassador to Turkey 1685–6. He wrote
'To the Author of *Sardanapalus* [i.e. John Oldham], upon that and his other
Writings' (in MS *c.*1681; printed in *EP* (1693)), in which he rebukes Oldham
for his roughness: 'From the *Boy*'s hand, take *Horace* into thine,/ And thy
rude Satires by his Rules refine./ See thy gross faults in *Boyleau's* faithful
glass,/ And get the sense, to know thy self an *Ass*' (*EP* 328).

The Art of Poetry

Written in French by the Sieur de Boileau,

Made English

Canto I

> Rash author, 'tis a vain presumptuous crime
> To undertake the sacred art of rhyme,
> If at thy birth the stars that ruled thy sense
> Shone not with a poetic influence:
> In thy strait genius thou wilt still be bound,
> Find Phoebus deaf, and Pegasus unsound.
>   You then, that burn with the desire to try
> The dangerous course of charming poetry,
> Forbear in fruitless verse to lose your time,
> Or take for genius the desire of rhyme:

5   (line 5)
10   (line 10)

¶79. *6. Phoebus*] Apollo, god of poetry.   *Pegasus*] the winged horse of
Greek mythology, often an image for poetic flights (cp. l. 39).   *unsound*]
i.e. of wind.

Fear the allurements of a specious bait,
And well consider your own force and weight.
   Nature abounds in wits of every kind,
And for each author can a talent find:
15   One may in verse describe an amorous flame,
Another sharpen a short epigram;
Waller a hero's mighty acts extol,
Spenser sing Rosalind in pastoral;
But authors that themselves too much esteem
20   Lose their own genius, and mistake their theme.
Thus in times past Du Bartas vainly writ,
Allaying sacred truth with trifling wit,
Impertinently, and without delight
Described the Israelites' triumphant flight,
25   And following Moses o'er the sandy plain,
Perished with Pharaoh in th' Arabian main.

17. Waller] Edmund Waller (1606–87) had written panegyrics to Charles I, Cromwell and Charles II, and in *Instructions to a Painter* (1665) he had celebrated the English naval exploits against the Dutch. Boileau refers to François de Malherbe (1555–1628), a writer of political poetry and an advocate of a pure, concise style.

18. Spenser] Edmund Spenser (1552–99); his *The Shepheardes Calender* (1579) had celebrated Rosalind. Boileau has Honorat de Bueil, Seigneur de Racan (1589–1670), writer of pastoral poetry.

21. 'Dubartas translated by Sylvester' (note in *1683*). Sylvester's translation of *Du Bartas his Divine Weekes and Works* (1592–1605) was one of D.'s favourite books in childhood, but in the Epistle Dedicatory to *The Spanish Friar* (1681) he cites him to show that 'when men affect a Vertue which they cannot reach, they fall into a Vice, which bears the nearest resemblance to it. Thus an injudicious Poet who aims at Loftiness runs easily into the swelling puffie style, because it looks like Greatness. I remember, when I was a Boy, I thought inimitable *Spencer* a mean Poet in comparison of *Sylvester's Dubartas*: and was rapt into an ecstasie when I read these lines: *Now, when the Winter's keener breath began/ To Chrystallize the Baltick Ocean;/ To glaze the Lakes, to bridle up the Floods,/ And periwig with Snow the bald-pate Woods:* I am much deceiv'd if this be not abominable fustian' (sig. A3ʳ). Boileau in a note here names Marc-Antoine de Gérard, Sieur de Saint-Amand (1594–1661), author of the epic poem *Moïse Sauvé* (1654).

23. Impertinently] inappropriately.

>   Whate'er you write of, pleasant or sublime,
>   Always let sense accompany your rhyme.
>   Falsely they seem each other to oppose:
> 30   Rhyme must be made with reason's laws to close,
>   And when to conquer her you bend your force,
>   The mind will triumph in the noble course;
>   To reason's yoke she quickly will incline,
>   Which far from hurting, renders her divine;
> 35   But if neglected, will as easily stray,
>   And master reason, which she should obey.
>   Love reason then, and let whate'er you write
>   Borrow from her its beauty, force and light.
>   Most writers, mounted on a resty Muse,
> 40   Extravagant and senseless objects choose;
>   They think they err, if in their verse they fall
>   On any thought that's plain or natural.
>   Fly this excess, and let Italians be
>   Vain authors of false glitt'ring poetry.
> 45   All ought to aim at sense, but most in vain
>   Strive the hard pass and slipp'ry path to gain:
>   You drown, if to the right or left you stray;
>   Reason to go has often but one way.
>   Sometimes an author, fond of his own thought,
> 50   Pursues his object till it's overwrought:
>   If he describes a house, he shows the face,
>   And after walks you round from place to place;

27. *sublime*] Also Boileau's word, alluding to Longinus' Περὶ ὕψους, which Boileau had translated as *Traité du Sublime* (1674). The examples of *sublime* in OED suggest that the word had not yet become established in English as a critical term (though Marvell uses it in 'On Mr. *Milton*'s Paradise lost' (1674) l. 53). Pulteney's translation of the *Traité* uses 'lofty' throughout. In his preface to the *Traité* Boileau explained what he understood by *sublime*: 'cet extraordinaire et ce merveilleux qui frape dans le discours, et qui fait qu'un ouvrage enleve, ravit, transporte' (45).

28. *sense*] This is another attempt to naturalize a French critical term: it translates *le bon sens*.

39. *resty*] restive.

43. *Italians*] such as Ariosto, criticized by Boileau in his *Dissertation sur la Joconde* (1669), and Tasso, described dismissively in *Satire* ix 176 and coolly in ll. 636–43 below.

51. *face*] façade (OED 12b).

Here is a vista, there the doors unfold,
Balconies here are balustered with gold:
55 Then counts the rounds and ovals in the halls,
'The festoons, friezes, and the astragals'.
Tired with his tedious pomp, away I run,
And skip o'er twenty pages to be gone.
Of such descriptions the vain folly see,
60 And shun their barren superfluity.
All that is needless carefully avoid,
The mind once satisfied is quickly cloyed.
He cannot write who knows not to give o'er:
To mend one fault he makes a hundred more.
65 A verse was weak: you turn it much too strong,
And grow obscure for fear you should be long.
Some are not gaudy, but are flat and dry;
Not to be low, another soars too high.
Would you of everyone deserve the praise?
70 In writing, vary your discourse and phrase.
A frozen style, that neither ebbs nor flows,
Instead of pleasing, makes us gape and doze.
Those tedious authors are esteemed by none
Who tire us, humming the same heavy tone.
75 Happy, who in his verse can gently steer
From grave to light, from pleasant to severe:
His works will be admired wherever found,
And oft with buyers will be compassed round.
In all you write, be neither low nor vile:
80 The meanest theme may have a proper style.
      The dull burlesque appeared with impudence,
And pleased by novelty, in spite of sense.

54. *Balconies*] accented on the second syllable in the seventeenth century.
56. 'Verse of Scudéry' (note in *1683*). Boileau satirizes a passage in Chant iii
of Georges de Scudéry's *Alaric*, though his supposed quotation ('Ce ne sont
que Festons, ce ne sont qu' Astragales') is invented.   *astragals*] mouldings
placed around columns.
71. For 'Un stile trop égal et toûjours uniforme'. The phrasing may be
influenced by Denham's description of his ideal style: 'O could I flow like
thee [the Thames]/ . . . Though deep, yet clear, though gentle, yet not dull,/
Strong without rage, without ore-flowing full' (*Cooper's Hill* (first printed
1642) ll. 189–92).
72. *gape*] yawn.
81. There had been a spate of French burlesques of Ovid and Virgil in the

All except trivial points grew out of date,
Parnassus spoke the cant of Billingsgate:
85 Boundless and mad disordered rhyme was seen,
Disguised Apollo changed to harlequin.
This plague, which first in country towns began,
Cities and kingdoms quickly overran;
The dullest scribblers some admirers found,
90 And the *Mock Tempest* was a while renown'd:
But this low stuff the town at last despised,
And scorned the folly that they once had prized,
Distinguished dull from natural and plain,
And left the villages to Flecknoe's reign.
95 Let not so mean a style your Muse debase,
But learn from Butler the buffooning grace,
And let burlesque in ballads be employed,
Yet noisy bombast carefully avoid;
Nor think to raise (though on Pharsalia's plain)
100 'Millions of mourning mountains of the slain':
Nor with Du Bartas bridle up the floods,
And periwig with wool the bald-pate woods.
Choose a just style, be grave without constraint,
Great without pride, and lovely without paint.

1640s and 1650s. Examples of English burlesques would be Cotton's *Scarronides* (1670), adapted from Paul Scarron's *Virgile Travesti* (1648–52), and two burlesques of *Ovid's Epistles*: Matthew Stevenson's *The Wits Paraphras'd* and Alexander Radcliffe's *Ovid Travestie* (both 1680).

84. cant of Billingsgate] language of the London fishmarket, proverbially foul.

90. '*The Mock Tempest*, a play written by Mr Duffett' (note in *1683*). Thomas Duffett's parody of *The Tempest* was performed at Drury Lane in 1674. Boileau refers to Charles Coypeau, Sieur d'Assoucy (1605–77), author of burlesques including *Ovide en belle humeur* (1650).

94. Flecknoe] See *MF* headnote. Boileau refers to Scarron's *Typhon ou le Gigantomachie* (1644), which inaugurated the fashion for parodies of the epic. Flecknoe's work is seen here as an inadvertent parody of the classics which he aims to emulate.

96. '*Hudibras*' (note in *1683*). Butler's poem had appeared in three parts from 1662 to 1678. Boileau refers to the 'élegant badinage' of Clément Marot (1496–1544), a writer chiefly of short, witty court poetry.

99. Boileau refers to *La Pharsale* (1655), an epic adapted from Lucan by Georges de Brébeuf (1618–61).

100. 'Verse of Brébeuf' (note in *1683*); translating 'Des morts et mourans cent montagnes plaintives'.

101–2. 'Verse of Dubartas' (note in *1683*). An addition to Boileau; see l. 21*n.*

105   Write what your reader may be pleased to hear,
       And for the measure have a careful ear.
       On easy numbers fix your happy choice;
       Of jarring sounds avoid the odious noise.
       The fullest verse and the most laboured sense
110   Displease us if the ear once take offence.
         Our ancient verse, as homely as the times,
       Was rude, unmeasured, only tagged with rhymes:
       Number and cadence, that have since been shown,
       To those unpolished writers were unknown.
115   Fairfax was he, who in that darker age
       By his just rules restrained poetic rage;

111. Editorial paragraph.

111–42. Though this passage on the development of English poetry is constrained by the need to follow Boileau, it nevertheless echoes two concerns which are evident in D.'s prose criticism: the refinement of English verse, and poetic succession. In *EDP* Eugenius says that earlier English poets 'can produce nothing so courtly writ, or which expresses so much the Conversation of a Gentleman, as Sir *John Suckling*; nothing so even, sweet, and flowing as Mr. *Waller*; nothing so Majestique, so correct as Sir *John Denham*; nothing so elevated, so copious, and full of spirit, as Mr *Cowley*' (*Works* xvii 14). In the Preface to *Fables* D. says that George Sandys (the translator of Ovid's *Met.* (1626)) was 'the best Versifier of the former Age. . . . For *Spencer* and *Fairfax* both flourish'd in the Reign of Queen *Elizabeth*: Great Masters in our Language; and who saw much farther into the Beauties of our Numbers, than those who immediately followed them. *Milton* was the Poetical Son of *Spencer*, and Mr. *Waller* of *Fairfax*; for we have our Lineal Descents and Clans, as well as other Families: *Spencer* more than once insinuates, that the Soul of *Chaucer* was transfus'd into his Body; and that he was begotten by him Two hundred years after his Decease. *Milton* has acknowledg'd to me, that *Spencer* was his Original; and many besides my self have heard our famous *Waller* own, that he deriv'd the Harmony of his Numbers from the *Godfrey of Bulloign*, which was turn'd into *English* by Mr. *Fairfax*'. D. later remarks on the imperfect metre of Chaucer's verse: 'he liv'd in the Infancy of our Poetry, and . . . nothing is brought to perfection at the first . . . even after *Chaucer* there was a *Spencer*, a *Harrington*, a *Fairfax*, before *Waller* and *Denham* were in being: And our Numbers were in their Nonage till these last appear'd' (edited by Kinsley ll. 27–38, 347–53).

115. 'Fairfax in his translation of Godfrey of Bullen' (note in *1683*). Edward Fairfax's translation of Tasso's *Gerusalemme Liberata* was published in 1600. Boileau refers to François Villon (*c.*1431 to after 1463).

Spenser did next in pastorals excel,
And taught the noble art of writing well;
To stricter rules the stanza did restrain,
120   And found for poetry a richer vein.
Then Davenant came, who with a new-found art
Changed all, spoiled all, and had his way apart:
His haughty Muse all others did despise,
And thought in triumph to bear off the prize,
125   Till the sharp-sighted critics of the times
In their mock-*Gondibert* exposed his rhymes;
The laurels he pretended did refuse,
And dashed the hopes of his aspiring Muse.
This head-strong writer, falling from on high,
130   Made following authors take less liberty.
Waller came last, but was the first whose art
Just weight and measure did to verse impart,
That of a well-placed word could teach the force,
And showed for poetry a nobler course.
135   His happy genius did our tongue refine,
And easy words with pleasing numbers join.
His verses to good method did apply,
And changed harsh discord to soft harmony.
All owned his laws, which, long approved and tried,
140   To present authors now may be a guide.

117. Spenser's *The Shepheardes Calender* (1579) actually preceded Fairfax's work. Boileau refers to Marot (see l. 96*n*).

121. Sir William Davenant (1606–68), author of *Gondibert* (1651). D. used the *Gondibert* stanza in *Heroic Stanzas* and *AM*. Boileau refers to Pierre de Ronsard (1524–85), writer of love poems, political poetry, and an unfinished epic, the *Franciade*.

126. Two collections of satires on *Gondibert* were published: *Certain Verses written by severall of the Authors Friends* (1653) and *The Incomparable Poem Gondibert, Vindicated* (1655).

127. pretended] claimed.

131. Waller is again matched with Malherbe. In the Epistle Dedicatory to *The Rival Ladies* (1664) D. says: 'the Excellence and Dignity of [rhyme] were never fully known till Mr. *Waller* taught it; He first made Writing easily an Art: First shew'd us to conclude the Sense, most commonly, in Distichs; which in the Verse of those before him, runs on for so many Lines together, that the Reader is out of Breath to overtake it. This sweetness of Mr. *Wallers* Lyrick Poesie was afterwards follow'd in the Epick by Sir *John Denham*, in his *Coopers-Hill*: a Poem which . . . for the Majesty of the Style, is, and ever will be the exact Standard of good Writing' (*Works* viii 100).

Tread boldly in his steps, secure from fear,
And be, like him, in your expressions clear.
If in your verse you drag, and sense delay,
My patience tires, my fancy goes astray,
145 And from your vain discourse I turn my mind,
Nor search an author troublesome to find.
There is a kind of writer pleased with sound,
Whose fustian head with clouds is compassed round;
No reason can disperse 'em with its light.
150 Learn then to think ere you pretend to write.
As your idea's clear, or else obscure,
Th' expression follows perfect, or impure.
What we conceive, with ease we can express,
Words to the notions flow with readiness.
155   Observe the language well in all you write,
And swerve not from it in your loftiest flight.
The smoothest verse and the exactest sense
Displease us if ill English give offence:
A barb'rous phrase no reader can approve,
160 Nor bombast, noise or affectation love.
In short, without pure language what you write
Can never yield us profit or delight.
Take time for thinking; never work in haste,
And value not yourself for writing fast.
165 A rapid poem with such fury writ
Shows want of judgement, not abounding wit.
More pleased we are to see a river lead
His gentle streams along a flowery mead,
Than from high banks to hear loud torrents roar
170 With foamy waters on a muddy shore.
Gently make haste, of labour not afraid;
A hundred times consider what you've said.
Polish, repolish, every colour lay,
And sometimes add, but oft'ner take away.
175 'Tis not enough, when swarming faults are writ,
That here and there are scattered sparks of wit;
Each object must be fixed in the due place,
And differing parts have corresponding grace,

144. fancy] imagination.
148. fustian] ridiculously lofty, bombastic.
165. fury] passion, impetuosity.
173. lay] lay on, apply.

       Till by a curious art disposed, we find
180   One perfect whole, of all the pieces joined.
       Keep to your subject close in all you say,
       Nor for a sounding sentence ever stray.
          The public censure for your writings fear,
       And to yourself be critic most severe.
185   Fantastic wits their darling follies love,
       But find you faithful friends that will reprove,
       That on your works may look with careful eyes,
       And of your faults be zealous enemies.
       Lay by an author's pride and vanity,
190   And from a friend a flatterer descry,
       Who seems to like, but means not what he says:
       Embrace true counsel, but suspect false praise.
       A sycophant will everything admire,
       Each verse, each sentence sets his soul on fire:
195   'All is divine! There's not a word amiss!'
       He shakes with joy, and weeps with tenderness;
       He overpowers you with his mighty praise.
       Truth never moves in those impetuous ways:
       A faithful friend is careful of your fame,
200   And freely will your heedless errors blame;
       He cannot pardon a neglected line,
       But verse to rule and order will confine;
       Reproves of words the too affected sound:
       'Here the sense flags, and your expression's round,
205   Your fancy tires, and your discourse grows vain,
       Your terms improper: make them just and plain.'
       Thus 'tis a faithful friend will freedom use,
       But authors, partial to their darling Muse,
       Think to protect it they have just pretence,
210   And at your friendly counsel take offence.
       'Said you of this that the expression's flat?
       Your servant, sir; you must excuse me that',

179. *curious*] careful.
182. *sounding*] having an imposing sound.   *sentence*] sententious phrase,
epigram.
183. Editorial paragraph.
190. Cp. 'Virgil's Ninth Eclogue' l. 45n.
203–4. *sound:/ . . . your expression's round*] *1683 corrected*; noise;/ . . . repetition
cloys *1683 uncorrected*.   *round*] blunt, crude (*OED* 13c).

He answers you. 'This word has here no grace.
Pray leave it out.' 'That, sir, 's the prop' rest place.'
215 'This turn I like not.' ''Tis approved by all.'
Thus, resolute not from a fault to fall,
If there's a syllable of which you doubt,
'Tis a sure reason not to blot it out.
Yet still he says you may his faults confute,
220 And over him your power is absolute.
But of his feigned humility take heed:
'Tis a bait laid to make you hear him read;
And when he leaves you, happy in his Muse,
Restless he runs some other to abuse,
225 And often finds: for in our scribbling times
No fool can want a sot to praise his rhymes.
The flattest work has ever in the court
Met with some zealous ass for its support;
And in all times a forward, scribbling fop
230 Has found some greater fool to cry him up.

Canto II

Pastoral

As a fair nymph, when rising from her bed,
With sparkling diamonds dresses not her head,
But without gold, or pearl, or costly scents
Gathers from neighb'ring fields her ornaments:
235 Such, lovely in its dress, but plain withal,
Ought to appear a perfect pastoral:
Its humble method nothing has of fierce,
But hates the rattling of a lofty verse:
There native beauty pleases and excites,
240 And never with harsh sounds the ear affrights.
But in this style a poet often spent
In rage throws by his rural instrument,
And vainly, when disordered thoughts abound,
Amidst the eclogue makes the trumpet sound:
245 Pan flies alarmed into the neighb'ring woods
And frighted nymphs dive down into the floods.

215. *turn*] translating *tour*; see 'Preface to *Sylvae*' l. 92.
242. 'Flute pipe' (note in *1683*).

Opposed to this, another, low in style,
Makes shepherds speak a language base and vile:
His writings flat and heavy, without sound,
250 Kissing the earth, and creeping on the ground;
You'd swear that Randal in his rustic strains
Again was quav'ring to the country swains,
And changing, without care of sound or dress,
Strephon and Phyllis into Tom and Bess.
255 'Twixt these extremes 'tis hard to keep the right:
For guides take Virgil, and read Theocrite.
Be their just writings, by the gods inspired,
Your constant pattern, practised and admired.
By them alone you'll eas'ly comprehend
260 How poets without shame may condescend
To sing of gardens, fields, of flowers and fruit,
To stir up shepherds, and to tune the flute;
Of love's rewards to tell the happy hour,
Daphne a tree, Narcissus made a flower,
265 And by what means the eclogue yet has power
To make the woods worthy a conqueror:
This of their writings is the grace and flight,
Their risings lofty, yet not out of sight.

Elegy

The elegy, that loves a mournful style,
270 With unbound hair weeps at a funeral pile;
It paints the lover's torments and delights,
A mistress flatters, threatens and invites.
But well these raptures if you'll make us see,
You must know love, as well as poetry.
275 I hate those lukewarm authors whose forced fire
In a cold style describes a hot desire;
That sigh by rule, and raging in cold blood
Their sluggish Muse whip to an amorous mood:

251. *Randal*] Thomas Randolph (also spelt 'Randal[l]') (1605–53), though (as Scott noted) the pastorals in his *Poems* (1638) are ornate rather than rough.
256. *Theocrite*] This keeps the French form of Theocritus' name.
266. 'Virg. Eclog. 4' (note in *1683*). Virgil's poem is dedicated to the consul and general Pollio.
268. Translating 'D'un ton un peu plus haut, mais pourtant sans audace' (ii 38), which is the first line of Boileau's section on elegy (Kinsley).

Their feigned transports appear but flat and vain,
280   They always sigh, and always hug their chain,
Adore their prison, and their suff'rings bless,
Make sense and reason quarrel as they please.
'Twas not of old in this affected tone
That smooth Tibullus made his amorous moan;
285   Nor Ovid, when instructed from above
By nature's rules he taught the art of love.
The heart in elegies forms the discourse.

Ode

The ode is bolder, and has greater force.
Mounting to heaven in her ambitious flight,
290   Amongst the gods and heroes takes delight;
Of Pisa's wrestlers tells the sinewy force,
And sings the dusty conqueror's glorious course;
To Simois' streams does fierce Achilles bring,
And makes the Ganges bow to Britain's King.
295   Sometimes she flies like an industrious bee,
And robs the flowers by nature's chemistry,
Describes the shepherds' dances, feasts and bliss,
And boasts from Phyllis to surprise a kiss,
When gently she resists with feigned remorse,
300   That what she grants may seem to be by force:
Her generous style at random oft will part,
And by a brave disorder shows her art.
Unlike those fearful poets whose cold rhyme
In all their raptures keep exactest time,
305   That sing th' illustrious hero's mighty praise
(Lean writers!) by the terms of weeks and days,
And dare not from least circumstances part,
But take all towns by strictest rules of art.

284. The Latin poet Albius Tibullus (*c.*55–48 BC to 19 BC), whose love elegies were renowned for their smooth finish and refined plainness.
285–7. A selection from Ovid's *Amores* was translated in *MP* under the title *Ovids Elegies.*
291. Probably ultimately from Virgil, who refers to chariot races at Pisa (*Geo.* iii 180).
293. Simois] the river at Troy.
294. Translating 'Ou fait fléchir l'Escaut sous le joug de Louïs'.
299–300. Boileau notes that this refers to Horace, *Carm.* II xii 25–8.

Apollo drives those fops from his abode,
310   And some have said that once the humorous god,
Resolving all such scribblers to confound,
For the short sonnet ordered this strict bound,
Set rules for the just measure, and the time,
The easy running, and alternate rhyme;
315   But above all, those licences denied
Which in these writings the lame sense supplied,
Forbad an useless line should find a place,
Or a repeated word appear with grace.
A faultless sonnet, finished thus, would be
320   Worth tedious volumes of loose poetry.
A hundred scribbling authors without ground
Believe they have this only phoenix found,
When yet th' exactest scarce have two or three
Among whole tomes from faults and censure free.
325   The rest, but little read, regarded less,
Are shovelled to the pastry from the press.
Closing the sense within the measured time,
'Tis hard to fit the reason to the rhyme.

Epigram

The epigram, with little art composed,
330   Is one good sentence in a distich closed.
These points, that by Italians first were prized,
Our ancient authors knew not, or despised;
The vulgar, dazzled with their glaring light,
To their false pleasures quickly they invite,
335   But public favour so increased their pride,
They overwhelmed Parnassus with their tide.
The madrigal at first was overcome,
And the proud sonnet fell by the same doom;
With these grave tragedy adorned her flights,
340   And mournful elegy her funeral rites;

---

310. humorous] moody, out of humour (*OED* 3b).
322. only] sole.
326. Cp. *MF* l. 101n.
330. distich] couplet.
331. points] witty turns of thought, or plays on words (*OED* 10).

A hero never failed 'em on the stage,
Without his point a lover durst not rage;
The amorous shepherds took more care to prove
True to their point than faithful to their love.

345 Each word, like Janus, had a double face,
And prose as well as verse allowed it place;
The lawyer with conceits adorned his speech,
The parson without quibbling could not preach.
At last affronted reason looked about,

350 And from all serious matters shut 'em out:
Declared that none should use 'em without shame,
Except a scattering in the epigram,
Provided that by art, and in due time,
They turned upon the thought, and not the rhyme.

355 Thus in all parts disorders did abate,
Yet quibblers in the court had leave to prate:
Insipid jesters and unpleasant fools,
A corporation of dull punning drolls.
'Tis not but that sometimes a dexterous Muse

360 May with advantage a turned sense abuse,
And on a word may trifle with address,
But above all avoid the fond excess,
And think not, when your verse and sense are lame,
With a dull point to tag your epigram.

365   Each poem his perfection has apart:
The British round in plainness shows his art;
The ballad, though the pride of ancient time,
Has often nothing but his humorous rhyme;

342. *his*] Eds; this *1683*.
348. *quibbling*] playing on words, punning.
358. *punning*] This is the *OED*'s first example; its first recorded use of *pun* is from D.'s *The Wild Gallant* (performed 1663; printed 1669) (*Works*).
drolls] buffoons, jesters.
366. 'An old way of writing, which began and ended with the same measure' (note in *1683*, wrongly attached to 'madrigal'). The line translates 'Le Rondeau né Gaulois a la naïveté'.

     The madrigal may softer passions move,
370 And breathe the tender ecstasies of love.

Satire

     Desire to show itself, and not to wrong,
     Armed virtue first with satire in its tongue.
     Lucilius was the man who, bravely bold,
     To Roman vices did this mirror hold,
375 Protected humble goodness from reproach,
     Showed worth on foot, and rascals in the coach.
     Horace his pleasing wit to this did add,
     And none uncensured could be fool or mad;
     Unhappy was that wretch whose name might be
380 Squared to the rules of their sharp poetry.
     Persius, obscure, but full of sense and wit,
     Affected brevity in all he writ;
     And Juvenal, learned as those times could be,
     Too far did stretch his sharp hyperbole;
385 Though horrid truths through all his labours shine,
     In what he writes there's something of divine;
     Whether he blames the Caprian debauch,
     Or of Sejanus' fall tells the approach,
     Or that he makes the trembling Senate come
390 To the stern tyrant to receive their doom,
     Or Roman vice in coarsest habits shows,
     And paints an empress reeking from the stews:
     In all he writes appears a noble fire.
     To follow such a master then desire.
395 Chaucer alone, fixed on this solid base,
     In his old style conserves a modern grace,
     Too happy if the freedom of his rhymes
     Offended not the method of our times.

370. Satire] Press correction moved this heading to follow l. 372, but this alteration seems to be misguided.

373. Lucilius] Gaius Lucilius (d. 102/1 BC) was the originator of Roman satire: see Horace, *Serm*. II i.

386–92. Juvenal treats Tiberius' debauchery on Capri and the fall of Sejanus in *Satire* x, the senators in iv, and Messalina in vi.

395. For D.'s later account of Chaucer see 'Preface to *Fables*' (edited by Kinsley ll. 218–600). Boileau refers to the satirist Mathurin Régnier (1573–1613).

396. conserves] keeps alive (OED 2).

The Latin writers decency neglect,
400 But modern readers challenge our respect,
And at immodest writings take offence
If clean expression cover not the sense.
I love sharp satire, from obsceneness free,
Not impudence that preaches modesty.
405 Our English, who in malice never fail,
Hence in lampoons and libels learned to rail;
Pleasant detraction, that by singing goes
From mouth to mouth, and as it marches grows!
Our freedom in our poetry we see,
410 That child of joy begot by liberty.
But, vain blasphemer, tremble when you choose
God for the subject of your impious Muse:
At last those jests which libertines invent
Bring the lewd author to just punishment.
415 Ev'n in a song there must be art and sense,
Yet sometimes we have seen that wine or chance
Have warmed cold brains, and given dull writers
mettle,
And furnished out a scene for Mr S——.
But for one lucky hit that made thee please,
420 Let not thy folly grow to a disease,
Nor think thyself a wit: for in our age
If a warm fancy does some fop engage,
He neither eats nor sleeps till he has writ,
But plagues the world with his adulterate wit.
425 Nay, 'tis a wonder if, in his dire rage,
He prints not his dull follies for the stage,
And in the front of all his senseless plays
Makes David Loggan crown his head with bays.

418. For Settle see *2AA* ll. 412–56n. Boileau refers to François Payot de Lignières (1626–1704), writer of satires against prominent members of the literary world.
428. 'D. Logan a graver' (note in *1683*). David Loggan (1635–1700) was a master of the engraved portrait. Boileau refers to the engraver Robert Nanteuil (1623–78). Cp. Oldham: '*But is it nought* (thou'lt say) *in Front to stand,/ With Lawrel crown'd by White, or Loggan's hand*' ('A Satyr Dissuading from Poetry' ll. 69–70; printed in *Poems, and Translations* (1683; advertised July)).

Canto III

Tragedy

There's not a monster bred beneath the sky
430 But, well disposed by art, may please the eye:
A curious workman, by his skill divine,
From an ill object makes a good design.
Thus, to delight us, tragedy in tears
For Oedipus provokes our hopes and fears;
435 For parricide Orestes asks relief,
And, to increase our pleasure, causes grief.
You then that in this noble art would rise,
Come, and in lofty verse dispute the prize.
Would you upon the stage acquire renown,
440 And for your judges summon all the town?
Would you your works for ever should remain,
And, after ages past, be sought again?
In all you write, observe with care and art
To move the passions, and incline the heart.
445 If in a laboured act the pleasing rage
Cannot our hopes and fears by turns engage,
Nor in our mind a feeling pity raise,
In vain with learnèd scenes you fill your plays:
Your cold discourse can never move the mind
450 Of a stern critic, naturally unkind,
Who, justly tired with your pedantic flight,
Or falls asleep or censures all you write.
The secret is attention first to gain,
To move our minds, and then to entertain,
455 That from the very opening of the scenes
The first may show us what the author means.
I'm tired to see an actor on the stage
That knows not whether he's to laugh or rage,
Who, an intrigue unravelling in vain,
460 Instead of pleasing keeps my mind in pain:

431. curious] skilful.
434. Oedipus] 'Writ by Mr Dryden' (note in *1683*). D. and Lee's *Oedipus* was
performed in 1678.
435. In Aeschylus' *Oresteia*, Orestes kills his mother Clytemnestra to avenge
her murder of his father.
452. Or ... or] Either ... or.

I'd rather much the nauseous dunce should say
Downright, 'My name is Hector in the play',
Than with a mass of miracles ill joined
Confound my ears, and not instruct my mind:
465 The subject's never soon enough expressed.
Your place of action must be fixed, and rest.
A Spanish poet may, with good event,
In one day's space whole ages represent;
There oft the hero of a wandering stage
470 Begins a child, and ends the play of age;
But we, that are by reason's rules confined,
Will that with art the poem be designed,
That unity of action, time and place
Keep the stage full, and all our labours grace.
475 Write not what cannot be with ease conceived:
Some truths may be too strong to be believed.
A foolish wonder cannot entertain;
My mind's not moved if your discourse be vain.
You may relate what would offend the eye;
480 Seeing, indeed, would better satisfy:
But there are objects that a curious art
Hides from the eyes, yet offers to the heart.
The mind is most agreeably surprised
When a well-woven subject, long disguised,
485 You on a sudden artfully unfold,
And give the whole another face and mould.
At first the tragedy was void of art,
A song, where each man danced and sung his part,
And of god Bacchus roaring out the praise
490 Sought a good vintage for their jolly days.
Then wine and joy were seen in each man's eyes,
And a fat goat was the best singer's prize.
Thespis was first, who, all besmeared with lee,
Began this pleasure for posterity,
495 And with his carted actors and a song
Amused the people as he passed along.
Next Aeschylus the different persons placed,
And with a better mask his players graced;

467. *event*] outcome, result.
487. 'The beginning and progress of tragedies' (note in *1683*).

Upon a theatre his verse expressed,
500   And showed his hero with a buskin dressed.
Then Sophocles, the genius of his age,
Increased the pomp and beauty of the stage,
Engaged the chorus' song in every part,
And polished rugged verse by rules of art.
505   He in the Greek did those perfections gain
Which the weak Latin never could attain.
Our pious fathers, in their priest-rid age,
As impious and profane abhorred the stage;
A troop of silly pilgrims, as 'tis said,
510   Foolishly zealous, scandalously played
(Instead of heroes and of love's complaints)
The angels, God, the Virgin and the saints.
At last right reason did his laws reveal,
And showed the folly of their ill-placed zeal,
515   Silenced those nonconformists of the age,
And raised the lawful heroes of the stage.
Only th' Athenian mask was laid aside,
And chorus by the music was supplied.
Ingenious love, inventive in new arts,
520   Mingled in plays, and quickly touched our hearts.
This passion never could resistance find,
But knows the shortest passage to the mind.
Paint then, I'm pleased my hero be in love,
But let him not like a tame shepherd move.
525   Let not Achilles be like Thyrsis seen,
Or for a Cyrus show an Artamen,
That struggling oft, his passions we may find
The frailty, not the virtue, of his mind.
Of romance heroes shun the low design,
530   Yet to great hearts some human frailties join:
Achilles must with Homer's heat engage:
For an affront I'm pleased to see him rage.

500. buskin] boot worn by actors in Greek tragedy.
507. in their priest-rid age] an addition to Boileau.
509. silly] simple, naive.
515. nonconformists] translating 'Docteurs preschans sans mission'.
525. Thyrsis] typical name for a shepherd in pastoral poetry.
526. 'Artamen, the name of Cyrus in Scudéry's *Romance*' (note in *1683*).
Madeleine de Scudéry (1607–1701); her romance was *Le Grand Cyrus* (1649–
53).

Those little failings in your hero's heart
Show that of man and nature he has part.
535   To leave known rules you cannot be allowed:
Make Agamemnon covetous and proud,
Aeneas in religious rites austere;
Keep to each man his proper character.
Of countries and of times the humours know;
540   From different climates differing customs grow:
And strive to shun their fault who vainly dress
An antique hero like some modern ass,
Who make old Romans like our English move,
Show Cato sparkish, or make Brutus love.
545   In a romance those errors are excused:
There 'tis enough that, reading, we're amused.
Rules too severe would then be useless found,
But the strict scene must have a juster bound.
Exact decorum we must always find.
550   If then you form some hero in your mind,
Be sure your image with itself agree,
For what he first appears he still must be.
Affected wits will naturally incline
To paint their figures by their own design.
555   Your bully poets bully heroes write: ⎫
Chapman in Bussy D'Ambois took delight,   ⎬
And thought perfection was to huff and fight. ⎭

---

539. *humours*] distinctive characters.
544. *sparkish*] like a witty gallant.
555. *bully*] blustering, swashbuckling (*OED* 3; first example 1688).
556. D. had commented on George Chapman's *Bussy D'Ambois* (1607) in the Epistle Dedicatory to *The Spanish Friar* (1681): 'I have sometimes wonder'd, in the reading, what was become of those glaring Colours which amaz'd me in *Bussy Damboys* upon the Theatre: but when I had taken up what I suppos'd, a fallen Star, I found I had been cozen'd with a Jelly: nothing but a cold dull mass, which glitter'd no longer than it was shooting: A dwarfish thought dress'd up in gigantick words, repetition in aboundance, looseness of expression, and gross Hyperboles; the Sense of one line expanded prodigiously into ten: and, to sum up all, uncorrect English, and a hideous mingle of false Poetry and true Nonsense; or, at best, a scantling of wit which lay gasping for life, and groaning beneath a Heap of Rubbish' (sig. A2ᵛ). Boileau refers to Juba, the hero of La Calprenède's romance *Cléopâtre* (12 vols, 1647).
557. *huff*] bluster (*OED* 4).

Wise nature by variety does please;
Clothe differing passions in a differing dress:
560 Bold anger in rough, haughty words appears,
Sorrow is humble, and dissolves in tears.
Make not your Hecuba with fury rage,
And show a ranting grief upon the stage,
Or tell in vain how the rough Tanais bore
565 His seven-fold waters to the Euxine shore.
These swoll'n expressions, this affected noise
Shows like some pedant that declaims to boys.
In sorrow you must softer methods keep,
And to excite our tears yourself must weep.
570 Those noisy words with which ill plays abound
Come not from hearts that are in sadness drowned.
The theatre for a young poet's rhymes
Is a bold venture in our knowing times:
An author cannot eas'ly purchase fame;
575 Critics are always apt to hiss and blame:
You may be judged by every ass in town,
The privilege is bought for half a crown.
To please, you must a hundred changes try,
Sometimes be humble, then must soar on high;
580 In noble thoughts must everywhere abound,
Be easy, pleasant, solid and profound.
To these you must surprising touches join,
And show us a new wonder in each line,
That all in a just method well designed
585 May leave a strong impression in the mind.
These are the arts that tragedy maintain.

The Epic

But the heroic claims a loftier strain.
In the narration of some great design,
Invention, art and fable all must join;

562. *Hecuba*] 'Seneca Trag.' (note in *1683*), referring to Seneca's *Troades*.
564–5. In *Troades* 8–9 Hecuba laments that Troy fell in spite of the aid of Rhesus, who drinks the waters of Tanais (the river Don) which flows into the Euxine (Black) Sea.
576–7. Cp. Oldham: 'Where every Sot, for paying half a Crown,/ Has the Prerogative to cry him down?' ('A Satyr Dissuading from Poetry' ll. 199–200; printed in his *Poems, and Translations* (*1683*)).

590   Here fiction must employ its utmost grace,
      All must assume a body, mind and face.
      Each virtue a divinity is seen,
      Prudence is Pallas, beauty Paphos' Queen.
      'Tis not a cloud from whence swift lightnings fly,
595   But Jupiter that thunders from the sky;
      Nor a rough storm that gives the sailor pain,
      But angry Neptune ploughing up the main.
      Echo's no more an empty airy sound,
      But a fair nymph that weeps, her lover drowned.
600   Thus in the endless treasure of his mind
      The poet does a thousand figures find;
      Around the work his ornaments he pours,
      And strows with lavish hand his opening flowers.
      'Tis not a wonder if a tempest bore
605   The Trojan fleet against the Libyan shore;
      From faithless Fortune this is no surprise,
      For every day 'tis common to our eyes;
      But angry Juno, that she might destroy
      And overwhelm the rest of ruined Troy,
610   That Aeolus with the fierce goddess joined
      Opened the hollow prisons of the wind,
      Till angry Neptune, looking o'er the main,
      Rebukes the tempest, calms the waves again,
      Their vessels from the dang'rous quicksands steers:
615   These are the springs that move our hopes and fears.
      Without these ornaments before our eyes
      Th' unsinewed poem languishes and dies;
      Your poet in his art will always fail
      And tell you but a dull insipid tale.
620   In vain have our mistaken authors tried
      These ancient ornaments to lay aside,
      Thinking our God, and prophets that he sent,
      Might act like those the poets did invent,
      To fright poor readers in each line with hell,
625   And talk of Satan, Ashtaroth and Bel.
      The mysteries which Christians must believe
      Disdain such shifting pageants to receive;

593. *Pallas*] Athena.   *Paphos' Queen*] Venus.
604–14. In Virgil's *Aen.*
620–59. D. was to discuss this argument by Boileau in 1693 in his 'Discourse Concerning Satire' (*Works* iv 17–18).

The gospel offers nothing to our thoughts
But penitence, or punishment for faults,
630   And mingling falsehoods with those mysteries
Would make our sacred truths appear like lies.
Besides, what pleasure can it be to hear
The howlings of repining Lucifer,
Whose rage at your imagined hero flies,
635   And oft with God himself disputes the prize?
Tasso, you'll say, has done it with applause:
It is not here I mean to judge his cause,
Yet though our age has so extolled his name,
His works had never gained immortal fame
640   If holy Godfrey in his ecstasies
Had only conquered Satan on his knees,
If Tancred, and Armida's pleasing form,
Did not his melancholy theme adorn.
'Tis not that Christian poems ought to be
645   Filled with the fictions of idolatry,
But in a common subject to reject
The gods, and heathen ornaments neglect,
To banish Tritons who the seas invade,
To take Pan's whistle, or the Fates degrade,
650   To hinder Charon in his leaky boat
To pass the shepherd with the man of note,
Is with vain scruples to disturb your mind,
And search perfection you can never find.
As well they may forbid us to present
655   Prudence or Justice for an ornament,
To paint old Janus with his front of brass,
And take from Time his scythe, his wings and glass,
And everywhere, as 'twere idolatry,
Banish descriptions from our poetry.
660   Leave 'em their pious follies to pursue,
But let our reason such vain fears subdue,
And let us not, amongst our vanities,
Of the true God create a god of lies.
In fable we a thousand pleasures see,
665   And the smooth names seem made for poetry:

636. Torquato Tasso's *Gerusalemme Liberata* (1575).
651. i.e. from transporting over the river Styx the humble shepherd as well as
the man of renown.

As Hector, Alexander, Helen, Phyllis,
Ulysses, Agamemnon and Achilles:
In such a crowd the poet were to blame
To choose King Chilperic for his hero's name.
670   Sometimes the name being well or ill applied
Will the whole fortune of your work decide.
Would you your reader never should be tired?
Choose some great hero, fit to be admired,
In courage signal, and in virtue bright,
675   Let ev'n his very failings give delight;
Let his great actions our attention bind,
Like Caesar, or like Scipio frame his mind,
And not like Oedipus his perjured race.
A common conqueror is a theme too base.
680   Choose not your tale of accidents too full—
Too much variety may make it dull:
Achilles' rage alone, when wrought with skill,
Abundantly does a whole *Iliad* fill.
Be your narrations lively, short and smart;
685   In your descriptions show your noblest art:
There 'tis your poetry may be employed,
Yet you must trivial accidents avoid.
Nor imitate that fool who, to describe
The wondrous marches of the chosen tribe,
690   Placed on the sides, to see their armies pass,
The fishes staring through the liquid glass;
Described a child, who with his little hand
Picked up the shining pebbles from the sand.
Such objects are too mean to stay our sight:
695   Allow your work a just and nobler flight.
Be your beginning plain, and take good heed
Too soon you mount not on the airy steed,
Nor tell your reader in a thundering verse:
'I sing the conqueror of the universe'.

---

669. *Chilperic*] A Frankish king. Boileau refers to Carel de Sainte-Garde's epic poem *Childebrand ou les Sarrasins chassez de France* (1666); in the 1679 edition the poem's title was changed to *Charles Martel*.
688. *that fool*] 'St Amant' (note in *1683*); the passage occurs in his *Moïse Sauvé* (1654).
699. 'The first line of Scudéry's *Alaric*' (note in *1683*): 'Je chante le Vainqueur des Vainqueurs de la terre'. Cp. l. 56n.

700   What can an author after this produce?
       The labouring mountain must bring forth a mouse.
       Much better are we pleased with his address
       Who, without making such vast promises,
       Says in an easier style and plainer sense:
705   'I sing the combats of that pious prince
       Who from the Phrygian coast his armies bore,
       And landed first on the Lavinian shore.'
       His opening Muse sets not the world on fire,
       And yet performs more than we can require:
710   Quickly you'll hear him celebrate the fame
       And future glory of the Roman name;
       Of Styx and Acheron describe the floods,
       And Caesar's wandering in th' Elysian woods;
       With figures numberless his story grace,
715   And everything in beauteous colours trace.
       At once you may be pleasing and sublime:
       I hate a heavy, melancholy rhyme.
       I'd rather read Orlando's comic tale
       Than a dull author always stiff and stale,
720   Who thinks himself dishonoured in his style
       If on his works the Graces do but smile.
       'Tis said that Homer, matchless in his art,
       Stole Venus' girdle to engage the heart;
       His works indeed vast treasures do unfold,
725   And whatsoe'er he touches turns to gold:
       All in his hands new beauty does acquire,
       He always pleases, and can never tire.
       A happy warmth he everywhere may boast,
       Nor is he in too long digressions lost.
730   His verses without rule a method find,
       And of themselves appear in order joined;
       All without trouble answers his intent,
       Each syllable is tending to th' event.
       Let his example your endeavours raise:
735   To love his writings is a kind of praise.
           A poem where we all perfections find
       Is not the work of a fantastic mind:

702. *his address*] 'Virgil's *Aeneids*' (note in *1683*).
714. *his story*] Boileau has 'vostre ouvrage'.
718. Ariosto's *Orlando Furioso*.
737. *fantastic*] too fanciful or extravagant (OED 4); Boileau has 'caprice'.

There must be care, and time, and skill and pains,
Not the first heat of unexperienced brains.
740 Yet sometimes artless poets, when the rage
Of a warm fancy does their minds engage,
Puffed with vain pride presume they understand,
And boldly take the trumpet in their hand;
Their fustian Muse each accident confounds,
745 Nor can she fly, but rise by leaps and bounds,
Till their small stock of learning quickly spent,
Their poem dies for want of nourishment.
In vain mankind the hot-brained fools decries,
No branding censures can unveil their eyes;
750 With impudence the laurel they invade,
Resolved to like the monsters they have made.
Virgil, compared to them, is flat and dry,
And Homer understood not poetry.
Against their merit if this age rebel,
755 To future times for justice they appeal;
But waiting till mankind shall do 'em right,
And bring their works triumphantly to light,
Neglected heaps we in by-corners lay,
Where they become to worms and moths a prey;
760 Forgot, in dust and cobwebs let 'em rest,
Whilst we return from whence we first digressed.

Comedy

The great success which tragic writers found
In Athens first the comedy renowned;
Th' abusive Grecian there by pleasing ways
765 Dispersed his natural malice in his plays:
Wisdom and virtue, honour, wit and sense
Were subject to buffooning insolence;
Poets were publicly approved, and sought,
That vice extolled and virtue set at nought;

740. *rage*] passion.
749. *their*] *Eds*; his *1683*.
761. Comedy] *Ed.*; *not in 1683*.
763. *renowned*] a verb: 'made famous'; i.e. 'the success of the tragedians made comedy famous too'.

770   And Socrates himself in that loose age
       Was made the pastime of a scoffing stage.
       At last the public took in hand the cause,
       And cured this madness by the power of laws,
       Forbad at any time or any place
775   To name the person or describe the face.
       The stage its ancient fury thus let fall,
       And comedy diverted without gall,
       By mild reproofs recovered minds diseased,
       And, sparing persons, innocently pleased.
780   Each one was nicely shown in this new glass,
       And smiled to think he was not meant the ass:
       A miser oft would laugh the first to find
       A faithful draft of his own sordid mind,
       And fops were with such care and cunning writ
785   They liked the piece for which themselves did sit.
       You then that would the comic laurels wear,
       To study nature be your only care:
       Whoe'er knows man, and by a curious art
       Discerns the hidden secrets of the heart,
790   He who observes, and naturally can paint
       The jealous fool, the fawning sycophant,
       A sober wit, an enterprising ass,
       A humorous Otter, or a Hudibras,
       May safely in these noble lists engage,
795   And make 'em act and speak upon the stage.
       Strive to be natural in all you write,
       And paint with colours that may please the sight.
       Nature in various figures does abound,
       And in each mind are different humours found:
800   A glance, a touch, discovers to the wise,
       But every man has not discerning eyes.
       All-changing time does also change the mind,
       And different ages different pleasures find.
       Youth, hot and furious, cannot brook delay,
805   By flattering vice is eas'ly led away;
       Vain in discourse, inconstant in desire,
       In censure rash, in pleasures all on fire.

770–1. In Aristophanes' *The Clouds*.
780–1. Echoes Soame's verses on Oldham (see headnote).
793. *Otter*] In Jonson's *Epicoene*.

The manly age does steadier thoughts enjoy,
Power and ambition do his soul employ;
810 Against the turns of fate he sets his mind,
And by the past the future hopes to find.
Decrepit age, still adding to his stores,
For others heaps the treasure he adores;
In all his actions keeps a frozen pace,
815 Past times extols, the present to debase;
Incapable of pleasures youth abuse,
In others blames what age does him refuse.
Your actors must by reason be controlled:
Let young men speak like young, old men like old.
820 Observe the town, and study well the court,
For thither various characters resort.
Thus 'twas great Jonson purchased his renown,
And in his art had born away the crown,
If less desirous of the people's praise
825 He had not with low farce debased his plays,
Mixing dull buffoon'ry with wit refined,
And Harlequin with noble Terence joined.
When in *The Fox* I see the tortoise hissed,
I lose the author of *The Alchemist.*
830 The comic wit, born with a smiling air,
Must tragic grief and pompous verse forbear,
Yet may he not, as on a market place,
With bawdy jests amuse the populace.
With well-bred conversation you must please,
835 And your intrigue unravelled be with ease:
Your action still should reason's rules obey,
Nor in an empty scene may lose its way.
Your humble style must sometimes gently rise,
And your discourse sententious be, and wise:
840 The passions must to nature be confined,
And scenes to scenes with artful weaving joined.

822–9. For D.'s earlier critique of Jonson see *EDP,* 'Epilogue to *2 Conquest of Granada*' ll. 3–6nn, and *Defence of the Epilogue* (*Works* xi 203–18).
825. For farce cp. *MF* l. 182n.
828–9. In *Volpone, or The Foxe* V iv, Sir Politique Would-bee disguises himself as a tortoise to escape three merchants. Boileau refers to Molière: 'Dans ce sac ridicule ou Scapin s'enveloppe,/ Je ne reconnois plus l'Auteur du Misanthrope'.
834. Cp. Dedication to *Marriage A-la-Mode* (*Works* xi 221).

Your wit must not unseasonably play,
But follow business, never lead the way.
Observe how Terence does this error shun:
845   A careful father chides his amorous son;
Then see that son, whom no advice can move,
Forget those orders and pursue his love.
'Tis not a well-drawn picture we discover,
'Tis a true son, a father and a lover.
850   I like an author that reforms the age,
And keeps the right decorum of the stage,
That always pleases by just reason's rule;
But for a tedious droll, a quibbling fool,
Who with low nauseous bawdry fills his plays,
855   Let him be gone, and on two trestles raise
Some Smithfield stage where he may act his pranks,
And make Jack Puddings speak to mountebanks.

Canto IV

In Florence dwelt a doctor of renown,
The scourge of God, and terror of the town,
860   Who all the cant of physic had by heart,
And never murdered but by rules of art.
The public mischief was his private gain:
Children their slaughtered parents sought in vain;
A brother here his poisoned brother wept;
865   Some bloodless died, and some by opium slept.
Colds at his presence would to frenzies turn,
And agues like malignant fevers burn.

842. unseasonably] Cp. D.'s comment that Ovid is 'frequently witty out of season' ('Preface to *Ovid's Epistles*' ll. 124–5).
844–9. In Terence's *Heautontimoroumenos.*
856. Smithfield] The London meat-market, where popular theatrical entertainments were performed at Bartholomew Fair. Boileau has 'le Pont Neuf'.
857. Jack Puddings] clowns, low buffoons; cp. 'Prologue to *Albumazar*' l. 38.
858. Though not named, Boileau's doctor is Claude Perrault (1613–88, brother of the poet Charles), who turned his hand to architecture and literature. Tonson said that the passage which starts here was reworked by D. (see headnote).
860–1. An addition to Boileau.
860. cant] jargon.
866. frenzies] states of delirium.
867. agues] fevers with cold and hot stages; used particularly of the cold stage.

Hated, at last his practice gives him o'er:
One friend, unkilled by drugs, of all his store,
870 In his new country house affords him place:
'Twas a rich abbot, and a building ass.
Here first the doctor's talent came in play;
He seems inspired, and talks like Wren or May:
Of this new portico condemns the face,
875 And turns the entrance to a better place;
Designs the staircase at the other end.
His friend approves, does for his mason send;
He comes; the doctor's arguments prevail.
In short, to finish this our humorous tale,
880 He Galen's dangerous science does reject,
And from ill doctor turn good architect.
     In this example we may have our part:
Rather be mason ('tis an useful art!)
Than a dull poet; for that trade accursed
885 Admits no mean betwixt the best and worst.
In other sciences, without disgrace
A candidate may a fill a second place;
But poetry no medium can admit,
No reader suffers an indifferent wit:
890 The ruined stationers against him bawl,
And Herringman degrades him from his stall.
Burlesque at least our laughter may excite,
But a cold writer never can delight.
The *Counter-Scuffle* has more wit and art
895 Than the stiff, formal style of *Gondibert*.
Be not affected with that empty praise
Which your vain flatterers will sometimes raise,

873. 'The King's Architects' (note in *1683*). Sir Christopher Wren (1632–1723) and Baptist May (1629–98). May was Wren's clerk of works at Windsor Castle, and undertook extensive alterations there in 1671 (*DNB*). Boileau has the architect François Mansard (1598–1666), who gave his name to the mansard roof.
880. Galen] the Roman physician (AD 129–?199), whose works had a profound effect on the practice of medicine into the Renaissance.
891. Herringman] the bookseller: see *MF* l. 105*n*.
894. Counter-Scuffle] Robert Speed's burlesque poem (published 1621 and reprinted seventeen times before 1700) describing a brawl at Woodstreet Counter (prison).

And when you read, with ecstasy will say,
'The finished piece! The admirable play!',
900   Which, when exposed to censure and to light,
Cannot endure a critic's piercing sight.
A hundred authors' fates have been foretold,
And Sh——ll's works are printed, but not sold.
Hear all the world, consider every thought:
905   A fool by chance may stumble on a fault.
Yet when Apollo does your Muse inspire,
Be not impatient to expose your fire,
Nor imitate the Settles of our times,
Those tuneful readers of their own dull rhymes,
910   Who seize on all th' acquaintance they can meet,
And stop the passengers that walk the street.
There is no sanctuary you can choose
For a defence from their pursuing Muse.
I've said before, be patient when they blame:
915   To alter for the better is no shame.
Yet yield not to a fool's impertinence:
Sometimes conceited sceptics, void of sense,
By their false taste condemn some finished part,
And blame the noblest flights of wit and art.
920   In vain their fond opinions you deride,
With their loved follies they are satisfied,
And their weak judgement, void of sense and light,
Thinks nothing can escape their feeble sight.
Their dangerous counsels do not cure, but wound; ⎤
925   To shun the storm they run your verse aground, ⎬
And thinking to escape a rock, are drowned.   ⎦
Choose a sure judge to censure what you write,
Whose reason leads, and knowledge gives you light,
Whose steady hand will prove your faithful guide,
930   And touch the darling follies you would hide:
He in your doubts will carefully advise,
And clear the mist before your feeble eyes;

---

903. *Sh——ll's*] *Ed.*; *Sh——le's 1683* (probably a confusion between *Shadwell*
and *Settle*). For Shadwell see *MF*, headnote and *passim*. Boileau has Jean Oger
de Gombauld (*c.* 1570–1666), a writer of elegies, sonnets and plays.
908. *Settles*] For Settle see *2AA* ll. 412–56n.
911. *passengers*] passers-by.
920. *fond*] foolish.

'Tis he will tell you to what noble height
A generous Muse may sometimes take her flight,
935 When, too much fettered with the rules of art,
May from her stricter bounds and limits part.
But such a perfect judge is hard to see,
And every rhymer knows not poetry;
Nay, some there are, for writing verse extolled,
940 Who know not Lucan's dross from Virgil's gold.
    Would you in this great art acquire renown?
Authors, observe the rules I here lay down.
In prudent lessons everywhere abound;
With pleasant join the useful and the sound.
945 A sober reader a vain tale will slight:
He seeks as well instruction as delight.
Let all your thoughts to virtue be confined,
Still offering noble figures to our mind.
I like not those loose writers who employ
950 Their guilty Muse good manners to destroy,
Who with false colours still deceive our eyes,
And show us vice dressed in a fair disguise.
Yet do I not their sullen Muse approve
Who from all modest writings banish love,
955 That strip the playhouse of its chief intrigue,
And make a murderer of Roderigue.
The lightest love, if decently expressed,
Will raise no vicious motions in our breast.
Dido in vain may weep, and ask relief;
960 I blame her folly, whilst I share her grief.
A virtuous author, in his charming art,
To please the sense needs not corrupt the heart;
His heat will never cause a guilty fire.
To follow virtue then be your desire.

940. For examples of D.'s critical comments on Lucan see *AM*, 'Account'
ll. 48–9, 160–1; 'Of Heroique Playes' (*Works* xi 11–12); 'Preface to *Fables*'
(edited by Kinsley ll. 293–5).
956. 'The *Cid*, translated into English' (note in *1683*, wrongly attached to
l. 957). Corneille's *Le Cid* (whose protagonist is Rodrigue) had been translated into English in 1637 by Joseph Rutter; as *The Valiant Cid* it was performed in London in 1662, 1666 and 1675.
957. *lightest*] most immoral.   *decently*] with decorum.
958. *vicious*] immoral.

965   In vain your art and vigour are expressed;
       Th' obscene expression shows th' infected breast.
       But above all, base jealousies avoid,
       In which detracting poets are employed.
       A noble wit dares liberally commend,
970   And scorns to grudge at his deserving friend.
       Base rivals who true wit and merit hate,
       Caballing still against it with the great,
       Maliciously aspire to gain renown
       By standing up, and pulling others down.
975   Never debase yourself by treacherous ways,
       Nor by such abject methods seek for praise.
       Let not your only business be to write:
       Be virtuous, just, and in your friends delight.
       'Tis not enough your poems be admired,
980   But strive your conversation be desired.
       Write for immortal fame, nor ever choose
       Gold for the object of a generous Muse.
       I know a noble wit may, without crime,
       Receive a lawful tribute for his time;
985   Yet I abhor those writers who despise
       Their honour, and alone their profit prize,
       Who their Apollo basely will degrade,
       And of a noble science make a trade.
       Before kind reason did her light display,
990   And government taught mortals to obey,
       Men, like wild beasts, did nature's laws pursue,
       They fed on herbs, and drink from rivers drew;
       Their brutal force, on lust and rapine bent,
       Committed murders without punishment.
995   Reason at last, by her all-conquering arts,
       Reduced these savages, and tuned their hearts;
       Mankind from bogs, and woods, and caverns calls,
       And towns and cities fortifies with walls:
       Thus fear of justice made proud rapine cease,
1000   And sheltered innocence by laws and peace.
             These benefits from poets we received,
       From whence are raised those fictions since believed,

972. *Caballing*] conspiring.
982. *generous*] noble.

That Orpheus by his soft harmonious strains
Tamed the fierce tigers of the Thracian plains;
1005 Amphion's notes, by their melodious powers,
Drew rocks and woods, and raised the Theban
    towers.
These miracles from numbers did arise,
Since which in verse heaven taught his mysteries,
And by a priest possessed with rage divine
1010 Apollo spoke from his prophetic shrine.
Soon after, Homer the old heroes praised,
And noble minds by great examples raised;
Then Hesiod did his Grecian swains incline
To till the fields, and prune the bounteous vine.
1015 Thus useful rules were by the poets' aid
In easy numbers to rude men conveyed,
And pleasingly their precepts did impart,
First charmed the ear, and then engaged the heart.
The Muses thus their reputation raised,
1020 And with just gratitude in Greece were praised;
With pleasure mortals did their wonders see,
And sacrificed to their divinity;
But want at last base flatt'ry entertained,
And old Parnassus with this vice was stained.
1025 Desire of gain dazzling the poets' eyes,
Their works were filled with fulsome flatteries.
Thus needy wits a vile revenue made,
And verse became a mercenary trade.
Debase not with so mean a vice thy art:
1030 If gold must be the idol of thy heart,
Fly, fly th' unfruitful Heliconian strand;
Those streams are not enriched with golden sand.
Great wits, as well as warriors, only gain
Laurels and honours for their toil and pain.
1035 But what? 'An author cannot live on fame,
Or pay a reck'ning with a lofty name;

1007. numbers] verse.
1009. rage] inspiration.
1013. Hesiod] Greek poet, *c.*700 BC, author of the *Works and Days*, which
gives advice on agriculture.
1016. rude] unsophisticated.
1031. Heliconian] Helicon was the home of the Muses.

A poet to whom Fortune is unkind,
Who when he goes to bed has hardly dined,
Takes little pleasure in Parnassus dreams,
1040   Or relishes the Heliconian streams.
    Horace had ease and plenty when he writ, ⎫
    And free from cares for money or for meat ⎬
    Did not expect his dinner from his wit.' ⎭
    'Tis true; but verse is cherished by the great,
1045   And now none famish who deserve to eat.
    What can we fear, when virtue, arts and sense
    Receive the stars' propitious influence,
    When a sharp-sighted Prince by early grants
    Rewards your merits, and prevents your wants?
1050   Sing then his glory, celebrate his fame,
    Your noblest theme is his immortal name.
    Let mighty Spenser raise his reverend head,
    Cowley and Denham start up from the dead,
    Waller his age renew, and off'rings bring,
1055   Our monarch's praise let bright-eyed virgins sing;
    Let Dryden with new rules our stage refine,
    And his great models form by this design.
    But where's a second Virgil, to rehearse
    Our hero's glories in his epic verse?
1060   What Orpheus sing his triumphs o'er the main,
    And make the hills and forests move again,
    Show his bold fleet on the Batavian shore,
    And Holland trembling as his cannons roar;

1049. prevents] anticipates.

1052–4. The references to Spenser, Cowley, Denham and Waller have no precise equivalent in Boileau, who writes about the dramatist Pierre Corneille (1606–84).

1056–7. The reference to D. corresponds to Boileau's lines on Racine: 'Que Racine enfantant des miracles nouveaux,/ De ses Heros sur lui forme tous les tableaux' (iv 197–8).   *by this design*] i.e. by copying Charles II (the Prince of l. 1048).

1058–9. Though they are a close translation from Boileau, these lines recall D.'s ambitions to write an epic poem, which he discusses in the Epistle Dedicatory to *Aureng-Zebe* (1676) sig. A4ʳ⁻ᵛ; in the 'Discourse Concerning Satire' (1693) he says that the project was abandoned, 'being encourag'd only with fair Words, by King *Charles* II, my little Sallary ill paid, and no prospect of a future Subsistance' (*Works* iv 23).

1062. The Dutch wars of 1665–7 and 1672–4.

Paint Europe's balance in his steady hand, ⎫
1065 Whilst the two worlds in expectation stand ⎬
Of peace or war, that wait on his command? ⎭
But, as I speak, new glories strike my eyes,
Glories which heaven itself does give and prize,
Blessings of peace, that with their milder rays
1070 Adorn his reign, and bring Saturnian days.
Now let rebellion, discord, vice and rage
That have in patriots' forms debauched our age,
Vanish with all the ministers of hell;
His rays their pois'nous vapours shall dispel.
1075 'Tis he alone our safety did create, ⎫
His own firm soul secured the nation's fate, ⎬
Opposed to all the boutefeux of the state. ⎭
Authors, for him your great endeavours raise,
The loftiest numbers will but reach his praise.
1080 For me, whose verse in satire has been bred,
And never durst heroic measures tread,
Yet you shall see me in that famous field
With eyes and voice my best assistance yield,
Offer you lessons that my infant Muse
1085 Learned when she Horace for her guide did choose,
Second your zeal with wishes, heart and eyes,
And afar off hold up the glorious prize.
But pardon, too, if zealous for the right,
A strict observer of each noble flight,
1090 From the fine gold I separate th' allay,
And show how hasty writers sometimes stray:
Apter to blame than knowing how to mend,
A sharp, but yet a necessary friend.

1068–77. This passage replaces Boileau's celebration of Louis XIV's military victories.

1070. *Saturnian days*] the golden age.

1072. *in patriots' forms*] See *AA* l. 179n.

1077. *boutefeux*] firebrands.

1090. *allay*] alloy.

Date and publication. Lee's play was first performed in early November 1683 (from Luttrell's date, below), by the United Company at Drury Lane, with a Prologue by Otway and an Epilogue by D. The Prologue and Epilogue were first printed in a folio half sheet headed *The Prologue and Epilogue, To the Last New Play; Constantine the Great* (1683; MS date 12 November on Luttrell's copy (Noyes)). Published by 'C. Tebroc' (i.e. 'C. Corbet'; this disguised imprint is also found on *A New Song* (1682) against Shaftesbury (Wing N744B); for Corbet see also ll. 40–5n); this was probably a pirated edition deriving from a shorthand transcription in the theatre (J. H. Smith, *PMLA* lxviii (1953) 257–8n). Tonson subsequently published *A True Coppy of the Epilogue to Constantine the Great. That which was first Published being false printed and surreptitious*, a folio half sheet (1684; MS date 14 November 1683 on Luttrell's copy (Noyes)). The Epilogue was also included in Lee's *Constantine the Great; A Tragedy* (1684) published by Bentley and Tonson. The 1683 text has several errors; the *1684 folio* text is followed here, emended at l. 13 from the *1684 play* text.

Epilogue

    Our hero's happy in the play's conclusion,
    The holy rogue at last has met confusion:
    Though Arius all along appeared a saint,
    The last act showed him a True Protestant.
5   Eusebius (for you know I read Greek authors)
    Reports that after all these plots and slaughters

¶80. *Title. Ed.*
1–4. At the end of the play Constantine accepts the marriage of his son Crispus to Fausta. Arius is revealed as a plotting hypocrite.
4. True Protestant] a designation adopted by the Whigs.
5–8. Eusebius (*c.*AD 260–*c.*AD 340) says in his *Life of Constantine* (ii 19) that after Constantine's defeat of Licinius 'all fear of those mischiefs wherewith all men had been heretofore opprest, was now taken away. And they who in times past had been dejected and sorrowfull, then lookt one upon another with smiling countenances and chearfull eyes. . . . There was an oblivion of past Afflictions, no remembrance of impiety; but an enjoyment of the present Blessings, and an expectation of more in future' (*The History of the Church* (1683) 557).
5. I] According to *1683* and *1684 play* the Epilogue was spoken by Mrs Cooke, who acted Serena (cp. 'Epilogue to *The Loyal Brother*').

The court of Constantine was full of glory,
And every Trimmer turned addressing Tory;
They followed him in herds as they were mad:
10 When Clause was king, then all the world was glad.
Whigs kept the places they possessed before,
And most were in a way of getting more;
Which was as much as saying, gentlemen,
Here's power and money to be rogues again.
15 Indeed, there were a sort of peaking tools,
Some call them modest, but I call 'em fools,
Men much more loyal, though not half so loud;
But these poor devils were cast behind the crowd.
For bold knaves thrive without one grain of sense,
20 But good men starve for want of impudence.
Besides all these, there were a sort of wights
(I think my author calls them Teckelites),
Such hearty rogues against the King and laws,
They favoured ev'n a foreign rebel's cause;
25 When their own damned design was quashed and awed,
At least they gave it their good word abroad:
As many a man who, for a quiet life,
Breeds out his bastard not to nose his wife.
Thus o'er their darling plot these Trimmers cry,⎤
30 And though they cannot keep it in their eye, ⎬
They bind it prentice to Count Teckely.   ⎦

7. Constantine] Constantine the Great (d. 337), the first Roman emperor to adopt Christianity.

8. Trimmer] See 'Epilogue to *The Duke of Guise*' l. 23n.   *addressing*] See 'Prologue to *Mithridates*' l. 4n.

10. Clause is elected king of the beggars in Beaumont and Fletcher's *The Beggar's Bush* (1647) II i.

13. as much as] *1684 play*; much as *1684 folio*.

15. peaking] sneaking, skulking (*OED*).

18. devils] monosyllabic.

21–3. The Hungarian Count Teckely led a revolt against the Austrian government which was persecuting his fellow-Protestants, and in 1683 joined the Turks who were besieging Vienna. The name 'Teckelites' was applied derisively to English Whigs, e.g. by L'Estrange in *The Observator* (29 August 1683).

28. breeds out] brings up elsewhere.   *nose*] confront.

> They believe not the last plot; may I be cursed
> If I believe they e'er believed the first;
> No wonder their own plot no plot they think—
> 35 The man that makes it never smells the stink.
> And, now it comes into my head, I'll tell
> Why these damned Trimmers loved the Turks so well.
> Th' orig'nal Trimmer, though a friend to no man,
> Yet in his heart adored a pretty woman:
> 40 He knew that Mahomet laid up for ever
> Kind black-eyed rogues for every true believer;
> And, which was more than mortal man e'er tasted,
> One pleasure that for threescore twelve-months lasted.
> To turn for this may surely be forgiven:
> 45 Who'd not be circumcised for such a heaven!

32. the last plot] The Whig Rye House Plot to murder the King, revealed in June 1683. The Whig leader Lord Russell was executed for his alleged part in it on 21 July, and the trial of Algernon Sidney was to begin on 21 November. Some Whigs denied that the plot was genuine.

33. the first] The Popish Plot, 'discovered' by Titus Oates and his Whig associates.

38–9. Probably Shaftesbury (Kinsley); for his alleged lechery cp. *The Medal* l. 37.

40–5. The Moslem paradise included 'Virgins sumptuous in apparel, and beautiful as the light . . . made on purpose to entertain the *Musulmin*' (Lancelot Addison, *The First State of Mahumedism* (1679) 121); cp. *HP* i 377–87. Richard Baxter wrote of some men's desire for 'a Mahometane Heaven of Leachery, and Wine, and Sports: A Heaven of Cards, and Dice, and Plays, and Jeasting' (*The Poor Man's Family Book* (1675) 109–10). The case of Teckely gave L'Estrange the chance for jibes about the 'Reconciling of the *True-Protestants*, and the *Mahometans*' (*The Observator* 23 October 1682; 29 August 1683). See also *A Letter from Count Teckely to the Salamanca Doctor* [i.e. Oates] (1683; published by Charles Corbet); *Dr Oats's last Legacy's and his Farewel Sermon. He being sent for to be high Priest to the Grand Turk* (1683); and *Great News from Count Teckely, or, An Account of some Passages 'twixt a True Protestant English Volunteer, and a Teckelytish Mahumetan in the Turkish Camp* (1684), where the True Protestant complains that Christianity 'gives no Incouragement to a good substantial Debauchery; no rewards to *Treason* and *Rebellion*; allows no Poligamy, nor a train of rampant Concubines'; the Teckelite says that 'your English Conventiclers I find differ not much from our *Mahometans*, only in Name; they jump together in Practice; and agree in all their Political Proceedings', to which the True Protestant replies: 'But I'me afraid they would not like circumcision?' (1–2).

44. turn] convert.

81 Ovid's Elegies, Book II Elegy the Nineteenth

Date and publication. Printed in 1684 in *MP* (advertised in *The Observator* 2 February; *SR* 4 February); reprinted 1692.

Context. This is one of a substantial selection from Ovid's *Amores* in *MP* (for a list see Appendix A). Oldham had included versions of three *Amores* in his *Poems, and Translations* (1683). D. made two other translations from the *Amores* which were published posthumously.

Sources. For the editions of Ovid used by D. see headnote to 'Preface to *Ovid's Epistles'*. There is no evidence that D. used previous translations (e.g. Marlowe's). D. renders Ovid's poem in the same number of lines (except for the final couplet), but often eschews close translation for paraphrase, using contemporary equivalents and a vigorous Restoration idiom.

Elegy the Nineteenth

If for thyself thou wilt not watch thy whore,
Watch her for me, that I may love her more;
What comes with ease we nauseously receive:
Who but a sot would scorn to love with leave?
5 With hopes and fears my flames are blown up higher:
Make me despair, and then I can desire.
Give me a jilt to tease my jealous mind;
Deceits are virtues in the female kind.
Corinna my fantastic humour knew,
10 Played trick for trick, and kept herself still new:

⌃

¶**81**. *1–8.* These lines, and ll. 37–62, are addressed to the husband of the woman addressed in ll. 19–36.
1. whore] for *puella* ('girl').
4. sot] fool; for *fereus* ('made of iron').
7. jilt] unfaithful woman.
8. D.'s addition.
10. For *quaque capi possem, callida norat opem* ('shrewdly recognized the means by which to snare me').

She, that next night I might the sharper come,
Fell out with me, and sent me fasting home;
Or some pretence to lie alone would take,
Whene'er she pleased her head and teeth would ache;
15   Till having won me to the highest strain,
She took occasion to be sweet again.
With what a gust, ye gods, we then embraced!
How every kiss was dearer than the last!
    Thou whom I now adore be edified,
20   Take care that I may often be denied.
Forget the promised hour, or feign some fright,
Make me lie rough on bulks each other night.
These are the arts that best secure thy reign,
And this the food that must my fires maintain.
25   Gross easy love does like gross diet pall;
In squeasy stomachs honey turns to gall.
Had Danae not been kept in brazen towers,
Jove had not thought her worth his golden showers.
When Juno to a cow turned Io's shape,
30   The watchman helped her to a second leap.
Let him who loves an easy Whetstone whore
Pluck leaves from trees, and drink the common shore.

11–16. D.'s paraphrase.

17. gust] keen relish (*OED* 4); cp. *AA* l. 20.

21. D.'s addition.

22. bulks] Stalls projecting from the front of a shop, a common sleeping-place for the destitute; Ovid has *in limine* ('on [your] threshold').

26. squeasy] easily upset.

27–8. Acrisius, to thwart the prophecy that his grandson would kill him, imprisoned his daughter Danae in a dungeon with brazen doors, but Zeus ('Jove' to the Romans) visited her in the form of a shower of gold, and she bore a son, Perseus.

29–30. Io, turned into a cow as a result of Hera's (Juno's) jealousy at her affair with Zeus, was guarded by Argus, the watchman with a hundred eyes. Kinsley notes that D. follows Heinsius' reading *dum nimium servat custos Iunonius Io* ('while Juno's watchman guarded Io too well') for the more usual *dum servat Iuno mutatam cornibus Io* ('while Juno guarded Io, changed to a horned beast').

30. helped her to a second leap] for *facta est . . . gratior illa Iovi* ('made her more pleasing to Jove').

31. Whetstone whore] There is no equivalent in Ovid. Whetstone Park was a resort of prostitutes: see 'Prologue to *The Wild Gallant* revived' l. 8n.

32. shore] sewer; for *e magno flumine* ('from the great river').

The jilting harlot strikes the surest blow,
A truth which I by sad experience know.
35 The kind, poor, constant creature we despise:
Man but pursues the quarry while it flies.
     But thou, dull husband of a wife too fair,
Stand on thy guard, and watch the precious ware;
If creaking doors, or barking dogs thou hear,
40 Or windows scratched, suspect a rival there;
An orange-wench would tempt thy wife abroad:
Kick her, for she's a letter-bearing bawd.
In short, be jealous as the devil in hell,
And set my wit on work to cheat thee well.
45 The sneaking City cuckold is my foe:
I scorn to strike, but when he wards the blow.
Look to thy hits, and leave off thy conniving;
I'll be no drudge to any wittol living.
I have been patient and forborn thee long,
50 In hope thou wouldst not pocket up thy wrong;
If no affront can rouse thee, understand
I'll take no more indulgence at thy hand.
What, ne'er to be forbid thy house and wife!
Damn him who loves to lead so dull a life.
55 Now I can neither sigh, nor whine, nor pray;
All those occasions thou hast ta'en away.
Why art thou so incorrigibly civil?
Do somewhat I may wish thee at the devil.

---

38. *watch the precious ware*] D.'s addition.
41. *orange-wench*] For *ancilla* ('slave girl'). Mary Meggs, chief orange-seller at
the Theatre Royal, often earned money as a messenger (Pepys viii 395, 598–
9).
45–6. D.'s addition.
45. *sneaking City cuckold*] For *stultus* ('fool'). Restoration drama often
represents the rakes regarding the wives of City merchants as fair
game.   *sneaking*] mean, contemptible (*OED* 2).
47. *Look to thy hits*] look after your own interests (*OED* hit 3b).
48. *drudge*] one who provides sexual services; not in *OED*, but cp. Rochester:
'Let the porter and the groom,/ . . . Drudge in fair Aurelia's womb' ('Song:
"Love a woman?"' ll. 5, 7), and D.'s 'The Sixth Satire of Juvenal' ll. 46–7,
496–7.   *wittol*] a cuckold complacently aware of his wife's infidelity.
50. *pocket up*] accept without resentment (*OED* 3a).
54, 61–2. D.'s additions.

For shame, be no accomplice in my treason:
60   A pimping husband is too much, in reason.
      Once more wear horns before I quite forsake her;
      In hopes whereof I rest thy cuckold-maker.

82 Amaryllis (from Theocritus' *Idyll* III)

Date and publication. Printed in 1684 in *MP* (*SR* 4 February; advertised in *The Observator* 2 February); reprinted 1692.

Context. Contemporary interest in Theocritus was slight compared with the enthusiasm for other classical poets, but an edition of the Greek text was published by John Fell in Oxford in 1676, and a selection with a parallel Greek and Latin text by George Sylvanus in 1683. Thomas Creech's complete translation of *The Idylliums of Theocritus*, prefaced by an abridged translation of René Rapin's *De Carmine Pastorali*, was published in 1684 (Dedication dated 12 July), with *Idyll* xvi dedicated 'To his very good Friend *John Dryden* Esquire'. *MP* includes one translation from Theocritus by Richard Duke, and one by William Bowles; *Sylvae* has eight more, three of them by D., two by William Bowles, the others anonymous. See also Gillespie 65.

Sources. D. translates Theocritus' *Idyll* iii. His version is freer than was his usual practice, so the notes below identifying D.'s additions are only approximate. D. used the 1604 edition of Theocritus by Daniel Heinsius, often taking ideas from Heinsius' Latin paraphrase (see Francis Pughe, *John Dryden's Übersetzungen aus Theokrit* (1894)). As Creech had already seen *MP* (to which he contributed) in time for him to quote Roscommon's and D.'s versions of the *Eclogues* in his translation of Rapin, the verbal parallels between Creech's version of *Idyll* iii and D.'s are probably borrowings by Creech. In the case of D.'s translations from Theocritus in *Sylvae*, we do not know exactly when they were written (see headnote to 'Preface to *Sylvae*'), nor when D. saw Creech's translations, so the occasional verbal parallels between the two versions cannot be accounted for with certainty; they may be fortuitous. D. said in 1699 that he had never read Creech's Theocritus (*Letters* 127). D.'s translations from Theocritus are discussed by Silvano Gerevini, *Dryden e Teocrito* (1966).

Amaryllis,
Or the Third *Idyllium* of Theocritus, Paraphrased

To Amaryllis love compels my way,
My browsing goats upon the mountains stray;

O Tityrus, tend them well, and see them fed ⎤
In pastures fresh, and to their watering led,   ⎬
5 And 'ware the ridgling with his butting head.⎦
Ah beauteous nymph, can you forget your love,
The conscious grottoes, and the shady grove,
Where stretched at ease your tender limbs were laid,
Your nameless beauties nakedly displayed?
10 Then I was called your darling, your desire,
With kisses such as set my soul on fire.
But you are changed; yet I am still the same,
My heart maintains for both a double flame:
Grieved but unmoved, and patient of your scorn,
15 So faithful I, and you so much forsworn!
I die, and death will finish all my pain;
Yet ere I die, behold me once again:
Am I so much deformed, so changed of late?
What partial judges are our love and hate!
20 Ten wildings have I gathered for my dear,
How ruddy like your lips their streaks appear!
Far off you viewed them with a longing eye
Upon the topmost branch (the tree was high);
Yet nimbly up, from bough to bough I swerved,
25 And for tomorrow have ten more reserved.
Look on me kindly, and some pity show,
Or give me leave at least to look on you.
Some god transform me by his heavenly power
Ev'n to a bee to buzz within your bower,
30 The winding ivy-chaplet to invade
And folded fern that your fair forehead shade.
Now to my cost the force of love I find,
The heavy hand he bears on human kind!
The milk of tigers was his infant food, ⎤
35 Taught from his tender years the taste of blood;   ⎬
His brother whelps and he ran wild about the wood.⎦
Ah nymph, trained up in his tyrannic court
To make the sufferings of your slaves your sport!

¶82. *5. ridgling*] animal with only one testicle (cp. 'Virgil's Ninth Eclogue'
l. 30).

7. conscious] witnessing human secrets (OED 2).

8–11, 13–15, 17, 19. D.'s additions.

20. wildings] wild apples (OED 1).

21, 23–4, 27–8, 35, 37–9, 42, 44–6. D.'s additions.

Plate *1*. The medal struck to celebrate the verdict of *ignoramus* in the case against the Earl of Shaftesbury, the occasion for Dryden's poem *The Medal*. Copyright British Museum.

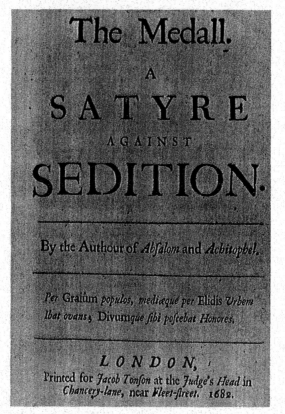

The Medall.

A

SATYRE

AGAINST

SEDITION.

By the Authour of *Abſalom* and *Achitophel*.

Per Graiûm *populos, mediæque per* Elidis *Urbem Ibat ovans; Divumque ſibi poſcebat Honores.*

LONDON,
Printed for *Jacob Tonſon* at the *Judge's Head* in *Chancery-lane,* near *Fleet-ſtreet.* 1682.

Plate *2*. Title page of the first edition of *The Medal* (1682), from a copy in the Brotherton Collection, Leeds University Library. Reproduced by permission of the Librarian.

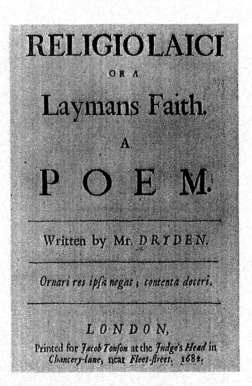

Plate 3. Title page of the first edition of *Religio Laici* (1682), from a copy in the Brotherton Collection, Leeds University Library. Reproduced by permission of the Librarian.

Plates 4 and 5. Dryden's poem 'To Mr L. Maidwell on his new method', from the unique text in Leeds University Library Brotherton Collection MS Lt 66 f. 1^{r-v}. Reproduced by permission of the Librarian.

To Mr Maidwell on his new method

Great is now of equal art become
To English men, since now the *gate* to Rome
A guide, our language, nothing is expert
grateful to each or to the Roman *art*
grammar is true on which this words must feed
Nor is it said to one *judgment* bred
... Then no Reverend Master be adored
And all our *gracefull* Bard his praise record
... not *...* myself get it from
From his examples and his precepts came.
Our Nobles using from this institution can
... the Senate and *...* the Bar
But above all the Muses need *...*
... been transplanted from us God *...*
Nor thou the learn whose *Judgman* has afford
And *...* that many which our Master *...*
grammar which are before the *ungratefull* past
Of our *...* years is made a *...*

Should appeal'd that *...* remain
... [Rule?] is useful each *...* places
... [even?] that by language is expert
Common distinguishing *...* man and *...*
See that the grammar make the *difference* more
Then man *...* then man *...* before

... is thy academy thou confirst
... it *...* *...* it would the the mind
Grow by degree are out of *...* brought
The Grammar only for its self is taught
Designed by that not for the end but ways
So *...* than doth our youth comely
From step to step by thy judicious care
... *...* out into knowledge are aware
Than at the last Historians they become
... know the deeds as well as words of Rome
Which then by sure *...* doth bind
For that *...* *...* in the mind
Thy *...* permits not more to say
So *...* thy own compendious ways
... is a more the *...* of pace
... *...* of the *...* *...* the race

Dryden

Circum renidenteis Lareis!
Hæc ubi locutus fænerator Alphius,
Jam jam futurus rusticus,
Omnem relegit Idibus pecuniam;
70   *Quærit Kalendis ponere.*

EPOD.

dinem notat: ut paſſim *examen apum*
dicimus pro nova illa ſobole, quæ ad
alias ſedes quærendas educitur. Cujus
ſimilitudine *juvenum rectus examen* dixit
Horat. lib. 1. Od. 35. *Examen domus.*]
Vernæ ſunt, quaſi examen apium, in di-
vitis domo.

66. *Circum renidenteis lares.*] Neque
ab renidenteis ad *lares*, ſed ad vernas re-
ferendum eſt, ut ſit ordo: *Vernas re-*
nidentis circum lares. Eſt autem Horatio
valde uſitata Synchuſis. Sic Od. 10.
lib. 1.

  Quin te Atridas duce te superbos
  Illo dives &c.
Non enim *duce te superbos*, ſed *duce te*
fefellit. Et in Tyreſia:

  Quando pauperiem missis ambagibus hor-
   res,
  Accipe qua ratione queas ditescere.
Pro, *Accipe missis ambagibus.* ut recte
vetus Comment. explicat. In arte:

  Qui variare cupit rem prodigialiter unam
  Delphinum sylvis appinget, &c.
Eſt enim *prodigialiter appinget*, non au-
tem *prodigialiter variare.* Alibi,

  — *quid est cur barbara minus*
  Venena Medeæ valent?
Subintellige, *quam, Quid est cur mea*
venena minus quam Medeæ valent? Græ-
ci felicius hoc per articulum; quo quia
Latini deſtituimur, magnæ plerumque
obſcuritatis cauſa eſt. Neque minus
obſcurum eſt quod ſequitur:

  Venena magnum fas nefasque non valent
  Convertere humanas vices.
Sed legendum eſt, *magicum fas nefas-*
que. Venena, inquit, quæ totum Ma-
gorum fas & nefas ſunt, humanas vices
convertere nequeunt. *Ruigersi. Reniden-*

tes Lares.] Circum Lares ſplendentes,
& hilares. vide Od.18.l.1.

67. *Hæc ubi loquutus.*] Fingit Horatius Alphium fœneratorem ſuperiora
omnia dixiſſe, quaſi is approbaret vitæ
ruſticæ jucunditatem, ſed ad ingenium
ſuum rediens, properat ad pecuniam in
fœnore collocandam. *Fœnerator Al-*
phius.] Scribe *Alfius*, ut in vetuſtis
membranis. Summa vero in eo facetia
eſt, quod ſub Alſii perſona hactenus vitam ruſticam laudavit Poëta, more hu-
mano fieri oſtendens, ut vel optime de
rebus ſentientes, aſſueta tamen non
relinquamus. *Torrent.*

69. *Omnem relegit.*] Multo plures me-
lioreſque codices *redegit* legunt, quod
exemplis firmat Cruquius. *Redigere* e-
nim verbum elegans, ut *cogere* quoque
nummos, argentum, aurum, &c. dicimus
unde & *coactores.* Torrent. *Relegit.*]
Omnem pecuniam congregavit, à debi-
toribus eam exigens Idibus, (id eſt, cir-
cà dimidiatum menſem) ſtudetque ite-
rum in fœnore collocare ſequentis
menſis Kalendis. *Idibus.*] Idibus, inquit
Lamb. nomina exigebant: Calendis autem & exigebant & collocabant. De
Idibus citat alterum Poëtæ locum ex
Sat.6. lib.1.

  Ibant octonis referentes Idibus æra.
De Calendis illum è Satyra 3.

  Qui nisi cum tristes misero venere Kalen-
   dæ.
Et priſci interpretis verba à me reperta,
paulo aliter quam Cruquius opponam:
Redegit Idibus, ut vitam agens rusticam;
sed cum venerunt Kalendæ, quia sunt se-
quenti die post Idus, quærebat ponere in usu-
ram. Torrent.

  1. *Olim.*]

Plate 6. Page 306 from *Q. Horatius Flaccus cum commentariis selectissimis,*
edited by Cornelius Schrevelius (Leiden, 1663), showing the various
interpretations of the end of Horace's *Epode* II. From a copy in the
Brotherton Collection, Leeds University Library, reproduced by
permission of the Librarian.

Unheeded ruin! treacherous delight!
40   O polished hardness softened to the sight!
Whose radiant eyes your ebon brows adorn,
Like midnight those, and these like break of morn!
Smile once again, revive me with your charms,
And let me die contented in your arms.
45   I would not ask to live another day,
Might I but sweetly kiss my soul away!
Ah, why am I from empty joys debarred,
For kisses are but empty, when compared!
I rave, and in my raging fit shall tear
50   The garland which I wove for you to wear,
Of parsley with a wreath of ivy bound,
And bordered with a rosy edging round.
What pangs I feel, unpitied and unheard!
Since I must die, why is my fate deferred?
55   I strip my body of my shepherd's frock;
Behold that dreadful downfall of a rock,
Where yon old fisher views the waves from high!
'Tis that convenient leap I mean to try.
You would be pleased to see me plunge to shore,
60   But better pleased if I should rise no more.
I might have read my fortune long ago,
When, seeking my success in love to know,
I tried th' infallible prophetic way,
A poppy-leaf upon my palm to lay;
65   I struck, and yet no lucky crack did follow,
Yet I struck hard, and yet the leaf lay hollow.
And which was worse, if any worse could prove,
The with'ring leaf foreshowed your with'ring love.

48. when compared] i.e. with a fuller pleasure; cp. 'Daphnis' ll. 5–6 (Kinsley).
56. downfall] precipice (*OED* 2).
64. poppy-leaf] for τηλέφιλον ('love-in-absence'); apparently, if the leaf, when placed on one hand and struck by the other, burst with a loud crack, it was a good omen.
65. From Heinsius' paraphrase: *telephilon allisum non edidit sonum* ('the love-in-absence when struck did not give out a sound') (*Works*).
67–9. D.'s addition.
67. Echoes 'And which is worse, if worse then this can be', from Orrery's *The Black Prince* (performed 1667) in his *Two New Tragedies* (1672) 18; it was parodied in Rochester's *Timon* (in MS 1674, printed 1680), ll. 117–18. D. echoes the line again in *HP* iii 1089.

Yet farther (ah, how far a lover dares!)
70 My last recourse I had to sieve and shears,
And told the witch Agreo my disease
(Agreo that in harvest used to lease,
But harvest done, to chare-work did aspire:
Meat, drink and twopence was her daily hire):
75 To work she went, her charms she muttered o'er, ⎫
And yet the resty sieve wagged ne'er the more. ⎬
I wept for woe, the testy beldame swore, ⎭
And foaming with her god foretold my fate:
That I was doomed to love, and you to hate.
80 A milk-white goat for you I did provide,
Two milk-white kids run frisking by her side,
For which the nut-brown lass Erithacis
Full often offered many a savoury kiss.
Hers they shall be, since you refuse the price:
85 What madman would o'erstand his market twice?
My right eye itches, some good luck is near, ⎫
Perhaps my Amaryllis may appear; ⎬
I'll set up such a note as she shall hear. ⎭
What nymph but my melodious voice would move?
90 She must be flint if she refuse my love.

---

70. The Greek practice of coscinomancy entailed holding a sieve on a pair of shears; the sieve trembled when the significant name was mentioned.

72. lease] glean.

73–8. D.'s addition.

73. chare-work] occasional work, odd jobs.

74. The average rate for an agricultural labourer was 3½d. a day in winter and 4½d. in summer, with meat and drink (Ogg 85).

76. resty] lazy, inactive (*OED* 2).

77. beldame] old woman.

81. D.'s addition.

82. nut-brown] for μελανόχρως ('dark-skinned'); traditionally used of girls with dark complexions (see *OED*).   *Erithacis*] Not understood as a proper name in Theocritus by modern scholars (ἐριθακὶς means 'a working woman'), but taken so by Heinsius: *filia Mermnonis nigella Erithacis* ('Erithacis the dark daughter of Mermnon') (*Works*).

83. D.'s addition.   *savoury*] pleasing to the taste (*OED* 1).

85. D.'s addition.   *o'erstand*] outstay (*OED* 2), i.e. miss a sale altogether by waiting too long for the best one.

89. D.'s addition.

Hippomenes, who ran with noble strife ⎤
To win his lady, or to lose his life,   ⎬
(What shift some men will make to get a wife!) ⎭
Threw down a golden apple in her way;

95 For all her haste she could not choose but stay:
Renown said 'run', the glittering bribe cried 'hold';
The man might have been hanged, but for his gold.
Yet some suppose 'twas love (some few indeed)
That stopped the fatal fury of her speed:

100 She saw, she sighed; her nimble feet refuse
Their wonted speed, and she took pains to lose.
A prophet some, and some a poet cry,
(No matter which, so neither of them lie),
From steepy Othrys' top to Pylus drove

105 His herd, and for his pains enjoyed his love.
If such another wager should be laid,
I'll find the man, if you can find the maid.
Why name I men, when love extended finds
His power on high, and in celestial minds?

110 Venus the shepherd's homely habit took,
And managed something else besides the crook;
Nay, when Adonis died, was heard to roar,
And never from her heart forgave the boar.
How blessed is fair Endymion with his moon,

115 Who sleeps on Latmos' top from night to noon!
What Jason from Medea's love possessed
You shall not hear, but know 'tis like the rest.

91–7. Atalanta raced with her suitors, and killed those she overtook. Hippomenes defeated her by dropping golden apples (provided by Aphrodite, goddess of love) which Atalanta stopped to pick up.

92–3, 95–9, 101. D.'s additions.

102. prophet . . . poet] Both are meanings of the Latin *vates*, which is used in Heinsius' paraphrase (*Works*).

103, 106–9. D.'s additions.

110–13. Venus (in Greek, Aphrodite) was in love with Adonis, who was killed by a wild boar.

110. Venus dresses like a hunter in Ovid's *Met.* x 536.

113. D.'s addition.

114–15. Endymion was loved by the moon-goddess Semele, who bore him fifty daughters; he slept eternally on Mount Latmos.

116. D. substitutes Jason for Theocritus' Iasion, lover of the goddess Demeter.

My aching head can scarce support the pain,
This cursèd love will surely turn my brain;
120 Feel how it shoots, and yet you take no pity:
Nay then 'tis time to end my doleful ditty.
A clammy sweat does o'er my temples creep,
My heavy eyes are urged with iron sleep:
I lay me down to gasp my latest breath,
125 The wolves will get a breakfast by my death;
Yet scarce enough their hunger to supply,
For love has made me carrion ere I die.

119–20, 122–3, 126–7. D.'s additions.
127. carrion] as lean as a skeleton, skin and bones (*OED* 9a).

83 The Tears of Amynta

Date and publication. Printed in 1684 in *MP* (*SR* 4 February; advertised in *The Observator* 2 February); reprinted 1692.

The Tears of Amynta for the Death of Damon
Song

1

On a bank, beside a willow,
Heaven her cov'ring, earth her pillow,
Sad Amynta sighed alone;
From the cheerless dawn of morning,
5   Till the dews of night returning,
Singing thus she made her moan:
    'Hope is banished,
    Joys are vanished,
Damon my beloved is gone!

2

10   Time, I dare thee to discover
Such a youth, and such a lover;
O so true, so kind was he!
Damon was the pride of nature,
Charming in his every feature,
15   Damon lived alone for me:
    Melting kisses
    Murmuring blisses,
Who so lived and loved as we?

¶83. *12. kind*] includes the meaning 'sexually compliant'.
15. alone] only.

3

Never shall we curse the morning,

20   Never bless the night returning,
Sweet embraces to restore:
Never shall we both lie dying,
Nature failing, love supplying
All the joys he drained before.

25   Death, come end me
To befriend me:
Love and Damon are no more.'

---

22. *dying*] a common seventeenth-century image for orgasm.

84 Virgil's Fourth Eclogue

Date and publication. Printed in 1684 in *MP* (*SR* 4 February; advertised in *The Observator* 2 February); reprinted 1692. Revised for inclusion in *The Works of Virgil* (1697); for the revisions see the notes.

Context. Earl Miner (*RES* xi (1960) 299–302; corrected by Winn 607) argues that the poem was designed to compliment Princess Mary, who had married George of Denmark on 26 July 1683, and was pregnant when the poem was published. The child was stillborn on 30 April 1684. For another possible poem on this marriage see headnote to 'Theocritus: Idyllium the Eighteenth'. Virgil had always been the most respected of the Roman poets in England, and D. shows a detailed knowledge of and strong affinity with Virgil throughout his career (see Reuben A. Brower, *PQ* xviii (1939) 211–17, *PMLA* lv (1940) 119–38, *ELH* xix (1952) 38–48; *Works* vi 843–53). *Astraea Redux* invokes a Virgilian precedent for the return of Charles II in 1660; *AM* has many Virgilian echoes, and a discussion of Virgil in the prefatory 'Account of the Ensuing Poem'; *MF* and 'To the Memory of Mr Oldham' make important use of *Aen.*; D. was to translate several passages from *Aen.* in *Sylvae*; and in 1697 he published his complete translation of Virgil's works. Among his contemporaries in the 1680s there was considerable interest in translating Virgil: it concerned the Roscommon circle (see 'To the Earl of Roscommon' l. 40*n*); Oldham's translation of *Ecl.* viii was published in his *Remains* (1684); *MP* includes a complete translation of the *Eclogues* by various hands (see Appendix A). For other translations of Virgil see Gillespie 66–7.

Sources. For his translations from Virgil D. generally used the edition by Ruaeus (1675, revised 1682): see Bottkol, and *Works* vi 859–60. D.'s only copy of Virgil to have survived is the 1636 edition by Heinsius (see Paul Hammond, *N & Q* ccxxix (1984) 344–5). For his possible use of the edition by Emmenessius (1680) see 'To the Memory of Mr Oldham' ll. 3*n*, 7*n*. English translators consulted by D. for *Ecl.* iv probably included John Beaumont, *Bosworth-Field* (1629), and John Bidle, *Virgil's Bucolicks Englished* (1634); there are occasional coincidences of rhyme-words with John Ogilby's *The Works of Publius Virgilius Maro* (1649, revised 1654). For D.'s use of his predecessors in translating the *Eclogues* see Arthur Sherbo, *SB* xxxviii (1985) 262–76.

Reception. Roscommon in his *Essay on Translated Verse* (1684) 3 compliments D. by alluding to this translation: 'But hear, oh hear, in what exalted streins/ *Sicilian Muses* through these happy Plains,/ Proclaim *Saturnian* Times, our own *Apollo* Reigns' (see H. A. Mason, *N & Q* ccxxxv (1990) 296). Creech's translation of Rapin's *De Carmine Pastorali* (included in his 1684 translation of Theocritus) quotes ll. 1–4 (23, 54).

The Fourth Eclogue
Pollio

The poet celebrates the birthday of Saloninus, the son of
Pollio, born in the consulship of his father after the taking of
Salonae, a city in Dalmatia. Many of the verses are translated
from one of the Sibyls, who prophesy of our Saviour's birth.

> Sicilian Muse, begin a loftier strain!
> Though lowly shrubs, and trees that shade the plain
> Delight not all, if thither I repair
> My song shall make 'em worth a consul's care.
> 5   The last great age foretold by sacred rhymes
> Renews its finished course; Saturnian times
> Roll round again, and mighty years, begun
> From their first orb, in radiant circles run.
> The base, degenerate iron offspring ends,
> 10 A golden progeny from heaven descends;
> O chaste Lucina, speed the mother's pains,
> And haste the glorious birth: thy own Apollo reigns!

¶84. *Headnote.* D.'s headnote is translated from that found in many seventeenth-century editions of Virgil. The traditional interpretation of this eclogue as a prophecy of the birth of Christ does not influence D.'s translation.
1. Cp. Bidle: 'Sicilian Muses Now.some Loftier strain' (*Works*).   *Sicilian*]
The Greek pastoral poet Theocritus was Sicilian.
3–4. Delight not all; *Sicilian* Muse, prepare / To make the vocal Woods
deserve a Consul's care. *1697.*
5. sacred rhymes] the Sibylline books, whose prophecies were consulted by the
Romans.
6. Saturnian times] the Golden Age, presided over by Saturn (see Ovid, *Met.* i
89–112); cp. epigraph to *Astraea Redux.*
8. D.'s addition.   *orb*] circle. D. has in mind the 'great year' or *annus
magnus platonicus*, the cycle completed when all the heavenly bodies simultaneously return to their original positions (see Alastair Fowler's note to *PL* v
583; and cp. *PL* v 861–2).
9. iron] The Iron Age was the last of the ages which succeeded the Golden
Age (*Met.* i 127–50).
10. Cp. Beaumont: 'progenies from lofty Heav'n descend' (*Works*).
11. Lucina] goddess of childbirth.

The lovely boy, with his auspicious face,
Shall Pollio's consulship and triumph grace;
15　Majestic months set out with him to their appointed
　　　race.
The father banished virtue shall restore,
And crimes shall threat the guilty world no more.
The son shall lead the life of gods, and be
By gods and heroes seen, and gods and heroes see.
20　The jarring nations he in peace shall bind,
And with paternal virtues rule mankind.
Unbidden earth shall wreathing ivy bring,
And fragrant herbs, the promises of spring,
As her first off'rings to her infant King.
25　The goats with strutting dugs shall homeward speed,
And lowing herds secure from lions feed.
His cradle shall with rising flowers be crowned;
The serpent's brood shall die; the sacred ground
Shall weeds and pois'nous plants refuse to bear,
30　Each common bush shall Syrian roses wear.
But when heroic verse his youth shall raise,
And form it to hereditary praise,
Unlaboured harvests shall the fields adorn,
And clustered grapes shall blush on every thorn;
35　The knotted oaks shall showers of honey weep,
And through the matted grass the liquid gold shall
　　　creep.
Yet of old fraud some footsteps shall remain,
The merchant still shall plough the deep for gain;
Great cities shall with walls be compassed round,
40　And sharpened shares shall vex the fruitful ground.

13, 73. auspicious] well-omened. D.'s addition; see *AM* l. *77n.*
25. strutting] swelling (*OED* 1).
30. roses] for Virgil's cardamom, a spice.
31. verse] D.'s addition, from *Poesim* in Ruaeus.
36. D.'s addition.
37. footsteps] i.e. traces.
38. merchant . . . for gain] D.'s addition; cp. 'Horace: *Odes* III xxix' ll. 89–93;
'Horace: *Epode* II' ll. 12–13.
40. vex] agitate, tear up (*OED* 6).

Another Tiphys shall new seas explore,
Another Argos on th' Iberian shore
Shall land the chosen chiefs;
Another Helen other wars create,
45   And great Achilles shall be sent to urge the Trojan fate.
But when to ripened manhood he shall grow,
The greedy sailor shall the seas forgo;
No keel shall cut the waves for foreign ware,
For every soil shall every product bear.
50   The labouring hind his oxen shall disjoin,
No plough shall hurt the glebe, no pruning-hook the
      vine,
Nor wool shall in dissembled colours shine;
But the luxurious father of the fold
With native purple or unborrowed gold,
55   Beneath his pompous fleece shall proudly sweat,
And under Tyrian robes the lamb shall bleat.
The Fates, when they this happy web have spun,
Shall bless the sacred clue, and bid it smoothly run.
Mature in years, to awful honours move,
60   O of celestial stem! O foster son of Jove!
See, labouring Nature calls thee to sustain
The nodding frame of heaven and earth and main;

41. *Tiphys*] helmsman of the *Argo*, which carried Jason and his men in search of the Golden Fleece.
42–3. Another *Argos* land the Chiefs upon th' *Iberian* Shore. *1697*.
45. And great *Achilles* urge the *Trojan* fate. *1697*.   *urge*] drive on (OED 6).
47. *greedy*] D.'s addition; cp. l. 38*n*.
50. *hind*] farm worker.
53. Translating *in pratis aries* ('the ram in the meadows'). This line seems to have had some currency in the Roscommon circle, for Knightly Chetwood in his life of Roscommon says: 'Mr Dryden, whom Lord Ros: look'd upon, as a naturall rather than a correct Poet, & therefore calls him somewhere, *The luxurious Father of the fold*' (Cambridge UL MS Mm 1.47 pp. 39–40; H. A. Mason, privately).
55. *pompous*] magnificent, splendid.
56. *Tyrian*] i.e. of Tyrian purple.
58. *clue*] thread of life (OED 3b, quoting this instance).
59. *awful*] awesome.   *awful*] ready *1697*.
60. *stem*] Seed *1697*.
62. *nodding*] tottering.

See to their base restored earth, seas and air,
And joyful ages from behind stand crowding to appear.
65 To sing thy praise, would heaven my breath prolong,
Infusing spirits worthy such a song,
Not Thracian Orpheus should transcend my lays,
Nor Linus crowned with never-fading bays,
Though each his heavenly parent should inspire,
70 The Muse instruct the voice, and Phoebus tune the lyre.
Should Pan contend with me, and thou my theme,
Arcadian judges should their god condemn.
Begin, auspicious boy, to cast about
Thy infant eyes, and with a smile thy mother single out;
75 Thy mother well deserves that short delight,
The nauseous qualms of ten long months and travail to
requite.
Then smile: the frowning infant's doom is read,
No god shall crown the board, nor goddess bless the
bed.

64. stand crowding to] in crowding Ranks *1697*.
67. Orpheus] the archetypal poet in Greek mythology.
68. Linus] in Greek mythology a young poet who met a violent death.
crowned . . . bays] D.'s addition.
70. Phoebus] Apollo, god of poetry.
71. Pan] the Arcadian god and piper.   *with me*] in Verse *1697*.

85 Virgil's Ninth Eclogue

Date and publication. Printed in 1684 in *MP* (*SR* 4 February; advertised in *The Observator* 2 February); reprinted 1692. Revised for inclusion in *The Works of Virgil* (1697); for the revisions see the notes.

Context. For contemporary interest in Virgil see headnote to 'Virgil's Fourth Eclogue'. The poem echoes D.'s own financial plight: his salary was four years in arrears, and in a letter to Lawrence Hyde, Earl of Rochester, probably written in March 1684, he asked for payment of half a year's salary; it continued to be in arrears (*Letters* 20–1; Winn 392–3, 530, 607). Cp. *The Art of Poetry* ll. 1058–9n. D.'s concern here may be echoed in the subtitle of Creech's translation of *Idyll* xvi in his 1684 Theocritus, a poem which he dedicated to D.: 'He complains that Poetry meets not a suitable Reward from Great Men, for that immortality which it bestows upon them'.

Sources. See headnote to 'Virgil's Fourth Eclogue'.

The Ninth Eclogue

When Virgil by the favour of Augustus had recovered his patrimony near Mantua, and went in hope to take possession, he was in danger to be slain by Arius the centurion, to whom those lands were assigned by the Emperor in reward of his service against Brutus and Cassius. This eclogue therefore is filled with complaints of his hard usage, and the persons introduced are the bailiff of Virgil, and his friend.

Lycidas, Moeris

Lyc.   Ho Moeris! whither on thy way so fast?
       This leads to town.
Moe.   O Lycidas, at last
       The time is come I never thought to see
       (Strange revolution for my farm and me),

¶85. *Headnote.* D.'s headnote is translated from that found in many seventeenth-century editions of Virgil.
4. revolution] alteration, change (*OED* 6); D.'s addition.

5   When the grim captain in a surly tone
            Cries out, 'Pack up, ye rascals, and be gone.'
            Kicked out, we set the best face on 't we could, ⎫
            And these two kids, to' appease his angry mood ⎬
            I bear, of which the devil give him good. ⎭

10 *Lyc.* Good gods! I heard a quite contrary tale,
            That from the sloping mountain to the vale
            And doddered oak, and all the banks along,
            Menalcas saved his fortune with a song.

   Moe. Such was the news, indeed, but songs and rhymes
15   Prevail as much in these hard iron times
            As would a plump of trembling fowl that rise
            Against an eagle sousing from the skies;
            And had not Phoebus warned me by the croak
            Of an old raven from a hollow oak
20   To shun debate, Menalcas had been slain,
            And Moeris not survived him to complain.

   Lyc. Now heaven defend! could barbarous rage prevail
            So far the sacred Muses to assail?

---

8. *to' appease*] The original punctuation is kept here because it indicates that the two vowels are to be run together, rather than one of them being completely elided. D.'s autograph MS of *Heroic Stanzas* uses a similar practice (see Introduction to Volume I, p. xix).

9. *devil*] Furies *1697*.

10. Your Country Friends were told another Tale *1697*.

12. *doddered oak*] translating *veteres fagos* ('old beeches').   *doddered*] Apparently D.'s coinage, meaning either 'decayed' or 'pollarded' (see *OED* for problematic sense and etymology). Thomas Sternberg suggests that the word had Northamptonshire associations (*The Dialect and Folk-Lore of Northamptonshire* (1851) 188–9).

15. *iron times*] like the degenerate iron age in Ovid, *Met.* i 127–50; translating *tela inter Martia* ('among the weapons of war').

16. *plump*] flock.

17. *sousing*] swooping down. For D.'s precise vocabulary for birds cp. *AM* ll. 341–8nn.

18. *Phoebus*] Apollo, god of poetry; D.'s addition.

22. *prevail*] induce *1697*.

23. The Brutal Son of *Mars*, t'insult the sacred Muse *1697*.   *the sacred Muses to assail*] D.'s translation of *solacia rapta* ('the consolations [of your music] torn from us').

Who then should sing the nymphs, or who
    rehearse
25   The waters gliding in a smoother verse?
Or Amaryllis praise—that heavenly lay
That shortened as we went our tedious way:
'O Tityrus, tend my herd and see them fed, ⎫
To morning pastures, evening waters led, ⎬
30   And 'ware the Libyan ridgel's butting head.' ⎭
    Moe. Or what unfinished he to Varus read:
'Thy name, O Varus, if the kinder powers
Preserve our plains, and shield the Mantuan
    towers
Obnoxious by Cremona's neighbouring crime,
35   The wings of swans, and stronger-pinioned
    rhyme
Shall raise aloft, and soaring bear above
Th' immortal gift of gratitude to Jove.'
    Lyc. Sing on, sing on, for I can ne'er be cloyed,
So may thy swarms the baleful yew avoid,
40   So may thy cows their burdened bags distend,
And trees to goats their willing branches bend;
Mean as I am, yet have the Muses made
Me free, a member of the tuneful trade;
At least the shepherds seem to like my lays,

28–30. Virgil adapts Theocritus, *Idyll* iii 3–5; see 'Amaryllis' ll. 3–5.

28. Tityrus] disyllabic here.

30. 'ware] beware.   *Libyan]* not in Virgil, but from Theocritus, *Idyll* iii 3–
5.   *ridgel]* animal with only one testicle (here a goat).

31. Varus] the land commissioner in Virgil's *Ecl.* vi 7.

33–4. The confiscation of territory around Cremona to supply land for
followers of Augustus after the battle of Philippi had encroached upon land
belonging to Mantua, Virgil's birthplace.

34. Obnoxious] exposed to harm.

35. swans] Mantua was famous for swans, which were associated with Apollo
and the Muses.   *pinioned]* winged.

39. baleful yew] Yew trees are associated with death; they may also cause
honey to be bitter: Virgil warns against placing beehives near them in *Geo.* iv
47.

41. D.'s addition.

43. free] invested with the rights of membership in a guild.

45   But I discern their flattery from their praise:
         I nor to Cinna's ears, or Varus' dare aspire,
         But gabble like a goose amidst the swan-like
            choir.
   Moe. 'Tis what I have been conning in my mind;
         Nor are they verses of a vulgar kind:
50   'Come Galatea, come, the seas forsake,
         What pleasures can the tides with their hoarse
            murmurs make?
         See on the shore inhabits purple spring,
         Where nightingales their love-sick ditty sing;
         See meads with purling streams, with flowers the ⎤
            ground,   ⎥
55   The grottoes cool with shady poplars crowned, ⎥
         And creeping vines to arbours weaved around. ⎦
         Come then, and leave the waves' tumultuous
            roar,
         Let the wild surges vainly beat the shore.'
   Lyc. Or that sweet song I heard with such delight,
60   The same you sung alone one starry night;
         The tune I still retain, but not the words.
   Moe. 'Why, Daphnis, dost thou search in old records

---

45. Translating *sed non ego credulus illis* ('but I do not believe them'). The phrasing is influenced by Boileau: 'Mais sçachez de l'Ami discerner le Flatteur' (*L'Art Poétique* (1674) i 189; D. revised Soame's translation for publication in 1683: see *The Art of Poetry* headnote).   *discern*] distinguish (*OED* 1).

46. *Cinna*] C. Helvius Cinna, lyric poet, murdered 44 BC.   *Varus*] L. Varius Rufus, poet and tragedian; member of Maecenas' circle; editor of *Aen.* after Virgil's death.

48. *conning*] studying, committing to memory (*OED* 3).

51. *hoarse murmurs*] Cp. Milton: 'as the sound of waters deep/ Hoarse murmur echoed to his words applause' (*PL* v 872–3; J. R. Mason).

52. *purple*] brightly coloured (*OED* 3); Virgil's *purpureum* here likewise probably means 'richly coloured'.

53. D.'s addition.

54. *purling*] flowing with whirling motion; murmuring (*OED*).

56. *to*] on 1697.

62. *search in old records*] D.'s addition.   *records*] accented on the second syllable.

To know the seasons when the stars arise?
See, Caesar's lamp is lighted in the skies,
65   The star whose rays the blushing grapes adorn,
And swell the kindly ripening ears of corn:
Under this influence graft the tender shoot;
Thy children's children shall enjoy the fruit.'
The rest I have forgot, for cares and time
70   Change all things, and untune my soul to rhyme.
I could have once sung down a summer's sun,
But now the chime of poetry is done.
My voice grows hoarse, I feel the notes decay,
As if the wolves had seen me first today.
75   But these, and more than I to mind can bring,
Menalcas has not yet forgot to sing.
   Lyc. Thy faint excuses but inflame me more,
And now the waves roll silent to the shore;
Hushed winds the topmost branches scarcely
        bend,
80   As if thy tuneful song they did attend.
Already we have half our way o'ercome:
Far off I can discern Bianor's tomb.
Here, where the labourer's hands have formed a
        bower
Of wreathing trees, in singing waste an hour.
85   Rest here thy weary limbs, thy kids lay down;
We've day before us yet to reach the town;
Of if ere night the gathering clouds we fear,
A song will help the beating storm to bear.
And that thou may'st not be too late abroad,
90   Sing, and I'll ease thy shoulders of thy load.

64. *Caesar's lamp*] the comet which appeared after the death of Julius Caesar.
66. *kindly*] thriving, goodly (*OED* 4).
69–70. Translating *omnia fert aetas, animum quoque* ('time robs us of all, even of memory').   *untune*] render unsuited (*OED*).
73. *I feel the notes decay*] D.'s addition.
80. D.'s addition.
82. *Bianor*] Servius, the fourth-century commentator on Virgil, identifies him with Ocnus, the legendary founder of Mantua; modern scholars doubt this, but disagree on alternative explanations.

Moe. Cease to entreat me, let us mind our way;
　　Another song requires another day.
　　When good Menalcas comes, if he rejoice
　　And find a friend at court, I'll find a voice.

91. entreat] request *1697.*
92. D.'s addition.
94. And find a friend at court] D.'s addition.

Date and publication. Thomas Southerne's play was first staged in April 1684 by the King's Company at the Theatre Royal, Drury Lane. D. had contributed the Prologue and Epilogue to Southerne's first play, *The Loyal Brother* (q.v.) in 1682. The present Prologue and Epilogue were published by E. Lucy in a folio half-sheet headed *Prologue To a New Play, Call'd, The Disappointment: Or, The Mother in Fashion* (1684; MS date 5 April on Luttrell's copy (Noyes)). The Prologue is anonymous, the Epilogue 'By Another Hand'. They were reprinted in Southerne's *The Disappointment, or The Mother in Fashion*, published by Hindmarsh in 1684 (*TC* June). The Prologue is attributed there to D., and the Epilogue to John Stafford. In *MP* (1702) the Epilogue is attributed to D., but almost certainly in error. The present text is from *1684 folio*.

Prologue to a new play called *The Disappointment, Or, The Mother in Fashion*

Spoken by Mr Betterton

> How comes it, gentlemen, that nowadays
> When all of you so shrewdly judge of plays,
> Our poets tax you still with want of sense?
> All prologues treat you at your own expense.
> 5 Sharp citizens a wiser way can go—
> They make you fools, but never call you so.
> They in good manners seldom make a slip,
> But treat a common whore with 'ladyship';
> But here each saucy wit at random writes,
> 10 And uses ladies as he uses knights.
> Our author, young, and grateful in his nature,
> Vows that from him no nymph deserves a satire;

¶86. *Title. Betterton*] See 'Prologue to *Troilus and Cressida*' Title *n*, and 'Prologue to the King and Queen' Title *n*.

10. knights] Cp. Wycherley: 'Their Predecessors were contented to make Serving-men only their Stage-Fools, but these Rogues must have Gentlemen, with a Pox to'em, nay Knights: and indeed you shall hardly see a Fool upon the Stage, but he's a Knight' (*The Country-Wife* (1675) III ii 107–10; Southerne edited by Jordan and Love).

Nor will he ever draw—I mean his rhyme—
Against the sweet partaker of his crime.
15 Nor is he yet so bold an undertaker
To call men fools; 'tis railing at their Maker.
Besides, he fears to split upon that shelf;
He's young enough to be a fop himself:
And if his praise can bring you all abed,
20 He swears such hopeful youth no nation ever bred.
Your nurses, we presume, in such a case ⎱
Your father chose because he liked the face; ⎬
And often they supplied your mother's place.⎰
The dry nurse was your mother's ancient maid,
25 Who knew some former slip she ne'er betrayed.
Betwixt 'em both, for milk and sugar candy,
Your sucking bottles were well stored with brandy.
Your father to initiate your discourse ⎱
Meant to have taught you first to swear and curse, ⎬
30 But was prevented by each careful nurse: ⎰
For leaving 'dad' and 'mam' as names too common,
They taught you certain parts of man and woman.
I pass your schools, for there when first you came
You would be sure to learn the Latin name.
35 In colleges you scorned their art of thinking,
But learned all moods and figures of good drinking.
Thence come to town, you practise play, to know
The virtues of the high dice and the low;
Each thinks himself a sharper most profound:
40 He cheats by pence—is cheated by the pound.
With these perfections, and what else he gleans, ⎱
The spark sets up for love behind our scenes, ⎬
Hot in pursuit of princesses and queens: ⎰
There, if they know their man, with cunning carriage,
45 Twenty to one but it concludes in marriage.
He hires some homely room love's fruits to gather,
And garret-high rebels against his father.

19. bring you all abed] draw out what you are (*OED*).
20. hopeful] promising.
30. prevented] anticipated.
38. the high dice and the low] loaded dice, contrived some for high and others
for low scores (Scott).
42. Cp. 'Epilogue to the King and Queen' l. 35*n*.

But he once dead——
Brings her in triumph with her portion down,
50   A twillet, dressing-box, and half a crown.
Some marry first, and then they fall to scouring,
Which is refining marriage into whoring.
Our women batten well on their good nature,
All they can rap and rend for the dear creature;
55   But while abroad so liberal the dolt is,
Poor spouse at home as ragged as a colt is.
Last, some there are who take their first degrees
Of lewdness in our middle galleries:
The doughty bullies enter bloody drunk,
60   Invade and grubble one another's punk;
They caterwaul and make a dismal rout,
Call 'sons of whores', and strike, but ne'er lug out:
Thus while for paltry punk they roar and stickle,
They make it bawdier than a conventicle.

49–50. Cp. *The Wild Gallant*: 'I'm glad with all my Heart this Minx is
prevented of her design. . . . His old Father in the Country would have given
him but little thank for't, to see him bring down a fine-bred Woman, with a
Lute, and a Dressing-box, and a handful of money to her Portion' (III ii 73–8;
Scott).
50. twillet] toilet: cloth cover for a dressing table (*OED* 2).
51. scouring] See 'Prologue to *The Spanish Friar*' l. 39n.
54. i.e. everything that the men can snatch and steal to provide for their
mistresses.
55–6. Reused by D. in 'Epilogue to *The Pilgrim*' (1700) ll. 41–2.   *ragged as
a colt*] proverbial (Tilley C521) (Jordan and Love).
58. middle galleries] Cp. 'Epilogue to the King and Queen' l. 12.
59. bullies] blustering gallants.
60. grubble] grope.
62. lug out] draw the sword.
63–4. stickle/ . . . conventicle] This rhyme occurs twice in *Hudibras* (I ii 437–8,
III ii 1387–9; Jordan and Love).
63. stickle] contend (*OED* 3).
64. On 23–5 March 1668 nonconformist apprentices attacked London brothels, motivated partly by the King's proclamation on 10 March outlawing
conventicles (nonconformist meetings) (see Tim Harris, *HJ* xxix (1986) 537–
56). For the association of brothels and conventicles see also Crowne's Prologue to *The Ambitious Statesman* (1679) l. 8 (Danchin no. 266). In *The
Vindication* (1683) 5 D. says that the playhouse has become 'more Seditious
than a *Conventicle*'.

87 To the Earl of Roscommon

Date and publication. This is the first of the commendatory poems in *An Essay on Translated Verse. By the Earl of Roscommon*, published by Jacob Tonson in 1684; second edition 1685.

Context. Wentworth Dillon, fourth Earl of Roscommon (1637–85) was born in Ireland and educated at the Protestant academy in Caen during the Commonwealth, returning to a place of favour at court after the Restoration. Around 1680 he formed an academy which was particularly concerned with translation and the refinement of the English language; members included the Marquis of Halifax (who began to translate Tacitus), Lord Maitland (who began to translate Virgil), the Earl of Dorset, and D. himself (see Carl Niemeyer, *MLN* xlix (1934) 432–7). Knightly Chetwood wrote that 'they aim'd at refining our Language, without abating the force of it, & therefore insted of making a laborious Dictionary, they proposed severally to peruse our best writers, & mark such words, as they thought vulgar, base, improper, or obsolete'; he also recorded that Roscommon thought D. 'a naturall rather than a correct Poet' (Life of Roscommon in Cambridge UL MS Mm 1.47 pp. 39–40). Roscommon himself published a translation of Horace's *Ars Poetica* in 1680 (reprinted 1684), a commendatory poem for the 1683 issue of D.'s *RL*, translations of Virgil's *Ecl.* vi and Horace's *Carm.* I xxii and III vi in *MP*, and other poems (for the canon see Carl Niemeyer, *SP* xxxvi (1939) 622–36). The other commendatory poems printed with the *Essay* were by D.'s son Charles (in Latin), Knightly Chetwood and J. Amherst. D. praised Roscommon in the 'Preface to *Ovid's Epistles*' ll. 255–6, the 'Preface to *Sylvae*' ll. 17–21, 225, 403 and the 'Dedication of the *Aeneis*' (*Works* v 325), and dedicated 'Horace: *Odes* I iii' to him. D. wrote to Tonson *c.* August 1684: 'For my Lord Roscommons Essay, I am of your opinion, that you shou'd reprint it, & that you may safely venture on a thousand more' (*Letters* 22–3). Roscommon's interest in translation in the early 1680s coincides with that shown by D. and Tonson in *Ovid's Epistles* (1680), *MP* (1684) and *Sylvae* (1685), and Roscommon specifically praises recent translations of Ovid, Theocritus and Horace (*Essay* 2, 4; see H. A. Mason, *N & Q* ccxxxv (1990) 296).

To the Earl of Roscommon on his Excellent *Essay on Translated Verse*

Whether the fruitful Nile, or Tyrian shore,
The seeds of arts and infant science bore,
'Tis sure the noble plant, translated first,
Advanced its head in Grecian gardens nursed.
5   The Grecians added verse, their tuneful tongue
Made nature first, and nature's God their song.
Nor stopped translation here: for conquering Rome
With Grecian spoils brought Grecian numbers home,

¶87. *1–10*. D. probably had in mind Denham's 'The Progress of Learning' (1668): 'From thence [Chaldaea] did Learning into *Ægypt* pass;/ . . . From *Ægypt* Arts their Progress made to *Greece*,/ . . . Flying from thence, to *Italy* it came,/ . . . Till both their Nation and their Arts did come/ A welcom Trophy to Triumphant *Rome*;/ Then wheresoe're her Conquering Eagles fled,/ Arts, Learning, and Civility were spread' (ll. 16, 21, 47, 49–52; *Poetical Works* 115–16).

2. science] learning.

3–4. The image is used by Roscommon: 'The noblest Fruits Transplanted, in our Isle/ With early Hope, and fragrant Blossoms smile' (2); cp. Amherst's commendatory poem: 'a generous understanding Muse/ Does richer fruits from happier Soils Translate' (sig. a2ʳ). The image goes back to Denham: 'Transplanted wit,/ All the defects of air and soil doth share' ('To Sir Richard Fanshaw upon his translation of *Pastor Fido*' (1648) ll. 10–11).

4. Grecian gardens] The Greeks often taught and debated outdoors.

6. nature] It was a contemporary commonplace that the Greek poets, particularly Homer, had a specially close contact with, and insight into, 'nature', in its wide sense of 'the fundamental principles of life': see Kirsti Simonsuuri, *Homer's Original Genius* (1979), and Pope: '*Nature* and *Homer* were, he found, the *same*' (*An Essay on Criticism* l. 135). D. uses the same idea in complimenting Shakespeare: 'All the Images of Nature were still present to him . . . he needed not the spectacles of Books to read Nature; he look'd inwards, and found her there' (*EDP* in *Works* xvii 55), and cp. 'Prologue to *The Tempest*' ll. 7–8.

7–8. Rome gained control of parts of Greece in 229 BC and completed her domination in 146 BC. Greek poets and philosophers had an important influence on their Roman successors. See also ll. 41–8*n*. Chetwood writes in his commendatory poem that Englishmen 'Search'd all the *Treasuries* of *Greece*, and *Rome*,/ And brought the *precious spoils* in Triumph *home*' (sig. A3ᵛ).

Enriched by those Athenian Muses more
10   Than all the vanquished world could yield before;
Till barb'rous nations, and more barb'rous times,
Debased the majesty of verse to rhymes:
Those rude at first, a kind of hobbling prose
That limped along, and tinkled in the close;
15   But Italy, reviving from the trance
Of Vandal, Goth, and monkish ignorance,
With pauses, cadence, and well-vowelled words,
And all the graces a good ear affords,
Made rhyme an art; and Dante's polished page
20   Restored a silver, not a golden age.
Then Petrarch followed, and in him we see ⎤
What rhyme improved in all its height can be: ⎬
At best a pleasing sound, and fair barbarity. ⎦
The French pursued their steps, and Britain last
25   In manly sweetness all the rest surpassed.
The wit of Greece, the gravity of Rome,
Appear exalted in the British loom;
The Muses' empire is restored again
In Charles his reign, and by Roscommon's pen.
30   Yet modestly he does his work survey,
And calls a finished poem an 'essay':

11–12. Rhyme was not used in classical poetry, and was introduced into Latin verse in the early Middle Ages. Milton, in his prefatory note in the second edition of *PL* (1674), calls rhyme 'the invention of a barbarous age, to set off wretched matter and lame metre'. In the *Essay* Roscommon says: 'Of many faults, *Rhyme* is (perhaps) the *Cause,/* Too *strict* to *Rhyme* We slight more *useful* Laws./ For *That,* in *Greece* or *Rome,* was never *known,/* 'Till By *Barbarian* Deluges oreflown' (23). In the second edition he adds a passage in blank verse in imitation of *PL* (24–5). D. had given up using rhyme in his plays with *All For Love* (1678).
15–23. D.'s admiration for the Italian language is expressed in the Preface to *Albion and Albanius* (1685) (*Works* xv 6–7) (Kinsley).
17. pauses] breaks in the line of verse, caesuras.   *cadence*] rhythm and metre.   *well-vowelled*] well supplied with vowels; OED quotes Playford (1662): 'The Italian language is more smooth and better vowelled than the English.'
19–21. Dante Alighieri (1265–1321) and Francesco Petrarch (1304–74) were instrumental in pioneering vernacular Italian poetry.
31. essay] accented on the second syllable; a tentative treatment, a rough draft (OED 7, 8).

For all the needful rules are scattered here,
Truth smoothly told, and pleasantly severe
(So well is art disguised, for nature to appear). }

35 Nor need those rules to give translation light:
His own example is a flame so bright
That he who but arrives to copy well
Unguided will advance, unknowing will excel.
Scarce his own Horace could such rules ordain,
40 Or his own Virgil sing a nobler strain.
How much in him may rising Ireland boast,
How much in gaining him has Britain lost!
Their island in revenge has ours reclaimed,
The more instructed we, the more we still are shamed.
45 'Tis well for us his generous blood did flow
Derived from British channels long ago,
That here his conquering ancestors were nursed,
And Ireland but translated England first:

32. needful rules] Rules were a feature of neo-classical literary criticism, which tended to develop and codify the principles offered less systematically by Aristotle and Horace. Contemporary interest in this approach is evident in the translations of Horace's *Ars Poetica* by Roscommon (1680), Oldham (1681) and Creech (1684), the translation of Boileau's *Art Poétique* by Soame and D. (1683), and Mulgrave's *An Essay upon Poetry* (1682).

36. His own example] See headnote.

37. arrives to] reaches his object (*OED*).

39. Roscommon had translated Horace (see headnote), and says in the *Essay* that he has 'serv'd him more than twenty years' (4).

40. Roscommon had translated Virgil (see headnote), and his reverence for Virgil is evident in the *Essay* (11–12).

41–8. Works notes that this passage is based on Horace's epistle to Augustus: *Graecia capta ferum victorem cepit et artes/ intulit agresti Latio* ('Greece, the captive, made her savage victor captive, and brought the arts into rustic Latium': *Epist.* II i 156–7).

41. Roscommon had estates in Ireland, but after spending a period there after the Restoration, he returned to England.

45–7. Roscommon's mother came from Yorkshire, and was the sister of the Earl of Strafford; his father's family had lived in Ireland for at least five generations, but had presumably come over as part of the Tudor settlement of Ireland.

45. generous] noble.

47. were] *1685*; was *1684*. Writing to Tonson D. said: 'pray let the printer mend his errour, & let the line stand thus, That heer his Conque'ring Ancestors were nursd' (*Letters* 23).

By this reprisal we regain our right,
50 Else must the two contending nations fight
A nobler quarrel for his native earth
Than what divided Greece for Homer's birth.
To what perfection will our tongue arrive,
How will invention and translation thrive,
55 When authors nobly born will bear their part,
And not disdain th' inglorious praise of art!
Great generals thus descending from command
With their own toil provoke the soldiers' hand.
How will sweet Ovid's ghost be pleased to hear
60 His fame augmented by an English peer;   *The Earl of*
How he embellishes his Helen's loves,   *Mulgrave*
Outdoes his softness, and his sense improves!
When these translate, and teach translators too,
Nor firstling kid, nor any vulgar vow
65 Should at Apollo's grateful altar stand: ⎫
Roscommon writes; to that auspicious hand,   ⎬
Muse, feed the bull that spurns the yellow sand. ⎭
Roscommon, whom both court and camps commend,
True to his Prince, and faithful to his friend;

49. *reprisal*] regaining, recovery (OED 3c).
52. Greek cities had contended for the honour of having been Homer's birthplace; Chios and Smyrna were the chief candidates.
53. The perfecting of the English language was one of the aims of Roscommon's academy (see headnote). For D.'s anxieties about the inexactitude and instability of English see his Dedication to *Troilus and Cressida* (1679) (*Works* xiii 222–4).
56. i.e. artistic achievement brings the artist no glory.
58. *provoke*] call forth, from the Latin *provocare* (*Works*).
60. John Sheffield, Earl of Mulgrave (1648–1721) was D.'s pátron. They had collaborated on 'Helen to Paris' in *Ovid's Epistles*. Roscommon's *Essay* begins with a compliment to Mulgrave, whose *Essay upon Poetry* 'Repairs so well our Old *Horatian* way' (1).   *English*] 1685; Brittish 1684.
64. *vow*] votive offering (OED 6).
65. *grateful*] pleasing (OED 1).
67. *Works* notes an echo of Virgil's *Ecl.* iii 86–7, where sacrifice is offered to the Roman general, critic and poet Pollio: *pascite taurum/ iam cornu petat et pedibus qui spargat harenam* ('feed a bull, able even now to butt with the horn and to churn up the sand with his hoofs').
68. Cp. Amherst: 'A Muse inur'd to Camps, in Courts refin'd' (sig. a2ᵛ).

70   Roscommon, first in fields of honour known, ⎫
       First in the peaceful triumphs of the gown, ⎬
       He both Minervas justly makes his own.   ⎭
       Now let the few beloved by Jove, and they
       Whom infused Titan formed of better clay,
75   On equal terms with ancient wit engage,
       Nor mighty Homer fear, nor sacred Virgil's page:
       Our English palace opens wide in state,
       And without stooping they may pass the gate.

70–1. Roscommon had held several military positions, and was now a captain in Arran's Regiment of Horse, and Master of the Horse to the Duchess of York. He had received honorary doctorates from both Cambridge and Oxford.

72. both Minervas] Minerva was goddess of wisdom and of war.

73–4. Cp. Roscommon: 'But, few, oh, few, Souls, praeordain'd by *Fate,/* The Race of *Gods,* have reach'd that *envy'd Height. /* No *Rebel-Titan's* sacrilegious *Crime,/* By heaping Hills on Hills can *thither climb'* (10–11).

74. D. echoes Juvenal, *Satire* xiv 34–5: *Forsitan haec spernant iuvenes, quibus arte benigna/ et meliore luto finxit praecordia Titan* ('Perhaps *one* youth, or *two,* untainted live,/ . . . whose hearts *Tytan* may/ Have fram'd with more art, and of better clay': Stapylton's translation (1647) 255) (Kinsley).   *infused*] divinely inspired; accented on the first syllable.   *Titan*] Prometheus, who according to Greek myth created mankind, and taught them arts and crafts.

75–8. D.'s lines are in tune with the ending of the *Essay*: Britain will be 'what *Rome* or *Athens* were *Before./* O may I Live to see that glorious Day,/ And sing loud *Paeans* through the Crowded way/ When in Triumphant state the *British Muse/* True to her *self* shall *Barb'rous* aid *refuse./* And in that *Roman Majesty* appear,/ Which none knows better and none *Comes* so *near'* (24).

78. Perhaps recalling Aeneas' entrance into the palace of Evander: 'stooping, through the Narrow Gate they press'd' ('The Eighth Book of the *Aeneis*' l. 475; Donald C. Mell, *PLL* xvii (1981) 153).

88 To Mr L. Maidwell

Date and publication. Probably written early in 1684. The poem survives uniquely in Leeds UL Brotherton Collection MS Lt 66 (see plates 4 and 5). It was first printed by John Barnard and Paul Hammond in *TLS* 25 May 1984 586. The MS is a MS Latin grammar by Lewis Maidwell, written in a fair copy by an immature hand, and probably intended to be shown to prospective patrons of Maidwell's school. D.'s is the first commendatory poem, and is followed by one from Nahum Tate.

Context. Lewis Maidwell (1650–1715) was an educationalist and private tutor who ran an academy in Hatton Gardens, London. Born in Northamptonshire (a few miles from D.'s home in Titchmarsh), he was educated at Westminster School and Cambridge (BA 1672). The Prologue to his play *The Loving Enemies* (1680) refers to the Rose Alley attack on D., but the only direct connection between the two men is D.'s reference to Maidwell as 'my Learn'd Friend' in the 'Discourse Concerning Satire' (1693) (*Works* iv 76). However, Albert Poyet (*Cahiers Élisabéthains* xxxi (1987) 63–4) has argued that D. alludes to Maidwell's *arbor conjugandi* (as 'the Grammar-Tree') in 'The Sixth Satire of Juvenal' l. 583. This shows that D. knew of this important and distinctive feature of Maidwell's way of teaching grammar, which was intended for inclusion in MS Lt 66 but not printed until 1707 in Maidwell's *Nova Grammatices Experimenta*. Tate's connection with Maidwell is clearer: he wrote a commendatory poem for the translation of Eutropius which was made by boys from Maidwell's academy and published in 1684 (*TC* February); Tate's two poems on Maidwell were printed in his *Poems Written on Several Occasions* (1684; *TC* May). D.'s association with Tate is also clear: he wrote for Tate a 'Prologue to *The Loyal General*' (1680); both men contributed to *Ovid's Epistles* (1680); Tate wrote commendatory verses to *AA* and *The Medal* and collaborated with D. on *2AA*; and both contributed memorial poems to Oldham's *Remains* (late 1684).

As G. J. Clingham shows (*EIC* xxxv (1985) 281–93) the present poem addresses several topics which are evident in other works by D. at this period, particularly its interest in 'the transmission of knowledge from the past to the present, and its assessment of grammar and translation as ways of civilizing language and the community's consciousness of what it possesses'. The concern with language and translation was shared by the members of Roscommon's academy in the early 1680s (see 'To the Earl of Roscommon', headnote), and in the Dedication to *Troilus and Cressida* (1679) D. says that in France Richelieu 'lay'd the foundations of so great a work: That he began it with a Grammar and a Dictionary; without which all those Remarques and Observations, which have since been made, had been perform'd to as little purpose as it wou'd be to consider the furniture of the Rooms before the contrivance of the House. . . . And as our *English* is a composition of the dead and living Tongues, there is requir'd a perfect knowledge, not onely of the

Greek and *Latine*, but of the Old *German*, the *French* and the *Italian*' (*Works* xiii 222).

Authorship. The MS attributes the poem to 'J. Drydon' (the spelling is insignificant). Corroboration of D.'s authorship is provided by the contextual evidence given above, and by parallels of thought and wording with other works by D. (see notes). The attribution is accepted by Winn 42. Alan Roper (*TLS* 22 June 1984 696) objected to the attribution of the poem to D. because (i) it is of poor quality; (ii) there were other J. Drydens who had been at Westminster (including the poet's cousin Jonathan and his son John); (iii) false attributions are common in Restoration poetry; (iv) there is no known link between D. and Maidwell before 1693. Point (i) is a matter of individual judgement, and great poets do not always write great poetry. (ii) Jonathan Dryden's only known poems are Latin verses from 1661–2, and in 1684 he was a clergyman in Yorkshire. D.'s son John was born in 1668, so was only 16 in 1684, too young to have written the poem unaided, though he was later to contribute a translation of *Satire* xiv to D.'s Juvenal (1693) and to write the play *The Husband his own Cuckold* (1696); collaboration between father and son cannot be dismissed. (iii) The question of a false attribution needs to be considered more closely, particularly since the accompanying poem by Tate is unquestionably genuine. If the attribution in the MS is wrong it must be either (a) deliberately fraudulent, (b) innocently mistaken, or (c) intended as a reference to another Dryden. (a) Since the grammar was evidently intended to be seen quite widely (whether in its present MS form, or in a printed version), with the prefatory poems conferring prestige, a deliberately fraudulent attribution would be foolish and unlikely. (b) The attribution cannot be an innocent error, since the MS was written for Maidwell, who would know the source of his poems. (c) Since the poem by 'J. Drydon' precedes one by Tate, the reader is evidently intended to assume that it is by the Poet Laureate. (iv) The common friendship with Tate provides a link between D. and Maidwell at this date. The circumstantial evidence and the parallels of thought and expression with other works by D. point to D.'s authorship, though this remains unproven.

To Mr L. Maidwell on his New Method

Latin is now of equal use become
To Englishmen, as was the Greek to Rome:
It guides our language, nothing is expressed
Graceful or true but by the Roman test.
5 Grammar's the base on which this work must stand,
Not to be laid by every vulgar hand.
Let then our reverend master be adored,
And all our grateful pens his praise record.
I dare not name myself, yet what I am
10 From his examples and his precepts came.
Our noblest wits from his instructive care
Have graced the senate, and have judged the bar;
But above all, the Muses' sacred band
Have been transplanted from his Eden land.

¶88. *Title. Method*] i.e. of teaching grammar.

1–4. In the Dedication to *Troilus and Cressida* (1679) D. says: 'I am often put to a stand, in considering whether what I write be the Idiom of the Tongue, or false Grammar . . . and have no other way to clear my doubts, but by translating my *English* into *Latine*, and thereby trying what sence the words will bear in a more stable language' (*Works* xiii 222). Maidwell shared D.'s interest in translation and the different properties of languages; in the preface to Eutropius he says to Sir John Lowther: 'The usefulness of Translation I know you much approve of . . . it procures two Languages, and discovers their proprieties the easiest and quickest way' (*A Breviary of Roman History* (1684) sig. A6ʳ).

2. For the Greek foundations of Roman culture cp. 'To the Earl of Roscommon' ll. 7–10.

5. Cp. Tate's poem: 'What Progress then in Learning must be made,/ When half the Building's in the *Basis* laid?' (*Poems* (1684) 168).

6. vulgar] ordinary, without any distinction (*OED* 10).

7. our reverend master] Richard Busby (1606–95), headmaster of Westminster School, where both D. and Maidwell were educated.

9–10. Cp. Jonson 'To William Camden', his schoolmaster: 'Camden, most reuerend head, to whom I owe/ All that I am in arts, all that I know,/ (How nothing's that?)' (ll. 1–3; *Ben Jonson* viii 31). Winn 552 notes a parallel with *RL* ll. 226–7.

14. For the image cp. 'To the Earl of Roscommon' ll. 1–4 (G. J. Clingham, *EIC* xxxv (1985) 281–93).

15 Nor thou the least, whose judgement has refined
    And milled that money which our master coined.
    Grammar, which was before th' ungrateful part
    Of our green years, is made a pleasing art:
    So filed, so polished, that no knots remain,
20 Each rule is useful, each example plain.
    As reason then by language is expressed,
    (Converse distinguishing 'twixt man and beast)
    So this thy grammar makes the difference more
    'Twixt man and man, than man and beast before.
25 Nor is thy academy thus confined,
    But as it teacheth words, it moulds the mind.

15–16. During the 1660s the old hammered coinage was being replaced by milled coins. David Yonge (*TLS* 8 June 1984 637) suggests that the image is of Busby's coins being melted down and reminted, though *refined* could also mean 'polished' (*OED* 4b). Davenant applies this image extensively to poetic wit in his Prologue to *The Wits* (*Works* (1673) 167–8); Cowley applies it to translation in 'The Adventures of Five hours' (*Poems* 440–1); and D. applies it to patronage in the Dedication to *Don Sebastian* (1690) (*Works* xv 59–60) and to language in 'Dedication of the *Aeneis*' (*Works* v 319, 334, 336). D. frequently argued that contemporary English culture was making advances on past achievements: in the refinement of the language compared with that of Shakespeare and Jonson (e.g. in 'Defence of the Epilogue', printed with *The Conquest of Granada* (1672) (*Works* xi 203–18)) and in the English versions of the classics (e.g. 'To the Earl of Roscommon' ll. 26–7, 75–8).   *refined/ . . . coined*] For the rhyme cp. 'joins/ . . . refines' in 'Epilogue to *The Wild Gallant*' ll. 19–20.

17. ungrateful] unpleasing.

22. Converse] discourse, exchange of thoughts; accented on the second syllable in the seventeenth century (*OED*); cp. 'To judge that language their converse refines' ('Epilogue to *The Wild Gallant*' l. 20).

24. Echoes 'Man differs more from man, than man from beast' (Rochester, *Satire against Reason and Mankind* (in MS, 1674, printed 1679) l. 221).

25–36. Maidwell discusses the importance of teaching history in his preface to the translation of Eutropius: 'I never found any motive more charming to a Youth to prosecute his Studies in any Language than History, which insensibly draws on the Student to gain the Tongue, and insinuating an Appetite from the beginning, continues it to the end. All our Learning terminates in it. . . . History [should be] rais'd up with the two Wings of Chronology, and Geography. . . . History cultivates the Memory, and improves the Judgment' (*A Breviary* sigs. A4ᵛ–A5ʳ).

25. academy] accented on the third syllable in the seventeenth century (*OED*).

Boys by degrees are out of nonage brought,
Nor grammar only for itself is taught,
Designed by thee not for the end, but way:
30 So artfully thou dost our youth convey
From step to step by thy judicious care,
And cheat'st 'em into knowledge ere aware,
That at the last, historians they become,
And know the deeds as well as words of Rome;
35 Which thou by sure chronology dost bind,
For that cements the story in the mind.
Thy modesty permits not more to say:
I'll imitate thy own compendious way.
Praise is a course: the speediness of pace
40 And shortness of the turning win the race.

27. *nonage*] infancy.

30–2. For the art of leading people into knowledge without seeming to do so, cp. 'To the Earl of Roscommon' ll. 32–4 (Clingham).

32. Echoes 'A man is to be cheated into passion, but to be reasoned into truth' (Preface to *RL* ll. 450–1; and cp. Maidwell's 'insensibly' in ll. 25–36*n*).

33–6. Clingham 285–6 notes that D.'s concern to 'distinguish between real knowledge of man and man's past, and mere verbalizing' and his interest in the method of imparting knowledge are also apparent in his comments on Plutarch: 'he learnt not the knowledge of things by words; but by the understanding and the use he had of things'; 'when the understanding is intent and fix'd on a single thing, it carries closer to the mark, every part of the object sinks into it, and the Soul receives it unmixt and whole'; ethics and politics 'teach by Argumentation and reasoning: Which rush as it were into the mind, and possess it with violence: But History rather allures than forces us to vertue. There is nothing of the Tyrant in Example; but it gently slides into us, is easie and pleasant in its passage' ('The Life of Plutarch' (1683) (*Works* xvii 245, 274, 275)).

37. D. also commends Roscommon's modesty ('To the Earl of Roscommon' l. 30; Clingham).

38–40. Cp. Tate: 'From thy own Stores thy Tribute we must raise;/ For who best learns thy Precepts, best can praise' (*Poems* 167). Clingham observes that this ending is similar to D.'s procedure in 'To the Memory of Mr Oldham', 'where he both imitates Oldham's thought and echoes his very words' (288).

39–40. For the movement of these lines cp. the final couplets of 'Upon the Death of the Lord Hastings' and 'Epitaph on the Marquis of Winchester'.

39. course] race (*OED* 3). For the image of poetic utterance as a race cp. 'Prologue to *Tyrannic Love*' ll. 22–3; 'To Mr Lee, on his *Alexander*' ll. 41–4 and 'To the Memory of Mr Oldham' ll. 7–10.

89 To the Memory of Mr Oldham

Date and publication. Printed in 1684 as the first of the memorial poems prefixed to *Remains of Mr. John Oldham in Verse and Prose,* published by Joseph Hindmarsh in 1684 (*TC* November; Wood's memorial poem is dated 26 May 1684); second edition 1687.

Context. John Oldham (1653–83) was born in Shipton Moyne, Gloucestershire, and educated at St Edmund Hall, Oxford. In 1676 he became an usher at Whitgift School, Croydon, where he is said to have 'received a Visit from the Earl of *Rochester,* the Earl of *Dorset,* Sir *Charles Sedley,* and other Persons of Distinction, merely upon the Reputation of some of his Verses, which they had seen in Manuscript' (anonymous life in Oldham's *Works* (1722) v). From 1679 to 1681 he was a tutor in the household of Sir Edward Thurland, and later tutor to the son of Sir William Hickes. At some stage, perhaps in 1682, he set up independently in London, and if he knew D. personally it would have been at this time. Oldham found a new patron in the Earl of Kingston, and died at his house at Holme Pierrepont, Nottinghamshire, being buried on 7 December 1683. Oldham's poetry includes pindaric verses in the manner of Cowley, erotic poems influenced by Rochester and his circle, the *Satyrs upon the Jesuits* inspired by the Popish Plot, poems which lament the poor status of the poet in Restoration England, and translations from Greek, Latin and French poetry. Some poems show the influence of D.'s poetry and heroic plays, and his transcript of *MF* (dated 1678) is preserved in BodL MS Rawl. Poet. 123. It is often assumed (e.g. in *Works* iii 385) that the race which D. says Oldham won (ll. 7–10) was for the publication of heroic satire on national themes, since his *Satyrs upon the Jesuits* (1681; *TC* November 1680) appeared a year before *AA.* But it is also possible (given D.'s special interest in translation in the early 1680s, and the markedly classical temper of this poem) that D. had in mind Oldham's translations. His versions of Horace's *Ars Poetica, Serm.* I ix, and *Carm.* I xxxi and II xiv appeared in *Some New Pieces* (1681), while his *Poems, and Translations* (1683) included versions of Juvenal's *Satires* III and XIII, and Boileau's *Satires* V and VIII; all these renderings transpose the setting to contemporary England. It may be no coincidence that it was in 1684 that D. began his serious work as a translator. There are several thematic and verbal parallels between this poem and D.'s other poems of 1684–5, notably those which discuss the writer's vocation ('Virgil's Ninth Eclogue', 'To the Earl of Roscommon' and 'To Mr L. Maidwell') and those which contemplate death ('Nisus and Euryalus', 'Lucretius: Against the Fear of Death'): for a discussion of the significance of this poem to D.'s understanding of himself as a writer see Dustin H. Griffin, *MLQ* xxxvii (1976) 133–50. For Oldham's work generally see his *Poems,* and Paul Hammond, *John Oldham and the Renewal of Classical Culture* (1983). The other contributors of memorial verses to *Remains* were Thomas Flatman, Nahum Tate, Thomas D'Urfey, Thomas Andrews, and Anon; and in the second edition Jacob Tonson (anonymously, first printed in *Sylvae*) and Robert Gould.

Sources. The poem is full of echoes (including echoes of D.'s own work), but no single source dominates. D. draws on two pieces in Oldham's *Poems, and Translations*: one celebrated a male friendship, 'David's Lamentation for the Death of Saul and Jonathan' and the other an English classical poet, 'Upon the Works of Ben. Johnson'. (Both poems are singled out for praise by other elegists in the *Remains*.) D. also draws on Milton's *Lycidas* (see Bruce King, *EA* xix (1966) 60–3) and on Cowley's *Davideis* and 'On the Death of Mr. William Hervey'. There are several echoes of Roman poetry too—appropriately, given Oldham's classical interests: see Hoffman 92–8 and R. G. Petersen, *MPh* lxvi (1969) 232–6. Two passages in Virgil came to D.'s mind: the story of Nisus and Euryalus from *Aen.* v and ix (see ll. 9–10, and ll. 3–4*n*, 7*n*); and the vision of Marcellus in *Aen.* vi (see l. 23*n*). These allusions counteract the note of Augustan promise which D. sounds in 'Virgil's Fourth Eclogue', but are in keeping with the almost despairing tone of 'Virgil's Ninth Eclogue'. Virgil's passage on Marcellus is an acknowledged masterpiece of the Latin literature of grief, and had probably inspired D.'s eulogy for the young Ossory in *AA* ll. 831–53. There may be another Latin source in the *Noctes Atticae* of Aulus Gellius: Leonard Moskovit (*N & Q* ccxvii (1972) 26–7) cites XIII ii 3–6 where Accius says, 'it is with the mind as it is with fruits; those which are at first harsh and bitter, later become mild and sweet; but those which at once grow mellow and soft, and are juicy in the beginning, presently become, not ripe, but decayed. Accordingly it has seemed to me that something should be left in the products of the intellect for time and age to mellow.' There are also several classical turns of phrase in the poem (see notes).

Reception. Apart from those cited in ll. 15–16*n*, there are no contemporary comments on this poem, but it was echoed by the anonymous author of 'The Vision' (BL MS Add 28276 f. 86ᵛ), and imitated by H. Hall in his memorial poem for Purcell (*Orpheus Britannicus* (1696) vi).

To the Memory of Mr Oldham

Farewell, too little and too lately known,
Whom I began to think and call my own;
For sure our souls were near allied, and thine
Cast in the same poetic mould with mine.
5 One common note on either lyre did strike,
And knaves and fools we both abhorred alike:
To the same goal did both our studies drive,
The last set out the soonest did arrive.

¶89. *1*. Echoes 'Too early seen unknown, and known too late' (*Romeo and Juliet* I v 141); cp. also Andrews: 'Fled e'er his Worth or Merit was half known;/ No sooner seen, but in a Moment gone' (*Remains* sig. A4ᵛ); and cp. Cowley, quoted in l. 11*n*. There is no evidence as to whether D. knew Oldham personally. The fact that all Oldham's work was published anonymously would have impeded recognition.

3–4. Echoes Oldham: 'Oh, dearer than my Soul! if I can call it mine,/ For sure we had the same, 'twas very thine' ('David's Lamentation' ll. 204–5). There are verbal parallels between ll. 3–5 here and 'Nisus and Euryalus' ll. 249–54. D. also echoes his own earlier line: 'For Noble Souls in Nature are alli'd' (*Aureng-Zebe* (1676) 50).   *souls*] Perhaps from *animae duae, animus unus* ('two souls, one soul'), the gloss on *Aen.* ix 182 in Emmenessius' edition (1680); see 'Nisus and Euryalus' ll. 11 and 249–54*n*.   *near allied*] Anna Battigelli points out that since Oldham and D. shared the same birthday of 9 August they would have shared the same astrological sign (*N & Q* ccxxxiii (1988) 174–5); however, we do not know that D. knew this.   *allied*] Echoes Oldham's 'Both excellent they were, both equally alli'd' ('David's Lamentation' l. 119).

5–6. Echoes Cowley: 'Thus when two *Brethren strings* are set alike,/ To *move* them *both*, but *one* of them we *strike*,/ Thus *Davids Lyre* did *Sauls* wild rage controul./ And tun'd the harsh disorders of his *Soul*' (*Davideis, Poems* 254).

7–10. D. echoes his earlier lines: 'It seems my soul then mov'd the quicker pace,/ Yours first set out, mine reach'd her in the race' (*The Indian Emperor* (1667) I ii 147–8), and he echoes these lines again in Evander's lament for his son Pallas, 'The Eleventh Book of the *Aeneis*' ll. 244–5. D. had used the image of the writer's life as a race in 'Prologue to *Tyrannic Love*' ll. 19–23 and 'To Mr Lee, on his *Alexander*' ll. 43–4, and writes of praise as a race in 'To Mr L. Maidwell' ll. 39–40. For the image of life as a race see Hebrews xii 1 and *OED* race 1c.

7. studies] Cp. *eorum studio flagrabant* ('they were inflamed with study'): Servius' gloss on *Aen.* ix 182, quoted in Emmenessius.

Thus Nisus fell upon the slippery place,
10   While his young friend performed and won the race.
O early ripe! to thy abundant store
What could advancing age have added more?

9–10. In *Aen.* v the young Euryalus wins a race as a result of his friend Nisus falling and impeding a rival; the allusion also implicitly evokes the death of the pair in *Aen.* ix. D. translated both passages in 1684 for *Sylvae* (see 'Nisus and Euryalus'); for verbal parallels with that translation see ll. 3–4*n*, 11*n*. The story had also been used as an example of friendship by Otway in a poem to Richard Duke in *MP* (1684) (see 'Nisus and Euryalus', headnote). Nisus here represents D., but, as Griffin notes, many readers momentarily assume that Nisus, being the fallen runner, stands for Oldham, which strengthens the suggestion that the two poets share a similar fate. Exactly why D. thought of himself as having fallen is unclear.

9. slippery] In Virgil the ground is wet with sacrificial blood, but D. probably retains the word here because it had become the standard epithet for the position of the courtier, deriving from Seneca's *Thyestes* ll. 391–2: *stet quicunque volet potens/ aulae culmine lubrico* ('Upon the slippery tops of humane State/ . . . Let others proudly stand': tr. Cowley, *Essays* 399–400). D. uses its connotations again in 'The slipp'ry state of human-kind,/ And fickle fortune' ('The Tenth Book of the *Aeneis*' ll. 225–6; cp. *Threnodia Augustalis* l. 400). The phrasing of the line thus associates D. with the slippery life of the courtier; for his growing distrust of such a role see 'Horace: *Epode* II' l. 15*n*.

11–14. Tonson speculated that Oldham would have equalled D. himself: 'Had Fate allow'd his Life a longer thread,/ Adding experience to that wondrous fraught/ Of Youthful vigour, how wou'd he have wrote!/ Equal to mighty *Pan*'s Immortal Verse, [marginal note: '*Mr. Dryden.*']/ He that now rules with undisputed sway' (*Sylvae* 472–3).

11. Echoes Cowley's 'On the Death of Mr. *William Hervey*': 'Wondrous young Man, why wert thou made so good,/ To be snatcht hence ere better *understood*?/ Snatcht before half of thee enough was seen!/ *Thou Ripe*, and yet thy *Life* but *Green*!' (*Poems* 36). D. uses Cowley's poem again in 'Nisus and Euryalus' ll. 251, 253. D. also adapts Oldham: 'Rich in thy self, to whose unbounded store/ Exhausted Nature could vouchsafe no more' ('Upon the Works of *Ben. Johnson*' ll. 171–2). For the sentiment and rhymes see D.'s addition to Virgil in 'Mezentius and Lausus' ll. 101–2. Cp. also *2AA* ll. 949–50; 'Lucretius: Against the Fear of Death' ll. 138–9.   *early ripe*] Thomas Sprat had described the young Cowley's talents as 'early-ripe' (*Works of Mr Abraham Cowley* (1668) sig. A2ʳ).

It might (what Nature never gives the young)
Have taught the numbers of thy native tongue;
15   But satire needs not those, and wit will shine
Through the harsh cadence of a rugged line:
·   A noble error, and but seldom made,
When poets are by too much force betrayed.

14. numbers] rhythm and metre. For discussions of D.'s understanding of
prosody see R. D. Jameson, *MPh* xx (1923) 241–53 and George McFadden,
Duquesne Studies, Philological Series v (1964) 87–109.
15–16. D. adapts Roscommon's *Essay on Translated Verse* (1684) 15: 'Be not
too fond of a Sonorous Line;/ *Good Sence* will through a *plain expression*
shine.' Raman Selden (*MLR* lxvi (1971) 264–72) suggests an echo of Horace's
verdict on Lucilius: *facetus,/ emunctae naris, durus componere versus* (*Serm.* I iv 7–
8: 'Witty he was, and of keen-scented nostrils, but harsh in framing his
verse'). Selden also observes that in associating satirical and metrical asperity
Oldham and D. were closer to the views of J. C. Scaliger and Joseph Hall
than to those of their Restoration colleagues. Oldham defended himself
against the charge of excessive harshness in the Advertisement to *Some New
Pieces*, saying that his work showed that he was capable of melodious verse
when it was appropriate, but that in satire 'I did not so much mind the
Cadence, as the Sense and expressiveness of my words' (ll. 82–3). In their
contributions to *Remains* D'Urfey and Andrews stress Oldham's ability at
both rough and 'easie Numbers', and Gould (perhaps replying to D.) objects
to such criticism: 'How wide shoot they, that strive to blast thy Fame,/ By
saying, that thy Verse was rough and lame?' (*Remains* (1687) sig. B5ᵛ). Tom
Brown said that D. here kicked over the milk he had given: 'you tell the
World that he was a very fine ingenious Gentleman, but still did not understand the cadence of the *English* Tongue' (*The Late Converts Exposed* (1690)
33). Tonson found Oldham's roughness to be artistically appropriate: 'Sometimes becoming negligence adorn'd/ His Verse, and nature shew'd they were
her own,/ Yet Art he us'd, where Art cou'd useful be,/ But sweated not to be
correctly dull' (*Sylvae* 472).
17–18. D. had praised Lee's vigour, defending him against criticisms that he
was too fiery, in 'To Mr Lee, on his *Alexander*' ll. 37–48; cp. also 'Prologue to
Tyrannic Love' l. 21. In the 'Dedication of the Georgics' (1697) D. says of
Virgil's description of a colt: 'His beginnings must be in rashness; a Noble
Fault: But Time and Experience will correct that Errour, and tame it into a
deliberate and well-weigh'd Courage; which knows both to be cautious and
to dare, as occasion offers' (*Works* v 140).
18. Echoes Roscommon: 'With how much ease is a *young Muse Betrayed*'
(*Essay* 7).

Thy generous fruits, though gathered ere their prime ⎫
20 Still showed a quickness; and maturing time   ⎬
But mellows what we write to the dull sweets of ⎪
   rhyme.   ⎭
Once more, hail and farewell; farewell thou young,
But ah too short, Marcellus of our tongue;
Thy brows with ivy, and with laurels bound;
25 But fate and gloomy night encompass thee around.

19–21. Echoes *Lycidas* ll. 3–8: 'I come to pluck your berries harsh and crude,/ And with forced fingers rude,/ Shatter your leaves before the mellowing year/ . . . For Lycidas is dead, dead ere his prime'. D'Urfey has a similar image: 'That *Oldham* honour'd for his early Worth,/ Was cropt, like a sweet Blossom from the earth' (*Remains* sig. A3ʳ). Cp. also *2AA* ll. 963–4.

19. generous] abundant (*OED* 4); strong, rich (a metaphor from wine; *OED* 5).

20. quickness] liveliness; sharpness of taste (*OED* 5).

21. sweets] pleasures (*OED* 3). Cp. 'Preface to *Sylvae*' l. 124.

22. Cp. Catullus ci 10: *in perpetuum, frater, ave atque vale* ('for ever, my brother, hail and farewell'). R. G. Petersen notes the Roman custom of bidding a triple farewell to a corpse.

23. Marcellus] The nephew and adopted son of Augustus, who died in 23 BC, his twentieth year, of great and unfulfilled promise. In *Aen.* vi 860–86 Aeneas sees the shade of Marcellus in the underworld. Anchises describes him as 'Admir'd when living, and Ador'd when lost!/ Mirror of ancient Faith in early Youth!/ Undaunted Worth, Inviolable Truth!' ('The Sixth Book of the *Aeneis*' ll. 1213–15). D. implies that Oldham was the lost heir to the classical tradition of English poetry, as Marcellus was the lost heir to Augustus. The same comparison is used by the anonymous contributor to *Remains* (sig. A5ᵛ).

24. ivy . . . laurels] In antiquity laurel denoted conquest, ivy immortality. Virgil awards Pollio this mixed crown in *Ecl.* viii 11–13; Petersen notes that in *Ecl.* vii 25 Virgil assigns ivy to a *crescentem poetam* ('rising poet'). Horace (*Carm.* I i 29) was responsible for the further association of ivy with learning; see also Ovid's elegy for Tibullus (*Amores* III xxix 61–2). For classical garlands see further J. B. Trapp, *JWCI* xxi (1958) 227–55.

25. Echoes Virgil: *sed nox atra caput tristi circumuolat umbra* (*Aen.* vi 866: 'But hov'ring Mists around his Brows are spread,/ And Night, with sable Shades, involves his Head': 'The Sixth Book of the *Aeneis*' ll. 1198–9). At *Aen.* vi 869 Fate allows Aeneas only a brief glimpse of Marcellus. D. uses 'compass him around' again in l. 1196; the phrasing is biblical: cp. 'The sorrows of hell compassed me about' (Psalm xviii 5). The ending not only offers no hope of Christian immortality, it also omits the injunction to fortitude common in classical elegies (e.g. Horace, *Carm.* I xxix).   *fate*] destiny (*OED* 1); death (*OED* 4b).

Date and publication. Sylvae: or, the Second Part of Poetical Miscellanies was
published by Tonson in 1685 (*SR* 10 January; advertised in *The Observator* 1
January); reprinted 1692 (some copies dated 1693). The translations of Lucretius and the part of the Preface discussing Lucretius were added as an appendix to the 1700 edition of Creech's *Lucretius and Manilius . . . Translated.* The
date of composition of the various pieces in *Sylvae* can be estimated approximately. D. would have written the Preface shortly before the publication of
Sylvae, so probably in November or December 1684. In the Preface (l. 1) he
assigns the translations to 'this last half year', i.e. roughly April–October
1684. D.'s statement in the Preface that he began with Theocritus and Horace, and proceeded to Lucretius and Virgil, is confirmed by his letter to
Tonson *c.* August 1684: 'You will have of mine four Odes of Horace, which I
have already translated, another small translation of forty lines from Lucretius: the whole story of Nisus & Eurialus, both in the fifth, & the ninth of
Virgils Eneids; & I care not who translates them beside me, for let him be
friend or foe, I will please my self, & not give off in consideration of any
man. there will be forty lines more of Virgil in another place; to answer those
of Lucretius; I meane those very lines which Montaign has compar'd in those
two poets: & Homer shall sleep on for me: I will not now meddle with him'
(*Letters* 23; for Montaigne see 'Venus to Vulcan', headnote). It would seem,
then, that the translations of Theocritus and Horace were made in the late
spring or early summer of 1684. There are some parallels between D.'s
translations of Theocritus and those by Creech, but the chronological prece-
dence of the two is unclear (see the headnote to 'Amaryllis'). There are also
verbal parallels between D.'s translations of Horace and those by Creech,
which were published in 1684 with a Dedication to D. dated 25 May. D.
could have seen these before making his own translations, but Creech's
statement that D. has thought Horace 'worthy your Study and Imitation'
(sig. A4^{r-v}) suggests that Creech knew of the existence of at least some
versions of Horace by D. at the time he was writing the Dedication. If Creech
had seen a MS, the verbal borrowings might be by Creech from D. rather
than vice versa. The question remains open. The translations from Lucretius
Book I and *Aen.* V, VIII, and IX would have been made in the summer of
1684, and those from *Aen.* X and the other parts of Lucretius in the autumn:
evidently these were not envisaged at the time of D.'s letter. It is possible that
D.'s 'Theocritus: Idyllium the Eighteenth' was composed in 1683 or early
1684: see headnote to that poem. For other aspects of the complicated chronology of D.'s work in 1684 see Edward L. Saslow, *MPh* lxxii (1975) 248–55.

Context. Sylvae is a volume of major importance in D.'s career (for its
contents see Appendix A). It is the second of the miscellanies published by
Tonson with some editorial supervision by D., the first being *MP* in 1684.
(For a bibliographical analysis of the way in which the two collections were

assembled see Paul Hammond, *PBSA* lxxxiv (1990) 402–12.) Whereas *MP* collected many items which had previously been published separately, *Sylvae* includes only new pieces; D. wrote to Tonson: 'Your opinion of the Miscellanyes is likewise mine: I will for once lay by the Religio Laici, till another time. But I must also add, that since we are to have nothing but new, I am resolvd we will have nothing but good, whomever we disoblige' (*Letters* 23). It begins with a substantial group of pieces by D.: the Preface, three translations from the *Aen.*, five from Lucretius, three from Theocritus and four from Horace; later in the volume there are two songs by D. The remaining pieces by other hands (including D.'s son Charles and his brother-in-law Sir Robert Howard) are mainly classical translations, though the volume also includes a poem on the translation of Fr Simon's *Critical History* (see headnote to *RL*), and Tonson's poem on the death of Oldham. *Sylvae* marks an important stage in the development of D.'s work as a translator, demonstrating a serious commitment which goes beyond that of *Ovid's Epistles* (see Stuart Gillespie, Cambridge PhD thesis 1987). It is partly a response to the interest which several gifted contemporaries had shown in poetic translation in the 1680s. Thomas Creech published his complete translation of Lucretius in 1682 to considerable acclaim, and followed it with a Horace and Theocritus, both in 1684. John Oldham had printed some fine translations of Horace in *Some New Pieces* (1681) and of Juvenal in *Poems, and Translations* (1683) (see Paul Hammond, *John Oldham and the Renewal of Classical Culture* (1983), and D.'s 'To the Memory of Mr Oldham'). The Earl of Roscommon and his circle were interested in translation, and the Earl published an *Essay on Translated Verse* in 1684 (see 'To the Earl of Roscommon'). Tonson seems to have taken a leading role in the promotion of poetic translation, and was particularly interested in publishing composite sets of classical translations: he followed *Ovid's Epistles* with a set of versions of Ovid's *Elegies*, Horace's *Odes* and Virgil's *Eclogues*, all in *MP*, while *Sylvae* has smaller collections of Ovid, Horace and Theocritus (see Stuart Gillespie, *Restoration* xii (1988) 10–19). D.'s translations in *Sylvae* share concerns and common influences. Recurring topics are the confrontation of death (with links to D.'s contemporary poem 'To the Memory of Mr Oldham'), the power of sexual desire, the corrupting influence on the soul of involvement in court and commerce, the attractions of the retired country life, and the need to make use of the present. There are many echoes between the poems, and when translating one piece D. frequently recalled other comparable passages in classical and Renaissance poetry, as H. A. Mason has shown (see headnotes to the Horatian translations). Besides the examples of Creech, Oldham and Roscommon, noted above, Cowley's *Essays* helped to shape D.'s thinking about freedom and retirement, and Milton is an influential presence (see J. R. Mason).

Sylvae: or, the Second Part of Poetical Miscellanies

*—Non deficit alter
Aureus; et simili frondescit virga metallo.*   Virg.

Preface

For this last half year I have been troubled with the
disease (as I may call it) of translation; the cold prose fits
of it (which are always the most tedious with me) were
spent in *The History of the League*, the hot (which suc-
5   ceeded them) in this volume of verse miscellanies. The
truth is, I fancied to myself a kind of ease in the change
of the paroxysm, never suspecting but that the humour
would have wasted itself in two or three pastorals of
Theocritus, and as many odes of Horace. But finding,
10   or at least thinking I found, something that was more
pleasing in them than my ordinary productions, I
encouraged myself to renew my old acquaintance with
Lucretius and Virgil, and immediately fixed upon some
parts of them which had most affected me in the read-

¶**90.** *Title.* The Latin *silvae* means 'woods'. It was used as the title of a
collection of poems by Statius. Jonson imitated this practice in calling his
collections *The Forrest* and *The Under-wood*, noting that 'the Ancients call'd
that kind of body *Sylva*, or Ὕλη, in which there were workes of divers
nature, and matter congested' (viii 126).
Epigraph. 'Another golden one will not be lacking, and a bough of the same
metal will grow' (Virgil, *Aen.* vi 143–4). This refers to the golden bough
which Aeneas breaks off and carries with him on his journey through the
underworld. Here the allusion to a second golden bough refers to the second
part of the Tonson miscellanies, but it also suggests that English writers are
producing a second, no less golden, version of the Latin poets.
1. this last half year] See headnote, '*Date and publication*'.
4. The History of the League] D. translated Louis Maimbourg's *Histoire de la
Ligue* at the command of Charles II. It was published in 1684 (advertised 16
April, appeared in late July; see Edward L. Saslow, *MPh* lxxii (1975) 248–55).
7. humour] temporary feeling, mood (*OED* 5).
12–13. old acquaintance with Lucretius and Virgil] D. would have known both
poets since his schooldays. He had used Virgil frequently in his poems (see
headnote to 'Virgil's Fourth Eclogue'); Lucretius is less prominent, but had

15   ing. These were my natural impulses for the undertaking, but there was an accidental motive, which was
full as forcible, and God forgive him who was the occasion of it. It was my Lord Roscommon's *Essay on
Translated Verse*, which made me uneasy till I tried
20   whether or no I was capable of following his rules, and
of reducing the speculation into practice. For many a fair
precept in poetry is like a seeming demonstration in the
mathematics, very specious in the diagram, but failing
in the mechanic operation. I think I have generally ob-
25   served his instructions; I am sure my reason is sufficiently convinced both of their truth and usefulness;
which, in other words, is to confess no less a vanity than
to pretend that I have at least in some places made
examples to his rules. Yet withal I must acknowledge
30   that I have many times exceeded my commission, for I
have both added and omitted, and even sometimes very
boldly made such expositions of my authors as no
Dutch commentator will forgive me. Perhaps, in such
particular passages, I have thought that I discovered
35   some beauty yet undiscovered by those pedants, which
none but a poet could have found. Where I have taken
away some of their expressions, and cut them shorter, it
may possibly be on this consideration, that what was
beautiful in the Greek or Latin would not appear so
40   shining in the English: and where I have enlarged them,
I desire the false critics would not always think that
those thoughts are wholly mine, but that either they are
secretly in the poet, or may be fairly deduced from him;

been used in several plays (see headnote to 'Lucretius: The Beginning of the
First Book').

18–19. Roscommon's Essay on Translated Verse] published in 1684 with a
commendatory poem by D. (q.v.).

23. specious] plausible.

24. mechanic] practical, applied (*OED* mechanical 2b).

28. pretend] claim.

30. exceeded my commission] Roscommon says: '*Excursions are inexpiably Bad,/
For 'tis much safer to leave out, than Add*' (14). D.'s translations in *Sylvae* do
adapt the originals with some freedom; see ll. 43*n*, 45–6*n*.

33. Dutch commentator] Many of the leading seventeenth-century editions of
classical texts were edited and annotated by Dutch scholars.

43. or may be fairly deduced from him] Cp. Denham: 'Where my expressions . . .

or at least, if both those considerations should fail, that
45 my own is of a piece with his, and that if he were living,
and an Englishman, they are such as he would probably
have written.

   For, after all, a translator is to make his author appear
as charming as possibly he can, provided he maintains
50 his character, and makes him not unlike himself.
Translation is a kind of drawing after the life, where
everyone will acknowledge there is a double sort of
likeness, a good one and a bad. 'Tis one thing to draw
the outlines true, the features like, the proportions
55 exact, the colouring itself perhaps tolerable, and another
thing to make all these graceful, by the posture, the
shadowings, and chiefly by the spirit which animates
the whole. I cannot without some indignation look on
an ill copy of an excellent original: much less can I

---

are fuller than his, they are but the impressions which the often reading of
him, hath left upon my thoughts; so that if they are not his own Conceptions,
they are at least the results of them' (Preface to *The Destruction of Troy* (1656);
Poetical Works 160).

45–6. if he were living, and an Englishman] The question of how much liberty
and modernization should be allowed in a translation was controversial.
Denham had argued that 'if *Virgil* must needs speak English, it were fit he
should speak not only as a man of this Nation, but as a man of this age' (160).
In the 'Preface to *Ovid's Epistles*' (ll. 318–22) D. had drawn back from the
'libertine way' of imitation, where the translator writes 'as he supposes the
author would have done, had he lived in our age, and in our country'. But
Oldham, in the Advertisement to *Some New Pieces* (1681) explained that in
translating Horace he had made him 'speak, as if he were living, and writing
now' (ll. 24–5), and transposed the scenes to England. He followed the same
practice with Juvenal in *Poems, and Translations* (1683). Creech rejected this
form of modernization, preferring 'to convey down the Learning of the
Ancients, than their thin Ghost imbody'd with some light Air of my own'
(*The Odes, Satyrs and Epistles of Horace* (1684) sig. A7ʳ). D.'s practice in *Sylvae*
is freer than in *Ovid's Epistles*, but he moves between different degrees of
modernization and of literal faithfulness. He continued to adhere to this
position in his later essays: see 'Dedication of the *Aeneis*' (*Works* v 330–1) and
'Preface to *Fables*' (edited by Kinsley ll. 519–24).

49. charming as] *1692*; charming at *1685*.

51–8. The comparison of poetry and painting interested D. throughout his
career, and he translated Du Fresnoy's *De Arte Graphica* in 1695, with a
Preface which developed 'a Parallel, Of *Poetry* and *Painting*'. Cp. also *Astraea
Redux* ll. 125–8.

60 behold with patience Virgil, Homer and some others,
whose beauties I have been endeavouring all my life
to imitate, so abused (as I may say to their faces) by
a botching interpreter. What English readers unacquainted with Greek or Latin will believe me or any
65 other man, when we commend those authors, and confess we derive all that is pardonable in us from their
fountains, if they take those to be the same poets whom
our Ogilbys have translated? But I dare assure them,
that a good poet is no more like himself in a dull trans-
70 lation, than his carcass would be to his living body.
There are many who understand Greek and Latin, and
yet are ignorant of their mother tongue. The proprieties
and delicacies of the English are known to few; 'tis
impossible even for a good wit to understand and prac-
75 tise them without the help of a liberal education, long
reading and digesting of those few good authors we
have amongst us, the knowledge of men and manners,
the freedom of habitudes and conversation with the best
company of both sexes, and, in short, without wearing
80 off the rust which he contracted while he was laying in a
stock of learning. Thus difficult it is to understand the
purity of English, and critically to discern not only
good writers from bad, and a proper style from a corrupt, but also to distinguish that which is pure in a good
85 author from that which is vicious and corrupt in him.

68. our Ogilbys] John Ogilby had translated Virgil (1649), the *Iliad* (1660) and
the *Odyssey* (1665); see *MF* l. 102 and *n*.

70. carcass] Echoing Denham: see 'Preface to *Ovid's Epistles*' ll. 362-5 and *n*.

72-3. The question of correct English had interested D. for many years; he
discussed it in the *Defence of the Epilogue* appended to *The Conquest of Granada*
(1672), and in the Dedication and Preface to *Troilus and Cressida* (1679); see
also 'To Mr L. Maidwell' ll. 1-4.

72. proprieties] special characteristics, correctness of diction (*OED* 5); fitness,
appropriateness (*OED* 6).

73-81. Kinsley cites D.'s Dedication to *Troilus and Cressida*: 'the perfect
knowledge of a Tongue was never attain'd by any single person. The Court,
the Colledge, and the Town, must be joyn'd in it' (*Works* xiii 222). Kinsley
also compares Boileau: 'Que les vers ne soient pas vostre éternel employ./
Cultivez vos amis, soyez homme de foy./ C'est peu d'estre agreable et
charmant dans un livre;/ Il faut sçavoir encore et converser et vivre' (*L' Art
Poétique* (1674) iv 121-4).

78. habitudes] intimacies, associations (*OED* 3).

And for want of all these requisites, or the greatest part
of them, most of our ingenious young men take up
some cried-up English poet for their model, adore him,
and imitate him as they think, without knowing where-
90   in he is defective, where he is boyish and trifling, wherein either his thoughts are improper to his subject, or
his expressions unworthy of his thoughts, or the turn of
both is unharmonious. Thus it appears necessary that a
man should be a nice critic in his mother tongue
95   before he attempts to translate a foreign language.
Neither is it sufficient that he be able to judge of words
and style, but he must be a master of them too. He must
perfectly understand his author's tongue, and absolutely
command his own: so that to be a thorough translator
100 he must be a thorough poet. Neither is it enough to give
his author's sense in good English, in poetical expressions, and in musical numbers: for, though all these
are exceeding difficult to perform, there yet remains an
harder task, and 'tis a secret of which few translators
105 have sufficiently thought. I have already hinted a word
or two concerning it: that is, the maintaining the
character of an author which distinguishes him from all
others, and makes him appear that individual poet
whom you would interpret. For example, not only the
110 thoughts but the style and versification of Virgil and
Ovid are very different, yet I see, even in our best poets
who have translated some parts of them, that they have

90. boyish] puerile. In the 'Preface to *Fables*' (edited by Kinsley l. 292) D.
coined the word 'boyisms' for the inopportune witticisms to which Ovid was
prone: this draws on the comment by the younger Seneca that Ovid descended *ad pueriles ineptias* ('to childish silliness': *Naturales Quaestiones* III xxvii
13; see David Hopkins in *Ovid Renewed*, edited by Charles Martindale (1988)
167–70). Rapin commented that Ovid's work frequently 'discovers his
youthfullnesse' whereas Virgil's 'does not fall into those childishnesses'
(*Observations on the Poems of Homer and Virgil*, tr. John Davies (1672) 80, 71).
92. turn] The repetition of a word in a new grammatical form to give rise to a
new idea. D. discusses this feature of verse in the 'Discourse Concerning
Satire' (*Works* iv 84–6).
94. nice] exact, subtle (*OED* 7b,c).
102. numbers] metrical rhythms.
110. versification] Watson notes that this is the first recorded use of the word
to mean 'metre' (antedating *OED*).

confounded their several talents, and by endeavouring
only at the sweetness and harmony of numbers, have
115 made them both so much alike that, if I did not know
the originals, I should never be able to judge by the
copies which was Virgil and which was Ovid. It was
objected against a late noble painter, that he drew many
graceful pictures, but few of them were like. And this
120 happened to him because he always studied himself
more than those who sate to him. In such translators I
can easily distinguish the hand which performed the
work, but I cannot distinguish their poet from another.
Suppose two authors are equally sweet, yet there is a
125 great distinction to be made in sweetness, as in that of
sugar and that of honey. I can make the difference more
plain by giving you (if it be worth knowing) my own
method of proceeding in my translations out of four
several poets in this volume: Virgil, Theocritus, Lucre-
130 tius and Horace. In each of these, before I undertook
them, I considered the genius and distinguishing
character of my author. I looked on Virgil as a succinct
and grave majestic writer, one who weighed not only
every thought but every word and syllable, who was
135 still aiming to crowd his sense into as narrow a compass
as possibly he could; for which reason he is so very
figurative that he requires (I may almost say) a grammar
apart to construe him. His verse is everywhere sounding the very thing in your ears whose sense it bears; yet
140 the numbers are perpetually varied to increase the
delight of the reader, so that the same sounds are never
repeated twice together. On the contrary, Ovid and
Claudian, though they write in styles differing from

113. several] separate, individual.

118. painter] probably Sir Peter Lely (1618–80).

121. sate] sat.

124. sweet] pleasing in artistic (esp. musical) effect (*OED* 4, 5); cp. 'To the Memory of Mr Oldham' l. 21.

131. genius] distinctive ability, particular cast of mind (*OED* 4).

138–9. sounding the very thing] Roscommon had advocated: 'The *sound* is still a Comment to the Sense' (22). The idea became common in the seventeenth century but goes back to Dionysius of Halicarnassus (Spingarn ii 357–8).

143. Claudian] Latin poet (d. *c*. AD 404), writer of political poems and panegyrics.

each other, yet have each of them but one sort of music
145   in their verses. All the versification and little variety of
Claudian is included within the compass of four or five
lines, and then he begins again in the same tenor, perpetually closing his sense at the end of a verse, and that
verse commonly which they call golden, or two sub-
150   stantives and two adjectives with a verb betwixt them
to keep the peace. Ovid, with all his sweetness, has as
little variety of numbers and sound as he: he is always as
it were upon the hand-gallop, and his verse runs upon
carpet-ground. He avoids like the other all synalœphas
155   (or cutting off one vowel when it comes before another
in the following word) so that minding only smoothness he wants both variety and majesty. But to return to
Virgil, though he is smooth where smoothness is
required, yet he is so far from affecting it that he seems
160   rather to disdain it, frequently makes use of synalœphas, and concludes his sense in the middle of his
verse. He is everywhere above conceits of epigrammatic wit and gross hyperboles: he maintains majesty in
the midst of plainness; he shines, but glares not, and is
165   stately without ambition, which is the vice of Lucan. I
drew my definition of poetical wit from my particular

---

153. hand-gallop] easy gallop.
154. carpet-ground] ground as smooth as a carpet (*OED* 5).   *synalœphas*] See
also D.'s Dedication to *EP* (*Works* iv 371–2).
162–3. above . . . epigrammatic wit] D. had contrasted Ovid and Virgil in this
respect in the 'Account' of *AM* ll. 156–201.
165. ambition] ostentation (*OED* 2).   *Lucan*] See *AM* 'Account' ll. 48–9.
166. my definition of poetical wit] In 'The Authors Apology for Heroique
Poetry; and Poetique Licence', prefixed to *The State of Innocence* (1677), D.
defines wit as 'a propriety of Thoughts and Words; or in other terms,
Thought and Words, elegantly adapted to the Subject' (sig. c2ᵛ). Later, in the
Preface to *Albion and Albanius* (1685) he says: 'If Wit has truly been defin'd a
propriety of Thoughts and Words, then that Definition will extend to all
sorts of Poetry. . . . Propriety of thought is that Fancy which arises naturally
from the Subject, or which the Poet adapts to it. Propriety of Words, is the
cloathing of those thoughts with such Expressions, as are naturally proper to
them: and from both these, if they are judiciously perform'd, the delight of
Poetry results' (*Works* xv 3). In his life of Lucian (1711) i 42 D. says that he
had imagined that he had originated this definition, but found it substantially
in Aristotle (*Poetics* 1450b) (Kinsley).

consideration of him, for propriety of thoughts and
words are only to be found in him, and where they are
proper they will be delightful. Pleasure follows of
170 necessity, as the effect does the cause, and therefore is
not to be put into the definition. This exact propriety of
Virgil I particularly regarded as a great part of his
character, but must confess to my shame that I have not
been able to translate any part of him so well as to make
175 him appear wholly like himself. For where the original
is close, no version can reach it in the same compass.
Hannibal Caro's in the Italian is the nearest, the most
poetical and the most sonorous of any translation of the
Aeneids; yet, though he takes the advantage of blank
180 verse, he commonly allows two lines for one of Virgil,
and does not always hit his sense. Tasso tells us in his
letters that Sperone Speroni, a great Italian wit who was
his contemporary, observed of Virgil and Tully that the
Latin orator endeavoured to imitate the copiousness of
185 Homer the Greek poet, and that the Latin poet made it
his business to reach the conciseness of Demosthenes
the Greek orator. Virgil therefore being so very sparing
of his words, and leaving so much to be imagined by
the reader, can never be translated as he ought in any
190 modern tongue. To make him copious is to alter his
character, and to translate him line for line is impossible, because the Latin is naturally a more succinct language than either the Italian, Spanish, French, or even
than the English, which by reason of its monosyllables
195 is far the most compendious of them; Virgil is much the
closest of any Roman poet, and the Latin hexameter has
more feet than the English heroic.

Besides all this, an author has the choice of his own
thoughts and words, which a translator has not; he is
200 confined by the sense of the inventor to those expressions which are the nearest to it: so that Virgil,
studying brevity and having the command of his own

---

176. close] compact, pithy (*OED* 13c).

177. Hannibal Caro's in the Italian] The translation of *Aen.* by Annibale Caro
(1581). D. was to be more critical of it in the 'Discourse Concerning Satire'
(1693) and the 'Dedication of the *Aeneis*' (*Works* iv 15, v 324).

181. Tasso tells us] in his *Discorsi del Poema Eroico* (1594) (Ker).

language, could bring those words into a narrow compass which a translator cannot render without circumlo-
205   cutions. In short, they who have called him the torture
of grammarians might also have called him the plague
of translators, for he seems to have studied not to be
translated. I own that endeavouring to turn his 'Nisus
and Euryalus' as close as I was able, I have performed
210   that episode too literally; that giving more scope to
'Mezentius and Lausus', that version which has more of
the majesty of Virgil has less of his conciseness; and all
that I can promise for myself is only that I have done
both better than Ogilby, and perhaps as well as Caro.
215   So that methinks I come like a malefactor to make a
speech upon the gallows, and to warn all other poets by
my sad example from the sacrilege of translating Virgil.
Yet by considering him so carefully as I did before my
attempt, I have made some faint resemblance of him,
220   and had I taken more time might possibly have succeeded better, but never so well as to have satisfied
myself.

He who excels all other poets in his own language,
were it possible to do him right, must appear above
225   them in our tongue, which, as my Lord Roscommon
justly observes, approaches nearest to the Roman in its
majesty: nearest, indeed, but with a vast interval
betwixt them. There is an inimitable grace in Virgil's
words, and in them principally consists that beauty
230   which gives so unexpressible a pleasure to him who best
understands their force. This diction of his, I must once
again say, is never to be copied, and since it cannot, he
will appear but lame in the best translation. The turns of
his verse, his breakings, his propriety, his numbers and
235   his gravity I have as far imitated as the poverty of our
language and the hastiness of my performance would

205–6. the torture of grammarians] Virgil was supposed to have introduced two
riddles near the end of *Ecl.* iii to torture the grammarians (*Works*).
225–6. Roscommon . . . observes] 'When in Triumphant state the *British Muse*/
True to her *self* shall *Barb'rous* aid *refuse*./ And in that *Roman Majesty* appear,/
Which none knows better and none *Comes* so *near*' (24).
227. nearest . . . interval] Echoing Virgil: *longo sed proximo interuallo* ('next,
but by a long interval'; *Aen.* v 320); cp. 'Nisus and Euryalus' l. 46.
234. breakings] probably caesuras.

allow. I may seem sometimes to have varied from his sense, but I think the greatest variations may be fairly deduced from him, and where I leave his commentators
240 it may be I understand him better: at least, I writ without consulting them in many places. But two particular lines in 'Mezentius and Lausus' I cannot so easily excuse; they are indeed remotely allied to Virgil's sense, but they are too like the trifling tenderness of Ovid, and
245 were printed before I had considered them enough to alter them. The first of them I have forgotten, and cannot easily retrieve, because the copy is at the press; the second is this:

When Lausus died, I was already slain.

250 This appears pretty enough at first sight, but I am convinced for many reasons that the expression is too bold, that Virgil would not have said it, though Ovid would. The reader may pardon it, if he please, for the freeness of the confession, and instead of that and the former
255 admit these two lines which are more according to the author:

Nor ask I life, nor fought with that design;
As I had used my fortune, use thou thine.

Having with much ado got clear of Virgil, I have in
260 the next place to consider the genius of Lucretius, whom I have translated more happily in those parts of him which I undertook. If he was not of the best age of Roman poetry, he was at least of that which preceded it; and he himself refined it to that degree of perfection,
265 both in the language and the thoughts, that he left an easy task to Virgil, who, as he succeeded him in time, so he copied his excellencies: for the method of the *Georgics* is plainly derived from him. Lucretius had chosen a subject naturally crabbed; he therefore adorned

---

246. The first of them] perhaps 'Mezentius and Lausus' l. 116.

249. When . . . slain] See 'Mezentius and Lausus' ll. 227–8*n*.

262. not of the best age] Lucretius (*c*.94–55 BC) preceded the great poets of Augustan Rome: Virgil (70–19 BC), Horace (65–8 BC) and Ovid (43 BC to AD 17).

269. a subject naturally crabbed] The subject of *De Rerum Natura* is a philosophical discussion of the physical phenomena of the natural world.

270   it with poetical descriptions, and precepts of morality in
      the beginning and ending of his books; which you see
      Virgil has imitated with great success in those four
      books, which in my opinion are more perfect in their
      kind than even his divine *Aeneids*. The turn of his verse
275   he has likewise followed, in those places which Lucre-
      tius has most laboured, and some of his very lines he has
      transplanted into his own works without much vari-
      ation. If I am not mistaken, the distinguishing character
      of Lucretius (I mean of his soul and genius) is a certain
280   kind of noble pride, and positive assertion of his
      opinions. He is everywhere confident of his own
      reason, and assuming an absolute command not only
      over his vulgar reader but even his patron Memmius.
      For he is always bidding him attend, as if he had the rod
285   over him, and using a magisterial authority while he
      instructs him. From his time to ours I know none so
      · like him as our poet and philosopher of Malmesbury.
      This is that perpetual dictatorship which is exercised by
      Lucretius, who though often in the wrong yet seems to
290   deal *bona fide* with his reader, and tells him nothing but
      what he thinks; in which plain sincerity I believe he
      differs from our Hobbes, who could not but be con-
      vinced, or at least doubt of, some eternal truths which
      he has opposed. But for Lucretius, he seems to disdain
295   all manner of replies, and is so confident of his cause
      that he is beforehand with his antagonists, urging for
      them whatever he imagined they could say, and leaving
      them, as he supposes, without an objection for the

273. more perfect] For D.'s admiration for *Geo.* above *Aen.* see *AM* 'Account'
ll. 218–19 and the 'Dedication of the *Georgics*' (*Works* v 137).
283. vulgar] unsophisticated (OED 10).   *Memmius*] the addressee of Lucretius' poem.
287. our poet and philosopher] Thomas Hobbes (1588–1679), born in Malmes-
bury, Wiltshire. Many contemporaries thought that Hobbes's manner of
arguing was too dogmatic. He was widely suspected of atheism.
293. doubt of] i.e. be doubtful about, instead of absolutely rejecting.   *some
eternal truths*] For example, Hobbes in *Leviathan* (1651) argued against the idea
of an immortal, incorporeal soul. His mechanist and materialist philosophy
has affinities with the Epicureanism of Lucretius, though D. does not equate
their systems as others did, e.g. Creech in the preface to his translation of
Lucretius (1682) sig. b3ᵛ (*Works*).

future. All this too with so much scorn and indignation
300 as if he were assured of the triumph before he entered
into the lists. From this sublime and daring genius of his
it must of necessity come to pass that his thoughts must
be masculine, full of argumentation, and that sufficiently warm. From the same fiery temper proceeds
305 the loftiness of his expressions, and the perpetual torrent of his verse, where the barrenness of his subject
does not too much constrain the quickness of his fancy.
For there is no doubt to be made but that he could have
been everywhere as poetical as he is in his descriptions
310 and in the moral part of his philosophy, if he had not
aimed more to instruct in his system of nature than to
delight. But he was bent upon making Memmius a
materialist, and teaching him to defy an invisible
power: in short, he was so much an atheist that he
315 forgot sometimes to be a poet. These are the considerations which I had of that author before I attempted to
translate some parts of him, and accordingly I laid by
my natural diffidence and scepticism for a while, to take
up that dogmatical way of his which, as I said, is so
320 much his character as to make him that individual poet.
As for his opinions concerning the mortality of the soul,
they are so absurd that I cannot if I would believe them.
I think a future state demonstrable even by natural arguments; at least, to take away rewards and punishments
325 is only a pleasing prospect to a man who resolves be-
forehand not to live morally. But on the other side, the
thought of being nothing after death is a burden unsup-
portable to a virtuous man, even though a heathen. We
naturally aim at happiness, and cannot bear to have
330 it confined to the shortness of our present being,
especially when we consider that virtue is generally
unhappy in this world, and vice fortunate. So that 'tis
hope of futurity alone that makes this life tolerable, in

313. *materialist*] one who believes that the world is composed entirely of
matter, without spirit.
318. *scepticism*] Here, the ability to see both sides of a question and to keep
different hypotheses in play (see Harth 5–9).
321. *mortality of the soul*] expounded in 'Lucretius: Against the Fear of Death'.
323–4. *by natural arguments*] From reasoning based on the laws of nature,
rather than from divine revelation; cp. *RL* ll. 54–61.

expectation of a better. Who would not commit all the
335 excesses to which he is prompted by his natural inclina-
tions, if he may do them with security while he is alive,
and be uncapable of punishment after he is dead! If he be
cunning and secret enough to avoid the laws, there is no
band of morality to restrain him, for fame and repu-
340 tation are weak ties: many men have not the least sense
of them; powerful men are only awed by them as they
conduce to their interest, and that not always when a
passion is predominant; and no man will be contained
within the bounds of duty when he may safely trans-
345 gress them. These are my thoughts abstractedly, and
without entering into the notions of our Christian faith,
which is the proper business of divines.

But there are other arguments in this poem, which I
have turned into English, not belonging to the mor-
350 tality of the soul, which are strong enough to a reasonable man to make him less in love with life, and consequently in less apprehensions of death. Such as are the
natural satiety proceeding from a perpetual enjoyment
of the same things, the inconveniencies of old age which
355 make him uncapable of corporeal pleasures, the decay
of understanding and memory which render him contemptible and useless to others; these and many other
reasons so pathetically urged, so beautifully expressed,
so adorned with examples, and so admirably raised by
360 the *prosopopeia* of Nature, who is brought in speaking
to her children with so much authority and vigour,
deserve the pains I have taken with them, which I hope
have not been unsuccessful, or unworthy of my author.
At least I must take the liberty to own that I was pleased
365 with my own endeavours, which but rarely happens to
me, and that I am not dissatisfied upon the review of
anything I have done in this author.

'Tis true, there is something, and that of some
moment, to be objected against my Englishing 'The
370 Nature of Love' from the fourth book of Lucretius; and

---

339. band] chain, fetter (*OED* 1).
360. prosopopeia] personification; Creech uses the word in the margin of his
translation (*Works*). Nature's speech forms ll. 123–62 in D.'s 'Lucretius:
Against the Fear of Death'.

I can less easily answer why I translated it than why
I thus translated it. The objection arises from the
obscenity of the subject, which is aggravated by the too
lively and alluring delicacy of the verses. In the first
375 place, without the least formality of an excuse, I own it
pleased me: and let my enemies make the worst they
can of this confession. I am not yet so secure from that
passion but that I want my author's antidotes against it.
He has given the truest and most philosophical account
380 both of the disease and remedy which I ever found in
any author, for which reasons I translated him. But it
will be asked why I turned him into this luscious English (for I will not give it a worse word); instead of an
answer, I would ask again of my supercilious adver-
385 saries whether I am not bound when I translate an
author to do him all the right I can, and to translate him
to the best advantage? If to mince his meaning, which I
am satisfied was honest and instructive, I had either
omitted some part of what he said, or taken from the
390 strength of his expression, I certainly had wronged him;
and that freeness of thought and words being thus cashiered in my hands, he had no longer been Lucretius. If
nothing of this kind be to be read, physicians must not
study nature, anatomies must not be seen, and some-
395 what I could say of particular passages in books, which
to avoid profaneness I do not name. But the intention
qualifies the act, and both mine and my author's were to
instruct as well as please. 'Tis most certain that barefaced bawdry is the poorest pretence to wit imaginable;
400 if I should say otherwise, I should have two great auth-

378. but that I want] that I do not need.
382. luscious] voluptuous, lascivious (OED 4). ·
384. supercilious] severe in judgement, censorious (OED 2).
387. mince] diminish, take away from (OED 3).
389. omitted some part] *Pace Works*, Creech had not omitted this portion of
Lucretius.
391. cashiered] made void, annulled (OED 4).
394. anatomies] dissected bodies (OED 2).
395. books] i.e. in the Bible.
398–9. barefaced bawdry] D. quotes the Earl of Mulgrave's *An Essay upon
Poetry* (published anonymously 1682): 'Bawdry barefac'd, that poor pretence
to Wit' (6).

orities against me: the one is the *Essay on Poetry*, which I
publicly valued before I knew the author of it, and with
the commendation of which my Lord Roscommon so
happily begins his *Essay on Translated Verse*; the other is
405 no less than our admired Cowley, who says the same
thing in other words, for in his 'Ode concerning Wit' he
writes thus of it:

> Much less can that have any place
> At which a virgin hides her face:
410 Such dross the fire must purge away; 'tis just
> The author blush, there where the reader must.

Here indeed Mr Cowley goes farther than the *Essay*,
for he asserts plainly that obscenity has no place in wit;
the other only says 'tis a poor pretence to it, or an ill sort
415 of wit which has nothing more to support it than barefaced ribaldry, which is both unmannerly in itself and
fulsome to the reader. But neither of these will reach
my case: for in the first place, I am only the translator,
not the inventor, so that the heaviest part of the censure
420 falls upon Lucretius before it reaches me; in the next
place, neither he nor I have used the grossest words, but
the cleanliest metaphors we could find to palliate the
broadness of the meaning, and, to conclude, have
carried the poetical part no farther than the philosophi-
425 cal exacted. There is one mistake of mine which I will
not lay to the printer's charge, who has enough to
answer for in false pointings; 'tis in the word 'viper': I
would have the verse run thus,

> The scorpion, love, must on the wound be bruised.

430 There are a sort of blundering half-witted people who
make a great deal of noise about a verbal slip, though
Horace would instruct them better in true criticism:

---

403. commendation] Roscommon's *Essay* begins: 'Happy that Author, whose
correct Essay/ *Repairs* so well our Old *Horatian* way' (1).
406. 'Ode concerning Wit'] Cowley's 'Ode. *Of Wit*' (*Poems* 16–18).
417. fulsome] offensive, disgusting (*OED* 6).   *reach*] affect, apply to (*OED*
7b).
427. pointings] punctuation.
429. The scorpion ... bruised] See 'Lucretius: Concerning the Nature of Love'
l. 26n.

—non ego paucis
offendor maculis, quas aut incuria fudit
435   aut humana parum cavit natura.

True judgement in poetry, like that in painting, takes a
view of the whole together, whether it be good or not,
and where the beauties are more than the faults, concludes for the poet against the little judge: 'tis a sign that
440   malice is hard driven when 'tis forced to lay hold on a
word or syllable; to arraign a man is one thing, and to
cavil at him is another. In the midst of an ill-natured
generation of scribblers, there is always justice enough
left in mankind to protect good writers, and they too
445   are obliged, both by humanity and interest, to espouse
each other's cause against false critics, who are the
common enemies. This last consideration puts me in
mind of what I owe to the ingenious and learned translator of Lucretius; I have not here designed to rob him
450   of any part of that commendation which he has so justly
acquired by the whole author whose fragments only fall
to my portion. What I have now performed is no more
than I intended above twenty years ago. The ways of
our translation are very different: he follows him more
455   closely than I have done, which became an interpreter
of the whole poem. I take more liberty, because it best
suited with my design, which was to make him as
pleasing as I could. He had been too voluminous had he
used my method in so long a work, and I had certainly

433–5. 'I do not take offence at a few blots which a careless hand has let drop,
or human frailty has failed to avert' (Horace, *Ars Poetica* ll. 351–3). D. omits
Horace's preceding conditional line ('where many good things shine in a
poem'), and so changes his subjunctive *offendar* to the indicative *offendor.*
Kinsley's silent emendation here is therefore wrong.

448. translator] Thomas Creech (1659–1700); his translation of Lucretius was
published in 1682 (reprinted three times in 1683); his Horace (dedicated to D.)
in 1684; and his Theocritus (with an abridged translation of René Rapin's *De
Carmine Pastorali*) in 1684, Idyll xvi being dedicated to D. He contributed
commendatory verses to *RL* in 1682. D. complimented him on his translations of Horace and Theocritus in the Preface to *Cleomenes* (1692). For D.
and Creech see also James Winn, *PQ* lxxi (1992) 47–68.

453. intended above twenty years ago] This intention is otherwise unknown. For
D.'s earlier interest in Lucretius see headnote to 'Lucretius: The Beginning of
the First Book'.

460   taken his had I made it my business to translate the
       whole. The preference then is justly his, and I join with
       Mr Evelyn in the confession of it, with this additional
       advantage to him, that his reputation is already estab-
       lished in this poet, mine is to make its fortune in the
465   world. If I have been anywhere obscure in following
       our common author, or if Lucretius himself is to be
       condemned, I refer myself to his excellent annotations,
       which I have often read, and always with some new
       pleasure.
470   My preface begins already to swell upon me, and
       looks as if I were afraid of my reader by so tedious
       a bespeaking of him, and yet I have Horace and Theocri-
       tus upon my hands; but the Greek gentleman shall
       quickly be dispatched, because I have more business
475   with the Roman.
           That which distinguishes Theocritus from all other
       poets, both Greek and Latin, and which raises him even
       above Virgil in his *Eclogues*, is the inimitable tenderness
       of his passions, and the natural expression of them in
480   words so becoming of a pastoral. A simplicity shines
       through all he writes: he shows his art and learning by
       disguising both. His shepherds never rise above their
       country education in their complaints of love: there is
       the same difference betwixt him and Virgil as there is
485   betwixt Tasso's *Aminta* and the *Pastor Fido* of Guarini.
       Virgil's shepherds are too well read in the philosophy of

462. Evelyn] John Evelyn (who had published a translation of *De Rerum
Natura* Book I in 1656) had written commendatory verses to the 1683 edition
of Creech's translation, along with Nahum Tate, Thomas Otway, Aphra
Behn, Richard Duke, Jacob Tonson and others.
472. bespeaking] addressing (*OED* 6).
480. so becoming of a pastoral] Renaissance commentators had argued about
whether pastoral ought to aim at lofty subjects and elegant expression. Rapin
said that Theocritus 'designdly makes his Shepherds discourse in the *Doric*
i.e. the Rustick Dialect, sometimes scarce true Grammar . . . that the Manners may the more exactly suit with the Persons . . . who of themselves are
rude and unpolish: And this proves that they scandalously err, who make
their Shepherds appear polite and elegant' (*De Carmine Pastorali*, tr. by
Creech in *The Idylliums of Theocritus* (1684) 32).
481–2. shows his art . . . by disguising] adapting the anonymous Latin tag *ars est
celare artem* ('the art lies in concealing the art').

Epicurus and of Plato, and Guarini's seem to have been bred in courts. But Theocritus and Tasso have taken theirs from cottages and plains. It was said of Tasso, in
490 relation to his similitudes, 'Mai esce del bosco': that he never departed from the woods, that is, all his comparisons were taken from the country. The same may be said of our Theocritus; he is softer than Ovid, he touches the passions more delicately, and performs all
495 this out of his own fond, without diving into the arts and sciences for a supply. Even his Doric dialect has an incomparable sweetness in its clownishness, like a fair shepherdess in her country russet talking in a Yorkshire tone. This was impossible for Virgil to imitate, because
500 the severity of the Roman language denied him that advantage. Spenser has endeavoured it in his *Shepherd's Calendar*, but neither will it succeed in English, for which reason I forbore to attempt it; for Theocritus writ to Sicilians, who spoke that dialect, and I direct this part
505 of my translations to our ladies, who neither understand nor will take pleasure in such homely expressions. I proceed to Horace.

Take him in parts, and he is chiefly to be considered in his three different talents, as he was a critic, a satirist
510 and a writer of odes. His morals are uniform, and run through all of them; for let his Dutch commentators say what they will, his philosophy was Epicurean, and he made use of gods and providence only to serve a turn in poetry. But since neither his criticisms (which are the

489. It was said] The source of this comment is unknown; *Works* suggests that it may have been an adaptation of J. C. Scaliger's comment on Virgil in *Poetices Libri Septem* (1561) 150.

495. fond] supply, store (*OED* 2).

496. dialect] D. discusses this again in his 'Dedication of Virgil's *Pastorals*' (*Works* v 6).

498. russet] garments made from coarse reddish brown cloth.

511. Dutch commentators] As *Works* notes, Daniel Heinsius in the essay 'De Satyra Horatiana' in his 1629 edition of Horace had argued that Horace was not an Epicurean but an Eclectic (206–18); for D.'s later view see his 'Discourse Concerning Satire' (*Works* iv 56).

512. Epicurean] For the philosophy of Epicurus see headnote to 'Lucretius: The Beginning of the First Book'.

514. his criticisms] Horace's critical writings are principally his *Ars Poetica*; *Serm.* I iv, I x, II i; and *Epist.* II i.

515   most instructive of any that are written in this art) nor
       his satires (which are incomparably beyond Juvenal's, if
       to laugh and rally is to be preferred to railing and dec-
       laiming) are any part of my present undertaking, I con-
       fine myself wholly to his odes. These are also of several
520   sorts: some of them are panegyrical, others moral, the
       rest jovial or (if I may so call them) Bacchanalian. As
       difficult as he makes it, and as indeed it is, to imitate
       Pindar, yet in his most elevated flights and in the sudden
       changes of his subject with almost imperceptible con-
525   nexions, that Theban poet is his master. But Horace is
       of the more bounded fancy, and confines himself
       strictly to one sort of verse or stanza in every ode. That
       which will distinguish his style from all other poets is
       the elegance of his words, and the numerousness of his
530   verse; there is nothing so delicately turned in all the
       Roman language. There appears in every part of his
       diction, or (to speak English) in all his expressions, a
       kind of noble and bold purity. His words are chosen
       with as much exactness as Virgil's, but there seems to
535   be a greater spirit in them. There is a secret happiness
       attends his choice, which in Petronius is called *curiosa*
       felicitas, and which I suppose he had from the *feliciter*
       audere of Horace himself. But the most distinguishing
       part of all his character seems to me to be his briskness,

516–18. D. returns to the comparison of Horace and Juvenal in the 'Discourse Concerning Satire' (*Works* iv 49–69).

517. rally] use good-humoured ridicule, banter.

523. Pindar] Greek lyric poet (518–438 BC). Cowley, imitating him in his
pindaric odes, had confessed: '*Pindar* is imitable by none' ('The Praise of
Pindar', *Poems* 178). The problem lay in Pindar's irregular verse, rhapsodic
style and obscure transitions.

529. numerousness] 'Probably a unique usage, meaning metrical perfection'
(Watson).

532. diction] choice of words (from Latin *dictio*; OED 4, citing D.'s *Fables*
(1700) as its first example). Although the word had been used before (e.g. in
Sidney's *Apology for Poetry* (1581)), D. may be (or may believe he is) innovat-
ing in applying it specifically to a poet's choice of vocabulary. (The OED is
insufficiently clear here.)

536–7. curiosa felicitas] 'careful felicity' (Petronius, *Satyricon* 118, applied to
Horace).

537–8. feliciter audere] 'to venture happily' (Horace, *Epist.* II i 166; actually
'*audet*').

540 his jollity, and his good humour, and those I have
chiefly endeavoured to copy; his other excellencies I
confess are above my imitation. One ode which infinitely pleased me in the reading I have attempted to
translate in pindaric verse: 'tis that which is inscribed to
545 the present Earl of Rochester, to whom I have particular
obligations which this small testimony of my gratitude
can never pay. 'Tis his darling in the Latin, and I have
taken some pains to make it my masterpiece in English;
for which reason I took this kind of verse, which allows
550 more latitude than any other. Everyone knows it was
introduced into our language in this age by the happy
genius of Mr Cowley. The seeming easiness of it has
made it spread, but it has not been considered enough to
be so well cultivated. It languishes in almost every hand
555 but his, and some very few whom (to keep the rest in
countenance) I do not name. He, indeed, has brought it
as near perfection as was possible in so short a time. But
if I may be allowed to speak my mind modestly, and
without injury to his sacred ashes, somewhat of the
560 purity of English, somewhat of more equal thoughts,
somewhat of sweetness in the numbers, in one word,
somewhat of a finer turn and more lyrical verse is yet
wanting. As for the soul of it, which consists in the
warmth and vigour of fancy, the masterly figures, and
565 the copiousness of imagination, he has excelled all
others in this kind. Yet if the kind itself be capable of
more perfection, though rather in the ornamental parts
of it than the essential, what rules of morality or respect
have I broken in naming the defects, that they may
570 hereafter be amended? Imitation is a nice point, and
there are few poets who deserve to be models in all they

542. *One ode*] 'Horace: *Odes* III xxix'.

545. *Earl of Rochester*] Laurence Hyde (see *AA* ll. 888–97n). D. had written to
him, probably in March 1684, in an attempt to have his salary paid (*Letters*
20–2; for the likely date see Edward L. Saslow, *MPh* lxxii (1975) 248–55). If
this succeeded it might explain the 'particular obligations' referred to here.
See also 'Virgil's Ninth Eclogue' headnote.

551–2. *introduced . . . by . . . Cowley*] Cowley had pioneered pindaric verse in
English through his translations and imitations of Pindar in his *Poems* (1653).

560. *equal*] adequate, fitting (*OED* 3).

write. Milton's *Paradise Lost* is admirable, but am I
therefore bound to maintain that there are no flats
amongst his elevations, when 'tis evident he creeps
575 along sometimes for above an hundred lines together?
Cannot I admire the height of his invention, and the
strength of his expression, without defending his anti-
quated words and the perpetual harshness of their
sound? 'Tis as much commendation as a man can bear,
580 to own him excellent; all beyond it is idolatry. Since
Pindar was the prince of lyric poets, let me have leave to
say that in imitating him our numbers should for the
most part be lyrical; for variety, or rather where the
majesty of the thought requires it, they may be
585 stretched to the English heroic of five feet, and to the
French Alexandrine of six. But the ear must preside,
and direct the judgement to the choice of numbers.
Without the nicety of this, the harmony of pindaric
verse can never be complete; the cadency of one line
590 must be a rule to that of the next, and the sound of the
former must slide gently into that which follows, without leaping from one extreme into another. It must be
done like the shadowings of a picture, which fall by
degrees into a darker colour. I shall be glad if I have so
595 explained myself as to be understood, but if I have not,
quod nequeo dicere et sentio tantum must be my excuse.
There remains much more to be said on this subject, but

572. Paradise Lost] Milton's poem had been published in 1667; D. had based
his opera *The State of Innocence* on it (written 1674, published 1677). Apart
from Marvell's prefatory poem to the 1674 edition of *PL*, and Lee's to *The
State of Innocence*, D.'s comments here form the first published literary criticism of *PL*. Roscommon was to add a passage on *PL* to the second edition of
his *Essay on Translated Verse* (1685) 25–6. D. returns to Milton in the 'Discourse Concerning Satire' (*Works* iv 14–15). For Milton's influence on *Sylvae*
see the notes, *passim*, and J. R. Mason.
580. idolatry] Echoing Jonson on Shakespeare: 'I lov'd the man, and doe
honour his memory (on this side Idolatry) as much as any' (*Ben Jonson* viii
583–4; Watson).
585. heroic] heroic line, iambic pentameter.
588. nicety] precision, subtlety.
589. cadency] cadence, rhythm.
593–4. See ll. 51–8n.
596. quod . . . tantum] 'What I cannot say, and only feel' (adapted from
Juvenal, *Satire* vii 56: *qualem nequeo monstrare* ['show'] *et sentio tantum*).

to avoid envy I will be silent. What I have said is the
general opinion of the best judges, and in a manner has
600 been forced from me by seeing a noble sort of poetry so
happily restored by one man, and so grossly copied by
almost all the rest. A musical ear, and a great genius, if
another Mr Cowley could arise, in another age may
bring it to perfection. In the mean time,

605   —fungar vice cotis, acutum
        reddere quae ferrum valet, expers ipsa secandi.

I hope it will not be expected from me that I should
say anything of my fellow undertakers in this miscellany. Some of them are too nearly related to me to be
610 commended without suspicion of partiality; others I am
sure need it not; and the rest I have not perused. To
conclude, I am sensible that I have written this too
hastily and too loosely; I fear I have been tedious, and,
which is worse, it comes out from the first draught, and
615 uncorrected. This I grant is no excuse, for it may be
reasonably urged, why did he not write with more
leisure, or, if he had it not (which was certainly my
case) why did he attempt to write on so nice a subject?
The objection is unanswerable, but in part of recom-
620 pense let me assure the reader that in hasty productions
he is sure to meet with an author's present sense, which
cooler thoughts would possibly have disguised. There
is undoubtedly more of spirit, though not of judgement, in these uncorrect essays, and consequently
625 though my hazard be the greater, yet the reader's
pleasure is not the less.

                                              John Dryden

605–6. fungar . . . secandi] 'I will play the part of a whetstone, which makes
steel sharp, but of itself cannot cut' (Horace, *Ars Poetica* ll. 304–5); previously
used by D. as the epigraph to *EDP* (Watson).
609. too nearly related] D.'s son Charles contributed the Latin verses *Horti
Arlingtoniani* ('On the Earl of Arlington's Gardens'), and his brother-in-law
Sir Robert Howard translated 'Of Natures Changes' from Lucretius.
618. nice] difficult to settle, demanding close consideration (*OED* 9).
624. essays] trials, attempts; rough drafts.

91 Nisus and Euryalus (from Virgil's *Aeneid* V and IX)

Date and publication. Printed in 1685 in *Sylvae* (*SR* 10 January; advertised in *The Observator* 1 January); reprinted 1692. Incorporated with revisions into D.'s 1697 translation of Virgil (printed here as a modernized parallel text). For possible date of composition see headnote to 'Preface to *Sylvae*'.

Context. The story of Nisus and Euryalus is referred to by D. in 'To the Memory of Mr Oldham' ll. 9–10, also composed in 1684, and there are verbal echoes between the two pieces (see notes). The death of a promising young man mourned by an elder is also presented in 'Mezentius and Lausus', which again has echoes of D.'s poem on Oldham (ll. 101–2n). The episode of Nisus and Euryalus was seen as an example of ideal male friendship by Thomas Otway in his verse letter to Richard Duke: 'Next *Nisus* and *Euryalus* we admire,/ Their gentle Friendship, and their Martial fire;/ We praise their valour 'cause yet matcht by none,/ And Love their Friendship, so much like our own' (published in *MP* (1684) 221).

Sources. D. translates *Aen.* v 286–361 and ix 174–449. For the editions and other translations which he used see headnote to 'Virgil's Fourth Eclogue'.

The entire episode of Nisus and Euryalus, translated from the Fifth and Ninth Books of Virgil's *Aeneids*

Connection of the first part of the episode in the fifth book with the rest of the foregoing poem:

Aeneas, having buried his father Anchises in Sicily, and setting sail from thence in search of Italy, is driven by a storm on the same coasts from whence he departed; after a year's wandering, he is hospitably received by his friend Acestes, King of that part of the island, who was born of Trojan parentage. He applies himself to celebrate the memory of his father with divine honours, and accordingly institutes funeral games, and appoints prizes for those who should conquer in them. One of these games was a foot race, in which Nisus and Euryalus were engaged amongst other Trojans and Sicilians.

From thence his way the Trojan hero bent,
Into a grassy plain with mountains pent,
Whose brows were shaded with surrounding wood;
Full in the midst of this fair valley stood
5   A native theatre, which rising slow
By just degrees, o'erlooked the ground below.
A numerous train attend in solemn state;
High on the new-raised turf their leader sate.
Here those who in the rapid race delight
10   Desire of honour and the prize invite;
The Trojans and Sicilians mingled stand
With Nisus and Euryalus, the foremost of the band:
Euryalus with youth and beauty crowned,
Nisus for friendship to the boy renowned.
15   Diores next, of Priam's regal race,
Then Salius, joined with Patron, took his place:
But from Epirus one derived his birth,
The other owed it to Arcadian earth.

Revised text from 1697 edition:

From thence his way the Trojan hero bent
Into the neighbouring plain, with mountains pent,
375   Whose sides were shaded with surrounding wood;
Full in the midst of this fair valley stood
A native theatre, which rising slow
By just degrees, o'erlooked the ground below.
High on a sylvan throne the leader sate;
380   A numerous train attend in solemn state.
Here those that in the rapid course delight
Desire of honour and the prize invite;
The rival runners without order stand,
The Trojans mixed with the Sicilian band.
385   First Nisus, with Euryalus, appears—
Euryalus a boy of blooming years,
With sprightly grace and equal beauty crowned—
Nisus for friendship to the youth renowned.
Diores next, of Priam's royal race,
390   Then Salius, joined with Patron, took their place;
(But Patron in Arcadia had his birth,
And Salius his from Acarnanian earth:)

¶91. *8.* Cp. Milton: 'High on a throne of royal state . . ./ Satan exalted sat'
(*PL* ii 1–5; J. R. Mason); cp. *MF* ll. 107–9.

      Then two Sicilian youths; the name of this
20 Was Helimus, of that was Panopes:
      Two jolly huntsmen in the forest bred,
      And owning old Acestes for their head;
      With many others of obscurer name
      Whom time has not delivered o'er to fame.
25 To these Aeneas in the midst arose,
      And pleasingly did thus his mind expose:
      'Not one of you shall unrewarded go; ⎫
      On each I will two Cretan spears bestow, ⎬
      Pointed with polished steel; a battle-axe too, ⎭
30 With silver studded; these in common share,
      The foremost three shall olive garlands wear;
      The victor who shall first the race obtain
      Shall for his prize a well-breathed courser gain,
      Adorned with trappings; to the next in fame
35 The quiver of an Amazonian dame,
      With feathered Thracian arrows well supplied,
      Hung on a golden belt, and with a jewel tied;

Revised text from 1697 edition:

      Then two Sicilian youths—the names of these
      Swift Helymus, and lovely Panopes
395 (Both jolly huntsmen, both in forests bred,
      And owning old Acestes for their head),
      With several others of ignobler name,
      Whom time has not delivered o'er to fame.
        To these the hero thus his thoughts explained,
400 In words which general approbation gained:
      'One common largess is for all designed,
      The vanquished and the victor shall be joined:
      Two darts of polished steel and Gnossian wood,
      A silvered, studded axe, alike bestowed.
405 The foremost three have olive-wreaths decreed,
      The first of these obtains a stately steed
      Adorned with trappings; and the next in fame,
      The quiver of an Amazonian dame,
      With feathered Thracian arrows well supplied: ⎫
410 A golden belt shall gird his manly side, ⎬
      Which with a sparkling diamond shall be tied. ⎭

33. *well-breathed*] sound of wind.

The third this Grecian helmet must content.'
He said. To their appointed base they went,
40 With beating hearts th' expected sign receive,
And starting all at once, the station leave.
Spread out as on the wings of winds they flew,
And seized the distant goal with eager view;
Shot from the crowd, swift Nisus all o'erpassed,
45 Not storms nor thunder equal half his haste:
The next, but though the next yet far disjoined,
Came Salius; then, a distant space behind,
Euryalus the third;
Next Helymus, whom young Diores plied,
50 Step after step, and almost side by side,
His shoulders pressing, and in longer space
Had won, or left at least a doubtful race.
Now spent, the goal they almost reach at last,
When eager Nisus, hapless in his haste,
55 Slipped first, and slipping fell upon the plain,
Moist with the blood of oxen lately slain;

Revised text from 1697 edition:

The third this Grecian helmet shall content.'
He said. To their appointed base they went,
With beating hearts th' expected sign receive,
415 And starting all at once, the barrier leave.
Spread out as on the wingèd winds they flew,
And seized the distant goal with greedy view;
Shot from the crowd, swift Nisus all o'erpassed,
Nor storms, nor thunder, equal half his haste:
420 The next, but, though the next, yet far disjoined,
Came Salius; and Euryalus behind;
Then Helymus, whom young Diores plied,
Step after step, and almost side by side,
His shoulders pressing, and in longer space
425 Had won, or left at least a dubious race.
    Now spent, the goal they almost reach at last,
When eager Nisus, hapless in his haste,
Slipped first, and slipping fell upon the plain,
Soaked with the blood of oxen newly slain;

38. Cp. Ogilby: 'This *Graecian* helmet shall the third content'.
48. Imitating Virgil's half-line: *tertius Euryalus* (l. 322).
52. Cp. Ogilby: 'or doubtfull left the race'.

The careless victor had not marked his way,
But treading where the treacherous puddle lay
His heels flew up, and on the grassy floor
60 He fell, besmeared with filth and holy gore.
Nor mindless then Euryalus of thee,
Nor of the sacred bonds of amity,
He strove th' immediate rival to oppose,
And caught the foot of Salius as he rose;
65 So Salius lay extended on the plain:
Euryalus springs out the prize to gain,
And cuts the crowd; applauding peals attend
The conqueror to the goal, who conquered through
  his friend.
Next Helymus, and then Diores came,
70 By two misfortunes now the third in fame;
But Salius enters, and exclaiming loud
For justice, deafens and disturbs the crowd,
Urges his cause may in the court be heard,
And pleads the prize is wrongfully conferred.

Revised text from 1697 edition:

430 The careless victor had not marked his way,
But treading where the treacherous puddle lay
His heels flew up, and on the grassy floor
He fell, besmeared with filth and holy gore.
Not mindless then Euryalus of thee,
435 Nor of the sacred bonds of amity,
He strove th' immediate rival's hope to cross,
And caught the foot of Salius as he rose;
So Salius lay extended on the plain:
Euryalus springs out the prize to gain,
440 And leaves the crowd; applauding peals attend
The victor to the goal, who vanquished by his friend.
Next Helymus, and then Diores came,
By two misfortunes made the third in fame.
 But Salius enters, and exclaiming loud
445 For justice, deafens and disturbs the crowd,
Urges his cause may in the court be heard,
And pleads the prize is wrongfully conferred.

70. *By two misfortunes*] D.'s addition, strengthening the role of Fortune:
similarly he adds 'Where Fortune placed it' and 'her errors to amend' (ll. 82–
3), and brings 'fortune' twice into ll. 93–4 where Virgil has it only once. For
the significance of Fortune for D. see 'Horace: *Odes* III xxix' ll. 73–87*n*.

75 But favour for Euryalus appears,
    His blooming beauty and his graceful tears
    Had bribed the judges to protect his claim:
    Besides, Diores does as loud exclaim,
    Who vainly reaches at the last reward
80 If the first palm on Salius be conferred.
    Then thus the Prince: 'Let no disputes arise;
    Where Fortune placed it, I award the prize.
    But give me leave her errors to amend,
    At least to pity a deserving friend.'
85 Thus having said,
    A lion's hide, amazing to behold,
    Pond'rous with bristles and with paws of gold
    He gave the youth, which Nisus grieved to view. ⎤
    'If such rewards to vanquished men are due,'   ⎬
90 Said he, 'and falling is to rise by you,   ⎦
    What prize may Nisus from your bounty claim,
    Who merited the first rewards and fame?
    In falling, both did equal fortune try;
    Would fortune make me fall as happily!'

Revised text from 1697 edition:

    But favour for Euryalus appears,
    His blooming beauty, with his tender tears
450 Had bribed the judges to protect his claim:
    Besides, Diores does as loud exclaim,
    Who vainly reaches at the last reward
    If the first palm on Salius be conferred.
    Then thus the Prince: 'Let no disputes arise;
455 Where Fortune placed it, I award the prize.
    But Fortune's errors give me leave to mend,
    At least to pity my deserving friend.'
    He said, and, from among the spoils, he draws
    (Ponderous with shaggy mane and golden paws)
460 A lion's hide: to Salius this he gives:
    Nisus with envy sees the gift, and grieves.
    'If such rewards to vanquished men are due,'
    He said, 'and falling is to rise by you,
    What prize may Nisus from your bounty claim,
465 Who merited the first rewards and fame?
    In falling, both an equal fortune tried;
    Would Fortune for my fall so well provide!'

95 With this he pointed to his face, and showed
    His hands and body all besmeared with blood.
    Th' indulgent father of the people smiled,
    And caused to be produced a massy shield
    Of wondrous art, by Didymaon wrought,
100 Long since from Neptune's bars in triumph brought.
    With this the graceful youth he gratified,
    Then the remaining presents did divide.

Revised text from 1697 edition:

    With this he pointed to his face, and showed
    His hands and all his habit smeared with blood.
470 Th' indulgent father of the people smiled,
    And caused to be produced an ample shield
    Of wondrous art, by Didymaon wrought,
    Long since from Neptune's bars in triumph brought.
    This given to Nisus, he divides the rest,
475 And equal justice in his gifts expressed.

Connection of the remaining part of the episode, translated out of the ninth book of Virgil's Aeneids, *with the foregoing part of the story:*

The war being now broken out betwixt the Trojans and Latins, and Aeneas being overmatched in numbers by his enemies, who were aided by King Turnus, he fortifies his camp, and leaves in it his young son Ascanius under the direction of his chief councillors and captains, while he goes in person to beg succours from King Evander and the Tuscans. Turnus takes advantage of his absence and assaults his camp; the Trojans in it are reduced to great extremities, which gives the poet the occasion of continuing this admirable episode, wherein he describes the friendship, the generosity, the adventures and the death of Nisus and Euryalus.

    The Trojan camp the common danger shared;
    By turns they watched the walls, and kept the nightly
       guard.

Revised text from 1697 edition:

    Commissioned by their absent Prince to share
    The common danger, and divide the care.
    The soldiers draw their lots, and, as they fall,
220 By turns relieve each other on the wall.

105 To warlike Nisus fell the gate by lot
     (Whom Hyrtacus on huntress Ida got,
     And sent to sea, Aeneas to attend);
     Well could he dart the spear, and shafts unerring send.
     Beside him stood Euryalus, his ever-faithful friend.

110 No youth in all the Trojan host was seen
     More beautiful in arms, or of a nobler mien;
     Scarce was the down upon his chin begun,
     One was their friendship, their desire was one;
     With minds united in the field they warred,

115 And now were both by choice upon the guard.
     Then Nisus thus:
     'Or do the gods this warlike warmth inspire,
     Or makes each man a god of his desire?
     A noble ardour boils within my breast,

120 Eager of action, enemy of rest,

Revised text from 1697 edition:

     Nigh where the foes their utmost guards advance,
     To watch the gate was warlike Nisus' chance.
     His father Hyrtacus, of noble blood;
     His mother was a huntress of the wood,

225 And sent him to the wars. Well could he bear
     His lance in fight, and dart the flying spear;
     But better skilled unerring shafts to send.
     Beside him stood Euryalus, his friend—
     Euryalus, than whom the Trojan host

230 No fairer face or sweeter air could boast:
     Scarce had the down to shade his cheeks begun.
     One was their care, and their delight was one:
     One common hazard in the war they shared,
     And now were both by choice upon the guard.

235   Then Nisus thus: 'Or do the gods inspire
     This warmth, or make we gods of our desire?
     A generous ardour boils within my breast,
     Eager of action, enemy to rest:

109. ever-faithful] The first of a series of additions through which D. emphasises the bond between the friends: others are l. 113 (translating *amor unus erat* ('their love was one'); 'those dear eyes' (l. 153); 'pious friends' (l. 154); 'I would not perish all' (l. 158); 'lover's' (l. 160); 'whom living he adored' (l. 428); 'lover' (l. 455, perhaps translating *amans* ('loving') instead of Virgil's *amens* ('mad')); l. 473; 'lover' (l. 482); 'on his dear breast' (l. 483).

117–18. Or . . . Or] Either . . . Or.

118. Cp. Ogilby (1649): 'Or makes each man a god of's own desire?'.

That urges me to fight, or undertake
Some deed that may my fame immortal make.
Thou seest the foe secure; how faintly shine
Their scattered fires, the most in sleep supine,
125 Dissolved in ease, and drunk with victory;
The few awake the fuming flaggon ply,
All hushed around. Now hear what I revolve
Within my mind, and what my labouring thoughts
    resolve.
Our absent lord both camp and council mourn;
130 By message both would hasten his return:
The gifts proposed if they confer on thee
(For fame is recompense enough to me)
Methinks beneath yon hill I have espied
A way that safely will my passage guide.'
135 Euryalus stood listening while he spoke,
With love of praise and noble envy struck;

Revised text from 1697 edition:

    This urges me to fight, and fires my mind
240 To leave a memorable name behind.
    Thou seest the foe secure; how faintly shine
    Their scattered fires; the most, in sleep supine
    Along the ground, an easy conquest lie:
    The wakeful few the fuming flagon ply:
245 All hushed around. Now hear what I revolve—
    A thought unripe—and scarcely yet resolve.
    Our absent Prince both camp and council mourn;
    By message both would hasten his return:
    If they confer what I demand on thee
250 (For fame is recompense enough for me)
    Methinks beneath yon hill I have espied
    A way that safely will my passage guide.'
      Euryalus stood listening while he spoke,
    With love of praise and noble envy struck;

---

122. may my fame immortal make] D.'s addition.
126. D.'s addition.

Then to his ardent friend exposed his mind: ⎫
'All this alone, and leaving me behind! ⎬
Am I unworthy, Nisus, to be joined? ⎭
140 Think'st thou my share of honour I will yield,
Or send thee unassisted to the field?
Not so my father taught my childhood arms,
Born in a siege, and bred amongst alarms:
Nor is my youth unworthy of my friend,
145 Or of the heaven-born hero I attend.
The thing called life with ease I can disclaim,
And think it oversold to purchase fame.'
To whom his friend:
'I could not think, alas, thy tender years
150 Would minister new matter to my fears:
Nor is it just thou shouldst thy wish obtain.
So Jove in triumph bring me back again
To those dear eyes, or if a god there be
To pious friends propitious more than he.
155 But if some one, as many sure there are,
Of adverse accidents in doubtful war,

Revised text from 1697 edition:

255 Then to his ardent friend exposed his mind: ⎫
'All this alone, and leaving me behind! ⎬
Am I unworthy, Nisus, to be joined? ⎭
Think'st thou I can my share of glory yield,
Or send thee unassisted to the field?
260 Not so my father taught my childhood arms,
Born in a siege, and bred among alarms:
Nor is my youth unworthy of my friend,
Nor of the heaven-born hero I attend.
The thing called life with ease I can disclaim,
265 And think it oversold to purchase fame.'
Then Nisus thus: 'Alas! thy tender years
Would minister new matter to my fears.
So may the gods who view this friendly strife,
Restore me to thy loved embrace with life,
270 Condemned to pay my vows (as sure I trust),
This thy request is cruel and unjust.
But if some chance—as many chances are,
And doubtful hazards, in the deeds of war—

145. *heaven-born hero*] Aeneas, son of the goddess Venus.

If one should reach my head, there let it fall
And spare thy life: I would not perish all.
Thy youth is worthy of a longer date.
160 Do thou remain to mourn thy lover's fate,
To bear my mangled body from the foe,
Or buy it back, and funeral rites bestow;
Or if hard Fortune shall my corpse deny,
Those dues with empty marble to supply.
165 O let not me the widow's tears renew,
Let not a mother's curse my name pursue;
Thy pious mother, who in love to thee
Left the fair coast of fruitful Sicily,
Her age committing to the seas and wind,
170 When every weary matron stayed behind.'
To this Euryalus: 'Thou plead'st in vain,
And but delay'st the cause thou canst not gain;
No more, 'tis loss of time.' With that he wakes
The nodding watch; each to his office takes.
175 The guard relieved, in company they went
To find the council at the royal tent.

Revised text from 1697 edition:

If one should reach my head, there let it fall,
275 And spare thy life: I would not perish all.
Thy bloomy youth deserves a longer date:
Live thou to mourn thy love's unhappy fate,
To bear my mangled body from the foe,
Or buy it back, and funeral rites bestow;
280 Or if hard Fortune shall those dues deny,
Thou canst at least an empty tomb supply.
O let not me the widow's tears renew,
Nor let a mother's curse my name pursue—
Thy pious parent, who for love of thee
285 Forsook the coasts of friendly Sicily,
Her age committing to the seas and wind,
When every weary matron stayed behind.'
To this Euryalus: 'You plead in vain,
And but protract the cause you cannot gain.
290 No more delays, but haste!' With that he wakes
The nodding watch; each to his office takes.
The guard relieved, the generous couple went
To find the council at the royal tent.

159. *date*] duration, term of life (*OED* 4).
165, 169. D.'s additions, strengthening the mother's role; cp. l. 264*n*.

Now every living thing lay void of care,
And sleep, the common gift of nature, share.
Meantime the Trojan peers in council sate, ⎫
180 And called their chief commanders to debate ⎬
The weighty business of th' endangered state: ⎭
What next was to be done, who to be sent
T' inform Aeneas of the foe's intent.
In midst of all the quiet camp they held
185 Nocturnal council; each sustains a shield
Which his o'erlaboured arm can hardly rear,
And leans upon a long projected spear.
Now Nisus and his friend approach the guard, ⎫
And beg admittance, eager to be heard, ⎬
190 Th' affair important, not to be deferred. ⎭
Ascanius bids them be conducted in,
Then thus, commanded, Nisus does begin:
'Ye Trojan fathers, lend attentive ears,
Nor judge our undertaking by our years.
195 The foes securely drenched in sleep and wine
Their watch neglect; their fires but thinly shine:

Revised text from 1697 edition:

All creatures else forgot their daily care,
295 And sleep, the common gift of nature, share;
Except the Trojan peers, who wakeful sate
In nightly council for th' endangered state.
They vote a message to their absent chief,
Show their distress, and beg a swift relief.
300 Amid the camp a silent seat they chose,
Remote from clamour, and secure from foes.
On their left arms their ample shields they bear,
The right reclined upon the bending spear.
Now Nisus and his friend approach the guard, ⎫
305 And beg admission, eager to be heard, ⎬
Th' affair important, not to be deferred. ⎭
Ascanius bids 'em be conducted in,
Ordering the more experienced to begin.
Then Nisus thus: 'Ye fathers, lend your ears;
310 Nor judge our bold attempt beyond our years.
The foe, securely drenched in sleep and wine,
Neglect their watch; the fires but thinly shine;

179. sate] sat.
187. projected] protruding.
195. securely] carelessly, without apprehension (*OED* 1).

And where the smoke in thickening vapours flies,
Covering the plain, and clouding all the skies,
Betwixt the spaces we have marked a way,
200   Close by the gate, and coasting by the sea;
This passage undisturbed and unespied
Our steps will safely to Aeneas guide;
Expect each hour to see him back again,
Loaded with spoils of foes in battle slain.
205   Snatch we the lucky minute while we may.
Nor can we be mistaken in the way,
For hunting in the vale we oft have seen
The rising turrets with the stream between,
And know its winding course, with every ford.'
210   He paused, and old Alethes took the word:
'Our country gods in whom our trust we place
Will yet from ruin save the Trojan race,
While we behold such springing worth appear
In youth so brave, and breasts so void of fear.'

Revised text from 1697 edition:

And where the smoke in cloudy vapours flies,
Covering the plain, and curling to the skies,
315   Betwixt two paths which at the gate divide, ⎫
Close by the sea, a passage we have spied, ⎬
Which will our way to great Aeneas guide. ⎭
Expect each hour to see him safe again,
Loaded with spoils of foes in battle slain.
320   Snatch we the lucky minute while we may.
Nor can we be mistaken in the way;
For hunting in the vale, we both have seen
The rising turrets, and the stream between,
And know the winding course, with every ford.'
325   He ceased; and old Alethes took the word:
'Our country gods in whom our trust we place
Will yet from ruin save the Trojan race,
While we behold such dauntless worth appear
In dawning youth, and souls so void of fear.'

200. *coasting*] skirting (*OED* 2).
210. *took the word*] began speaking (*OED* 28).
211. *country*] country's (the noun is frequently used attributively: *OED* 13).
213. *springing*] rising, developing (*OED* 1b).

215 With this he took the hand of either boy,
   Embraced them closely both, and wept for joy.
   'Ye brave young men, what equal gifts can we,
   What recompense for such desert, decree?
   The greatest, sure, and best you can receive
220 The gods, your virtue and your fame will give:
   The rest our grateful general will bestow,
   And young Ascanius till his manhood owe.'
   'And I, whose welfare in my father lies,'
   Ascanius adds, 'by all the deities,
225 By our great country, and our household gods,
   By hoary Vesta's rites and dark abodes,
   Adjure you both; on you my fortune stands:
   That and my faith I plight into your hands.
   Make me but happy in his safe return
230 (For I no other loss but only his can mourn),
   Nisus, your gift shall two large goblets be
   Of silver, wrought with curious imagery,

Revised text from 1697 edition:

330 Then into tears of joy the father broke: ⎫
   Each in his longing arms by turns he took,   ⎬
   Panted and paused; and thus again he spoke: ⎭
   'Ye brave young men, what equal gifts can we,
   In recompense of such desert, decree?
335 The greatest, sure, and best you can receive,
   The gods and your own conscious worth will give.
   The rest our grateful general will bestow,
   And young Ascanius, till his manhood, owe.'
      'And I, whose welfare in my father lies,'
340 Ascanius adds 'by the great deities,
   By my dear country, by my household gods,
   By hoary Vesta's rites and dark abodes,
   Adjure you both; on you my fortune stands:
   That and my faith I plight into your hands.
345 Make me but happy in his safe return,
   Whose wanted presence I can only mourn,
   Your common gift shall two large goblets be
   Of silver, wrought with curious imagery,

217. *equal*] adequate (*OED* 3).
226. *hoary*] venerable, time-honoured (*OED* 1c).   *Vesta*] Roman goddess
of the hearth.
232. *curious*] elaborate, carefully worked (*OED* 7).

And high embossed, which when old Priam reigned
My conquering sire at sacked Arisba gained;
235   And more, two tripods cast in antique mould,
With two great talents of the finest gold;
Besides a bowl which Tyrian art did grave,
The present that Sidonian Dido gave.
But if in conquered Italy we reign,
240   When spoils by lot the victors shall obtain,
Thou saw'st the courser by proud Turnus pressed:
That and his golden arms, and sanguine crest
And shield, from lot exempted, thou shalt share;
With these, twelve captive damsels young and fair,
245   Male slaves as many, well appointed all
With vests and arms, shall to thy portion fall:
And last, a fruitful field to thee shall rest,
The large demesnes the Latian king possessed.

Revised text from 1697 edition:

And high embossed, which when old Priam reigned
350   My conquering sire at sacked Arisba gained;
And more, two tripods cast in antique mould,
With two great talents of the finest gold;
Beside a costly bowl, engraved with art,
Which Dido gave, when first she gave her heart.
355   But if in conquered Italy we reign,
When spoils by lot the victor shall obtain,
Thou saw'st the courser by proud Turnus pressed:
That, Nisus, and his arms, and nodding crest,
And shield, from chance exempt, shall be thy share; ⎫
360   Twelve labouring slaves, twelve handmaids young and ⎬
      fair,   ⎪
All clad in rich attire, and trained with care;   ⎭
And, last, a Latian field with fruitful plains,
And a large portion of the king's domains.

236. *talents*] The talent was a Greek and Roman weight; its value varied, but
was commonly approx. 80lb.
238. *Sidonian Dido*] Queen of Carthage, daughter of the King of Tyre, a city
south of Sidon on the coast of Phoenicia.
246. *vests*] clothing (*OED* 1d).
247. *rest*] remain due.

But thou, whose years are more to mine allied,
250 No fate my vowed affection shall divide
From thee, O wondrous youth: be ever mine,
Take full possession, all my soul is thine;
My life's companion, and my bosom friend,
One faith, one fame, one fate shall both attend.
255 My peace shall be committed to thy care,
And to thy conduct my concerns in war.'
Then thus the bold Euryalus replied:
'Whatever fortune, good or bad, betide,
The same shall be my age, as now my youth;
260 No time shall find me wanting to my truth.
This only from your bounty let me gain
(And this not granted, all rewards are vain):

Revised text from 1697 edition:

But thou, whose years are more to mine allied,
365 No fate my vowed affection shall divide
From thee, heroic youth: be wholly mine,
Take full possession, all my soul is thine;
One faith, one fame, one fate, shall both attend:
My life's companion, and my bosom friend.
370 My peace shall be committed to thy care,
And to thy conduct my concerns in war.'
    Then thus the young Euryalus replied:
'Whatever fortune, good or bad, betide,
The same shall be my age, as now my youth;
375 No time shall find me wanting to my truth.
This only from your goodness let me gain
(And this ungranted, all rewards are vain):

249–54. D. elaborates and heightens Virgil: *te uero, mea quem spatiis propriori-bus aetas/ insequitur, uenerande puer, iam pectore toto/ accipio et comitem casus complector in omnis./ nulla meis sine te quaeretur gloria rebus* (*Aen.* ix 275–8: 'you indeed, who approach my age more closely, revered youth, I now receive with my whole heart, and embrace you as my companion in all that may chance. I shall never seek any glory without you'). D.'s passage has similari-ties with 'To the Memory of Mr Oldham': *allied, soul* and the rhymes *mine/ thine* recur in ll. 3–4, and with l. 254 here cp. l. 5.

251. *wondrous*] An emotive translation of *uenerande* ('revered'), recalling Cowley's 'Wondrous young Man' in his 'On the Death of Mr. *William Hervey*' (*Poems* 36); cp. 'To the Memory of Mr Oldham' l. 11*n.*

253. Cp. Cowley: 'My sweet *Companion*, and my gentle *Peere*' (*Poems* 33).

Of Priam's royal race my mother came,
And sure the best that ever bore the name,
265 Whom neither Troy nor Sicily could hold
From me departing, but o'erspent and old
My fate she followed; ignorant of this
Whatever danger, neither parting kiss
Nor pious blessing taken, her I leave,
270 And in this only act of all my life deceive.
By this your hand and conscious night I swear,
My youth so sad a farewell could not bear.
Be you her patron, fill my vacant place
(Permit me to presume so great a grace),
275 Support her age, forsaken and distressed:
That hope alone will fortify my breast
Against the worst of fortunes and of fears.'
He said; th' assistants shed presaging tears,

Revised text from 1697 edition:

Of Priam's royal race my mother came,
And sure the best that ever bore the name,
380 Whom neither Troy nor Sicily could hold
From me departing, but o'erspent and old
My fate she followed; ignorant of this
Whatever danger, neither parting kiss
Nor pious blessing taken, her I leave,
385 And in this only act of all my life deceive.
By this right hand and conscious night I swear,
My soul so sad a farewell could not bear.
Be you her comfort, fill my vacant place
(Permit me to presume so great a grace),
390 Support her age, forsaken and distressed:
That hope alone will fortify my breast
Against the worst of fortunes and of fears.'
He said. The moved assistants melt in tears.

264. D.'s addition; cp. ll. 165, 169*n*.
266. *o'erspent*] worn out, exhausted (*OED* 1).
267-9. i.e. 'I leave her unaware of the danger which I am about to incur (whatever that may be) without having received a parting kiss or blessing from her.'
271. *conscious*] knowing human secrets (*OED* 2).
278. *assistants*] bystanders (*OED* 1).

But above all, Ascanius, moved to see
280   That image of paternal piety;
Then thus replied:
'So great beginnings in so green an age
Exact that faith which firmly I engage;
Thy mother all the privilege shall claim
285   Creusa had, and only want the name.
Whate'er event thy enterprise shall have,
'Tis merit to have borne a son so brave.
By this my head a sacred oath I swear
(My father used it): what returning here,
290   Crowned with success, I for thyself prepare,
Thy parent and thy family shall share.'
He said; and weeping while he spoke the word,
From his broad belt he drew a shining sword,
Magnificent with gold: Lycaon made,
295   And in an ivory scabbard sheathed the blade.

Revised text from 1697 edition:

Then thus Ascanius, wonder-struck to see
395   That image of his filial piety:
'So great beginnings in so green an age
Exact the faith which I again engage;
Thy mother all the dues shall justly claim
Creusa had, and only want the name.
400   Whate'er event thy bold attempt shall have,
'Tis merit to have borne a son so brave.
Now by my head a sacred oath I swear
(My father used it): what returning here,
Crowned with success, I for thyself prepare,
405   That, if thou fail, shall thy loved mother share.'
He said; and weeping while he spoke the word,
From his broad belt he drew a shining sword,
Magnificent with gold: Lycaon made,
And in an ivory scabbard sheathed the blade.

---

280. paternal piety] that reverence for the gods, nation and family (Latin *pietas*)
characteristic of his father Aeneas.
282. D.'s addition.
285. Creusa] trisyllabic; Ascanius' mother.
286. event] outcome.
289–90. i.e. 'those rewards which I prepare for your successful return here'.

This was his gift, while Mnestheus did provide ⎞
For Nisus' arms a grisly lion's hide,   ⎟
And true Alethes changed with him his helm of ⎬
   temper tried.   ⎠
Thus armed they went: the noble Trojans wait
300 Their going forth, and follow to the gate.
With prayers and vows above the rest appears
Ascanius, manly far above his years,
And messages committed to their care,
Which all in winds were lost, and empty air.
305 The trenches first they passed, then took their way
Where their proud foes in pitched pavilions lay,
To many fatal ere themselves were slain.
The careless host dispersed upon the plain
They found, who drunk with wine supinely snore;
310 Unharnessed chariots stand upon the shore:
Midst wheels, and reins, and arms, the goblet by,
A medley of debauch and war they lie.
Observing, Nisus showed his friend the sight,
Then thus: 'Behold a conquest without fight.

Revised text from 1697 edition:

410 This was his gift. Great Mnestheus gave his friend
A lion's hide, his body to defend;
And good Alethes furnished him, beside,
With his own trusty helm, of temper tried.
   Thus armed they went: the noble Trojans wait
415 Their issuing forth, and follow to the gate
With prayers and vows. Above the rest appears
Ascanius, manly far beyond his years,
And messages committed to their care,
Which all in winds were lost, and flitting air.
420   The trenches first they passed, then took their way
Where their proud foes in pitched pavilions lay,
To many fatal ere themselves were slain.
·They found the careless host dispersed upon the plain,
Who, gorged, and drunk with wine, supinely snore.
425 Unharnessed chariots stand along the shore:
Amidst the wheels and reins, the goblet by,
A medley of debauch and war they lie.
Observing, Nisus showed his friend the sight:
'Behold a conquest gained without a fight.

298. *of temper tried*] of proven temper.
314. *Behold . . . fight*] D.'s addition.

315 Occasion calls the sword to be prepared:
    Our way lies there; stand thou upon the guard,
    And look behind, while I securely go
    To cut an ample passage through the foe.'
    Softly he spoke, then stalking took his way
320 With his drawn sword where haughty Rhamnes lay,
    His head raised high, on tapestry beneath,
    And heaving from his breast he puffed his breath:
    A king and prophet by King Turnus loved,
    But fate by prescience cannot be removed.
325 Three sleeping slaves he soon subdues, then spies
    Where Rhemus with his proud retinue lies:
    His armour-bearer first, and next he kills
    His charioteer, entrenched betwixt the wheels
    And his loved horses; last invades their lord:
330 Full on his neck he aims the fatal sword,
    The gasping head flies off, a purple flood
    Flows from the trunk that wallows in the blood,

Revised text from 1697 edition:

430 Occasion offers, and I stand prepared:
    There lies our way: be thou upon the guard,
    And look around, while I securely go
    And hew a passage through the sleeping foe.'
    Softly he spoke, then striding took his way
435 With his drawn sword where haughty Rhamnes lay,
    His head raised high, on tapestry beneath,
    And heaving from his breast he drew his breath:
    A king and prophet by King Turnus loved,
    But fate by prescience cannot be removed.
440 Him and his sleeping slaves he slew; then spies
    Where Rhemus with his rich retinue lies.
    His armour-bearer first, and next he kills
    His charioteer, entrenched betwixt the wheels
    And his loved horses; last invades their lord:
445 Full on his neck he drives the fatal sword,
    The gasping head flies off, a purple flood
    Flows from the trunk that welters in the blood,

326. *retinue*] accented on the second syllable in the seventeenth century.
329. *invades*] sets upon, assaults (*OED* 5).

Which by the spurning heels dispersed around,
The bed besprinkles, and bedews the ground.
335 Then Lamyrus with Lamus, and the young
Serranus, who with gaming did prolong
The night: oppressed with wine and slumber lay ⎤
The beauteous youth, and dreamt of lucky play— ⎬
More lucky had it been protracted till the day. ⎦
340 The famished lion thus with hunger bold
O'erleaps the fences of the nightly fold,
The peaceful flock devours, and tears, and draws;
Wrapped up in silent fear they lie, and pant beneath his
paws.
Nor with less rage Euryalus employs
345 The vengeful sword, nor fewer foes destroys;
But on th' ignoble crowd his fury flew,
Which Fadus, Hebesus and Rhaetus slew,
With Abaris. In sleep the rest did fall,
But Rhaetus waking, and observing all,

Revised text from 1697 edition:

Which by the spurning heels dispersed around,
The bed besprinkles, and bedews the ground.
450 Lamus the bold and Lamyrus the strong,
He slew, and then Serranus fair and young.
From dice and wine the youth retired to rest,
And puffed the fumy god from out his breast:
Ev'n then he dreamt of drink and lucky play—
455 More lucky, had it lasted till the day.
The famished lion thus with hunger bold
O'erleaps the fences of the nightly fold,
And tears the peaceful flocks: with silent awe
Trembling they lie, and pant beneath his paw.
460 Nor with less rage Euryalus employs
The wrathful sword, or fewer foes destroys;
But on th' ignoble crowd his fury flew:
He Fadus, Hebesus and Rhœtus slew.
Oppressed with heavy sleep the former fall,
465 But Rhœtus wakeful, and observing all,

333. *spurning*] kicking.
341. Cp. Milton: 'Leaps o'er the fence with ease into the fold' (*PL* iv 187; J. R. Mason); cp. 'Horace: *Odes* I iii' ll. 32–3*n*.
343. D. elaborates Virgil's *mutum metu* ('silent with fear').

350   Behind a mighty jar he slunk for fear:
      The sharp-edged iron found and reached him there;
      Full as he rose he plunged it in his side,
      The cruel sword returned in crimson dyed.
      The wound a blended stream of wine and blood
355   Pours out; the purple soul comes floating in the flood.
      Now where Messapus quartered they arrive,
      The fires were fainting there, and just alive;
      The warlike horses tied in order fed.
      Nisus the discipline observed, and said:
360   'Our eagerness of blood may both betray:
      Behold the doubtful glimmering of the day,
      Foe to these nightly thefts: no more, my friend,
      Here let our glutted execution end;
      A lane through slaughtered bodies we have made.'
365   The bold Euryalus, though loath, obeyed;
      Rich arms and arras which they scattered find,
      And plate, a precious load they leave behind.

                  Revised text from 1697 edition:

      Behind a spacious jar he slinked for fear:
      The fatal iron found and reached him there;
      For, as he rose, it pierced his naked side,
      And, reeking, thence returned in crimson dyed.
470   The wound pours out a stream of wine and blood;
      The purple soul comes floating in the flood.
          Now where Messapus quartered they arrive,
      The fires were fainting there, and just alive;
      The warrior-horses tied in order fed.
475   Nisus observed the discipline, and said:
      'Our eager thirst of blood may both betray:
      And see, the scattered streaks of dawning day,
      Foe to nocturnal thefts: no more, my friend,
      Here let our glutted execution end;
480   A lane through slaughtered bodies we have made.'
      The bold Euryalus, though loath, obeyed.
      Of arms, and arras, and of plate, they find
      A precious load: but these they leave behind.

355. *flood*] stream (OED 2).
366. *arras*] tapestry.

Yet fond of gaudy spoils, the boy would stay
To make the proud caparisons his prey,
370 Which decked a neighbouring steed.
Nor did his eyes less longingly behold
The girdle studded o'er with nails of gold
Which Rhamnes wore: this present long ago
On Remulus did Caedicus bestow,
375 And absent joined in hospitable ties.
He dying to his heir bequeathed the prize,
Till by the conquering Rutuli oppressed
He fell, and they the glorious gift possessed.
These gaudy spoils Euryalus now bears,
380 And vainly on his brawny shoulders wears:
Messapus' helm he found amongst the dead,
Garnished with plumes, and fitted to his head.
They leave the camp and take the safest road.
Meantime a squadron of their foes abroad,
385 Three hundred horse, with bucklers armed, they spied,
Whom Volscens by the King's command did guide:

Revised text from 1697 edition:

Yet fond of gaudy spoils, the boy would stay ⎫
485 To make the rich caparison his prey, ⎬
Which on the steed of conquered Rhamnes lay. ⎭
Nor did his eyes less longingly behold
The girdle-belt, with nails of burnished gold.
This present Cædicus the rich bestowed
490 On Remulus, when friendship first they vowed,
And, absent, joined in hospitable ties;
He dying to his heir bequeathed the prize,
Till by the conquering Ardean troops oppressed
He fell, and they the glorious gift possessed.
495 These glittering spoils (now made the victor's gain)
He to his body suits, but suits in vain.
Messapus' helm he finds among the rest,
And laces on, and wears the waving crest.
Proud of their conquest, prouder of their prey,
500 They leave the camp, and take the ready way.
But far they had not passed, before they spied
Three hundred horse, with Volscens for their guide.

To Turnus these were from the city sent,
And to perform their message sought his tent.
Approaching near their utmost lines they draw,
390   When bending t'wards the left their captain saw
The faithful pair, for through the doubtful shade ⎤
His glittering helm Euryalus betrayed,   ⎬
On which the moon with full reflection played. ⎦
   ' 'Tis not for nought' cried Volscens from the crowd,
395   'These men go there', then raised his voice aloud:
'Stand, stand! why thus in arms? and whither bent?
From whence, to whom, and on what errand sent?'
Silent they make away, and haste their flight
To neighbouring woods, and trust themselves to
     night.
400   The speedy horsemen spur their steeds to get
'Twixt them and home, and every path beset,
And all the windings of the well-known wood;
Black was the brake, and thick with oak it stood,
With fern all horrid, and perplexing thorn,
405   Where tracks of bears had scarce a passage worn.

Revised text from 1697 edition:

The Queen a legion to King Turnus sent, ⎤
But the swift horse the slower foot outwent, ⎬
505   And now, advancing, sought the leader's tent. ⎦
They saw the pair; for, through the doubtful shade, ⎤
His shining helm Euryalus betrayed,   ⎬
On which the moon with full reflection played. ⎦
   ' 'Tis not for nought' cried Volscens from the crowd,
510   'These men go there', then raised his voice aloud:
'Stand, stand! why thus in arms? and whither bent?
From whence, to whom, and on what errand sent?'
Silent they scud away, and haste their flight
To neighbouring woods, and trust themselves to night.
515   The speedy horse all passages belay,
And spur their smoking steeds to cross their way,
And watch each entrance of the winding wood.
Black was the forest: thick with beech it stood,
Horrid with fern, and intricate with thorn:
520   Few paths of human feet, or tracks of beasts, were worn.

404. *horrid*] bristling.   *perplexing*] entangling.

The darkness of the shades, his heavy prey,
And fear, misled the younger from his way;
But Nisus hit the turns with happier haste,
Who now, unknowing, had the danger passed,
410   And Alban lakes (from Alba's name so called)
Where King Latinus then his oxen stalled;
Till turning at the length he stood his ground,
And vainly cast his longing eyes around
For his lost friend.
415   'Ah wretch!' he cried, 'where have I left behind,
Where shall I hope th' unhappy youth to find?
Or what way take?' Again he ventures back,
And treads the mazes of his former track
Through the wild wood; at last he hears the noise
420   Of trampling horses, and the riders' voice.
The sound approached, and suddenly he viewed
His foes enclosing, and his friend pursued,
Forelaid, and taken, while he strove in vain
The covert of the neighbouring wood to gain.

Revised text from 1697 edition:

The darkness of the shades, his heavy prey,
And fear, misled the younger from his way;
But Nisus hit the turns with happier haste,
And thoughtless of his friend, the forest passed,
525   And Alban plains (from Alba's name so called)
Where King Latinus then his oxen stalled;
Till turning at the length he stood his ground,
And missed his friend, and cast his eyes around.
'Ah wretch!' he cried, 'where have I left behind
530   Th' unhappy youth? where shall I hope to find?
Or what way take?' Again he ventures back,
And treads the mazes of his former track.
He winds the wood, and, listening, hears the noise
Of trampling coursers, and the riders' voice.
535   The sound approached, and suddenly he viewed
The foes enclosing, and his friend pursued,
Forelaid, and taken, while he strove in vain
The shelter of the friendly shades to gain.

423. *Forelaid*] waylaid, ambushed.

425 What should he next attempt, what arms employ
With fruitless force to free the captive boy?
Or tempt unequal numbers with the sword,
And die by him whom living he adored?
Resolved on death, his dreadful spear he shook,
430 And casting to the moon a mournful look,
'Fair Queen', said he, 'who dost in woods delight, ⎱
Grace of the stars, and goddess of the night, ⎰
Be present, and direct my dart aright. ⎰
If e'er my pious father for my sake
435 Did on thy altars grateful offerings make,
Or I increased them with successful toils,
And hung thy sacred roof with savage spoils,
Through the brown shadows guide my flying spear
To reach this troop.' Then poising from his ear
440 The quivering weapon with full force he threw:
Through the divided shades the deadly javelin flew;
On Sulmo's back it splits, the double dart
Drove deeper onward and transfixed his heart.

Revised text from 1697 edition:

What should he next attempt, what arms employ,
540 What fruitless force, to free the captive boy?
Or desperate should he rush and lose his life,
With odds oppressed, in such unequal strife?
Resolved at length, his pointed spear he shook,
And casting on the moon a mournful look,
545 'Guardian of groves, and goddess of the night!
Fair Queen!' he said, 'direct my dart aright.
If e'er my pious father for my sake
Did grateful offerings on thy altars make,
Or I increased them with my sylvan toils,
550 And hung thy holy roofs with savage spoils,
Give me to scatter these.' Then from his ear
He poised, and aimed, and launched the trembling spear.
The deadly weapon, hissing from the grove,
Impetuous on the back of Sulmo drove;
555 Pierced his thin armour, drank his vital blood,
And in his body left the broken wood.

427. *tempt*] attempt.
431. *Queen*] Diana, the moon, and goddess of hunting.
433. *dart*] spear.
437. *savage*] wild; i.e. the spoils from hunting wild beasts.
438. *brown*] dark (*OED* 1).

He staggers round, his eyeballs roll in death,
445 And with short sobs he gasps away his breath.
All stand amazed; a second javelin flies
From his stretched arm, and hisses through the skies.
The lance through Tagus' temples forced its way,
And in his brain-pan warmly buried lay.
450 Fierce Volscens foams with rage, and gazing round
Descried no author of the fatal wound,
Nor where to fix revenge. 'But thou' he cries
'Shalt pay for both', and at the prisoner flies
With his drawn sword. Then, struck with deep
        despair,
455 That fatal sight the lover could not bear,
But from his covert rushed in open view,
And sent his voice before him as he flew:
'Me, me, employ your sword on me alone;
The crime confessed; the fact was all my own.
460 He neither could nor durst, the guiltless youth,
Ye moon and stars bear witness to the truth;
His only fault, if that be to offend,
Was too much loving his unhappy friend.'

Revised text from 1697 edition:

He staggers round, his eyeballs roll in death,
And with short sobs he gasps away his breath.
All stand amazed; a second javelin flies
560 With equal strength, and quivers through the skies.
This through thy temples, Tagus, forced the way,
And in the brain-pan warmly buried lay.
Fierce Volscens foams with rage, and gazing round
Descried not him who gave the fatal wound,
565 Nor knew to fix revenge. 'But thou' he cries
'Shalt pay for both,' and at the prisoner flies
With his drawn sword. Then, struck with deep despair,
That cruel sight the lover could not bear,
But from his covert rushed in open view,
570 And sent his voice before him as he flew:
'Me! me!' he cried, 'turn all your swords alone
On me—the fact confessed, the fault my own.
He neither could nor durst, the guiltless youth—
Ye moon and stars, bear witness to the truth!
575 His only crime (if friendship can offend)
Is too much love to his unhappy friend.'

459. *fact*] deed.

Too late, alas, he speaks:
465　The sword, which unrelenting fury guides,
　　Driven with full force had pierced his tender sides.
　　Down fell the beauteous youth, the gaping wound
　　Gushed out a crimson stream, and stained the ground.
　　His nodding neck reclines on his white breast,
470　Like a fair flower in furrowed fields oppressed
　　By the keen share, or poppy on the plain,
　　Whose heavy head is overcharged with rain.
　　Disdain, despair, and deadly vengeance vowed
　　Drove Nisus headlong on the hostile crowd;
475　Volscens he seeks, at him alone he bends,
　　Born back and pushed by his surrounding friends,
　　He still pressed on, and kept him still in sight,
　　Then whirled aloft his sword with all his might.
　　Th' unerring weapon flew, and winged with death
480　Entered his gaping mouth and stopped his breath.
　　Dying he slew, and staggering on the plain
　　Sought for the body of his lover slain;

Revised text from 1697 edition:

Too late he speaks: the sword, which fury guides,
　　Driven with full force, had pierced his tender sides.
　　Down fell the beauteous youth: the yawning wound
580　Gushed out a purple stream, and stained the ground.
　　His snowy neck reclines upon his breast,
　　Like a fair flower by the keen share oppressed,
　　Like a white poppy sinking on the plain,
　　Whose heavy head is overcharged with rain.
585　Despair, and rage, and vengeance justly vowed,
　　Drove Nisus headlong on the hostile crowd;
　　Volscens he seeks, on him alone he bends,
　　Borne back and bored by his surrounding friends,
　　Onward he pressed, and kept him still in sight,
590　Then whirled aloft his sword with all his might:
　　Th' unerring steel descended while he spoke,
　　Pierced his wide mouth, and through his weazon broke.
　　Dying, he slew; and staggered on the plain,
　　With swimming eyes he sought his lover slain;

473. D.'s addition.
475. bends] aims (*OED* 17).
480. his] i.e. Volscens'.

Then quietly on his dear breast he fell,
Content in death to be revenged so well.
485 O happy pair! For if my verse can give
Eternity, your fame shall ever live:
Fixed as the Capitol's foundation lies,
And spread where'er the Roman eagle flies.

Revised text from 1697 edition:

595 Then quiet on his bleeding bosom fell,
Content in death to be revenged so well.
O happy friends! For if my verse can give
Immortal life, your fame shall ever live:
Fixed as the Capitol's foundation lies,
600 And spread where'er the Roman eagle flies.

485–6. D. uses the Latin original of these lines as the epigraph to *Threnodia Augustalis*.

485. *happy*] Translating *Fortunati*; D. avoids 'fortunate' because its connotations for him are largely malevolent (see 'Horace: *Odes* III xxix' ll. 73–87*n*), and chooses *happy* because of its philosophical connotations (see 'Horace: *Epode* II' l. 1*n*).

487. *Capitol*] the national temple of the Romans, dedicated to Jupiter.

92 Mezentius and Lausus (from Virgil's *Aeneid* X)

Date and publication. Printed in 1685 in *Sylvae* (SR 10 January; advertised in *The Observator* 1 January); reprinted 1692. Incorporated with revisions into D.'s 1697 translation of Virgil (printed here as a modernized parallel text). For possible date of composition see headnote to 'Preface to *Sylvae*'.

Context. See headnote to 'Nisus and Euryalus'.

Sources. D. translates *Aen.* x 755–908. For the editions and other translations which he used see headnote to 'Virgil's Fourth Eclogue'.

The entire episode of Mezentius and Lausus, translated out of the Tenth Book of Virgil's *Aeneids*

Connection of the episode with the foregoing story:

Mezentius was King of Etruria, or Tuscany, from whence he was expelled by his subjects for his tyrannical government and cruelty, and a new king elected. Being thus banished he applies himself to King Turnus, in whose court he and his son Lausus take sanctuary. Turnus for the love of Lavinia making war with Aeneas, Mezentius engages in the cause of his benefactor, and performs many great actions, particularly in revenging himself on his late subjects, who now assisted Aeneas out of hatred to him. Mezentius is everywhere described by Virgil as an atheist; his son Lausus is made the pattern of filial piety and virtue; and the death of those two is the subject of this noble episode.

Thus equal deaths are dealt, and equal chance;
By turns they quit their ground, by turns advance;
Victors and vanquished in the various field,
Nor wholly overcome, nor wholly yield.
5   The gods from heaven survey the doubtful strife,
And mourn the miseries of human life.
Above the rest two goddesses appear,
Concerned for each: here Venus, Juno there.
Amidst the crowd infernal Ate shakes
10   Her scourge aloft, and hissing crest of snakes.
Once more Mezentius, with a proud disdain,
Brandished his spear, and rushed into the plain,
Where towering in the midmost ranks he stood,
Like vast Orion stalking o'er the flood,
15   When with his brawny breast he cuts the waves,
His shoulders scarce the topmost billow laves;
Or like a mountain ash, whose roots are spread
Deep fixed in earth, in clouds he hides his head:

Revised text from 1697 edition:

Thus equal deaths are dealt with equal chance:
By turns they quit their ground, by turns advance;
Victors and vanquished in the various field,
Nor wholly overcome, nor wholly yield.
1075   The gods from heaven survey the fatal strife,
And mourn the miseries of human life.
Above the rest two goddesses appear,
Concerned for each: here Venus, Juno there.
Amidst the crowd infernal Ate shakes
1080   Her scourge aloft, and crest of hissing snakes.
Once more the proud Mezentius, with disdain,
Brandished his spear, and rushed into the plain,
Where towering in the midmost ranks he stood,
Like tall Orion stalking o'er the flood,
1085   When with his brawny breast he cuts the waves,
His shoulders scarce the topmost billow laves;
Or like a mountain ash, whose roots are spread
Deep fixed in earth, in clouds he hides his head.

¶**92**. *3. various*] changeable (*OED* 1); cp. 'Horace: *Odes* III xxix' l. 77*n*.
4. Nor . . . nor] Neither . . . nor.
8. Throughout *Aen.* Venus favours the Trojans while Juno opposes them.
9. Ate] disyllabic; Infatuation, goddess of mischief in Greek mythology.
14. Orion] the giant hunter of Greek mythology.
16. laves] washes.

Thus armed, he took the field.
20   The Trojan Prince beheld him from afar
With joyful eyes, and undertook the war.
Collected in himself, and like a rock
Poised on his base, Mezentius stood the shock
Of his great foe: then measuring with his eyes
25   The space his spear could reach, aloud he cries:
'My own right hand and sword assist my stroke
(Those only gods Mezentius will invoke);
His armour from the Trojan pirate torn
Shall by my Lausus be in triumph worn.'
30   He said; and straight with all his force he threw
The massy spear, which hissing as it flew
Reached the celestial shield; that stopped the course,
But glancing thence the yet unbroken force
Took a new bent obliquely, and betwixt
35   The side and bowels famed Anthores fixed.

Revised text from 1697 edition:

The Trojan Prince beheld him from afar,
1090   And dauntless undertook the doubtful war.
Collected in his strength, and like a rock
Poised on his base, Mezentius stood the shock.
He stood, and, measuring first with careful eyes
The space his spear could reach, aloud he cries:
1095   'My strong right hand and sword assist my stroke
(Those only gods Mezentius will invoke);
His armour from the Trojan pirate torn
By my triumphant Lausus shall be worn.'
He said; and with his utmost force he threw
1100   The massy spear, which hissing as it flew
Reached the celestial shield; that stopped the course,
But glancing thence the yet unbroken force
Took a new bent obliquely, and betwixt
The side and bowels famed Anthores fixed.

20. Trojan Prince] Aeneas.
22. Collected in himself] Cp. Milton's description of Satan: 'Stood in himself collected' (*PL* ix 673; J. R. Mason).
27. D.'s elaboration; in Virgil Mezentius simply calls his right hand his god (*dextra mihi deus*).
32. celestial shield] In *Aen.* viii the god Vulcan forges a shield for Aeneas on which are depicted the deeds of his descendants; see 'The Speech of Venus to Vulcan'.

Anthores had from Argos travelled far,
Alcides' friend, and brother of the war,
Till, tired with toils, fair Italy he chose,
And in Evander's palace sought repose;
40 Now falling by another's wound, his eyes
He casts to heaven; on Argos thinks, and dies.
The pious Trojan then his javelin sent;
The shield gave way, through treble plates it went
Of solid brass, of linen trebly rolled,
45 And three bull hides which round the buckler fold;
All these it passed with unresisted course,
Transpierced his thigh, and spent its dying force.
The gaping wound gushed out a crimson flood:
The Trojan, glad with sight of hostile blood,
50 His falchion drew, to closer fight addressed,
And with new force his fainting foe oppressed.
His father's danger Lausus viewed with grief;
He sighed, he wept, he ran to his relief.

Revised text from 1697 edition:

1105 Anthores had from Argos travelled far,
Alcides' friend, and brother of the war,
Till, tired with toils, fair Italy he chose,
And in Evander's palace sought repose;
Now falling by another's wound, his eyes
1110 He casts to heaven; on Argos thinks, and dies,
      The pious Trojan then his javelin sent;
The shield gave way, through treble plates it went
Of solid brass, of linen trebly rolled,
And three bull hides which round the buckler fold;
1115 All these it passed, resistless in the course,
Transpierced his thigh, and spent its dying force.
The gaping wound gushed out a crimson flood:
The Trojan, glad with sight of hostile blood,
His falchion drew, to closer fight addressed,
1120 And with new force his fainting foe oppressed.
      His father's peril Lausus viewed with grief;
He sighed, he wept, he ran to his relief.

48. *flood*] stream.
50. *falchion*] sword.

And here, O wondrous youth, 'tis here I must
55   To thy immortal memory be just,
And sing an act so noble and so new,
Posterity shall scarce believe it true.
Pained with his wound, and useless for the fight,
The father sought to save himself by flight;
60   Encumbered, slow he dragged the spear along,
Which pierced his thigh, and in his buckler hung.
The pious youth, resolved to undergo   ⎫
The lifted sword, springs out to face his foe, ⎬
Protects his father, and prevents the blow.   ⎭
65   Shouts of applause ran ringing through the field
To see the son the vanquished father shield.
All fired with noble emulation strive,
And with a storm of darts to distance drive
The Trojan chief, who held at bay, from far
70   On his Vulcanian orb sustained the war.

Revised text from 1697 edition:

And here, heroic youth, 'tis here I must
To thy immortal memory be just,
1125   And sing an act so noble and so new,
Posterity will scarce believe 'tis true.
Pained with his wound, and useless for the fight,
The father sought to save himself by flight;
Encumbered, slow he dragged the spear along,
1130   Which pierced his thigh, and in his buckler hung.
The pious youth, resolved on death, below   ⎫
The lifted sword, springs forth to face the foe, ⎬
Protects his parent, and prevents the blow.   ⎭
Shouts of applause ran ringing through the field
1135   To see the son the vanquished father shield.
All fired with generous indignation strive,
And with a storm of darts to distance drive
The Trojan chief, who held at bay, from far
On his Vulcanian orb sustained the war.

---

54. *wondrous*] for *memorande* ('memorable'); cp. 'Nisus and Euryalus' l. 251*n*.
62. *pious*] having filial piety: see D.'s headnote.   *undergo*] pass underneath
(*OED* 3).
68. *darts*] spears.
70. *orb*] anything circular (*OED* 1), here the shield (cp. *PL* vi 254–5).

As when thick hail comes rattling in the wind,
The ploughman, passenger and labouring hind
For shelter to the neighbouring covert fly,
Or housed, or safe in hollow caverns lie;
75   But that o'erblown, when heaven above 'em smiles,
Return to travel, and renew their toils:
Aeneas thus o'erwhelmed, on every side   ⎫
The storm of darts undaunted did abide,   ⎪
And thus to Lausus loud with friendly threatening ⎬
    cried: ⎭
80   'Why wilt thou rush to certain death, and rage
In rash attempts beyond thy tender age,
Betrayed by pious love?' Nor thus forborne
The youth desists, but with insulting scorn
Provokes the lingering Prince, whose patience tired
85   Gave place, and all his breast with fury fired.
For now the Fates prepared their cruel shears,
And lifted high the conquering sword appears,

Revised text from 1697 edition:

1140   As when thick hail comes rattling in the wind,
The ploughman, passenger, and labouring hind
For shelter to the neighbouring covert fly,
Or housed, or safe in hollow caverns lie;
But that o'erblown, when heaven above 'em smiles,
1145   Return to travel, and renew their toils:
Aeneas thus o'erwhelmed on every side   ⎫
The storm of darts undaunted did abide,   ⎬
And thus to Lausus loud with friendly threatening cried, ⎭
'Why wilt thou rush to certain death, and rage
1150   In rash attempts beyond thy tender age,
Betrayed by pious love?' Nor thus forborne
The youth desists, but with insulting scorn
Provokes the lingering Prince, whose patience tired
Gave place, and all his breast with fury fired.
1155   For now the Fates prepared their cruel shears,
And lifted high the flaming sword appears,

72. *passenger*] traveller (OED 1).   *hind*] farm worker.
76. *travel*] also in the sense 'travail'.
82. *forborne*] kept back (OED 7).

Which full descending with a fearful sway ⎫
Through shield and cuirass forced th' impetuous way ⎬
90   And buried deep in his fair bosom lay. ⎭
The springing streams through the thin armour strove,
And drenched the golden coat his careful mother
    wove;
And life at length forsook his heaving heart,
Loath from so sweet a mansion to depart.
95   But when, with blood and paleness all bespread,
The pious Prince beheld young Lausus dead,
He grieved, he wept; the sight an image brought
Of his own filial love, a sadly pleasing thought;
Then stretched his hand to raise him up, and said:
100   'Poor hapless youth, what praises can be paid
To love so great, to such transcendent store
Of early worth, and sure presage of more!

Revised text from 1697 edition:

Which full descending with a frightful sway ⎫
Through shield and corselet forced th' impetuous way ⎬
And buried deep in his fair bosom lay. ⎭
1160   The purple streams through the thin armour strove,
And drenched th' embroidered coat his mother wove;
And life at length forsook his heaving heart,
Loath from so sweet a mansion to depart.
    But when, with blood and paleness all o'erspread,
1165   The pious Prince beheld young Lausus dead,
He grieved, he wept; the sight an image brought
Of his own filial love, a sadly pleasing thought;
Then stretched his hand to hold him up, and said:
'Poor hapless youth, what praises can be paid
1170   To love so great, to such transcendent store
Of early worth, and sure presage of more!'

88. sway] sweeping movement (*OED* 2).
89. impetuous] rapid, violent (*OED* 1).
94. D.'s addition.
98. a sadly pleasing thought] D.'s addition.
101–2. D.'s addition. For the sentiment and the rhymes cp. 'To the Memory of Mr Oldham' ll. 11–12.   *sure presage of more*] from Servius' gloss *imago virtutis futurae* ('image of future virtue'), found in many seventeenth-century editions.

Accept whate'er Aeneas can afford:
Untouched thy arms, untaken be thy sword,
105   And all that pleased thee living still remain
Inviolate, and sacred to the slain.
Thy body on thy parents I bestow ⎫
To please thy ghost—at least, if shadows know ⎬
Or have a taste of human things below. ⎭
110   There to thy fellow ghosts with glory tell,
" 'Twas by the great Aeneas' hand I fell.' "
With this he bids his distant friends draw near,
Provokes their duty, and prevents their fear;
Himself assists to raise him from the ground,
115   His locks deformed with blood that welled from out
his wound.
Meantime the father, now no father, stood
And washed his wounds by Tiber's yellow flood;
Oppressed with anguish, panting and o'erspent,
His fainting limbs against a tree he leant;

Revised text from 1697 edition:

Accept whate'er Aeneas can afford:
Untouched thy arms, untaken be thy sword,
And all that pleased thee living still remain
1175   Inviolate, and sacred to the slain.
Thy body on thy parents I bestow ⎫
To rest thy soul—at least, if shadows know ⎬
Or have a sense of human things below. ⎭
There to thy fellow ghosts with glory tell,
1180   " 'Twas by the great Aeneas' hand I fell.' "
With this, his distant friends he beckons near,
Provokes their duty, and prevents their fear;
Himself assists to lift him from the ground,
With clotted locks, and blood that welled from out the wound.
1185   Meantime his father, now no father, stood
And washed his wounds by Tiber's yellow flood;
Oppressed with anguish, panting and o'erspent,
His fainting limbs against an oak he leant;

107–8. Because the Romans believed that the spirits of the dead could not be admitted to the underworld unless they had been given proper burial.
113. D.'s addition.   *Provokes*] calls forth (*OED* 1).   *prevents*] acts in anticipation of (*OED* 1).
116. now no father] D.'s addition. This may be the line regretted by D. in 'Preface to *Sylvae*' l. 246.
118. D.'s addition.   *o'erspent*] exhausted.

120   A bough his brazen helmet did sustain,
      His heavier arms lay scattered on the plain;
      Of youth a chosen troop around him stand,
      His head hung down, and rested on his hand;
      His grizzly beard his pensive bosom sought,
125   And all on Lausus ran his restless thought.
      Careful, concerned his danger to prevent,
      Much he enquired, and many a message sent
      To warn him from the field; alas, in vain:
      Behold his mournful followers bear him slain
130   On their broad shields; still gushed the gaping wound
      And drew a bloody trail along the ground.
      Far off he heard their cries, far off divined
      The dire event with a foreboding mind.
      With dust he sprinkled first his hoary head,   ⎫
135   Then both his lifted arms to heaven he spread;   ⎬
      Last, the dear corpse embracing, thus he said: ⎭
      'What joys, alas, could this frail being give,
      That I have been so covetous to live?

Revised text from 1697 edition:

      A bough his brazen helmet did sustain,
1190 His heavier arms lay scattered on the plain;
      A chosen train of youth around him stand,
      His drooping head was rested on his hand;
      His grizzly beard his pensive bosom sought,
      And all on Lausus ran his restless thought.
1195 Careful, concerned his danger to prevent,
      He much enquired, and many a message sent
      To warn him from the field; alas, in vain:
      Behold his mournful followers bear him slain:
      O'er his broad shield still gushed the yawning wound,
1200 And drew a bloody trail along the ground.
          Far off he heard their cries, far off divined
      The dire event with a foreboding mind.
      With dust he sprinkled first his hoary head,   ⎫
      Then both his lifted hands to heaven he spread; ⎬
1205 Last, the dear corpse embracing, thus he said: ⎭
      'What joys, alas, could this frail being give,
      That I have been so covetous to live?

124. pensive] mournful, gloomy (*OED* 3).
126. Careful] full of care for his son.
131. D.'s addition.

To see my son, and such a son, resign
140   His life a ransom for preserving mine!
And am I then preserved, and art thou lost?
How much too dear has that redemption cost!
'Tis now my bitter banishment I feel:
This is a wound too deep for time to heal.
145   My guilt thy growing virtues did defame,
My blackness blotted thy unblemished name.
Chased from a throne, abandoned, and exiled
For foul misdeeds, were punishments too mild:
I owed my people these, and from their hate
150   With less injustice could have borne my fate.
And yet I live, and yet support the sight
Of hateful men, and of more hated light!
But will not long.' With that he raised from ground
His fainting limbs that staggered with his wound.
155   Yet with a mind resolved, and unappalled
With pains or perils, for his courser called,

Revised text from 1697 edition:

To see my son, and such a son, resign
His life a ransom for preserving mine!
1210   And am I then preserved, and art thou lost?
How much too dear has that redemption cost!
'Tis now my bitter banishment I feel:
This is a wound too deep for time to heal.
My guilt thy growing virtues did defame,
1215   My blackness blotted thy unblemished name.
Chased from a throne, abandoned, and exiled
For foul misdeeds, were punishments too mild:
I owed my people these, and from their hate
With less resentment could have borne my fate.
1220   And yet I live, and yet sustain the sight
Of hated men, and of more hated light!
But will not long.' With that he raised from ground
His fainting limbs that staggered with his wound.
Yet with a mind resolved, and unappalled
1225   With pains or perils, for his courser called,

142, 145. D.'s additions.
156. courser] horse.

Well-mouthed, well-managed, whom himself did   ⎫
    dress   ⎪
With daily care, and mounted with success;   ⎬
His aid in arms, his ornament in peace.   ⎭

160 Soothing his courage with a gentle stroke,
    The horse seemed sensible while thus he spoke:
    'O Rhaebus, we have lived too long for me
    (If 'long' and 'life' were terms that could agree!);
    This day thou either shalt bring back the head
165 And bloody trophies of the Trojan dead;
    This day, thou either shalt revenge my woe
    For murthered Lausus on his cruel foe;
    Or if inexorable Fate deny
    Our conquest, with thy conquered master die:
170 For after such a lord, I rest secure
    Thou wilt no foreign reins or Trojan load endure.'

Revised text from 1697 edition:

Well-mouthed, well-managed, whom himself did dress ⎫
With daily care, and mounted with success;   ⎬
His aid in arms, his ornament in peace.   ⎭
    Soothing his courage with a gentle stroke,
1230 The steed seemed sensible, while thus he spoke:
    'O Rhaebus, we have lived too long for me
    (If 'life' and 'long' were terms that could agree!);
    This day thou either shalt bring back the head
    And bloody trophies of the Trojan dead;
1235 This day thou either shalt revenge my woe,
    For murthered Lausus on his cruel foe;
    Or if inexorable Fate deny
    Our conquest, with thy conquered master die:
    For after such a lord, I rest secure,
1240 Thou wilt no foreign reins or Trojan load endure.'

---

157. Well-mouthed] well trained to the use of the bit.   *dress*] groom (*OED*
13e).
160. courage] liveliness (*OED* 3).
161. sensible] endowed with feeling (*OED* 7).
163. i.e. 'if anything in human life could be considered "long"'.
168. D.'s addition.
170. secure] certain (*OED* 2).

He said; and straight th' officious courser kneels
To take his wonted weight; his hands he fills
With pointed javelins; on his head he laced
175   His glittering helm, which terribly was graced
With crested horsehair, nodding from afar;
Then spurred his thundering steed amidst the war.
Love, anguish, wrath, and grief to madness wrought,
Despair, and secret shame, and conscious thought
180   Of inborn worth, his labouring soul oppressed,
Rolled in his eyes, and raged within his breast.
Then loud he called Aeneas thrice by name,
The loud repeated voice to glad Aeneas came.
'Great Jove' said he 'and the far-shooting god
185   Inspire thy mind to make thy challenge good.'
He said no more, but hastened to appear,
And threatened with his long protended spear.
To whom Mezentius thus: 'Thy vaunts are vain,
My Lausus lies extended on the plain;

Revised text from 1697 edition:

He said; and straight th' officious courser kneels
To take his wonted weight. His hands he fills
With pointed javelins; on his head he laced
His glittering helm, which terribly was graced
1245   With waving horsehair, nodding from afar;
Then spurred his thundering steed amidst the war.
Love, anguish, wrath, and grief to madness wrought,
Despair, and secret shame, and conscious thought
Of inborn worth, his labouring soul oppressed,
1250   Rolled in his eyes, and raged within his breast.
Then loud he called Aeneas thrice by name,
The loud repeated voice to glad Aeneas came.
'Great Jove' he said, 'and the far-shooting god
Inspire thy mind to make thy challenge good.'
1255   He spoke no more, but hastened, void of fear,
And threatened with his long protended spear.
  To whom Mezentius thus: 'Thy vaunts are vain,
My Lausus lies extended on the plain;

172. *officious*] dutiful (*OED* 2).
181. D.'s addition.
184. *the far-shooting god*] Apollo.
187. *protended*] stretched out (*OED* 1).

190 He's lost; thy conquest is already won:
    This was my only way to be undone.
    Nor fate I fear, but all the gods defy!   ⎫
    Forbear thy threats: my business is to die. ⎬
    But first receive this parting legacy.'   ⎭
195 He said; and straight a whirling dart he sent,
    Another after, and another went.
    Round in a spacious ring he rides the field, ⎫
    And vainly plies th' impenetrable shield.   ⎬
    Thrice rode he round, and thrice Aeneas wheeled, ⎭
200 Turned as he turned; the golden orb withstood
    The strokes, and bore about an iron wood.
    Impatient of delay, and weary grown
    Still to defend, and to defend alone,
    To wrench the darts that in his buckler light,
205 Urged and o'erlaboured in unequal fight,
    At last resolved, he throws with all his force
    Full at the temples of the warlike horse:
    Betwixt the temples passed th' unerring spear,
    And piercing stood transfixed from ear to ear.

Revised text from 1697 edition:

        He's lost; thy conquest is already won:
1260   The wretched sire is murthered in the son.
        Nor fate I fear, but all the gods defy!   ⎫
        Forbear thy threats: my business is to die. ⎬
        But first receive this parting legacy.'   ⎭
        He said; and straight a whirling dart he sent,
1265   Another after, and another went.
        Round in a spacious ring he rides the field,   ⎫
        And vainly plies th' impenetrable shield.   ⎬
        Thrice rode he round, and thrice Aeneas wheeled, ⎭
        Turned as he turned; the golden orb withstood
1270   The strokes, and bore about an iron wood.
        Impatient of delay, and weary grown
        Still to defend, and to defend alone,
        To wrench the darts which in his buckler light,
        Urged and o'erlaboured in unequal fight,
1275   At length resolved, he throws with all his force
        Full at the temples of the warrior-horse.
        Just where the stroke was aimed, th' unerring spear
        Made way, and stood transfixed through either ear.

192. fate] death (*OED* 4b).
205. Urged] constrained (*OED* 4).

210   Seized with the sudden pain, surprised with fright,
      The courser bounds aloft and stands upright;
      He beats his hoofs a while in air, then pressed ⎫
      With anguish, floundering falls the generous beast ⎬
      And his cast rider, with his weight oppressed. ⎭
215   From either host the mingled shouts and cries
      Of Trojans and Rutulians rend the skies.
      Aeneas hastening waved his fatal sword
      High o'er his head, with this reproachful word:
      'Now, where are now thy vaunts, the fierce disdain
220   Of proud Mezentius, and the lofty strain?'
      Struggling, and wildly staring on the skies,
      With scarce recovered breath he thus replies:
      'Why these insulting threats, this waste of breath,
      To souls undaunted and secure of death?
225   'Tis no dishonour for the brave to die,
      Nor came I here with hope of victory;

Revised text from 1697 edition:

        Seized with unwonted pain, surprised with fright,
1280   The wounded steed curvets, and raised upright,
        Lights on his feet before; his hoofs behind
        Spring up in air aloft, and lash the wind.
        Down comes the rider headlong from his height;
        His horse came after with unwieldy weight,
1285   And, floundering forward, pitching on his head,
        His lord's encumbered shoulder overlaid.
          From either host, the mingled shouts and cries
        Of Trojans and Rutulians rend the skies.
        Aeneas hastening waved his fatal sword
1290   High o'er his head, with this reproachful word:
        'Now, where are now thy vaunts, the fierce disdain
        Of proud Mezentius, and the lofty strain?'
          Struggling, and wildly staring on the skies
        With scarce recovered sight, he thus replies:
1295   'Why these insulting words, this waste of breath,
        To souls undaunted and secure of death?
        'Tis no dishonour for the brave to die,
        Nor came I here with hope of victory;

212. pressed] afflicted (*OED* 6b).
213. generous] courageous, spirited (*OED* 2).

Nor ask I life, nor fought with that design;
As I had used my fortune, use thou thine.
My dying son contracted no such band,
230   Nor would I take it from his murderer's hand.
For this, this only favour let me sue:
If pity to a conquered foe be due,
Refuse not that, but let my body have
The last retreat of human kind—a grave.
235   Too well I know my injured people's hate:
Protect me from their vengeance after fate.
This refuge for my poor remains provide, ⎫
And lay my much-loved Lausus by my side.' ⎬
He said; and to the sword his throat applied. ⎭
240   The crimson stream distained his arms around,
And the disdainful soul came rushing through the
wound.

Revised text from 1697 edition:

Nor ask I life, nor fought with that design;
1300   As I had used my fortune, use thou thine.
My dying son contracted no such band,
The gift is hateful from his murderer's hand.
For this, this only favour let me sue:
If pity can to conquered foes be due,
1305   Refuse it not; but let my body have
The last retreat of human kind—a grave.
Too well I know th' insulting people's hate:
Protect me from their vengeance after fate.
This refuge for my poor remains provide, ⎫
1310   And lay my much-loved Lausus by my side.' ⎬
He said, and to the sword his throat applied. ⎭
The crimson stream distained his arms around,
And the disdainful soul came rushing through the wound.

227–8. D.'s addition. Following D.'s directions in the 'Preface to *Sylvae*', these lines replace those originally printed: 'But, with a glorious Fate, to end my pain;/ When *Lausus* fell, I was already slain:/ Nor ask I life,/'.
229. contracted no such band] made no such agreement; extracted no such promise.
236. fate] death (*OED* 4b).
240. distained] stained.

93 The Speech of Venus to Vulcan (from Virgil's *Aeneid* VIII)

Date and publication. Printed in 1685 in *Sylvae* (SR 10 January; advertised in *The Observator* 1 January); reprinted 1692. Incorporated with revisions into D.'s 1697 translation of Virgil (printed here as a modernized parallel text). For possible date of composition see headnote to 'Preface to *Sylvae*'.

Context. The choice of this extract was suggested by Montaigne's association of it with the opening of Lucretius Book I in his 'Sur des Vers de Virgile' (*Essais* III v); cp. 'Lucretius: The Beginning of the First Book', and headnote to 'Preface to *Sylvae*'.

Sources. D. translates *Aen.* viii 369–406. For the editions and other translations which D. used for Virgil see headnote to 'Virgil's Fourth Eclogue'.

The Speech of Venus to Vulcan

Wherein she persuades him to make arms for her son Aeneas, then engaged in a war against the Latins and King Turnus. Translated out of the eighth book of Virgil's *Aeneids*.

> Now night with sable wings the world o'erspread,
> But Venus, not in vain surprised with dread
> Of Latian arms, before the tempest breaks
> Her husband's timely succour thus bespeaks,
> 5 Couched in his golden bed;
> And, that her pleasing speech his mind may move,
> Inspires it with diviner charms of love:

> *Revised text from 1697 edition:*
> Now night had shed her silver dews around,
> 485 And with her sable wings embraced the ground,
> When love's fair goddess, anxious for her son
> (New tumults rising, and new wars begun),
> Couched with her husband in his golden bed,
> With these alluring words invokes his aid—
> 490 And, that her pleasing speech his mind may move,
> Inspires each accent with the charms of love:

'While adverse Fate conspired with Grecian powers
To level with the ground the Trojan towers,
10   I begged no aid th' unhappy to restore,
Nor did thy succour, nor thy art implore;
Nor sought their sinking empire to sustain,
To urge the labour of my lord in vain;
Though much I owed to Priam's house, and more
15   The dangers of Aeneas did deplore:
But now, by Jove's command and Fate's decree,
His race is doomed to reign in Italy,
With humble suit I ask thy needful art,
O still propitious power, O sovereign of my heart.
20   A mother stands a suppliant for a son:
By silver-footed Thetis thou wert won
For fierce Achilles, and the rosy morn
Moved thee with arms her Memnon to adorn;
Are these my tears less powerful on thy mind?
25   Behold what warlike nations are combined

Revised text from 1697 edition:

'While cruel Fate conspired with Grecian powers
To level with the ground the Trojan towers,
I asked not aid th' unhappy to restore,
495   Nor did the succour of thy skill implore;
Nor urged the labours of my lord in vain,
A sinking empire longer to sustain:
Though much I owed to Priam's house, and more
The dangers of Aeneas did deplore:
500   But now by Jove's command and Fate's decree,
His race is doomed to reign in Italy,
With humble suit I beg thy needful art,
O still propitious power, that rules my heart!
A mother kneels a suppliant for her son.
505   By Thetis and Aurora thou wert won
To forge impenetrable shields, and grace
With fated arms a less illustrious race.
Behold, what haughty nations are combined
Against the relics of the Phrygian-kind;

¶93. *12. sinking empire to sustain*] D.'s addition.
17. doomed] destined.
21–3. Vulcan (in Greek myth Hephaestus) had made armour for Achilles and
Memnon at the request of their mothers Thetis and Aurora (*Iliad* xviii).

With fire and sword my people to destroy,
And twice to triumph over me and Troy.'
She said; and straight her arms of snowy hue
About her unresolving husband threw:
30 Her soft embraces soon infuse desire,
His bones and marrow sudden warmth inspire, }
And all the godhead feels the wonted fire.
Not half so swift the rolling thunder flies,
Or streaks of lightning flash along the skies.
35 The goddess, pleased with her successful wiles,
And conscious of her conquering beauty, smiles.
Then thus the good old god, soothed with her charms,
Panting, and half dissolving in her arms:
'Why seek you reasons for a cause so just,
40 Or your own beauty, or my love distrust?
Long since, had you required my helpful hand,
You might the artist and his art command

Revised text from 1697 edition:

510 With fire and sword my people to destroy,
And conquer Venus twice, in conquering Troy.'
She said; and straight her arms of snowy hue
About her unresolving husband threw:
Her soft embraces soon infuse desire,
515 His bones and marrow sudden warmth inspire, }
And all the godhead feels the wonted fire.
Not half so swift the rattling thunder flies,
Or forky lightnings flash along the skies.
The goddess, proud of her successful wiles,
520 And conscious of her form, in secret smiles.
Then thus the power, obnoxious to her charms,
Panting, and half dissolving in her arms:
'Why seek you reasons for a cause so just,
Or your own beauties or my love distrust?
525 Long since, had you required my helpful hand,
Th' artificer, and art, you might command,

29. *unresolving*] irresolute.
31. *inspire*] breathe in (*OED* 3 used figuratively).
37–8. Translating *tum pater aeterno fatur deuinctus amore* ('then the father, overcome by eternal love, spoke').
38. *dissolving*] See 'Lucretius: Concerning the Nature of Love' l. 82*n*.
42. D.'s addition.

To arm your Trojans; nor did Jove or Fate
Confine their empire to so short a date:
45 And if you now desire new wars to wage,
My care, my skill, my labour I engage;
Whatever melting metals can conspire,
Or breathing bellows, or the forming fire,
I freely promise; all your doubts remove,
50 And think no task is difficult to love.'
He said; and eager to enjoy her charms
He snatched the lovely goddess to his arms;
Till all infused in joy he lay possessed
Of full desire, and sunk to pleasing rest.

       To labour arms for Troy; nor Jove, nor Fate,
       Confined their empire to so short a date.
       And if you now desire new wars to wage,
530   My skill I promise, and my pains engage:
       Whatever melting metals can conspire,
       Or breathing bellows, or the forming fire,
       Is freely yours: your anxious fears remove,
       And think no task is difficult to love.'
535   Trembling he spoke; and, eager of her charms,
       He snatched the willing goddess to his arms;
       Till, in her lap infused, he lay possessed
       Of full desire, and sunk to pleasing rest.

53. infused] steeped (*OED* 2), translating *infusus*. Montaigne, commenting on the comparable passage in Lucretius, writes of 'cette noble *circunfusa*, mere du gentil *infusus*' (850).

94 Lucretius: The Beginning of the First Book

Date and publication. Printed in 1685 in *Sylvae* (*SR* 10 January; advertised in *The Observator* 1 January); reprinted 1692; reprinted as an appendix to Creech's *Lucretius . . . and Manilius . . . Translated* (1700). For the likely date of composition see headnote to 'Preface to *Sylvae*'.

Context. De Rerum Natura ('On the Nature of Things'), the only work of Titus Lucretius Carus (94–55 BC), is a poem on the phenomena of the physical world, following the philosophy of Epicurus. This philosophy attracted renewed interest in England in the mid-seventeenth century (see Howard Jones, *The Epicurean Tradition* (1989); T. H. Mayo, *Epicurus in England 1650–1725* (1934); C. T. Harrison, *Harvard Studies in Classical Philology* xlv (1934) 1–79). This revival was particularly aided by the work of Pierre Gassendi, e.g. his *De Vita et Moribus Epicuri* (1647). The materialism of Epicurus, and his teaching that pleasure is the highest good, shocked Christian moralists (see *RL* ll. 18–19n) and encouraged the vulgar idea that he advocated mere libertinism; but, as Gassendi showed, Epicurus thought of pleasure as a state of tranquillity in which the mind was untroubled by passions and desires. This view of Epicureanism was promoted by Walter Charleton in *Epicurus' Morals* (1656) (for D. and Charleton see 'To Dr Charleton', headnote). An example of Epicurus' philosophy is provided in his epistle to Menoeceus, translated by Charleton: 'when we say; that Pleasure in the Generall is the end of a happy life, or the Chiefest Good; we are very far from understanding those Pleasures, which are so much admired, courted and pursued by men wallowing in Luxury, or any other pleasures that are placed in the meer motion or action of Fruition [i.e. sex], wereby, the sense is pleasantly tickled . . . but onely this . . . Not to be pained in body, nor perturbed in Mind. For, it is not perpetuall Feastings and Drinkings; it is not the love of, and Familiarity with beautifull boyes and women; it is not the Delicacies of rare Fishes, sweet meats, rich Wines, nor any other Dainties of the Table, that can make a Happy life: But, it is Reason, with Sobriety, and consequently a serene Mind; investigating the Causes, why this Object is to be Elected, and that to be Rejected; and chasing away those vain, superstitious and deluding opinions, which would occasion very great disquiet in the mind' (23). This philosophy is apparent in the passages which D. has selected from Lucretius, which particularly stress two of the chief disturbances to the tranquillity of the mind: the fear of death, and sexual desire. D.'s selection is consistent with his other classical translations in *Sylvae*, which also urge moderate, contented enjoyment of nature's gifts, and the need for freedom from anxiety and care. For D.'s own comment on his selection see 'Preface to *Sylvae*' ll. 278–425.

Lucretius had never been one of the most popular classical poets in England, but his reputation grew during the seventeenth century. He was translated by Lucy Hutchinson (MS in BL) and John Evelyn (MS of Books i and iii–vi in Christ Church, Oxford; Book i printed 1656). Creech's complete translation was published in 1682 and reprinted three times in 1683. Rochester translated two fragments from Book i, and D. refers to Rochester's interest in Lucretius when writing to him in 1673 (*Letters* 9). Sir Robert Howard published a translation from part of Book v in *Sylvae*. Although D. had been interested in the Epicurean atomic theory as early as 1660 (see 'To Sir Robert Howard' ll. 29–34), and may have planned a translation of Lucretius then (see 'Preface to *Sylvae*' ll. 452–3), his reading of Lucretius first becomes evident in *Tyrannic Love* (1669), where arguments drawn from Lucretius are debated between St Catharine and the Romans (see III i 40–73; IV i 380–406). In *Aureng-Zebe* (1676) the Emperor voices a debased version of Epicureanism (Act III), while lines from Nature's speech in Book iii are adapted in Act IV (see 'Lucretius: Against the Fear of Death' ll. 126–34*n*). In the Dedication of *Aureng-Zebe* to the Earl of Mulgrave (sigs A3ᵛ–A4ʳ) D. quotes *De Rerum Natura* ii 1–4 (see 'Lucretius: The Beginning of the Second Book' ll. 1–4) and says: 'I am sure his Master *Epicurus*, and my better Master *Cowley*, prefer'd the solitude of a Garden, and the conversation of a friend to any consideration, so much as a regard, of those unhappy People, whom in our own wrong, we call the great. True greatness, if it be any where on Earth, is in a private Virtue; removed from the notion of Pomp and Vanity, confin'd to a contemplation of it self, and centring on it self: *Omnis enim per se Divum natura, necesse est/ Immortali aevo summa cum pace fruatur;/ . . . Cura semota, metuque/ Ipsa suis pollens opibus*' (from ii 646–50: 'For the very nature of divinity must necessarily enjoy immortal life in the deepest peace . . . remote from care and fear, mighty through its own resources'; 'remote from care and fear' is D.'s alteration of the Latin, taken from ii 19 and consonant with the recurring stress on this point throughout *Sylvae*). He continues: 'If this be not the life of a Deity, because it cannot consist with Providence; 'tis at least a godlike life: I can be contented . . . with an humbler station in the Temple of Virtue, than to be set on the Pinacle of it', and quotes ii 9–10 (see ll. 10–11 in D.'s version). There are several echoes of Lucretius in *The State of Innocence* (1677) and in *Oedipus* (see headnote to 'Lucretius: Against the Fear of Death'). *RL* takes issue with Epicureanism (see ll. 18–33*nn*). D. alludes to Lucretius' theory of creation in the Dedication to *Plutarchs Lives* (1683) (*Works* xvii 227). There is also an undated letter in which D. adjudicates in a dispute about the sense of some lines in Creech's translation (*Letters* 14–16). For D.'s aims and methods in his translations from Lucretius see Paul Hammond, *MLR* lxxviii (1983) 1–23, and for their association with the seventeenth-century tradition of poems on the theme of the 'Happy Man' see Maren-Sofie Røstvig, *The Happy Man* (1962) 229–310.

As for D.'s choice of the opening of Book i, he told Tonson (*Letters* 23; quoted in headnote to 'Preface to *Sylvae*') that this was influenced by Montaigne's praise of its vigorous language in 'Sur des Vers de Virgile' (*Essais* III v), where he compares it with the lines in *Aen.* viii which D. translated for *Sylvae* as 'The Speech of Venus to Vulcan': 'Ce que Virgile dict de Venus et

de Vulcan, Lucrece l'aviot diet plus sortablement d'une jouissance desrobée
d'elle et de Mars . . . [quotes *De Rerum Natura* i 32–40] Quand je rumine ce
"*rejicit, pascit, inhians, molli, fovet medullas, labefacta, pendet, percurrit*", et cette
noble "*circunfusa*", mere du gentil "*infusus*", j'ay desdain de ces menues
pointes et allusions verballes qui nasquirent depuis. A ces bonnes gens, il ne
falloit pas d'aigüe et subtile rencontre; leur langage est tout plein et gros d'une
vigueur naturelle et constante; ils sont tout epigramme, non la queuë seule-
ment, mais la teste, l'estomac et les pieds. Il n'y a rien d'efforcé, rien de
treinant, tout y marche d'une pareille teneur. . . . Ce n'est pas une eloquence
molle et seulement-sans offence: elle est nerveuse et solide, qui ne plaict pas
tant comme elle remplit et ravit; et ravit le plus les plus forts espris. Quand je
voy ces braves formes de s'expliquer, si vifves, si profondes, je ne dicts pas
que c'est bien dire, je dicts que c'est bien penser. C'est la gaillardise de
l'imagination qui esleve et enfle les parolles' (850–1). Rochester had translated
ll. 1–5 of this book (not printed until 1953). D. returned to this passage in
Lucretius for parts of Palamon's speech to Venus in 'Palamon and Arcite' iii
129–44.

Sources. D. translates *De Rerum Natura* i 1–40. For his translations from
Lucretius D. relied chiefly upon the edition by Lambinus (1570) and the
translation by Creech (1682). He often drew upon the Latin glosses in Lambinus, and took words, phrases and rhymes from Creech. Other minor parallels suggest that he may also have consulted the French translation by Marolles (1650). For this translation from Book i D. turned to the adaptation of
the passage by Spenser in *FQ* IV x 44–7, and the translation of Book i
published by Evelyn in 1656.

Lucretius:
The Beginning of the First Book

Delight of human kind and gods above,
Parent of Rome, propitious Queen of love,

¶94. *1–2.* These lines are echoed in Palamon's prayer to Venus: 'Creator
Venus, Genial Pow'r of Love,/ The Bliss of Men below, and Gods above'
('Palamon and Arcite' iii 129–30).
1. Delight of human kind] Cp. *AA* l. 318n.   *Delight*] thus Creech.
2. Parent of Rome] thus Creech.   *propitious*] D.'s addition, perhaps from
Evelyn's note.

Whose vital power air, earth and sea supplies,
And breeds whate'er is born beneath the rolling skies—
5 For every kind, by thy prolific might,
Springs, and beholds the regions of the light—
Thee, goddess, thee the clouds and tempests fear,
And at thy pleasing presence disappear;
For thee the land in fragrant flowers is dressed,
10 For thee the ocean smiles, and smooths her wavy
    breast,
And heaven itself with more serene and purer light is
    blessed.
For when the rising spring adorns the mead,
And a new scene of nature stands displayed,
When teeming buds and cheerful greens appear,
15 And western gales unlock the lazy year,
The joyous birds thy welcome first express,
Whose native songs thy genial fire confess;

3–5. J. R. Mason compares *PL* xi 336–8: 'his omnipresence fills/ Land, sea, and air, and every kind that lives,/ Fomented by his virtual power and warmed'.

3. *vital*] life-giving. In Milton the Holy Spirit at creation 'vital virtue infused, and vital warmth' (*PL* viii 236; J. R. Mason).

5. *every kind*] The phrase is biblical: 'And God made the beast of the earth after his kind, and cattle after their kind, and every thing that creepeth upon the earth after his kind' (Genesis i 25).   *prolific*] generative.

6. *regions of the light*] from *regiones luminis* in Lambinus' gloss on l. 22.

7. Cp. Spenser: 'Thee goddesse, thee the winds, the clouds doe feare' (*FQ* IV x 44; *Works*); and Adam to Eve: 'Thee, Goddess, thee th' Eternal did ordain/ His softer Substitute on Earth to Reign' (*The State of Innocence* (1677) 13); and Palamon to Venus: 'Thee, Goddess, thee the Storms of Winter fly' (iii 135).

10. *smooths her wavy breast*] D.'s addition.

11. *serene*] from *serenum* in Lambinus.   *purer*] D.'s addition; Milton writes of 'purest light' (*PL* ii 137, vi 660).

13. *scene*] D.'s image.

14. D.'s addition.

15. *unlock the lazy year*] D.'s adaptation of *reserata aura* ('loosened [or unlocked] wind'); *reserare annum* was used of the formal opening of a year. Cp. 'Thy Month reveals the Spring, and opens all the Year' ('Palamon and Arcite' iii 134).

16. *joyous birds*] Spenser uses this phrase in his description of the Bower of Bliss (*FQ* II xii 71) and the Garden of Adonis (III vi 42). J. R. Mason notes the phrase in *PL* viii 515.

17. *genial*] pertaining to procreation (*OED* 1).

Then salvage beasts bound o'er their slighted food,
Struck with thy darts, and tempt the raging flood:
20 All nature is thy gift, earth, air and sea;
Of all that breathes, the various progeny
Stung with delight, is goaded on by thee.
O'er barren mountains, o'er the flowery plain,
The leavy forest, and the liquid main
25 Extends thy uncontrolled and boundless reign:
Through all the living regions dost thou move,
And scatter'st where thou goest the kindly seeds of
    love.
Since then the race of every living thing
Obeys thy power, since nothing new can spring
30 Without thy warmth, without thy influence bear,
Or beautiful or lovesome can appear,
Be thou my aid: my tuneful song inspire,
And kindle with thy own productive fire;
While all thy province, nature, I survey,
35 And sing to Memmius an immortal lay
Of heaven and earth, and everywhere thy wondrous
    power display;

18–19. Cp. Spenser: 'Then doe the saluage beasts begin to play/ Their pleasant friskes, and loath their wonted food/ . . . tempt the deepest flood' (*FQ* IV
x 46).

18. salvage] wild.   *their slighted food*] i.e. the meadows.   *slighted*] as
Lambinus explains, *neglegunt* ('they neglect').

19. Struck with thy darts] For *capta lepore* ('held captive by your charm'). D. is
thinking of Cupid's darts; for the violence cp. l. 22.

20–2. Translating the line which Lambinus prints after l. 15: *Inlecebrisque tuis
omnis natura animantum* ('and with your charms the whole nature of living
things'), which modern editors omit.

22. Stung] 'Sting' is used for sexual desire in *FQ* II xii 39, III viii 25.

25. D.'s addition.

26–7. For *omnibus incutiens blandum per pectora amorem,/ efficis ut cupide genera-
tim saecla propagent* ('striking alluring love into the breasts of all creatures, you
cause them greedily to beget their generations after their kind').

27. kindly] natural (*OED* 1); favourable to growth (*OED* 4).

30. For *sine te* ('without you').   *influence*] infusion of heavenly power
(*OED* 3).

31. lovesome] lovely, beautiful (*OED* 2).

33. D.'s addition; cp. 'To John Hoddesdon' ll. 7–10.

36. D.'s addition.   *wondrous*] Used by Milton of God's works in *PL* iii
663, v 155, viii 68.

To Memmius, under thy sweet influence born,
Whom thou with all thy gifts and graces dost adorn.
The rather, then, assist my Muse and me,
40   Infusing verses worthy him and thee.
Meantime on land and sea let barbarous discord cease,
And lull the listening world in universal peace.
To thee mankind their soft repose must owe,
For thou alone that blessing canst bestow,
45   Because the brutal business of the war
Is managed by thy dreadful servant's care,
Who oft retires from fighting fields to prove
The pleasing pains of thy eternal love,
And panting on thy breast supinely lies,
50   While with thy heavenly form he feeds his famished
      eyes,
Sucks in with open lips thy balmy breath,
By turns restored to life, and plunged in pleasing death.
There while thy curling limbs about him move,
Involved and fettered in the links of love,
55   When wishing all he nothing can deny,
Thy charms in that auspicious moment try;
With winning eloquence our peace implore,
And quiet to the weary world restore.

39–40. Translating *quo magis aeternum da dictis, diva, leporem* ('all the more grant to my speech, goddess, an eternal charm').

42. D.'s addition.

43–58. Cp. 'The Speech of Venus to Vulcan'.

46. thy dreadful servant] i.e. Mars; from Lambinus' gloss *qui tibi, vt amans, seruit* ('who serves you as a lover').

47. D.'s addition.   *prove*] experience.

49. Cp. Creech: 'Where on thy bosome he supinely lies'.   *supinely*] lazily (*OED* 2).

50. heavenly form] Milton's phrase for Eve (*PL* ix 457; J. R. Mason).   *feeds his famished eyes*] Cp. Evelyn: 'feeds his amorous eyes'.   *famished*] Lambinus' note on *inhians* ('gaping') includes *esurientibus* ('starving').

52. D.'s addition.   *death*] a common seventeenth-century image for orgasm.

54–6. D.'s additions.

54. Involved] entangled.

58. to the weary world] for *Romanis* ('to Romans').

95 Lucretius: The Beginning of the Second Book

Date and publication. Printed in 1685 in *Sylvae* (*SR* 10 January; advertised in *The Observator* 1 January); reprinted 1692; reprinted as an appendix to Creech's *Lucretius . . . and Manilius . . . Translated* (1700). For the likely date of composition see headnote to 'Preface to *Sylvae*'.

Context. For D.'s Lucretian translations generally, and his previous use of this passage in the Dedication to *Aureng-Zebe*, see headnote to 'Lucretius: The Beginning of the First Book'. The opening of Book ii had been translated in Tottel's Miscellany (1557), by Amyot in the preface to his Plutarch (1568; tr. North 1579), and by Bacon in his essay 'Of Truth' (*Essays* (1625)).

Sources. D. translates *De Rerum Natura* ii 1–61. For the editions and translations used by D. see headnote to 'Lucretius: The Beginning of the First Book'.

Lucretius:
The Beginning of the Second Book

Suave mari magno, etc.

'Tis pleasant safely to behold from shore
The rolling ship, and hear the tempest roar:
Not that another's pain is our delight,
But pains unfelt produce the pleasing sight.
5   'Tis pleasant also to behold from far
The moving legions mingled in the war;
But much more sweet thy labouring steps to guide ⎤
To virtue's heights, with wisdom well supplied, ⎬
And all the magazines of learning fortified: ⎦

¶95. *1–4.* D. had adapted these lines in Lucretius for St Catharine's speech in *Tyrannic Love* (1670): 'No happiness can be where is no rest:/ Th' unknown, untalk'd of man is only blest./ He, as in some safe Cliff, his Cell does keep,/ From thence he views the labours of the Deep:/ The Gold-fraught Vessel which mad tempests beat,/ He sees now vainly make to his retreat:/ And, when from far, the tenth wave does appear,/ Shrinks up in silent joy, that he's not there' (III i 46–53).
1–2. Cp. *Threnodia Augustalis* ll. 191–2.
1. 'Tis pleasant] thus Creech.
2. rolling ship] D.'s addition.
5. Cp. Creech: ' 'Tis also pleasant to behold from far'.
7. thy labouring steps to guide] D.'s addition.

10   From thence to look below on human kind,
       Bewildered in the maze of life, and blind;
       To see vain fools ambitiously contend
       For wit and power, their lost endeavours bend
       T' outshine each other, waste their time and health
15   In search of honour, and pursuit of wealth.
       O wretched man! in what a mist of life,
       Enclosed with dangers and with noisy strife
       He spends his little span, and overfeeds
       His crammed desires with more than nature needs:
20   For nature wisely stints our appetite,
       And craves no more than undisturbed delight,
       Which minds unmixed with cares and fears obtain,
       A soul serene, a body void of pain.

10–11. D. returns to this idea of attaining a wise viewpoint on human error in 'Of the Pythagorean Philosophy' ll. 213–20.

11. Bewildered] lost in pathless places; this is the *OED*'s first example, but see *RL* l. 189.

16–17. Cp. Creech: 'Blind, *Wretched* Man! in what dark paths of strife/ We walk this little journey of our life'.

16. mist] A favourite image in Webster: 'Their life a general mist of error' (*The Duchess of Malfi* IV ii 188; cp. V vi 94; *The White Devil* V vi 260).

18–20. and overfeeds . . . our appetite] D.'s addition.

19. crammed] Repeated in 'Lucretius: Against the Fear of Death' l. 131. *more than nature needs*] Echoes 'Allow not nature more than nature needs,/ Man's life is cheap as beast's' (*King Lear* III i 266–7).

20. wisely] See 'Horace: *Odes* III xxix' l. 45n.

21–3. Translating *nil aliud sibi naturam latrare, nisi utqui/ corpore seiunctus dolor absit, mente fruatur/ iucundo sensu cura semota metuque* ('Nature demands nothing except that pain be removed away out of the body, and that the mind, kept away from care and fear, enjoy a feeling of delight').

21. delight] For Epicurus' understanding of pleasure see the quotation in the headnote to 'Lucretius: The Beginning of the First Book'.

22. unmixed] D. often returns to the idea that human happiness is mixed with care: see *AM* l. 833n.

23. A soul serene] D.'s addition is in the spirit of seventeenth-century poems of contemplative retirement (see Maren-Sofie Røstvig, *passim*), but it is also faithful to Epicurus (see quotation in headnote to 'Lucretius: The Beginning of the First Book').   *soul*] This rendering of *mente* (usually 'mind') is not necessarily a Christianising of Lucretius, for Epicurus uses ψυχή and Lucretius himself elsewhere uses *animus*, both of which can be translated 'soul' or 'mind'.

So little this corporeal frame requires,
25   So bounded are our natural desires,
That wanting all, and setting pain aside,
With bare privation sense is satisfied:
If golden sconces hang not on the walls
To light the costly suppers and the balls,
30   If the proud palace shines not with the state
Of burnished bowls, and of reflected plate,
If well-tuned harps, nor the more pleasing sound
Of voices, from the vaulted roofs rebound;
Yet on the grass beneath a poplar shade
35   By the cool stream our careless limbs are laid,
With cheaper pleasures innocently blessed,
When the warm spring with gaudy flowers is dressed.
Nor will the raging fever's fire abate
With golden canopies and beds of state,
40   But the poor patient will as soon be sound
On the hard mattress, or the mother ground.
Then since our bodies are not eased the more
By birth, or power, or Fortune's wealthy store,
'Tis plain, these useless toys of every kind
45   As little can relieve the labouring mind:

25. D.'s addition.

26. wanting all] Modern editors of Lucretius print l. 22 as *delicias quoque uti multas sustenere possint* ('and can also spread for our use many delights'); D. follows Lambinus in rejecting *multas* ('many') in favour of *nullas* ('none'). *wanting*] lacking (not 'desiring').

27. privation] i.e. absence both of benefits and pain. The word comes from Lambinus, who notes: *qui dolore careat, summa voluptate perfrui: denique omnis doloris priuatione summam voluptatem terminari* ('he who lacks pain enjoys the highest pleasure; so the highest pleasure is said to be the absence [*priuatione*] of pain'). Lambinus is quoting Cicero, *De Finibus* I xi 38.

28. sconces] bracket candlesticks.

32–3. nor . . . voices] D.'s addition; cp. '& des voix' in Marolles.

33. Cp. Creech: 'from the roofs rebound'.

35. careless] See 'Horace: *Odes* III xxix' l. 10*n.*

36. innocently] D.'s addition. For the stress on pastoral innocence see also 'Horace: *Epode* II' l. 54.

37. spring with gaudy flowers] from Creech.   *gaudy*] bright.

41. For *in plebeia veste* ('on the poor man's blanket').

43. Fortune's wealthy store] Translating *gazae* ('treasures'). For Fortune see 'Horace: *Odes* III xxix' ll. 73–87*n.*

44. D.'s addition.   *toys*] trifles.

Unless we could suppose the dreadful sight
Of marshalled legions moving to the fight
Could with their sound and terrible array
Expel our fears, and drive the thoughts of death away;
50 But since the supposition vain appears,
Since clinging cares, and trains of inbred fears,
Are not with sounds to be affrighted thence,
But in the midst of pomp pursue the prince,
Not awed by arms, but in the presence bold,
55 Without respect to purple or to gold;
Why should not we these pageantries despise,
Whose worth but in our want of reason lies?
For life is all in wandering errors led;
And just as children are surprised with dread,
60 And tremble in the dark, so riper years
Ev'n in broad daylight are possessed with fears,
And shake at shadows fanciful and vain
As those which in the breasts of children reign.
These bugbears of the mind, this inward hell
65 No rays of outward sunshine can dispel;
But nature and right reason must display
Their beams abroad, and bring the darksome soul to
day.

46–8. D. follows Lambinus in omitting ll. 42–3 (*subsidiis . . . animatas*) and
the spurious line about a fleet found in other Renaissance editions. D.'s l. 48
adapts Lambinus' note *perterritae armorum sonitu, & telorum horrore* ('terrified
with the sound of arms, and the bristling of weapons').   *dreadful . . .*
terrible array] J. R. Mason compares Milton on the opposing armies in heaven:
'a dreadful interval, and front to front/ Presented stood in terrible array' (*PL*
vi 105–6).
56–7. Translating *quid dubitas quin omni' sit haec rationi potestas?* ('why do you
doubt that this power [to remove care] belongs wholly to reason?'). D.
concentrates instead on our unnecessary intimidation by the trappings of
power.
58. in wandering errors] for *in tenebris* ('in the dark'); a tautology (as in *PL* vii
302).
64. bugbears] See 'Lucretius: Against the Fear of Death' l. 1n.   *inward hell*]
for *tenebras* ('darkness'); Milton stresses 'the hell within' (*PL* iv 20, 75).
66–7. For *natura species ratioque* ('the aspect and law of nature').
66. right reason] reason, properly informed, acting as a guide to behaviour; cp.
'Of the Pythagorean Philosophy' l. 221. For Restoration uses of the idea see
R. W. McHenry, *Mosaic* vii (1974) 69–86 and John Spurr, *JHI* xlix (1988)
563–85.

96 Lucretius: Against the Fear of Death (from Book III)

Date and publication. Printed in 1685 in *Sylvae* (*SR* 10 January; advertised in *The Observator* 1 January); reprinted 1692; reprinted as an appendix to Creech's *Lucretius . . . and Manilius . . . Translated* (1700). For the likely date of composition see headnote to 'Preface to *Sylvae*'.

Context. For D.'s Lucretian translations generally, see headnote to 'Lucretius: The Beginning of the First Book'. D. had previously taken some material from this portion of Lucretius for speeches in *Oedipus* (1679) III i 41–65. Montaigne had used the passage extensively in his essay 'Que Philosopher, c'est apprendre à mourir'. George Sandys had translated ll. 972–1010 in the commentary to his *Ovid's Metamorphosis Englished* (1632) 163–4. Lines 843–52 were quoted by Charles Blount in his *Anima Mundi* [1679] 11–12. Lines 894–6 were translated by Thomas Flatman in his *Poems and Songs* (1682) 140. Lucretius' denial of the immortality of the soul made this a controversial passage, particularly since churchmen were currently campaigning against atheism (for contexts see Michael Hunter, *TRHS* xxxv (1985) 135–57, chiefly on the early seventeenth century, and Gillian Manning, *SC* viii (1993) 99–121 on Rochester and the current religious debate). In the 'Preface to *Sylvae*' ll. 321–47 D. rejects Lucretius' dismissal of the immortality of the soul, and in this he is following Renaissance commentators otherwise sympathetic to Epicureanism, such as Lucretius' editor Lambinus. Mortalism was not unknown in England: it was espoused by Milton and other radicals (see Christopher Hill, *Milton and the English Revolution* (1977) 317–23), by Hobbes, and by Rochester in his translation from Seneca's *Troades* (*c.* 1674). But, as D. says in the 'Preface to *Sylvae*', it was possible to believe in the immortality of the soul and still find the passage valuable as a *consolatio*, a dissuasion from the fear of death and an encouragement to the proper use of the gifts of nature. For such reasons the passage figured prominently in Walter Charleton's *Epicurus' Morals* (1656) even though Charleton was simultaneously staging a debate with Lucretius in *The Immortality of the Human Soul Demonstrated* (1656), which used arguments from natural philosophy of the kind to which D. refers in the 'Preface to *Sylvae*' ll. 323–4.

Sources. D. translates *De Rerum Natura* iii 830–1094. For the editions and translations used by D. see headnote to 'Lucretius: The Beginning of the First Book'.

Translation of the Latter Part of the Third Book of Lucretius: Against the Fear of Death

What has this bugbear death to frighten man,
If souls can die, as well as bodies can?
For, as before our birth we felt no pain
When Punic arms infested land and main,
5   When heaven and earth were in confusion hurled
For the debated empire of the world,
Which awed with dreadful expectation lay,
Sure to be slaves, uncertain who should sway:
So, when our mortal frame shall be disjoined,
10 The lifeless lump uncoupled from the mind,
From sense of grief and pain we shall be free;
We shall not feel, because we shall not *be*.
Though earth in seas, and seas in heaven were lost,
We should not move, we only should be tossed.
15 Nay, ev'n suppose when we have suffered fate,
The soul could feel in her divided state,
What's that to us? for we are only we
While souls and bodies in one frame agree.

¶96. *Title. Against the Fear of Death*] thus Creech (margin).
1. bugbear] Object of needless (especially superstitious) terror; Eurydice calls death a bugbear in *Oedipus* (1679) III i 75.
2. The distinction between soul and body is added by D.; Lucretius has: *quandoquidem natura animi mortalis habetur* ('since the nature of the mind [or 'soul'] is understood to be mortal'). *souls can die*] thus Creech.
4–8. The three Punic Wars in which Rome and Carthage contended for supremacy in the western Mediterranean (264–241, 218–201 and 149–146 BC).
6–8. Translating *in dubioque fuere utrorum ad regna cadendum/ omnibus humanis esset* ('and was in doubt under which domination all men were destined to fall'). For D.'s stress on fear and slavery in the poems in *Sylvae* cp. 'Horace: *Epode* II' ll. 16–17n.
9. Cp. 'Let the frame of things disjoint' (*Macbeth* III ii 16).
10. lifeless lump] for *corporis* ('body'). *lump*] see *AA* l. 172n.
11, 14. D.'s additions.
15–17. Cp. Creech: 'But now suppose the *Soul*, when separate,/ Could live, and think, in a *divided state:*/ Yet what is that to *us*'.
15. fate] death, destruction (*OED* 4b,c).

Nay, though our atoms should revolve by chance,
20   And matter leap into the former dance;
Though time our life and motion could restore,
And make our bodies what they were before,
What gain to us would all this bustle bring?
The new-made man would be another thing;
25   When once an interrupting pause is made,
That individual being is decayed.
We, who are dead and gone, shall bear no part
In all the pleasures, nor shall feel the smart,
Which to that other mortal shall accrue,
30   Whom of our matter time shall mould anew.
For backward if you look on that long space
Of ages past, and view the changing face
Of matter, tossed and variously combined
In sundry shapes, 'tis easy for the mind
35   From thence t' infer, that seeds of things have been
In the same order as they now are seen:
Which yet our dark remembrance cannot trace,
Because a pause of life, a gaping space
Has come betwixt, where memory lies dead,
40   And all the wandering motions from the sense are fled.
For whosoe'er shall in misfortunes live
Must *be* when those misfortunes shall arrive;
And since the man who *is* not, feels not woe
(For death exempts him, and wards off the blow,

19. revolve] turn back again. *OED* quotes Sir Thomas Herbert (1665): 'And the four Elements . . . shall maintain a dreadful fight, so long and so fiercely . . . that at last all will be revolved into a dark confusion.'
20. leap . . . dance] D.'s images; cp. *RL* ll. 18–19, and 'Song for St Cecilia's Day' ll. 3–9.
24, 26. D.'s additions.
28. From Lambinus' gloss: *aut me ulla voluptate, vel molestia afficit* ('affects me with either any pleasure or hurt').
30. D. translates *Quos de materia nostra proferet aetas,* which modern editors omit.
32. face] With biblical overtones: 'And the earth was without form, and void; and darkness was upon the face of the deep' (Genesis i 2); cp. Milton, *PL* vii 278, 316, 636.
35. seeds] literal translation of *semina,* Lucretius' word for atoms.
39. where memory lies dead] D.'s addition.
40. sense] consciousness (*OED* 6b); also at ll. 55, 113–14, and cp. *senseless* (l. 67).

45 Which we the living only feel and bear),
     What is there left for us in death to fear?
     When once that pause of life has come between,
     'Tis just the same as we had never been.
     And therefore if a man bemoan his lot,
50 That after death his mouldering limbs shall rot,
     Or flames, or jaws of beasts devour his mass,
     Know he's an unsincere, unthinking ass.
     A secret sting remains within his mind,
     The fool is to his own cast offals kind;
55 He boasts no sense can after death remain,   ⎤
     Yet makes himself a part of life again: ⎬
     As if some other he could feel the pain.   ⎦
     If while he live this thought molest his head,
     'What wolf or vulture shall devour me dead?',
60 He wastes his days in idle grief, nor can
     Distinguish 'twixt the body and the man;
     But thinks himself can still himself survive,
     And what when dead he feels not, feels alive.
     Then he repines that he was born to die,
65 Nor knows in death there is no other he;
     No living he remains his grief to vent,
     And o'er his senseless carcass to lament.

48. Cp. 'Who are perished as though they had never been' (Ecclesiasticus xliv 9).

52. unsincere] unsound (*OED* 2).   *unthinking ass]* D.'s addition. Cp. 'our sphere of action is life's happiness/ And he who thinks beyond thinks like an ass' (Rochester, *Satire against Reason and Mankind* (in MS *c.*1674; printed 1679) ll. 96–7).

54. D.'s addition.   *offals]* carrion; also (opprobriously) the bodies of the slain (*OED* 2b).

57. D.'s addition.

58. this thought molest his head] J. R. Mason compares Milton: 'nor with perplexing thoughts/ To interrupt the sweet of life, from which/ God hath bid dwell far off all anxious cares,/ And not molest us, unless we our selves/ Seek them with wandering thoughts, and notions vain' (*PL* viii 183–7). Cp. 'Horace: *Odes* III xxix' ll. 45, 49*n*; 'Horace: *Epode* II' l. 55*n*; 'Lucretius: Concerning the Nature of Love' l. 19.   *molest]* cp. also l. 28*n*.

60. idle] futile.

64. Cp. Creech: 'And hence he grieves, that he was born to dye'.   *repines]* complains.

If after death 'tis painful to be torn
By birds and beasts, then why not so to burn,
70 Or drenched in floods of honey to be soaked,
Embalmed to be at once preserved and choked;
Or on an airy mountain's top to lie
Exposed to cold and heaven's inclemency,
Or crowded in a tomb to be oppressed
75 With monumental marble on thy breast?
But to be snatched from all thy household joys,
From thy chaste wife, and thy dear prattling boys,
Whose little arms about thy legs are cast,
And climbing for a kiss prevent their mother's haste,
80 Inspiring secret pleasure through thy breast;
All these shall be no more: thy friends oppressed
Thy care and courage now no more shall free:
'Ah wretch', thou criest, 'ah! miserable me,
One woeful day sweeps children, friends, and wife,
85 And all the brittle blessings of my life!'
Add one thing more, and all thou say'st is true:
Thy want and wish of them is vanished too,
Which well considered were a quick relief
To all thy vain imaginary grief.
90 For thou shalt sleep and never wake again,
And quitting life, shall quit thy living pain.
But we thy friends shall all those sorrows find
Which in forgetful death thou leav'st behind;
No time shall dry our tears, nor drive thee from our
      mind.

68–9. Cp. Creech: 'But if 'tis miserable to be torn/ By Beasts when dead,
why is't not so to burn?'.
72. D.'s addition.
73–4. Creech has: 'expos'd to cold' and 'To be opprest'.
76–9. Cp. Creech: 'Ay, but he now is snatch'd from all his joys:/ No more
shall his chast wife, and pratling boyes/ Run to their Dad with eager hast, and
strive/ Which shall have the first kiss, as when alive.'
78. D.'s addition.
79. prevent] anticipate.
84–5. children . . . life] for Lucretius' tot praemia vitae ('so many prizes of life').
91. quitting] giving up, letting go of (OED 5).
92. Future tense because Lambinus prints deflebimus ('we shall lament') where
modern editors have deflevimus ('we have lamented').

95   The worst that can befall thee, measured right,
     Is a sound slumber, and a long good night.
     Yet thus the fools, that would be thought the wits,
     Disturb their mirth with melancholy fits,
     When healths go round, and kindly brimmers flow,
100 Till the fresh garlands on their foreheads glow,
     They whine, and cry, 'Let us make haste to live,
     Short are the joys that human life can give'.
     Eternal preachers, that corrupt the draught,
     And pall the god that never thinks with thought;
105 Idiots with all that thought, to whom the worst
     Of death is want of drink, and endless thirst,
     Or any fond desire as vain as these.
     For ev'n in sleep, the body wrapped in ease
     Supinely lies, as in the peaceful grave,
110 And wanting nothing, nothing can it crave.

97–8. D.'s addition. Lucretius is attacking mere hedonism, false 'epicurean-ism'. D.'s *wits* suggests a reference to Restoration rakes, who combined sensual indulgence with versifying and moralising (cp. ll. 103–5n), though the word can also mean 'men of intelligence', as in Tillotson's attack on Epicureans who 'assume to themselves to be the *Men of Reason*, the *great Wits* of the World, the onely *cautious* and wary persons, that hate to be imposed upon, that must have convincing evidence for every thing, and can assent to nothing without a clear Demonstration for it' (*The Wisdom of Being Religious* (1664) 16). See further Gillian Manning, *SC* viii (1993) 105–6.

99. Cp. 'whilst frequent Healths go round' (Creech).   *brimmers*] brimming cups (perhaps a vogue word, since *OED*'s first example is from 1663).

101. whine] D. makes Lucretius' sarcasm explicit.   *make haste to live*] from Cowley: 'None ever yet, made Haste enough to Live' ('Mart. Lib. 2. Ep. 90', *Essays* 455).

103–5. Eternal . . . thought] D.'s addition. D. may be alluding to works such as Rochester's *Satire against Reason and Mankind*, which attempts to correct the relationship between reason and appetite: 'His wisdom did his happiness destroy,/ Aiming to know that world he should enjoy/ . . . The pleasure past, a threatening doubt remains/ That frights th'enjoyer with succeeding pains./ . . . But thoughts are given for action's government;/ Where action ceases, thought's impertinent' (ll. 33–4, 39–40, 94–5).

104. pall] particularly, to make wine flat or stale (*OED* 8).   *god*] Bacchus, god of wine.

107. fond] foolish.

108. wrapped in ease] Cp. Cowley: 'wrapt in th' Arms of Quiet' ('Seneca, ex Thyeste, Act. 2. Chor.', *Essays* 400).   *ease*] see *AA* l. 168n.

110. wanting] lacking.

Were that sound sleep eternal, it were death;
Yet the first atoms then, the seeds of breath
Are moving near to sense, we do but shake
And rouse that sense, and straight we are awake.
115   Then death to us, and death's anxiety
Is less than nothing, if a less could be.
For then our atoms, which in order lay,
Are scattered from their heap, and puffed away,
And never can return into their place,
120   When once the pause of life has left an empty space.
And last, suppose great Nature's voice should call
To thee, or me, or any of us all,
'What dost thou mean, ungrateful wretch, thou vain,
Thou mortal thing, thus idly to complain,
125   And sigh and sob, that thou shalt be no more?
For if thy life were pleasant heretofore,
If all the bounteous blessings I could give ⎫
Thou hast enjoyed, if thou hast known to live, ⎬
And pleasure not leaked through thee like a sieve, ⎭
130   Why dost thou not give thanks as at a plenteous feast,
Crammed to the throat with life, and rise and take thy
        rest?

---

112. Translating *primordia* ('first beginnings'). Cp. Lambinus' note: *corpora prima, ex quibus animus noster constat* ('the first beginnings, from which our soul [or 'breath'] is made up').

123. ungrateful wretch . . . vain] D.'s addition.

126–34. D. had already adapted this passage in *Aureng-Zebe* (1676): 'If you have liv'd, take thankfully the past:/ Make, as you can, the sweet remembrance last./ If you have not enjoy'd what Youth could give,/ But life sunk through you like a leaky Sieve,/ Accuse yourself you liv'd not while you might' (58).

126. pleasant] pleasing (*OED* 1, stronger than in twentieth-century usage); merry (*OED* 2).

128. known to live] D.'s addition. Lambinus' note on l. 961 cites the parallel passage in Horace, *Epistulae* II ii 213–16, including *vivere si recte nescis, decede peritis* ('if you do not know how to live, make way for those who do'). *live*] The emphatic positioning of this word stresses its importance for D.; for other strong uses of *live* see 'Horace: *Odes* III xxix' l. 68 and 'Palamon and Arcite' iii 1114: 'Possess our Souls, and while we live, to live'.

130–1. Cp. Creech: 'Why dost thou not then like a *thankful* Guest/ Rise chearfully from *Life's abundant* Feast,/ And with a *quiet* mind go take thy *rest*?'.

But if my blessings thou hast thrown away,
If indigested joys passed through and would not stay,
Why dost thou wish for more to squander still?
135 If life be grown a load, a real ill,
And I would all thy cares and labours end,
Lay down thy burden, fool, and know thy friend.
To please thee I have emptied all my store,
I can invent, and can supply no more,
140 But run the round again, the round I ran before.
Suppose thou art not broken yet with years,
Yet still the self-same scene of things appears,
And would be ever, could'st thou ever live;
For life is still but life, there's nothing new to give.'
145 What can we plead against so just a bill?
We stand convicted, and our cause goes ill.
But if a wretch, a man oppressed by fate,
Should beg of Nature to prolong his date,
She speaks aloud to him with more disdain,
150 'Be still thou martyr fool, thou covetous of pain.'
But if an old decrepit sot lament,
'What thou', she cries, 'who hast outlived content!
Dost thou complain, who hast enjoyed my store?
But this is still th' effect of wishing more!
155 Unsatisfied with all that Nature brings,
Loathing the present, liking absent things;

133. D.'s addition, adapting Lambinus' gloss: *sin ea omnia . . . tibi e memoria effluxerunt, vel te non expleuerunt* ('if all things . . . passed out of your memory, or did not fill you').
136–7. D. expands Lucretius' *non potius vitae finem facis atque laboris?* ('why not rather make an end of life and trouble?'). burden] from Creech.
138–40. Translating *nam tibi praeterea quod machiner inveniamque,/ quod placeat, nil est: eadem sunt omnia semper* ('for there is nothing else I can devise and invent to please you: everything is always the same'). Cp. *To His Sacred Majesty* ll. 21–2; 'To the Memory of Mr Oldham' ll. 11–12.
140. Cp. Creech: 'My *Pleasures* always in a *Circle* run'.
144. D.'s addition.
145. bill] charge, indictment.
147. Cp. Creech: 'But if a *Wretch*, if one *opprest* by fate'.
148. date] allotted span of life (*OED* 4).
150–2. D. follows the order of lines in Lambinus (*aufer . . ./ grandior . . ./ omnia . . .*) which differs in modern editions.
150. martyr . . . covetous of pain] D.'s additions, adapting Lambinus' gloss *avidissime* ('very covetous').

From hence it comes thy vain desires at strife
Within themselves, have tantalized thy life,
And ghastly death appeared before thy sight
160   Ere thou had'st gorged thy soul and senses with
    delight.
Now leave those joys unsuiting to thy age
To a fresh comer, and resign the stage.'
Is Nature to be blamed if thus she chide?
No, sure; for 'tis her business to provide,
165   Against this ever-changing frame's decay,
New things to come, and old to pass away.
One being worn, another being makes,
Changed but not lost; for Nature gives and takes:
New matter must be found for things to come,
170   And these must waste like those, and follow Nature's
    doom.
All things, like thee, have time to rise and rot,
And from each other's ruin are begot;
For life is not confined to him or thee—
'Tis giv'n to all for use, to none for property.
175   Consider former ages past and gone,
Whose circles ended long ere thine begun,

157–8. Translating *imperfecta tibi elapsast ingrataque vita* ('life has slipped by for you incomplete and ungratifying').   *at strife/ Within themselves*] For D.'s stress on the mind divided against itself cp. l. 269, and 'Lucretius: Concerning the Nature of Love' l. 114.   *tantalized*] D.'s only use of this word; see ll. 185–8.

161–2. Cp. Creech: 'Yet leave these toyes, that not befit thine age,/ *New* Actors now come on; *resign* the Stage.' D. applies this advice to himself in 'To Mr Granville' (1698) ll. 1–10.

163. if thus she chide] from Creech.

164–74. D. returns to the universal processes of change in 'Of the Pythagorean Philosophy', esp. ll. 374–97.

166, 168. Cp. 'The Lord geueth, and the Lord taketh awaie . . . so cummeth thynges to passe' (Job i 21; text from the burial service in the pre-1662 Book of Common Prayer).

170. doom] judgement, decision.

171. rise and rot] Cp. 'we ripe and ripe,/ And then from hour to hour we rot and rot' (*As You Like It* II v 26–7).

173. D.'s addition.

174. property] *proprietas* is Lambinus' gloss for Lucretius' *mancipium* ('right of ownership').

176. circles] D.'s addition; cp. 'Virgil's Fourth Eclogue' l. 8.

Then tell me fool, what part in them thou hast?
Thus may'st thou judge the future by the past.
What horror seest thou in that quiet state,
180   What bugbear dreams to fright thee after fate?
No ghost, no goblins that still passage keep,
But all is there serene in that eternal sleep.
For all the dismal tales that poets tell
Are verified on earth, and not in hell.
185   No Tantalus looks up with fearful eye,
Or dreads th' impending rock to crush him from on
    high:
But fear of chance on earth disturbs our easy hours,
Or vain imagined wrath, of vain imagined powers.
No Tityus torn by vultures lies in hell, ⎫
190   Nor could the lobes of his rank liver swell ⎬
To that prodigious mass for their eternal meal; ⎭
Not though his monstrous bulk had covered o'er ⎫
Nine spreading acres, or nine thousand more; ⎬
Not though the globe of earth had been the giant's ⎪
    floor; ⎭
195   Nor in eternal torments could he lie,
Nor could his corpse sufficient food supply.
But he's the Tityus, who by love oppressed, ⎫
Or tyrant passion preying on his breast, ⎬
And ever-anxious thoughts is robbed of rest. ⎭

180–1. D.'s addition.

180. fate] death.

181. goblins] demons.   *passage*] [transition to] death (*OED* 2).   *keep*]
guard.

184. verified] made true.

185–6. Lucretius follows the version of the legend in which Tantalus is
punished for stealing the gods' nectar and ambrosia by having a large stone
suspended over him, for fear of which he dares not drink.

186. impending] hanging threateningly (*OED* 2).

188. Lucretius has: *divom metus urget inanis mortalis* ('the fear of gods oppresses
mortals without cause').

189. Two vultures fed eternally on the liver of Tityos, who had tried to rape
Leto (*Odyssey* xi 576–81).

190. lobes] the technical term for the divisions of the liver (*OED* 1a).

198. tyrant] D.'s addition. Cowley frequently calls a passion a tyrant (e.g.
Essays 388, 390, 442).

199. ever-anxious thoughts] A close translation, but also a recurring topic in

200   The Sisyphus is he, whom noise and strife
       Seduce from all the soft retreats of life,
       To vex the government, disturb the laws,
       Drunk with the fumes of popular applause;
       He courts the giddy crowd to make him great,
205   And sweats and toils in vain to mount the sovereign
           seat.
       For still to aim at power, and still to fail,
       Ever to strive and never to prevail,
       What is it, but in reason's true account
       To heave the stone against the rising mount;
210   Which urged, and laboured, and forced up with pain,
       Recoils and rolls impetuous down, and smokes along
           the plain?
       Then still to treat thy ever-craving mind
       With every blessing, and of every kind,
       Yet never fill thy ravening appetite,
215   Though years and seasons vary thy delight,
       Yet nothing to be seen of all the store,
       But still the wolf within thee barks for more:

Sylvae: see 'Lucretius: Concerning the Nature of Love' l. 114 and 'Horace: *Odes* III xxix' l. 10*n*.

200–5. D. expands from *qui petere a populo fasces saevasque secures/ imbibit et semper victus tristisque recedit* ('athirst to solicit from the people the lictor's rods and cruel axes, and always retiring defeated and full of gloom').

200. Sisyphus] D. described himself as 'the *Sisyphus* of the Stage' in the Dedication to *Aureng-Zebe* (1676) sig. A4ʳ. He returns to the character of the ambitious man in the Dedication to *Don Sebastian* (1690) (*Works* xv 60).

203. D. repeats this line in *HP* iii 1092.

204–5. Cp. *The Medal* ll. 271–2.

204. giddy] D.'s epithet for the Jews in *AA* l. 216.

206–11. Cp. Creech: 'For still to seek, and still in Hopes devour,/ But never to enjoy desired Power,/ What is it, but to roll a *mighty* stone/ Against the *hill*, which streight will tumble down?/ Almost at *top*, it must *return* again,/ And with *swift* force roll thro the *humble* Plain'.

210–11. Lucretius (ll. 1000–2, following *Odyssey* xi 598) also makes his rhythm appropriate to the ascent and descent of the stone.

211. impetuous] with violent motion (*OED* 1).   *smokes*] moves rapidly (*OED* 2c, where the first example is from 'The Seventh Book of the *Aeneis*' l. 909); sends up dust (*OED* 2). Homer says that dust rose up from the head of Sisyphus (*Odyssey* xi 600).

214. Cp. Creech: 'And never fills the *greedy* Appetite'.

217. D.'s image.

This is the fable's moral which they tell
Of fifty foolish virgins damned in hell
220 To leaky vessels, which the liquor spill—
To vessels of their sex, which none could ever fill.
As for the dog, the Furies, and their snakes,
The gloomy caverns, and the burning lakes,
And all the vain infernal trumpery,
225 They neither are, nor were, nor e'er can be.
But here on earth the guilty have in view
The mighty pains to mighty mischiefs due:
Racks, prisons, poisons, the Tarpeian rock,
Stripes, hangmen, pitch, and suffocating smoke,
230 And last, and most, if these were cast behind,
Th' avenging horror of a conscious mind,
Whose deadly fear anticipates the blow,
And sees no end of punishment and woe,
But looks for more, at the last gasp of breath:
235 This makes an hell on earth, and life a death.
Meantime, when thoughts of death disturb thy head,
Consider, Ancus great and good is dead;

219. The Danaids were condemned to carry water in perforated vessels as a
punishment for murdering their husbands on their wedding night.   foolish
virgins] The phrasing recalls the parable in Matthew xxv 1–13 of the girls
who made improvident use of the oil in their lamps.
220. leaky vessels] The image had been applied to insatiable desire by Plato:
'that part of the soul in foolish people where the desires reside . . . he likened
to a leaky jar, because it can never be filled' (Gorgias 493). Cp. 'Lucretius:
Concerning the Nature of Love' l. 20; RL l. 35.
221. D.'s addition.
222. dog] Cerberus, who guarded the entrance to the underworld.   snakes]
Not in Lucretius, but the Furies were regularly depicted as or with snakes,
e.g. in Aeschylus, Choephoroi l. 1049.
223. burning lakes] not in Lucretius; see Revelation xix 20 and PL i 210.
224. D.'s addition.
225. This line is reused in 'The Cock and the Fox' l. 332.
228. Racks] numella (l. 1015, an alternative reading to luella ('punishment')) is
glossed by Lambinus as a wooden machine for torturing criminals.   Tarpeian rock] a cliff in Rome from which murderers and traitors were thrown to
their deaths.
229. Stripes] lashes from a whip.
231. conscious] guilty (OED 4b).
237. Ancus] according to tradition, the fourth king of Rome.

Ancus, thy better far, was born to die,
And thou, dost thou bewail mortality?
240 So many monarchs with their mighty state,
Who ruled the world, were overruled by fate.
That haughty king, who lorded o'er the main,
And whose stupendous bridge did the wild waves
    restrain
(In vain they foamed, in vain they threatened wreck,
245 While his proud legions marched upon their back),
Him death, a greater monarch, overcame,
Nor spared his guards the more, for their immortal
    name.
The Roman chief, the Carthaginian dread,   ⎫
Scipio, the thunderbolt of war is dead,   ⎬
250 And like a common slave by Fate in triumph led. ⎭
The founders of invented arts are lost,
And wits who made eternity their boast;
Where now is Homer who possessed the throne?
Th' immortal work remains, the mortal author's gone.

---

239. D.'s addition.

241. overruled by fate] D.'s addition.

242. Xerxes, King of Persia, who in 480 BC built a wooden bridge across the Hellespont to attack Greece.

243. stupendous bridge] from *PL* x 351 (J. R. Mason).

244–5. wreck/ . . . back/] a perfect rhyme in seventeenth-century pronunciation.

244. they²] *1700*; thy *1685, 1692*.

245. upon their back] D.'s addition, prompted by *dorso* in Lambinus' quotation here from *Geo.* iii 116.

247. D.'s addition. The 10,000 men of the royal Persian bodyguard were known as the Immortals because their number was kept constantly replenished.

249. Scipio] Roman general (236–184/3 BC) who defeated the Carthaginian armies in Spain and North Africa.

250. Cp. Creech: 'like the meanest *common* Slave'.   *by Fate in triumph led*] D.'s addition.

251. invented arts] From Virgil, *Aen.* vi 663: *inuentas aut qui uitam excoluere per artis* ('or those who refined life through the arts they invented').

252. Cp. Creech: '*Wits*, and *Poets* too, that give,/ *Eternity* to others'. See ll. 97–8*n.*

254. D.'s addition.

255   Democritus perceiving age invade,
       His body weakened, and his mind decayed,
       Obeyed the summons with a cheerful face,
       Made haste to welcome death, and met him half the
            race.
       That stroke ev'n Epicurus could not bar,   ⎤
260   Though he in wit surpassed mankind as far   ⎬
       As does the midday sun the midnight star.   ⎦
       And thou, dost thou disdain to yield thy breath,
       Whose very life is little more than death?
       More than one half by lazy sleep possessed,   ⎤
265   And when awake, thy soul but nods at best,   ⎬
       Day-dreams and sickly thoughts revolving in thy   ⎦
            breast.
       Eternal troubles haunt thy anxious mind,
       Whose cause and cure thou never hop'st to find;
       But still uncertain, with thyself at strife,
270   Thou wander'st in the labyrinth of life.
       O, if the foolish race of man, who find
       A weight of cares still pressing on their mind,
       Could find as well the cause of this unrest,
       And all this burden lodged within the breast,
275   Sure they would change their course, nor live as now,
       Uncertain what to wish or what to vow.
       Uneasy both in country and in town,
       They search a place to lay their burden down.
       One restless in his palace walks abroad,
280   And vainly thinks to leave behind the load;
       But straight returns, for he's as restless there,
       And finds there's no relief in open air.

---

255. *Democritus*] Philosopher of the fifth century BC who was an early
proponent of the atomic theory of the universe. He advised living cheerfully
within bounds, and counselled against the fear of death.
257–8. Translating *sponte sua leto caput obvius obtulit ipse* ('of his own free will
himself offered his head to death'). For the image of the race as 'the course of
life' (*OED* 1c) cp. 'To the Memory of Mr Oldham' ll. 7–10*n*.
257. Cp. Creech: 'obey thy *summons*'.
260. *wit*] intelligence.
269. *with thyself at strife*] D.'s addition; cp. ll. 157–8*n*.
270. *labyrinth*] D.'s image.
277. D.'s addition.

Another to his villa would retire,
And spurs as hard as if it were on fire;
285   No sooner entered at his country door,
But he begins to stretch, and yawn, and snore,
Or seeks the city which he left before.
Thus every man o'erworks his weary will
To shun himself, and to shake off his ill;
290   The shaking fit returns and hangs upon him still.
No prospect of repose, nor hope of ease,
The wretch is ignorant of his disease,
Which known would all his fruitless trouble spare,
For he would know the world not worth his care:
295   Then would he search more deeply for the cause,
And study nature well, and nature's laws:
For in this moment lies not the debate,
But on our future, fixed, eternal state,
That never-changing state which all must keep
300   Whom Death has doomed to everlasting sleep.
Why are we then so fond of mortal life,
Beset with dangers and maintained with strife?
A life which all our care can never save;
One fate attends us, and one common grave.
305   Besides we tread but a perpetual round,
We ne'er strike out, but beat the former ground,
And the same mawkish joys in the same track are
    found.

290. D.'s addition.

294. Translating *rebus relictis* ('having abandoned his business'). Cp. 'Believe me, Son, and needless trouble spare;/ 'Tis a base World, and is not worth our care' (*Aureng-Zebe* (1676) 36); and 'The World's not worth my care' (*All for Love* (1678) I i 123).

295–6. Translating *naturam primum studeat cognoscere rerum* ('first study to learn the nature of things'). The stress on the *laws* of nature is D.'s own; cp. 'Happy the Man, who, studying Nature's Laws,/ Thro' known Effects can trace the secret Cause' ('The Second Book of the *Georgics*' ll. 698–9, translating *felix qui potuit rerum cognoscere causas* ('happy he who can understand the causes of things': *Geo.* ii 490)); and 'To learn the Laws/ Of Nature, and explore their hidden Cause' ('Of the Pythagorean Philosophy' ll. 8–9).

303. D.'s addition; cp. 'whosoever will save his life shall lose it', Mark vii 35.

307 mawkish] nauseating (*OED* 2; first example 1697). The *OED*'s first examples for the adjective, in the sense 'inclined to sickness' or 'without appetite' (*OED* 1a, b) are both from D. The word comes from *mawk*, a maggot.

For still we think an absent blessing best,
Which cloys, and is no blessing when possessed; ⎫
310   A new arising wish expels it from the breast. ⎬
The feverish thirst of life increases still, ⎭
We call for more and more, and never have our fill;
Yet know not what tomorrow we shall try,
What dregs of life in the last draught may lie.
315   Nor, by the longest life we can attain,   ⎫
One moment from the length of death we gain; ⎬
For all behind belongs to his eternal reign.   ⎭
When once the Fates have cut the mortal thread,
The man as much to all intents is dead
320   Who dies today, and will as long be so,
As he who died a thousand years ago.

308–12. D. had adapted these lines from Lucretius in *Tyrannic Love* (1670):
'You roam about, and never are at rest,/ By new desires, that is, new
torments, still possest;/ Qualmish and loathing all you had before,/ Yet with
a sickly appetite to more./ As in a fev'rish dream you still drink on;/ And
wonder why your thirst is never gone' (IV i 384–9).

308. Lambinus, annotating l. 1082, quotes Horace, *Carm.* III xxix 41–4 (see
'Horace: *Odes* III xxix' ll. 65–9).

314. D.'s addition, adapting Rochester's description of love: 'That cordial
drop Heaven in our cup has thrown/ To make the nauseous draught of life go
down' (*Artemisia to Chloe* (in MS 1674; printed 1679) ll. 44–5).

318. D.'s addition.

97 Lucretius: Concerning the Nature of Love (from Book IV)

Date and publication. Printed in 1685 in *Sylvae* (*SR* 10 January; advertised in *The Observator* 1 January); reprinted 1692; reprinted as an appendix to Creech's *Lucretius . . . and Manilius . . . Translated* (1700). For the likely date of composition see headnote to 'Preface to *Sylvae*'.

Context. For D.'s Lucretian translations generally, see headnote to 'Lucretius: The Beginning of the First Book'. See also D.'s discussion of this passage in 'Preface to *Sylvae*' ll. 368–425. As he says there, one of the attractions of this part of the poem was its argument against being enslaved to sexual desire, and many of D.'s additions and emphases underline the powerful force of love and the mental agitation which it provokes. George Sandys had translated ll. 1074–113 in the commentary to his *Ovid's Metamorphosis Englished* (1632) 160.

Sources. D. translates *De Rerum Natura* iv 1052–287. For the editions and translations used by D. see headnote to 'Lucretius: The Beginning of the First Book'.

Lucretius: The Fourth Book Concerning the Nature of Love

Beginning at this line,
Sic igitur, Veneris qui telis accipit ictum, etc.

> Thus therefore, he who feels the fiery dart
> Of strong desire transfix his amorous heart,
> Whether some beauteous boy's alluring face,
> Or lovelier maid with unresisted grace
> 5 From her each part the wingèd arrow sends,
> From whence he first was struck he thither tends;

¶97. *1–2*. For *sic igitur Veneris qui telis accipit ictus* ('so, therefore, he who receives a blow from the weapons of Venus').
3. Cp. Creech: '*beauteous* face'.   *alluring face*] rendering *membris mulieribus* ('girlish limbs').
4. *unresisted*] irresistible; D.'s addition.

Restless he roams, impatient to be freed,
And eager to inject the sprightly seed.
For fierce desire does all his mind employ,
10   And ardent love assures approaching joy.
Such is the nature of that pleasing smart
Whose burning drops distil upon the heart,
The fever of the soul shot from the fair,
And the cold ague of succeeding care.
15   If absent, her idea still appears,
And her sweet name is chiming in your ears;
But strive those pleasing phantoms to remove,
And shun th' aerial images of love
That feed the flame: when one molests thy mind
20   Discharge thy loins on all the leaky kind;
For that's a wiser way than to restrain
Within thy swelling nerves that hoard of pain.
For every hour some deadlier symptom shows,
And by delay the gathering venom grows

7. D.'s addition.
8. sprightly] lively; cp. l. 29n.
9. D.'s addition.
12. distil] trickle down (OED 1).
13. D.'s addition.
15. idea] mental image (OED 8a).
18. aerial] imaginary; trisyllabic, and always stressed on the second syllable in D.'s poetry, as in l. 62.
19. molests] From Lambinus' amoris molestias ('vexations of love'); cp. also 'Lucretius: Against the Fear of Death' l. 58n.
20. Discharge thy loins] From Marolles' se decharger; translating iactere umorem conlectum ('cast the collected liquid').   all the leaky kind] i.e. women, but Lucretius has corpora quaeque ('any body').   leaky] (i) talkative (OED 1c); the Wife of Bath says: 'Like leaky Sives no Secrets we can hold' ('The Wife of Bath her Tale' l. 155); (ii) menstruating (cp. 'as leaky as an unstanched wench', Shakespeare, The Tempest I i 47–8, kept in the version by D. and Davenant); (iii) sexually insatiable (cp. 'Lucretius: Against the Fear of Death' ll. 219–21).
22. swelling nerves] D.'s addition. Here and at l. 84 D. may be using nerve in the modern physiological sense, or to mean 'sinew' (OED 1a), but he elsewhere uses nerve for 'penis', which is one sense of the Latin nervus (see OED 1b; 'The Sixth Satire of Juvenal' l. 285; 'The Fourth Satire of Persius' l. 108n). For the plural cp. Lucretius l. 1043: in loca conveniens nervorum certa ('gathering in fixed parts in the loins').

25 When kindly applications are not used;
    The scorpion, love, must on the wound be bruised:
    On that one object 'tis not safe to stay,
    But force the tide of thought some other way:
    The squandered spirits prodigally throw,
30 And in the common glebe of nature sow.
    Nor wants he all the bliss that lovers feign,
    Who takes the pleasure and avoids the pain;
    For purer joys in purer health abound,
    And less affect the sickly than the sound.
35 When love its utmost vigour does employ,
    Ev'n then, 'tis but a restless wandering joy:
    Nor knows the lover in that wild excess,
    With hands or eyes what first he would possess;
    But strains at all, and fastening where he strains,
40 Too closely presses with his frantic pains;
    With biting kisses hurts the twining fair,
    Which shows his joys imperfect, unsincere:
    For stung with inward rage he flings around,
    And strives t' avenge the smart on that which gave the
        wound.
45 But love those eager bitings does restrain,
    And mingling pleasure mollifies the pain.

26. *scorpion*] D.'s image. *1685* reads *Viper*, but D. corrects this in the Preface
(ll. 427–9). *Works* cites the cure for scorpion stings in Thomas Muffet's *The
Theatre of Insects*: 'Lay on a Scorpion bruised, to recall/ The venome' (in
Edward Topsell, *The History of Four-footed Beasts and Serpents* (1658) 1057).
29–30. D.'s adaptation of *volgivagaque vagus Venere* ('wandering with roving
love').
29, 86, 123. *spirits*] fluids supposed to permeate the blood and organs of the
body (*OED* 16); cp. 'The Second Book of the *Georgics*' ll. 155–8: 'For when
his Blood no Youthful Spirits move,/ He languishes and labours in his Love./
And when the sprightly Seed should swiftly come,/ Dribling he drudges, and
defrauds the Womb.' For the specifically sexual senses see Hugh Ormsby-
Lennon, *Swift Studies* iii (1988) 9–78, and cp. 'Epilogue to *The Loyal Brother*'
l. 12*n*, and Shakespeare, *Sonnet* cxxix l. 1.
30. *common glebe*] lands held in common; here meaning prostitutes.
31. *wants*] lacks.
34. *sickly*] i.e. the love-sick.
42. *unsincere*] not unmixed, not pure (*OED* 2), translating *non pura*; cp. *AM*
l. 833.

For ardent hope still flatters anxious grief,
And sends him to his foe to seek relief:
Which yet the nature of the thing denies,
50   For love, and love alone of all our joys,
By full possession does but fan the fire;
The more we still enjoy, the more we still desire.
Nature for meat and drink provides a space,
And when received they fill their certain place;
55   Hence thirst and hunger may be satisfied,
But this repletion is to love denied:
Form, feature, colour, whatsoe'er delight
Provokes the lover's endless appetite,
These fill no space, nor can we thence remove
60   With lips, or hands, or all our instruments of love:
In our deluded grasp we nothing find
But thin aerial shapes that fleet before the mind.
As he who in a dream with drought is cursed,
And finds no real drink to quench his thirst,
65   Runs to imagined lakes his heat to steep,
And vainly swills and labours in his sleep;
So love with phantoms cheats our longing eyes,
Which hourly seeing never satisfies;
Our hands pull nothing from the parts they strain,
70   But wander o'er the lovely limbs in vain:
Nor when the youthful pair more closely join,
When hands in hands they lock, and thighs in thighs
     they twine,

47. For *namque in eo spes est* ('here lies the hope').   *anxious*] see l. 114n.
grief] pain, suffering (*OED* 1).
56–62. D.'s expansion of *ex hominis vero facie pulchroque colore/ nil datur in corpus praeter simulacra fruendum/ tenuia; quae vento spes raptast saepe misella* ('But from man's aspect and beautiful bloom nothing comes into the body to be enjoyed but thin images; and this poor hope is often snatched away by the wind').
62. *fleet*] float, drift (*OED* 3), dissolve, vanish (*OED* 9).   *mind*] Possibly a misprint for *wind*, since its equivalent in Lucretius is *vento*, but D. could have settled on *mind* after beginning with the literal translation.
68. *hourly*] D.'s addition.
69. *strain*] clasp tightly (*OED* 2).
72. Lucretius has *membris conlatis* ('with limbs joined').

Just in the raging foam of full desire,
When both press on, both murmur, both expire,
75   They gripe, they squeeze, their humid tongues they
          dart,
As each would force their way to t' other's heart—
In vain; they only cruise about the coast,
For bodies cannot pierce, nor be in bodies lost:
As sure they strive to be, when both engage
80   In that tumultuous momentany rage;
So tangled in the nets of love they lie,
Till man dissolves in that excess of joy.
Then, when the gathered bag has burst its way,
And ebbing tides the slackened nerves betray,
85   A pause ensues; and nature nods a while,
Till with recruited rage new spirits boil;
And then the same vain violence returns,

73. Replaces ll. 1106–7 ('when the body foretastes its joy, and Venus is on the point of sowing the woman's field').   *foam*] a traditional metaphor, from its being a sign of fury or madness. *OED* (1b) cites Bonner (1555): 'the fome or rage of concupiscence'.

75. *gripe*] clutch (*OED* 3a); enclose in a tight embrace (*OED* 3c).

76. D.'s addition.

77. *cruise about the coast*] D.'s addition.

80. D.'s addition.   *momentany*] momentary.

81. *tangled in the nets*] D.'s image, adapting Lambinus' gloss *vinculis* ('chains'), and perhaps recalling the net in which Vulcan caught his wife Venus making love to Mars. See also l. 133.

82–8. D. makes this passage refer specifically to the man (whereas Lucretius writes of the couple), and increases the physiological precision.

82. *dissolves*] A common Restoration word for achieving orgasm: cp. 'In liquid raptures I dissolve all o'er' (Rochester, 'The Imperfect Enjoyment' l. 15, a male speaker; also in l. 10); Oldham, 'The Passion of Byblis' l. 69, where the woman says: 'I all dissolv'd in reeking pleasures lay!'; and cp. D.'s 'The Speech of Venus to Vulcan' l. 38.

83. *gathered bag*] For *conlecta cupido* ('gathered desire'); cp. Rochester: 'Nor do you think it worth your care/ How empty and how dull/ The heads of your admirers are,/ So that their bags be full' ('To a Lady in a Letter' (printed 1676) ll. 21–4).

84–6. D.'s addition, apart from *A pause ensues*.

84. *nerves*] see l. 22n.

86. *recruited*] For the specifically sexual usage cp. P.M., *The Cimmerian Matron* (1668): 'with a thousand parting kisses [she] dismiss'd him to recruit his spirits lost in the conflict' (*Restoration Prose Fiction*, edited by C. C. Mish (1970) 155).   *spirits*] see l. 29n.

With flames renewed th' erected furnace burns.
Again they in each other would be lost,
90 But still by adamantine bars are crossed;
All ways they try, successless all they prove,
To cure the secret sore of lingering love.
Besides——
They waste their strength in the venereal strife,
95 And to a woman's will enslave their life;
Th' estate runs out, and mortgages are made, ⎫
All offices of friendship are decayed, ⎬
Their fortune ruined, and their fame betrayed. ⎭
Assyrian ointment from their temples flows,
100 And diamond buckles sparkle at their shoes;
The cheerful emerald twinkles on their hands,
With all the luxury of foreign lands,
And the blue coat that with embroidery shines
Is drunk with sweat of their o'er-laboured loins.
105 Their frugal fathers' gains they misemploy,
And turn to point, and pearl, and every female toy.
French fashions, costly treats are their delight;
The Park by day, and plays and balls by night.

88. D.'s addition.
89–90. For *cum sibi quod cupiunt ipsi contingere quaerunt,/ nec reperire malum id possunt quae machina vincat:/ usque adeo incerti tabescunt volnere caeco* ('when they seek to attain what they desire, and can find no device to master the trouble: in such uncertainty do they pine with their secret wound').
90. adamantine] impenetrable (from 'adamant', a very hard rock).
93–4. Cp. Creech: 'Besides, they wast their *strength*'. Creech has several lines consisting solely of 'Besides' in Books iv and v.
95. For *alterius sub nutu degitur aetas* ('one lives at the nod of another'): D.'s stress continues to be on the man's experience.   *enslave]* For D.'s concern with freedom and enslavement in *Sylvae* see 'Horace: *Epode* II' ll. 16–17n, and 'Lucretius: Against the Fear of Death' ll. 6–8n.
96. mortgages] closely translates *vadimonia* in Lambinus' text; modern editors print *Babylonica*.
97. offices] kindnesses, attentions (*OED* 1); duties (*OED* 2); translating *officia*. *of friendship]* D.'s addition.
99–100. For *unguenta et pulchra in pedibus Sicyonia rident* ('Fine Siconian slippers laugh on his mistress' perfumed feet').
102. D.'s addition.
103. that with embroidery shines] D.'s addition.
106–8. D. finds approximate modern equivalents.   *point]* lace.   *toy]* trifle.   *Park]* i.e. St James's Park, London, a place of fashionable resort.

In vain——
110 For in the fountain where their sweets are sought,
     Some bitter bubbles up, and poisons all the draught.
     First guilty conscience does the mirror bring,
     Then sharp remorse shoots out her angry sting,
     And anxious thoughts within themselves at strife
115 Upbraid the long misspent, luxurious life.
     Perhaps the fickle fair one proves unkind,   ⎫
     Or drops a doubtful word that pains his mind,   ⎬
     And leaves a rankling jealousy behind.   ⎭
     Perhaps he watches close her amorous eyes,
120 And in the act of ogling does surprise,
     And thinks he sees upon her cheeks the while   ⎫
     The dimpled tracks of some foregoing smile;   ⎬
     His raging pulse beats thick, and his pent spirits boil. ⎭
     This is the product ev'n of prosperous love;
125 Think then what pangs disastrous passions prove!
     Innumerable ills: disdain, despair,
     With all the meagre family of care.
     Thus, as I said, 'tis better to prevent
     Than flatter the disease, and late repent;
130 Because to shun th' allurement is not hard
     To minds resolved, forewarned, and well prepared:

110. sweets] pleasures.
111. bitter] bitterness (*OED* B1).   *draught*] for the image of a drink (D.'s
addition) cp. 'Lucretius: Against the Fear of Death' l. 314*n*.
112–15. For *cum conscius ipse animus se forte remordet/ desidiose agere aetatem
lustrisque perire* ('when his conscious mind chances to sting him with the
thought that he is passing his life in sloth and perishing in debauches').
114. For D.'s stress on anxiety see 'Horace: *Odes* III xxix' l. 10*n*, and for the
mind at strife within itself see 'Lucretius: Against the Fear of Death' ll. 157–
8*n*, 199.
116, 119. D.'s additions.
120. ogling] *OED*'s first example is from Shadwell (1682), who glosses it as 'a
foolish Word among the Canters for glancing'.
123. D.'s addition.
124–5. Cp. Creech: 'Such mischeifs happen e'en in *prosperous* Love,/ But
those that *cross*, and *adverse* passion prove'.
125. prove] experience, suffer (*OED* 3).
127. D.'s addition.   *meagre*] emaciated (*OED* 1b); cp. 'Horace: *Odes* I iii'
l. 42.
129. D.'s addition.   *flatter*] soothe, gloss over (*OED* 6).
131. D.'s addition.

But wondrous difficult, when once beset,
To struggle through the straits, and break th'
    involving net.
Yet thus ensnared, thy freedom thou may'st gain,
135   If, like a fool, thou dost not hug thy chain;
If not to ruin obstinately blind,   ⎫
And wilfully endeav'ring not to find   ⎬
Her plain defects of body and of mind.   ⎭
For thus the bedlam train of lovers use
140   T' enhance the value, and the faults excuse.
And therefore 'tis no wonder if we see
They dote on dowdies and deformity;
Ev'n what they cannot praise, they will not blame,
But veil with some extenuating name:
145   The sallow skin is for the swarthy put,
And love can make a slattern of a slut;
If cat-eyed, then a Pallas is their love,
If freckled she's a particoloured dove.
If little, then she's life and soul all o'er,
150   An Amazon, the large two-handed whore.
She stammers, O what grace in lisping lies!
If she says nothing, to be sure she's wise.

133. *straits*] Lucretius' *rete* ('net') may have recalled *fretum* ('strait').   *involv-ing*] wrapping round, entangling; D.'s addition.

135. *hug thy chain*] D.'s image.

136. D.'s addition.

139. *bedlam*] mad.   *use*] are accustomed.

142. *dowdies*] implies both plain features and shabby dress.

143–4. Replaces ll. 1157–9, which Lambinus marks for possible omission.

145. Here Lucretius begins a list of pet names borrowed from Greek.

146. *slattern*] untidy, slovenly woman.   *slut*] like *slattern*, but with the additional implication 'prostitute' (*OED*). The two words were virtually interchangeable in Restoration usage.

147. Homer's epithet for Pallas Athene is γλαυκῶπις ('grey-blue eyed, bright-eyed').

148. Lucretius has *nervosa et lignea dorcas* ('the sinewy and wooden a "gazelle"'). D. adopts the variant *naevosa* ('freckled'), noted but rejected by Lambinus.

149. *life and soul*] D.'s addition, recalling the phrase ζωή καί ψυχή; cp. 'The Sixth Satire of Juvenal' l. 278.

150. *two-handed*] bulky, strapping (*OED* 3).

If shrill, and with a voice to drown a choir,
Sharp-witted she must be, and full of fire.
155 The lean, consumptive wench with coughs decayed,
Is called a pretty, tight, and slender maid.
Th' o'er-grown, a goodly Ceres is expressed,
A bed-fellow for Bacchus at the least.
Flat-nose the name of satyr never misses,
160 And hanging blubber lips but pout for kisses.
The task were endless all the rest to trace:
Yet grant she were a Venus for her face
And shape, yet others equal beauty share,
And time was you could live without the fair:
165 She does no more, in that for which you woo,
Than homelier women full as well can do.
Besides she daubs, and stinks so much of paint,
Her own attendants cannot bear the scent,
But laugh behind, and bite their lips to hold;
170 Meantime excluded, and exposed to cold,
The whining lover stands before the gates,
And there with humble adoration waits,
Crowning with flowers the threshold and the floor,
And printing kisses on th' obdurate door;
175 Who if admitted in that nick of time,
If some unsavoury whiff betray the crime,
Invents a quarrel straight, if there be none,
Or makes some faint excuses to be gone;
And calls himself a doting fool to serve,
180 Ascribing more than woman can deserve:
Which well they understand like cunning queans,
And hide their nastiness behind the scenes

---

156. *tight*] lively (OED 3); smart, shapely (OED 4).
157. *o'er-grown*] for *tumida et mammosa* ('swollen, with large breasts').
Ceres] goddess of the crops.
158. *Bacchus*] god of wine.
159. Because satyrs were depicted with flat noses (Lambinus).
163. Cp. Creech: 'yet others *equal* beauties'.
165–6. D.'s innuendo; Lucretius has 'she does all the same things as the ugly woman does' (i.e. painting and perfuming).
172. D.'s addition.
177–8. Cp. Creech: 'none,/ But seeks some *fit excuses* to be gone'.
177. D.'s addition, adapting *querela* ('complaint') in l. 1182.
181. *like cunning queans*] D.'s addition.   *queans*] prostitutes.

From him they have allured and would retain;
But to a piercing eye 'tis all in vain,
185 For common sense brings all their cheats to view,
And the false light discovers by the true:
Which a wise harlot owns, and hopes to find
A pardon for defects that run through all the kind.
Nor always do they feign the sweets of love,
190 When round the panting youth their pliant limbs they
    move,
And cling, and heave, and moisten every kiss;
They often share, and more than share the bliss:
From every part, ev'n to their inmost soul,
They feel the trickling joys, and run with vigour to the
    goal.
195 Stirred with the same impetuous desire,
Birds, beasts, and herds, and mares their males require:
Because the throbbing nature in their veins
Provokes them to assuage their kindly pains:
The lusty leap th' expecting female stands,
200 By mutual heat compelled to mutual bands.
Thus dogs with lolling tongues by love are tied,
Nor shouting boys, nor blows their union can divide;
At either end they strive the link to loose—
In vain, for stronger Venus holds the noose:
205 Which never would those wretched lovers do, ⎫
But that the common heats of love they know; ⎬
The pleasure therefore must be shared in common too. ⎭
And when the woman's more prevailing juice
Sucks in the man's, the mixture will produce
210 The mother's likeness; when the man prevails,
His own resemblance in the seed he seals.
But when we see the new-begotten race
Reflect the features of each parent's face,

---

187. D.'s addition.
188. the kind] the female sex.
196. require] invite (*OED* 3e); seek for (*OED* 9).
198. D.'s addition.   *kindly*] natural.
201. with lolling tongues] D.'s addition.
202. D.'s addition.

Then of the father's and the mother's blood
215   The justly tempered seed is understood:
When both conspire, with equal ardour bent,
From every limb the due proportion sent,
When neither party foils, when neither foiled,
This gives the blended features of the child.
220   Sometimes the boy the grandsire's image bears,
Sometimes the more remote progenitor he shares,
Because the genial atoms of the seed
Lie long concealed ere they exert the breed,
And after sundry ages past produce
225   The tardy likeness of the latent juice.
Hence families such different figures take,
And represent their ancestors in face, and hair and
        make:
Because of the same seed the voice, and hair,   ⎫
And shape, and face, and other members are,   ⎬
230   And the same antique mould the likeness does prepare. ⎭
Thus oft the father's likeness does prevail
In females, and the mother's in the male.
For since the seed is of a double kind,
From that where we the most resemblance find
235   We may conclude the strongest tincture sent,
And that was in conception prevalent.
Nor can the vain decrees of powers above
Deny production to the act of love,
Or hinder fathers of that happy name,
240   Or with a barren womb the matron shame;
As many think, who stain with victims' blood
The mournful altars, and with incense load,
To bless the showery seed with future life,
And to impregnate the well-laboured wife.
245   In vain they weary heaven with prayer, or fly
To oracles, or magic numbers try:

216. *conspire*] combine to effect something (*OED* 3); also, evoking its Latin
root, 'breathe together' (*OED* 6).
222. *genial*] generative.
223. *exert*] exhibit, reveal (*OED* 1b).
224–5. D.'s addition.
227. *make*] build (*OED* 2b).
230. D.'s addition.
244. *well-laboured*] thoroughly tilled; for the metaphor cp. l. 283.

For barrenness of sexes will proceed
Either from too condensed or watery seed;
The watery juice too soon dissolves away,
250   And in the parts projected will not stay;
The too condensed, unsouled, unwieldly mass
Drops short, nor carries to the destined place:
Nor pierces to the parts, nor, though injected home,
Will mingle with the kindly moisture of the womb.
255   For nuptials are unlike in their success:
Some men with fruitful seed some women bless,
And from some men some women fruitful are,
Just as their constitutions join or jar;
And many seeming barren wives have been,
260   Who after matched with more prolific men
Have filled a family with prattling boys;
And many not supplied at home with joys
Have found a friend abroad to ease their smart,
And to perform the sapless husband's part.
265   So much it does import, that seed with seed
Should of the kindly mixture make the breed;
And thick with thin, and thin with thick should join,
So to produce and propagate the line.
Of such concernment too is drink and food,
270   T' incrassate or attenuate the blood.
Of like importance is the posture too,
In which the genial feat of love we do:
For as the females of the four-foot kind
Receive the leapings of their males behind,
275   So the good wives, with loins uplifted high,
And leaning on their hands the fruitful stroke may try:
For in that posture will they best conceive,
Not when supinely laid they frisk and heave;

250. *the parts projected*] the parts into which it has been thrown forward.
251. *unsouled*] unanimated; lacking life.   *unwieldly*] variant form of 'unwieldy'.
254, 266. *kindly*] favourable to growth (*OED* 5b).
258. D.'s addition.
262–4. D.'s addition, replacing ll. 1254–6 on husbands who eventually find a fruitful mate.
270. *incrassate*] thicken; Lucretius has the adjective *crassus* here.
274, 276, 278. D.'s additions.

For active motions only break the blow,
280   And more of strumpets than of wives they show,
When answering stroke with stroke, the mingled
    liquors flow.
Endearments eager, and too brisk a bound,
Throws off the ploughshare from the furrowed
    ground;
But common harlots in conjunction heave,
285   Because 'tis less their business to conceive
Than to delight, and to provoke the deed—
A trick which honest wives but little need.
Nor is it from the gods, or Cupid's dart,
That many a homely woman takes the heart;
290   But wives well-humoured, dutiful, and chaste,
And clean, will hold their wandering husbands fast;
Such are the links of love, and such a love will last.
For what remains, long habitude and use
Will kindness in domestic bands produce,
295   For custom will a strong impression leave;
Hard bodies which the lightest stroke receive,
In length of time will moulder and decay,
And stones with drops of rain are washed away.

280. D.'s addition.
291. *hold their wandering husbands fast*] For *facile insuescat te secum degere vitam* ('easily accustoms you to live with her').
292. D.'s addition.
293–4. For *quod superest, consuetudo concinnat amorem* ('moreover, it is habit that breeds love').
295. D.'s addition.

98 From Lucretius: Book the Fifth

Date and publication. Printed in 1685 in *Sylvae* (*SR* 10 January; advertised in *The Observator* 1 January); reprinted 1692; reprinted as an appendix to Creech's *Lucretius . . . and Manilius . . . Translated* (1700). For the likely date of composition see headnote to 'Preface to *Sylvae*'.

Context. For D.'s Lucretian translations generally, see headnote to 'Lucretius: The Beginning of the First Book'. For D.'s interest in the growth of the child cp. 'Palamon and Arcite' iii 1066–73, and 'Of the Pythagorean Philosophy' ll. 324–41. Charles Blount quotes exactly this passage from Lucretius in *Anima Mundi* [1679] 57.

Sources. D. translates *De Rerum Natura* v 222–34. For the editions and translations used by D. see headnote to 'Lucretius: The Beginning of the First Book'.

From Lucretius: Book the Fifth

Tum porro puer, etc.

Thus like a sailor by the tempest hurled
Ashore, the babe is shipwracked on the world:
Naked he lies, and ready to expire,
Helpless of all that human wants require;
5 Exposed upon unhospitable earth
From the first moment of his hapless birth.
Straight with foreboding cries he fills the room,
Too true presages of his future doom.
But flocks, and herds, and every savage beast
10 By more indulgent Nature are increased.
They want no rattles for their froward mood,
Nor nurse to reconcile them to their food

¶98. *3. ready to expire*] D.'s addition.
4. Helpless of] destitute of (an apparently rare construction: *OED* 1b).
5. D.'s addition.   *unhospitable*] stressed on the second syllable in the seventeenth century.
6. hapless] unlucky.
8. doom] destiny (*OED* 4).
10. D.'s addition.
11. want] need.   *froward*] perverse, hard to please.
12. to reconcile them to their food] D.'s addition.

With broken words; nor winter blasts they fear,
Nor change their habits with the changing year;
15 Nor for their safety citadels prepare,
Nor forge the wicked instruments of war:
Unlaboured Earth her bounteous treasure grants,
And Nature's lavish hands supplies their common
    wants.

13. nor winter blasts they fear] D.'s addition.
14. habits] clothes.
17. Unlaboured] uncultivated.
18. hands supplies] *1685*; hand supplies *Kinsley*; hands supply *Works*. A plural subject with a singular verb is a common seventeenth-century usage, though a misprint is possible.

99 Theocritus: Idyllium the Eighteenth (The Epithalamium of Helen and Menelaus)

Date and publication. Printed in 1685 in *Sylvae* (*SR* 10 January; advertised in *The Observator* 1 January); reprinted 1692.

Context. Stuart Gillespie (*RES* xli (1990) 365–9) suggests that this translation was made as a complimentary poem for the marriage of Princess Anne (daughter of the Duke of York) to Prince George of Denmark on 28 July 1683. The marriage could have provided a politically uncontroversial heir for James, but instead the princess's pregnancy resulted in a still birth on 30 April 1684. The poem might have been written in 1683 for the marriage, or early in 1684 in anticipation of a birth (cp. D.'s additions at ll. 36, 86–7), and printed in 1685 without any topical allusions since the moment for celebration had passed.

Sources. See headnote to 'Amaryllis'.

Theocrit. Idyllium the 18th
The Epithalamium of Helen and Menelaus

Twelve Spartan virgins, noble, young and fair,
With violet wreaths adorned their flowing hair,
And to the pompous palace did resort,
Where Menelaus kept his royal court.
5 There hand in hand a comely choir they led,
To sing a blessing to his nuptial bed,
With curious needles wrought, and painted flowers
    bespread.
Jove's beauteous daughter now his bride must be,
And Jove himself was less a god than he.

¶**99**. *3. pompous*] magnificent.
6. D.'s addition.
7. For νεογράπτω ('newly painted').   *curious*] careful, skilful (*OED* 7).
8. Jove's beauteous daughter] Helen was the daughter of Leda and Zeus.
9–10. D.'s addition.

10   For this their artful hands instruct the lute to sound,
     Their feet assist their hands and justly beat the ground.
     This was their song: 'Why, happy bridegroom, why
     Ere yet the stars are kindled in the sky,
     Ere twilight shades or evening dews are shed,
15   Why dost thou steal so soon away to bed?
     Has Somnus brushed thy eyelids with his rod, ⎤
     Or do thy legs refuse to bear their load,   ⎬
     With flowing bowls of a more generous god? ⎦
     If gentle slumber on thy temples creep
20   (But, naughty man, thou dost not mean to sleep),
     Betake thee to thy bed, thou drowsy drone,
     Sleep by thyself, and leave thy bride alone:
     Go leave her with her maiden mates to play
     At sports more harmless till the break of day;
25   Give us this evening: thou hast morn and night
     And all the year before thee for delight.
     O happy youth! to thee among the crowd
     Of rival princes Cupid sneezed aloud,
     And every lucky omen sent before
30   To meet thee landing on the Spartan shore.
     Of all our heroes thou canst boast alone
     That Jove, whene'er he thunders, calls thee son.

---

11. justly] precisely (*OED* 5).   *beat the ground*] Cp. Milton: 'Come, knit hands, and beat the ground' (*A Masque* l. 143; J. R. Mason).

13–14. D.'s addition.

15. In Theocritus Menelaus is asked why he has fallen asleep so early.

16. D.'s image.   *Somnus*] the god of sleep (see Ovid, *Met.* xi 586).

18. generous] rich and strong (of wine) (*OED* 5).   *god*] i.e. Bacchus, god of wine.

20. D.'s addition.

28. A sneeze was regarded as an omen (e.g. *Odyssey* xvii 541).   *Cupid*] D.'s addition.

30. landing on the . . . shore] D.'s addition, perhaps facilitating an allusion to Prince George.

Betwixt two sheets thou shalt enjoy her bare, ⎫
With whom no Grecian virgin can compare: ⎬
35 So soft, so sweet, so balmy and so fair. ⎭
A boy like thee would make a kingly line,
But O, a girl like her must be divine.
Her equals we in years, but not in face,
Twelve score viragos of the Spartan race,
40 While naked to Eurotas' banks we bend,
And there in manly exercise contend,
When she appears are all eclipsed and lost,
And hide the beauties that we made our boast.
So when the night and winter disappear,
45 The purple morning rising with the year
Salutes the spring, as her celestial eyes
Adorn the world, and brighten all the skies:
So beauteous Helen shines among the rest,
Tall, slender, straight, with all the graces blessed.
50 As pines the mountains, or as fields the corn,
Or as Thessalian steeds the race adorn,
So rosy-coloured Helen is the pride
Of Lacedaemon, and of Greece beside.
Like her no nymph can willing osiers bend ⎫
55 In basket-works which painted streaks commend; ⎬
With Pallas in the loom she may contend. ⎭
But none, ah none can animate the lyre,
And the mute strings with vocal souls inspire;
Whether the learned Minerva be her theme,
60 Or chaste Diana bathing in the stream;

33. For ὑπὸ τὰν μίαν ἵκετο χλαῖναν ('she has come to you under the same mantle').

35–6. D.'s addition. Line 36 may allude to the English succession.

40. Eurotas] the river of Sparta.

49. D.'s addition.

51. Thessalian steeds] the most famous breed of horses in Greece.

54–5. For Theocritus' οὔτε τις ἐκ ταλάρω πανίσδεται ἔργα τοιαῦτα ('no one wound such yarn from her basket').

56. D. adds the comparison between Helen and Pallas Athene, probably recalling the weaving contest between Athene and Arachne (Ovid, *Met.* vi 1–145).

58. D.'s addition.

59–60. Minerva . . . Diana] D. substitutes the Roman equivalents for the Greek goddesses Athene and Artemis.

None can record their heavenly praise so well
As Helen, in whose eyes ten thousand Cupids dwell.
O fair, O graceful! yet with maids enrolled,
But whom tomorrow's sun a matron shall behold:
65 Yet ere tomorrow's sun shall show his head, ⎫
The dewy paths of meadows we will tread   ⎬
For crowns and chaplets to adorn thy head: ⎭
Where all shall weep, and wish for thy return,
As bleating lambs their absent mother mourn.
70 Our noblest maids shall to thy name bequeath
The boughs of lotus, formed into a wreath;
This monument, thy maiden beauties' due,
High on a plane tree shall be hung to view:
On the smooth rind the passenger shall see
75 Thy name engraved, and worship Helen's tree.
Balm from a silver box distilled around
Shall all bedew the roots and scent the sacred ground;
The balm, 'tis true, can agèd plants prolong,
But Helen's name will keep it ever young.
80 Hail bride, hail bridegroom, son-in-law to Jove!
With fruitful joys Latona bless your love;
Let Venus furnish you with full desires,
Add vigour to your wills, and fuel to your fires.
Almighty Jove augment your wealthy store,
85 Give much to you, and to his grandsons more.
From generous loins a generous race will spring,
Each girl, like her, a queen; each boy, like you, a king.
Now sleep, if sleep you can; but while you rest
Sleep close, with folded arms, and breast to breast.

---

62. For τὰς πάντες ἐπ' ὄμμασιν ἵμεροι ἐντί ('in whose eyes is all desire'); cp. Creech: 'And Thousand *Cupids* wanton in her Eyes'.

71. lotus] Theocritus' λωτῷ seems to mean 'trefoil', but D. evidently has in mind the lotus tree (see *OED* 1–4 for various plants of this name).

74. rind] bark.   *passenger*] traveller, passer-by.

76. distilled] spread in minute drops (*OED* 2).

78–9. D.'s addition.

81. Latona] goddess of childbirth.

83, 86–7. D.'s addition. For ll. 86–7 see headnote.

86. generous] noble (*OED* 1); the first instance also has connotations of 'liberal' (*OED* 4), 'strong' (cp. *OED* 5, 6) and 'fertile' (cp. *OED* 3b).

88. if sleep you can] D.'s addition.

90   Rise in the morn, but O, before you rise
      Forget not to perform your morning sacrifice.
      We will be with you ere the crowing cock
      Salutes the light, and struts before his feathered flock.
      Hymen, O Hymen, to thy triumphs run,
95   And view the mighty spoils thou hast in battle won.'

---

91. D.'s addition.
93. struts before his feathered flock] D.'s addition.
94. Hymen] god of marriage.
95. D.'s addition.

100 Theocritus: Idyllium the Twenty-third (The Despairing Lover)

Date and publication. Printed in 1685 in *Sylvae* (SR 10 January; advertised in *The Observator* 1 January); reprinted 1692. For possible date of composition see headnote to 'Preface to *Sylvae*'.

Sources. See headnote to 'Amaryllis'. The main change which D. makes to Theocritus' *Idyll* xxiii is to change its subject from a homosexual to a heterosexual love (unlike Creech: *pace Works* iii 287).

Idyllium the 23d
The Despairing Lover

With inauspicious love a wretched swain
Pursued the fairest nymph of all the plain;
Fairest indeed, but prouder far than fair,
She plunged him hopeless in a deep despair:
5 Her heavenly form too haughtily she prized,
His person hated, and his gifts despised;
Nor knew the force of Cupid's cruel darts,
Nor feared his awful power on human hearts;
But either from her hopeless lover fled,
10 Or with disdainful glances shot him dead;
No kiss, no look to cheer the drooping boy,
No word she spoke—she scorned ev'n to deny.
But as a hunted panther casts about
Her glaring eyes, and pricks her listening ears to scout,
15 So she to shun his toils her cares employed,
And fiercely in her savage freedom joyed.

¶**100.** *1. inauspicious*] ill-omened, unlucky.
8. awful] awesome.
13. panther] for θήρ, 'wild beast'.
14. pricks her listening ears to scout] D.'s addition.
15–16. D.'s addition.
15. toils] nets, traps.
16. savage] wild, untamed.

Her mouth she writhed, her forehead taught to frown,
Her eyes to sparkle fires to love unknown;
Her sallow cheeks her envious mind did show,
20 And every feature spoke aloud the curstness of a
        shrew.
Yet could not he his obvious fate escape:
His love still dressed her in a pleasing shape,
And every sullen frown and bitter scorn
But fanned the fuel that too fast did burn.
25 Long time unequal to his mighty pain
He strove to curb it, but he strove in vain;
At last his woes broke out, and begged relief
With tears, the dumb petitioners of grief,
With tears so tender as adorned his love,
30 And any heart but only hers would move.
Trembling before her bolted doors he stood,
And there poured out th' unprofitable flood;
Staring his eyes, and haggard was his look,
Then, kissing first the threshold, thus he spoke:
35   'Ah, nymph more cruel than of human race,
Thy tigress heart belies thy angel face;
Too well thou show'st thy pedigree from stone,
Thy grandame's was the first by Pyrrha thrown.
Unworthy thou to be so long desired,
40 But so my love, and so my fate required.
I beg not now (for 'tis in vain) to live,
But take this gift, the last that I can give.
This friendly cord shall soon decide the strife
Betwixt my lingering love and loathsome life;

17. *writhed*] twisted, distorted (*OED* 5b).
19. *envious*] malicious, spiteful (*OED* 2).
20–1. D.'s addition.
20. *curstness*] ill temper, fierceness (*OED* 4).
21. *obvious*] waiting in his path (*OED* 1).
25–6, 29–30, 33. D.'s additions.
37–8. Developing λάϊνε πᾶι, 'boy of stone'. After mankind had been destroyed in the flood, Pyrrha and Deucalion recreated the race by throwing stones over their shoulders, which became human beings.
38. *grandame's*] grandmother's.
40–1. D.'s addition.
43–4. Developing βρόχον, 'halter'.

45   This moment puts an end to all my pain;
       I shall no more despair, nor thou disdain.
       Farewell, ungrateful and unkind, I go
       Condemned by thee to those sad shades below;
       I go th' extremest remedy to prove,
50   To drink oblivion, and to drench my love;
       There happily to lose my long desires:
       But ah, what draught so deep to quench my fires!
       Farewell, ye never-opening gates, ye stones
       And threshold guilty of my midnight moans:
55   What I have suffered here ye know too well;
       What I shall do, the gods and I can tell.
       The rose is fragrant, but it fades in time,
       The violet sweet, but quickly past the prime;
       White lilies hang their heads and soon decay,
60   And whiter snow in minutes melts away:
       Such is your blooming youth, and withering so;
       The time will come, it will, when you shall know
       The rage of love; your haughty heart shall burn
       In flames like mine, and meet a like return.
65   Obdurate as you are, O hear at least
       My dying prayers, and grant my last request!
       When first you ope your doors, and passing by
       The sad, ill-omened object meets your eye,
       Think it not lost, a moment if you stay;
70   The breathless wretch—so made by you—survey:
       Some cruel pleasure will from thence arise,
       To view the mighty ravage of your eyes.
       I wish (but O, my wish is vain, I fear)
       The kind oblation of a falling tear.
75   Then loose the knot, and take me from the place,
       And spread your mantle o'er my grisly face;
       Upon my livid lips bestow a kiss:
       O envy not the dead, they feel not bliss!
       Nor fear your kisses can restore my breath:
80   Ev'n you are not more pitiless than death.
       Then for my corpse a homely grave provide,
       Which love and me from public scorn may hide.

45, 47, 54–5, 71–3, 80. D.'s additions.
81. *homely*] plain, simple.

Thrice call upon my name, thrice beat your breast,
And hail me thrice to everlasting rest.
85 Last, let my tomb this sad inscription bear:
"A wretch whom love has killed lies buried here:
O passengers, Aminta's eyes beware." '
   Thus having said, and furious with his love,
He heaved with more than human force, to move
90 A weighty stone (the labour of a team),
And raised from thence he reached the neighbouring
   beam:
Around its bulk a sliding knot he throws,
And fitted to his neck the fatal noose;
Then spurning backward took a swing, till death
95 Crept up, and stopped the passage of his breath.
The bounce burst ope the door; the scornful fair
Relentless looked, and saw him beat his quivering feet
   in air;
Nor wept his fate, nor cast a pitying eye,
Nor took him down, but brushed regardless by;
100 And as she passed, her chance or fate was such
Her garments touched the dead, polluted by the touch.
Next to the dance, thence to the bath did move:
The bath was sacred to the god of love,
Whose injured image with a wrathful eye
105 Stood threatening from a pedestal on high;
Nodding a while, and watchful of his blow,
He fell, and falling crushed th' ungrateful nymph
   below.
Her gushing blood the pavement all besmeared,
And this her last expiring voice was heard:
110   'Lovers, farewell; revenge has reached my scorn;
   Thus warned, be wise, and love for love return.'

---

84. hail] OED records this only as a greeting, not a farewell. D. may be
thinking of the Latin ave, which is both, esp. to the dead.
87. passengers] passers-by.   Aminta] D.'s addition.
88. furious] mad, frantic.
94. spurning] kicking.
95–6, 106. D.'s additions.
106. Nodding] tottering.

101 Daphnis (from Theocritus' *Idyll* XXVII)

Date and publication. Printed in 1685 in *Sylvae* (*SR* 10 January; advertised in *The Observator* 1 January); reprinted 1692. For possible date of composition see headnote to 'Preface to *Sylvae*'.

Sources. See headnote to 'Amaryllis'.

Daphnis
From Theocritus Idyll 27

Daphnis	The shepherd Paris bore the Spartan bride
	By force away, and then by force enjoyed;
	But I by free consent can boast a bliss,
	A fairer Helen, and a sweeter kiss.
5 *Chloris*	Kisses are empty joys, and soon are o'er.
Daphnis	A kiss betwixt the lips is something more.
Chloris	I wipe my mouth, and where's your kissing then?
Daphnis	I swear you wipe it to be kissed again.
Chloris	Go tend your herd, and kiss your cows at home;
10	I am a maid, and in my beauties' bloom.
Daphnis	'Tis well remembered: do not waste your time,
	But wisely use it ere you pass your prime.
Chloris	Blown roses hold their sweetness to the last,
	And raisins keep their luscious native taste.
15 *Daphnis*	The sun's too hot; those olive shades are near:
	I fain would whisper something in your ear.

¶**101.** *1–2.* These lines are given to the woman in modern editions of Theocritus, but to Daphnis in Heinsius.

1. the Spartan bride] Helen.

5. Chloris] For Theocritus' Acrotime; Chloris is a common name in Restoration pastoral.

6. For ἔστι καὶ ἐν κενεοῖσι φιλάμασιν ἁδέα τέρψις ('even in empty kisses there is sweet delight').

Chloris	'Tis honest talking where we may be seen;
	God knows what secret mischief you may mean.
	I doubt you'll play the wag, and kiss again.

20　Daphnis　At least beneath yon elm you need not fear;
　　　　　　My pipe's in tune, if you're disposed to hear.

　　　Chloris　Play by yourself: I dare not venture thither;
　　　　　　You and your naughty pipe go hang together.

　　　Daphnis　Coy nymph beware, lest Venus you offend.

25　Chloris　I shall have chaste Diana still to friend.

　　　Daphnis　You have a soul, and Cupid has a dart.

　　　Chloris　Diana will defend, or heal my heart.
　　　　　　Nay, fie; what mean you in this open place!
　　　　　　Unhand me, or I swear I'll scratch your face.

30　　　　　　Let go, for shame, you make me mad for spite;
　　　　　　My mouth's my own, and if you kiss I'll bite.

　　　Daphnis　Away with your dissembling female tricks;
　　　　　　What, would you scape the fate of all your sex?

　　　Chloris　I swear I'll keep my maidenhead till death,

35　　　　　　And die as pure as Queen Elizabeth.

　　　Daphnis　Nay, mum for that; but let me lay thee down:
　　　　　　Better with me, than with some nauseous clown.

　　　Chloris　I'd have you know, if I were so inclined
　　　　　　I have been wooed by many a wealthy hind,

40　　　　　　But never found a husband to my mind.

17–19. For οὐκ ἐθέλω· καὶ πρίν με παρήπαφες ἀδει μύθῳ ('No thank you; you won me over before with your pretty story').

19. doubt] suspect (*OED* 6b).　　*play the wag*] be mischievous.

23, 28. D.'s additions.

29–31. I swear . . . my own] D.'s addition.

30. spite] annoyance, irritation (*OED* 4c).

32–7. D.'s addition.

36. mum for that] not a word about that.

37. clown] peasant, boor (*OED* 1).

39. hind] steward, bailiff (*OED* 2c).

Daphnis	But they are absent all, and I am here.	⎫
Chloris	The matrimonial yoke is hard to bear,	⎬
	And 'marriage' is a woeful word to hear.	⎭
Daphnis	A scarecrow, set to frighten fools away;	
45	Marriage has joys, and you shall have a say.	
Chloris	Sour sauce is often mixed with our delight;	
	You kick by day more than you kiss by night.	
Daphnis	Sham stories all; but say the worst you can,	
	A very wife fears neither God nor man.	
50 *Chloris*	But childbirth is, they say, a deadly pain;	
	It costs at least a month to knit again.	
Daphnis	Diana cures the wounds Lucina made;	
	Your goddess is a midwife by her trade.	
Chloris	But I shall spoil my beauty if I bear.	
55 *Daphnis*	But 'Mam' and 'Dad' are pretty names to hear.	
Chloris	But there's a civil question used of late:	
	Where lies my jointure, where your own estate?	
Daphnis	My flocks, my fields, my wood, my pastures take,	
	With settlement as good as law can make.	

43–4. D.'s addition.

45. *you shall have a say*] D.'s addition.

46–7. For ναὶ μάν φασι γυναικᾶς ἑοὺς τρομέειν παρακοίτας ('yes, but they say that wives fear their bedfellows').

48. D.'s addition.

49. For τί καὶ τρομέουσι γυναῖκες; ('what should wives fear?').   *very*] true.

51. D.'s addition.

52. *Lucina*] goddess of childbirth.

53. D.'s addition.

56–7. For καὶ τί μοι ἕδνον ἄγεις γάμου ἄξιον, ἢν ἐπινεύσω; ('what wedding gift will you bring me, worth the marriage, if I agree?'). The grounds for the financial arrangements between husband and wife were currently the subject of debate and lawsuits: see Susan Staves, *Players' Scepters* (1979) 145–60.   *civil*] polite (*OED* 9); legal (*OED* 17, 19). Staves discusses the debate over whether marriage was subject to civil or ecclesiastical regulation. *jointure*] the wife's legal interest in an estate.

59. D.'s addition.

60	*Chloris*	Swear then you will not leave me on the common,
		But marry me, and make an honest woman.
	Daphnis	I swear by Pan (though he wears horns, you'll say),
		Cudgelled and kicked, I'll not be forced away.
	Chloris	I bargain for a wedding bed at least,
65		A house, and handsome lodging for a guest.
	Daphnis	A house well furnished shall be thine to keep,
		And for a flock-bed I can shear my sheep.
	Chloris	What tale shall I to my old father tell?
	Daphnis	'Twill make him chuckle thou'rt bestowed so well.
70	*Chloris*	But after all, in troth I am to blame,
		To be so loving ere I know your name.
		A pleasant-sounding name's a pretty thing.
	Daphnis	Faith, mine's a very pretty name to sing:
		They call me Daphnis; Lycidas my sire;
75		Both sound as well as woman can desire.
		Nomæa bore me; farmers in degree,
		He a good husband, a good housewife she.
	Chloris	Your kindred is not much amiss, 'tis true,
		Yet I am somewhat better born than you.
80	*Daphnis*	I know your father and his family,
		And, without boasting, am as good as he—
		Menalcas, and no master goes before.

60. on the common] i.e. destitute. *OED* cites Hinde (1641): '[Some] deale no better with their impotent and old servants than to turne them off their hands to live on a Commons or dye in a ditch.'

61. D.'s addition.

62. though he wears horns, you'll say] D.'s addition. The goat-god Pan has horns; so too does the devil, who is not to be trusted. There is a further play on the cuckold's horns.

67. For τὰ δὲ πώεα καλὰ νομεύω ('the flocks of sheep which I feed are fine'). *flock-bed*] bed stuffed with wool.

70–1. For οὔνομα σὸν λέγε τῆνο ('tell me your name').

73, 75. D.'s additions.

76–7. farmers . . . she] D.'s addition.   *degree*] social status.   *husband*] husbandman.

81–2. D.'s expansion of 'Menalcas'.   *Menalcas*] *Eds*; Menelaus *1685*.

Chloris	Hang both our pedigrees, not one word more;
	But if you love me, let me see your living,
85	Your house and home: for seeing is believing.
Daphnis	See first yon cypress grove, a shade from noon.
Chloris	Browse on, my goats, for I'll be with you soon.
Daphnis	Feed well, my bulls, to whet your appetite,
	That each may take a lusty leap at night.
90 *Chloris*	What do you mean, uncivil as you are,
	To touch my breasts, and leave my bosom bare?
Daphnis	These pretty bubbies first I make my own.
Chloris	Pull out your hand, I swear, or I shall swoon.
Daphnis	Why does thy ebbing blood forsake thy face?
95 *Chloris*	Throw me at least upon a cleaner place:
	My linen ruffled, and my waistcoat soiling,
	What, do you think new clothes were made for spoiling?
Daphnis	I'll lay my lambskins underneath thy back.
Chloris	My headgear's off: what filthy work you make!
100 *Daphnis*	To Venus first I lay these offerings by.
Chloris	Nay, first look round that nobody be nigh:
	Methinks I hear a whispering in the grove.
Daphnis	The cypress trees are telling tales of love.
Chloris	You tear off all behind me, and before me,
105	And I'm as naked as my mother bore me.

<hr/>

83, 89. D.'s addition.

92. *bubbies*] *OED*'s first example is from 1686.

95–7. For βάλλεις εἰς ἀμάραν με καὶ εἵματα καλὰ μιαίνεις ('you are throwing me into the ditch, and soiling my fine clothes').

99. *headgear*] for μίτραν (either 'girdle' or 'headband', 'snood').

	Daphnis	I'll buy thee better clothes than these I tear,
		And lie so close I'll cover thee from air.
	Chloris	Y' are liberal now, but when your turn is sped,
		You'll wish me choked with every crust of bread.
110	*Daphnis*	I'll give thee more, much more than I have told;
		Would I could coin my very heart to gold.
	Chloris	Forgive thy handmaid, huntress of the wood,
		I see there's no resisting flesh and blood!
	Daphnis	The noble deed is done: my herds I'll cull;
115		Cupid, be thine a calf, and Venus, thine a bull.
	Chloris	A maid I came, in an unlucky hour,
		But hence return without my virgin flower.
	Daphnis	A maid is but a barren name at best;
		If thou canst hold, I bid for twins at least.

120   Thus did this happy pair their love dispense
         With mutual joys, and gratified their sense;
         The god of love was there a bidden guest,
         And present at his own mysterious feast.
         His azure mantle underneath he spread,
125   And scattered roses on the nuptial bed;
         While folded in each other's arms they lay, ⎫
         He blew the flames, and furnished out the   ⎬
             play,   ⎪
         And from their foreheads wiped the balmy   ⎭
             sweat away.
         First rose the maid, and with a glowing face
130   Her downcast eyes beheld her print upon the
             grass;
         Thence to her herd she sped herself in haste: ⎫
         The bridegroom started from his trance at last, ⎬
         And piping homeward jocundly he passed.   ⎭

107, 110, 113–14, 119. D.'s additions.

119. hold] retain the seed, conceive (*OED* 15d).

122–8. D.'s addition.

128. balmy sweat] Cp. Milton: 'I found me laid/ In balmy sweat' (*PL* viii 254–5; J. R. Mason).

130. D.'s addition.

Date and publication. Printed in 1685 in *Sylvae* (*SR* 10 January; advertised in *The Observator* 1 January); reprinted 1692. See headnote to 'Preface to *Sylvae*' for possible date of composition.

Context. Horace had been popular with translators throughout the seventeenth century; in the Restoration the composite translation of *The Poems of Horace*, edited by Alexander Brome, appeared in 1666 (revised 1671, 1680), and Creech's complete translation was published in 1684. Writers who translated some of Horace's *Carm.* included Cowley, Oldham and Roscommon. For details see Gillespie's 'Checklist'. D.'s translation of *Carm.* I iii is influenced partly by his revulsion from the political turmoil of the previous years: the emphasis here on the destructive consequences of ambition and audacity echo his charges against the Whig leaders in *AA* l. 198*n*, ll. 304–9; *The Medal passim*.

Sources. It is not easy to establish which editions of Horace D. used, since the textual variants are minimal, and editors take their notes from one another. Bottkol came to no conclusion; *Works* speculated (without evidence) that D. used Heinsius' 1629 edition. The present notes to the four Horatian translations from *Sylvae* show that D. used the Latin prose interpretation and glosses in the editions by Lubinus (1612) and Schrevelius (1653; a page from the 1663 reprint is illustrated in Plate 6), and the French edition and translation by Dacier (1681–9); other minor evidence suggests that he may also have consulted Cruquius (1578). For further evidence of D.'s use of particular editions of Horace see Paul Hammond in *Horace Made New*, edited by Charles Martindale and David Hopkins (1993) 127–47, 294–7, esp. 294. D. evidently used as many previous translations as he could find, and the following seem to have supplied him with occasional words (including rhymes): John Ashmore, *Certain Selected Odes of Horace Englished* (1621), Alexander Brome (ed.), *The Poems of Horace* (1666, revised 1671 and 1680), Richard Fanshawe, *Selected Parts of Horace, Prince of Lyricks* (1652), J. H[arrington], *The Odes and Epodes of Horace* (1684), Thomas Hawkins, *Odes of Horace, the Best of Lyrick Poets* (1635), Barten Holyday, *Horace, the Best of Lyrick Poets* (1652), Henry Rider, *All the Odes and Epodes of Horace* (1638). There are also parallels between D.'s versions and those of Creech, *The Odes, Satyrs, and Epistles of Horace* (1684), which have previously (and probably rightly) been taken to be D.'s borrowings, but the relative dates of the two translations are uncertain (see headnote to 'Preface to *Sylvae*').

Horat. Ode 3. Lib. 1.

Inscribed to the Earl of Roscommon, on his intended voyage to Ireland

So may th' auspicious Queen ȍf love,
And the twin stars (the seed of Jove),
And he who rules the raging wind,
To thee, O sacred ship, be kind;
5   And gentle breezes fill thy sails,
Supplying soft Etesian gales,
As thou, to whom the Muse commends
The best of poets and of friends,
Dost thy committed pledge restore,
10   And land him safely on the shore;
And save the better part of me
From perishing with him at sea.
Sure he who first the passage tried ⎫
In hardened oak his heart did hide, ⎬
15   And ribs of iron armed his side! ⎭
Or his at least in hollow wood,
Who tempted first the briny flood;
Nor feared the winds' contending roar,
Nor billows beating on the shore,

¶102. *Title.* For Roscommon see 'To the Earl of Roscommon' headnote. Roscommon was born in Ireland. The occasion of the proposed voyage is not known. Horace's poem is addressed to Virgil on his voyage to Greece.

1. auspicious Queen of love] Venus. Cp. 'Lucretius: The Beginning of the First Book' l. 2*n.*   *auspicious*] D.'s addition; see *AM* l. 77*n.*

2. twin stars] Castor and Pollux, protectors of sailors.   *seed of Jove*] D.'s addition; cp. Lubinus' *Iovis . . . filij* ('sons of Jove').

3. he who rules] Aeolus, master of the winds.

6. Etesian] Classically, north-west winds; in seventeenth-century England the term was more loosely used for winds from any particular quarter (*OED*).

7–8. D.'s expansion, where Horace names Virgil.

7. commends] Cp. *commendatum* in Lubinus and Cruquius.

10. Cp. Creech: 'And land him on the *Attick* shore' (*Works*).

11. the better part of me] For *animae dimidium meae* ('half of my soul'); cp. 'thou art all the better part of me' (Shakespeare, *Sonnet* xxxix 2; cp. lxxiv 8).

12. D.'s expansion.

20   Nor Hyades portending rain,
        Nor all the tyrants of the main.
        What form of death could him affright,
        Who unconcerned, with steadfast sight,
        Could view the surges mounting steep,
25   And monsters rolling in the deep?
        Could through the ranks of ruin go,
        With storms above, and rocks below!
        In vain did Nature's wise command
        Divide the waters from the land,
30   If daring ships and men profane
        Invade th' inviolable main,
        Th' eternal fences overleap,
        And pass at will the boundless deep.
        No toil, no hardship can restrain
35   Ambitious man inured to pain;
        The more confined, the more he tries,
        And at forbidden quarry flies.
        Thus bold Prometheus did aspire,
        And stole from heaven the seed of fire;

20. Hyades] Trisyllabic; stars in the constellation Taurus, whose rising and
setting were thought to indicate rain.
21. D. generalises Horace's description of Notus (the South wind) as ruler of
the Adriatic.   *tyrants*] In *Carm.* II xvii 19 Horace calls Capricorn *tyrannus*
of the ocean.
28. Nature] for Horace's *deus* ('god').
32–3. D.'s addition, echoing Satan's invasion of Paradise: 'Leaps o'er the
fence' (*PL* iv 187; J. R. Mason); cp. 'Nisus and Euryalus' l. 341. D. had
already adapted this for Lucifer's speech in *The State of Innocence* (1677) 3: 'T'
o'erleap th' Eternal Fence, or if so high/ We cannot climb, to undermine his
Skie'. D. was prompted here by Horace's *transiliunt* ('they leap over').
boundless deep] from Milton, *PL* i 177, vii 168 (J. R. Mason).
36. D.'s addition.
38–9. aspire/ . . . fire/] For the rhyme cp. Jonson's reference to Prometheus in
'An Ode. To Himself' ll. 27–8.
39. seed of fire] Horace just has *ignem* ('fire'), but *semina flammae* (or *ignis*) is a
common classical phrase (e.g. Lucretius vi 201 etc; Virgil, *Aen.* vi 6; Ovid,
Met. xv 347); cp. *AM* l. 866.

40   A train of ills, a ghastly crew
        The robber's blazing track pursue:
        Fierce Famine, with her meagre face,
        And fevers of the fiery race
        In swarms th' offending wretch surround,
45   All brooding on the blasted ground;
        And limping Death, lashed on by Fate,
        Comes up to shorten half our date.
        This made not Dedalus beware
        With borrowed wings to sail in air;
50   To hell Alcides forced his way,
        Plunged through the lake, and snatched the prey.
        Nay, scarce the gods or heavenly climes
        Are safe from our audacious crimes;
        We reach at Jove's imperial crown,
55   And pull th' unwilling thunder down.

40–1. D.'s addition.

40. A train of ills] Zeus punished the theft by sending Pandora with a box full of diseases.   *ghastly*] causing terror (*OED* 1); corpse-like (*OED* 2). *crew*] Adam is shown a 'monstrous crew' of diseases in *PL* xii 474 (J. R. Mason).

42. D.'s expansion of *macies* ('leanness'), possibly from Lubinus' glosses *fames* ('famine') and *pallor*.   *meagre*] emaciated.

43–5. D.'s expansion of *nova febrium terris incubuit cohors* ('a new battalion of fevers dwelt on the earth').

46–7. D.'s expansion of *semotique prius tarda necessitas leti corripuit gradum* ('the slow necessity of a previously remote death quickened her pace').   *date*] term of life (*OED* 4).

50–1. Hercules stole Cerberus from the underworld.

54. imperial crown] D.'s addition.

55. unwilling] D.'s addition.

103 Horace: *Odes* I ix

Date and publication. Printed in 1685 in *Sylvae* (*SR* 10 January; advertised in *The Observator* 1 January); reprinted 1692. See headnote to 'Preface to *Sylvae*' for possible date of composition.

Context. See headnote to 'Horace: *Odes* I iii'.

Sources. For the editions and translations of Horace used by D. see headnote to 'Horace: *Odes* I iii'. For an account of D.'s methods and aims in this translation see H. A. Mason, *CQ* xiv (1985) 205–39.

Horace Lib. 1. Ode 9

I

Behold yon mountain's hoary height
   Made higher with new mounts of snow;
Again behold the winter's weight
   Oppress the labouring woods below;
5   And streams with icy fetters bound,
   Benumbed and cramped to solid ground.

II

With well-heaped logs dissolve the cold,
   And feed the genial hearth with fires;
Produce the wine that makes us bold,
10   And sprightly wit and love inspires:
   For what hereafter shall betide,
   God, if 'tis worth his care, provide.

¶**103.** *1. mountain*] Horace specifically writes of Soracte.   *hoary*] greyish white (*OED* 2); venerable (*OED* 1c).
4. labouring] burdened (*OED* 15), i.e. with snow; from Horace's *laborantes*.
5–6. fetters . . . ground] D.'s expansion of *constiterint* ('stand').   *bound*] thus Creech.
7. dissolve] translating *dissolve*.
8. genial] festive (*OED* 2). On the significance of *genial* (which combines religious and joyful feelings about the hearth as the focus of the good life) see H. A. Mason 213–22. For a parallel with this passage see 'The Fifth Satire of Persius' ll. 220–3.
9–10. that . . . inspires] D.'s addition. D. gives no equivalent for Horace's address to Thaliarchus.
11–12. Translating *permitte divis cetera* ('entrust the rest to the gods').

III

Let him alone with what he made,
  To toss and turn the world below;
15 At his command the storms invade,
  The winds by his commission blow;
Till with a nod he bids 'em cease,
And then the calm returns, and all is peace.

IV

Tomorrow and her works defy,
20   Lay hold upon the present hour,
And snatch the pleasures passing by,
  To put them out of Fortune's power;
Nor love, nor love's delights disdain:
Whate'er thou get'st today is gain.

V

25 Secure those golden early joys
  That youth unsoured with sorrow bears,
Ere with'ring time the taste destroys
  With sickness and unwieldy years!
For active sports, for pleasing rest, ⎫
30 This is the time to be possessed;   ⎬
The best is but in season best.   ⎭

---

13. D.'s addition.

14. Biblical: Isaiah xxii 18 says that God 'will surely violently turn and toss thee' (H. A. Mason).

19. Translating *quid sit futurum cras fuge quaerere* ('forbear to ask what tomorrow will be').

20–3. Translating *quem Fors dierum cumque dabit lucro/ appone* ('credit to your account whatever days Fortune gives you'). Cp. 'Horace: *Odes* III xxix' ll. 50–1, and l. 73*n.* H. A. Mason 222 suggests an influence from Horace's *Carm.* III viii: *dona praesentis rape laetus horae ac/ linque severa* ('snatch joyfully what the present hour gives, and leave gloomier matters to the future'), and compares 'The Seventh Book of the *Aeneis*' ll. 179–82.

24. Cp. Dacier: 'comme si vous aviez dû mourir aujourd'huy, comtez que vous gagnez' (Stuart Gillespie, privately).

28. unwieldy] feeble, infirm (*OED* 1).

30–1. D.'s elaboration of *nunc . . . nunc* ('now . . . now').

30. Probably not 'now is the time to possess such blessings' (*Works*) but 'this is the time which we must possess' (cp. the tag *carpe diem* ('seize the time') and l. 20).

VI

The pointed hour of promised bliss,
   The pleasing whisper in the dark,
The half-unwilling, willing kiss,
35   The laugh that guides thee to the mark,
When the kind nymph would coyness feign,
And hides but to be found again:
These, these are joys the gods for youth ordain.

32. pointed] appointed (*OED*).
34. half-unwilling, willing] for *male pertinaci* ('hardly resisting').   *willing*] in Creech.
35. that . . . mark] D.'s addition. Cp. Denham: 'Not a Spark/ Left to light me to the mark' ('Martial. Epigram' ll. 14–15, *Poems and Translations* (1668)).
36–8. D.'s addition.

Date and publication. Printed in 1685 in *Sylvae* (*SR* 10 January; advertised in *The Observator* 1 January); reprinted 1692. See headnote to 'Preface to *Sylvae*' for possible date of composition. In the present text the indentation has been regularized to reflect the number of syllables in each line.

Context. For Restoration translations of Horace generally see headnote to 'Horace: *Odes* I iii'. Buckingham translated ll. 46–64 of *Carm.* III xxix in 1680 (BL MS Add 34362).

Sources. For the editions and translations used by D. see headnote to 'Horace: *Odes* I iii'. In addition, Cowley's *Essays*, with their stress on liberty and retirement, are an important influence on this poem. For an account of the aims and methods of D.'s translation see H. A. Mason, *CQ* x (1981) 91–129.

Horat. Ode 29. Book 3.
Paraphrased in Pindaric Verse
and
Inscribed to the Right Honourable
Laurence, Earl of Rochester

I

Descended of an ancient line
That long the Tuscan sceptre swayed,

¶**104.** *Title. Paraphrased*] This indicates that D. is not attempting a close translation; he actually blends Roman and contemporary references. See further 'Preface to *Ovid's Epistles*' ll. 237–42.   *Pindaric Verse*] See 'Preface to *Sylvae*' ll. 549–606.   *Laurence, Earl of Rochester*] Laurence Hyde (1641–1711), second son of Edward Hyde, Earl of Clarendon (see *To My Lord Chancellor*); previously celebrated in *AA* (see ll. 888–97n); see 'Preface to *Sylvae*' ll. 545–7.

1–2. Works comments that these lines apply awkwardly to Rochester's family, since his father had been ennobled only in 1660. But D. does not refer specifically to membership of the peerage, and Clarendon had served Charles I (if not actually swayed his sceptre) since before the Civil War, and served his son since 1645, first as his guardian and subsequently as Lord Chancellor. The original is addressed to Horace's patron Maecenas, a member of the ancient Etruscan (hence 'Tuscan') aristocracy; he was a friend and confidant of Augustus.

1. From Dacier's 'qui descendez d'une des plus anciennes Familles' (H. A. Mason).

Make haste to meet the generous wine
Whose piercing is for thee delayed:
5   The rosy wreath is ready made,
And artful hands prepare
The fragrant Syrian oil that shall perfume thy hair.

II

When the wine sparkles from afar,
And the well-natured friend cries, 'Come away',
10   Make haste, and leave thy business and thy care;
No mortal interest can be worth thy stay.

III

Leave for a while thy costly country seat,
And, to be great indeed, forget
The nauseous pleasures of the great:

3. generous] rich and strong (*OED* 5); the English application of the word to
wine comes from Horace's use of *generosus* in *Epist.* I xv 18.
4. piercing] To *pierce* (*OED* 2) was to broach a cask. Creech has 'pierc'd' and
Dacier 'percé'.
7. Syrian] not named by Horace, but suggested by Schrevelius.
8–11. D.'s addition.
10. thy business and thy care] This translates Lubinus' gloss *curis ac negotijs*.
These are key words for D. in *Sylvae.* He frequently mentions the burdens of
business (often aware of the element 'busy'): cp. ll. 19, 52; 'Horace: *Epode* II'
ll. 4, 59; 'Lucretius: The Beginning of the First Book' l. 45. Business is seen as
a curse in Cowley's *Essays* (e.g. 387–8, 390). Stuart Gillespie (in *Horace Made
New*, edited by Charles Martindale and David Hopkins (1993) 298) notes that
business means both 'professional duties' (*OED* 12) and 'anxiety, care' (*OED*
5). For its opposite, *ease*, see *AA* l. 168*n*. D. returns to the need for release
from anxious care in 'Horace: *Epode* II' ll. 12, 55, 60; 'Lucretius: The Beginning of the Second Book' ll. 22, 35, 51; 'Lucretius: Against the Fear of Death'
ll. 82, 136, 199, 272, 294, 303; 'Lucretius: Concerning the Nature of Love'
l. 127.
11. interest] This word had been used frequently by D. for the narrow self-
interest pursued by the Whigs at the expense of public peace (e.g. in *AA*
ll. 501, 724; *The Medal* ll. 88–9).   *worth thy stay*] Another leading idea in
Sylvae is the question of what is worth man's attention: cp. 'Lucretius:
Against the Fear of Death' l. 294; 'Horace: *Odes* I ix' l. 12.
13. D.'s addition.

15   Make haste and come;
            Come and forsake thy cloying store,
            Thy turret that surveys from high
            The smoke, and wealth and noise of Rome,
            And all the busy pageantry
20   That wise men scorn, and fools adore:
        Come, give thy soul a loose, and taste the pleasures of
            the poor.

                            IV
            Sometimes 'tis grateful to the rich to try
        A short vicissitude, and fit of poverty;
            A savoury dish, a homely treat,
25   Where all is plain, where all is neat,
            Without the stately spacious room,
        The Persian carpet, or the Tyrian loom,
        Clear up the cloudy foreheads of the great.

16. cloying store] from Harrington.

17. turret] from *turrim* ('tower') in Lubinus and Schrevelius; in Horace this is Maecenas' town house.

18. Cp. 'The Wealth, the noise, and smoak of *Rome*' (Creech). Contemporaries were concerned at the atmospheric pollution in London; Evelyn proposed remedies in *Fumifugium: or The Inconvenience of the Aer and Smoak of London Dissipated* (1661).

19–21. D.'s addition.

21. give . . . a loose] give freedom, allow free rein (*OED* 3b, first example); perhaps translating *solveret animum* from Horace's *Serm.* II vi 83 (David Hopkins in *Horace Made New* 118).

22. grateful] pleasing, welcome (*OED* 1).

23. vicissitude] change (*OED* 3); from *vices* in Horace and *vicissitudines* in Lubinus and Cruquius.   *fit*] short period (*OED* 4d).

24. savoury] appetising (*OED* 1).   *a homely treat*] thus Creech.

26–7. Cp. Cowley: 'Behind a hanging in a spacious room,/ The richest work of *Mortclakes* noble Loom*' ('The Country Mouse'; *Essays* 415; Stuart Gillespie, privately).

27. Cp. Creech: 'Purple wrought in *Tyrian* Looms'.

28. cloudy foreheads] cp. 'clouded forhead' (Rider).   *cloudy*] darkened by trouble, frowning (*OED* 6).

V

The sun is in the lion mounted high;

30
The Sirian star
Barks from afar,

And with his sultry breath infects the sky;

The ground below is parched, the heavens above us
fry.

The shepherd drives his fainting flock

35
Beneath the covert of a rock;
And seeks refreshing rivulets nigh:

The Sylvans to their shades retire,

Those very shades and streams, new shades and
streams require,

And want a cooling breeze of wind to fan the raging
fire.

VI

40
Thou, what befits the new Lord Mayor,
And what the City faction dare,
And what the Gallic arms will do,
And what the quiver-bearing foe,
Art anxiously inquisitive to know;

---

29. lion] the sign of Leo.

30–1. Sirius the dog-star, associated with hot, sultry summer weather.

33–4. parched . . . fainting] Many translators have these words.

33. fry] suffer intense heat, burn (*OED* 4).

36. rivulets] Probably pronounced 'riv'lets'; cp. *AM* l. 624*n*.

37. Sylvans] wood spirits.

38. require] seek (*OED* 9).

39. want] lack (translating *caret*).

40–3. D. finds modern equivalents for Horace's topical allusions. For this practice see 'Preface to *Sylvae*' ll. 45–6.

40–1. Lord Mayor . . . City faction] London politics, dominated by the Whigs, had an important effect on national affairs: see *AA* ll. 513*n*, 584–629*n*; 'Prologue to *The Duke of Guise*' l. 3*n*.

42. Gallic arms] Louis XIV was conducting a vigorous military campaign against Spain and the Holy Roman Empire, and achieved a dominating position in Europe by the Truce of Ratisbon (August 1684).

43. quiver-bearing foe] Possibly the Turks, whose invasion of Europe had been halted at the gates of Vienna in 1683. Creech has 'quiver'd *Persian*'.

44. anxiously] From Lubinus' *anxius*; cp. 'Horace: *Epode* II' l. 55*n*; *RL* l. 35.

45   But God has wisely hid from human sight
        The dark decrees of future fate,
        And sown their seeds in depth of night;
        He laughs at all the giddy turns of state,
        When mortals search too soon, and fear too late.

                        VII
50   Enjoy the present smiling hour,
        And put it out of Fortune's power.
        The tide of business, like the running stream,
        Is sometimes high, and sometimes low,
        A quiet ebb, or a tempestuous flow,
55   And always in extreme:
        Now with a noiseless, gentle course
        It keeps within the middle bed;
        Anon it lifts aloft the head,
        And bears down all before it with impetuous force,

45, 49. wisely hid from human . . . search . . . fear] D. takes several words from
Raphael's speeches to Adam in *PL* viii (which themselves draw on this ode in
Horace): cp. 'To ask or search I blame thee not' (66); 'the rest/ From man or
angel the great architect/ Did wisely to conceal' (71–3); 'Solicit not thy
thoughts with matters hid,/ Leave them to God above, him serve and fear'
(167–8); 'God to remove his ways from human sense' (119); and cp. vii 118–
25 (J. R. Mason).
47. sown their seeds] D.'s addition. For his interest in the unknowable origins
of events cp. *AM* ll. 865–6.
48. at all the giddy turns of state] D.'s addition.
49. Translating *si mortalis ultra fas trepidat* ('if a mortal is alarmed beyond what
is lawful').
50–1. Translating *quod adest memento componere aequus* ('be sure to deal calmly
with what is at hand'); cp. 'Horace: *Odes* I ix' ll. 20–2. D. may have been
prompted by Schrevelius' glosses: *futura in nostra non sunt potestate* ('future
things are not in our power'), *quod praesens est* ('what is present'), and *nihil
fortunae tribuere* ('give nothing to Fortune': gloss on l. 42). D. returns to this
topic in the Dedication to *Don Sebastian* (*Works* xv 60) and 'Palamon and
Arcite' iii 1096.   *present . . . hour*] Creech has 'present Hours'.   *Fortune*]
D.'s addition; see ll. 73–87n.
52. Cp. Cowley: 'The stream of Business does begin,/ And a Spring-Tide of
Clients is come in' ('Ode. Upon Liberty', *Essays* 389; Stuart Gillespie).
business] translating *cetera* ('other things'); cp. l. 10n.
53–5, 58–9. D.'s addition.
59. impetuous] violent (*OED* 1).

60   And trunks of trees come rolling down,
      Sheep and their folds together drown;
    Both house and homestead into seas are borne,
    And rocks are from their old foundations torn,
And woods made thin with winds their scattered
    honours mourn.

                  VIII

65   Happy the man, and happy he alone,
      He who can call today his own:
      He who secure within can say,
    'Tomorrow do thy worst, for I have lived today.
      Be fair, or foul, or rain, or shine,
70   The joys I have possessed, in spite of Fate, are mine:
    Not heaven itself upon the past has power,
    But what has been has been, and I have had my
      hour.'

63. from their old foundations torn] D.'s addition. Cp. 'The First Book of the *Georgics*' l. 455: 'The Rocks are from their old Foundations rent'.
64. Translating *clamore vicinaeque silvae* ('the roar of the neighbouring wood'). *honours*] ornaments (*OED* 6b).
65–7. Translating *ille potens sui/ laetus deget, cui licet in diem/ dixisse* ('he lives happy and master of himself, who can say each day'). For the phrasing cp. Cowley: 'He's no small Prince who every day/ Thus to himself can say' ('Ode. Upon Liberty', *Essays* 390).
65. he alone] D.'s addition; Creech has 'alone'.
66. The phrasing recalls Cowley: 'The ground he holds, if he his own, can call' ('Martial. Lib. 2.', *Essays* 386); cp. 'Horace: *Epode* II' l. 9*n.*
68. Translating *vixi* ('I have lived'); cp. Creech: 'for I have liv'd to day', and Cowley: 'To morrow let my Sun his beams display,/ Or in clouds hide them; I have liv'd to Day' ('Of My self', *Essays* 457; H. A. Mason). For the strong force of *lived* see 'Lucretius: Against the Fear of Death' l. 128*n.*
70. in spite of Fate] D.'s addition, perhaps from Schrevelius' *non pendet ex fortunae inconstantia* ('it does not depend upon the inconstancy of Fortune').
71. Cp. Dacier: 'la Fortune n'a aucun pouvoir sur le passé' (H. A. Mason).

IX

Fortune, that with malicious joy
Does man her slave oppress,

75

Proud of her office to destroy
Is seldom pleased to bless;
Still various and unconstant still,
But with an inclination to be ill,
Promotes, degrades, delights in strife,

80

And makes a lottery of life.
I can enjoy her while she's kind,
But when she dances in the wind
And shakes her wings, and will not stay,
I puff the prostitute away:

85 The little or the much she gave is quietly resigned;

Content with poverty, my soul I arm,
And virtue, though in rags, will keep me warm.

73–87. Fortune] Fortune is a significant figure in D.'s translations from Horace (cp. ll. 50–1; 'Horace: *Odes* I ix' l. 23), and in his poetry generally (e.g. *Heroic Stanzas* ll. 29–32; *AM* ll. 797–800; *AA* ll. 252–61). She stands for the capricious power of chance, but also for the world of transitory and beguiling material rewards. See Paul Hammond, *MLR* lxxx (1985) 769–85.

73–80. Translates *Fortuna saevo laeta negotio et/ ludum insolentem ludere pertinax/ transmutat incertos honores,/ nunc mihi, nunc alii benigna* ('Fortune is pleased with her savage work, and persists in playing her insolent game, changes her untrustworthy honours, kind now to me, now to another').

73–5. Cp. 'Sigismonda and Guiscardo' ll. 187–8 (Stuart Gillespie).

73. malicious] Creech has 'maliciously'.

74. For D.'s stress on man's servility cp. 'Horace: *Epode* II' l. 17.

75. office] duty, function.

77. Adapted from Virgil's *varium et mutabile semper femina* ('woman is a fickle and changeable thing': *Aen.* iv 569).

81–2. kind/ . . . wind/] a perfect rhyme in seventeenth-century pronunciation.

82, 84. D.'s additions. For the idea of Fortune as a prostitute cp. Machiavelli, who describes her as a mistress (see *Heroic Stanzas* ll. 29–30*n*).

86. I arm] D.'s addition, from Schrevelius' *munio*.

X
What is't to me,
Who never sail in her unfaithful sea,
90   If storms arise, and clouds grow black;
If the mast split and threaten wrack,
Then let the greedy merchant fear
For his ill-gotten gain,
And pray to gods that will not hear,
95   While the debating winds and billows bear
His wealth into the main.
For me, secure from Fortune's blows
(Secure of what I cannot lose),
In my small pinnace I can sail,
100   Contemning all the blustering roar,
And running with a merry gale,
With friendly stars my safety seek
Within some little winding creek,
And see the storm ashore.

89. D.'s addition.   *unfaithful*] A common classical epithet for the sea (e.g.
freta perfida: Seneca, *Medea* l. 302). Cowley has 'faithless main' in his translation from Virgil's *Geo.* ii (*Essays* 410).
91. *wrack*] Ed.; wreck *1685*. The two words were close in pronunciation and
meaning.
93. *ill-gotten*] D.'s addition.
95. *debating*] fighting, quarrelling (*OED* 1).
97–8. D.'s addition.
100. *Contemning*] despising, scorning.
103–4. D.'s addition. For the idea of watching a storm from shore cp.
'Lucretius: The Beginning of the Second Book' ll. 1–4. D. returns to the
image in the 'Dedication of the Georgics' (1697) (*Works* v 143).
104. *ashore*] Ed.; a shore *1685*.

105 Horace: *Epode* II

Date and publication. Printed in 1685 in *Sylvae* (*SR* 10 January; advertised in *The Observator* 1 January); reprinted 1692. The indentation used here follows that in *Sylvae* (with some adjustments), which marks out the rhyme scheme. See headnote to 'Preface to *Sylvae*' for possible date of composition.

Context. For Restoration interest in Horace see headnote to 'Horace: *Odes* I iii'. Horace's poem was a major source for the seventeenth-century tradition of celebrating rural retirement as an alternative to the corruptions of life in the city or at court; see Maren-Sofie Røstvig, *The Happy Man* (1954; second edition 1962). As Cowley's *Essays* and Marvell's 'The Garden' illustrate, the subject continued to fascinate Restoration writers. Recent instances which D. would have known include Creech's Dedication to his Theocritus (1684), and several poems in *MP*: Roscommon's translation of Horace's *Carm.* I xxii and III vi; Otway's 'Epistle To *R.D.* from *T.O.*'; Chetwood's translation of *Carm.* II xv; Otway's translation of *Carm.* II xvi; and an anonymous version of *Epode* I. D.'s own 'Horace: *Odes* III xxix' explores similar themes of seeking integrity through retirement.

Sources. For the editions and translations used by D. see headnote to 'Horace: *Odes* I iii'. In addition, for *Epode* II D. consulted O. van Veen's *Q. Horatii Flacci Emblemata* (1612), Jonson's translation in his *Under-wood* (1640), and Cowley's in his *Essays* (published in the 1668 *Works*). He also turned to various writers on the pleasures of country life, and to Milton's account of the garden of Eden, to guide him in his careful choice of vocabulary. The aims and methods of D.'s translation are discussed by H. A. Mason, *CQ* viii (1978) 11–55 and ix (1980) 218–71.

From Horace,
Epod. 2d

How happy in his low degree,
How rich in humble poverty is he
Who leads a quiet country life!

¶105. *1–4.* Cp. 'To John Driden of Chesterton' ll. 1–2.

1. How happy] Translating *Beatus* ('blessed'). Most English translators have 'happy', which is a recurring epithet in the poems explored by Røstvig, e.g. Sir Henry Wotton's 'How *happy* is he born and taught,/ That serveth not an others *will*?' ('The Character of a Happy Life' in *Reliquiae Wottonianae* (1651) 522), and Cowley's 'Happy the Man, who his whole time doth bound/ Within th'enclosure of his little ground' ('Claudian's Old Man of Verona', *Essays* 447). *in his low degree*] D.'s addition. *degree*] social status.

2–3. D.'s addition. He also explores the idea of living content with little in 'Lucretius: The Beginning of the Second Book'; 'Horace: *Odes* III xxix'; *HP* ii 675–9; 'The Wife of Bath her Tale' ll. 464–84; and 'Baucis and Philemon'. H. A. Mason notes that an illustration of Baucis and Philemon is provided in van Veen, opposite quotations from *Epode* ii.

2. poverty] not destitution, but the state of having just the necessities of life (like the Latin *paupertas*).

3. quiet] This word is common in the seventeenth-century tradition of 'Happy Man' poems, and associates the aural peace of the countryside with man's mental, spiritual and emotional peace. Cp. Cowley: 'Here wrapt in th'Arms of Quiet let me ly' ('Seneca, ex Thyeste, Act. 2. Chor.', *Essays* 400; translating *dulcis quies* in Seneca); and D.'s 'easie Quiet, a secure Retreat' in 'The Second Book of the *Georgics*' l. 655 (translating *secura quies* in *Geo.* ii 467).

Discharged of business, void of strife,
5 And from the griping scrivener free.
   (Thus ere the seeds of vice were sown,
   Lived men in better ages born,
   Who ploughed with oxen of their own
   Their small paternal field of corn.)
10 Nor trumpets summon him to war,
   Nor drums disturb his morning sleep,
   Nor knows he merchants' gainful care,
   Nor fears the dangers of the deep.

4. discharged] unburdened; for *procul* ('far from'), probably from 'déchargé d'affaires' in van Veen (H. A. Mason). *business*] thus Jonson, Cowley and Creech; see 'Horace: *Odes* III xxix' l. 10*n*. *void of strife*] D.'s addition; used again in 'The Second Book of the *Georgics*' l. 688. *void of*] free from (*OED* 11b); thus Brome.
5. Cp. 'Free from the griping Scriveners bands' (Sir Richard Fanshawe, 'An Ode Vpon occasion of His Majesties Proclamation in the yeare 1630' in *Il Pastor Fido* (1648) 228). *griping*] clutching, grasping; many translators have this. 'Gripe' is the name of the scrivener in James Howard's *The English Mounsieur* (1674). *scrivener*] money-lender (*OED* 3); cp. 'Prologue to Amboyna' ll. 1–2.
6–7. For *ut prisca gens mortalium* ('like the first race of mortals').
6. seeds] Cp. 'Horace: *Odes* III xxix' l. 47*n*. D. echoes Spenser: 'the wicked seede of vice/ Began to spring which shortly grew full great' (*FQ* V i 1), and *semina nequitiae* in Ovid (*Amores* III iv 9; *Tristia* ii 279) (H. A. Mason).
7. Added from *magnanimi heroes nati melioribus annis* ('great heroes born in better times'; Virgil, *Aen.* vi 649); and cp. *RL* l. 80; (H. A. Mason).
9. small] D.'s addition, perhaps from Cowley: 'The ground he holds, if he his own can call,/ He quarrels not with Heaven because 'tis small' ('Martial. Lib. 2.', *Essays* 386); cp. 'Horace: *Odes* III xxix' l. 66*n*. *field of corn*] for *rura* ('country'); cp. Cowley: 'A Field of Corn, a Fountain and a Wood,/ Is all the Wealth by Nature understood' ('A Paraphrase on an ode in Horace', *Essays* 442).
11. D.'s addition.
12. D.'s addition, possibly from Lubinus' *lucri spe* ('hope of gain'); cp. 'Horace: *Odes* III xxix' ll. 10*n*, 92–3; 'Virgil's Fourth Eclogue' l. 38.

The clamours of contentious law,
15   And court and state he wisely shuns,
Nor bribed with hopes nor dared with awe
To servile salutations runs:
But either to the clasping vine
Does the supporting poplar wed,
20   Or with his pruning hook disjoin
Unbearing branches from their head,
And grafts more happy in their stead;
Or climbing to a hilly steep
He views his herds in vales afar,
25   Or sheers his overburdened sheep;

14–15. For *forumque vitat* ('he avoids the forum'). The forum was a market place, as well as a place for public assemblies and lawcourts.

14. Cp. Shadwell, *The Libertine* (1676) where the shepherds dismiss 'the clamorous Courts of tedious Law' (Act IV; Shadwell, *Works* iii 75).

15. court] Though Horace seems to be thinking of lawcourts, D.'s singular *court* refers rather to the King's entourage. Although D. praised Charles II and many courtiers, there is a notable element in his work which rejects the corruption and strife associated with court politics: see Dedication to *Marriage A-la-Mode* (1672; *Works* xi 221–3); 'Epilogue at Oxford, 1674' ll. 1–6; Dedication to *Aureng-Zebe* (1676); Dedication to *All for Love* (1678; *Works* xiii 8–9); Dedication to *Don Sebastian* (1690; *Works* xv 60); Dedication of the *Georgics* (*Works* v 141–4).

16–17. For *superba civium/ potentiorum limina* ('the proud thresholds of powerful citizens'), with hints from Lubinus' *tanquam cliens & adulator* ('like a client and flatterer'). For other cases where D. stresses the servility of those who pay court to great men see *All for Love* III i 141–2; and 'The Tenth Satire of Juvenal' ll. 144–7.

16. dared] dazed, paralysed (*OED* 5); larks are 'dared' with mirrors in order to catch them (see ll. 51–2, and cp. *AM* l. 780).

17. salutations] H. A. Mason notes that D. has recalled the parallel passage in Virgil's *Geo.* ii 462: *mane salutantum totis uomit aedibus undam* ('a tide of clients spews in to greet him in the morning').

18. clasping] Cp. the 'clasping ivy' in Milton's paradise (*PL* ix 217; J. R. Mason).

21. Unbearing] unfruitful (*OED* has no example between 1200 and this one).

23. D.'s addition, from Lubinus' *ex editiore loco* ('from a loftier place'). *steep*] slope of a hill, cliff.

24. Pace Works, not an addition.

25. overburdened sheep] thus Holyday and Hawkins.

Or mead for cooling drink prepares
    Of virgin honey in the jars.
Or in the now declining year,
    When bounteous Autumn rears his head,
30 He joys to pull the ripened pear,
    And clustering grapes with purple spread.
The fairest of his fruit he serves,
    Priapus, thy rewards;
Sylvanus too his part deserves,
35   Whose care the fences guards.
Sometimes beneath an ancient oak,
    Or on the matted grass he lies;
No god of sleep he need invoke,
    The stream that o'er the pebbles flies
40   With gentle slumber crowns his eyes.

26. D.'s addition. Mead was declining in importance in late-seventeenth-century London, with tea, coffee, chocolate, wine and spirits becoming more fashionable, but it remained popular in the countryside, and enjoyed a revival among the gentry after the Restoration. Sir Kenelm Digby collected fifty-six recipes for mead (Jennifer Stead, privately; C. Anne Wilson, *Food and Drink in Britain* (1973) 403). *cooling*] Sir Kenelm Digby called it 'a most pleasant, quick, cooling, smoothing drink' (*The Closet of the Eminently Learned Sir Kenelme Digby Kt Opened* (1671) 93; H. A. Mason).
27. virgin honey] 'Virgin-honey . . . is the best . . . [it comes] of Bees that swarmed the Spring before, and are taken up in Autumn; and it is made best by chusing the whitest Combs of the Hive, and then letting the Honey run out of them lying on a Seive, without pressing it, or breaking of the Combs' (Digby 4; H. A. Mason 47–8); cp. *AM* l. 578.
28. D.'s addition.
29. his] Autumnus is masculine in Latin.
31. clustering grapes] Cp. 'clustering vine' in *PL* vii 320 (J. R. Mason).
32. D.'s addition. *fairest . . . fruit*] Cp. 'goodliest trees loaden with fairest fruit' (*PL* iv 147, and cp. ix 851; J. R. Mason).
33. Priapus] the god of procreation; also of gardens and vineyards, where his statue was placed.
34. Sylvanus] the god of the woods.
38. D.'s addition. The god of sleep, Morpheus, comes from Ovid's *Met.* xi.
39. o'er the pebbles] D.'s addition, perhaps from Virgil, *Ecl.* v 84, where the rivers flow through stony valleys (*saxosas uallis*: 'the scarce cover'd Pebbles'; 'Virgil's Fifth Pastoral' l. 132).
40. D.'s addition. *crowns*] blesses (*OED* 11). H. A. Mason notes an echo of Shakespeare: 'on your eyelids crown the god of sleep' (*I Henry IV* IV i 210).

The wind that whistles through the sprays
    Maintains the consort of the song,
And hidden birds with native lays
    The golden sleep prolong.
45 But when the blast of winter blows,
    And hoary frost inverts the year,
Into the naked woods he goes,
    And seeks the tusky boar to rear
    With well-mouthed hounds and pointed spear;
50 Or spreads his subtle nets from sight,
    With twinkling glasses to betray
The larks that in the meshes light,
    Or makes the fearful hare his prey.
Amidst his harmless easy joys
55   No anxious care invades his health,
Nor love his peace of mind destroys,
    Nor wicked avarice of wealth.

41–2. D.'s addition. H. A. Mason notes an echo of 'How, with their drowsie tone, the whistling Air/ (Your sleep to tempt) a Consort does prepare!' (Virgil, *Ecl.* i, tr. John Caryll in *MP* (1684) 6). Mason also observes that the sound of the wind contributes to the music of several paradisal scenes in Tasso, and in Spenser's Bower of Bliss (*FQ* II xii 70–1). Cp. also Cowley: 'The whistling Winds add their less artful strains' (Verses in 'The Garden', *Essays* 424).

42. Maintains] supports (*OED* 11, 12).   *consort*] harmony (*OED* 3), perhaps from *concert* in Dacier.

44. prolong] D.'s addition. He also adds the idea that a voice prolongs sleep in 'Virgil's First Pastoral' l. 76.

46. inverts the year] D. adapts *inversum annum* 'the inverted [i.e. completed] year') from Horace's *Serm.* I i 36 (H. A. Mason).

47. D.'s addition.

48. rear] rouse from covert (*OED* 4b): the technical term for dislodging a boar (Nicholas Cox, *The Gentleman's Recreation* (1677) 10).

49. well-mouthed] capable of baying loudly; thus Cowley.   *and pointed spear*] D.'s addition.

50. subtle] of fine texture (*OED* 2); thus Jonson.

51–2. D.'s addition, replacing Horace's thrushes with larks; cp. l. 16n.

51. glasses] mirrors.

54–6. For *quis non malarum, quas amor curas habet,/ haec inter obliviscitur?* ('who, amongst such things, would not forget the ills and cares which love brings?').

54. harmless] D.'s addition, stressing the innocence of the pastoral life. He adds the same word in 'The Second Book of the *Georgics*' l. 656.   *easy*] see *AA* l. 168n.

55. anxious care] Cp. 'God hath bid dwell far off all anxious cares' (*PL* viii 185;

But if a chaste and pleasing wife,
To ease the business of his life,
60   Divides with him his household care,
Such as the Sabine matrons were,
Such as the swift Apulian's bride,
Sunburnt and swarthy though she be,
Will fire for winter nights provide,
65   And without noise will oversee
His children and his family,
And order all things till he come
Sweaty and overlaboured home;
If she in pens his flocks will fold,
70   And then produce her dairy store,
With wine to drive away the cold,
And unbought dainties of the poor;
Not oysters of the Lucrine lake
My sober appetite would wish,
75   Nor turbot, or the foreign fish
That rolling tempests overtake,
And hither waft the costly dish;

J. R. Mason); and cp. 'Horace: *Odes* III xxix' ll. 10*n*, 44; 'To John Driden of Chesterton' l. 2.

57, 59. D.'s additions.

59. business] See 'Horace: *Odes* III xxix' l. 10*n*.

61. Cp. Creech: 'Such as the ancient *Sabines* were'. The Sabines lived northeast of Rome, where Horace had his farm.

62. The Apulians lived in south-east Italy.

68. sweaty and overlaboured] for *lassi* ('tired').

69. Cp. Milton: 'The folded flocks penned in their wattled cotes' (*A Masque* l. 343; and cp. *PL* iv 185–7; J. R. Mason).

73. Lucrine lake] a shallow lagoon off the Bay of Naples, famous for its oysters.

75. turbot] Exactly translating *rhombus*. Turbot caught near Tynemouth were conveyed in tanks on board ship to the London market, so it was an expensive fish (Wilson, *Food and Drink in Britain* 47; Jennifer Stead, privately).   *the foreign fish*] for Horace's *scar*, a fish much prized by the Romans.

Not heathpout, or the rarer bird
　　Which Phasis or Ionia yields,
80　More pleasing morsels would afford
　　Than the fat olives of my fields,
　　Than shards or mallows for the pot,
　　　That keep the loosened body sound;
　　Or than the lamb that falls by lot
85　　To the just guardian of my ground.
　　Amidst these feasts of happy swains,
　　　The jolly shepherd smiles to see
　　His flock returning from the plains;
　　　The farmer is as pleased as he
90　To view his oxen, sweating smoke,
　　Bear on their necks the loosened yoke;
　　To look upon his menial crew
　　　That sit around his cheerful hearth,
　　And bodies spent in toil renew
95　　With wholesome food and country mirth.

78. heathpout] grouse.　　*rarer bird*] In Horace, the heath-cock. After the passing of the 1671 Act restricting the killing of game, these would have been rarities in London (Wilson 108; Stead).

79. Phasis] not in Horace; an area in Colchis (east of the Black Sea) noted for pheasants.　　*Ionia*] part of Asia Minor on the Aegean Sea.

82. shards] chard beet: ' 'Tis of quality Cold and Moist, and naturally somewhat *Laxative*' (John Evelyn, *Acetaria: A Discourse of Sallets* (1699) 11; Stead). *mallows*] the marsh mallow: held by Pythagoras to reduce the passions and cleanse both stomach and mind; also a laxative (Evelyn 35–6; Stead).

85. guardian] Terminus, the god of boundaries. D. omits Horace's kid snatched from the wolf.

90. sweating smoke] D.'s addition.　　*smoke*] steam (*OED* 3).

92. menial] household, domestic (*OED* 1; not derogatory).　　*crew*] company (*OED* 3).

94–5. D.'s addition.

This Morecraft said within himself,
  Resolved to leave the wicked town
  And live retired upon his own;
    He called his money in:
100 But the prevailing love of pelf
  Soon split him on the former shelf,
    And put it out again.

96–102. Some translators (e.g. Cowley) omit the ironic ending to Horace's poem, where it is revealed that this eloquent praise of the country life is spoken by a moneylender. In order to preserve the element of surprise which both Horace and D. have, the inverted commas which should mark out ll. 1–95 as Morecraft's speech are not added in this edition. For editors' comments on the ending of Horace's poem see Plate 6.

96–7. Echoes Oldham's 'A Satyr in Imitation of the Third of Juvenal' ll. 35–6, where the character who is about to move from the town to the country says: ''Tis my Resolve to quit the nauseous Town./ Let thriving *Morecraft* chuse his dwelling there' (published in *Poems, and Translations* (1683)).

96. Morecraft] the usurer in Beaumont and Fletcher's *The Scornful Lady*; cp. 'Prologue to *Marriage A-la-Mode*' l. 29n.

97–8. For *iam iam futurus rusticus* ('already a future countryman').

98. his own] his own resources, own estate.

99. Thus Creech.

100–1. D.'s addition. Cp. '*This love of Pelf,/ Makes this vile Slave an enemy to himself*' (Horace, *Serm.* I ii, tr. Brome (1666) 192).

100. pelf] money (*OED* 3; generally derogatory).

101. For the religious connotations of the image cp. Jonson: 'God wisheth, none should wracke on a strange shelf' ('To Sir Robert Wroth' l. 95), and *RL* ll. 425–6.   *split*] wrecked (*OED* 1).   *shelf*] sandbank; submerged ledge of rock (*OED* 1).

106 A New Song ('Sylvia the fair')

Date and publication. Printed in 1685 in *Sylvae* (*SR* 10 January; advertised in *The Observator* 1 January); reprinted 1692. Also printed in *Wit's Cabinet* [1699] with an extra stanza unlikely to be by D. Anonymous Latin translation in *The Gentleman's Journal* September 1693.

A New Song

I

Sylvia the fair, in the bloom of fifteen,
Felt an innocent warmth as she lay on the green;
She had heard of a pleasure, and something she guessed
By the tousing and tumbling and touching her breast;
5   She saw the men eager, but was at a loss
What they meant by their sighing and kissing so close,
     By their praying and whining,
     And clasping and twining,
     And panting and wishing,
10   And sighing and kissing,
     And sighing and kissing so close.

II

'Ah', she cried, 'ah, for a languishing maid
In a country of Christians to die without aid!
Not a Whig or a Tory, or Trimmer at least,
15   Or a Protestant parson or Catholic priest
To instruct a young virgin that is at a loss
What they meant by their sighing and kissing so close!
     By their praying and whining,
     And clasping and twining,
20   And panting and wishing,
     And sighing and kissing,
     And sighing and kissing so close.'

¶**106**. *4. tousing*] pulling a woman about roughly (*OED* 1c).
14. Trimmer] See 'Epilogue to *The Duke of Guise*' l. 23*n*.

III

Cupid in shape of a swain did appear,
He saw the sad wound, and in pity drew near;
25   Then showed her his arrow, and bid her not fear,
For the pain was no more than a maiden may bear.
When the balm was infused she was not at a loss
What they meant by their sighing and kissing so close,
    By their praying and whining,
30   And clasping and twining,
    And panting and wishing,
    And sighing and kissing,
    And sighing and kissing so close.

107 Song ('Go tell Amynta, gentle swain')

Date and publication. Printed in 1685 in *Sylvae* (*SR* 10 January; advertised in *The Observator* 1 January); reprinted 1692. Setting by Robert King in *The Theater of Music* (1685; facsimile in Day 74), *A Collection of Twenty Four Songs* (1685) and *Wit and Mirth* (1700). Setting by Henry Purcell (from 1686) in various MSS (see Beal 416–17) printed in *Orpheus Britannicus* (1706).

Song

I

Go tell Amynta, gentle swain,
I would not die, nor dare complain;
Thy tuneful voice with numbers join,
Thy words will more prevail than mine;
5 To souls oppressed and dumb with grief
The gods ordain this kind relief,
That music should in sounds convey
What dying lovers dare not say.

II

A sigh or tear perhaps she'll give,
10 But love on pity cannot live.
Tell her that hearts for hearts were made,
And love with love is only paid.
Tell her my pains so fast increase
That soon they will be past redress;
15 But ah! the wretch that speechless lies
Attends but death to close his eyes.

108 Threnodia Augustalis

Date and publication. Charles II died on 6 February 1685. *Threnodia Augustalis: A Funeral-Pindarique Poem Sacred to the Happy Memory of King Charles II. By John Dryden, Servant to His late Majesty, and to the Present King*, was published by Jacob Tonson in 1685 (MS date 9 March on BL copy; advertised in *The Observator* 14 March); Macdonald 20a, siglum here: *1685a*. The second edition (Macdonald 20b; *1685b*) followed quickly upon the first (advertised 25 March); it was printed from the same setting of type, with some changes which were introduced at different stages during the printing, and are therefore not present in all copies. The substantive changes in *1685b* are almost certainly authorial revisions, whereas the alterations to accidentals may derive either from D. or from a proof-reader in the printing house. The poem was reprinted at Dublin in 1685 (Macdonald 20c), and in London in 1685 in a smaller typeface (20d). The position of 20d in the sequence of editions is uncertain: Kinsley believed it to be the first edition, but *Works* is probably correct in assuming that the more handsome edition, 20a, is more likely to be the first, with 20d being a hasty reprint. The poem was not subsequently reprinted in D.'s lifetime. The present text is based on *1685a*, emended from *1685b* where that edition makes substantive changes (ll. 126, 164, 288, 371, 484, 494). The indentation in *1685a* follows the line lengths in sig. A, but is lacking from B to the end; the present edition indents throughout according to the length of the lines.

Context. The death of Charles II at the age of 54 was unexpected. He suddenly fell ill on the morning of Monday 2 February, probably of a kidney disease. After emergency treatment his condition improved, and on Tuesday he was thought to be out of danger, but there was a relapse on Wednesday evening. His doctors treated him through blood-letting, blistering, and the use of cantharides, which caused considerable pain. The death-bed was attended by the King's brother James, Duke of York, his wife Queen Catherine, and his various illegitimate children, together with many court officials. On the Thursday night Charles was secretly received into the Roman Catholic Church and given the last sacrament by Father Richard Hudleston, who had helped him in his escape from the Battle of Worcester in 1651. He died at noon on Friday 6 February. The King's illness was announced in the *London Gazette* mmv (2–5 February 1685), and his death in issue mmvi (5–9 February): 'On Monday last in the morning our late Gracious Soveraign King *Charles* the Second was seized with a violent Fit, by which his Speech and Senses were for some time taken from him, but upon the immediate application of fitting Remedies He returned to such a condition as gave some hopes of His Recovery till Wednesday night, at which time the Disease returning upon him with greater violence, he expired this day about Noon'. A good account of the King's death is provided by Evelyn's *Diary* for 4–6 February. Contemporary descriptions are used as the foundation for Raymond Crawfurd's narrative, *The Last Days of Charles II* (1909). Not used by

Crawfurd is the anonymous *A True Relation of the Late Kings Death* [1685], which is primarily interested in the King's receiving of the Roman Catholic sacrament from Fr Hudleston.

Sources. Little information about Charles's illness and death would have been available to D. in print: the *London Gazette*'s account is brief, and the exact date of *A True Relation* is uncertain. But he would have had good contacts at court through which he could have obtained a vivid impression of the events. The poem shares imagery with many of the other elegies for the King, and the comparatively late appearance of D.'s poem makes it possible that he drew on these (though their dates are uncertain); however, images which D.'s poem shares with others are probably best regarded as coming from a common stock of tropes, rather than being cases of conscious borrowing. An exception is Tate's poem, which D. deliberately responds to in ll. 1–8. *Works* drew attention to the similarities between D.'s poem and the collection of elegies from Cambridge, *Moestissimae ac Laetissimae Academiae Cantabrigiensis Affectus* (1685), which includes a pastoral *Ecloga* by D.'s son Charles (sigs K2ʳ–K3ʳ). *Works* imagines that D. showed his poem to his son, who in turn showed it to the score of contributors whose poems have parallels with it; however, the influence could be the other way round, or the parallels could be coincidental, since most of the ideas shared by D. and the Cambridge elegists are also found in other poems. For a list of elegies on Charles see John Alden, *The Muses Mourn* (1958).

Threnodia Augustalis:
A Funeral Pindaric Poem
Sacred to the Happy Memory of
King Charles II

fortunati ambo, si quid mea carmina possunt,
nulla dies unquam memori vos eximet aevo!

¶**108**. *Title. Threnodia*] lament for the dead (a Greek noun).   *Augustalis*] relating to the Roman Emperor Augustus (a Latin adjective). There is a precedent for this macaronic title in Fitzpayne Fisher's *Threnodia Triumphalis* for Cromwell (1658). For the association of Charles II with Augustus see ll. 385–7n, and *Astraea Redux* ll. 322–3n; discussed by Howard Erskine-Hill, *The Augustan Idea in English Literature* (1983).
Epigraph. Aen. ix 446–7: 'O happy Friends! for if my Verse can give/ Immortal Life, your Fame shall ever live;' (D.'s 'The Ninth Book of the *Aeneis*' ll. 597–8). The pair of friends are Nisus and Euryalus: see 'Nisus and Euryalus' ll. 485–6.

I

Thus long my grief has kept me dumb:
Sure there's a lethargy in mighty woe,
Tears stand congealed, and cannot flow,
And the sad soul retires into her inmost room:
5   Tears for a stroke foreseen afford relief,
But unprovided for a sudden blow
Like Niobe we marble grow,
And petrify with grief.
Our British heaven was all serene,

1–8. Over a month elapsed between the King's death and the publication of
Threnodia, during which period many other writers issued memorial poems.
Nahum Tate had called upon D. to publish something: 'Wake Britains *Hor-
ace*, wake from thy fresh Shroud,/ To tune our Sorrows and instruct the
Crowd,/ Our *CHARLES* his Fame and Fate *thy Numbers* crave,/ Such Flame
as thine methinks should warm the Grave./ Less streins may well on
common Shrines be worn,/ And meaner Muses meaner Theams Adorn,/
May suit some bloody Conqueror's Decease,/ But not the *Arbiter* of Europe's
Peace./ How well has *Asaph*'s Muse our *David* stil'd?/ His Form so God-like,
and His Reign so mild./ She Sung His Troubles, now His latest Breath/ Let
Her record, and Constancy in Death' (*On the Sacred Memory of our late Sovereign*, second edition (1685) 3). In styling D. 'Asaph' (which means 'one that
assembles or completes') Tate is giving D. the name of King David's
recorder, as he had done in *2AA* ll. 938, 1037–64.
2. D. echoes Tate: 'If yet the Common Lethargy of Grief,/ And Nation's
Apoplex can bear Relief,/ Let now their Art condoling Muses show,/ And
teach our *Sorrows* standing-Tide to flow' (1).
7. Niobe] Trisyllabic; Niobe, weeping for the death of her children, was
transformed into marble, which continued to shed tears (Ovid, *Met.* vi 306–
12).
9–15. Since the end of the Exclusion Crisis in 1683 the country had enjoyed
domestic peace, and was not involved in the wars conducted by various
European nations against Louis XIV or the Turks.
9–11, 16, 24–5. Several elegists commented on the lack of portents. Aphra
Behn exclaimed: '*Impossible!* (I raving Cry)/ That such a *Monarch!* such a *God*
should dye!/ And no *Dire Warning* to the World be given:/ No *Hurricanes* on
Earth! no *Blazing Fires* in Heaven!' (*A Pindarick on the Death of our Late
Sovereign* (1685) 2). Cp. also *Ireland's Tears* (1685) 6 and Sir F[rancis] F[ane],
A Pindarick Ode (1685) 6.
9. British heaven] A translation of *Coelum Britannicum*, the title of Thomas
Carew's masque of 1633, which probably influenced *Albion and Albanius*, on
which D. had recently been working (see Paul Hammond in *The Court
Masque*, edited by David Lindley (1984) 178).

10   No threatening cloud was nigh,
                Not the least wrinkle to deform the sky;
                We lived as unconcerned and happily
                As the first age in nature's golden scene;
                   Supine amidst our flowing store
15   We slept securely, and we dreamt of more:
                When suddenly the thunder-clap was heard
                It took us unprepared and out of guard,
                   Already lost before we feared.
                Th' amazing news of Charles at once were spread,
20   At once the general voice declared
                      Our gracious Prince was dead.
                No sickness known before, no slow disease
                   To soften grief by just degrees,
                But like a hurricane on Indian seas
25   The tempest rose;
                   An unexpected burst of woes,
                   With scarce a breathing space betwixt,
                This now becalmed, and perishing the next:
                   As if great Atlas from his height
30   Should sink beneath his heavenly weight,

---

13. For the golden age see Ovid, *Met.* i 89–112 (ll. 113–43 in D.'s translation
'The First Book of Ovid's *Metamorphoses*' in *EP*). In *Astraea Redux* D. had
represented the return of Charles II as inaugurating a new golden age (see
Astraea Redux Title *n*).

14. Supine] D. frequently uses this word for the relaxed enjoyment of ease:
cp. *Astraea Redux* l. 107; *MF* l. 28.   *flowing*] Ovid writes that in the golden
age *flumina iam lactis, iam flumina nectaris ibant,/ flavaque de viridi stillabant ilice
mella* (*Met.* i 111–12: 'Streams of milk and streams of sweet nectar flowed,
and yellow honey was distilled from the verdant oak'). In Exodus iii 8 God
promises Moses that he will lead the Israelites into 'a land flowing with milk
and honey'. Richard Duke said that Charles had 'made the Land with Milk
and Honey flow!' (*Moestissimae* sig. Dd3ʳ).

17. out of guard] off guard (*OED* 5c, last example).

19. news] Originally a plural noun, but the now usual understanding of it as a
singular dates from the sixteenth century.

29–30. Atlas was the giant in Greek mythology who supported the heavens
on his shoulders. Alexander Ross wrote: 'A King is the *Atlas* of his
Common-wealth, both for strength and greatnesse . . . by means of his
knowledge and providence the Kingdome is supported' (*Mystagogus Poeticus*
(1647) 33; *Works*).

And with a mighty flaw, the flaming wall
(As once it shall)
Should gape immense and rushing down o'erwhelm
this nether ball;
So swift and so surprising was our fear:
35   Our Atlas fell indeed; but Hercules was near.

II

His pious brother, sure the best
Who ever bore that name,
Was newly risen from his rest,
And with a fervent flame
40   His usual morning vows had just addressed

31–3. Cp. the apocalyptic passages in 'To the Memory of Anne Killigrew'
ll. 178–95 and 'A Song for St Cecilia's Day' ll. 55–63 (*Works*).
31. flaw] blast of wind; uproar, tumult (*OED* flaw² 1, 2).   *flaming wall*]
From Lucretius: *flammantia moenia mundi* ('the flaming walls of the world'; *De
Rerum Natura* i 73; Christie); the Latin phrase is used by James Montagu in his
elegy in *Moestissimae* sig. B2ᵛ.
32. once] one day in the future (*OED* 5).
35. Hercules] Hercules temporarily relieved Atlas of his burden while the
latter obtained the golden apples of the Hesperides for him. Hercules as a
figure for James anticipates D.'s stress on him as a 'warlike Prince' (l. 429
etc). Ross explains that Hercules is 'the type of a good king, who ought to
subdue all monsters, cruelty, disorder, and oppression in his kingdom, who
should support the heaven of the Church with the shoulders of authoritie'
(*Mystagogus Poeticus* 116; *Works*). The image of the King as Atlas had previously been used for Charles I by Abraham Markland, *Poems on His Majesties
Birth and Restauration* (1667): 'Thou didst not *CHARLES*, but Piety behead:/
Who cuts off *Atlas* head does pull down Heaven' (3). The comparison of
Charles II and James II with Atlas and Hercules is very common amongst the
elegists. Ed. Brown wrote: *Sic, ubi lassatus grandi subduxit Olympo/ Brachia, &
effœtis tremuit cervicibus*, Atlas;/ *Fortior* Alcides *tergo nutantia fulsit/ Pondera* ('So
when Atlas, weary in his arms from holding up mighty Olympus, began to
tremble in his shoulders, stronger Hercules took the tottering weight on his
back'; *Moestissimae* sig. L4ᵛ); cp. George Stepney: 'Which eas'd our *Atlas* of
his glorious weight/ Since stronger *Hercules* Supports the State' (*Moestissimae*
sig. Gg4ᵛ); the image is also used in *Moestissimae* sigs A4ʳ, C3ʳ, E4ᵛ, M1ʳ,
P4ᵛ, Q2ʳ; *Ireland's Tears* 3; Fane 3.
36. pious] devout (*OED* 1); faithful to the duties owed to family and state
(*OED* 2), a sense influenced by the Latin *pius*, often applied by Virgil to
Aeneas; D. uses the word in this way for Charles II in *AM* l. 958.
39. flame] passion (*OED* 6a).

For his dear sovereign's health,
And hoped to have 'em heard
In long increase of years,
In honour, fame and wealth.
45   Guiltless of greatness thus he always prayed,
Nor knew nor wished those vows he made
On his own head should be repaid.
Soon as th' ill-omened rumour reached his ear
(Ill news is winged with fate, and flies apace),
50   Who can describe th' amazement in his face!
Horror in all his pomp was there,
Mute and magnificent without a tear;
And then the hero first was seen to fear.
Half unarrayed he ran to his relief,
55   So hasty and so artless was his grief:
Approaching greatness met him with her charms
Of power and future state,
But looked so ghastly in a brother's fate,
He shook her from his arms.
60   Arrived within the mournful room he saw
A wild distraction, void of awe,
And arbitrary grief, unbounded by a law.

49. A proverbial idea (Tilley N 148).
51. *his*] i.e. horror's.
54. James came so hastily to the King's bedchamber that he was wearing one slipper and one shoe (Crawfurd 29).
56–9. Cp. Antony in *All for Love*: 'purple greatness met my ripen'd years./ . . . Fate could not ruine me; till I took pains/ And work'd against my Fortune, chid her from me,/ And turn'd her loose' (I i 298–306; *Works*).
62. Whigs had accused Charles of aiming at arbitrary government unbounded by law, and suspected James of similar ambitions; D. insists that only the people's grief knows no bounds.

> God's image, God's anointed lay
> Without motion, pulse or breath,
65 A senseless lump of sacred clay,
> An image now of death.
> Amidst his sad attendants' groans and cries,
> The lines of that adored, forgiving face,
> Distorted from their native grace,
70 An iron slumber sate on his majestic eyes.
> The pious Duke—forbear, audacious Muse,
> No terms thy feeble art can use
> Are able to adorn so vast a woe:
> The grief of all the rest like subject-grief did show,
75 His like a sovereign did transcend;
> No wife, no brother such a grief could know,
> Nor any name, but friend.

63. The King was regarded by Tory theorists (reviving early Stuart and Tudor thinking) as having two bodies, the one sacred and eternal, the other physical and mutable (for applications of this to Charles II see Paul Hammond in *Culture, Politics and Society in Britain 1660–1800*, edited by Jeremy Black and Jeremy Gregory (1991) 13–48; and for the earlier doctrines see E. H. Kantorowicz, *The King's Two Bodies* (1957)). The King was not only God's anointed deputy, but also his image on earth: 'Kings are petty Gods. . . . Their Soveraignty is an Image of his Soveraignty, their Majesty the Figure of his Majesty, and their Empire a similitude of his Empire, they are Supream on Earth as he is in Heaven' (George Hickes, *A Discourse of the Soveraign Power* (1682) 7).

65. lump] often used of the material of the body when not animated by spirit: cp. *AA* l. 172n.

70. iron slumber] from Virgil's *ferreus somnus* (*Aen.* x 745–6; H. J. Todd). *sate*] sat.

74–7. Evelyn records that James 'was almost continually kneeling by his bed side, & in tears'.

77. friend] The friendship between the two brothers is stressed by many elegists. William Ayloffe wrote: 'Ye kindest Brothers, and ye best of Men,/ Born to redeem the name of Friend agen!' (*Moestissimae* sig. Ee2ʳ); cp. Fane: Charles 'shew'd himself not *more a Monarch*, than a *Friend./ Friendship* like this the World did never know,/ Save what the *King* of *Heav'n* did show' (3); and cp. also *Moestissimae* sigs Aa1ʳ, Cc4ᵛ; *Ireland's Tears* 3; W[illiam] P[enn], *The Quakers Elegy* (1685) 3. The importance of friendship for D. is attested by his studies of the strong bonds between Antony and Dollabella in *All for Love*, between the two young men in 'Nisus and Euryalus', and Dorax and Sebastian in *Don Sebastian*; and by the warmth of his celebration of literary friendships in 'To the Memory of Mr Oldham', 'To the Earl of Roscommon', 'To

III

O wondrous changes of a fatal scene,
Still varying to the last!
80   Heaven, though its hard decree was past
Seemed pointing to a gracious turn again,
And death's uplifted arm arrested in its haste.
Heaven half repented of the doom,
And almost grieved it had foreseen
85   What by foresight it willed eternally to come.
Mercy above did hourly plead
For her resemblance here below,
And mild forgiveness intercede
To stop the coming blow.
90   New miracles approached th' etherial throne,
Such as his wondrous life had oft and lately known,
And urged that still they might be shown.

My Dear Friend Mr Congreve', and the Epistle Dedicatory to *The Assignation*.

83. doom] judgement, decision (*OED* 2); fate, destiny (*OED* 4).

84–5. D. seems here to envisage God's foreknowledge as constituting a willing of the event (unlike Milton in *PL* iii 117–19, where God's foreknowledge has no influence on events).

86. mercy] Cp. ll. 257–60. Mercy is represented as characteristic of Charles by D. in *Astraea Redux* ll. 258–65, *To My Lord Chancellor* ll. 55–60, *AM* ll. 1054–7 and *AA* ll. 146, 939, as well as by many of the elegists. *Ireland's Tears* exclaims: 'Clemency!/ Herein he was Heav'ns Parallel' (3); and cp. Wood 5; *Moestissimae* sigs E1ᵛ, S3ʳ, Bb1ʳ, Cc3ᵛ. Otway, however, thought that too much mercy could be dangerous to the stability of the state: 'Mercy's indeed the Attribute of Heav'n,/ For Gods have Pow'r to keep the balance ev'n,/ Which if Kings loose, how can they govern well?/ Mercy shou'd pardon, but the sword compell./ Compassion's else a Kingdom's greatest harm,/ Its Warmth engenders Rebels till they swarm' (*Windsor Castle* (1685) 3).

90. miracles] D. would expect readers to see as miracles such events as Charles's escape after the Battle of Worcester in 1651, his restoration in 1660 (see *Astraea Redux* l. 241), the course taken by the Fire of London (see *AM* l. 1081*n*), and the discovery of the Rye House Plot to assassinate the King in 1683; cp. *AA* l. 320. *Ireland's Tears* said: 'How Dear to Heav'n its Champion was . . ./ Let the long Chain of Miracles convince' (4). *A True Relation* represents Charles himself as seeing his life as a succession of miracles: 'The K. seeing Mr. *H.* [i.e. the Catholic priest Father Hudleston] cryed out, *Almighty God, what good Planet governs me, that all my Life is Wonders and Miracles? When, O Lord, I consider my Infancy, my Exile, my Escape at* Worcester, *my Preservation in the Tree, with the Assistance of this good Father; and now to

On earth his pious brother prayed and vowed,
Renouncing greatness at so dear a rate,
95 Himself defending what he could
From all the glories of his future fate.
With him th' innumerable crowd
Of armèd prayers
Knocked at the gates of heaven, and knocked
aloud,
100 The first, well-meaning rude petitioners:
All for his life assailed the throne,
All would have bribed the skies by offering up their
own.
So great a throng not heaven itself could bar,
'Twas almost borne by force as in the giants' war.
105 The prayers at least for his reprieve were heard;
His death, like Hezekiah's, was deferred.

have him again to preserve my Soul: O Lord, my wonderful Restoration, my great
Danger in the late Conspiracy; and last of all, to be raised from Death to Life, and to
have my Soul preserved by the Assistance of this Father, whom I see, O good Lord,
that thou hast created for my Good.'
97–9. Evelyn records: 'Prayers were solemnly made in all the Churches,
especially in both the Court Chapells, where the Chaplaines relieved one
another every halfe quarter of an houre, from the time he began to be in
danger, til he expir'd'.
100. rude] lacking experience or skill (OED 2b).   petitioners] Since
'petitions' were demands presented to the King by Whigs, whereas the Tory
equivalents were known as 'addresses' (see 'Prologue Spoken at Mithridates'
l. 4n), D. may be implying here that Whigs prayed fervently for the King's
recovery (as, indeed, they had good reason to do, since Monmouth was in
exile abroad, and James poised to succeed).
104. the giants' war] In revenge for Zeus having confined their brothers the
Titans in Tartarus, the giants besieged Mount Olympus (Ovid, Met. i 151–5;
Hesiod, Theogony 617–735).
106. When the righteous and successful King Hezekiah was 'sick unto death',
his prayers were answered by an assurance of fifteen further years of life; the
sign of this reprieve was that the shadow on the sundial went back ten
degrees (2 Kings xx 1–11).

       Against the sun the shadow went
       Five days, those five degrees were lent
       To form our patience and prepare th' event.
110   The second causes took the swift command,
       The med'cinal head, the ready hand,
       All eager to perform their part,
  All but eternal doom was conquered by their art.
       Once more the fleeting soul came back
115   T' inspire the mortal frame,
       And in the body took a doubtful stand,
       Doubtful and hovering like expiring flame
  That mounts and falls by turns, and trembles o'er
    the brand.

IV

      The joyful short-lived news soon spread around,
120   Took the same train, the same impetuous bound:
     The drooping town in smiles again was dressed,
       Gladness in every face expressed,
      Their eyes before their tongues confessed.

108. lent] For life as something lent by God rather than given, cp. Jonson, 'On my First Sonne': 'Seuen yeeres tho'wert lent to me, and I thee pay,/ Exacted by thy fate, on the iust day' (ll. 3–4), and 'To Sir Robert Wroth': 'Thou maist thinke life, a thing but lent.' (l. 106) (*Ben Jonson* viii 41, 100). *Ireland's Tears* asks: 'The Prince whose Death you so bemoan,/ Was he not th' Almighties Loan?' (7). The idea is classical in origin: see Richmond Lattimore, *Themes in Greek and Latin Epitaphs* (1942) 170–1.

109. event] outcome.

110. second causes] human agents, as distinct from the 'first cause', God, who is the creator or prime mover.

111. med'cinal] This is the spelling in *1685*, repeated at l. 170; the pronunciation is probably disyllabic (thus balancing 'ready'), as it is in 'The Twelfth Book of the *Aeneis*' l. 620: 'With Juice of med'cnal herbs prepar'd to bathe the Wound' (cp. also Milton, *Samson Agonistes* l. 627).

116. doubtful] apprehensive, fearful (*OED* 5), as well as 'undecided'.

119. On the Tuesday messengers were sent out into every county carrying news of the King's recovery, in order to prevent political disturbances (Crawfurd 31). The announcement in the *London Gazette* for 2–5 February, published on the Thursday morning, said that the King was now 'in a condition of Safety, and that He will in a few days be freed from His Distemper'.

120. train] course (*OED* 12).

Men met each other with erected look,
125   The steps were higher that they took;
Friends to congratulate their friends made haste,
And long inveterate foes saluted as they passed.
Above the rest heroic James appeared
Exalted more, because he more had feared:
130   His manly heart, whose noble pride
Was still above
Dissembled hate or varnished love,
Its more than common transport could not hide,
But like an eagre rode in triumph o'er the tide.
135   Thus in alternate course
The tyrant passions, hope and fear,
Did in extremes appear,
And flashed upon the soul with equal force.
Thus, at half ebb, a rolling sea
140   Returns, and wins upon the shore;
The watery herd, affrighted at the roar,
Rest on their fins awhile, and stay,
Then backward take their wondering way:
The prophet wonders more than they
145   At prodigies but rarely seen before,
And cries, 'A king must fall, or kingdoms change
their sway.'
Such were our counter-tides at land, and so
Presaging of the fatal blow
In their prodigious ebb and flow.

124. erected] uplifted.
126. Friends . . . their friends] *1685b*; Each . . . his friend *1685a*.
132. varnished] pretended, simulated (*OED* 2b).
134. 'An eagre is a tide swelling above another tide, which I have myself observed on the River Trent' (D.'s note).
136. tyrant passions] Cowley describes the passions of ambition, avarice and lust as 'Tyrants' in his 'Ode. *Upon Liberty*' (*Essays* 388); cp. also 'Lucretius: Against the Fear of Death' l. 198.
139–43. Cp. Serapion's account of the prodigies in Egypt: 'Our fruitful *Nile*/ Flow'd ere the wonted Season, with a Torrent/ So unexpected, and so wondrous fierce,/ That the wild Deluge overtook the haste/ Ev'n of the Hinds that watch'd it . . ./ Then, with so swift an Ebb, the Floud drove backward,/ It slipt from underneath the Scaly Herd' (*All for Love* I i 2–10) (*Works*).
147–9. It seems unclear whether D. is referring here to actual disturbances in the tides seen at this time, or whether he is continuing the simile which compares the oscillating emotions in the people to the ebb and flow of tides.

150   The royal soul, that like the labouring moon
                 By charms of art was hurried down,
             Forced with regret to leave her native sphere,
                 Came but awhile on liking here:
                 Soon weary of the painful strife,
155   And made but faint essays of life:
                     An evening light
                     Soon shut in night,
             A strong distemper, and a weak relief,
             Short intervals of joy, and long returns of grief.

                                    V

160   The sons of art all med'cines tried,
             And every noble remedy applied;
                 With emulation each essayed
                 His utmost skill; nay more, they prayed:
             Never was losing game with better conduct played.
165   Death never won a stake with greater toil,
                 Nor e'er was Fate so near a foil:
                 But like a fortress on a rock,
             Th' impregnable disease their vain attempts did
                 mock;
                 They mined it near, they battered from afar,
170   With all the cannon of the med'cinal war;
                 No gentle means could be essayed,
                 'Twas beyond parley when the siege was laid.

150–1. Magicians were said to have power over the moon; cp. *PL* ii 665–6, where the witches dance 'while the labouring moon/ Eclipses at their charms'.   *labouring*] eclipsed (*OED* 3b, Latinate usage).
152. sphere] recalling the Ptolemaic universe of concentric celestial spheres.
153. liking] approval.
155. essays] attempts.
156–8. The King suffered a relapse on Wednesday evening, and his doctors noticed that the symptoms had grown worse each night (Crawfurd 32).
158. distemper] illness (*OED* 4).
160–4. The King was attended by a large group of doctors, who tried a variety of remedies; the details were recorded by Sir Charles Scarburgh (see Crawfurd 52–80).
164. Never was] *1685b*; Was never *1685a*.
166. foil] repulse, defeat (*OED* 2).

Th' extremest ways they first ordain,
Prescribing such intolerable pain
175   As none but Caesar could sustain;
Undaunted Caesar underwent
The malice of their art, nor bent
Beneath whate'er their pious rigour could invent:
In five such days he suffered more
180   Than any suffered in his reign before;
More, infinitely more, than he
Against the worst of rebels could decree,
A traitor or twice-pardoned enemy.
Now art was tired without success,
185   No racks could make the stubborn malady confess.
The vain insurancers of life,
And he who most performed, and promised less,
Ev'n Short himself forsook th' unequal strife.

173–4. After the initial convulsions Sir Edmund King promptly removed sixteen ounces of blood from the King's arm. When the other doctors assembled, their initial prescription was fearsome: 'They ordered cupping-glasses to be applied to his shoulders forthwith, and deep scarification to be carried out, by which they succeeded in removing another eight ounces of blood. A strong antimonial emetic was administered . . . [and] a full dose of Sulphate of Zinc. Strong purgatives were given, and supplemented by a succession of clysters. The hair was shorn close and pungent blistering agents applied all over his head; and as though this were not enough, the red-hot cautery was requisitioned as well' (Crawfurd 28).

186. insurancers] those who give insurance or assurance (*OED*'s first example).

188. Short] Thomas Short (1635–85), Roman Catholic physician. Richard Duke praises Short in his translation of Theocritus xi: 'Who both in Physick's sacred Art excell,/ And in Wit's Orb among the brightest shine,/ The Love of *Phoebus*, and the tunefull nine' (*MP* 253–4; Kinsley). Short was commemorated by 'Philophilus' in the poem *On the Universally Lamented Death of the Incomparable Dr. Short* (1685). *himself*] 1685ab; and *Hobbs* 1701 *folio*. This alteration refers to Thomas Hobbs (*c.*1647–98), who attended Charles in his last illness, and was also D.'s physician in the 1690s: he is thanked by D. in the 'Postscript to the *Aeneis*' (*Works* vi 810). For Hobbs see further *Works* vi 1112–13, and G. C. R. Morris, *N & Q* ccxx (1975) 558–9. It is more likely that a grateful D. made this tribute to Hobbs in a revised copy of the poem which he gave to Tonson (thus Morris and *Works* vi 1113), than that Tonson made the change himself (as Kinsley and *Works* iii 308 suggest).

Death and despair was in their looks,
190   No longer they consult their memories or books;
Like helpless friends who view from shore
The labouring ship, and hear the tempest roar,
So stood they with their arms across,
Not to assist, but to deplore
195   Th' inevitable loss.

VI

Death was denounced; that frightful sound
Which ev'n the best can hardly bear;
He took the summons void of fear,
And unconcernedly cast his eyes around,
200   As if to find and dare the grisly challenger.
What death could do he lately tried,
When in four days he more than died.
The same assurance all his words did grace,
The same majestic mildness held its place,
205   Nor lost the monarch in his dying face.
Intrepid, pious, merciful and brave,
He looked as when he conquered and forgave.

VII

As if some angel had been sent
To lengthen out his government,
210   And to foretell as many years again
As he had numbered in his happy reign,
So cheerfully he took the doom
Of his departing breath;
Nor shrunk, nor stepped aside for death,
215   But with unaltered pace kept on,
Providing for events to come
When he resigned the throne.

189. *was*] A plural subject with a singular verb is common seventeenth-century grammar.
191–2. Echoes 'Lucretius: The Beginning of the Second Book' ll. 1–2.
194. *deplore*] weep for, mourn.
196. *denounced*] To 'denounce' is to give official warning of an imminent calamitous event (*OED* 1b).
198. *He*] Charles.
201. *tried*] found out (*OED* 5).
216–28. Charles 'gave his breeches & Keys to the Duke . . . he also rec-

Still he maintained his kingly state,
And grew familiar with his fate.
220   Kind, good and gracious to the last,
On all he loved before, his dying beams he cast.
O truly good, and truly great,
For glorious as he rose, benignly so he set!
All that on earth he held most dear
225   He recommended to his care
To whom both heaven
The right had given
And his own love bequeathed supreme command.
He took and pressed that ever-loyal hand,
230   Which could in peace secure his reign,
Which could in wars his power maintain,
That hand on which no plighted vows were ever
vain.
Well for so great a trust he chose
A prince who never disobeyed,
235   Not when the most severe commands were laid;
Nor want nor exile with his duty weighed:
A prince on whom, if heaven its eyes could close,
The welfare of the world it safely might repose.

---

ommended to him the care of his natural Children, all except the D: of
Monmoth, now in Holland, & in his displeasure; he intreated the Queene to
pardon him. . . . He spake to the Duke to be kind to his Concubines the DD:
of *Cleveland*, & especially *Portsmouth*, & that *Nelly* might not sterve' (Evelyn).
223. D. had used the image of the setting sun for Charles I in *To My Lord
Chancellor* l. 87.
225. his] James's.
230–5. There are several echoes here of Marvell's lines on Cromwell in the
'Horatian Ode': 'The same *Arts* that did *gain*/ A *Pow'r* must it *maintain*'; 'How
good he is, how just,/ And fit for highest Trust:/ Nor yet grown stiffer with
Command/ . . . How fit he is to sway/ That can so well obey' (ll. 119–20,
79–84). For D.'s earlier uses of this poem see *To My Lord Chancellor* ll. 39–
42n.
236. exile] James was exiled to Brussels and then to Scotland from March
ᵗ679 to April 1682.

VIII

That King who lived to God's own heart
240   Yet less serenely died than he:
Charles left behind no harsh decree
For schoolmen with laborious art
            To salve from cruelty:
Those for whom love could no excuses frame,
245   He graciously forgot to name.
Thus far my Muse, though rudely, has designed
Some faint resemblance of his godlike mind,
But neither pen nor pencil can express
The parting brothers' tenderness:
250   Though that's a term too mean and low
(The blessed above a kinder word may know);
But what they did, and what they said,
The monarch who triumphant went,
The militant who stayed,
255   Like painters when their heightening arts are
            spent,
            I cast into a shade.

239–40. The dying King David (about whom Samuel had said to Saul, 'the Lord hath sought him a man after his own heart' (1 Samuel xiii 14; cp. *AA* l. 7)), charged his son Solomon to wreak vengeance on Joab and Shimei (1 Kings ii 1–9).

242. *schoolmen*] scholars, academic theologians.

243. *salve*] explain away, excuse (*OED* 2b).

244–5. Charles made no mention of Monmouth: see ll. 216–28n. For his affection for Monmouth cp. *AA* ll. 31–2.

246. *rudely*] awkwardly.

247. *godlike*] as in *AA* ll. 14, 237.

248, 255–6. The comparison between poetry and painting is one which fascinated D. throughout his career: cp. *Astraea Redux* ll. 125–30; 'To Sir Godfrey Kneller'; and 'A Parallel, of Poetry and Painting' (1695; *Works* xx 38–77). In Du Fresnoy's *De Arte Graphica* (tr. D. 1695) the painter is advised: 'the Lights and the Shadows . . . are so dextrously to be manag'd, that you may make the Bodies appear enlighten'd by the Shadows which bound the sight . . . take care to place those shadowings round about [the limbs], thereby to heighten the parts' (*Works* xx 96–8).

253–4. The church distinguishes between 'the church triumphant', those Christians in heaven, and 'the church militant', those on earth.

That all-forgiving King,
The type of him above,
That inexhausted spring
260   Of clemency and love;
Himself to his next self accused,
And asked that pardon which he ne'er refused:
For faults not his, for guilt and crimes
Of godless men, and of rebellious times,
265   For an hard exile, kindly meant,
When his ungrateful country sent
Their best Camillus into banishment,
And forced their sovereign's act—they could not his
consent.
O how much rather had that injured chief
270   Repeated all his sufferings past,
Than hear a pardon begged at last
Which given could give the dying no relief.

258. type] In Christian usage, a symbol which prefigures something to be
definitively revealed later (*OED* 1).

261–79. Scarburgh describes the scene thus: James, 'moved by the deepest
affection for the King and by a more than brotherly love, was so anxious for
his recovery, that he scarcely ever had the heart to leave the prostrate King's
bedside, at times completely overwhelmed with grief, at times watching
attentively the following out of the Physicians' instructions, at other times
imploring Heaven's Arch-Healer for help and succour with most earnest
prayers and vows and with repeated lamentations, so that it was clear to all
that he preferred to enjoy the comradeship of his Most Distinguished
Brother, rather than the Sceptre, but to no purpose, for the Fates were
arrayed against him' (tr. Crawfurd 79).

261. his next self] i.e. James. For the phrase cp. Shakespeare, *Sonnet* cxxxiii,
where 'my next self' (meaning 'my nearest and dearest self') is applied to the
Friend.

262–7. 'Charles thanked James for having always been the best of brothers
and friends, and asked pardon for any hardship he might have inflicted on
him from time to time, and for the risks of fortune he had run on his account'
(Crawfurd 45).

267. Camillus] M. Furius Camillus, a Roman general and 'a most devout
Person in point of Religion', went into exile rather than submit to an unjust
fine. He was 'the greatest Man both in War and Peace, before he was
banished; more famous in his banishment; . . . being restored to his Country,
he restored the Country to itself at the same time. For which reason he was
afterward . . . lookt upon as worthy to be stiled the *Second Founder* of the
City, after *Romulus*' (Livy v 32; tr. as *The Roman History* (1686) 142, 149, 175;
Kinsley).

He bent, he sunk beneath his grief,
His dauntless heart would fain have held
275   From weeping, but his eyes rebelled.
Perhaps the godlike hero in his breast
Disdained, or was ashamed to show
So weak, so womanish a woe,
Which yet the brother and the friend so plenteously
confessed.

IX

280   Amidst that silent shower the royal mind
An easy passage found,
And left its sacred earth behind:
Nor murmuring groan expressed, nor labouring
sound,
Nor any least tumultuous breath;
285   Calm was his life, and quiet was his death,
Soft as those gentle whispers were
In which th' Almighty did appear:
By the still voice the prophet knew him there.

285. Accounts agree on the calmness and courage with which Charles faced
death. D. had praised Charles's calmness in *To His Sacred Majesty* ll. 91–2.
Although (or perhaps because) Charles's early life was spent amid the turmoil
of the Civil War, and his reign was troubled by wars, plots and factional
disputes, he put a high value on his personal ease and quiet. Assiduous in
certain of his royal duties, particularly public ceremonial and attendance at
Privy Council meetings, he was impatient of detail and paperwork, and
valued his relaxations (see Ronald Hutton, *Charles the Second* (1989) 447–55).
Halifax commented that 'the *love* of *Ease* exercise[d] an entire Sovereignty in
his Thoughts' (Halifax, *Works*, edited by Mark N. Brown, 3 vols (1989) ii
501). *Works* notes that in 1687 D. wrote to Etherege that James II would do
well to emulate the ease of his brother: 'Oh that our Monarch wou'd encourage noble idleness by his own example, as he of blessed memory did before
him for my minde misgives me, that he will not much advance his affaires by
Stirring' (*Letters* 27).
286–8. God spoke to the prophet Elijah in 'a still small voice' (1 Kings xix
12).
288. voice] *1685b*; Sound *1685a*. The alteration brings the poem closer to the
biblical phrasing. Charles Montague said of Charles that 'In the *still gentle
Voice* He lov'd to speak' (*Moestissimae* sig. Bb4').

That peace which made thy prosperous reign to
  shine,
290   That peace thou leav'st to thy imperial line,
    That peace, O happy shade, be ever thine!

X

For all those joys thy restoration brought,
    For all the miracles it wrought,
    For all the healing balm thy mercy poured
295   Into the nation's bleeding wound,
    And care that after kept it sound,
    For numerous blessings yearly showered,
    And property with plenty crowned,
    For freedom still maintained alive,
300   Freedom which in no other land will thrive,
    Freedom, an English subject's sole prerogative,

---

289. peace] The importance to D. of peaceful government is evident in a range of works: see his praise of Cromwell's achievements in *Heroic Stanzas* ll. 141–5; his hopes for the new reign in *Astraea Redux* ll. 312–13 and *To His Sacred Majesty* l. 136; his compliments to Clarendon's skills in the arts of peace in *To My Lord Chancellor* ll. 105–7; his attack in *AA* (*passim*) on the threat to domestic peace posed by the Whigs; the stress in *RL* l. 450 on the need to avoid disputes caused by religious differences; and, in mythological terms, in 'The Speech of Venus to Vulcan'.

290. imperial] This word was part of the official designation of the monarchy, and the proclamation of James as King referred to 'the Imperial Crowns of England, Scotland, France and Ireland' (*London Gazette* mmvi (5–9 February 1685)); cp. l. 317.

291. D. had similarly wished Cromwell peaceful rest after giving peace to the nation: *Heroic Stanzas* l. 145.

297. showered] rhymes with *poured* (l. 294); for the pronunciation cp. 'Prologue to His Royal Highness' ll. 34–5.

298–9. property . . . freedom] These are loaded words in the political debates of the Exclusion Crisis: see *AA* ll. 499n, 51–6n.

301. prerogative] There had been much debate over Charles's use of the royal prerogative, e.g. in issuing the 1672 Declaration of Indulgence suspending the penal laws against dissenters, as this was seen by many as infringing the power of Parliament and thus the rights of the subject. D.'s use of the word here claims that Charles had used his royal powers to preserve the fundamental liberties of the English people, rather than to abridge them, as many Whigs would have argued.

>   Without whose charms e'en peace would be
>   But a dull, quiet slavery;
>   For these and more accept our pious praise:
> 305   'Tis all the subsidy
>   The present age can raise;
>   The rest is charged on late posterity.
>   Posterity is charged the more
>   Because the large abounding store
> 310   To them and to their heirs is still entailed by thee.
>   Succession, of a long descent
>   Which chastely in the channels ran,
>   And from our demi-gods began,
>   Equal almost to time in its extent,
> 315   Through hazards numberless and great,
>   Thou hast derived this mighty blessing down,
>   And fixed the fairest gem that decks th' imperial
>   crown.

305. subsidy] A tax agreed by Parliament to raise money for the King for special needs. For the image cp. Rochester: [on account of the blessing of love] 'God might raise/ In lands of atheists, subsidies of praise' (*Artemisia to Chloe* (1679) ll. 46–7).

307. late posterity] D. seems to envisage posterity as coming up behind the people of the present, coming later; he repeats the phrase *late posterity* in 'The Second Book of the *Georgics*' l. 82, and Thomas Flatman also uses it in his poem *On the Death of our late Sovereign Lord King Charles II* (1685) 7, as had Thomas Sprat in *Three Poems upon the Death of his late Highnesse Oliver* (1659) 29. *OED* gives no example of such usage of the adjective *late*, but as a rare meaning of the adverb ('behind the others, in the rear') cites D.'s 'The Third Book of the *Georgics*', where a sheep is said 'late to lag behind' (l. 708).

310. entailed] i.e. the blessings conferred by Charles's reign are to be passed on inalienably to subsequent generations, like an estate which is entailed so that it cannot be split up or passed out of the direct line of descent.

311–17. The direct line of succession to the crown was preserved by Charles when he resisted Whig attempts to exclude James. The long descent of Charles is charted by Giles Fleming in *Stemma Sacrum, The Royal Progeny* (1660) (*Works*).

313. The origins of the British monarchy were traced back to Brutus, great-grandson of Aeneas, who was himself the son of the goddess Venus (see Geoffrey of Monmouth, *Historia Regum Britanniae* i 3). D. was using material from early British history in the semi-opera *King Arthur*, on which he was working in 1684.

316. derived] handed down by descent (*OED* 4b); the original meaning of *derive* is 'conduct [a stream] from its source' (cp. l. 312).

Not faction, when it shook thy regal seat,
Not senates, insolently loud,
320   (Those echoes of a thoughtless crowd),
Not foreign or domestic treachery,
Could warp thy soul to their unjust decree.
So much thy foes thy manly mind mistook,
Who judged it by the mildness of thy look:
325   Like a well-tempered sword, it bent at will,
But kept the native toughness of the steel.

XI
Be true, O Clio, to thy hero's name!
      But draw him strictly, so
That all who view the piece may know
330   He needs no trappings of fictitious fame.
      The load's too weighty: thou may'st choose
      Some parts of praise, and some refuse:
Write, that his annals may be thought more lavish than
the Muse.
      In scanty truth thou hast confined
335   The virtues of a royal mind,
      Forgiving, bounteous, humble, just and kind;

318–22. During the Exclusion Crisis the Whig party (or *faction*, from D.'s viewpoint) pursued its demands vociferously in Parliament (here, *senate*), particularly in the Commons but also in the Lords, backed by street demonstrations; domestic plots against Charles included the work of Shaftesbury in organizing the Whig campaign, and the Rye House Plot to assassinate the King and others. Foreign treachery is more difficult to gloss factually, though suspicions of interference by foreign agents abounded, and Louis XIV funded both opposition and court politicians; the French ambassador Barillon maintained contacts with opposition figures, and passed information to and from the republican Algernon Sidney (see Jonathan Scott, *Algernon·Sidney and the Restoration Crisis, 1677–1683* (1991) *passim*). Additionally, Holland was a base for Whig exiles, and the source of their long-term hopes for a Protestant monarchy under (or guaranteed by) William of Orange.
327. Clio] the Muse of history.
331–2. Echoes Horace: *sumite materiam vestris, qui scribitis, aequam/ viribus et versate diu, quid ferre recusent,/ quid valeant umeri* ('writers, take a subject equal to your strength, and ponder long what your shoulders refuse, and what they can bear': *Ars Poetica* ll. 38–40).
333. annals] D. describes *annals* as 'naked History: Or the plain relation of matter of fact, according to the succession of time, devested of all other Ornaments' ('The Life of Plutarch'; *Works* xvii 271).

His conversation, wit and parts,
His knowledge in the noblest, useful arts,
Were such dead authors could not give,
340   But habitudes of those who live;
Who lighting him did greater lights receive:
He drained from all, and all they knew;
His apprehension quick, his judgement true,
That the most learned with shame confess
345   His knowledge more, his reading only less.

XII

Amidst the peaceful triumphs of his reign,
What wonder if the kindly beams he shed
Revived the drooping arts again,
If Science raised her head,
350   And soft Humanity that from rebellion fled;

337–45. Halifax commented: 'His Wit consisted chiefly in the *Quickness* of his *Apprehension*. . . . His Wit was not acquired by *Reading*; that which he had above his original Stock by Nature, was from Company' (Halifax, *Works* ii 495–6).

340. habitudes] familiarities, associations (*OED* 3): i.e. Charles gained his knowledge and understanding not from books but from associating with intelligent people.

347. kindly] nurturing (*OED* 5b).

348–50. For the revival of the arts at Charles's restoration cp. *To My Lord Chancellor* ll. 17–23. Many elegists cited Charles's encouragement of the arts as a distinctive feature of his reign: William Bowles wrote: 'To His Protection improv'd Arts we owe,/ And solid knowledge does from Tryal grow;/ (All subject Nature ours) new Worlds are found,/ And Sciences disdain their antient bound.' (*Moestissimae* sig. Cc4ʳ); and Thomas Wood: 'Under his shade the *Tuneful* Tribe did long retreat,/ There did the Muses meet . . ./ Each *Science* tho' in *Russet* clad/ To th' Court their Journeys made' (4); cp. *Ireland's Tears* 3; Fane 3.

349. Science] philosophy, esp. the investigation of the natural world; cp. *EDP*: 'Is it not evident, in these last hundred years (when the Study of Philosophy has been the business of all the *Virtuosi* in *Christendome*) that almost a new Nature has been reveal'd to us? that . . . more useful Experiments in Philosophy have been made, more Noble Secrets in Opticks, Medicine, Anatomy, Astronomy, discover'd . . . so true it is that nothing spreads more fast than Science, when rightly and generally cultivated' (*Works* xvii 15).

350. Humanity] literature and literary scholarship (*OED* 4).

Our isle, indeed, too fruitful was before,
       But all uncultivated lay,
   Out of the solar walk, and heaven's high way,
       With rank Geneva weeds run o'er,
355 And cockle, at the best, amidst the corn it bore:
       The royal husbandman appeared,
       And ploughed, and sowed and tilled,
   The thorns he rooted out, the rubbish cleared,
       And blessed th' obedient field;
360   When straight a double harvest rose,
       Such as the swarthy Indian mows,
       Or happier climates near the line,
   Or paradise manured and dressed by hands divine.

XIII
   As when the new-born phoenix takes his way
365   His rich paternal regions to survey,

353. From Virgil: *extra anni solisque vias* (*Aen.* vi 796: 'beyond the paths of the year and of the sun'; Christie); Virgil refers to the new territory into which Augustus will extend Roman rule.
354. Geneva] the city of Calvin.
355. cockle] a weed growing in cornfields; see *AA* l. 195*n.*
360. double harvest] seen as characteristic of exotic lands: cp. 'Cinyras and Myrrha' l. 18.
362. line] equator.
363. manured] cultivated (*OED* 2).   *dressed*] cultivated (*OED* 13c).
364–7. The phoenix was a standard image for the monarch (for its medieval history see Kantorowicz, *The King's Two Bodies* 385–95), and seemed especially appropriate to Charles II. A medal of 1649 represented him as a phoenix (Kantorowicz fig. 23), and Thomas Heynes wrote: 'Like as the solitary Bird that moves/ Her pinion o're the tall *Arabian* Groves,/ Doth from the Ashes of her Dam advance,/ And to herself that noble kind inhance:/ So the pure Flames of our late Soveraign's Urn/ Did to this most puissant Monarch turn;' (*The Triumphs of Royalty* (1683) 2). The phoenix image was useful to political thinkers who wished to stress the unbroken continuity of monarchy: 'The King of *England* is Immortal; and the young *Phoenix* stays not to rise from the spicy ashes of the old one, but the Soul of Royalty by a kind of *Metempsychosis* passes immediately out of one body into another' (John Nalson, *The Common Interest of King and People* (1677) 117–18). The image was used of the succession from Charles II to James II by Ephraim Howard and George Stepney (*Moestissimae* sigs Cc2ᵛ, Gg4ᵛ). D. had compared the Duchess of York with the phoenix in the 'Verses to her Highness the Duchess' (prefixed to *AM*) ll. 52–7 (see *n*).

        Of airy choristers a numerous train
        Attend his wondrous progress o'er the plain;
           So rising from his father's urn
           So glorious did our Charles return;
370   Th' officious Muses came along,
     A gay, harmonious choir like angels ever young.
      (The Muse that mourns him now his happy triumph
        sung.)
        Ev'n they could thrive in his auspicious reign,
         And such a plenteous crop they bore
375   Of purest and well-winnowed grain,
         As Britain never knew before.
        Though little was their hire, and light their gain,
         Yet somewhat to their share he threw;
         Fed from his hand they sung and flew,
380   Like birds of paradise that lived on morning dew.
        O never let their lays his name forget!
        The pension of a prince's praise is great.
        Live then, thou great encourager of arts,
         Live ever in our thankful hearts;

370. officious] zealous in performing their duty (*OED* 2).

371. like] *1685b*; of *1685a*.

372. D. had celebrated Charles's triumphant return to England in 1660 in *Astraea Redux*.

373. auspicious] well-omened; cp. *AM* l. 77*n*.

377. D.'s own pension from the King was small, and irregularly paid; at the time of Charles's death it was four years in arrears (Winn 530). In 1693, in his 'Discourse Concerning Satire', D. recalled that 'being encourag'd only with fair Words, by King *Charles* II, my little Sallary ill paid, and no prospect of a future Subsistance', he was discouraged from writing an epic poem (*Works* iv 23).

380. John Swan wrote that the birds of paradise are supposed to 'nourish themselves, and maintain their lives by the dew that falleth, and the flowers of the spices' (*Speculum Mundi* (1635) 419; *Works*).

385   Live blessed above, almost invoked below,
           Live and receive this pious vow,
           Our patron once, our guardian angel now.
           Thou Fabius of a sinking state,
           Who didst by wise delays divert our fate,
390   When faction like a tempest rose
             In death's most hideous form;
           Then art to rage thou didst oppose,

385–7. Cp. Virgil's praise of Augustus: *da facilem cursum atque audacibus adnue coeptis,/ ignarosque uiae mecum miseratus agrestis/ ingredere et uotis iam nunc adsuesce uocari* (*Geo.* i 40–2: 'But thou, propitious *Caesar,* guide my Course,/ And to my bold Endeavours add thy Force./ Pity the Poet's and the Plough-man's Cares,/ Int'rest thy Greatness in our mean Affairs,/ And use thy self betimes to hear and grant our Pray'rs.': D.'s 'The First Book of the *Georgics'* ll. 59–63). For D.'s association of Charles II with Virgil's praise of Augustus in the opening of *Geo.* i see H. A. Mason, *CQ* xx (1991) 223–57.

385. almost invoked] The invocation of saints for aid is part of Catholic prayer, but is not Protestant usage.

388–98. Addressing the King in the Dedication to *The History of the League* (1684), D. wrote: 'By weathering of which Storm [the Exclusion Crisis] . . . You have perform'd a Greater and more Glorious work than all the Con-quests of Your Neighbours . . . to be press'd with wants, surrounded with dangers, Your Authority undermined in Popular Assemblies, Your Sacred Life attempted by a Conspiracy, Your Royal Brother forc'd from Your Arms, in one word to Govern a Kingdom which was either possess'd, or turn'd into a *Bedlam,* and yet in the midst of ruine to stand firm, undaunted, and resolv'd, and at last to break through all these difficulties, and dispell them, this is indeed an Action which is worthy the Grandson of *Henry* the Great' (*Works* xviii 6; *Works*).

388. Fabius] Quintus Fabius Maximus Verrucosus (d. 203 BC), was elected dictator after the disastrous defeat of the Romans by Hannibal at Lake Trasi-mene; he restored the people's morale through religious observances, and was responsible for the strategy of wearing down Hannibal and defeating him through exhaustion rather than in pitched battles; this won him the nickname 'Cunctator' ('the delayer').

389. Charles delayed the moment when he would have to give or refuse his assent to an Exclusion Bill by adroit use of his powers to summon, prorogue and dissolve Parliament. After the Commons had passed an Exclusion Bill, the King prorogued Parliament on 27 May 1679 to reassemble in August, but he dissolved it before it could meet. The new Parliament met on 7 October, but was immediately prorogued, and did not meet again until 21 October 1680; after the Commons had again passed an Exclusion Bill in November, Parliament was prorogued on 10 January 1681, and then dissolved; the new Parliament met at Oxford on 21 March 1681 and was dissolved on 28 March, after the Commons had begun work on a third Exclusion Bill.

To weather out the storm:
Not quitting thy supreme command,
395   Thou held'st the rudder with a steady hand,
Till safely on the shore the bark did land:
The bark that all our blessings brought,
Charged with thyself and James, a doubly royal
fraught.

                                XIV
O frail estate of human things,
400   And slippery hopes below!
Now to our cost your emptiness we know,
(For 'tis a lesson dearly bought)
Assurance here is never to be sought.
The best, and best beloved of kings,
405   And best deserving to be so,
When scarce he had escaped the fatal blow
Of faction and conspiracy,
Death did his promised hopes destroy:
He toiled, he gained, but lived not to enjoy.
410   What mists of providence are these
Through which we cannot see!
So saints, by supernatural power set free
Are left at last in martyrdom to die;
Such is the end of oft-repeated miracles.
415   Forgive me, heaven, that impious thought,
'Twas grief for Charles, to madness wrought,
That questioned thy supreme decree!
Thou didst his gracious reign prolong,
Ev'n in thy saints' and angels' wrong,
420   His fellow-citizens of immortality:

395–8. For the image of the ship of state cp. *AA* ll. 159–62*n*.
398. *fraught*] cargo (*OED* 2).
399. *estate*] condition (*OED* 1).
400. *slippery*] insecure, unreliable (*OED* 3); see 'To the Memory of Mr Oldham' l. 9*n*.
406. Charles had escaped assassination in the Rye House Plot in the spring of 1683.
414. *miracles*] rhymes with *these* (l. 410) (Christie); cp. 'To the Memory of Anne Killigrew' l. 52, where it rhymes with *bees*.
416. *grief . . . to madness wrought*] echoes 'Mezentius and Lausus' l. 178.

For twelve long years of exile borne
Twice twelve we numbered since his blessed
return:
So strictly wert thou just to pay,
Ev'n to the driblet of a day.
425   Yet still we murmur and complain
The quails and manna should no longer rain;
Those miracles 'twas needless to renew:
The chosen flock has now the promised land in
view.

XV

A warlike Prince ascends the regal state,
430   A Prince long exercised by Fate;
Long may he keep, though he obtains it late.
Heroes in heaven's peculiar mould are cast,

421. As *Works* notes, D.'s reckoning seems to depend on the old-style (OS) dating then current, by which the year ended on 24 March: Charles was proclaimed King in Scotland on 4 February 1648 OS (1649 NS), and returned from exile in May 1660; he died on 6 February 1684 OS (1685 NS). His death was *the driblet of a day* later than the anniversary of his proclamation in Scotland.

424. driblet] small sum of money, tiny debt (*OED*).

426–8. The Israelites (God's 'chosen people'), delivered from their exile in Egypt by Moses, journeyed through the wilderness for forty years, and were sustained by the miraculous appearance of manna and quails (Exodus xvi). Moses died before reaching the promised land himself, and they were led there by the warrior Joshua. Other elegists used this comparison: Aphra Behn wrote: 'Like *Moses*, he had led the Murm'ring Crowd,/ Beneath the *Peaceful Rule* of his Almighty Wand;/ Pull'd down the *Golden Calf* to which they bow'd,/ And left 'em *safe*, entring the promis'd Land;/ And to *good JOSHUA*, now resigns his sway,/ *JOSHUA*, by *Heaven* and *Nature* pointed out to lead the way' (4); cp. also Penn 3; *Moestissimae* sig. S1^{r-v}.

429. warlike] James served with the French army 1652–5, and with the Spanish forces 1657–8; from the beginning of Charles's reign he took an active interest in naval matters, and in 1665 fought in the naval battles against the Dutch (cp. *AM* ll. 73–4). D. celebrates James as 'a Warlike Loyal Brother' in *Albion and Albanius* (1685) III i 196–9; see also 'To Mr Northleigh' l. 10. James's warlike qualities are stressed *passim* in *Moestissimae.*   *state*] throne (*OED* 20).

430. Echoes Anchises' speech to Aeneas: *Iliacis exercite fatis* (Virgil, *Aen.* iii 182: 'much tried by Ilium's fate'; Christie).   *exercised*] harassed (*OED* 4b).

432. peculiar] particular, very own (*OED* 1).

They and their poets are not formed in haste;
Man was the first in God's design, and man was made
   the last.
435   False heroes, made by flattery so,
     Heaven can strike out, like sparkles, at a blow;
     But ere a Prince is to perfection brought,
     He costs omnipotence a second thought.
          With toil and sweat,
440   With hardening cold and forming heat
      The Cyclops did their strokes repeat,
     Before th' impenetrable shield was wrought.
     It looks as if the Maker would not own
        The noble work for his,
445   Before 'twas tried and found a masterpiece.

               XVI
     View then a monarch ripened for a throne.
      Alcides thus his race began,
      O'er infancy he swiftly ran,
     The future god at first was more than man.
450   Dangers and toils, and Juno's hate,
      Ev'n o'er his cradle lay in wait,
      And there he grappled first with Fate:
     In his young hands the hissing snakes he pressed,
     So early was the deity confessed:
455   Thus by degrees he rose to Jove's imperial seat.
Thus difficulties prove a soul legitimately great.
      Like his, our hero's infancy was tried;
     Betimes the Furies did their snakes provide,

436. strike out] produce by a blow (*OED* 83c).
439–42. The Cyclops made an impenetrable shield for Aeneas (*Aen.* vii 439–53).
447–55. Hercules (*Alcides*) was the son of Jupiter by Alcmene; Juno jealously thwarted her husband's attempt to make him ruler of the House of Perseus, but Jupiter persuaded Juno to agree that after performing twelve labours, Hercules should become a god. Juno sent two snakes to kill Hercules in his cradle, but the child strangled one with each hand.
454. confessed] revealed, made manifest (*OED* 5).
457–64. The parallel between Hercules and James is that as the infant Hercules was attacked in his cradle by snakes, so the infant James was attacked by the parliamentarians in arms against his father; this formed a prelude to the

And to his infant arms oppose
460   His father's rebels and his brother's foes.
The more oppressed, the higher still he rose.
Those were the preludes of his fate
That formed his manhood to subdue
The hydra of the many-headed, hissing crew.

XVII

465   As after Numa's peaceful reign
The martial Ancus did the sceptre wield,
Furbished the rusty sword again,
Resumed the long-forgotten shield,
And led the Latins to the dusty field;
470   So James the drowsy genius wakes
Of Britain, long entranced in charms,
Restive, and slumbering on its arms:
'Tis roused, and with a new-strung nerve the spear
already shakes.
No neighing of the warrior steeds,
475   No drum or louder trumpet needs
T' inspire the coward, warm the cold;
His voice, his sole appearance makes 'em bold.

---

confrontation between the mature James and the Whigs who demanded his
exclusion from the succession. (*Works* wrongly assumes that three attacks are
referred to by D., and invents a childhood illness to explain one of them.)
The *hydra* (a many-headed snake) is a traditional image for a rebellious
populace (cp. *AA* l. 541*n*). Hercules killed the hydra as his second labour.
The elegists refer to both Charles and James as conquering the hydra of
rebellion: Wood says of Charles: 'Our *Hercules*, our guardian God/ An *Hydra*
tam'd, he tam'd the *multitude*' (3); cp. *Moestissimae* sigs D1ᵛ, H2ʳ⁻ᵛ, O4ᵛ.
461. Palms were thought to flourish when weighted down; this is depicted in
the frontispiece to *Eikon Basilike* (1649) as an emblem of Charles I's sufferings. Cp. *Heroic Stanzas* l. 57*n*. James Saunderson noted: Virtus/ Vulnere
virescit, *durisque oppressa triumphat* ('*Virtue flourishes when wounded*, and
triumphs when oppressed by hardships': *Moestissimae* sig. C1ᵛ).
465–6. Numa, traditionally the second king of Rome, was credited with
having established peace (Livy i 19, 22). He was succeeded by Tullus, and
then by Ancus, who conducted a war against the Latins (Livy i 32–3). Cp.
'Of the Pythagorean Philosophy' ll. 712–20.
472. Restive] inactive (*OED* 1).
473. nerve] sinew (*OED* 1).

Gaul and Batavia dread th' impending blow,
Too well the vigour of that arm they know;
480   They lick the dust, and crouch beneath their fatal
foe.
Long may they fear this awful Prince,
And not provoke his lingering sword;
Peace is their only sure defence,
Their best security his word:
485   In all the changes of his doubtful state,
His truth, like heaven's, was kept inviolate:
For him to promise is to make it fate.
His valour can triumph o'er land and main;
With broken oaths his fame he will not stain,
490   With conquest basely bought, and with inglorious
gain.

478. *Gaul and Batavia*] France and Holland. Other elegists similarly envisaged
James making war: William Villiers said: *tacete/ Vos*, Galli, *& Batavi, dum
tremetis pavidi* ('Be silent, France and Holland, so long as you shake with fear':
Moestissimae sig. B4^v; cp. B2^v–B3^r). In fact, James refused to join the alliance
against Louis XIV, with whom he maintained close, confidential relations,
and from whom he received financial subsidies. He was too well aware of the
hopes which many English Protestants invested in William of Orange to
antagonize him, and kept up a polite correspondence with him.
481. *awful*] awesome.
484–7. James was regarded by contemporaries as a man of his word. The Earl
of Ailesbury called him 'a prince that had all the moral virtues . . . the most
honest and sincere man I ever knew' (David Ogg, *England in the Reigns of
James II and William III* (1955) 140). D. draws a longer portrait of James along
these lines in 'Epilogue to *Albion and Albanius*' and *HP* iii 906–37.
484. *Their*] 1685b; There 1685a.
488. *triumph*] The verb was often accented on the second syllable in the
seventeenth century: cp. *RL* l. 56n.

XVIII

For once, O heaven, unfold thy adamantine book,
  And let his wondering senate see
  If not thy firm, immutable decree,
  At least the second page, of strong contingency,
495 Such as consists with wills originally free:
   Let them with glad amazement look
   On what their happiness may be;
  Let them not still be obstinately blind,
  Still to divert the good thou hast designed,
500   Or with malignant penury
  To starve the royal virtues of his mind.
  Faith is a Christian's, and a subject's test,
 O give them to believe, and they are surely blessed!
  They do, and with a distant view I see
505 Th' amended vows of English loyalty.

491. *adamantine*] incapable of being altered.

492. *senate*] Parliament, which James summoned shortly after his accession.

493–5. i.e. they will be shown not the decrees of God himself, but an account of how those decrees will be worked out by human agents, acting according to their own free will in the world of second causes (cp. l. 110).

494. *strong*] *1685b*; great *1685a*.

500. *penury*] D. touches on a topical and sensitive issue. Since the customs and excise had been granted to Charles only for his lifetime, James was financially dependent upon the decision of the new Parliament, which would determine the level of tax revenues for the duration of his reign. On 9 February he had issued a proclamation ordering the continued payment of customs duties and the subsidies of tonnage and poundage as they applied in the previous reign, pending the assembling of a new Parliament, but this move was of doubtful legality. It had been Charles II's financial difficulties which had forced him to summon Parliament during the Exclusion Crisis, in the hope of obtaining extra revenue; his problems were solved when Louis XIV gave him a secret grant which was substantial enough for him to dissolve the Oxford Parliament in March 1681 and dispense with Parliament altogether for the remainder of his reign. Louis made half a million livres available to James, and the Commons granted him for life the revenues which Charles had received, along with some additional duties.

501. *sterve*] starve (variant spelling).

502–3. D. repeats this point in 'Epilogue to *Albion and Albanius*' ll. 23–32 (*Works*).

And all beyond that object there appears
The long retinue of a prosperous reign,
A series of successful years,
In orderly array, a martial, manly train.
510   Behold, ev'n to remoter shores
A conquering navy proudly spread,
The British cannon formidably roars;
While starting from his oozy bed
Th' asserted ocean rears his reverend head
515   To view and recognise his ancient lord again,
And with a willing hand restores
The fasces of the main.

506–17. Echoes *Astraea Redux* ll. 292–303 *(Works)*.

507. retinue] accented on the second syllable in the seventeenth century *(OED)*.

513–17. The appearance of a sea or river god, rearing his head above the waves, is a common image: cp. Virgil, *Aen*. i 124–7; *Geo*. iv 363–73; Claudian, *De Sexto Consulatu Honorii Augusti* ll. 159–61; Silius Italicus, *Punica* vii 254–9. *(Works)*.

514. asserted] claimed *(OED's* first example, though the meaning 'lay claim to' is a common seventeenth-century usage of the verb); cp. *Heroic Stanzas* l. 85.

516–17. Echoes *Astraea Redux* l. 249 (see *n*). Thomas Hesilrige wrote: *Nunc Pius aequoreas Moderatur vela per Undas/ Ipse Maris Dominus, nostri spes altera Regni,/ JACOBUS; facilem cui spondent Numina cursum;/ Submittasque volens proprium*, Neptune, *Tridentem* ('Now the pious lord of the sea himself directs his sails through the waves of the sea: James, our kingdom's other hope. The gods promise an easy course for him, and you willingly submit your own trident to him, Neptune'; *Moestissimae* sig. C2ᵛ); and cp. John Naylor: *Tibi laeta suos submisit ut Anglia fasces* ('England joyfully lowers her fasces to you': *Moestissimae* sig. d3ᵛ). D. celebrates James as 'Lord of Land and Main' in *Albion and Albanius* III i 219.

109 Prologue, Epilogue and Songs from *Albion and Albanius*

Date and publication. The opera was staged before Charles late in 1684, but after his death on 6 February 1685 it was revised, and performed publicly at Dorset Garden on 3 June 1685. *Albion and Albanius: An Opera* was published by Tonson in 1685 (advertised in *The Observator* 8 June); reprinted 1691. The Prologue and Epilogue were not printed with the opera, but were issued separately on a single folio half-sheet (Macdonald no. 104), which is often found bound into copies of the opera. Luttrell dated his copy of the opera (now at Yale) 3 June, and the leaf containing the Prologue and Epilogue 6 June (J. M. Osborn, *MPh* xxxix (1941) 91). It is possible that the Prologue and Epilogue were printed separately for distribution at performances. An edition of the words and music was published by William Nott in 1687.

Context. The opera was originally intended as the prologue to *King Arthur*, which was eventually completed and staged in 1691. It shows Albion and Albanius (Charles and James) overcoming opposition, first at the Restoration in 1660, and then through the defeat of the Whigs in the 1680s. The music was by the French composer Louis Grabu. For a discussion of the iconography see Paul Hammond in *The Court Masque*, edited by David Lindley (1984) 169–83, and for the musical settings see Winn, *When Beauty* 254–73.

Prologue to the Opera

Full twenty years and more our labouring stage
Has lost on this incorrigible age:
Our poets, the John Ketches of the nation,
Have seemed to lash ye, ev'n to excoriation;
5 But still no sign remains, which plainly notes
You bore like heroes, or you bribed like Oates.
What can we do, when mimicking a fop,
Like beating nut trees, makes a larger crop?

¶**109**. *Prologue.*
3. John Ketches] hangmen.
4. excoriation] flaying.
5. notes] signifies (*OED* 5).
6. bribed like Oates] Titus Oates was alleged to have bribed the hangman to be lenient in administering the whipping which he suffered in May 1685.
8. Proverbial (Tilley W 644).

Faith, we'll e'en spare our pains, and to content you
10   Will fairly leave you what your maker meant you.
Satire was once your physic, wit your food,
One nourished not, and t' other drew no blood.
We now prescribe, like doctors in despair,
The diet your weak appetites can bear.
15   Since hearty beef and mutton will not do,
Here's julep dance, ptisan of song and show:
Give you strong sense, the liquor is too heady;
You're come to farce, that's ass's milk, already.
Some hopeful youths there are, of callow wit,
20   Who one day may be men, if heaven think fit;
Sound may serve such ere they to sense are grown,
Like leading strings till they can walk alone:
But yet to keep our friends in count'nance, know
The wise Italians first invented show;
25   Thence into France the noble pageant passed,
'Tis England's credit to be cozened last.
Freedom and Zeal have choused you o'er and o'er; ⎫
Pray give us leave to bubble you once more;   ⎬
You never were so cheaply fooled before.   ⎭
30   We bring you change to humour your disease,
Change for the worse has ever used to please:
Then 'tis the mode of France, without whose rules
None must presume to set up here for fools:
In France the oldest man is always young,   ⎫
35   Sees operas daily, learns the tunes so long   ⎬
Till foot, hand, head keep time with every song.   ⎭
Each sings his part, echoing from pit and box,
With his hoarse voice, half harmony, half pox.

---

16. *julep*] a sweet drink with comforting or mildly stimulating properties
(*OED*).   *ptisan*] a slightly medicinal barley-water drink (*OED*).
18. *ass's milk*] an invalid's diet.
19. *hopeful*] promising.
22. *leading strings*] child's reins.
24. In his Preface D. says that the Italians 'have not only invented, but
brought to perfection, this sort of Dramatique Musical Entertainment . . . all
Europe has been enriched out of their Treasury' (*Works* xv 5).
27. *Freedom and Zeal*] In the opera the opposition to Albion includes Demo-
cracy (i.e. mob rule) and Zelota ('Feigned Zeal').   *choused*] cheated.
28. *bubble*] cheat.

'*Le plus grand Roi du monde*' is always ringing,
40 They show themselves good subjects by their singing.
On that condition, set up every throat,
You Whigs may sing, for you have changed your note.
Cits and citesses raise a joyful strain,
'Tis a good omen to begin a reign:
45 Voices may help your charter to restoring,
And get by singing what you lost by roaring.

Epilogue to the Opera

After our Aesop's fable shown today,
I come to give the moral of the play.
Feigned Zeal, you saw, set out the speedier pace,
But, the last heat, Plain Dealing won the race.
5 Plain Dealing for a jewel has been known,
But ne'er till now the jewel of a crown.
When heaven made man, to show the work divine
Truth was his image stamped upon the coin,
And when a king is to a god refined,
10 On all he says and does he stamps his mind:
This proves a soul without allay and pure;
Kings, like their gold, should every touch endure.
To dare in fields is valour, but how few
Dare be so throughly valiant to be true!
15 The name of great let other kings affect,
He's great indeed, the prince that is direct.
His subjects know him now, and trust him more
Than all their kings and all their laws before.

39. Le plus grand Roi du monde] 'The greatest king in the world'; used of Louis XIV.
43. cits] citizens.   *citesses*] female citizens (*OED*'s only example).
45–6. The enforced surrender of the City of London's charter in October 1683 marked the King's victory in his campaign for control of civic appointments (cp. 'Prologue to *The Duke of Guise*' headnote, ll. 3*n*, 43*n*).
46. roaring] riotous behaviour (*OED* 2).

Epilogue. For D.'s praise of James II's virtues cp. *AA* ll. 353–60*n*; *Threnodia Augustalis* ll. 429–90, esp. ll. 484–90 on James's reputation for keeping his word.
12. touch] testing of gold by a touchstone (*OED* 5).

What safety could their public Acts afford?
20   Those he can break, but cannot break his word.
So great a trust to him alone was due,
Well have they trusted whom so well they knew.
The saint who walked on waves securely trod
While he believed the beck'ning of his God;
25   But when his faith no longer bore him out
Began to sink, as he began to doubt.
Let us our native character maintain,
'Tis of our growth to be sincerely plain.
T' excel in truth we loyally may strive,
30   Set privilege against prerogative;
He plights his faith, and we believe him just;
His honour is to promise, ours to trust.
Thus Britain's basis on a word is laid,
As by a word the world itself was made.

Songs

I

I

Albion.   Then Zeal and Commonwealth infest
My land again;
The fumes of madness that possessed
The people's giddy brain,
5   Once more disturb the nation's rest,
And dye rebellion in a deeper stain.

2

Will they at length awake the sleeping sword,
And force revenge from their offended lord?

---

19. Acts] Acts of Parliament.
23–6. St Peter: Matthew xiv 22–33.
30. privilege] the rights of Parliament (*OED* 4).   *prerogative*] the rights of
the sovereign (*OED* 1a).
34. Genesis i 3; John i 1.

Songs. The choice of songs from an opera which is sung throughout is
difficult; those selected here are mostly set out as songs in the printed text.
Songs I–IV are from Act II, Songs V–VII from Act III.

How long, ye gods, how long
10   Can royal patience bear
Th' insults and wrong
Of madmen's jealousies and causeless fear?

3

I thought their love by mildness might be gained,
By peace I was restored, in peace I reigned;
15   But tumults, seditions,
And haughty petitions
Are all the effects of a merciful nature;
Forgiving and granting
Ere mortals are wanting
20   But leads to rebelling against their creator.

II
1

Apollo. All hail, ye royal pair!
The gods' peculiar care:
Fear not the malice of your foes,
Their dark designing
5   And combining
Time and truth shall once expose:
Fear not the malice of your foes.

2

My sacred oracles assure
The tempest shall not long endure,
10   But when the nation's crimes are purged away
Then shall you both in glory shine,
Propitious both, and both divine,
In lustre equal to the god of day.

III

Thames. Old father Ocean calls my tide,
'Come away, come away';
The barks upon the billows ride,
The master will not stay;

5   The merry boatswain from his side
       His whistle takes to check and chide
       The lingering lads' delay,
       And all the crew aloud has cried,
       'Come away, come away'.

10   See the god of seas attends thee,
       Nymphs divine, a beauteous train,
       All the calmer gales befriend thee
       In thy passage o'er the main;
       Every maid her locks is binding,
15   Every Triton's horn is winding,
       Welcome to the watery plain.

IV

Two nymphs and Triton sing.

1

Ye nymphs, the charge is royal,
    Which you must convey;
Your hearts and hands employ all,
    Hasten to obey;
5   When earth is grown disloyal,
Show there's honour in the sea.

2

Sports and pleasures shall attend you
    Through all the watery plains,
        Where Neptune reigns:
10 Venus ready to defend you,
And her nymphs to ease your pains.
    No storm shall offend you
        Passing the main;
Nor billow threat in vain
15   So sacred a train,
Till the gods that defend you
    Restore you again.

3

See at your blessed returning
    Rage disappears;

20   The widowed isle in mourning
                  Dries up her tears,
          With flowers the meads adorning,
                  Pleasure appears,
          And love dispels the nation's causeless fears.

                            V

          Nereids rise out of the sea and sing; Tritons dance.
                            I
          From the low palace of old father Ocean,
          Come we in pity your cares to deplore;
          Sea-racing dolphins are trained for our motion,
          Moony tides swelling to roll us ashore.

                            2
5   Every nymph of the flood, her tresses rending,
          Throws off her armlet of pearl in the main;
          Neptune in anguish his charge unattending,
          Vessels are found'ring, and vows are in vain.

                           VI
                            I
Proteus. Albion, loved of gods and men,
          Prince of peace too mildly reigning,
          Cease thy sorrow and complaining,
          Thou shalt be restored again:
5   Albion, loved of gods and men.

                            2
          Still thou art the care of heaven,
          In thy youth to exile driven;
          Heaven thy ruin then prevented,
          Till the guilty land repented;
10   In thy age, when none could aid thee,
          Foes conspired and friends betrayed thee;

Song V.
3. racing . . . trained] *1685 errata*; spouting . . . tam'd *1685*; a possible revision.

To the brink of danger driven,
Still thou art the care of heaven.

VII

1

Venus.   Albion, hail; the gods present thee
All the richest of their treasures,
Peace and pleasures
To content thee,
5   Dancing their eternal measures.

                    Graces and Loves dance an entry.

2

But above all human blessing
Take a warlike loyal brother;
Never prince had such another:
Conduct, courage, truth expressing,
10   All heroic worth possessing.

                    Here the heroes' dance is performed.

110 To Mr Northleigh

Date and publication. The poem appeared in John Northleigh's *The Triumph of our Monarchy, over the Plots and Principles of our Rebels and Republicans*, which was published by Benjamin Tooke in 1685 (a note on an unsigned preliminary page says that the book was almost completely printed before the licensing Act was revived (24 June)).

Context. Northleigh (1657–1705), lawyer and physician, had previously written *The Parallel* (1682), which compared the Whig Association with the Solemn League and Covenant of 1643 (see *The Medal*, 'Epistle to the Whigs' ll. 82–3n and 'Prologue to *The Duke of Guise*' ll. 1–2n). Commendatory verses for *The Triumph* were also supplied by Thomas Flatman. His book is a critique of five Whig or republican works of political theory.

To My Friend Mr J. Northleigh, Author of *The Parallel*, On his *Triumph of the British Monarchy*

So Joseph, yet a youth, expounded well ⎫
The boding dream, and did th' event foretell, ⎬
Judged by the past, and drew the parallel. ⎭
Thus early Solomon the truth explored,
5   The right awarded, and the babe restored.
Thus Daniel, ere to prophecy he grew, ⎫
The perjured presbyters did first subdue, ⎬
And freed Susannah from the canting crew. ⎭
Well may our monarchy triumphant stand
10   While warlike James protects both sea and land,

¶110. *1–2*. Joseph expounded Pharaoh's dreams foretelling seven years of plenty followed by seven of famine (Genesis xli).
2. event] outcome.
4–5. Solomon asked God for wisdom, since he was 'but a little child'; his judgement between two women who claimed the same baby resulted in the restoration of the child to its true mother (1 Kings iii 7, 16–28).
6–8. In the apocryphal book of Susannah, the young Daniel intervenes to prevent the execution of Susannah, falsely accused of adultery by two elders who lusted after her.
7. presbyters] a title adopted by nonconformist ministers.
10. James II had succeeded to the throne on 6 February 1685. D. stressed his military reputation in *Threnodia Augustalis* ll. 429–90.

And under covert of his seven-fold shield
Thou send'st thy shafts to scour the distant field.
By law thy powerful pen has set us free:
Thou studiest that, and that may study thee.

⌣

11–12. As Teucer fought under cover of Ajax's shield (*Iliad* viii 266–72; cp.
'To Sir Godfrey Kneller' l. 78; Kinsley).
12. *scour*] range about in search of an enemy.
13. Northleigh stresses the benefits of monarchical rule by law, and the law
of succession (*Works*).

Appendix A
The Contents of *Miscellany Poems* and *Sylvae*

While this edition presents Dryden's translations in the context of his other poems, they were initially read as part of a different canon in the miscellanies and composite translations published by Tonson. Although *Sylvae* was published in facsimile in 1973, these early volumes are not easy for modern readers to find, and so a list of their contents is provided here. Many writers contributed to more than one collection, and there was evidently a group of translators recruited by Dryden and Tonson (often with a common Cambridge connection) for the various composite translations which were published in the 1680s and 1690s. For studies of the compilation of these miscellanies see W. J. Cameron, 'Miscellany Poems 1684–1716' (unpublished PhD thesis, Reading 1957); Arthur Sherbo, *EA* xxxii (1979) 262–76; Stuart Gillespie, *Restoration* xii (1988) 10–19, and PhD thesis; Paul Hammond, *PBSA* lxxxiv (1990) 405–12.

Attributions are supplied inside square brackets where the original publication was anonymous.

Miscellany Poems (1684)
This list is based upon the contents page, with some normalization of titles.

Mac Flecknoe	[John Dryden] (This and the following two poems were attributed to Dryden on the contents page of the 1692 edition, but not in the text.)
Absalom and Achitophel	[John Dryden]
The Medal	[John Dryden]

Several of Ovid's Elegies: *Book the First:*

Elegy I	[John] Cooper
II	Thomas Creech
IV	Sir Carr Scrope
V	Richard Duke
VIII	Sir Charles Sedley

Out of the Second Book:

Elegy I	Mr Adams (Gillespie (thesis

278) identifies him with the T.
Adams to whom a
commendatory poem on *The
Medal* is attributed in the 1716
edition of *Miscellany Poems*: but
he could be the John Adams
(1662–1720), then BA, and later
Provost, of King's College,
Cambridge, who is credited by
Winn (*PQ* lxxi (1992) 62, 64–6)
with commendatory poems to
Creech's Lucretius (1682) and
Aphra Behn's *Poems on Several
Occasions* (1684).)

V	Sir Charles Sedley
VI	Thomas Creech
VII	Thomas Creech
VIII	Thomas Creech
VIII	'The same by another hand'
IX	John Wilmot, Earl of Rochester
XII	Thomas Creech
XV	Mr Adams
XIX	John Dryden

Out of the Third Book:

Elegy IV	Sir Charles Sedley
V	Anon
VI	Thomas Rymer
IX	[George] Stepney
XIII	Nahum Tate
XIII	'The same elegy by another hand'

Part of Virgil's Fourth *Georgic*	E[arl] of M[ulgrave]
The Parting of Sireno and Diana	Sir Carr Scrope
Lucretia out of Ovid, *De Fastis*	Thomas Creech
On Mr Dryden's *Religio Laici*	Earl of Roscommon
Upon Mr Dryden's *Religio Laici*	Anon

Odes *of Horace*

Odes I xxii	Earl of Roscommon
III vi	Earl of Roscommon

I iv	Anon
II iv	Richard Duke
II viii	Richard Duke
III ix	Richard Duke
III ix	'The same by another hand'
IV ix	[George] Stepney
II xv	[Knightley Chetwood] (attributed in 1692 edition)
II xvi	Thomas Otway
The first *Epode* of Horace	[Knightley Chetwood] (attributed in 1716 edition)
Propertius, *Elegy* I iii	Mr Adams
'Foeda est in coitu' out of Petronius	Anon
Epistle from T.O. to R.D.	T[homas] O[tway]
A Letter to a Friend	Anon (R. G. Ham, *Otway and Lee* (1931) 179, attributes the poem to Otway, but without evidence; not in Ghosh.)
An elegy out of the Latin of Francis Remond	Anon
Amaryllis [from Theocritus III]	John Dryden
Pharmaceutra [from Theocritus II]	William Bowles
The Cyclop [from Theocritus XI]	Richard Duke
To absent Caelia	Richard Duke
Prologue at Oxford, 1673	John Dryden
Epilogue at Oxford, 1673	John Dryden
Prologue at Oxford, 1674	John Dryden
Epilogue at Oxford, 1674	John Dryden
Prologue at Oxford, 1679	John Dryden
Prologue at Oxford, 1676	John Dryden
Epilogue at Oxford, 1674	John Dryden
Prologue at Oxford, 1680	John Dryden
Prologue to *Albumazar*	John Dryden
Prologue to *Arviragus* revived	John Dryden
Prologue [to *Wit without Money*]	John Dryden
Prologue Spoken by the Women	John Dryden
Prologue at the Opening of the New House	John Dryden
Epilogue at the Opening of the New House	John Dryden

Epilogue ('Where you but half so wise . . .')	John Dryden
Epilogue [to *The Unhappy Favourite*]	John Dryden
Prologue to *The Princess of Cleves*	John Dryden
Epilogue to *The Princess of Cleves*	John Dryden
A Poem spoken to the Queen at Trinity College in Cambridge	Richard Duke
Floriana, a Pastoral	Richard Duke
The Tears of Amynta	John Dryden
The Praises of Italy (from Virgil, *Geo.* II)	Knightley Chetwood
Epilogue to *Calisto*	[John Dryden] (attributed in 1702 edition: see headnote to the poem)

Virgil's Eclogues *Translated by Several Hands*

Eclogue I	John Caryll
II	Nahum Tate
II	Thomas Creech
III	Thomas Creech
IV	John Dryden
V	Richard Duke
VI	Earl of Roscommon
VII	Mr Adams
VIII	[John] Stafford (Macdonald 160–1)
VIII	Knightley Chetwood
IX	[John Dryden] (attributed in 1692 edition)
X	[John] Stafford
X	[Sir William Temple] (attributed in 1716 edition)

Sylvae (1685)

This list is based upon the contents page, with some normalization of titles.

Preface	John Dryden
Nisus and Euryalus	John Dryden
Mezentius and Lausus	John Dryden
The Speech of Venus to Vulcan	John Dryden
Lucretius: The Beginning of the	

First Book	John Dryden
Lucretius: The Beginning of the Second Book	John Dryden
Lucretius: Against the Fear of Death	John Dryden
Lucretius: Concerning the Nature of Love	John Dryden
From Lucretius: Book the Fifth	John Dryden
Theocritus: Idyllium the Eighteenth	John Dryden
Theocritus: Idyllium the Twenty-third	John Dryden
Daphnis (from Theocritus' *Idyll* XXVII)	John Dryden
Horace: *Odes* I iii	John Dryden
Horace: *Odes* I ix	John Dryden
Horace: *Odes* III xxix	John Dryden
Horace: *Epode* II	John Dryden
Part of Virgil's *Georgics* IV	'By an unknown hand' (attributed to Thomas Creech in 1702 edition, though William Frost (*N & Q* ccxxvii (1982) 511–13) points out that it is identical with Lauderdale's translation)
Tibullus, *Elegy* I vi	Anon (Ham 179 attributes it without evidence to Otway; not in Ghosh)
Ovid's Dream	Anon
Prologue intended for *A Duke and No Duke*	Anon (see Danchin no. 346)
Horace: *Odes* II xiv	[John Potenger: see his *Private Memoirs* (1841) 73]
Theocritus: *Idyll* I	Anon
Theocritus: *Idyll* X	William Bowles
Theocritus: *Idyll* XII	Anon
Theocritus: *Idyll* XIX	Anon
The Complaint of Ariadna out of Catullus	William Bowles
Theocritus: *Idyll* XX	William Bowles
To Lesbia, out of Catullus	Anon
To Lesbia	Anon

To Lesbia, a petition to be freed from love	Anon
Ovid: *Elegies* II xii	Anon
Ovid: *Elegies* II xvi	Anon
Ovid: *Elegies* III xix	Anon
Of Nature's Changes, from Lucretius Book V	[Sir Robert Howard; attributed in 1716 edition; said in *1685* to be 'by a person of quality']
Horace: *Odes* IV vii	'by an unknown hand'
Horace: *Odes* II x	Anon
Horace: *Epistle* I xviii	Anon
Horace: *Satire* I ii	[John] Stafford
Ovid: *Elegy* II iv	Anon
Ovid: *Tristia* V xi	Anon
An Ode sung before the King on New Year's Day	[James (or Jacob) Allestry (or Allestree); attributed in 1702 edition]
Upon the Late Ingenious Translation of Père Simon's *Critical History* by H.D. Esq.	Anon
Horti Arlingtoniani	Charles Dryden
A New Song	[John Dryden] (attributed in 1692 edition)
A Song	[John Dryden] (attributed in 1692 edition)
On the Death of Mr Oldham	[Jacob Tonson: see Sarah Clapp, *Jacob Tonson in ten letters by and about him* (1948) 11–12]
On the King's House now building at Winchester	Anon
The Episode of the Death of Camilla, from Virgil, *Aeneid* XI	[John] Stafford

Appendix B

Commendatory Poems on *The Medal* and *Religio Laici*

The Medal

The first edition of *The Medal* included two commendatory poems, both unsigned. The first was reprinted in Nahum Tate's *Poems Written on Several Occasions* (1684), and the second was attributed to T. Adams in *MP* (1716); for Adams see pp. 431–2 above.

Upon the Author of the following Poem

> Once more our awful poet arms, t' engage
> The threat'ning hydra-faction of the age;
> Once more prepares his dreadful pen to wield,
> And every Muse attends him to the field:
> 5 By art and nature for this task designed,
> Yet modestly the fight he long declined,
> Forbore the torrent of his verse to pour,
> Nor loosed his satire till the needful hour.
> His sovereign's right, by patience half betrayed,
> 10 Waked his avenging genius to its aid.
> Blessed Muse, whose wit with such a cause was
>   crowned,
> And blessed the cause that such a champion found.
> With chosen verse upon the foe he falls,
> And black sedition in each quarter galls;
> 15 Yet like a prince with subjects forced t' engage,
> Secure of conquest he rebates his rage;
> His fury not without distinction sheds,
> Hurls mortal bolts, but on devoted heads;
> To less infected members gentle found,
> 20 Or spares, or else pours balm into the wound.
> Such gen'rous grace th' ingrateful tribe abuse,
> And trespass on the mercy of his Muse;
> Their wretched doggerel rhymers forth they bring
> To snarl and bark against the poet's King;
> 25 A crew that scandalize the nation more
> Than all their treason-canting priests before.

On these he scarce vouchsafes a scornful smile,
But on their powerful patrons turns his style:
A style so keen, as ev'n from faction draws
30   The vital poison, stabs to th' heart their cause.
Take then, great bard, what tribute we can raise;
Accept our thanks, for you transcend our praise.

[Nahum Tate]

To the Unknown Author of the following Poem, and that of *Absalom and Achitophel*

Thus pious ignorance with dubious praise
Altars of old to gods unknown did raise;
They knew not the loved deity, they knew
Divine effects a cause divine did show:
5   Nor can we doubt, when such these numbers are,
Such is their cause, though the worst Muse shall dare
Their sacred worth in humble verse declare.
    As gentle Thames, charmed with thy tuneful song,
Glides in a peaceful majesty along,
10   No rebel stone, no lofty bank does brave
The easy passage of his silent wave;
So, sacred poet, so thy numbers flow,
Sinewy, yet mild as happy lovers' woe;
Strong, yet harmonious too as planets move,
15   Yet soft as down upon the wings of love.
How sweet does virtue in your dress appear!
How much more charming when much less severe!
Whilst you our senses harmlessly beguile
With all th' allurements of your happy style,
20   Y' insinuate loyalty with kind deceit,
And into sense th' unthinking many cheat.
So the sweet Thracian with his charming lyre
Into rude nature virtue did inspire;
So he the savage herd to reason drew,
25   Yet scarce so sweet, so charmingly as you.
O that you would with some such powerful charm
Enervate Albion to just valour warm!
Whether much-suffering Charles shall theme afford,

Or the great deeds of godlike James' sword;
30 Again fair Gallia might be ours, again
Another fleet might pass the subject main,
Another Edward lead the Britons on,
Or such an Ossory as you did moan;
While in such numbers you in such a strain
35 Inflame their courage, and reward their pain.
    Let false Achitophel the rout engage,
Talk easy Absalom to rebel rage;
Let frugal Shimei curse in holy zeal,
Or modest Corah more new plots reveal;
40 Whilst constant to himself, secure of fate,
Good David still maintains the royal state;
Though each in vain such various ills employs,
Firmly he stands, and ev'n those ills enjoys;
Firm as fair Albion midst the raging main
45 Surveys encircling danger with disdain.
In vain the waves assault the unmoved shore,
In vain the winds with mingled fury roar,
Fair Albion's beauteous cliffs shine whiter than before.
    Nor shalt thou move, though hell thy fall conspire,
50 Though the worse rage of zeal's fanatic fire,
Thou best, thou greatest of the British race,
Thou only fit to fill great Charles' place.
    Ah wretched Britons! Ah too stubborn isle!
Ah stiff-necked Israel on blessed Canaan's soil!
55 Are those dear proofs of heaven's indulgence vain,
Restoring David and his gentle reign?
Is it in vain thou all the goods dost know
Auspicious stars on mortals shed below,
While all thy streams with milk, thy lands with honey
    flow?
60 No more, fond isle, no more thyself engage
In civil fury and intestine rage;
No rebel zeal thy duteous land molest,
But a smooth calm soothe every peaceful breast,
While in such charming notes divinely sings
65 The best of poets, of the best of kings.

[T. Adams]

Religio Laici

The first edition of *Religio Laici* included two commendatory poems;
the first was anonymous (perhaps by John, Lord Vaughan: see
Richard H. Perkinson, *PQ* xxviii (1949) 517); the second was signed
by Thomas Creech (for whom see 'Preface to *Sylvae*' l. 448n and
Appendix A). A third poem, by the Earl of Roscommon, was added
in the third edition (1683; Macdonald no. 16c); for Roscommon see
'To the Earl of Roscommon', headnote. Roscommon's poem was
reprinted in *MP* (1684), along with a further anonymous poem 'To
Mr Dryden on his *Religio Laici*', which begins 'Those Gods the pious
Ancients did adore'.

To Mr Dryden, on his Poem called *Religio Laici*

Great is the task, and worthy such a Muse,
To do faith right, yet reason disabuse.
How cheerfully the soul does take its flight
On faith's strong wings, guided by reason's light!
5   But reason does in vain her beams display,
Showing to th' place, whence first she came, the way,
If Peter's heirs must still hold fast the key.
The house which many mansions should contain,
Formed by the great, wise architect in vain,
10   Of disproportion justly we accuse
If the strait gate still entrance must refuse.
The only free, enriching port God made
What shameful monopoly did invade!
One factious company engrossed the trade.
15   Thou to the distant shore hast safely sailed,
Where the best pilots have so often failed.
Freely we now may buy the pearl of price,
The happy land abounds with fragrant spice,
And nothing is forbidden there but vice.
20   Thou best Columbus to the unknown world!
Mountains of doubt that in thy way were hurled,
Thy generous faith has bravely overcome,
And made heaven truly our familiar home.
Let crowds impossibilities receive,
25   Who cannot think ought not to disbelieve.
Let 'em pay tithes, and hood-winked go to heaven,

But sure the Quaker could not be forgiven,
Had not the clerk who hates lay-policy
Found out to countervail the injury
30 Swearing, a trade of which they are not free.
Too long has captived reason been enslaved,
By visions scared, and airy phantasms braved,
Listening t' each proud enthusiastic fool,
Pretending conscience but designing rule;
35 Whilst law, form, interest, ignorance, design
Did in the holy cheat together join.
Like vain astrologers gazing on the skies,
We fell, and did not dare to trust our eyes.
'Tis time at last to fix the trembling soul,
40 And by thy compass to point out the pole;
All men agree in what is to be done,
And each man's heart his table is of stone
Where he the God-writ character may view;
Were it as needful, faith had been so too.
45 O that our greatest fault were humble doubt,
And that we were more just, though less devout!
What reverence should we pay thy sacred rhymes,
Who in these factious too-believing times
Hast taught us to obey, and to distrust,
50 Yet to ourselves, our King, and God prove just.
Thou want'st not praise from an ensuring friend,
The poor to thee on double interest lend.
So strong thy reasons, and so clear thy sense,
They bring, like day, their own bright evidence:
55 Yet whilst mysterious truths to light you bring,
And heavenly things in heavenly numbers sing,
The joyful younger choir may clap the wing.

To Mr Dryden, on *Religio Laici*

'Tis nobly done, a layman's creed professed
When all our faith of late hung on a priest,
His doubtful words like oracles received,
And when we could not understand, believed.
5 Triumphant faith now takes a nobler course,
'Tis gentle, but resists intruding force:
Weak reason may pretend an awful sway,

And consistories charge her to obey;
(Strange nonsense, to confine the sacred dove, ⎫
10   And narrow rules prescribe how she shall love, ⎬
And how upon the barren waters move) ⎭
But she rejects and scorns their proud pretence,
And whilst those grovelling things depend on sense
She mounts on certain wings, and flies on high, ⎫
15   And looks upon a dazzling mystery ⎬
With fixed and steady and an eagle's eye. ⎭
Great King of verse, that dost instruct and please,
As Orpheus softened the rude savages,
And gently freest us from a double care,
20   The bold Socinian and the papal chair:
Thy judgement is correct, thy fancy young,
Thy numbers, as thy generous faith, are strong,
Whilst through dark prejudice they force their way
Our souls shake off the night and view the day.
25   We live secure from mad enthusiasts' rage,
And fond tradition now grown blind with age.
Let factious and ambitious souls repine, ⎫
Thy reason's strong, and generous thy design, ⎬
And always to do well is only thine. ⎭

Thomas Creech

On Mr Dryden's *Religio Laici*

Begone you slaves, you idle vermin go,
Fly from the scourges, and your master know:
Let free, impartial men from Dryden learn
Mysterious secrets of a high concern,
5   And weighty truths, solid convincing sense,
Explained by unaffected eloquence.
     What can you, reverend Levi, here take ill?
Men still had faults, and men will have them still;
He that hath none, and lives as angels do
10   Must be an angel; but what's that to you?
     While mighty Louis finds the Pope too great,
And dreads the yoke of his imposing seat,
Our sects a more tyrannic power assume,
And would for scorpions change the rods of Rome.
15   That church detained the legacy divine;

Fanatics cast the pearls of heaven to swine.
What then have honest thinking men to do,
But choose a mean between th' usurping two?
    Nor can th' Egyptian patriarch blame a Muse
20 Which for his firmness does his heat excuse;
Whatever councils have approved his creed,
The preface sure was his own act and deed.
Our church will have that preface read (you'll say):
'Tis true, but so she will th' Apocrypha,
25 And such as can believe them freely may.
    But did that God, so little understood,
Whose darling attribute is being good,
From the dark womb of the rude chaos bring
Such various creatures, and make man their king,
30 Yet leave his favourite, man, his chiefest care,
More wretched than the vilest insects are?
    O how much happier and more safe are they,
If helpless millions must be doomed a prey
To yelling Furies, and for ever burn
35 In that sad place from whence is no return,
For unbelief in one they never knew,
Or for not doing what they could not do!
    The very fiends know for what crime they fell,
And so do all their followers that rebel:
40 If then a blind, well-meaning Indian stray,
Shall the great gulf be showed him for the way?
    For better ends our kind redeemer died,
Or the fall'n angels' rooms will be but ill supplied.
    That Christ, who at the great deciding day
45 (For he declares what he resolves to say)
Will damn the goats for their ill-natured faults,
And save the sheep for actions, not for thoughts,
Hath too much mercy to send men to hell
For humble charity, and hoping well.
50   To what stupidity are zealots grown,
Whose inhumanity profusely shown
In damning crowds of souls may damn their own!
    I'll err at least on the securer side,
A convert free from malice and from pride.

                       Roscommon

Index of Titles

Index of First Lines